3/6/'95
Van Nuys,
Cal,

Learn and teach
and have fun....

Love
Jack

Hemp & The Marijuana Conspiracy:

THE EMPEROR WEARS NO CLOTHES

BY JACK HERER

— 1991 Edition Designed & Edited By Chris Conrad —

First printing, May, 1985. Second printing, Sept. 1990. Revised editions: © 1985, © 1986. ISBN # 1-878125-00-1.

First fully revised, updated and re-documented edition: © March, 1990, first printing, Sept. 1990, second printing. HEMP Publishing, 5632 Van Nuys Blvd., Van Nuys, CA 91401.

Production courtesy of the Business Alliance for Commerce in Hemp (BACH).

Revised 1991 seventh edition: © April, 1991

Reprint Acknowledgments:

The Author would like to acknowledge the kind permission of the Portland, OR, The Oregonian; Larry Sloman *(Reefer Madness)*; High Times Magazine; Dean Latimer *(Flowers in the Blood)*; Lindsey Bradshaw *(Tar Baby)*; and Harper and Row Publishers *(The Dope Chronicles)* for allowing us to reprint or excerpt so many of their essays, articles and commentaries.

We apologize if any copyrights have been infringed regarding any article, photograph or graphic in this book or its appendices, and hasten to add that great pains have been expended to locate present copyright owners of the several hundred separate items which appear herein. We have endeavored to give credit whenever possible, and will pay an appropriate use fee upon presentation of copyright ownership and documentation.

Our Thanks to the Following:

F. Alexander Magoun, *The Frigate Constitution*; Bettman Archives; Harper and Row; San Francisco Examiner; San Francisco Chronicle; Chicago Herald-Examiner; Chicago Tribune; N.Y. Herald; L.A. Times; L.A. Herald-Examiner; L.A. Daily News; Rolling Stone magazine; Popular Mechanics magazine; Hearst Publishing Company; High Times Encyclopedia; Readers' Digest; Colliers Encyclopedia; New World Encyclopedia; Encyclopaedia Brittanica; Science Digest; Omni magazine; N.Y. News Service; Robert McThomas; James J. Kirkpatrick; Mike Royko; Rick Hampson; Jess Riggenbach; Deb DeMoss; Art Harris; Phillip Hager; Playboy magazine; USA Today; Trevor McKlatchy News Service; UPI; AP; Universal Press; L.A. Times/Washington Post News Service; CNN; Tribune Media; ABC-TV News; NBC-TV News; CBS-TV News; Newsweek, Time, Science Digest, In These Times, Greenpeace magazine, The Guardian, Reason magazine, San Jose Mercury News, Orange County Register, Garry Trudeau, Civil Liberties, Wall Street Journal, Ann Landers, Oklahoma City Times, Athens Messenger, Athens News, Athens Post, National Enquirer, Cato Institute, Security magazine, Christic Institute, Common Sense for American, Public Citizen, and all the rest of the media and researchers that document our "American Experience," from which we learn—or must repeat.

And to Those Who Helped on Past Editions of The Emperor

For my friends who have especially supported this work and me for years: Captain Edwin Adair III; my friend "A" or "C," a.k.a. John Jay Greenfields; J.R.; P; Dobie Don; David & Debbie; Jay Lynn, who may be the world's most brilliant and interesting etymologist and philologist; and to my sons, who kept me going for two years of sabbatical so I could research, write and re-write this book. And finally, I dedicate this work to the hundreds of individual California Marijuana Initiative and Oregon Marijuana Initiative petitioners arrested between 1980-85 while petitioning legally to put this issue on the ballot.

Special acknowledgement to Bruce Anderson and Hans Georg Behr for incredible insights into some of the far corners of world class scholarship on hemp and darn near anything else. To Bryce Garner for his day-to-day dedication given to this endeavor in incredibly selfless doses for months; including editorship and comment. For proofreading and editing assistance: Carolee Wilson, Jim Carner, Rachel Shepard, Daryl Mauer, Susan O'Donnell-Church, Bob Chieger, Mary Balleta, Andy Kowl, Clark Jones, Eddy Gordon and Tod Mikuriya, M.D. To manuscript typists Vanetta Mayo and Laurie Weiner. John Zimmer for typesetting. Ben Masel and Dana Beal for their belief in this project, Howard for the space to do this work in, and Stephan for the memories.

Special 1990 Dedication for The Emperor

To my three youngest children: River, Chanci and B.J., and to a future in which natural things are not outlawed—so that they *have* a future.

INTRODUCTION TO THE 1991 EDITION OF
THE EMPEROR WEARS NO CLOTHES

Dedicated to all the Prisoners of Conscience and of Consciousness from this war on a plant, and to the spirit of mankind to endure and to seek and know the truth and to let old lies, hatreds, bigotries, inquisitions, and ethnocentricities to be thrown asunder so that people can continue to live on the surface of the Earth with all their favorite natural plants and substances.

The purpose of this book is to revive the authoritative historical, social and economic perspective needed to ensure comprehensive legal reforms, abolish cannabis hemp/marijuana prohibition laws, and save the Earth's life systems.

I wrote my first book on marijuana, *G.R.A.S.S.*, in early 1973. At that time I had no idea this plant could do anything, except maybe make rope, let alone that it was earth's most important resource for paper, fiber, fuel, etc.

I first wrote the *Emperor* in 1985, after 12 years of recording hemp information. It was meant to be the culmination of a highly focused personal crusade with my long-time friend and associate, Captain Ed Adair, to win the right to smoke marijuana for ourselves and our friends. It was Captain Ed who, since 1973, constantly encouraged me to record and compile the facts I obtained about marijuana and hemp.

As I gathered a fact here and a fact there, a bigger picture of cannabis hemp and its suppression came together —one that I had not originally expected.

What came together, fact after empirical fact was a picture of a world being destroyed by a malicious conspiracy to suppress, not a "killer-weed" but the world's premier renewable natural resource, for the benefit of a handful of wealthy and powerful individuals and corporations.

Over the years since the first publication of *Emperor*, thousands of more facts have surfaced, corroborating the information that was originally gathered, correcting some minor details and adding substance, fact and insight to the hazier areas of my work. Esoteric details of conspiracy aginst mankind started to fall into place like the filling in of a giant jig-saw puzzle.

The entire text has been revised. Whole new sections and side bars have been added. This information has never been denied by the U.S. government and has been ignored by the media.

And more and more of my friends have been locked away in prison and/or had their homes, jobs and businesses taken from them as part of this escalating "War on Drugs" prohibition. This has become a draconian nightmare for many of our best citizens who, with trust in their own intellect and responsibility for their own health, have defied this bad public policy and have become prisoners of conscience; prisoners of war. I hope after reading this book you will stand up with me and recognize them, not as outlaws, but as the heroes who saved the seed that will save the planet.

New people have been drawn in to work on this project, giving this project a scope and dimension I could only have hoped for at the beginning. They have brought with them skills and information that have been a major contribution to this effort. No egos surfaced as 4 or 5 of us stayed up night after night only the best from each mind was brought forth.

When you write a book like the original *Emperor,* because the information which should be common knowledge, is virtually unknown to our teachers and citizens, you always hope someone of great energy and intellect will read it, make it their own and join in teaching others.

Over the years, hundreds, perhaps thousands of people who have read *The Emperor Wears No Clothes* have thanked me for writing one of their favorite books. At a "Grateful Dead" show one Yale graduate even thanked and hugged me as his favorite author of all time and was thrilled that I was still alive—he had first heard his mother read him *The Emperor* when he was a small boy (probably thinking of the 19th century children's story, *The Emperors New Clothes*, by Hans Christian Anderson).

One day in early 1989 Chris Conrad, of Los Angeles, CA, read *The Emperor*. He became my ally. With his endless energies, editing and publishing talents and willingness to work 40 hours per week for almost five months, all the while holding down full-time resonsibilities as production manager at a major weekly newspaper, as well as many other responsibilities for numerous organizations and causes. During all this time his girlfriend, Mikki Norris, lent her support in so many ways to this project.

Chris did all this without any compensation, yet he worked like he was getting paid a million for it. Chris is one of the most powerful, energetic, skilled and organized human beings I have ever known. He is a light bulb for all mankind. He designed every inch of this book and was its main editor and enthusiast.

Also, we want to extend endless thanks to the rest of our dedicated entourage:

Thanks to Chris' and my associate editor and contributing writer, Lynn Osburn, who is both a great writer and marijuana/hemp energy scientist. Lynn set out to see and learn if, indeed, hemp was one of earth's primary renewable energy resources. He researched the technology needed to bring clean, renewable energy into use on the planet. His brilliant endeavor can be found throughout almost every page of this work. And an excerpt from his paper, *Energy Farming In America*, can be found in the appendix. Lynn's work will teach people all over the world the beauty, neccesity and easiness of energy farming and conversion.

While Lynn was researching this work he was arrested for a

arijuana cultivation violation. He continued to work on this roject day and night until Jan. 2, 1990, when he was incarcerted in Ventura County, CA for a period of one year. He contined to actively edit this book from behind bars.

To another one of my great associate editors and contributing riters, Lynn's wife, Judy Osburn. Judy has, out of neccesity nd outrage become a noted authority and author on seizure nd forfeiture law. The neccesity arose from the government's eizure and attempt to forfeit the home of the Osburn family, ho worked out, with me, a scheme to save our children and lanet. Judy's book, *Spectre of Forfeiture* is state-of-the-art conerning this information and can be ordered through a coupon the back of this book.

To Shan Clark, for his active participation: editing, cataloguig, inputting and for pushing this project and me forward hen it or I might otherwise have stalled.

To my assistant thoughout the last year and a half, Maria arrow, who has accompanied me from the Library of Congress the Smithsonian Institution to the U.S. Department of griculture, as we tracked down and interviewed dozens of overnment officials about hemp and hunted down hundreds of ocuments about hemp and the cover-up.

To Dana Beal, for all his work and research brillance in conecting the *DuPont Dynasties* by Jerry Colby with the informaon on the outlawing of hemp.

To Jerry Colby for his brave ingenious work, which awakened s to the meglomania of the DuPonts. To Ben Masel, for his ard critiques and great assistance and research into the more soteric abstracts on hemp cultivation world-wide and more....

To Julie Kershenbaum, for her excellent editorial assistance nd proof-reading. To D.S.H., for his editorial assistance and eticulous concern for accuracy and readability. To Brenda Kershenbaum and Doug McVay, for proof-reading and editorial omment.

To Steve Hager, John Holmstrom and their whole crew for heir editorial assistance and total support, not only of this proect but of their idea that the Earth could be saved and that ach one of us can become a "Freedom Fighter" for this cause.

To the *Wiz Kids* from KnoWare, Ron Lawrance and Vicki Marshal, who of their own volition, scanned into Mac computrs the old version of *Emperor* so when I came back from my all, 1989 college hemp speaking tour, they handed me, as a urprise gift: the old book in word-processing form, which gave ne the jump start I needed for this huge undertaking.

To Timothy Leary, who encouraged them and me to do this ob. To George Clayton Johnson, who for four years constantly rought me fresh edits of *Emperor* and loving encouragement o update and republish this book.

To the selflessness of my landlords, Ed and Esther, who exended me so much in deferred payments, so that this project which they believed in would not cease or bog down because of ack of money.

To my friends, Doctors Tod Mikuriya and Fred Oerther, for heir critique of the medical sections.

To Loey Glover, office manager at national NORML, for her onstant support and warm encouragement.

To Gatewood Galbraith and Mark Brennamen, of Lexington, Kentucky, for all their remarkable research on behalf of cannabis and their fight for Kentucky citizen's birthrights and potential.

To Barry for his extensive hemp archives which he made available to the hemp movement and ultimately, to this project.

To my dear friends, Ron and Vicki Linker, of Starseed Collections of Athens, Ohio, who elequently taught state senators and representatives and the people of Athens how ignorant (not knowing) they were about hemp and marijuana. Ron and Vicki are the truest of freedom fighters, who with Paul, Kevin and Cliff and the Ohio University Ecology Club have educated the citizens of Athens, as no other city in America.

On November 19, 1989, Ron Linker began serving a two year federal prison term for importing traditional Hindu smoking pipes, as he had for the past 15 years with the approval of Customs. The federal judge at sentencing said, after refusing any hemp information to be admitted at trial, "I only wish I could sentence you longer for all the lives you have destroyed with these [traditional Hindu] pipes." Ron and Vicki know the hemp information and the injustice of his punishment.

And to others who believed in this work and extended encouragment, money and credit even when it hurt. They are: David and Gloria Smith, Marco, Allan and Regina, Jon and Carol, David and Debbie, Steve and Chuquette, Roger, Gary H., Rooster, Dudley, to Jim, Rose and Chris, Gail and Billy, the Friendly Stranger--Ed, Steve and Andrew DeAngelo, Rick Pfrommer, Peter A., Larry G., Floyd, Jean Michel Eribon, Ron Tisbert, Richard M., T.C., Mitchel from New Jersey, Beau and Rachael, Jonathan Drewel (who brought us all his incredible energy from Southern MO Univ.), and to everyone who has read or contributed to this work that I may have left out.

Finally, I hope that this book helps everyone understand the true nature of cannabis hemp and that you, dear reader, decide to become active in the effort to end this crime against man and nature: marijuana prohibition. This book is meant to provide you with the tools, the sense of outrage and the empowerment needed to overcome the forces of personal repression.

We have tried to be as factual and accurate as humanly possible, but there will always be revisions and corrections needed. Please send me copies of any documents and materials that will make the next edition of Emperor even stronger.

We have already won the day; only no one knows it yet.

And once again to my 1991 readers and partners in discovery: thanks for all the documents, clippings and tips you, all our cannabis fans, have sent to us over the past year; keep sending us all the bits and tidbits that help us put the puzzle together for future editions. To my four associate editors, Chris Conrad, Lynn and Judy Osburn, and Shan Clark for again being the most outstanding editors, patriots and hempsters one could ever wish to work with to illuminate the human race with knowledge, integrity and perseverance.

Sincerely,

Jack Herer

Jack Herer
National Director and Founder
Help End Marijuana Prohibition. (HEMP)

PROLOGUE

Marijuana has been known to humankind for untold thousands of years. Government has attempted to prohibit its use for the past 50.

As with all previous attempts at prohibition, the attempt has been a dismal failure: people are simply not deterred from marijuana usage because of its illegality. Yet the prohibition continues and vast amounts of time, energy, and money are spent in the effort.

In Josephine County, Oregon, 20% of the felony cases processed through the Circuit Court involved marijuana; 75% of those cases involved marijuana possessed or grown for personal consumption. This reflects national trends, i.e., 600,000 arrested in 1984 alone.

We must ask at this point, if it is worth the effort.

Only in the light of knowledge, are we able to answer such questions. This enlightening book details the history of marijuana, the history of its prohibition, and the present state of the pharmacological facts about the herb.

In the calm light of understanding, we realize that the effort to prohibit marijuana—born in hysteria and racism, continued in self-righteousness and repression—has no substantial basis whatsoever: no fact, whether political, economic, medical, moral, or correctional, can justify the effort.

This book is well-documented, often startling, and sometimes outrageous, but never less than fascinating, and above all, a thoroughly enjoyable, not to mention educational experience.

— **Michael E. Rose**
Attorney at Law
May 2, 1985

— PREFACE —

By George Clayton Johnson
Author of eight Twilight Zone episodes, Twilight Zone
(The Movie), *Logan's Run* (book and movie), Star Trek,
Oceans Eleven, Kung Fu, etc.

February 22, 1990

Jack Herer has done it.

With incredible precision, backed by voluminous research, he has placed his finger on the point where all of the trends that threaten to overwhelm the world come together. And at the core of these complexities, he has found HEMP.

The premise of Jack Herer's book, *The Emperor Wears No Clothes,* is fanciful in the extreme: That the diverse properties of the scorned and condemned marijuana plant could provide sufficient clothing, oil, medicine, fuel, food, and shelter for all the peoples of the world, if completely legalized and commercialized; and that hemp might prove to be the means of saving the planet (us) from acid rain, global warming and the depletion of our precious forests and fossil fuels.

Further—that the dangers of marijuana smoking pale before the many advantages that are potential in the free commerce in hemp and its byproducts.

Now that Jack has pointed out these facts to a changing world searching for truth—the people, of course, will quickly set things right by renouncing the 1961 Single Convention Treaty on drugs and marijuana, and tooling up to produce a wealth of quality, ecologically sound goods for an upwardly mobile society.

As a science fiction writer, this view of an altered world of clean skies and lush forests, filled with freedom-loving people living in hemp houses, driving their hemp-fueled hemp cars down hemp-lined freeways, dressed in their hemp finery, eating their hemp tofu salad is very appealing to me.

Jack makes a very good case for it being possible. And in my reading his informative book I find that I am charmed.

— EDITOR'S NOTE —

To the 1991 Edition of Emperor

In 1989, when I first read Jack Herer's 1985 version of *Emperor*, I knew I had uncovered a diamond in the rough, and resolved to polish it up. Since then, I've been honored to work with a dedicated core of talented people to bring out the many faceted gem within.

We refined, expanded and consolidated the text, and organized the information into four major sections: the text, the bibliography/index, a smorgasbord of documents in the appendix, and numerous order forms and resources in the back.

The release of the 1990 edition of Emperor sent shock waves across the nation and has changed forever the way people think—and talk—about the cannabis hemp plant.

It has been gratifying to see the incredible information that has been uncovered in the past year, as well as the development of my editorial associates, Lynn and Judy Osburn and Shan Clark, whose research and support have made this 1991 revision possible.

So much has changed over the past year that what began as a modest update became almost a total rewrite of the book. Many people who own previous editions of *Emperor* will want to give away their old copy to get this new, even more powerful resource. This year's edition has fewer illustrations, so as to make room for new material and still keep the information as accessible and readable as possible.

Using the appendix may seem difficult at first. There was so much to include that we have had to shrink some of the documents down to where you need a magnifying glass or enlarged copies to read them. We tried this ourselves, and it worked quite well. We regret the poor quality of some documents we included, but these copies are the best we could locate, and many have been virtually lost elsewhere. Almost daily updates have been incorporated into the text to make it as current as possible.

The amount of new information on hemp that is being developed borders on overwhelming; but if you have any documented tidbits for future editions of *Emperor*, or better copies of documents found in the appendix, please share them with us.

So, let me again thank everyone who helped compile and authenticate this information (you know who you are). May there never be the need for such a task again.

And thank you for taking the time to read this important book. We hope this startling information gets you active in changing this gross injustice, hemp prohibition.

Together we shall carry the day.

Sincerely,

Chris Conrad,
Founder and Director, Business Alliance for Commerce in Hemp
April 10, 1991

— TABLE OF CONTENTS —

HEMP

THE MARIJUANA CONSPIRACY

HEMP

THE MARIJUANA CONSPIRACY

Chapter 1

OVERVIEW OF THE HISTORY OF CANNABIS HEMP

For the Purpose of Clarity in this Book:

Asterisk (*) explanations or documentations are listed at the end of the related paragraph(s). Other sources for facts, anecdotes, histories, studies, etc., are cited for brevity in the body of the text. Numbered footnotes are at the end of each chapter. Reproductions of selected critical source materials are incorporated into the body of the text or included in the appendices.

The facts cited herein are generally verifiable in the Encyclopaedia Britannica, which was printed primarily on paper produced with cannabis hemp for over 150 years. However, any encyclopedia (no matter how old) or good dictionary will do for general verification purposes.

CANNABIS HEMP

Also known as: Hemp, cannabis hemp, Indian (India) hemp, true hemp, muggles, pot, marijuana, reefer, grass, ganja, bhang, "the kind," dagga, herb, etc., all refer to exactly the same plant.

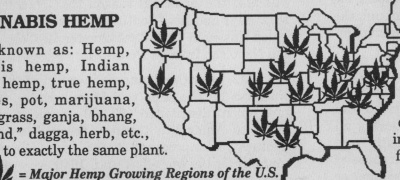

🌿 = *Major Hemp Growing Regions of the U.S.*

WHAT'S IN A NAME?

(US. Geography)

HEMPstead, Long Island; HEMPstead County, Arkansas; HEMPstead County, Texas; HEMPhill, North Carolina, among others, were named after cannabis growing regions, or after family names derived from hemp growing.

AMERICAN HISTORICAL NOTES

In 1619, America's first marijuana law was enacted at Jamestown Colony, Virginia, "ordering" all farmers to "make tryal of" (grow) Indian hemp seed. More mandatory (must-grow) hemp cultivation laws were enacted in Massachusetts in 1631, in Connecticut in 1632 and in the Chesapeake Colonies into the mid-1700s.

Even in England, the much-sought-after prize of full British citizenship was bestowed by a decree of the crown on foreigners who would grow cannabis, and fines were often levied against those who refused.

Cannabis hemp was legal tender (money) in most of the Americas from 1631 until the early 1800s. Why? To encourage American farmers to grow more.[1]

You could pay your taxes with cannabis hemp throughout America for over 200 years.[2]

You could even be jailed in America for not growing cannabis during several periods of shortage, e.g., in Virginia between 1763 and 1767.

(Herndon, G.M., *Hemp in Colonial Virginia*, 1963; *The Chesapeake Colonies*, 1954; L.A. Times, August 12, 1981; et al.)

George Washington and Thomas Jefferson grew cannabis on their plantations. Jefferson, while envoy to France, went to great expense—and even considerable risk to himself and his secret agents—to procure particularly good hemp seeds smuggled illegally into Turkey from China. The Chinese Mandarins (political rulers) so valued their hemp seeds that they made their exportation a capital offense.

(See the diaries of George Washington and Thomas Jefferson; Jefferson's Farm Books; Abel, Ernest, *Marijuana: The First 12,000 Years*, Plenum Press, NY, 1980; M. Aldrich, et al.)

Benjamin Franklin started one of America's first paper mills with cannabis. This allowed America to have a free colonial press without having to beg or justify paper and books from England.

The United States Census of 1850 counted 8,327* hemp "plantations" (minimum 2,000 acre farms) growing cannabis hemp for cloth, canvas and even the cordage used for baling cotton. Most of these plantations were located in the South or in the border states, primarily because of the cheap slave-labor available prior to 1865 for the labor-intensive hemp industry.

(U.S. Census, 1850; Allen, James Lane, *The Reign of Law, A Tale of the Kentucky Hemp Fields*, MacMillan Co., NY, 1900; Roffman, Roger. Ph.D., *Marijuana as Medicine*, Mendrone Books, WA, 1982.)

* This figure does not include the tens of thousands of smaller farms growing cannabis, nor the hundreds of thousands—if not millions—of family hemp patches in America; nor does it take into account that 80% of America's hemp consumption for 200 years *still* had to be imported from Russia, Hungary, Czechoslovakia and Poland well into this century.

Benjamin Franklin started one of America's first paper mills with cannabis. This allowed America to have a free colonial press without having to beg or justify paper and books from England.

In addition, varying marijuana and hashish extracts were the second or third most prescribed medicines in the United States from 1842 until the 1890s. Its legal medicinal use continued through the 1930s for humans and figured even more prominently in veterinary medicines during this time.

Cannabis extract medicines were produced by Eli Lilly, Parke-Davis, Tildens, Brothers Smith (Smith Brothers), Squibb and many other American and European companies and apothecaries. During all this time there was not one reported death from cannabis extract medicines, and virtually no abuse or mental disorders reported, except for first-time or novice-users occasionally becoming disoriented or overly introverted.

(Mikuriya, Tod, M.D., *Marijuana Medical Papers*, Medi-Comp Press, CA, 1973; Cohen, Sidney & Stillman, Richard, *Therapeutic Potential of Marijuana*, Plenum Press, NY, 1976.)

WORLD HISTORICAL NOTES

"The earliest known woven fabric was apparently of hemp, which began to be worked in the eighth millenium (8,000-7,000 B.C.)." (The Columbia History of the World, 1981, page 54.)

The body of literature (archaeologists, anthropologists, philologists, economists, historians, etc.) is in general agreement that, at the very least:

From more than 1,000 years before the time of Christ until 1883 A.D., cannabis hemp—indeed, marijuana—was our planet's largest agricultural crop and most important industry for thousands upon thousands of products and enterprises; producing the overall majority of earth's fiber, fabric, lighting oil, paper, incense and medicines as well as a primary source of protein for humans and animals alike.

And according to virtually every anthropologist and university in the world, marijuana was also used in most of our religions and cults as one of the seven, or so, most widely used mood-, mind- or pain-altering drugs taken as psychotropic, psychedelic (mind-manifesting or -expanding) sacraments.

These sacred (drug) experiences inspired our superstitions, amulets, talismans, religions, prayers, and language codes, almost without exception. (See chapter 10 on "Religions and Magic.")

(Wasson, R. Gordon, *Soma, Divine Mushroom of Immortality*; Allegro, J.M., *Sacred Mushroom & the Cross*, Doubleday, NY, 1969; Pliny; Josephus; Herodotus; Dead Sea Scrolls; Gnostic Gospels; the Bible; *Ginsberg Legends Kaballah*, c. 1860; Paracelsus; British Museum; Budge; Ency. Brittanica, "Pharmacological Cults;" Schultes & Wasson, *Plants of the Gods*; Research of: Schultes, R.E., Harvard Botanical Dept.; Wm. EmBoden, Cal State U., Northridge; et al.)

GREAT WARS WERE FOUGHT TO INSURE THE AVAILABILITY OF HEMP.

For example, one of the primary reasons for the War of 1812 (that America fought with Great Britain) was access to Russian cannabis hemp. Russian hemp was also the principal reason that Napoleon (our 1812 ally) and his "Continental Systems" allies invaded Russia in 1812. (See chapter 12, "War of 1812 and Napoleon Invades Russia.")

In 1942, after the Japanese invasion of the Philippines cut off the supply of Manila hemp, the U.S. government distributed 400,000 pounds of cannabis seeds to American farmers from Wisconsin to Kentucky, who produced 42,000 tons of hemp fiber annually for the war effort until 1946.

WHY HAS CANNABIS HEMP/MARIJUANA BEEN SO IMPORTANT IN HISTORY?

Because cannabis hemp is, overall, the strongest, most-durable, longest-lasting natural soft-fiber on the planet. Its leaves and flower tops (marijuana) were—depending on the culture—the first, second or third most important and most-used medicines for two-thirds of the world's people for at least 3,000 years, until the turn of this century.

Botanically, hemp is a member of the most advanced plant family on Earth. It is a dioecious (i.e., having male, female and sometimes hermaphroditic [male and female on same plant]) woody, herbaceous annual that uses the sun more efficiently than virtually any other plant on our planet, reaching a robust 12 to 20 feet or more in one short growing season. It can be grown in virtually any climate or soil condition on Earth, even marginal ones.

Hemp is, by far, Earth's premier, renewable natural resource. This is why hemp is so important.

Footnotes:
1. Clark, V.S., *History of Manufacture in the United States,* McGraw Hill, NY 1929, Pg. 34.
2. Ibid.

PEASANTS HARVESTING HEMP AT THE BEGINNING OF THE 20TH CENTURY

Whole families came out together to harvest the hemp fields at the height of the flowering season, all over the world for thousands upon thousands of years, never dreaming that it would one day be banned from the face of the earth, in favor of fossil fuels, timber and petrochemicals.

For the past half-century the United States has not only discouraged the use of hemp, but adopted a policy of forced extinction upon this species of plant.... The impact of accidentally destroying any single life form has never been fully considered, let alone the effect of this concerted attack upon what is arguably the Earth's primary renewable resource; one that has literally thousands of critical uses—especially in replacing the majority of uses of fossil fuels, timber and petrochemicals.

THERE WERE AT LEAST 60 TONS OF HEMP ON THE U.S.S. CONSTITUTION ALONE.

Ensigns
Sails
Rigging
Oakum (sealant)

HEMP

Pennants
Flags
Maps / Bibles
Logs

HEMP

THE CONSTITUTION FRIGATE

(A.K.A. "Old Ironsides")

Partial list of rigging (rope) required for the 1927 restoration of the U.S.S. Constitution and other Historic Ships". by F. Alexander Magoun, S.B., S.M. The Southworth Press. ©1928 by The Marine Research Society. Boston, Massachusetts. Pgs. 96 and 97.

Each mast (fore, mizen, main, etc.) required lifts, braces, reefs, jiggers, tackles, etc.
The Constitution carried well over four miles of hemp rope.

Standing Rigging, Hard Laid Hemp

Item	Circumference
Mainstay	12 inches
Forestay	12 "
Pendants	9½ "
Fore and main shrouds	9½ "
Mizen shrouds	7 "
Topmast backstays	9 "
Topmast stays	8 "
Topgallant backstays	5 "
Topgallant stays	4 "
Royal stays	2½ "

Running Rigging, Soft Laid Hemp

Item	Circumference	Gross Length
Truss tackles	2½ Inches	260 Feet
Jeer fall	4½ "	350 "
Pendant tackles	3¼ "	1200 "
Lifts	3½ "	470 "
Braces	4 "	608 "
Tacks	4 "	400 "
Sheets	4½ "	400 "
Clew garnets	3 "	400 "
Main Bowline	3¼ "	120 "
Reef tackles	3¼ "	350 "
Buntlines	2½ "	530 "
Leechlines	2½ "	432 "
Clew jiggers	2 "	520 "
Top burtons	3 "	1060 "
Topsail tye halliards	3¼ "	1440 "
Topsail lifts	4¼ "	360 "
Topsail braces	3¼ "	600 "
Best bower anchor cable	22½ "	720
Messenger	14 "	600
Gun breeching (each)	7 "	24
Out-haul tackles (each)	2½ "	60

Clothes / Uniforms

Papers

CONTINENTAL SOLDIER

Chapter Two

A BRIEF SUMMARY OF THE USES OF HEMP

OUR CHALLENGE TO THE WORLD: TRY TO PROVE US WRONG

If all fossil fuels and their derivatives, as well as the deforestation of trees for paper and agriculture are banned from use in order to save the planet, and reverse the greenhouse effect:

Then there is only one known renewable natural resource able to provide the overall majority of our paper, textiles and food, meet all the world's transportation, home and industrial energy needs, reduce pollution, rebuild the soil and clean the atmosphere—all at the same time—our old stand-by that did it all before: **Cannabis Hemp ...Marijuana!**

1. SHIPS AND SAILORS

Ninety percent* of all ships' sails (since before the Phoenicians, from at least the Fifth Century B.C. until long after the invention and commercialization of steam ships [mid- to late-19th century]) were made from hemp. (See picture.)

* The other 10% were usually flax or minor fibers like ramie, sisal, jute, abaca.

(Abel, Ernest, *Marijuana: The First 12,000 Years*; Plenum Press, 1980; Herodotus, *Histories*, 5th century B.C.; Frazier, Jack, *The Marijuana Farmers*, 1972; U.S. Agricultural Index, 1916-1982; USDA film, *Hemp for Victory*, 1942.)

The word "canvas"[1] is the Dutch pronunciation (twice removed, from French and Latin) of the Greek word "Kannabis."*

* Kannabis—of the (Hellenized) Mediterranean Basin Greek language, derived from the Persian and earlier Northern Semitics (Quanuba, Kanabosm, Cana?, Kanah?) which scholars have now traced back to the new-found dawn of the 6,000-year-old, Indo-Semitic-European language family base of the Sumerians and Accadians. The early Sumerian/Babylonian word K(a)N(a)B(a), or Q(a)N(a)B(a) is one of man's longest surviving root words.[1] (KN means cane and B means two--two reeds or two sexes.)

In addition to the canvas sails, virtually all of the rigging, anchor ropes, cargo nets, fishermen's nets, flags, shrouds, and oakum (the main sealant for ships against salt water for use between loose or green beams) were made from the stalk of the marijuana plant until this century.

Even the sailors' clothing, right down to the stitching in the seamen's rope-soled and (sometimes) "canvas" shoes were crafted from cannabis.*

* An average cargo, clipper, whaler, or naval ship of the line, in the 16th, 17th, 18th, or 19th centuries carried 50 to 100 tons of cannabis hemp rigging, not to mention the sails, nets, etc. and needed it all replaced every year or two, due to salt rot. (Ask the U.S. Naval Academy, or see the construction of the USS Constitution, a.k.a. "Old Ironsides," Boston Harbor.)

(Abel, Ernest, *Marijuana, The First 12,000 Years*, Plenum Press, 1980; Ency. Brittanica; Magoun, Alexander, *The Frigate Constitution*, 1928; USDA film *Hemp for Victory*, 1942.)

Additionally, the ships' charts, maps, logs, and Bibles were generally made of hemp-fiber paper from the time of Columbus (15th century) until the early 1900s in the Western European/American World, and by the Chinese from the first century A.D. on. Hemp paper lasted 50 to 100 times longer than most preparations of papyrus, and was a hundred times easier and cheaper to make.

Nor was hemp use restricted to the briny deep.

2. TEXTILES AND FABRICS

Eighty percent of all mankind's textiles and fabrics for clothes, tents, linens,* rugs, drapes, quilts, bed sheets, towels, diapers, etc., including our flag, "Old Glory," were made principally from cannabis fibers until the 1820s in America and until the 20th century in most of the rest of the world.

For hundreds, if not thousands, of years (until the 1830s) Ireland made the finest linens and Italy made the world's finest cloth for clothing with hemp.

* The 1893, 1910 Encyclopaedia Britannicas indicate—and in 1938, Popular Mechanics estimated—that at least half of all the material that has been called linen was not made from flax, but from cannabis. Herodotus (c. 450 B.C.) describes the hempen garments made by the Thracians as equal to linen in fineness and that "none but a very experienced person could tell whether they were of hemp or flax."

The fact that hemp is softer than cotton, warmer than cotton, more water absorbent than cotton, has three times the tensile strength of cotton and is many times more durable than cotton, was well known to our forebearers.

Homespun cloth was almost always spun from the family hemp patch into the early l900s.

In fact, when the patriotic, real life, 1776 mothers of our present day blue-blood "Daughters of the American Revolution" (the D.A.R.) of Boston and New England organized "spinning bees" to clothe Washington's soldiers, the majority of the thread was spun from hemp fibers. Were it not for the historically forgotten (or censored) and currently disparaged marijuana plant, the Continental Army would have frozen to death at Valley Forge, Pennsylvania.

The common use of hemp in the economy of the early republic was important enough to occupy the time and thoughts of our first U.S. Treasury Secretary Alexander Hamilton, who wrote in a Treasury notice from the 1790s, "Flax and Hemp: Manufacturers of these articles have so much affinity to each other, and they are so often blended, that they may with advantage be considered in conjunction. Sailcloth should have 10% duty."

(Herndon, G.M., *Hemp in Colonial Virginia,* 1963; D.A.R. histories; Able, E, *Marijuana, the First 12,000 Years;* also see the 1985 film *Revolution* with Al Pacino.)

The covered wagons went west (to Kentucky, Indiana, Illinois, Oregon, and California*) covered with sturdy hemp canvas tarpaulins;[2] while ships sailed around the "Horn" to San Francisco on hemp sails and ropes.

* The original, heavy-duty, famous Levi pants were made for the California '49ers out of hempen sailcloth and rivets. This way the pockets wouldn't rip when filled with gold panned from the sediment.[3]

Homespun cloth was almost always spun from the "family" hemp patch until after the Civil War, and into the early l900s, by Americans and people all over the world.*

* In the 1930s, Congress was told by the Federal Bureau of Narcotics that many Polish-Americans still grew pot in their backyards to make their winter "long johns" and work clothes, and greeted the agents with shotguns for stealing their next year's clothes.

If a farmer wanted soft linen-quality fibers he

would harvest his cannabis at two or three months; twine or cordage at 3-4 months; and heavy canvas o rope at six months. The density of the patch also in fluences the quality of the fiber.

As a rule of thumb, if you plan for medical or recreational use you plant one seed per five squar yards. When planted for seed: fou to five feet apart.

(Univ. of KY Ag. Ext. leaflet, March 1943.)

Two hundred seeds to the squar yard are planted for rough cordag or coarse cloth. Finest linen o lace is grown 900 plants to the square yard.

Farm Crop Reports, USDA internationa abstracts.

Were it not for the marijuana plant, the Continental Army would have frozen to death at Valley Forge.

By the late 1820s, the new American hand cotton gins (invented by Eli Whitney in 1793) were largely replaced by European-made "industrial" looms and cotton gins ("gin" is just short for engine), because of Europe's primary equipment-machinery-technology (tool and die making) lead over America.

For the first time, light cotton clothing could be produced at less cost than hand retting (rotting) and hand separating hemp fibers to be handspun on spinning wheels and jennys.[4]

However, because of its strength, softness, warmth and long-lasting qualities, hemp continued to be the second most used natural fiber* until the 1930s.

* In case you're wondering, there is no THC or "high" in hemp fiber. That's right, you can't smoke your shirt! In fact, attempting to smoke hemp fabric—or any fabric, for that matter—could be fatal!

After the 1937 Marijuana Tax law, hemp was replaced mostly by new DuPont "plastic fibers" under license of 1936 German I.G. Corporation patents, with patent surrenders as part of Germany's reparation payments to America from World War I. (Some 30% of Hitler's I.G. Corps, e.g., Farben, were owned and financed by America's DuPont.) Hemp was also replaced by Nylon, (invented in 1935) when it was patented and brought to market by DuPont in 1938.

(DuPont Dynasties)

Finally, it must be noted that approximately 50% of all chemicals used in American agriculture today are used in cotton growing. Hemp needs no chemicals, has virtually no weed or insect enemies—except for

#1 Fiber, 1776

SPINNING WHEEL

SPINNING JENNY

Vertical spindles

Belt

Roller

Roving bobbins

Movable tension bar

(Cavender, Jim, Professor of Botany, Ohio University, *"Authorities Examine Pot Claims,"* Athens News, November 16, 1989.)

3. FIBER & PULP PAPER

From 75-90% of all paper in the world was made with cannabis hemp fiber until 1883: books, Bibles, maps, paper money, stocks and bonds, newspapers, etc., including the Gutenberg Bible (15th century); Pantagruel and the Herb Pantagruelion, Rabelais 16th century); King James Bible (17th century); Thomas Paine's pamphlets, "The Rights of Man," "Common Sense," "The Age of Reason" (18th century); the works of Fitz Hugh Ludlow, Mark Twain, Victor Hugo, Alexander Dumas, Lewis Carroll's Alice in Wonderland (19th century); and just about everything else was printed on hemp paper.

The first draft of the Declaration of Independence (June 28, 1776) was written on Dutch [hemp] paper, as was the second draft completed on July 2, 1776. This was the document actually agreed to on that day and announced and released on July 4, 1776. ..On July 19, 1776, Congress ordered the Declaration be copied and engrossed on parchment (a prepared animal skin) and this was the document actually signed by the delegates on August 2, 1776.

Hemp fiber or rag paper can be torn when wet but returns to its full strength when dry. Rag paper is stable for centuries, barring extreme conditions. It will almost never wear out.

What we (the colonial Americans) and the rest of the world used to make all our paper from was the discarded sails and ropes sold by ship owners as scrap for recycling into paper.

The rest of our paper came from our worn-out clothes, sheets, diapers, curtains and rags* sold to scrap dealers made primarily from hemp and sometimes flax.

* Hence the term "rag paper."

Our ancestors were too thrifty to just throw anything away, so, until the 1880s, any remaining scraps and clothes were mixed together and recycled into paper. U.S. government papers were written, by law, in hempen rag paper until the 1920s.[5]

It is generally believed by scholars that the early Chinese knowledge, or art, of hemp paper making First Century A.D.—800 years before Islam discovered how, and 1,200 to 1,400 years before Europe) was one of the two chief reasons that Oriental knowledge and science were vastly superior to that of the West for 1,400 years. Thus, the art of long-lasting hemp papermaking allowed the Orientals' accumulated knowledge to be passed on, built upon, investi-

gated, refined, challenged and changed, for generation after generation (in other words, cumulative and comprehensive scholarship).

Hemp paper lasted 50 to 100 times longer than most preparations of papyrus, and was a hundred times easier and cheaper to make.

The other reason that Oriental knowledge and science sustained superiority to that of the West for 1,400 years was that the Roman Catholic Church forbade reading and writing for 95% of Europe's people; in addition, they burned, hunted down, or prohibited all foreign or domestic books—including their own Bible!—for over 1,200 years under the penalty and often-used punishment of death. Hence, historians term this period "The Dark Ages." (See chapter 10 on Sociology.)

4. ROPE, TWINE, AND CORDAGE

Virtually every city and town (from time out of mind) in the world had an industry making hemp rope.[6] Russia, however, was the world's largest producer and best-quality manufacturer, supplying 80% of the Western world's hemp from 1740 until 1940.

Thomas Paine outlined four essential natural resources for the the new nation in *Common Sense* (1776): "cordage, iron, timber and tar."

Chief among these was hemp for cordage. He wrote, "Hemp flourishes even to rankness, we do not want for cordage." Then he went on to list the other essentials necessary for war with the British navy: cannons, gunpowder, etc.

From 70-90% of all rope, twine, and cordage was made from hemp until 1937. It was then replaced mostly by petrochemical fibers (owned principally by DuPont under license from Germany's I.G. Corporation patents) and by Manila (Abaca) Hemp, with steel cables often intertwined for strength —brought in from our "new" far-Western Pacific Philippines possession, seized from Spain as reparations for the Spanish American War in 1898.

5. ART CANVAS

"Hemp is the perfect archival medium."[7]

The paintings of Rembrandt, Van Gogh, Gainsborough, etc., were primarily painted on hemp canvas, as were practically all canvas paintings.

A strong, lustrous fiber, hemp withstands heat, mildew, insects and is not damaged by light. Oil paintings on hemp canvas have stayed in fine condition for centuries.

6. PAINTS AND VARNISHES

For thousands of years, virtually all good paints and varnishes were made with hemp seed oil and/or linseed oil.

For instance, in 1935 alone, 116 million pounds (58,000 tons*) of hemp seed were used in America just for paint and varnish. The hemp drying oil business went principally to DuPont petro-chemicals.[8]

*National Institute of Oilseed Products congressional testimony *against* the 1937 Marijuana Transfer Tax Law.

Congress and the Treasury Department were assured through secret testimony given by DuPont in 1935-37 directly to Herman Oliphant, Chief Counsel for the Treasury Dept., that hemp seed oil could be replaced with synthetic petro-chemical oils made principally by DuPont.

Oliphant was solely responsible for drafting the Marijuana Tax Act that was submitted to Congress.[9] (See complete story in chapter 4, "The Last Days of Legal Cannabis.")

* As a comparison, consider that the U.S. Drug Enforcement Agency (DEA), along with all America's state and local police agencies, claim to have seized for all of 1988, 651.5 tons of American-grown marijuana—seed, plant, root, dirt clump and all.
(National Narcotics Intelligence Consumers Committee, NNICC Report, 1988 DEA office release, El Paso, TX, April, 1989.)

7. LIGHTING OIL

Until about 1800, hemp seed oil was the most consumed lighting oil in America and the world. From then until the 1870s, it was the second most consumed lighting oil, exceeded only by whale oil.

In fact, the celebrated botanist Luther Burbank stated, "The seed of [cannabis] is prized in other countries for its oil, and its neglect here illustrates the same wasteful use of our agricultural resources."
(Burbank, Luther, *How Plants Are Trained To Work For Man: Useful Plants,* P. F. Collier & Son Co., NY, Vol. 6, pg. 48.)

Hemp seed oil lit the lamps of Aladdin, Abraham the prophet and Abraham Lincoln and was the brightest lamp oil.*

*Canadian Report to the Ontario Department of Agriculture, 1977.

Hemp seed oil for lamps was replaced by petroleum kerosene, etc., after the 1859 Pennsylvania oil discovery and "Rockefeller's" 1870-on national petroleum stewardship. (See chapter 9 on "Economics.")

8. BIOMASS ENERGY

In the early 1900s, Henry Ford and other futuristic organic, engineering geniuses, (as their intellectual, scientific heirs still do today) recognized an important point—that up to 90% of all fossil fuel use in the world today (coal, oil, natural gas, etc.) should long ago have been replaced with biomass such as: cornstalks, cannabis, waste paper and the like.

When considered on a planet-wide, soil-wide, climate-wide basis, cannabis is at least four times and, more likely, 50 times richer in renewable biomass/ cellulose potential than its nearest rivals on the planet—cornstalks, trees, surgarcane, kenaf, etc.

Biomass can be converted to methane and methanol at a fraction of the current cost of oil, coal, or nuclear energy—especially when environmental costs are factored in—and its mandated use would automatically cleanse our air, end sulfur-based smog and reverse the atmospheric carbon dioxide imbalance on our planet.*

* Government and oil and coal companies, etc., will insist that burning biomass fuel is no better than using up our fossil fuel reserves, as far as pollution goes; but this is patently untrue.

WHEN HEMP SAVED GEORGE BUSH'S LIFE

One more example of the importance of hemp: Five years after cannabis hemp was outlawed in 1937, it was promptly re-introduced for the World War II effort in 1942.

So, when the young pilot George Bush bailed out of his burning airplane after a battle over the Pacific, little did he know:

• Parts of his aircraft engine were lubricated with cannabis hemp seed oil;

• 100% of his life-saving parachute webbing was made from U.S. grown cannabis hemp;

• Virtually all the rigging and ropes of the ship that pulled him in were made of cannabis hemp;

• The firehoses on the ship (as were those in the schools he had attended) were woven from cannabis hemp; and,

• Finally, as young George Bush stood safely on the deck, his shoes' durable stitching was of cannabis hemp, as it is in all good leather and military shoes to this day.

Yet Bush has spent a good deal of his career eradicating the cannabis plant and enforcing laws to make certain that no one will learn this information—possibly including himself....

(USDA film, *Hemp for Victory*, 1942; U. of KY Agricultural Ext. Service Leaflet 25, March, 1943; Galbraith, Gatewood, *Kentucky Marijuana Feasibility Study*, 1977.)

Why? Because, unlike fossil fuel, biomass comes from living (not extinct) plants that continue to remove carbon dioxide pollution from our atmosphere as they grow, through photosynthesis. Furthermore, biomass fuels do not contain sulfur.

This can be accomplished if hemp is grown for biomass and then converted through pyrolysis (charcoalizing) or biochemical composting into fuels to replace fossil fuel energy products.*

* Remarkably, when considered on a planet-wide, climate-wide, soil-wide basis, cannabis is at least four and could be many more times richer in sustainable, renewable biomass/cellulose potential than its nearest rivals on the planet—cornstalks, surgarcane, kenaf, trees, etc. Solar Gas, 1980; Omni, 1983: Cornell University; Science Digest, 1983: etc.). Also see chapter 9 on Economics.

One product of pyrolysis, methanol, is today used by most race cars and was used by American farmers and auto drivers routinely with petroleum/methanol options starting in the 1920s, through the 1930s, and even into the mid-1940s to run tens of thousands of auto, farm and military vehicles until the end of World War II.

Methanol can be converted to gasoline and save 50% of the storage space required.

9. MEDICINE

From 1842 and through the 890s, extremely strong marijuana (then known as cannabis extractums) and hashish extracts, tinctures and elixirs were routinely the second and third most-used medicine in America for humans (from birth, through childhood, to old age) and in veterinary medicine until the 1920s and longer. (See chapter 6 on "Medicine," and chapter 13 on the "19th Century.")

As stated earlier, for at least 3,000 years, prior to 842, widely varying marijuana extracts (buds, leaves, roots, etc.) were the most commonly used real medicine in the world for the majority of mankind's illnesses.

However, in Western Europe, the Roman Catholic Church forbade use of cannabis or any medical treatment, except for alcohol or blood letting, for 1200-plus years. (See chapter 10 on "Sociology.")

The U.S. Pharmacopoeia indicated cannabis should be used for treating such ailments as: fatigue, fits of coughing, rheumatism, asthma, delirium tremens, migraine headaches and the cramps and depressions associated with menstruation. (Professor William Imboden, Professor of Narcotic Botany, California

State University, Northridge.)

Queen Victoria used cannabis resins for her menstrual cramps and PMS, and her reign (1837-1901) paralleled the enormous growth of the use of Indian cannabis medicine in the English-speaking world.

In this century, cannabis research has demonstrated therapeutic value—and complete safety—in the treatment of many health problems including asthma, glaucoma, nausea, tumors, epilepsy, infection, stress, migraines, anorexia, depression, rheumatism, arthritis and possibly herpes. (See chapter 7, "Therapeutic Uses of Cannabis.")

10. FOOD OILS AND PROTEIN

Hemp seed was regularly used in porridge, soups, and gruels by virtually all the people of the world up until this century. Monks were required to eat hemp seed dishes three times a day, to weave their clothes of it and to print their Bibles on paper made with its fiber.

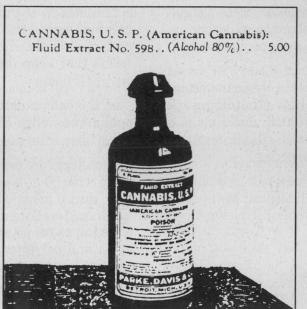

CANNABIS, U. S. P. (American Cannabis):
Fluid Extract No. 598. . (Alcohol 80%) . . 5.00

(See Rubin, Dr. Vera, "Research Institute for the Study Of Man;" Eastern Orthodox Church; Cohen & Stillman, *Therapeutic Potential of Marijuana*, Plenum Press, 1976; Abel, Ernest, *Marijuana, The First 12,000 Years*, Plenum Press, NY, 1980; Encyclopaedia Brittanica.)

Hemp seed can either be pressed for its vegetable oil, leaving a high-protein seed cake as a byproduct, or it can be sprouted (malted) and used like any other seed for salads or cooking.

Sprouting any seed improves its nutritional value, and was even recommended in the Essene gospels almost 2000 years ago as a way to increase the life-giving power of seed grains. Marijuana "seed" protein is one of mankind's finest, most complete and available-to-the-body vegetable proteins. (See discussion of edistins, chapter 8.)

Hemp seed was—until the 1937 prohibition law—the world's number-one bird seed, for both wild and domestic birds. It was their favorite* of any seed food on the planet; four million pounds of hemp seed for songbirds were sold at retail in the U.S. in 1937. Birds will pick hemp seeds out and eat them first from a pile of mixed seed. Birds in the wild live longer and breed more with hemp seed in their diet, using the oil for their feathers and their overall health. (More in chapter 8 "Hemp as a Basic World Food.")

* Congressional testimony, 1937: "Song birds won't sing without it," the bird food companies told Congress. Result: sterilized cannabis

seeds continues to be imported into the U.S. from Italy, China and other countries.

The hemp seed produces no observable high for humans or birds: only the most minute traces of THC are in the seed.

(Frazier, Jack, *The Marijuana Farmers*, Solar Age Press, New Orleans, LA, 1972)

11. BUILDING MATERIALS AND HOUSING

Because one acre of hemp produces as much cellulose fiber pulp as 4.1 acres of trees,* hemp is the perfect material to replace trees for pressed board, particle board and for concrete construction molds.

* Dewey & Merrill, *Bulletin #404*, U.S. Dept. of Ag., 1916.

Practical, inexpensive construction material which is fire resistant, with excellent thermal and sound insulating qualities, can be made using a process called Environcore.° This process, developed by Mansion Industries, applies heat and compression to agricultural fiber to create strong construction paneling, replacing dry wall and plywood. (See Appendix p. 172.)

Hemp has been used throughout history for carpet backing. Hemp fiber has potential in the manufacture of strong, rot resistant carpeting—eliminating the poisonous fumes of burning synthetic materials in a house or commercial fire, along with allergic reactions associated with new synthetic carpeting.

Plastic plumbing pipe (PVC pipes) can be manufactured using renewable hemp cellulose as the chemical feedstocks, replacing non-renewable petroleum-based chemical feedstocks.

So we can envision a house of the future built, plumbed, painted and furnished with the world's number one renewable resource —hemp.

12. ECONOMIC STABILITY, PROFIT & FREE TRADE

We believe that in a competitive market with all facts known, people will rush to buy long-lasting biodegradable Pot Tops or Mary Jeans.

It's time we put capitalism to the test and let the unrestricted market of supply and demand as well as "Green" ecological consciousness decide the future of the planet.

A cotton shirt in 1776 cost $100 to $200, while a hemp shirt cost $.50 to $1. By the 1830s, cooler lighter cotton shirts were on par in price with the warmer, heavier, hempen shirts, providing a competitive choice.

People were able to choose their garments based upon the particular qualities they wanted in a fabric. Today we have no such choice.

The role of hemp and other natural fibers should be determined by the market of supply and demand and personal tastes and values, not by the undue influence of prohibition laws, federal subsidies and huge tariffs that keep the natural fabrics from replacing synthetic fibers.

Yet this manipulation has occurred with virtually no public knowledge of the incredible potential of the hemp fiber or its uses.

When legal, by using 100% hemp or mixing 20-50% hemp with 50-80% cotton, you will be able to pass on your shirts, pants and other clothing to your grandchildren. Intelligent spending could essentially replace the use of petrochemical synthetic fibers such as nylon and polyester with tougher, cheaper, cool, absorbent, breathing, biodegradable, natural fibers.

China, Italy and Eastern European countries such as Hungary, Romania, Czechoslovakia, Poland, Russia and Georgia currently make millions of dollars worth of sturdy hemp and hemp/cotton textiles—and could be making billions of dollars—annually.

These countries build upon their traditional farming and weaving skills, while the U.S. tries to force the extinction of this plant to prop up destructive synthetic technologies.

Even cannabis/cotton blend textiles are still not cleared for direct sale in the U.S. to this day. The Chinese, for instance, are forced—by tacit agreement—to send us inferior ramie/cottons.

(National Import/Export Textile Company of Shanghai, Personal communication with author, April and May, 1983.)

Coincidentally, as the 1990 edition of *Emperor* went to press garments containing at least 55% cannabis hemp arrived from China—with a huge import fee at-

...ached. To import true hemp from China, one must first import it into Hong Kong and then re-export it to the U.S.—with quotas and a huge protective tariff to shield American synthetic fiber industries from competing with imported natural fibers such as hemp.

And, of course, you are not allowed to grow hemp domestically. This kind of run-around is nothing but obstructionism hidden behind bureaucratic legalese.

As Eastern bloc nations make their way toward market capitalism and democracy, they deserve a level playing field in which to market their wares.

And let the consumer decide.

13. SMOKING, LEISURE & CREATIVITY

The American Declaration of Independence recognizes the "inalienable rights" of "life, liberty and the pursuit of happiness." Subsequent court decisions have inferred the rights to privacy and choice from this, the U.S. Constitution and its Amendments.

Many artists and writers have used cannabis for creative stimulation—from the writers of the world's religious masterpieces to our most irreverent satirists. These include Lewis Carroll and his hookah smoking caterpillar in *Alice in Wonderland*, plus Victor Hugo and Alexander Dumas; such jazz greats as Louis Armstrong, Cab Calloway, Duke Ellington and Gene Krupa; and the pattern continues right up to modern day artists and musicians such as the Beatles, the Rolling Stones, the Eagles, the Doobie Brothers, Jefferson Airplane, Willie Nelson, Buddy Rich, Country Joe & the Fish, Joe Walsh, David Carradine, Ryan O'Neal, David Bowie, Iggy Pop, Lola Falana, Neil Diamond, Hunter Thompson, Linda Blair, Peter Tosh and the Grateful Dead.

Of course, smoking marijuana only enhances creativity for some and not for others.

But throughout history, various prohibition and "temperance" groups have attempted and occasionally succeeded in banning the preferred relaxational substances of others, like alcohol, tobacco or cannabis.

Abraham Lincoln responded to this kind of repressive mentality in December, 1840, when he said:

"Prohibition...goes beyond the bounds of reason in that it attempts to control a man's appetite by legislation and makes a crime out of things that are not crimes.... A prohibition law strikes a blow at the very principles upon which our government was founded."

IN CONCLUSION,

We must reiterate our original premise with our challenge to the world to prove us wrong:

1. Top of male plant in flower
2. Top of female plant in fruit
3. Seedling
4. Leaflet from a large leaf
5. Portion of a staminate in florescence, with buds and mature male flower
6. female flowers, with stigmas protruding from hairy bract
7. Fruit enclosed in persistent hairy bract
8. Fruit, lateral view
9. Fruit, end view
10. Glandular hair with multicellular stalk
11. Glandular hair with short, one-celled invisible stalk
12. Non glandular hair containing a cystolith.

Cannabis sativa L.

Drawing by E.W. Smith

If all fossil fuels and their derivatives, as well as the deforestation of trees for paper and agriculture, are banned from use in order to save the planet and reverse the greenhouse effect:

Then there is only one known renewable natural resource able to provide the overall majority of our paper, textiles and food, meet all the world's transportation, home and industrial energy needs, to reduce pollution, rebuild the soil and clean the atmosphere—all at the same time—our old stand-by that did it all before: Cannabis Hemp ...Marijuana!

Footnotes:

1. Oxford English Dictionary; Encyclopaedia Brittanica, 11th edition, 1910; U.S.D.A. film, *Hemp for Victory*, 1942.

2. Ibid.

3. Levi-Strauss & Company of San Francisco, CA, author's personal communication with Gene McClaine, 1985.

4. Ye Olde Spinning Jennys and Wheels were principally used for fiber in this order: cannabis hemp, flax, wool, cotton, and so forth.

5. Frazier, Jack, *The Marijuana Farmers*, Solar Age Press, New Orleans, LA, 1974; U.S. Library of Congress; National Archives; U.S. Mint; etc.

6. Adams, James T., editor, *Album of American History*, Charles Scribner's Sons, NY, 1944, pg. 116.

7. Frazier, Jack, *The Marijuana Farmers*, Solar Age Press, New Orleans, LA, 1974; U.S. Library of Congress; National Archives.

8. Sloman, Larry, *Reefer Madness*, Grove Press, New York, NY, 1979, pg. 72.

9. Bonnie, Richard and Whitebread, Charles, *The Marijuana Conviction*, Univ. of Virginia Press, 1974.

WHY NOT USE HEMP TO REVERSE THE GREENHOUSE EFFECT & SAVE THE WORLD?

In early 1989, Jack Herer and Maria Farrow put this question to Steve Rawlings, the highest ranking officer in the U.S. Department of Agriculture who was in charge of reversing the Greenhouse Effect, at the USDA world research facility in Beltsville, MD.

First, we introduced ourselves and told him we were writing for Green political party newspapers. Then we asked Rawlings, "If you could have any choice, what would be the ideal way to stop or reverse the Greenhouse Effect?"

He said, "Stop cutting down trees and stop using fossil fuels."

"Well, why don't we?"

"There's no viable substitute for wood for paper, or for fossil fuels."

"Why don't we use an annual plant for paper and for biomass to make fuel?"

"Well, that would be ideal," he agreed. "Unfortunately there is nothing you can use that could produce enough materials."

"Well, what would you say if there *was* such a plant that could substitute for all wood pulp paper, all fossil fuels, would make most of our fibers naturally, make everything from dynamite to plastic, grows in all 50 states and that one acre of it would replace 4.1 acres of trees, and that if you used about 6% of the U.S. land to raise it as an energy crop—even on our marginal lands, this plant would produce all 75 quadrillion billion BTUs needed to run America each year? Would that help save the planet?"

"That would be ideal. But there is no such plant."

"We think there is."

"Yeah? What is it?"

"Hemp."

"Hemp!" he mused for a moment. "I never would have thought of it.... You know, I think you're right. Hemp could be the plant that could do it. Wow! That's a great idea!"

We were excited as we outlined this information and delineated the potential of hemp for paper, fiber, fuel, food, paint, etc., and how it could be applied to balance the world's ecosystems and restore the atmosphere's oxygen balance with almost no disruption of the standard of living to which most Americans have become accustomed.

In essence, Rawlings agreed that our information was probably correct and could very well work.

He said, "It's a wonderful idea, and I think it might work. But, of course, you can't use it."

"You're kidding?" We responded. "Why not?"

"Well, Mr. Herer, did you know that hemp is also marijuana?"

"Yes, of course I know, I've been writing about it for about 40 hours a week for the past 17 years."

"Well, you know marijuana's illegal, don't you? You can't use it."

"Not even to save the world?"

"No. It's illegal," he sternly informed me. "You cannot use something illegal."

"Not even to save the world?" we asked, stunned.

"No, not even to save the world. It's illegal. You can't use it. Period."

"Don't get me wrong. It's a great idea," he went on, "But they'll never let you do it."

"Why don't you go ahead and tell the Secretary of Agriculture that a crazy man from California gave you documentation that showed that hemp might be able to save the planet and that your first reaction is that he might be right and it needs some serious study. What would he say?"

"Well, I don't think I'd be here very long after I did that. After all, I'm an officer of the government."

"Well, why not call up the information on your computer at your own USDA library. That's where we got the information in the first place."

He said, "I can't sign out that information."

"Well, why not? We did."

"Mr. Herer, you're a citizen. You can sign out for anything you want. But *I* am an officer of the Department of Agriculture. Someone's going to want to know why I want all this information. And then I'll be gone."

Finally, we agreed to send him all the information we got from the USDA library, if he would just look at it.

He said he would, but when we called back a month later, he said that he still had not opened the box that we sent him and that he would be sending it back to us unopened because he did not want to be responsible for the information now that the Bush administration was replacing him with their own man.

We asked him if he would pass on the information to his successor, and he replied, "Absolutely not."

In May, 1989, we had virtually the same conversation and result with his cohort, Dr. Gary Evans of the U.S. Department of Agriculture and Science, the man in charge of stopping the global warming trend.

In the end, he said, "If you really want to save the planet with hemp, then you (hemp/marijuana activists) would find a way to grow it without the narcotic (sic.) top—and then you can use it."

This is the kind of frightened (and frightening) irresponsibility we're up against in our government.

Chapter Three:

FEBRUARY 1938: POPULAR MECHANICS MAGAZINE:

"NEW BILLION DOLLAR CROP"

FEBRUARY 1938: MECHANICAL ENGINEERING MAGAZINE:

"THE MOST PROFITABLE & DESIREABLE CROP THAT CAN BE GROWN"

Modern technology was about to be applied to hemp production, making it the number one agricultural resource in America. Two of the most respected and influential journals in the nation, Popular Mechanics and Mechanical Engineering, forecast a bright future for American hemp. Thousands of new products creating millions of new jobs heralded the end of the Great Depression. Instead hemp was persecuted, outlawed and forgotten at the bidding of W. R. Hearst who branded hemp the "Mexican killer weed, marijuana."

As early as 1901 and continuing to 1937, the U.S. Department of Agriculture repeatedly predicted that, once machinery capable of harvesting, stripping and separating the fiber from the pulp was invented or engineered, hemp would again be America's Number One farm crop.

This was reaffirmed in the popular press when **Popular Mechanics** published its February, 1938 article "Billion-Dollar Crop." The first reproduction of this article in over 50 years was in the original edition of this book. The article is reproduced here exactly as it was printed in 1938.

Because of the printing deadline, this article was prepared in the Spring of 1937, when cannabis hemp for fiber, paper, dynamite and oil, was still legal to grow and was, in fact, an incredibly fast growing industry.

Also reprinted on these pages is an excerpt from the **Mechanical Engineering** article about hemp, published the same month. It originated as a paper presented a year earlier at the Feb. 26, 1937 Agricultural Processing Meeting of the American Society of Mechanical Engineers, New Brunswick, New Jersey.

Reports from the USDA during the 1930s and Congressional testimony in 1937 showed that cultivated hemp acreage had been doubling in size in America almost every year from the time it hit its bottom acreage, 1930—when 1,000 acres were planted in the U.S.—to 1937—when 14,000 acres were cultivated—with plans to continue to *double* that acreage annually in the forseeable future.

KENTUCKY HEMP FIELDS

For an incredible delineation of hemp's role during the period 1782-1900, read *The Reign of Law: A Tale of the Kentucky Hemp Fields*, James Lane Allen, published by McMillan & Co., 1900.*

* Pay special attention to pages 1 through 23 and the picture on page 25. These pages are entirely reproduced in our appendix.

As you will see in these articles, the newly mechanized cannabis hemp industry was in its infancy, but well on its way to again becoming America's largest agriculture crop. And, in light of subsequent developments (e.g., biomass energy technology, etc.), we now know that hemp is potentially the world's largest industry and most important ecological tool.

The Popular Mechanics article was the very first time in American history that the term "billion-dollar"* was ever applied to any U.S. agricultural crop.

* Equivalent to $20-$40 billion now.

Experts today conservatively estimate that, once fully restored in America, hemp industries will generate $500 billion to a trillion dollars per year, and will save the planet and civilization from fossil fuels and their derivatives—and from deforestation!

If Anslinger, DuPont, Hearst and their paid-for (know it or not) politicians had not outlawed hemp—under the pretext of marijuana (see chapter 4, "Last Days of Legal Cannabis")—and suppressed hemp knowledge from our schools, researchers and even scientists, the glowing predictions in these articles would already have come true by now—and more benefits than anyone could then envision—as new technologies continue to develop.

As one colleague so aptly put it:

"These articles were the last honest word spoken on hemp's behalf for over 40 years...."

POPULAR MECHANICS
February, 1938

NEW

AMERICAN farmers are promised a new cash crop with an annual value of several hundred million dollars, all because a machine has been invented which solves a problem more than 6,000 years old. It is hemp, a crop that will not compete with other American products. Instead, it will displace imports of raw material and manufactured products produced by underpaid coolie and peasant labor and it will provide thousands of jobs for American workers throughout the land.

The machine which makes this possible is designed for removing the fiber-bearing cortex from the rest of the stalk, making hemp fiber available for use without a prohibitive amount of human labor.

Hemp is the standard fiber of the world. It has great tensile strength and durability. It is used to produce more than 5,000 textile products, ranging from rope to fine laces, and the woody "hurds" remaining after the fiber has been removed contain more than seventy-seven per cent cellulose, and can be used to produce more than 25,000 products, ranging from dynamite to Cellophane.

Machines now in service in Texas, Illinois, Minnesota and other states are producing fiber at a manufacturing cost of half a cent a pound, and are finding a profitable market for the rest of the stalk. Machine operators are making a good profit in com-

Top, sailing the seas with sails and rope made of hemp. Bottom, hemp fiber being delivered from machine ready for baling. Pile of pulverized hurds beside machine is seventy-seven per cent cellulose

238

BILLION-DOLLAR CROP

petition with coolie-produced foreign fiber while paying farmers fifteen dollars a ton for hemp as it comes from the field.

From the farmers' point of view, hemp is an easy crop to grow and will yield from three to six tons per acre on any land that will grow corn, wheat, or oats. It has a short growing season, so that it can be planted after other crops are in. It can be grown in any state of the union. The long roots penetrate and break the soil to leave it in perfect condition for the next year's crop. The dense shock of leaves, eight to twelve feet above the ground, chokes out weeds. Two successive crops are enough to reclaim land that has been abandoned because of Canadian thistles or quack grass.

Under old methods, hemp

(Continued to page 144A)

Top, modern version of linen duster made from hemp. Bottom, harvesting hemp with a grain binder. Hemp grows luxuriously in Texas

239

New Billion-Dollar Crop

(Continued from page 239)

was cut and allowed to lie in the fields for weeks until it "retted" enough so the fibers could be pulled off by hand. Retting is simply rotting as a result of dew, rain and bacterial action. Machines were developed to separate the fibers mechanically after retting was complete, but the cost was high, the loss of fiber great, and the quality of fiber comparatively low. With the new machine, known as a decorticator, hemp is cut with a slightly modified grain binder. It is delivered to the machine where an automatic chain conveyor feeds it to the breaking arms at the rate of two or three tons per hour. The hurds are broken into fine pieces which drop into the hopper, from where they are delivered by blower to a baler or to truck or freight car for loose shipment. The fiber comes from the other end of the machine, ready for baling.

From this point on almost anything can happen. The raw fiber can be used to produce strong twine or rope, woven into burlap, used for carpet warp or linoleum backing or it may be bleached and refined, with resinous by-products of high commercial value. It can, in fact, be used to replace the foreign fibers which now flood our markets.

Thousands of tons of hemp hurds are used every year by one large powder company for the manufacture of dynamite and TNT. A large paper company, which has been paying more than a million dollars a year in duties on foreign-made cigarette papers, now is manufacturing these papers from American hemp grown in Minnesota. A new factory in Illinois is producing fine bond papers from hemp. The natural materials in hemp make it an economical source of pulp for any grade of paper manufactured, and the high percentage of alpha cellulose promises an unlimited supply of raw material for the thousands of cellulose products our chemists have developed.

It is generally believed that all linen is produced from flax. Actually, the majority comes from hemp—authorities estimate that more than half of our imported linen fabrics are manufactured from hemp fiber. Another misconception is that burlap is made from hemp. Actually, its source is usually jute, and practically all of the burlap we use is woven by laborers in India who receive only four cents a day. Binder twine is usually made from sisal which comes from Yucatan and East Africa.

All of these products, now imported, can be produced from home-grown hemp. Fish nets, bow strings, canvas, strong rope, overalls, damask tablecloths, fine linen garments, towels, bed linen and thousands of other everyday items can be grown on American farms. Our imports of foreign fabrics and fibers average about $200,000,000 per year; in raw fibers alone we imported over $50,000,000 in the first six months of 1937. All of this income can be made available for Americans.

The paper industry offers even greater possibilities. As an industry it amounts to over $1,000,000,000 a year, and of that eighty per cent is imported. But hemp will produce every grade of paper, and government figures estimate that 10,000 acres devoted to hemp will produce as much paper as 40,000 acres of average pulp land.

One obstacle in the onward march of hemp is the reluctance of farmers to try new crops. The problem is complicated by the need for proper equipment a reasonable distance from the farm. The machine cannot be operated profitably unless there is enough acreage within driving range and farmers cannot find a profitable market unless there is machinery to handle the crop. Another obstacle is that the blossom of the female hemp plant contains marijuana, a narcotic, and it is impossible to grow hemp without producing the blossom. Federal regulations now being drawn up require registration of hemp growers, and tentative proposals for preventing narcotic production are rather stringent.

However, the connection of hemp as a crop and marijuana seems to be exaggerated. The drug is usually produced from wild hemp or locoweed which can be found on vacant lots and along railroad tracks in every state. If federal regulations can be drawn to protect the public without preventing the legitimate culture of hemp, this new crop can add immeasurably to American agriculture and industry.

¶Popular Mechanics Magazine can furnish the name and address of the maker of, or dealer in, any article described in its pages. If you wish this information, write to the Bureau of Information, inclosing a stamped, self-addressed envelope.

MECHANICAL ENGINEERING
February 26, 1937

"Flax and Hemp: From the Seed to the Loom" was published in the February 1938 issue of Mechanical Engineering magazine. It was originally presented at the Agricultural Processing Meeting of the American Society of Mechanical Engineers in New Brunswick, NJ of February 26, 1937 by the Process Industries Division.

FLAX AND HEMP: FROM THE SEED TO THE LOOM   by George A. Lower

THE MOST PROFITABLE AND DESIREABLE CROP THAT CAN BE GROWN

This country imports practically all of its fibers except cotton. The Whitney gin, combined with improved spinning methods, enabled this country to produce cotton goods so far below the cost of linen that linen manufacture practically ceased in the United States. We cannot produce our fibers at less cost than can other farmers of the world. Aside from the higher cost of labor, we do not get as large production. For instance, Yugoslavia, which has the greatest fiber production per acre in Europe, recently had a yield of 883 lbs. Comparable figures for other countries are Argentina, 749 lbs.; Egypt 616 lbs.; and India, 393 lbs.; while the average yield in this country is 383 lbs.

To meet world competition profitably, we must improve our methods all the way from the field to the loom.

Flax is still pulled up by the roots, retted in a pond, dried in the sun, broken until the fibers separate from the wood, then spun, and finally bleached with lye from wood ashes, potash from burned seaweed, or lime. Improvements in tilling, planting, and harvesting mechanisms have materially helped the large farmers and, to a certain degree, the smaller ones, but the processes from the crop to the yarn are crude, wasteful, land injurious. Hemp, the strongest of the vegetable fibers, gives the greatest production per acre and requires the least attention. It not only requires no weeding, but also kills off all the weeds and leaves the soil in splendid condition for the following crop. This, irrespective of its own monetary value, makes it a desirable crop to grow.

In climate and cultivation, its requisites are similar to flax and, like flax, should be harvested before it is too ripe. The best time is when the lower leaves on the stalk wither and the flowers shed their pollen.

Like flax, the fibers run out where leaf stems are on the stalks and are made up of laminated fibers that are held to-

gether by pectose gums. When chemically treated like flax, hemp yields a beautiful fiber so closely resembling flax that a high-power microscope is needed to tell the difference -- and only then because in hemp, some of the ends are split. Wetting a few strands of fiber and holding them suspended will definitely identify the two because, upon drying, flax will be found to turn to the right or

Early International Harvester mule drawn mechanical hemp reaper provided a tremendous savings in human labor. Mechanical harvesting was a major step in making American hemp a competitive natural fiber.

clockwise, and hemp to the left or counterclockwise.

Before [World War I], Russia produced 400,000 tons of hemp, all of which is still hand-broken and hand-scutched. They now produce half that quantity and use most of it themselves, as also does Italy from whom we had large importations.

In this country, hemp, when planted one bu. per acre, yields about three tons of dry straw per acre. From 15 to 20 percent of this is fiber, and 80 to 85 percent is woody material. The rapidly growing market for cellulose and wood flour for plastics gives good reason to believe that this hitherto wasted material may prove sufficiently profitable to pay for the crop, leaving the cost of the fiber sufficiently low to compete with 500,000 tons of hard fiber now imported annually.

Hemp being from two to three times as strong as any of the hard fibers, much less weight is required to give the same yardage. For instance, sisal binder twine of 40-lb. tensile strength runs 450 ft. to the lb. A better twine made

MECHANICAL ENGINEERING
February 26, 1937

of hemp would run 1280 ft. to the lb. Hemp is not subject to as many kinds of deterioration as are the tropical fibers, and none of them lasts as long in either fresh or salt water.

While the theory in the past has been that straw should be cut when the pollen starts to fly, some of the best fiber handled by Minnesota hemp people was heavy with seed. This point should be proved as soon as possible by planting a few acres and then harvesting the first quarter when the pollen is flying, the second and third a week or ten days apart, and the last when the seed is fully matured. These four lots should be kept separate and scutched and processed separately to detect any difference in the quality and quantity of the fiber and seed.

International hemp harvester cut the hemp and laid it out in thin layered rows to begin the natural dew retting process near Mason City, Iowa.

Several types of machine are available in this country for harvesting hemp. One of these was brought out several years ago by the International Harvester Company. Recently, growers of hemp in the Middle West have rebuilt regular grain binders for this work. This rebuilding is not particularly expensive and the machines are reported to give satisfactory service.

Degumming of hemp is analogous to the treatment given flax. The shards probably offer slightly more resistance to digestion. On the other hand, they break down readily upon completion of the digestion process. And excellent fiber can, therefore, be obtained from hemp also. Hemp, when treated by a known chemical process, can be spun on cotton, wool, and worsted machinery, and has as much absorbance and wearing quality as linen.

Several types of machine for scutching the hemp stalks are also on the market. Scutch mills formerly operating in Illinois and Wisconsin used the system that consisted of a set of eight pairs of fluted rollers, through which the dried straw was passed to break up the woody portion. From there, the fiber with adhering shards -- or hurds, as they are called -- was transferred by an operator to an endless-chain conveyor. This carries the fiber past two revolving single drums in tandem, all having beating blades on their periphery, which beat off most of the hurds as well as the fibers that do not run the full length of the stalks. The proportion of line fiber to tow is 50 percent each. Tow or short tangled fiber then goes to a vibrating cleaner that shakes out some of the hurds. In Minnesota and Illinois, another type has been tried out. This machine consists of a feeding table upon which the stalks are placed horizontally. Conveyor chains carry the stalks along until they are grasped by a clamping chain that grips them and carries them through half of the machine.

A pair of intermeshing lawnmower-type beaters are placed at a 45-degree angle to the feeding chain and break the hemp stalks over the sharp edge of a steel plate, the object being to break the woody portion of the straw and whip the hurds from the fiber. On the other side and slightly beyond the first set of lawnmower beaters is another set, which is placed 90-degrees from the first pair and whips out the hurds.

The first clamping chain transfers the stalks to another to scutch the fiber that was under the clamp at the beginning. Unfortunately, this type of scutcher makes even more tow than the so-called Wisconsin type. This tow is difficult to reclean because the hurds are broken into long slivers that tenaciously adhere to the fiber.

Another type passes the stalks through a series of graduated fluted rollers. This breaks up the woody portion into hurds about 3/4 inch long, and the fiber then passes on through a series of reciprocating slotted plates working between stationary slotted plates.

Adhering hurds are removed from the fiber which continues on a conveyor to the baling press. Because no beating of the fiber against the grain occurs, this type of scutcher makes only line fiber. This is then processed by the same methods as those for flax.

Paint and lacquer manufacturers are interested in hempseed oil which is a good drying agent. When markets have been developed for the products now being wasted, seed and hurds, hemp will prove, both for the farmer and the public, the most profitable and desirable crop that can be grown, and one that can make American mills independent of importations.

Recent floods and dust storms have given warnings against the destruction of timber. Possibly, the hitherto waste products of flax and hemp may yet meet a good part of that need, especially in the plastic field which is growing by leaps and bounds.

THE MANY USES OF HEMP

The World's Most Valuable & Versatile Natural Resource

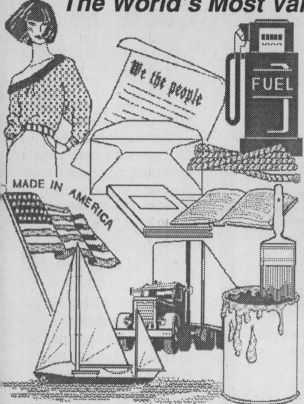

SEEDS FOR OIL & FOOD: Hemp seeds produce oil for cooking, lubrication, fuel, etc. Hemp seed is an excellent source of protein. Its leaves and flowers are also edible.

STEMS FOR FABRIC, FUEL, PAPER & COMMERCIAL USE. Hemp is dried and broken down into two parts: threadlike fibers and bits of "hurd," or pulp. Each of these products has its own distinct applications:

The fiber strands are spun into thread, which is either made into rope or woven into durable, high quality textiles and made into clothing, sails, fine linens and fabrics of all types and textures.

The fragments of dried stalk that remain are hurds—77% cellulose—that can be made into tree-free, dioxin-free paper; non-toxic paints and sealants; industrial fabrication materials; construction materials; plastics; and much, much more! Hemp is the best source of plant pulp for biomass fuel to make gas, charcoal, methanol, gasoline or even produce electricity.

MU9103

FOLIAGE FOR MEDICINE, FOOD & RELAXATION. Hemp has long-recognized medical value for easing pain, relieving stress and treating illnesses from glaucoma to asthma to nausea and beyond. Cannabis flowers and leaves are also smoked or eaten for many therapeutic, religious and relaxational purposes.

ROOTED IN AMERICA: Even hemp roots play an important role: they anchor and invigorate the soil to control erosion and mudslides. Hemp can save family farms, create jobs, reduce acid rain and chemical pollution, and reverse the Greenhouse effect.

UNITED STATES DEPARTMENT OF AGRICULTURE

BULLETIN No. 404

Contribution from the Bureau of Plant Industry
WM. A. TAYLOR, Chief

Washington, D.C.   PROFESSIONAL PAPER   October 14, 1916

HEMP HURDS AS PAPER-MAKING MATERIAL

By LYSTER H. DEWEY, *Botanist in Charge of Fiber-Plant Investigations*, and JASON L. MERRILL, *Paper-Plant Chemist, Paper-Plant Investigations*.

CONTENTS

In preparing the report on the manufacture of paper from hemp hurds it became evident that a short discussion of the agricultural aspects of this material should be included in the publication. Such an article was prepared, therefore, and the two reports are here presented together.

THE PRODUCTION AND HANDLING OF HEMP HURDS.

By LYSTER H. DEWEY, *Botanist in Charge of Fiber-Plant Investigations*

WHAT HEMP HURDS ARE.

The woody inner portion of the hemp stalk, broken into pieces and separated from the fiber in the processes of breaking and scutching, are called hemp hurds. These hurds correspond to shives in flax, but are much coarser and are usually softer in texture.

When the USDA published Bulletin 404 in 1916, it used for the first time hemp pulp paper (as opposed to hemp fiber paper) to demonstrate the outstanding qualities of using hemp hurds for pulp instead of using tree pulp; not only to reduce the cutting of trees but also to reduce the need for sulphuric acid compounds to break down the plant for the making of paper.

The frontal piece over the cover of the bulletin (reproduced above) tells you that the document is printed on hemp pulp paper, although the frontal piece itself was *not* printed on hemp pulp.

One acre of hemp equals 4.1 acres of forest land.

Cannabis Sativa (l.) at three months.

THE LAST DAYS OF LEGAL CANNABIS

As you now know, the industrial revolution of the 19th century was a setback for hemp in world commerce, due to the lack of mechanized harvesting and breaking technology needed for mass production. But this natural resource was far too valuable to be relegated to the back burner of history for very long.

By 1916, U.S.D.A. Bulletin 404 predicted that a decorticating and harvesting machine would be developed, and hemp would again be America's largest agricultural industry. In 1938, Popular Mechanics, Mechanical Engineering and others introduced a new generation of investors the first fully operational hemp decorticating devices; bringing us to this next bit of history:

BREAKTHROUGH IN PAPERMAKING

If hemp was legally cultivated using 20th Century chnology, it would be the single largest agricultur- crop in the United States and world today.

Popular Mechanics February 1938; Mechanical Engineering, bruary 1938; U.S. Department of Agriculture.)

In fact, when the preceeding two articles ere prepared early in 1937, hemp was ill legal to grow; and those who predict- l billions of dollars in new cannabis sinesses did not consider income from edicines, energy (fuel), food and paints hich would now add another trillion llars or more—about what oil brings 1991. Relaxational smoking would ld only a relatively minor amount to is figure.

he most important reason that the 38 magazine articles projected billions new income was hemp for "pulp paper" (as posed to fiber or rag paper). Other reasons re its fiber, seed and many other pulp uses.

his remarkable new hemp pulp technology for pa- rmaking was invented in 1916 by our own U.S. partment of Agriculture chief scientists, botanist ster Dewey and chemist Jason Merrill.

As the USDA bulletin suggested, this process had stay in the laboratory until the invention of decor- ating and harvesting machinery allowed for its onomical utilization.

Until this time, hemp paper had only been made m rags and stalk fibers while the fiber and cellu- e-rich hurds were burnt to fertilize the soil.

A PLAN TO SAVE OUR FORESTS

Some cannabis plant strains regularly reach tree-like heights of 20 feet or more in one growing season.

The new paper process used hemp "hurds"—77% of the hemp stalk's weight, which was then a wasted by-product of the fiber stripping process.

If the hemp pulp paper process of 1916 were in use today, it could replace 40 to 70% of all pulp paper, including corrugated boxes, computer printout paper and paper bags.

In 1916, USDA Bulletin No. 404 (see picture), reported that one acre of cannabis hemp, in annual rotation over a 20-year period, would produce as much pulp for paper as 4.1 acres of trees being cut down over the same 20-year period. This process would use only 1/4 to 1/7 as much polluting sulfur-based acid chemicals to break down the glue-like lignin that binds the fibers of the pulp, or even none at all using soda ash. The problem of dioxin contamination of rivers is avoided in the hemp paper making process, which does not need to use chlorine bleach (as the wood pulp paper making process requires) but instead safely substitutes hydrogen peroxide in the bleaching process.

All this lignin must be broken down to make pulp paper. Hemp pulp is only 4% lignin, while trees are 18-30% lignin. Thus hemp provides four times as much pulp with at least four to seven times less pollution (and yet, today is essentially illegal, as it has been for the last half-century).

As we have seen, this hemp pulp-paper potential depended on the invention and the engineering of new machines for stripping the hemp by modern technology. This would also lower demand for lumber and reduce the the cost of housing, while at the same time helping re-oxygenate the planet.[1]

As an example: If the new (1916) hemp pulp paper process were legal today, it would soon replace about 70% of all wood pulp paper, including computer printout paper, corrugated boxes and paper bags.

Pulp paper made from rags or machined from 60% to 100% hemp hurds is stronger and more flexible than paper made from wood pulp and makes a less expensive, more ecological paper—and a better one.

(Dewey & Merrill, *Bulletin #404*, U.S.D.A., 1916; New Scientist, 1980; Kimberly Clark production from its giant French hemp-fiber paper subsidiary De Mauduit, 1937 through 1984.)

CONSERVATION & SOURCE REDUCTION

Source reduction is a cost-cutting waste control method often called for by environmentalists: reduction of the source of pollution, usually from manufacturing with petrochemicals or their derivatives.

Whether the source of pollution is CFCs (chloro-flouro-carbons) from spray cans, computers and refrigeration, or tritium and plutonium produced for military uses, or the sulfuric acids used by paper-makers, reducing the source of pollution is the goal.

In the supermarket when you are asked to choose paper or plastic for your bags, you are faced with an environmental dilemma; paper from trees that were cut, or plastic bags made from fossil fuel and chemicals. With a third choice available—hemp hurd paper —one could choose a biodegradable, durable paper from an annually renewable source, the hemp plant.

The environmental advantages of harvesting hemp annually—leaving the trees in the ground!—make papermaking from hemp hurds critical for source reduction, along with using hemp to replace fossil fuel as an energy source.

A CONSPIRACY TO WIPE OUT THE NATURAL COMPETITION

When mechanical hemp fiber stripping machines and machines to conserve hemp's high-cellulose pulp finally became state-of-the-art, available and affordable in the mid-1930s, the enormous timber acreage and businesses of the Hearst Paper Manufacturing Division, Kimberly Clark (USA), St. Regis—and virtually all other timber, paper and large newspaper holding companies—stood to lose billions of dollars and perhaps go bankrupt.

Coincidentally, DuPont had just patented processes to make plastics from oil and coal, as well as new sul-

fate/sulfite processes to make paper from wood pulp in 1937 which would, according to their own corporate records and historians,* account for over 80% of all its railroad carloadings for the next 50 years.

* Author's research & communications with DuPont, 1985.

The environmental advantages of harvesting hemp annually—leaving the trees in the ground!—make papermaking from hemp hurds critical for source reduction.

If hemp had not been made illegal, 80% of DuPont business would never have come to be; nor would the great majority of the pollution which has been inflicted on our Northwestern and Southeastern rivers have ever occurred.

In an open marketplace, hemp would have saved the majority of America's vital family farms and would probably have boosted their numbers, despite the Great Depression of the 1930s.

Competing against the environmentally-sane hemp-paper and natural plastic technology would have jeopardized the lucrative financial schemes of Hearst, DuPont and DuPont's chief financial backer, Andrew Mellon of the Mellon Bank of Pittsburgh.

"SOCIAL REORGANIZATION"

A series of secret meetings were held.

ANNUAL REPORT 1937

Mellon, in his role as Hoover's Secretary of the Treasury, in 1930 appointed his future nephew-in-law Harry J. Anslinger to be head of the newly re-organized Federal Bureau of Narcotics and Dangerous Drugs (FBNDD), a post he held for the next 31 years.

These industrial barons and financiers knew that machinery to cut, bale, decorticate (to separate the fiber from the high-cellulose hurd), and process hemp into paper or plastics was becoming available in the mid-1930s. Cannabis hemp would have to go.

In DuPont's 1937 Annual Report to its stockholders, the company strongly urged action (investment) despite the economic chaos of the Great Depression. DuPont was anticipating "radical changes" from "the revenue raising power of government...converted into

MAN-MADE FIBER ...
THE TOXIC ALTERNATIVE TO NATURAL FIBERS.

The late 1920s and 1930s saw continuing consolidation of power into the hands of a few large steel, oil and chemical (munitions) companies. The U.S. federal government placed much of the textile production for the domestic economy in the hands of their chief munitions maker, DuPont.

The processing of nitrating cellulose into explosives is very similar to the process for nitrating cellulose into synthetic fibers and plastics. Rayon, the first synthetic fiber, is simply stabilized guncotton, or nitrated cloth, the basic explosive of the 19th century.

"Synthetic plastics find application in fabricating a wide variety of articles, many of which in the past were made from natural products," beamed Lammot DuPont (Popular Mechanics, June 1939, pg. 805).

"Consider our natural resources," the president of DuPont continued, "The chemist has aided in conserving natural resources by developing synthetic products to supplement or wholly replace natural products."

DuPont's scientists were the world's leading researchers into the processes of nitrating cellulose and were in fact the largest processor of cellulose in the nation in this era.

The February, 1938 Popular Mechanics article stated "Thousands of tons of hemp hurds are used every year by one large powder company for the manufacture of dynamite and TNT." History shows that Dupont had largely cornered the market in explosives by buying up and consolidating the smaller blasting companies in the late 1800s. By 1902 they controlled about two-thirds of industry output.

They were the largest powder company, supplying 40% of the munitions for the allies in WWI. As cellulose and fiber researchers, DuPont's chemists knew hemp's true value better than anyone else. The value of hemp goes far beyond line fibers; although recognized for linen, canvas, netting and cordage, these long fibers are only 20% of the hemp-stalks' weight. 80% of the hemp is in the 77% cellulose hurd, and this was the most abundant, cleanest resource of cellulose (fiber) for paper, plastics and even rayon.

The empirical evidence in this book shows that the federal government—through the 1937 Marijuana Tax Act—allowed this munitions maker to supply synthetic fibers for the domestic economy without competition. The proof of a successful conspiracy among these corporate and governing interests is simply this: In 1991 DuPont was still the largest producer of man-made fibers, while no citizen has legally harvested a single acre of textile grade hemp in over 50 years.

An almost unlimited tonnage of natural fiber and cellulose would have become available to the American farmer in 1937, the year DuPont patented nylon and the polluting wood-pulp paper sulfide process. All of hemp's potential value was lost.

Simple plastics of the early 1900s were made of nitrated cellulose, directly related to DuPont's munitions-making processes. Celluloid, acetate and rayon were the simple plastics of that era, and hemp was well known to cellulose researchers as the premier resource for this new industry to use. Worldwide, the raw material of simple plastics, rayon and paper could be best supplied by hemp hurds.

Nylon fibers were developed between 1926-1936 by the noted Harvard chemist Wallace Carothers, working from German patents. These polyamides are long fibers based on observed natural products. Carothers, supplied with an open-ended research grant from DuPont, made a comprehensive study of natural cellulose fibers. He duplicated natural fibers in his labs and polyamides—long fibers of a specific chemical process—were developed.

Coal tar and petroleum based chemicals were employed, and different devices, spinnerets and processes were patented. This new type of textile, nylon, was to be controlled from the raw material stage, as coal, to the completed product; a patented chemical product. The chemical company centralized the production and profits of the new "miracle" fiber.

The introduction of nylon, the introduction of high-volume machinery to separate hemp's long fiber from the cellulose hurd, and the outlawing of hemp as "marijuana" all occurred simultaneously.

The new man-made fibers (MMF's) can best be described as war material. The fiber making process has become one based on big factories, smokestacks, coolants and hazardous chemicals, rather than one of stripping out the abundant, naturally available fibers.

Coming from a history of making explosives and munitions, the old "chemical dye plants" now produce hosiery, mock linens, mock canvas, latex paint and synthetic carpets. Their polluting factories make imitation leather, upholstery and wood surfaces, while an important part of the natural cycle stands outlawed.

The standard fiber of world history, America's traditional crop, hemp, could provide our textiles, paper and be the premier source for cellulose. The war industries—DuPont, Allied Chemical, Monsanto, etc.,—are protected from competition by the marijuana laws. They make war on the natural cycle and the common farmer.

—*Shan Clark*

Sources:

Encyclopedia of Textiles 3rd Edition by the editors of American Fabrics and Fashions Magazine, William C. Legal, Publisher Prentice-Hall, Inc. Englewood Cliffs, N.J. 1980; *The Emergence of Industrial America Strategic Factors in American Economic Growth Since 1870*, Peter George State University, NY; DuPont (a corporate autobiography published periodically by E.I. DuPont De Nemours and Co., Inc. Wilmington, Del.); *The Blasting Handbook*, E.I. DuPont De Nemours & Co. Inc., Wilmington, DE; *Mechanical Engineering Magazine*, Feb. 1938; *Popular Mechanics*, Feb. 1938; *Journal of Applied Polymer Science*, Vol. 47, 1984; *Polyamides, the Chemistry of Long Molecules* (author unknown) U.S. Patent #2,071,250 (Feb. 16, 1937), W.H Carothers., *DuPont Dynasties*, Jerry Colby; The American Peoples Encyclopedia, the Sponsor Press, Chicago, 1953.

an instrument for forcing acceptance of sudden new ideas of industrial and *social* reorganization." (Our emphasis.)*

* (DuPont Company, annual report, 1937.)

In *The Marijuana Conviction* (U. of Virginia press, 1974), Richard Bonnie and Charles Whitebread II detailed this process:

"By the fall of 1936, Herman Oliphant (general counsel to the Treasury Department) had decided to employ the taxing power [of the federal government], but in a statute modeled after the National Firearms Act and wholly unrelated to the 1914 Harrison [narcotics] Act. Oliphant himself was in charge of preparing the bill. Anslinger directed his army to turn its campaign toward Washington.

"The key departure of the marijuana tax scheme from that of the Harrison Act is the notion of the prohibitive tax. Under the Harrison Act, a non-medical user could not legitimately buy or possess narcotics.

"To the dissenters in the Supreme Court decisions upholding the act, this clearly demonstrated that Congress' motive was to prohibit conduct rather than raise revenue. So in the National Firearms Act, designed to prohibit traffic in machine guns, Congress "permitted" anyone to buy a machine gun, but required him to pay a $200 transfer tax and carry out the purchase on an order form.*

"The Firearms Act, passed in June 1934, was the first act to hide Congress' motives behind a "prohibitive" tax. The Supreme Court unanimously upheld the anti-machine gun law on March 29, 1937. Oliphant had undoubtedly been awaiting the Court's decision, and the Treasury Department introduced its marihuana tax bill two weeks later, April 14, 1937."

Thus, DuPont's decision to invest in new technologies based on "forcing acceptance of sudden new ideas of industrial and social reorganization" makes sense.

* About $4,000 in 1991 dollars.

A QUESTION OF MOTIVE

This prospect was alluded to during the 1937 Senate hearings by Matt Rens, of Rens Hemp Company:

Mr. Rens: Such a tax would put all small producers out of the business of growing hemp, and the proportion of small producers is considerable... The real purpose of this bill is not to raise money, is it?

Senator Brown: Well, we're sticking to the proposition that it is.

Mr. Rens: It will cost a million.

Senator Brown: Thank you. (Witness dismissed.)

HEARST, HIS HATRED & HYSTERICAL LIES

Concern about the effects of hemp smoke had already led to two major governmental studies. The British governor of India released the *Report of the Indian Hemp Drugs Commission 1893-1894* on heavy bhang smokers in the subcontinent.

And in 1930, the U.S. government sponsored the Siler Commission study on the effects of off-duty smoking of marijuana by American servicemen in Panama. Both reports concluded that marijuana was not a problem and recommended that no criminal penalties apply to its use.

In early 1937, Assistant U.S. Surgeon General Walter Treadway told the Cannabis advisory subcommittee of the League of Nations that, "It may be taken for a relatively long time without social or emotional breakdown. Marihuana is habit-forming... in the same sense as...sugar or coffee."

But other forces were at work. The war fury that led to the Spanish American war in 1898 was ignited and fanned by William Randolph Hearst through his nationwide newspaper chains, marking the beginning of "yellow journalism"* as a force in American politics.

* Webster's dictionary defines "yellow journalism" as the use of cheaply sensational or unscrupulous methods in newspapers and other media to attract or influence the readers.

In the 1920s and 30s, Hearst's newspaper chain led the deliberate new yellow journalism campaign to have hemp outlawed. From 1916 to 1937, as an example, the story of a car accident in which a marijuana cigarette was found would dominate the headlines for weeks, while alcohol-related car accidents (which outnumbered marijuana-connected accidents by more than 1,000 to 1) made only the back pages.

This same theme of marijuana-related car accidents was burned into the minds of Americans over and over again (1936-1938) by showing marijuana related car accident headlines in movies such as "Reefer Madness" and "Marijuana— Assassin of Youth."

BIGOTRY AND APARTHEID

Starting with the 1898 Spanish American War, the Hearst newspaper had denounced Spaniards, Mexican-Americans and Latinos.

After the seizure of 800,000 acres of Hearst's prime Mexican timberland by the "marihuana" smoking army of Pancho Villa,* these slurs intensified.

* The song "La Cucaracha" tells the story of one of Villa's men looking for his stash of "marijuana por fumar!" (to smoke!)

Non-stop for the next for three decades, Hearst painted the picture of the lazy pot-smoking Mexican—still one of our most insidious prejudices.

He also did a similar racist smear campaign against the "Yellow Peril" of the Chinese.

Hearst, through pervasive and repetitive use, brought the word 'marijuana' into English.

Hearst papers from 1910 to 1920 would say the majority of Negroes raping white women could be traced directly to cocaine. This continued for 10 years until Hearst decided it was not cocaine crazed Negroes raping white women—it was now marijuana crazed Negroes raping white women.

Hearst and other sensational tabloids ran hysterical headlines atop stories portraying Negroes and Mexicans as frenzied beasts under the influence of marijuana, who played anti-white "voodoo-satanic" music (jazz) and heaped disrespect and "viciousness" onto the predominantly white readership. This Jim Crow (apartheid) crime wave included: stepping on white men's shadows, looking white people directly in the eye for three seconds or more, looking at a white woman twice, laughing at a white person, etc.

For such "crimes," hundreds of thousands of Mexicans and Negroes spent, in aggregate, millions of years in prisons and on chain gangs, under brutal segregation laws in effect throughout the U.S. until the 1950s and 60s. Hearst, through pervasive and repetitive use, pounded the obscure Mexican slang word 'marijuana' into the English-speaking American consciousness. 'Hemp' was discarded. 'Cannabis,' the scientific term, was ignored or buried.

The actual Spanish word for hemp is 'cáñamo.' But using a Mexican Sonoran colloquialism—marijuana, often Americanized as 'marihuana'—guaranteed that no one would realize the world's chief natural medicine and premier industrial resource had been outflanked, outlawed and pushed out of the language.

THE PROHIBITIVE MARIJUANA TAX

In the secret Treasury Department meetings conducted between 1935 and 1937 prohibitive tax laws were drafted and strategies plotted. 'Marijuana,' was not banned outright: it called for an "Occupational excise tax upon dealers, and a transfer tax upon dealings in marijuana."

Importers, manufacturers, sellers and distributors had to register with the Secretary of the Treasury and pay the occupational tax. Transfers were taxed at $1 an ounce; $100 an ounce if the dealer was unregistered. Sales to an unregistered taxpayer were prohibitively taxed. At the time, "raw drug" cannabis sold for one dollar an ounce.[2] The year was 1937. New York State had exactly one narcotics officer.*

* Now it has a network of thousands of officers, agents, spies and paid informants—and 20 times the penal capacity.

A Roundup of Hearst's Hysterical Headlines:

This is what current hemp laws are based on.

MARIHUANA MAKES FIENDS OF BOYS IN 30 DAYS: HASHEESH GOADS USERS TO BLOOD-LUST

Physicians Called On to Urge Harding Bid All Nations Meet to Throttle Dope At Its Source; United States Laws Too Lenient

"The Federal Government, operating under the Harrison Act, and the amending Jones-Miller bill, employs one hundred and seventy-three narcotic enforcement agents. For their year's labors Congress appropriates the sum of $750,000. The country is divided into thirteen districts under as many district chiefs, and their agents must cover the country. It is a feeble appropriation and a woefully light brigade." —Sidney Howard in current issue of Hearst's International.

In the mid-1930s, Harry Anslinger went around the country giving his speeches to judges, police, unions, etc., on the evils of marijuana.

Circled here is one of his favorite marijuana metaphors, which he assured his naive, supportive audiences, was *not* an overstatement!

Crusade Against Marihuana

A NATIONWIDE crusade of American women against the menace of marihuana smoking has been launched by the Women's National Exposition of Arts and Industries in New York City.

H. J. Anslinger, head of the Federal Narcotics Bureau, explained to the group the urgent necessity of NATIONAL ACTION.

Declaring that marihuana smoking is "taking our youth like a furnace," Mr. Anslinger said:

"If the hideous monster Frankenstein came face to face with the monster marihuana he would drop dead of fright."

This is not overstatement.

Users of the marihuana weed are committing a large percentage of the atrocious crimes blotting the daily picture of American life.

It is reducing thousands of boys to CRIMINAL INSANITY.

And ONLY TWO STATES have effective laws to protect their people against it.

The marihuana weed, according to Mr. Anslinger, is grown, sold and USED in every State in the Union.

He charges, and rightly, that this is not a responsibility of one State, but OF ALL—and of the Federal Government.

American women, aroused to this DANGER, will GET ACTION.

In New York State organized groups of women are GETTING ACTION by demanding enactment of the McNaboe bill creating a State Narcotics Bureau. That Bureau would replace the existing one-man Narcotics Division, which is powerless to cope with the fact that eighty per cent of New York's criminals are narcotic addicts.

HOOVER SEES END OF JAZZ IN RADIO

Better Programmes Held Big Need at Present.

NEW DOPE LURE, MARIJUANA, HAS MANY VICTIMS

Dubbed "Silly Smoke," Winifred Black Says It Soon Becomes Habit

JAZZ DANCING SOON TO PASS, SAYS COOLIDGE

—President's Philosophical Address After Keynote Political Address

Hotel Clerk Identifies Marihuana Smoker As 'Wild Gunman' Arrested for Shootings

A hungry-looking transient picked off the street was linked Friday to the strange shootings two week ends in a row of two elderly hotel clerks.

He was identified as John Kelly Stephens, 30, a onetime state hospital inmate and admitted marihuana user.

He was held on two charges under $15,000 bail, assault with intent to rob and assault with intent to kill.

tives Bob McKeown and Joseph Biewitt. Stephens admitted he had been drinking heavily, used

marihuana, and could not remember all his actions.

A foot patrolman, Fred Sutterfield, plucked Stephens off the street Thursday afternoon as a likely suspect in the attempted holdup Wednesday night of Powers & Estes drug store, 724 S. W. Washington street.

Sutterfield told detectives he was convinced Stephens "fitted closely enough to be brought in and checked."

Witnesses 'Pick' Him

After the Supreme Court decision of March 29, 1937, upholding the prohibition of machine guns through taxation, Herman Oliphant made his move.

"This bill is too all inclusive. This bill is a world encircling measure. This bill brings the activities—the crushing of this great industry under the supervision of a bureau—which may mean its suppression."

On April 14, 1937 he introduced the bill directly to the House Ways and Means Committee instead of to other appropriate committees such as food and drug, agriculture, textiles, commerce, etc.

The reason may have been that Ways and Means is the only committee to send its bills directly to the House floor without the act having to be debated upon by other committees.

Ways and Means Chairman Robert L. Doughton,* a key DuPont ally, quickly rubber-stamped the secret Treasury bill and sent it sailing through Congress to the President.

* Per Jerry Colby, author of *DuPont Dynasties*, Lyle Steward, 1984.

"DID ANYONE CONSULT THE A.M.A.?"

However, even within his controlled Committee hearings, many expert witnesses spoke out against the passage of these *unusual* tax laws.

Dr. James Woodward, for instance, who was both a physician and an attorney, testified on behalf of the American Medical Association (AMA).

He said in effect, the whole fabric of federal testimony was tabloid sensationalism! No real testimony was being used in its passage! This law could possibly in ignorance deny the world a potential medicine, especially now that the medical world was just beginning to find which ingredients in cannabis were active.

He stated to the committee that the whole reason the AMA hadn't come out against the marijuana tax law sooner was that marijuana had been described in the press for 20 years as "killer weed from Mexico."

The AMA doctors had just realized, "two days before" these Spring, 1937 hearings, that the plant Congress intended to outlaw was known medically as cannabis—the benign substance used in scores of illnesses, for 100 years in America, with perfect safety.

"We cannot understand yet, Mr. Chairman, why this bill should have been prepared in secret for two years without any intimation, even to the profession," protested Woodward, "that it was being prepared."

He and the AMA* were quickly denounced by Anslinger and the entire congressional committee, and curtly excused.[3]

* The A.M.A. and the Roosevelt administration were strong antag nists in 1937.

When the Marijuana Tax Act bill came up for or report, discussion, and vote on the floor of Congres only one pertinent question was asked from the floo "Did anyone consult with the AMA and get thei opinion?"

Representative Vinson answering for the Ways an Means Committee replied, "Yes, we have, a D Wharton [mistaken pronunciation of Woodward?] an [the AMA] are in complete agreement!"

With this memorable lie, the bill passed, and be came law in September, 1937. A federal police forc was created, able to demand millions of wasted year in jail and even the deaths of individual Americans i order to save poison, polluting industries, and to rein force some white politicians' policies of racial hatred.

(Mikurya, Tod, M.D., *Marijuana Medical Papers*, 1972; Sloma Larry, *Reefer Madness*, Grove Press, 1979; Lindsmith, Alfred, *Th Addict and the Law*, Indiana U. Press; Bonnie & Whitebread; *Th Marijuana Conviction*, U. of VA Press; U.S. Cong. Records; et al.)

OTHERS SPOKE OUT, TOO

Also lobbying *against* the Tax Act with all its ene gy was the National Oil Seed Institute, representin the high quality machine lubrication producers a well as paint manufacturers. Speaking to the Hous Ways and Means Committee in 1937, their genera counsel, Ralph Loziers, testified eloquently about th hemp seed oil that was to be, in effect, outlawed:

"Respectable authorities tell us that in the Orient, a least 200 million people use this drug; and when u take into consideration that for hundreds, yes, thou sands of years, practically that number of people hav been using this drug. It is significant that in Asia an elsewhere in the Orient, where poverty stalks abroad o every hand and where they draw on all the plant re sources which a bountiful nature has given that domai —it is significant that none of those 200 million peopl has ever, since the dawn of civilization, been found us ing the seed of this plant or using the oil as a drug.

"Now, if there were any deleterious properties or prin ciples in the seed or oil, it is reasonable to suppose tha these Orientals, who have been reaching out in thei poverty for something that would satisfy their morbi appetite, would have discovered it....

"If the committee please, the hemp seed, or the seed o the cannabis sativa l., is used in all the Oriental nation and also in a part of Russia as food. It is grown in thei fields and used as oatmeal. Millions of people every da are using hemp seed in the Orient as food. They hav been doing that for many generations, especially in per ods of famine....

"The point I make is this—that this bill is too all in clusive. This bill is a world encircling measure. This bi brings the activities—the crushing of this great industr

nder the supervision of a bureau—which may mean its
uppression. Last year, there was imported into the U.S.
~2,813,000 pounds of hemp seed. In 1935 there was im-
~orted 116 million pounds...."

PROTECTING SPECIAL INTERESTS

Testimony before Congress in 1937 for the purpose
~f outlawing hemp consisted almost entirely of
Hearst's and other sensational and racist newspaper
articles read aloud by Harry J. Anslinger,* director of
~he Federal Bureau of Narcotics (FBN). (This agency
~as since evolved into the Drug Enforcement Admin-
~stration [DEA]).

* Harry J. Anslinger was director of the new Federal Bureau of
Narcotics from its inception in 1931 for the next 31 years, and was
~nly forced into retirement in 1962 by President John F. Kennedy af-
~er Anslinger tried to censor the publications and publishers of Pro-
~essor Alfred Lindsmith (_The Addict and the Law_, Washington Post,
~961) and to blackmail and harass his employer, Indiana University.

Anslinger had come under attack for racist remarks as early as
~934 by a U.S. senator from Pennsylvania, Joseph Guffey, for such
~hings as referring to "ginger-colored niggers" in letters circulated to
~is department heads on FBN stationery.

Prior to 1931, Anslinger was Assistant U.S. Com-
~issioner for Prohibition. Anslinger, remember, was
~and-picked to head the new Federal Bureau of
Narcotics by his uncle-in-law, Andrew Mellon,
Secretary of the Treasury under President Herbert
Hoover. The same Andrew Mellon was also the owner
and largest stockholder of the sixth largest bank (in
~937) in the United States, the Mellon Bank in
Pittsburgh, one of only two bankers for DuPont*
~rom 1928 to the present.

* DuPont has borrowed money from banks only twice in its entire
~70-year history, once to buy control of General Motors in the 1920s.
~ts banking business is the prestigious plum of the financial world.

In 1937, Anslinger testified before Congress saying,
"Marijuana is the most violence causing drug in the
~istory of mankind."

This, along with Anslinger's outrageous racist
statements and beliefs, was made to the Southern-
~ominated congressional committee and is now an
~mbarrassment to read in its entirety.

For instance, Anslinger kept a "Gore File," culled
~lmost entirely from Hearst and other sensational
~abloids—e.g., stories of axe murders, where one of
~he participants reportedly smoked a joint four days
~efore committing the crime.

Anslinger pushed on Congress as a factual state-
~ent that about 50% of all violent crime committed
~n the U.S. were committed by Spaniards, Mexican-
~mericans, Latin Americans, Filipinos, Negroes, and
~reeks and that these crimes could be traced directly
~o marijuana.

(From Anslinger's own records given to the University of Pennsyl-
~ania, Li Cata Murders, etc.)

Not one of Anslinger's marijuana "Gore Files" of the

1930s is believed to be true by scholars who have
painstakingly checked the facts.[4]

SELF-PERPETUATING LIES

In fact, F.B.I. statistics, had Anslinger bothered to
check, showed at least 65% to 75% of all murders in
the U.S. were then—and still are—alcohol related.

As an example of his racist statement, Anslinger
read into U.S. Congressional testimony (without objection) stories about "coloreds" with big lips, luring
white women with jazz music and marijuana.

He read an account of two Negro students at the
University of Minnesota doing this to a white coed
"with the result of pregnancy." The Congressmen of
1937 gasped at this and at the fact that this drug
seemingly caused white women to touch or even look
at a "Negro."

Virtually no one in America other than a handful of
rich industrialists and their hired cops knew that
their chief potential competitor—hemp—was being
outlawed under the name marijuana.

That's right. Marijuana was most likely just a pretext for hemp prohibition and economic suppression.

The water was further muddied by the confusion of
marijuana with Loco Weed (Jimson Weed). The situation was not clarified by the press, which continued
to print the disinformation into the 1960s.

And even at the dawn of the 1990s, the most ex-
travagant and ridiculous attacks on the hemp plant
draw national media attention—such as a study
widely reported by health journals in 1989 that
claimed marijuana smokers put on about a half a
pound of weight per day....

(American Health, July/August, 1989.)

Meanwhile, serious discussions of the health, civil
liberties and economic aspects of the hemp issue are
frequently dismissed as being nothing but an "excuse
so that people can smoke pot"—as if people need an
'excuse' to state the facts about any matter.

One must concede that, as a tactic, lying to the public about the beneficial nature of hemp and confusing
them as to its relationship with "marijuana" has
been very successful.

Footnotes

1. Dewey & Merrill, _Bulletin 404_, US Department of Agriculture
1916; "Billion-Dollar Crop," Popular Mechanics, 1938; U.S.
Agricultural Indexes, 1916 through 1982; New Scientist, November
13, 1980.

2. Uelmen & Haddox, _Drug Abuse and the Law_, 1974.

3. Bonnie, Richard & Whitebread, Charles, _The Marijuana
Conviction_, Univ. of Virginia Press, 1974; Congressional testimony,
1937 (See full testimony in Appendix); et al.

4. Sloman, Larry; _Reefer Madness_, 1979; Bonnie and Whitebread,
The Marijuana Conviction, Univ. of Virginia Press, 1974.

Chapter Five:

MARIJUANA PROHIBITION

Anslinger got his marijuana law...

"Should we believe self-serving, ever-growing drug enforcement/drug treatment bureaucrats, whose pay and advancement depends on finding more and more people to arrest and 'treat'?

"More Americans die in just one day in prisons, penetentiaries, jails and stockades than have ever died from marijuana throughout history. Who are they protecting? From what?"

—Fred Oerther, M.D., Portland Oregon, September, 1986.

MOVING TO CRUSH DISSENT

After the 1938-1944 New York City "LaGuardia Marijuana Report" refuted his argument, by reporting that marijuana caused no violence at all and citing other positive results; Harry J. Anslinger, in public tirade after tirade, denounced Mayor Fiorella LaGuardia, the New York Academy of Medicine and the doctors who researched the report.

Anslinger proclaimed that these doctors would never again do marijuana experiments or research without his personal permission, or be sent to jail!

He then used the full power of the United States government, illegally, to halt virtually all research into marijuana while he blackmailed the American Medical Association (AMA)* into denouncing the New York Academy of Medicine and its doctors for the research they had done.

* Why, you ask, was the AMA now on Anslinger's side in 1944-45 after being against the Marijuana Tax Act in 1937? Answer: since Anslinger's FBN was responsible for prosecuting doctors who prescribed narcotic drugs for what he, Anslinger, deemed illegal purposes, they (the FBN) had prosecuted more than 3,000 AMA doctors for illegal prescriptions through 1939. In 1939, the AMA made specific peace with Anslinger on marijuana. The results: Only three doctors were prosecuted for illegal drugs of any sort from 1939 to 1949.

The 1938-1944 New York City "LaGuardia Marijuana Report" refuted the idea that marijuana caused violence, and cited other positive results.

To refute the LaGuardia report, the AMA, at Anslinger's personal request, conducted a 1944-45 study showing that 34 Negro GI's (and one white GI for statistical "control") who smoked marijuana became disrespectful of white soldiers and officers in the segregated military. (See Appendix p.111, "Army

Study of Marijuana," Newsweek, Jan. 15, 1945.)

This technique of biasing the outcome of a study is known among researchers as "gutter science."

POT & THE THREAT OF PEACE

However, between 1948 to 1950, Anslinger stopped feeding the press the story that marijuana was violence causing and began "Red Baiting," typical of the McCarthy era.

Now the frightened American public was told that this was a much more dangerous drug than originally thought. Testifying before a strongly anti-Communist Congress in 1948—and thereafter continually in the press—Anslinger proclaimed that marijuana caused its users to become so peaceful—and pacifistic!—that the Communists could and would use marijuana to weaken our American fighting men's will to fight.

This was a 180-degree turnaround of the original pretext on which cannabis was outlawed in 1937.

Undaunted, however, Congress now voted to continue the marijuana law—based on the exact opposite reasoning they had used to outlaw cannabis in the first place.

It is interesting and even absurd to note that Anslinger and his biggest supporters—Southern congressmen and his best senatorial friend, Senator Joseph McCarthy* of Wisconsin—from 1948 on, constantly received press coverage on the scare.

* According to Anslinger's autobiographical book, *The Murderers* and confirmed by former FBN agents, Anslinger had been supplying morphine illegally to a U.S. senator—Joseph McCarthy—for years.

The reason given by Anslinger in his book? So the communists would not be able to blackmail this Great American Senator for his drug-dependency weakness. (Dean Latimer, Flowers In The Blood, Harry Anslinger, *The Murderers*.)

The communists had the potential to sell marijuana to American boys to sap their will to fight—to make us a nation of zombie pacifists. Of course, the communists of Russia and China ridiculed this American marijuana paranoia every chance they got—in the press and at the United Nations.

In 1943, marijuana extracts were discontinued by Anslinger's group as America's first truth serum because it didn't work all the time. People being interrogated would often giggle or laugh hysterically at their captors, get paranoid, or have insatiable desires for food.

Unfortunately, the idea of pot and pacifism got so much sensational world press for the next decade that eventually Russia, China, and the Eastern Bloc communist countries (who grew large amounts of cannabis) outlawed marijuana for fear that America would sell or give it to their peoples to make their soldiers pacifists.

This was strange because Russia, Eastern Europe, and China had been growing and ingesting cannabis as a medical drug, relaxant and work tonic for hundreds and even thousands of years, with no thought of marijuana laws.

(The J.V. Dialogue Soviet Press Digest, Oct., 1990 reported a flourishing illegal hemp business, despite the frantic efforts by Soviet law enforcement agencies to stamp it out. "In Kirghizia alone hemp plantations occupy some 3,000 hectares." In another area Russians are traveling three days into the "one of the more sinister places in the Moiyn-Kumy desert," to harvest a special high grade, drought resitant variety of hemp or known locally as anasha.)

THE BUSH/QUAYLE/LILLY PHARMACEUTICAL SELL OUT

In America, marijuana's most outspoken opponent is none other than President George Bush, former Director of the CIA under Gerald Ford (1975-1977) and past director of President Reagan's "Drug Task Force" (1981-1988).

After leaving the CIA in 1977, Bush was made director of Eli Lilly by none other than Dan Quayle's father and family, who owned controlling interest in the Lilly company and the Indianapolis Star. Dan Quayle later acted as go-between for drug kingpins, gun runners and government officials in the Iran-Contra scandals.

The entire Bush family were large stockholders in Lilly, Abbott, Bristol and Pfizer, etc. After Bush's disclosure of assets in 1979, it became public that Bush's family still has a large interest in Pfizer and substantial amounts of stock in the other aforementioned drug companies.

In fact, Bush actively lobbied illegally both within and without the Administration as Vice President in 1981 to permit drug companies to dump more unwanted, obsolete or especially domestically-banned substances on unsuspecting Third World countries.

While Vice President, Bush continued to illegally act on behalf of pharmaceutical companies by personally going to the IRS for special tax breaks for certain drug companies (e.g. Lilly) manufacturing in Puerto Rico. In 1982, Vice President Bush was personally ordered to stop lobbying the IRS on behalf of the drug companies by the U.S. Supreme Court itself.

He did—but they (the pharmaceuticals) still received a 23% additional tax break for their companies in Puerto Rico who make these American outlawed drugs for sale to Third World countries.

OUTRAGEOUS!!

(Financial disclosure statements; Bush 1979 tax report; "Bush Tried to Sway A Tax Rule Change But Then Withdrew" NY Times, May 19, 1982 (see Appendix page 147); misc. corporate records; Christic Institute "La Penca" affidafit; Lilly 1979 Annual Report.)

A SECRET PROGRAM TO CONTROL MINDS & CHOICES

Through a report released in 1983 under the Freedom of Information Act, it was discovered (after 40 years of secrecy) that Anslinger was appointed in 1942 to a top-secret committee to create a "truth serum" for the OSS, Office of Strategic Services, which evolved into the CIA, the Central Intelligence Agency. (Rolling Stone, August 1983.)

Anslinger and his spy group picked, as America's first truth serum, "honey oil," a much purer, almost tasteless form of hash oil, to be administered in food to: spies, saboteurs, military prisoners and the like, to "spill the truth," without their knowledge.

Fifteen months later, in 1943, marijuana extracts were discontinued by Anslinger's group as America's first truth serum because it was noted that they didn't work all the time.

The people being interrogated would often giggle or laugh hysterically at their captors, get paranoid, or have insatiable desires for food (the munchies?). Also, the report noted that American OSS agents and other interrogation groups started using the honey oil illegally themselves, and would not give it to the spies. In Anslinger's OSS group's final report on marijuana as a truth-serum, there was no mention of violence caused by the drug! In fact, the opposite was indicated. The OSS and later the CIA continued the search and tried other drugs as a truth serum; psilocybe or amanita mushrooms and LSD, to name a few.

The CIA secretly tested these concoctions on American agents for 20 years.

— 29 —

Unsuspecting subjects jumped from buildings, or thought they'd gone insane.

Our government finally admitted to doing all this to its own people in the 1970s—after 25 years of denials: drugging innocent, non-consenting, unaware citizens, soldiers and government agents—all in the name of national security, of course.

These American "security" agencies constantly threatened individuals, families and organizations that suggested the druggings had ever occurred.

Anslinger supplied illegal morphine to U.S. Senator Joseph McCarthy for years.

It was three decades before the Freedom of Information Act forced the CIA to admit their lies through exposure on TV by CBS's 60 Minutes and others.

However, on April 16, 1985 the U.S. Supreme Court ruled that the CIA did not have to reveal the identities of either the individuals or institutions involved in this travesty.

The court said, in effect, that the CIA could decide what was or was not to be released under the Freedom of Information Act, and that the courts could not overrule the agency's decision.

As an aside, repealing this Freedom of Information Act is one of the prime goals of the Reagan/Bush Quayle Administration.

(L.A. Times, The Oregonian, etc. editorials 1984; The Oregonian January 21, 1985; Lee, Martin & Shlain, Bruce, *Acid Dreams*, Grove Press, NY, 1985.)

However, before Anslinger would start the pacifis zombie-marijuana scare in 1948, he publicly use jazz music, violence, and the "gore files" for five t seven more years (1943-50) in the press, at conven tions, lectures, and Congressional hearings.

CRIMINAL MISCONDUCT

We now know that on the subject of marijuana Anslinger was a bureaucratic police liar.

For over 50 years now Americans have been grow ing up with and accepting Anslinger's statements or the herb—from violence to evil pacifism and finally t the corrupting influence of music.

Whether this was economically or racially inspired or even because of up-beat music or some kind of syn ergistic (combined) hysteria; it is impossible to know for sure. But we do know that the U.S. Government information disseminated on cannabis was then, and continues to be, a deliberate deception.

As you will see in the following chapters, the weight of empirical fact and large amounts of corroborating evidence indicate that the Bush/Quayle administra tion, along with their unique pharmaceutical connec tions (see "Bush/Quayle/Lilly Pharmaceutical Sell out" sidebar in this chapter), have probably conspired at the highest levels to withhold information and to disinform the public, resulting in the avoidable and needless deaths of tens of thousands of Americans.

And they did it, it seems, intending to save their own investment—and their friends'—in the pharma ceutical, energy and paper industries; and to give these poisonous, synthetic industries an insane ad vantage over natural hemp and protect the billions of dollars in annual profits that they stood to lose if the hemp plant and marijuana were legal!

As a result, millions of years in jail time have been wasted, and millions of lives have been and continue to be ruined by what started out as Hearst's, Anslinger's and DuPont's shameful economic lies, vi cious racial libels and bigoted musical taste.

Footnotes:

1. Abel, Ernest, *Marijuana, The First 12,000 Years*, Plenum Press, NY, 1980, pg. 73 & 99.

2. Sloman, Larry, *Reefer Madness*, Grove Press, Inc., New York 1979, pg. 40.

3. Ibid, pg. 196, 197.

4. Research of Dr. Michael Aldrich, Richard Ashley, Michael Horowitz, et al.; The High Times Encyclopedia of Recreational Drugs, pg. 138.

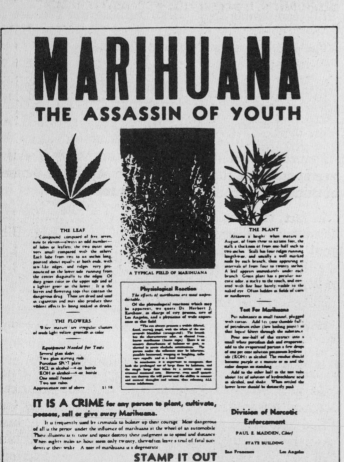

THE BODY OF MEDICAL LITERATURE ON
CANNABIS MEDICINE

*Our authority here is the 'Body of Literature,' starting with ancient materia medicas.
Chinese and Hindu pharmacopeias, Near Eastern cuneiform tablets all the way into this
century, through the 1966-76 U.S. rennaisance of cannabis studies: some 10,000 separate
studies on medicines and effects from the hemp plant.*

*Comprehensive compendia of these works are designated as the prime sources
for this medical chapter, as well as ongoing personal interviews with many
researchers.*

AFFORDABLE, AVAILABLE HERBAL HEALTH CARE

For more than 3,500 years, cannabis/hemp/marijuana has been, depending on the culture or nation, either the most used or one of the most widely used plants for medicines. This includes: China, India, the Middle and Near East, Africa, and pre-Roman Catholic Europe (prior to 400 A.D.).

Dr. Raphael Mechoulam, NORML, High Times and Omni magazine (September 1982) all indicate that, if marijuana were legal, it would replace immediately 10% to 20% of all pharmaceutical prescription medicines and therapy (based on current—through 1976—research). And, probably, Mechoulam estimates, 40% to 50% of all medicines, including patent medicines, could contain some extract from the cannabis plant when fully researched.

(Read the U.S. government sponsored research as outlined by Cohen & Stillman, *Therapeutic Potential of Marijuana*, 1976; Roffman, Roger, *Marijuana as Medicine*, 1980; Mikuriya, Tod, M.D., *Marijuana Medical Papers*, 1972; Also, the work of Dr. Norman Zinberg; Dr. Andrew Weill; Dr. Lester Grinspoon; and the U.S. Government's Presidential Commission reports [Shafer Commission] from 1969 through 1972; Dr. Raphael Mechoulam, Tel Aviv/Jerusalem Univ., 1964-84; W.B. O'Shaugnessy monograph, 1839; and the long-term Jamaican studies I & II, 1968-74; Costa Rican studies through 1982; U.S. Coptic studies, 1981; Ungerlieder; U.S. military studies since the 1950s and 60s.)

During all this time (pre-1000 B.C. to 1940s A.D.), researchers, doctors and drug manufacturers (Lilly, Parke-Davis, Squibb, etc.) had no idea as to what the active ingredients were in cannabis, nor which ones would work.

SUPERSTAR OF THE 19TH CENTURY

Marijuana was America's number one analgesic for 60 years before the re-discovery of aspirin around 1900. From 1842 to 1900 cannabis made up half of all medicine sold, with virtually no fear of its high.

The Committee on Cannabis Indica for the Ohio State Medical Society concluded, "the gall and vinegar, or myrrhed wine, offered to our Saviour immediately before his crucifixion was, in all probability, a preparation of Indian hemp."

The 1839 report on the uses of cannabis by Dr. W.B. O'Shaugnessy, one of the most respected members of the Royal Academy of Science, was just as important to mid-19th century Western medicine as the discoveries of antibiotics (like penicillin and Terramycin) were to mid-20th century medicine.

From 1850 to 1937, cannabis was prescribed as the prime medicine for more than 100 separate illnesses or diseases in American U.S. pharmacopeia.

In fact, the Committee on Cannabis Indica for the Ohio State Medical Society concluded that "High Biblical commentators [scholars]" believe "that the gall and vinegar, or myrrhed wine, offered to our Saviour immediately before his crucifixion was, in all probability, a preparation of Indian hemp."

(Transcripts, Ohio State Medical Society 15th annual meeting, June 12-14, 1860, pg. 75-100.)

20TH CENTURY RESEARCH

As outlined in the previous chapters, the American Medical Association (AMA) and drug companies testified *against* the 1937 Marijuana Tax Act because cannabis was known to have so much medical potential and had never caused any observable addictions or death by overdose.

They argued the possibility existed that, once the active ingredients in cannabis (such as THC Delta-9) were synthesized and correct dosages established, cannabis could become a miracle drug.

Research revealed positive indications when using cannabis for asthma, glaucoma, nausea from chemotherapy, anorexia, and tumors, as well as a general use antibiotic; epilepsy, Parkinson's disease, anorexia, multiple sclerosis, dystrophy, and tumors—all these merited further clinical studies.

Twenty-nine years, however, would pass before American scientists could begin to even look into cannabis medicine again.

THC Delta-9 was synthesized by Dr. Raphael Mechoulam at the University of Tel Aviv in 1964, confirming the work of Professor Taylor of Princeton, who had lead the research and identification of natural THC Delta-9 precursors in the 1930s. Kahn, Adams and Loewe also worked with the structure of cannabis' active ingredients in 1944.

Since 1964, more than 400 separate compounds have been isolated in cannabis, at least 60 of which are therapeutic, from over a thousand suspected compounds. The United States, however, forbade this type of research through the bureaucratic authority of Harry Anslinger until 1961, when he was forced to retire. (Omni magazine, September 1982.)

GROWING ACCEPTANCE

By 1966, millions of young Americans were using marijuana. Concerned parents and government, wanting to know the dangers their children were risking, started funding dozens and later hundreds of marijuana health studies.

Entrenched in the older generation's minds were 30 years of Anslinger/Hearst scare stories: Murder, atrocity, rape, and even zombie pacifism.

Federally sponsored research results began to ease Americans' fears of cannabis causing violence or zombie pacifism, and hundreds of new studies suggested that hidden inside the hemp plants' chemistry lay a medicinal array of incredible therapeutic potential. The government funded more and more studies.

Soon, legions of American researchers had positive indications using cannabis with asthma, glaucoma, nausea from chemotherapy, anorexia, and tumors, as well as a general use antibiotic. Cumulative results showed evidence or favorable anomalies occurring, for epilepsy, Parkinson's disease, anorexia, multiple sclerosis, dystrophy and tumors, plus thousands of

anecdotal stories all merited further clinical study.

Prior to 1976, reports of positive effects and new therapeutic indications for cannabis were almost a weekly occurrence in medical journals and the national press.

NATIONAL CONFERENCE PRAISED CANNABIS THERAPY POTENTIAL

In November 1975, virtually all of America's leading researchers on marijuana met at the Asilomar Conference Center, Pacific Grove, California. These seminars were sponsored by the National Institute of Drug Abuse (NIDA) to address a compendium of their studies from the earliest to their most recent findings.

When the seminars were over, practically all the participants (scientists) concluded that the federal government, with the hard evidence collected so far on the therapeutic potential of marijuana, should be rushing to invest tax money into more research.

They felt the taxpayers should be informed there was every legitimate reason for the field of public health to continue large scale research on cannabis medicine and therapies. All the participants, it seems, believed this. Many of them (such as Mechoulam) believed that cannabis would be one of the world's major medicines by the mid-1980s.

MARIJUANA RESEARCH BANNED

However, in 1976, just as multi-disciplined marijuana research should have been going into its second- third- and fourth-generation studies (see *Therapeutic Potential of Marijuana* and NORML federal files), a "surprise" United States government policy again forbade all promising federal research into marijuana's therapeutic effects.

This time, the research ban was accomplished when American pharmaceutical companies successfully petitioned the federal government to be allowed to finance and judge 100% of the research.

The previous 10 years of research had indicated a tremendous promise for the therapeutic uses of natural cannabis, and this potential was quietly turned over to corporate hands—not for the benefit of the public, but to suppress the information.

This plan, the drug manufacturers petitioned, would allow our private drug companies time to come up with patentable synthetics of the cannabis molecules at no cost to the federal government, and a promise of "no highs."

In 1976 the Ford Administration, NIDA and the DEA said, in effect, no American independent (read: university) research or federal health program would be allowed to again investigate natural cannabis derivatives for medicine. This agreement was made without any safeguards guaranteeing integrity on the part of the pharmaceutical companies; they were allowed to regulate themselves.

Private pharmaceutical corporations were allowed to do some "no high" research but it would be only for Delta-9 THC research, not any of the 400 other potentially therapeutic isomers in cannabis.

To summarize: Why did the drug companies conspire to take over marijuana? Because recent research (1966-1976) had indicated or confirmed through hundreds of studies that even "natural" crude cannabis was the "best and safest medicine of choice" for many serious health problems.

1988: DEA JUDGE RULES THAT CANNABIS HAS MEDICAL VALUE

The DEA's own conservative administrative law judge, Francis Young, after taking medical testimony for 15 days and reviewing hundreds of DEA/NIDA documents posed against the evidence introduced by marijuana reform activists concluded in September, 1988 that "marijuana is one of the safest therapeutically active substances known to man."

But despite this preponderance of evidence, DEA Director John Lawn ordered on December 30, 1989, that cannabis remain listed as a Schedule One narcotic: As having no known medical use.

WELL, IF IT'S KNOWN ALL THIS SINCE 1975, WHAT'S THE GOVERNMENT WAITING FOR?

PROTECTING PHARMACEUTICAL COMPANIES' PROFITS

NORML, High Times and Omni (September, 1982) indicate that Eli Lilly Co.; Abbott Labs; Pfizer; Smith, Kline & French; and others would lose hundreds of millions to billions of dollars annually if marijuana were legal in the U.S.* and lose even more billions in Third World countries.

* Remember, these drug companies, at their own insistence, specifically by lobbying, got the Federal Government to prevent all positive research into medical marijuana in 1976, the last year of the Ford Administration.

PUTTING THE FOX INTO THE HEALTH CARE CHICKEN COOP

In return, the drug companies took over all research and financing into analogs of synthetic THC, CBD, CBN, etc., promising "no high" before allowing the products on the market. Eli Lilly came out with Nabilone, a synthetic second cousin of THC Delta 9 and promised the government great results.

Omni magazine, in 1982, stated that after nine years, Nabilone was still considered virtually useless when compared with real, home-grown THC-rich marijuana buds.

Some 500,000 people are poisoned each year in Third World countries by drugs, pesticides, etc. that are sold to them by American companies, but which are banned from sale in the U.S.

Marijuana users agree, they do not like the effects of Lilly's Nabilone.

Why? You have to get three or four times as high on Nabilone for it to produce the same benefits as smoking one cigarette of good cannabis bud.

Omni also states that after tens of millions of dollars and nine years of research on medical marijuana synthetics, "these drug companies are totally unsuccessful," even though raw, organic cannabis is a "superior medicine" which works so well naturally, on so many different illnesses.

Omni also suggested that the drug companies petition the government to allow "crude drug extracts" on the market in the real interest of public health. The government and the drug companies, to date, have not responded. Or rather they have responded by ignoring it. However, the Reagan/Bush/Quayle Administration is absolutely refusing to allow resumption of real (university) cannabis research, except under the worthless pharmaceutical synthetic studies.

Omni suggests, and NORML and High Times concur, that the reason the drug companies and Reagan/Bush/Quayle want only synthetic THC legal is that simple extractions of the hundreds of ingredients from the cannabis crude drug would be enjoyed without pharmaceutical company patents which generate windfall monopolized profits.

UNDERMINING THE NATURAL MEDICINES COMPETITION

Eli Lilly, Pfizer and others stand to lose a third of their entire, highly profitable, patent monopoly on drugs including Darvon; to take losses in their Tuinal and Seconal lines (as well as other patent lines ranging from muscle ointments to burn ointments, to thousands of other uses already known in 1966-1976) from a plant anyone can grow: cannabis hemp.

Isn't it curious that American drug companies and pharmacist groups* supply almost half the funding for the 4000 "Families Against Marijuana" type organizations in America? The other half is supplied by Action, a federal VISTA agency, and by liquor and beer makers like Anhauser Busch, Coors, Philip

AN UNFAIR RAP FOR HEMP

After 20 years of study, the California Research Advisory Panel (RAP) in 1989 broke with the state Attorney General's office (A.G.), under which it works, and called for the re-legalization of cannabis.

"There is no point to continuing unmodified, much less intensified, the policies and laws that have so obviously failed to control the individual and societal damages associated with drug use," summarized Vice Chairman Frederick Meyers, M.D., in a letter released with the group's recommendations after the attorney general had suppressed the report and panel members elected to publish it at their own expense.

This was a complete turnaround from the RAP's long history of suppressing medical usage. The long term impact of this shift remains to be seen.

Chairman Edward P. O'Brien, Jr, appointed by the A.G., who dissented from the panel's conclusions, had for years dominated this group, rigidly controlling what research could be performed—and limiting those applications to control of nausea and vomiting that is secondary to cancer chemotherapy.

Under O'Brien, the panel systematically welched on its mandate to provide compassionate medicinal access to cannabis. Any applications for using cannabis including the control of pain, spastic neurological disorders, etc., have been rejected. Cannabis used to be the treatment of choice for vascular or migraine headache. (Osler, 1916; O'Shaugnessey, 1839)

Cannabis has the unique characteristic of affecting the vascular circulation of the covering of the brain—the meninges. The reddened eyes of the marijuana user are a reflection of this action.

Unlike other drugs, however, cannabis has no apparent affect on the vascular system in general, except for a slight speeding up of the heart during the onset of the effects of the drug.

RAP has discouraged the use of smoking cannabis in favor of synthetic Delta-9 THC capsules, despite crude cannabis' favorable comparative results reported to the Food and Drug Administration.

This has been frankly misrepresented in their reports to the legislature and testimony in the NORML vs. DEA case. Additionally, these memoranda favorably comparing smoked marijuana to oral THC have been buried in appendices to their reports—available in only four locations in the entire state of California!

On September 30, 1989, the medical marijuana program quietly expired, based on the staff's assessment that not enough people had been treated to justify its extension.

—*Tod Mikuriya, M.D.*
Berkeley, CA, 1990

Morris, etc., or as a 'public service' by the ad agencies who represent them.

* Pharmacists Against Drug Abuse, etc. See appendices.

POISONING THE THIRD WORLD

Colombia's largest newspaper, Periodical el Tiempo (Bogota) reported in 1983— and was not disputed by the U.S. government or American pharmaceutical companies—that these same anti-marijuana crusading American pharmaceutical companies are guilty of a practice known as product dumping, wherein they "sell on the over-the-counter markets of Colombia, Mexico, Panama, Chile, El Salvador, Honduras and Nicaragua, over 150 different illegal, dangerous drugs."

Some of these drugs have been forbidden by the FDA for sale or use in the U.S. or its counterparts in Europe because they are known to cause malnutrition, deformities and cancer. Yet they are sold over the counter to unsuspecting illiterates!

The World Health Organization backs up this story with a conservative estimate: They say that some 500,000 people are poisoned each year in Third World countries by items (drugs, pesticides, etc.) sold by American companies but which are banned from sale in the U.S.

Mother Jones magazine, 1979, "Unbroken Circle" June, 1989; The Progressive, April, 1991; et al.

DESTROYING THE PUBLIC RECORD

Some 10,000 studies were done on cannabis, 4,000 in the U.S. and only about a dozen have shown any negative results and these were unreplicated. The Reagan/Bush Administration put a soft "feeler" out in September of 1983, for all American universities and researchers to destroy all 1966-76 cannabis research work, including compendiums in libraries.

Scientists and doctors so ridiculed this unparalleled censorship move that the plans were dropped...for the moment.

However, we know that large amounts of information have since disappeared, including the original copy of the USDA's own pro-marijuana film *Hemp for Victory*. Worse yet, even the merest mention of the film was removed from the official record back to 1956 and has had to be painstakingly re-established as part of our national archives. Many archival and resource copies of USDA *Bulletin 404* have disappeared.

How much more irreplaceable knowledge has already been lost?

Chapter Seven:

THERAPEUTIC USE OF CANNABIS

There are 60 or more therapeutic compounds in cannabis that are healing agents in medical and herbal treatments. The primary known one is THC, and the effectiveness of therapy is directly proportionate to the herb's potency or concentration of THC. Recent DEA reports of more potent marijuana therefore represent a major medical advance; but, incredibly, the government uses these very numbers to solicit bigger budgets and harsher penalties.

Here's how people will benefit once the judgement and freedom of choice of doctor and patient are once again respected:

THIS WRITER, RESPONSIBLE SCIENTISTS AND DOCTORS WANT TO WARN YOU:
There is no pharmacological free lunch in cannabis or any drug. Negative reactions can result. A small percentage of people have negative or allergic reactions to marijuana. Heart patients could have problems, even though cannabis generally relieves stress, dilates the arteries, and in general lowers the diastolic pressure. A small percentage of people get especially high heart rates and anxieties with cannabis. These persons should not use it. Some bronchial asthma sufferers benefit from cannabis; however, for others it may serve as an additional irritant.
For the overwhelming majority of people, cannabis has demonstrated literally hundreds of therapeutic uses. Among them:

1. ASTHMA

More than 15 million Americans are affected by asthma. Smoking cannabis, (what the AMA called the 'raw drug') would be beneficial for 80% of them and add 30 to 60 million person-years in the aggregate of extended life to current asthmatics over presently legal toxic medicines—especially theophyline for children.

"Taking a hit of marijuana has been known to stop a full blown asthma attack." (Personal communication with Dr. Donald Tashkin, December 12, 1989.) The use of cannabis for asthmatics goes back thousands of years in literature; American doctors of the last century wrote in medical papers that asthma sufferers of the world would "bless" Indian Hemp (cannabis) all their lives.

Today, no Californian (or American, for that matter) receives or uses legal cannabis for asthma.

(Tashkin, Dr. Donald, UCLA Pulmonary Studies, 1969-90; Ibid., asthma studies, 1969-1976; Cohen, Sidney, & Stillman, *Therapeutic Potential of Marijuana, 1976*; Life Insurance Actuarial rates; Life shortening effects of childhood asthma, 1983.)

2. GLAUCOMA

Fourteen percent of all blindness in America is from glaucoma, a progressive loss of vision. Cannabis smoking would benefit 90% of our 2,500,000 glaucoma victims, and is two to three times as effective as any current medicines for reducing ocular pressure. Additionally, cannabis use has no toxic side effects to the liver and kidneys, or the occasional sudden death

syndromes associated with the legal pharmaceutical glaucoma drugs/drops. Most California eye doctors will advise their patients, usually discreetly and illegally, to use "street" marijuana in addition to (or to mitigate) their toxic legal glaucoma medicines.

(Harvard; Hepler & Frank, 1971, UCLA; Medical College of Georgia; University of North Carolina School of Medicine, 1975; Cohen & Stillman, *Therapeutic Potential of Marijuana*, UCLA, 1976; National Eye Institute.)

3. TUMORS

A tumor is a mass of swollen tissue. Researchers at the Medical College of Virginia discovered that cannabis is an incredibly successful herb for reducing many types of tumors, both benign and malignant (cancerous).

The DEA and other federal agencies had ordered these tumor studies studies done after hearing of erroneous reports of possible immunicological problems associated with cannabis smoke. When, instead of health problems, an apparent medical breakthrough occurred in 1975 and successful tumor reductions were recorded, orders were handed down by the DEA and the National Institute of Health to defund all further cannabis/tumor research and reporting.[1]

4. NAUSEA RELIEF (E.G., AIDS, CANCER THERAPY, SEA SICKNESS)

Chemotherapy treatment can help control cancer and AIDS, but it has some bad side effects, including nausea. "Marijuana is the best agent for control of nausea in cancer chemotherapy," according to Dr.

Thomas Ungerleider, who headed California's Marijuana for Cancer research program from 1979 to 1984. This is also true in AIDS and even the unsettled stomache common in motion sickness.

Pharmaceutical nausea control drugs come in pills that are often swallowed and simply thrown back up by the patient. Because cannabis can be ingested as smoke, it stays in the system and keeps working even after vomiting occurs.

Throughout the state's 10 year Compassionate Marijuana Medical law, George Deukmejian, both as attorney general and as governor, made it virtually impossible for any dying cancer patients to get cannabis, with no regard for their suffering.

The next attorney general, John Van DeKamp, continued harassing medical users and punishing growers and would not even look into the history of medical cannabis or accept a copy of the *Marijuana as Medicine* report at a KABC radio talk show in August 1983.

5. EPILEPSY, M.S., BACK PAIN & MUSCLE SPASMS.

Cannabis is beneficial for 60% of all epileptics. It is definitely the best treatment for many, but not all types of epilepsy, and for victims' post-seizure mental traumas. Cannabis users' epileptic seizures are of less intensity than the more dangerous seizures experienced by users of pharmaceuticals. Similarly, smoking cannabis has proven to be a major source of relief for multiple sclerosis, which affects the nervous system and is characterized by muscular weakness, tremors, etc.

Cannabis, smoked or applied as a herbal pack or poultice, is also the best muscle relaxant, back spasm medicine and antispasmodic medication on our planet, short of morphine.

ONE MAN'S DETERMINATION

Patric Mayers, with his testimony and personal lobbying, was instrumental in getting the California Legislature to pass a state law allowing cannabis for medical use. Mayers' life was saved in 1976 when his doctors illegally advised him to use marijuana for his chemotherapy nausea. At this point, Mayers weighed only 93 pounds. The easily smoked cannabis eased Patric's nausea and gave him an appetite for food. This lifesaving function of Cannabis, if developed in a laboratory, would be hailed around the globe and in every medical publication, it would be Nobel Prize material, but there is instead a forced silence because there is no money to be made on it.

Mayers received the "best flower tops of Thai and sinsemilla" free from dealers and students in his San Francisco law school where Mayers was class president when stricken with cancer in 1975.

Healthy and happily married in L.A., Mayers was shocked in 1981 to learn that the state attorney general, in charge of the medical cannabis program, refused to supply federally grown or even police-impounded contraband marijuana to cancer patients; cannabis to which he had legal access for doctors to prescribe or obtain for dying patients.

In 1982, Mayers got mad and caused the L.A. Times, other media, and Willie Brown, Speaker of the California Assembly to demand compliance with the state's 1979 marijuana law.

Following a few months of visible compliance, the policy to block medical access was back in full force. After 10 years of run arounds, refusals and harrassment, the well intended "Compassionate Marijuana" program lapsed automatically.

(Cohen & Stillman, *Therapeutic Potential of Marijuana*, 1976 Consult U.S. Pharmacopoeia prior to 1937; Mikuriya, Tod H., M.D. *Marijuana Medical Papers, 1839-1972*.)

6. ANTIBIOTIC/ANTIBACTERIAL CBD DISINFECTANTS

Young, un-budded, hemp plants provide extractions of CBDs (cannabidiolic acids). There are many antibiotic uses of the cannabidiols, including treatment for gonorrhea. A 1990 Florida study indicated its use in treating herpes.

The acid side of tetrahydrocannabinol, cannabidiols occur inversely to the amount of the plant's THC and is therefore more acceptable to prohibitionists because "it won't get you high." For virtually any disease or infection that can be treated with terramycin, cannabis derivatives did better in Czechoslovakian studies, 1952-1955.[3] The Czechs in 1989 still publish farm crop reports on strategies to grow Cannabidiol rich hemp.

(Also see Cohen & Stillman *Therapeutic Potential of Marijuana*; Mikuriya, Tod H., M.D. *Marijuana Medical Papers*; Roffman, *Marijuana as Medicine* 1982; International Farm Crop abstracts.)

7. ARTHRITIS HERPES, CYSTIC FIBROSIS, & RHEUMATISM

Cannabis is a topical analgesic.[2] Until 1937, virtually all fistulas, corn plasters, mustard plasters muscle ointments, and fibrosis poultices were made from or with cannabis extracts. Rheumatism was treated throughout South America until the 1960s with hemp leaves and/or flower tops heated in water or alcohol and placed on painful joints. In fact, this form of herbal medicine is still widely used in rural areas of Mexico, Central and South America, and by California Latinos for relief of arthritis pain.

Direct contact with THC killed herpes virus in a University of South Florida (Tampa) 1990 research study by Dr. Gerald Lancz, who warns that "smoking marijuana will not cure herpes." However, anecdotal reports indicate a faster drying and healing of the outbreak after topical application of strong bud," soaked in rubbing alcohol and crushed into paste.

8. LUNG CLEANER & EXPECTORANT

Cannabis is the best natural expectorant to clear the human lungs of smog, dust and the phlegm associated with tobacco use.

Marijuana smoke effectively dilates the airways of the lungs, the bronchi, opening them to allow more oxygen into the lungs. It is also the best natural dilator of the tiny airways of the lungs, the bronchial tubes—making cannabis the best overall bronchial dilator for 80% of the population (the remaining 20% sometimes show minor negative reactions.)

Marijuana could replace more than 50% of Valium, Librium, Thorazine, Stelazine, other "-zine" drugs and most sleeping pills.

(See section on asthma—a disease that closes these passages in spasms—UCLA Tashkin studies, 1969-83; U.S. Costa Rican, 1980-82; Jamaican studies 1968-74.)

Statistical evidence—showing up consistently as anomalies in matched populations—indicates that people who smoke tobacco cigarettes are usually better off and will live longer if they smoke cannabis moderately, too. (Jamaican, Costa Rican studies.)

Millions of Americans have given up or avoided

COMPASSIONATE CANNABIS & CRUEL COPS

From 1979 to 1989, California had a law that was supposed to help people get cannabis for medical purposes. Many states now have doctors in charge of their own, independent cannabis programs. (L.A. Times, 1982, et al.) However, instead of putting the California "compassionate cannabis" program under the health department, it was given to the attorney general—the state prosecutor.

As far as we know, no Californian receives or has received legal cannabis for glaucoma, even though California law allowed for experimental cannabis medicine for 10 years (from 1979 to 1989). Its use in any illness other than chemotherapy nausea is rare due to the current federal government's natural-medical marijuana prohibition.

Both as state Attorney General and governor, George Deukmejian deliberately and consciously thwarted doctors' and researchers' attempts to acquire federal cannabis from him and refused to carry out the program passed by California legislators. When the state's bill authorizing medical cannabis lapsed in July, 1989 almost no one had benefited from it—and no legislator even bothered to try to extend or implement it.

The federal government has had no coordinating program since 1976 to deal with the 30 states whose legislators have passed medical marijuana laws (over federal and DEA objections). Even worse, the Feds give these patients and doctors, consciously and with malice aforethought, the worst possible, harshest and least therapeutic cannabis: the broad leaf.

Healing agents and therapeutic compounds are concentrated in the flower tops. For these patients to buy top-grade "grass" on the black market costs anywhere from $200 to $400 per ounce. When the 1937 Marijuana Tax Act was passed, one ounce of cannabis, (what the AMA called the 'raw drug,') was available from the drugstore for one dollar.

---

smoking tobacco products in favor of cannabis, which is not good news to the powerful tobacco lobby—Senator Jesse Helms and his cohorts. A turn of the century grandfather clause in U.S. tobacco law, allows 400 to 6000 additional chemicals to be added. Additions since then to the average tobacco cigarette are unknown, and the public in the U.S. has "no right" to know what they are.

Many joggers and marathon runners feel cannabis use cleans their lungs, allowing better endurance.

The evidence indicates cannabis use will probably increase these outlaw American marijuana-users' lives by about one to two years—but can lose their rights, property, children, state licenses, etc., for using that safest of substances: Cannabis.

9. SLEEP & RELAXATION

Cannabis lowers blood pressure, dilates the arteries and reduces body temperature an average of 1/2 degree, thereby relieving stress. Evening cannabis smokers in general report more restful sleep.

Using cannabis allows most people a more complete rest with the highest amount of "alpha time" possible in sleep as compared to prescription or sleep-inducing patent sedatives.

Prescription sleeping pills (the so called 'legal, safe and effective' drugs) are often just synthesized analogs of truly dangerous plants like mandrake, henbane and belladonna. As we go to press in 1991, doctors, pharmacists and drug companies are fighting off new legislation to restrict these often abused compounds (L.A. Times, April 2, 1991).

Unlike Valium, cannabis does not potentiate the effects of alcohol. It is estimated that cannabis could replace more than 50% of Valium, Librium, Thorazine, Stelazine, other "-zine" drugs and most sleeping pills.

But where are they to defend the physician and patients' cannabis medical rights?

It is unconscionable that, over the past two decades, tens of thousands of parents have committed their own children, aged 11 to 17, to be treated by massive doses of so-called "-zine" drugs in order to get them off pot, at the urging of parent groups, the Feds and administrators and doctors from federally approved, private and high-profit drug rehabilitation centers.

Often, "-zine" drugs *do* work to stop these youths from using pot. They also stop a kid from loving his or her dog, too—and the child stands a one-in-four chance of suffering from uncontrollable shaking for the rest of their lives.* But at least they're not high.

* The U.S. Center for Disease Control in Atlanta said that 20% to 40% of "-zine" drug users have or will develop permanent lifetime palsies (shakes), November, 1983. These prescription neurotoxins are chemically related to pesticide.

Hundreds of private drug-rehabilitation centers and their leaders keep this policy alive and in front of the media, often quoting discredited reports from NIDA or DEA (see chapter 16, debunking)—because they earn fat profits selling their useless or destructive 'marijuana treatment' of children.

After all, a relapse just means using marijuana again after a number of bouts with an 'authority.' This is mind-control and an attempt to destroy individual free will.

10. THERAPEUTIC EMPHYSEMA POTENTIAL

Medical research indicates that light cannabis smoking might be useful for a majority of mild emphysema victims. It would improve the quality of life for millions of sufferers and extend their lifespans.

The U.S. government and DEA (since 1976) say the side effect, being 'high,' is not acceptable.

No matter how many years or lives it saves; even though some 60 million Americans have tried marijuana and 25 to 30 million smoke marijuana relaxationally or as a responsible form of daily self-medication, without one single death from overdose—ever.

All research into the oxygen blood transfer effects caused by cannabis indicates that the chest (lung) pains, extremity pains, shallowness of breath, and headaches we may experience on heavy smog days are usually alleviated by light cannabis smoking throughout the day. However, heavy pot smoking works no better—and may have ill effects.

Dr. Donald Tashkin, the U.S. government's leading scientist on pulmonary research, told us in December, 1989* that you cannot get or potentiate emphysema with cannabis smoking.

* See Tashkin's marijuana pulmonary research, UCLA, 1969-1989. This author has personally taken part in these studies for 10 years and has continuously interviewed Tashkin on cannabis's medical indications.

11. SUPERIOR RELIEF FOR STRESS AND MIGRAINES

Most of all: it is best for the world's number one killer—stress. It can safely curtail or replace Valium, Librium or alcohol for millions of Americans.

While marijuana intoxication varies with psychological set and social setting, "the most common response is a calm, mildly euphoric state in which time slows and a sensitivity to sights, sounds and touch is enhanced."[4]

In contrast to marijuana'a safe therapeutic action, [benzo]diazepines (valium) abuse is the number one drug [ab]use problem in the country, and is responsible for [m]ore emergency room admissions in the United [S]tates than either cocaine-related problems or mor[p]hine- and heroin-related admissions combined.[6]

While tobacco constricts arteries, cannabis dilates [th]em. Because migraine headaches are the result of [a]rtery spasms combined with over-relaxation of [v]eins, the vascular changes cannabis causes in the [co]vering of the brain (the meninges)s usually make [m]igraines disappear.

Evidence of vascular change caused by cannabis [c]an be seen in the user's red eyes, which are exten[s]ions of the brain. However, unlike most other drugs, [c]annabis has no apparent effect on the vascular sys[t]em in general, except for a slight increased heart [r]ate during the onset of the high.

12. TO INCREASE THE APPETITE,

Marijuana users often (but not always) get "the [m]unchies," a stimulated appetite for food, which [m]akes cannabis the very best medicine on the planet [t]o date for anorexia.

Hundreds of thousands of Americans in old age, [c]onvalescent wards or hospital situations have [a]norexia. Most could be helped by cannabis—yet [t]hese Americans are being denied a healthy life by [g]overnmental policy dictated by government police!

This effect can also extend the lives of victims of [p]ancreatic cancer (eat or die); however, the DEA and [U].S. Government prevented any research or use of [c]annabis in pancreatic cancer therapy since 1976.

They have collectively allowed tens of thousands of [p]eople to die each year, denied the right to live rela[t]ively normal, healthy and productive lives.

13. TO REDUCE SALIVA

Marijuana smoking can help dry your mouth for [t]he dentist: this is the best way to dry the mouth's [s]aliva non-toxically in what is known among smokers [a]s its "cotton mouth" effect.

It could replace the highly toxic Probathine com[p]ounds produced by Searle & Co., the Canadian [B]oard of Dentistry reported in studies conducted in [t]he 1970s. This may also indicate that cannabis could [b]e good for treating peptic ulcers.

AIDS, DEPRESSION & HUNDREDS OF OTHER PRIME MEDICAL USES

One well known effect of THC is to lift the spirit, or [m]ake you "high." Cannabis users in Jamaica praise ganja's benefits for meditation, concentration, consciousness-raising and promoting a state of well-being and self assertiveness.[5] This kind of attitude adjustment, along with a healthier appetite and better rest, often represents the difference between "dying of" AIDS and "living with" AIDS.

Cannabis also eases small pains and some big ones and helps senior citizens live with aches and pains like arthritis, insomnia and debilitating infirmities, and enjoy life in greater dignity and comfort. Legend has it, and medical evidence indicates, that cannabis is the best overall treatment for dementia, senility, and maybe Alzheimer's disease, for long-term memory "gain" and hundreds of other benefits.

U.S. statistics indicate that you will live eight to 24 years longer if you substitute daily cannabis use for daily tobacco and alcohol use. New research is outlawed, of course.

ACCEPTABLE RISKS

Every U.S. Commission or federal judge who has studied the evidence has agreed that cannabis is one of the safest drugs known. With all its therapeutic uses, it has only one side effect that has been exaggerated as a concern: the "high." The DEA says this is not acceptable, so cannabis continues to be totally illegal in utter disrespect for both doctor and patient.

Every day we entrust physicians to determine whether the risks associated with therapeutic, yet potentially dangerous, drugs are acceptable for their patients. Yet, doctors are not allowed to prescribe the herb that Judge Francis Young called the "safest therapeutically active substance known to man."

We don't put our doctors in charge of stopping violent crimes: The police and prosecutors should not be in charge of which herbal therapies people may use to treat their peronal health problems.

Footnotes:

1. Cohen & Stillman, *Therapeutic Potential of Marijuana*, UCLA, 1976; personal interviews with researchers who did this study in Washington, D.C., November, 1982.

2. Cohen & Stillman, *Therapeutic Potential of Marijuana*, UCLA, 1976; Mikuriya, Tod H., M.D., *Marijuana Medical Papers 1839-1972*, Medi-Comp Press, Oakland, CA, 1973.

3. The Antibiotic Effect of Cannabis Indica, 1952-53-55. The Antibacterial Effect of Cannabis Indica, 1955, from *Marijuana Medical Papers;* Cohen & Stillman, *Therapeutic Potential of Marijuana*, UCLA, 1976

4. Harvard Medical School *Mental Health Letter*, Vol. 4, No. 5, November, 1987.

5. Ruben, Vera & Comitas, Lambros, *Ganja in Jamaica, A Medical Anthropological Study of Chronic Marijuana Use*, Mouton & Co., The Hague and Paris, Anchor Books, U.S.A., 1976.

6. *Stopping Valium* Public Citizen Health Research Group, 2000 P St. NW, Washington, D.C.

CANNABIS (Marijuana)
Over 60 synergistic compounds in one natural medication

Available:
Cigarettes (350 mg.–500 mg. r.d.)
Concentrated cannabis oil (grass oil)
Concentrated cannabis pollen (kif)
Concentrated cannabis resin (hashish)

Description:
Cannabis is the crude vegetable preparation of the plants *Cannabis sativa L.* and *Cannabis indica*. The pharmacologically active components of the drug are cannabinoids, including delta-9 trans-tetrahydrocannabinol, cannabidiol, cannabinol, tetrahydrocannabivarin and perhaps 60 other cannabinoids of varying pharmacological properties. Unique both in botany and pharmacological action, cannabinoids are not nitrogenous alkaloids, and their site and mode of action in the body are unknown, though they clearly modify neurotransmission in the CSN. Cannabinoids work synergistically, in that the effects of delta-9 trans-tetrahydrocannabinol in isolation, for example, are very greatly modified by its interaction in crude cannabis with cannabidiol, which antagonizes some effects of the tetrahydrocannabinol and potentiates others. Cannabis also necessarily comprises a broad variety of nonpharmacological substances common to vegetable matter in general; however, most or all of these extraneous materials can be substantially eliminated, before the drug is ingested, by appropriate filtering devices.

Precautions:
Cannabis is proscribed under the Uniform Controlled Dangerous Substances Act of 1972. Its possession is a felony under federal law and physicians who facilitate its use by patients are subject to prosecution under conspiracy statutes; merely advising a patient where he or she might obtain cannabis renders a physician liable to arrest. Patients who use cannabis should be advised of the risk of prosecution and imprisonment and the material health hazards posed thereby.

Contraindications:
Persons suffering from viral or bacterial pulmonary infections should not ingest cannabis by inhalation until remission of the infection. Extended and regular administration to persons with emphysema and lung fibrosis may aggravate these conditions.

Adverse Reactions:
Idiosyncratic anxiety crises, dysphoric dissociation and depersonalization syndromes may occur in a very few patients experiencing acute onset of cannabis's mental effects for the first time; dosage should be lowered and an attempt should be made to determine the root emotional cause of the reaction. If the reaction persists long after the drug wears off or dependably occurs with succeeding administrations, a preexisting premorbid psychotic condition may be suspected and therapy should be discontinued.

Raw cannabis contains significant levels of mutagenic hydrocarbon condensates, toxins that irritate pharyngo-laryngeal, bronchial and alveolar tissues; water-soluble cytotoxins exist in cannabis that inhibit the bactericidal activity of alveolar macrophages; and the heat of the smoke from a cigarette depresses the activity of ciliated esophageal cells. While none of these effects poses any material hazard to patients free from pulmonary dysfunction or disease, the use of smoking devices that both filter and cool the smoke is recommended over cigarettes for therapeutic administration. Oral administration of cannabis has shown considerable effectiveness, particularly with glaucoma and antiemesis; but the physician cannot determine the dosage dependably when cannabis is eaten, since the drug is absorbed very unevenly through the G.I. tract and its decarboxylation there by HCI may alter its psychic and physiological effects in ways not yet adequately studied. The minimal untoward effects of cannabis upon lung function and tissues renders inhalation of its smoke a superior route of administration for therapeutic purposes; the patient is able to self-titrate the dosage, inhalation by inhalation, until the precise therapeutic effect is achieved.

Tachycardia, showing a pulse-rate increase of 30 to 60 percent, dependably occurs during the drug's onset in patients previously unexposed to cannabis; this usually persists 30 to 45 minutes. The rise and decline in heart action is smooth and uniform. Cannabis-induced tachycardia may render the drug inadvisable for use with patients who are receiving Digitalis in cardiac therapy.

Cannabis commonly promotes lassitude and drowsiness and has been shown to significantly prolong reaction time in human subjects. Patients receiving it should be advised not to drive or operate heavy machinery.

Drug Interactions:
While the site and nature of cannabis's mental effects in the CSN are largely unknown, it appears to raise the free levels of serotonin in the intersynaptic gap, probably by blocking its reuptake into the presynaptic neuron. Thus it appears to intensify and facilitate the effects of tricyclic antidepressants by promoting a higher intersynaptic ratio of serotonin to norepinephrine and dopamine. Its interaction with monoamine oxidase inhibitors is similarly felicitous, since both medications work to raise free serotonin levels. With the benzodiazepines, it has been suggested that cannabis may exert some yet-undetermined influence on the brain hormone GABA (gamma-aminobutyric acid) to facilitate the penetration of benzodiazepine metabolites into brain tissue and to potentiate their anxiety-alleviating action there. (*Note*: By itself, cannabis is not an antidepressant but a potentiator of moods. As an adjunct to antidepressant therapy, it should be employed only by physicians as part of a broad program of personal counseling.)

Cannabis has no known adverse reactions with any other drug. Suspicion exists, however, that in the liver cannabis metabolites may react with alcohol metabolites to promote an unwholesome modification of both drugs' psychotropic effects.

Dosage and Administration:
Psychophysiological responses to cannabis are greatly dependent on the individual patient's experience with the drug: After an initial period of three to five weeks of regular administration, a subject will exhibit a measure of habituation to some acute effects such as euphoria and tachycardia, while other effects, such as intraocular pressure reduction and antiemesis, will remain constant. Therefore it is advisable in most cases to have the patient determine the dosage for himself until the desired therapeutic effect is realized. Inhaling cannabis smoke is the most dependable known way to accomplish this.

Due to the nature of cannabis as a crude vegetable material, a standard uniform dose is virtually impossible to establish. The erratic provenance of street cannabis, which can originate from anywhere in the world, complicates it even further. Cannabis grown in northern latitudes, as a rule, will generally produce a pronounced sedative effect and its physical effects will typically be muted though prolonged. Equatorial cultivars of cannabis, by contrast, may exert a decided tonic effect with immediate and conspicuous physical effects of relatively brief duration per single dose. Of the cannabis cultivars most widely available on the street market to patients in the United States, the commonest commercial Colombian cultivar—"Santa Marta gold"—probably has the most dependable uniform effect per dose.

Usage in pregnancy:
Cannabis has no proven teratogenic properties. Due to the illegal status of the drug, however, no longitudinal epidemiological statistics are available in this regard. The United States Department of Health, Education and Welfare has imposed an arbitrary cannabis-testing ban on all women "who are or may become pregnant," rendering it impossible to scientifically investigate the influence on this or any other health concerns unique to women. The antiemetic properties of cannabis have been widely exploited by pregnant women to counteract morning nausea, but until more is known of its precise action in the body, it should not be recommended for regular use during pregnancy. Recent research has suggested that all psychotropic drugs may exert some measure of subtle teratogeny, and there is no substantive reason to believe that cannabis escapes this category. ◘

(Reprinted from High Times, July, 1980.)

Chapter Eight

CANNABIS HEMP SEED AS A BASIC WORLD FOOD

Ralph Loziers, general counsel of the National Institute of Oilseed Products, told the Congressional committee studying marijuana prohibition in 1937 that, "Hemp seed... is used in all the Oriental nations and also in a part of Russia as food. It is grown in their fields and used as oatmeal. Millions of people every day are using hemp seed in the Orient as food. They have been doing this for many generations, especially in periods of famine."

Today, we should again recognize hemp as a vital, primary link in the food chain which sustains life: Earth's premier renewable food source.

HOW AND WHY WOULD YOU EAT CANNABIS HEMP?

The cannabis hemp seed is a complete source of vegetable protein. Although soybeans contain a higher percentage of protein, the composition of the protein in hemp seed is unique in the vegetable kingdom. Sixty-five percent of hemp seed's protein content is in the form of globulin edestin.[1] (The word edestin comes from the Greek "edestos," meaning edible.)

The exceptionally high edestin content of hemp seed combined with albumin, another globular protein contained in all seeds, means hemp seed protein is readily available in the form found in human blood plasma—the fluid portion of blood which supplies nutrients to tissue.[2]

Because hemp seed contains human tissue proteins in similar proportions found in blood plasma, hemp seed may well be the most complete vegetable source of protein* on earth.

* No!, like the shirts, hemp seeds will not get you high.

Cannabis seed protein even allows a body with nutrition-blocking tuberculosis, or almost any other nutrition-blocking ailment, to get maximum nourish-ment.* Hemp leaves can also be brewed into a healthy tea and used medicinally or consumed as a beverage.

*Cohen & Stillman, *Therapeutic Potential of Marijuana*, Plenum Press, NY, 1976; Czech. Tubercular Nutritional Study, 1955.

USDA food comparisons found hempseed oil (which comprises 30% of the seed) lower in saturated fats than any other cooking oil, including soybean and canola. The byproduct of pressing hemp seed for its vegetable oil is a high protein seed cake. Hemp seed cake was one of the world's principal animal feeds until this century.*

*U.S. Agricultural Index; Frazier, Jack, *The Marijuana Farmers*, Solar Age Press, New Orleans, LA, 1972.

Hemp seed extracts, like soybeans, can be spiced to taste like chicken, steak, or pork and can be used to make tofu-type curd and margarine, at less cost than soybeans. Sprouting any seed improves its nutritional value and hemp can be sprouted and used like any other seed sprout for salads or cooking.

Hemp seed can be ground into meal, cooked, then sweetened and combined with milk to produce a nutritional breakfast cereal—like oatmeal or cream of wheat. This type of porridge is known as a gruel.

"Hemp is a favorite [bird seed] because of its nourishing oily content." (Margaret McKenny, *Birds in the Garden*, Reynal & Hitchcock, NY, 1939.) Incredibly, when cannabis hemp is grown for seed, half the weight of the mature, harvested female plant is seed!

One almost-instant potential benefit is that all domesticated animals (dogs, cats), farm animals and poultry could be fed a nearly complete diet with just protein and fat (oil) extracted from hemp seed.

These two factors alone will allow animals maximum weight gain for less than current costs without any artificial growth steroids or other drugs currently poisoning the human race and food chain.

SPECTRE OF WORLDWIDE FAMINE

By itself, widespread use of hemp seed food protein could save many of the world's children now dying of protein starvation! An estimated 60% of all children born in Third World countries (about 12-20 million a year) will die this way before reaching five years of age. Many times that number have their lives dramatically shortened and/or their brains decimated.[3]

Remember, hemp is a hearty plant that grows almost anywhere, even in adverse conditions. As have many countries throughout history, Australia survived two prolonged famines in the 19th century using nothing but hemp seeds for protein and hemp leaves for roughage.[4]

Furthermore, recent studies indicate that depletion of the ozone layer threatens to reduce world soya production by a substantial amount—up to 30% or even 50%, depending on the fluctuation of the density of the ozone shield. But hemp, on the other hand, resists the damage caused by increasing ultraviolet radiation and actually flourishes in it by producing more cannabinoids which provide protection from ultraviolet light.[5]

It's no wonder that some Central and South Americans hate America and want us out: They see us as ignorant killers. For years, our government demanded the paraquat poisoning of their lands; lands these farmers had grown cannabis on by law since 1564, when King Philip of Spain ordered it grown throughout his empire to provide food, sails, rope, towels, sheets and shirts—as well as providing one of the people's most important folk medicines for fever, childbirth, epilepsy, and poultices for rheumatism.

Today, if anyone is caught growing their old staple, cannabis, their U.S. supported government/military expropriates their lands. The leaders then qualify for more American foreign and military aid in exchange for adopting this policy of wiping out marijuana—one of their peoples' oldest livelihoods, folk medicines, food staples and joys.

A FUNDAMENTAL BIOLOGICAL LINK IN THE FOOD CHAIN

Our politicians who made these marijuana prohibition laws based on years of disinformation, may have doomed not only birds but also the human race to extinction from another direction.

Many animals eat birds and their eggs. Birds in the wild are essential to the food chain; and they continue to diminish in population due to—among other things, such as petrochemical pesticides—the lack of hemp seed! With hemp seed in their diet, birds will

live 10-20% longer. And their feathers will have mor oil, allowing longer flight.

Prior to 1937, there were more than 10 million acre of seed-laden cannabis hemp growing wild in the U.S Hundreds of millions of birds fed off them as their fa vorite and most necessary food until our governmen began its policy of total eradication of this most pr mary link in the food chain.

Oblivious to these inherent biocide (killing all life dangers, our government (Reagan/Bush/Quayle/Ran gel/Biden/Bennett/DuPont/Martinez, et al.) continue to escalate these programs of extinction, unabated both here and abroad, at the insistence of the DEA.

And not only have they tried to eradicate the hem plant (read planet savior), DuPont and other compa nies have created strains of grain—for example wheat—that only grow with *their* petro-chemical fer tilizers.

Their intention is to eradicate the surviving natura wheat and rye seeds, in the name of their persona corporate profits, leaving humanity solely at thei corporate mercy for their hybrid strains which *must* have their petro-chemical fertilizers and pesticides Corn is already so hybridized that it is not expected to last 50 years without human cultivation. If for any reason these hybrids die out—as hybrids are apt to do—we will be without wheat forever!

IF LEGALIZED AS A FOOD SOURCE:

• Hemp protein would provide the basic nutritiona building block for a variety of tasty new foods.

• The marijuana seed would be medical science' food of choice for treating nutrition blocking illnesse such as tuberculosis.

• Hemp would supply domesticated animals cheap er and better proteins, thereby producing highe quality meats and healthier pets.

• Hemp would save the starving children around the world from brain damage, physical deformity o death.

• It would help restore our world bird population.

Footnotes:

1. Walker, David W. , Ph.D., "Can Hemp Save Our Planet?", citing St. Angelo, A.J., E.J. Conkerton, J.M. Dechary, and A.M. Altschul 1966, *Biochimica et Biophysica Acta*, vol. 121, pp. 181; St. Angelo, A... L.y. Yatsu. and A.M. Altschul. 1968, *Archives of Biochemistry and Biophysics*, vol. 124, pp. 199-205; Stockwell, D.M., J.M. Dechary, and A.M. Altschul, 1964, *Biochimica Biophysica Acta*, vol. 82, pp. 221

2. Morroson, R.T. *Organic Chemistry*, 1960; Kimber, Gray Stackpole, *Textbook of Anatomy and Physiology*, 1943.

3. World Hunger Project, Save the Children, EST, Forum.

4. Frazier, Jack, *The Marijuana Farmers*, Solar Age Press, New Orleans, LA, 1972; also see Australian history books.

5. Teramura, Alan, University of MD study, Discover magazine September, 1989; Congressional testimony of Ralph Loziers, National Oil Seed Institute, before House Ways and Means Committee, 1937.

ECONOMICS: ENERGY, ENVIRONMENT & COMMERCE

We have explained what hemp has historically meant for this country's economy. Now, we must also consider the future of hemp.

We predict that the net effect of the re-legalization and deregulation of American hemp trades will be "ripple effect" economics—the spreading out of America's jobs and wealth into the hands of the community: Farmers, smaller businesses and entrepreneurs like yourself.

We now ask you to look at...

ENERGY AND THE ECONOMY

The book Solar Gas (1980), Science Digest, Omni Magazine, The Alliance for Survival, the "Green arty" of West Germany and others put the total figure of our energy costs at 80% of the total dollar exnse of living for each human being.

n validation; 82% of the total value of all issues aded on the New York Stock Exchange, other world ck exchanges, etc, are tied directly to:

• Energy supply companies (Exxon, Shell, etc.) ells/coal mines, (Con Edison, and so forth);

• Energy transportation, (pipeline companies, oil ipping and delivery companies) or;

• Refineries and retail sales (Exxon, Mobil, Shell, . Calif. Edison, NY Edison, et al.)

Eighty-two percent of all your money means that ughly into 33 of every 40 hours you work going to y for the ultimate energy cost in the goods and serces you purchase, whichever way (transportation, ating, cooking, lighting). Americans—5% of world pulation—in their drive for more 'net worth' and roductivity' use 25% to 40% of the worlds' energy. he hidden cost to the environment cannot be meaured.

Our current fossil energy sources also supply about % of the solid and airborne pollution which is slow- poisoning the planet. (See U.S. EPA report 1983-89 coming world catastrophe from carbon dioxide imalance caused by burning fossil fuels). The cheapest ubstitute for these expensive and wasteful energy ethods is not wind or solar panels, nuclear, geo-

thermal, and the like, but using the evenly distributed light of the sun to grow biomass.

On a global scale, the most energy efficient plant is hemp, an annually renewable resource able to replace all fossil fuels.

The early Oil Barons (Rockefeller of Standard; Rothschild of Shell; et al), paranoically aware in the Twenties of the possibilities of Ford's methanol scheme* and its cheapness, dropped and kept oil prices incredibly low, between $1 to $4 per barrel (there are 42 gallons in an oil barrel) for almost 50 years until 1970. So low, in fact, that no other energy source could compete with them...then once they were sure of the lack of competition, the price jumped to almost $40 per barrel in the next 10 years.

When hemp is grown for biomass as an energy crop, CO_2 is breathed in by the living plants, then when the hemp biomass is burned for energy the CO_2 is released back into the air. The CO_2 cycle is balanced.

---

* Henry Ford even grew marijuana on his estate after 1937, possibly to prove the cheapness of methanol production at Iron Mountain. He even made plastic cars with wheatstraw, hemp and sisal. (Popular Mechanics, Dec. 1941, "Pinch Hitters for Defense.") (See photo, page 47.) Meanwhile, Rudolph Diesel invented the diesel engine, which he intended to fuel "by a variety of fuels, especially vegetable and seed oils."

Until, suddenly, for whatever reason, we are now in an era when oil is not only prohibitively expensive, but embargoes or wars by foreign nations can virtually hold the U.S. hostage; that's how dependent we are on foreign sources of polluting petroleum products. Biomass conversion to fuels should begin immediately to both stop planetary pollution and make us energy independent.

By the year 2000, the U.S. will have burned 80% of its petroleum resources, while our coal reserves may last 100 years or so longer. But the decision to continue burning coal has serious drawbacks. This high-sulfur coal is responsible for our acid rain, which already kills 50,000 Americans and 5,000 to 10,000 Canadians annually.

(Brookhaven National Laboratory, 1986.)

CLEAN, RENEWABLE FUEL SOURCE

Fuel is not synonymous with petroleum. Biomass energy systems can supply a sustainable source of fuel and will create millions of new jobs. Hemp biomass can replace every type of fossil fuel energy product.

When hemp is grown for biomass as a renewable energy crop, CO_2 (carbon dioxide) is breathed in by the living plants to build cell structure; the left over oxygen is breathed out replenishing earth's air supply. Then when the carbon rich hemp biomass is burned for energy the CO_2 is released back into the air. The CO_2 cycle is balanced when the crop is grown the next year. This is the true meaning of maintaining environmental balance.

Biomass conversion through pyrolysis (applying high heat to organic material in the absence of air or in reduced air) will make charcoal to replace coal.

Charcoal contains no sulfur, so when it is burned for industry no sulfur is emitted from the process. Sulfur is the primary cause of acid rain. The rainfall in New England often falls between household vinegar and lemon juice in its acidity on the -ph scale. This is bad for every cell membrane it contacts, doing the most harm to the simplest life forms.

The biomass "cracking" process also produces non-sulfur fuel oil to replace fossil fuels. Again, no sulfur is released and the net CO_2 doesn't rise when harvested biomass is used for fuel.

Pyrolysis uses the *same* "cracking" technology employed by the petroleum industry in processing fossil fuels. The gasses that remain after the charcoal and fuel oils are extracted from hemp can be used for driving electric power co-generators, too!

This biomass conversion process can be adjusted to produce charcoal and oils for fuel, or methanol as well as chemicals important to industry: acetone, ethyl acetate, tar, pitch and creosote. The Ford Motor Co. successfully operated a biomass 'cracking' plant in the 1930s at Iron Mountain, Michigan.

"Progress in Biomass Conversion" Vol. 1, Sarkanen & Tillman, ed-itors; *Energy Farming in America*, Osburn, Lynn, BACH pub., 1989

Hemp seed contains 30% (by volume) oil. This o makes high grade diesel fuel oil and aircraft engin and precision machine oil. Remember, throughou history, hemp seed was made into fuel oil: the genie lamp burned hemp seed oil, as did Abraham th prophet's and Abraham Lincoln's. Only whale o came near hemp seed oil in popularity for fuel.

BIOMASS FOR ENERGY ABUNDANCE

The hemp plant is 80% hurds (pulp byproduct afte the hemp fiber is removed from the plant). Hem hurds are 77% cellulose—a primary chemical fee stock (industrial raw material) used in the produc tion of chemicals, plastics and fibers. Depending o which U.S. agricultural report is correct, an acre o full grown hemp plants can sustainably provide fron four to 50 or even 100 times the cellulose found i cornstalks, kenaf, or sugar cane—the planet's nex highest annual cellulose plants.

In most places, hemp can be harvested twice a yea and, in warmer areas such as Southern Californi Texas, Florida and the like, it could be a "year roun crop. Hemp has a short growing season and can b planted after food crops have been harvested.

An independent, semi-rural network of efficient an autonomous farmers will become the key economi player in the production of energy in this country.

The United States government pays (in cash or i "kind") for farmers to refrain from growing on 89 mi lion acres of farmland each year, called the soil bank And ten million to 89 million acres of hemp or othe woody annual biomass planted on this restricted, un planted fallow farmland (our Soil Bank) would mak energy a whole new ball game and be a real attemp at doing something to save the Earth.

Each acre of hemp would yield 1000 gallons c methanol. Hemp fuel derivatives, along with the re cycling of paper, etc., would be enough to ru America virtually without oil.

FAMILY FARMS OR FOSSIL FUEL?

In about 10 years, when our petroleum resource have dwindled to 20% of their original size, Americ will have four choices:

- Burn all our poisonous coal;

- Go to war over foreign oil;

- Cut down our forests for fuel; or

- Grow and process a variety of environmentall safe fuels from biomass.

Farming only 6% of continental U.S. acreage wit

…omass would provide all of America's gas and oil …ergy needs and end dependence on fossil fuels.

…Manahan, Stanley E., *Environmental Chemistry*, 4th edition.

'…llegal' Hemp is Earth's #1 biomass resource; it is …pable of producing 10 tons per acre in four months. …emp is easy on the soil,* sheds its lush foliage …roughout the season, adding mulch to the soil and …lping retain moisture. Hemp is an ideal crop for …e semi-arid west and open range land.

…Adam Beatty, vice president of the Kentucky Agricultural …iety, reported instances of good crops of hemp on the same ground …14 years in a row without a decline in yield. Beatty, A., "Southern …riculture," C.M. Saxton & Co., NY; 1843, pg. 113.

…Iemp is the only biomass source available that is …pable of making the U.S. energy independent. …timately, the world has no other rational environ-…ental choice but to give …o fossil fuels.

…But what about 'mari-…ana?' Well, farmers in …e Soviet Union, who are …ee to grow hemp, re-…rt* that people do occa-…onally snatch hemp …ranches —but they never …me back for more.

*Institute for Hemp (MN) meet-…g with a group of Soviet agricul-…re and bast crop representa-…es, March 3, 1991.

SO, WHAT'S THE CATCH?

The "catch" is obvious: …he energy companies! …hey own most of the …etro-chemicals, pharma-…utical, liquor, and tobac-… companies, and are in-…rtwined with insurance …mpanies and banks.

…Many politicians now in …ower, according to the …ress, are bought and …aid for by the energy …mpanies, and their U.S. …overnment arm is the …IA—"The Company"—…Robert Ludlum, etc.). The …ush/Quayle administration is uniquely tied to oil, …ewspapers, pharmaceuticals—and the CIA.

The world struggle for money is actually a struggle …r energy, as it is through energy that we may pro-…ace food, shelter, transportation and entertainment. … is this struggle which often erupts into open war. If

we remove the cause, these conflicts may never occur.

(Carl Sagan; and U.S. EPA prediction, 1983, of world-wide disaster in the making within 30 to 50 years.)

ENERGY SECURITY

At this point, we can tell OPEC goodbye forever. The national balance of payments deficit is cast by the wayside and your personal energy bills can be cut by at least 50%, and perhaps as much as 90% with biomass from hemp and recycled waste.

No more elderly or poor people freezing to death or living in misery in the winter.

If introduced to Third World nations, hemp biomass could drastically cut our overseas aid and reasons for war, while raising the quality of life there by quantum leaps.

New, non-polluting industries will spring up everywhere. The world economy will boom like never before. The race of man would at last be betting on environmental survival instead of indulging in the lemming-like consumption of fossil fuel, which threatens all life on the planet.

FREE ENTERPRISE & HIGH PROFIT

There are many other areas of the economy that would benefit from the re-legalization of hemp and de-regulation of commerce in non-smoking hemp, according to the non-profit Business Alliance for Commerce in Hemp (BACH).

Legal hemp would return billions of dollars worth of natural resource potential back to the farmers and bring millions of good jobs in ener-gy production to America's heartland. Hemp energy farmers will become our producers of raw materials for many of the nation's needs.

Family farms will be saved. Crops can be tailored to the needs of the nation. Biomass can be grown for fuel at about $30 per ton or seed crops can be

---

World War II:

THE MOST RECENT TIME AMERICA ASKED ITS FARMERS TO GROW MORE MARIJUANA

Our national energy needs are an undeniable national security priority. Look what Uncle Sam can do when pushed into action:

In 1942 Japan cut off our supplies of vital hemp and coarse fibers. Marijuana, which had been outlawed as the 'Assassin of Youth' just four years earlier was suddenly safe enough for our government to ask the kids in the Kentucky 4-H club to grow the nation's 1943 seed supply. The youths were urged to grow at least half an acre but preferably two acres of hemp each.

(U. of KY Ag. Extension Leaflet 25, Mar., 1943)

In 1942-43 farmers were made to attend showings of the USDA film *'Hemp for Victory,'* sign that they had seen the film and read a hemp cultivation booklet. Hemp harvesting machinery was made available at low or no cost. Five dollar tax stamps were available and 350,000 acres of cultivated hemp was the goal by 1943. (See transcript p. 104.)

Farmers from 1942 through 1945 who agreed to grow hemp were waived from serving in the military, along with their sons; that's how vitally important hemp was to America during World War II.

pressed for oil; the left over seed cake makes a high protein raw food resource.

Hemp grown for fiber will bring the paper and textile industry out of the hands of the multinational corporations, and back to the local communities.

Research by this Los Angeles based business association indicates there are around 50,000 non-smoking commercial uses for hemp that are economically viable and market competitive. These include:

A CHANGE IN HIGH FASHION

The arrival of newly imported hemp-cotton blended clothing from China* in 1989 signals the beginning of a new era for the rapidly changing world of fashion.

* Joint Venture Hempery and the Hemp Colony imports of shirts and shorts with the Stoned Wear® label can be found at a number of retail outlets or ordered by using the form in the back of this book.

Drawing on hemp fiber's special attributes —absorbency, insulation and strength—clothing manufacturers and designers will once again put hemp into linen to produce new lines of durable and attractive clothing and textiles.

Outerwear, warm bedsheets, soft towels (hemp is more water absorbent than cotton), diapers (even disposable ones that you don't have to cut down trees to make), upholstery, wall coverings, natural rugs—all these can now be designed and made from hemp: generally better, cheaper and ecologically safer.

Trade barriers and laws restricting the use of imported cannabis fibers need to be removed.

Right now textiles and apparel are the biggest share of imports into the U.S., at 59%. In 1989 textile imports accounted for 21% of the U.S. merchandise trade deficit. Foreign governments often subsidize their textile industries and do not require companies to follow environmental and health regulations.* Hardy hemp does not cause the environmental problems associated with cotton.

*The Washington Spectator, Vol. 17, No. 4, Feb. 15, 1991

The United States imports more textiles than anything else, yet the government obstructs hemp textile and apparel importation. Hemp textiles will not be fully cost competitive until hemp fiber can be grown and processed domestically, to avoid bloated federal import fees and lower the costs of transportation.

STURDY PAPER PRODUCTS

The devastated environments and job markets of the American Northwest and other timber regions stand to make a dramatic comeback once hemp is reintroduced to the domestic paper industry.

And, as in the case of soybeans, recent studies indicate that depletion of the ozone layer threatens substantially reduce world loblolly pine productic (the major source of pulp for paper)—by up to 30% even 50%, depending on the fluctuation of the dens ty of the ozone shield. But hemp not only resists tl damage caused by increased ultraviolet radiatic —it actually flourishes in it.

* Increased UV radiation causes hemp to produce more glandul oils and increases the weight of the plant. (Teramura, Ala University of MD study, Discover magazine, September, 1989.)

Paper mills can return to full production levels ar loggers will find new work in hemp trades.

Truck drivers can continue to haul pulp to tl mills, and lumber for construction, although the pri of lumber will go down as other demands on our tin ber resources are reduced by substituting farn grown hemp for forest-grown wood pulp. (Orego Hemp Products Inc., Jim Evans, Ashland, Oregon.)

There will also still be a lot of work to do in r forestation. Our rivers will go through a period of r covery following the 60-80% reduction of paper mal ing chemicals being dumped into them when hem replaces wood pulp in the paper industry.

This means more fish and more fishing, as well a increased camping and tourism in the beautiful an vital new-growth forest regions—and the spared ol growth forests.

A BIODEGRADABLE REPLACEMENT FOR PLASTIC

Hemp paper bags would be stronger and hav greater folding endurance than wood pulp pape bags,* eliminating the need for non-biodegradabl plastic bags at the supermarket.

* Dewey & Merrill, Bulletin #404, U.S. Dept. of Ag., 1916.

Hemp hurds are also the most efficient source cellulose, which can be polymerized for making pla tics including cellophane and celluloid or engineere into any number of plastic items.

These can be treated or rendered biodegradable; a least, as biodegradable as any other plastic—a topi still surrounded in controversy.

SPIN-OFF TRADES & TAXES

Hemp cellulose and oils can be used for literall tens of thousands of other uses from paints to dyna mite. Each application means new opportunities.

As each new hemp trade develops, money will flo from it to re-energize seemingly unrelated areas the economy. The American worker and soon-to-b rich entrepreneurs will bring millions of new job and new products to the marketplace.

FROM THE GROUND UP
HENRY *FORD'S THERMOCHEMICAL REACTOR*

Henry Ford and the hemp fueled and fabricated car he "grew from the soil" are shown in this photo with the original caption as appeared in *Popular Mechanics*, Dec., 1941.

The flow chart below illustrates various paths by which chemical feedstocks, transportation fuels, electricity and heat for industrial use are derived. Hemp is ideal for pyrolitic conversion into all the products illustrated in the center of the chart. The

Here is the auto Henry Ford "grew from the soil." Its plastic panels, with impact strength 10 times greater than steel, were made from flax, wheat, hemp, spruce pulp

same basic thermochemical decomposition process is used to refine both biomass and fossil fuels. Municipal and agricultural wastes are also suitable for this process, and as a supplemental resource can supply up to ten percent of our energy needs.

High moisture herbaceous plants, such as sugar cane and corn, are best suited for biochemical conversion. The resulting fermented alcohols are valuable chemical feedstocks. Bacterial digestion can also produce methane rich biogas, an excellent boiler fuel.

BIOMASS
vs
FOSSIL FUELS

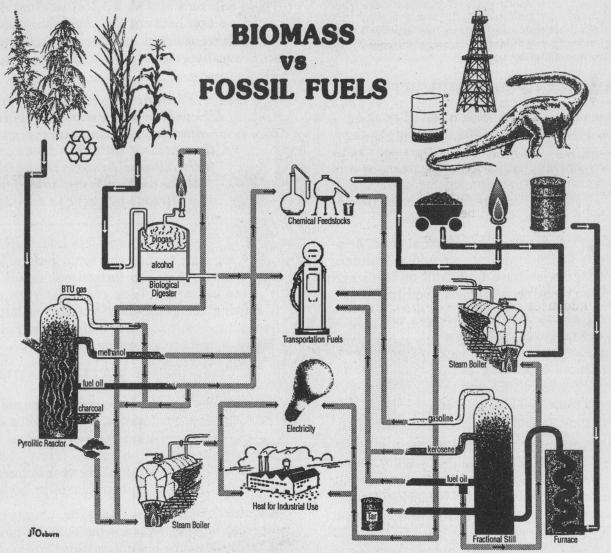

Biomass derived fuels can provide all U.S. energy needs currently supplied by fossil fuels. America has consumed 80% of her known oil and gas reserves. The use of biomass derived fuels will reduce acid rain and reverse the greenhouse effect.

Cont. From Pg. 46

They will also buy thousands of homes, cars and other non-hemp goods, thus stimulating a real economic expansion based on the ripple effect, rather than trickle-down economics—pumping money directly into the bloodstream of the American heartland and benefiting all of society.

Revived farms mean more purchases of equipment and each new business creates spin-off jobs in the shipping, marketing and commodities areas.

Farms, banks and investment houses would also realize large profits, and the billions of hemp-dollars in the legitimate economy would increase tax revenues and increase the liquid capital available for investment and purchasing of consumer goods.

Federal, state and local governments would realize a windfall of hundreds of millions of dollars in tax revenues without raising taxes.*

* "If the marijuana, cocaine and heroin markets were legal, state and federal governments would collect billions of dollars annually," assistant professor of politics at Princeton University, Ethan Nadleman said. "Instead, they expend billions in what amounts to a subsidy of organized criminals." (L.A. Times, November 20, 1989, pg. A-18.)

BALANCING THE BUDGET

Lots of money is already being made off smoking marijuana; $41.5 billion in 1988, according to the DEA. Add to that the huge (but suppressed) home growing and smoking accessories industries, as well as the necessary farm equipment for non-smoking production, looms, etc, and hemp could erase the national debt in a matter of a few short years.

Land values will rise in depressed rural areas, helping to rescue farmers, developers and speculators who might otherwise have to default on loans and further worsen the savings and loan (S&L) crisis.

An obvious comparison can be drawn between the federal government's low-end estimate of the national black market economy exceeding $41.5 billion in marijuana in 1988 and the plan to spend some $50 billion on an S&L bailout plan in 1989.

With billions more to be made from licensed hash bars and brand-name products, the marijuana industry will soon be as big as beer. If America is serious about balancing its budget, there is clearly a common sense economic option that needs to be addressed.

LAND & SOIL RECLAMATION

Land reclamation is another compelling economic and ecological argument for hemp cultivation.

Until this century, our pioneers and ordinary American farmers used cannabis to clear fields for planting, as a fallow year crop, and after forest fire to prevent mudslides and loss of watershed.

Hemp seeds put down a 10- to 12-inch root in only 30 days, compared to the one-inch root put down by the rye or barley grass presently used by the U.S. Government.

Southern California, Utah and other states used cannabis routinely in this manner until about 1915. It also breaks up compacted, overworked soil.

In the formerly lush Himalaya region Bangladesh, Nepal and Tibet there is now only a light moss covering left as flash floods wash millions of tons of topsoil away.

In 1964, Bangladesh (from bhang-cannabis-la-land, desh-people) signed an 'anti-drug' agreement with the U.S. not to grow hemp. Since that time the 'marijuana-land-people' have suffered disease, starvation and decimation, due to unrestrained flooding.

Farming only 6% of the continental U.S. with biomass would provide all of America's oil and gas energy needs, thus ending our dependence on fossil fuels. 'Illegal' hemp is the #1 biomass source on Earth: capable of producing 10 tons per acre in four months.

Hemp seeds sown free from airplanes flying over eroding soil could reclaim land the world over. The farmed out desert regions can be brought back year after year, not only slowing the genocide of starvation but easing threats of war and violent revolution.

NATURAL GUARD

Instead of a National Guard, why not establish a Natural Guard of environmental soldiers to be our front line for survival—planting trees, harvesting biomass (eg., hemp) from marginal farm lands?

A Natural Guard of electricians, plumbers, engineers and laborers who are put to work re-building the infra-structure of America: our roads, bridges, dams, canals, sewers, railroad tracks, etc.

Isn't this the humane, civilized and socially responsible way to use our human resources, rather than warehousing people like animals in prisons?

MYTH, MAGIC & MEDICINE:

A LOOK AT THE SOCIOLOGY OF CANNABIS USE THROUGHOUT WORLD HISTORY

Contrary to popular conception, "marijuana" is not a phenomenon rooted in the 1960s.

Cannabis hemp is part of our heritage and was the backbone of our most stable and longest surviving cultures.

Recent psycho-pharmacological studies have discovered THC has its own unique receptor sites in the brain indicating man and marijuana have a pre-cultural relationship—indeed, human culture could very well prove to be the blossom of our symbiosis with cannabis.

WHAT'S IN A NAME (PART 2)

The following is derived from the 1913 U.S.D.A. Agriculture arbook section on hemp by Lyster Dewey, p. 283- 293:

The name "hemp," derived from the Old English anf," came into use in Middle English by 1,000 D. and still belongs primarily to cannabis sativa. It also used to designate the long fiber obtained from at plant: the earliest, best-known and, until recent- the most widely used textile fiber on Earth.

It has long been regarded as the standard among ng fibers. As such, its name has come to be used as generic term for all long fibers. Now commodity arkets list names like "Manila hemp," abacá; "sisal emp," sisal and henequen; "Mauritius hemp," for rcraea fiber, "New Zealand hemp," phormium; unn hemp," Crotalaria; and "India hemp," for jute. l these plants are unlike true hemp in appearance d in economic properties. Curiously, the name is ver applied to flax, which is more nearly like hemp an any other commercial fiber.

True hemp is known in different languages by the llowing names: *cannabis*, Latin; *chanvre*, French; ñamo, Spanish; *canhamo*, Portuguese; *canapa*, alian; *canep*, Albanian; *konopli*, Russian; *konopi* d *penek*, Polish; *kemp*, Belgian; *hanf*, German; nnup, Dutch; *hamp*, Swedish; *hampa*, Danish; nevir, Bulgarian; *ta-ma*, *si-ma* and *tse-ma*, hinese; *asa*, Japanese; *nasha*, Turkish; *kanabira*, rian; *kannab*, Arabic.

FIRST KNOWN CANNABIS USERS

Ancient and modern historians, archaeologists, anropologists, philologists and the physical evidence ey cite (artifacts, relics, textiles, cuneiform, lan-guages, etc.) indicate that cannabis is one of mankind's oldest cultivated crops. The weaving of hemp fiber as an industry began 10,000 years ago, at approximately the same time as pottery making and prior to metal working.*

* Columbia History of the World, Harper & Row, NY, 1981.

From at least the 27th century B.C. until this century, cannabis was incorporated into virtually all cultures of the Middle East, Asia Minor, India, China, Japan, Europe, & Africa.

By the 27th century B.C., the Chinese cultivated "Ma" (cannabis hemp) for fiber, medicine and herbal use. 3,700 years later (circa 1000 A.D.), China called cannabis "Ta-Ma," or "great hemp," to differentiate it from the minor fiber plants, which were grouped under the generic fiber term "Ma." Their pictogram for true hemp is a large "man," indicating the strong relationship between man and hemp.

(Shen Nung Pharmacopoeia; Ponts'ao Ching; Han Dynasty classics; et al.)

BETWEEN 2300 B.C. AND 1000 B.C.:

Nomadic tribes, probably from central Asia and Persia (Iran and Iraq), and referred to in legend as Aryans, invaded and overran virtually everywhere in the Mediterranean and Middle East and over the Caucasus and west into Europe.

In the course of these movements and invasions the nomads introduced cannabis and its various uses north and west through Greece, Europe, the Middle East, to Egypt (and possibly even Africa) and south and East "over" the Himalayas to India.

Cannabis was incorporated into the cultures of the Middle East and India for its vast food, oil and fiber uses. Not only was hemp a staple of everyday livelihood; hemp drugs were a ritual link to the Gods.*

* Generally, those who grew and/or used hemp for everyday industrial uses did not know and was not taught (by religious law/threat/taboo) that his priest/shaman/witchdoctor/etc. used different extractions of the exact same plant for sacrament, medicine, unguent, etc.

HEMP AND THE SCYTHE...

Cannabis was undoubtedly used by the Scythians for many reasons. For example, the ancient Scythians grew hemp and harvested it with a hand reaper that we still call a scythe. Cannabis inhalation by the Scythians in funeral rituals was recorded by the Greek Historian Herodotus (Circa 450 B.C.), a custom apparently introduced to the Scythians by the Thracians in the early Sixth century B.C. The nomadic Scythians carried it on to other races...

(Emboden, W.A., Jr., *Flesh of the Gods*, Praeger Press, NY, 1974.)

HAREM LADY IN HER TRADITIONAL POSE
Circa 1876.

THREAD OF CIVILIZATION

From at least the 27th century B.C. up until this ce tury, cannabis was incorporated into virtually all t cultures of the Middle East, Asia Minor, Indi China, Japan, Europe, and Africa for its superi fiber, medicines, oils, food and for its meditative, e phoric, and relaxational uses.

Hemp was one of our ancestors' most importa overall industries, along with toolmaking, anim husbandry and farming.

HEMP TO ENFORCE THE LAW

The hemp plant has had a curious relationship wi the world's legal codes throughout the ages. As not before, it has variously been illegal to grow hemp a not to grow it at different times. But hemp has al played a direct role in law enforcement.

For example: The most serious punishment/rehab itation meted out in many African tribes for capit crimes was forcing the transgressor to smoke ma sive amounts of dagga (cannabis) non-stop for hou on end in a small, enclosed hut until he pass out—literally unconscious from inhaling the fum The equivalent of a year or two's supply for a hea American smoker is consumed in just an hour or Does it work? African users say the rate of repe criminal offenses after dagga treatment is virtua non-existent.

European and American cultures used hemp to e force their laws in a more terminal form of capit punishment: the hangman's noose* of hempen rope

* "Merry boys are we/As e're did sing/ In a hempen string/ Un the gallows tree." John Fletcher *Rollo, Duke of Normandy*; Act III, 3; 1639. "We're bound to stop this business, or hang you to a m For we've hemp and hand enough in town to hang the whole da clan." From a horse thief's tombstone in Rapid City, SD, 18 Shushan, E.R.; Grave Matters; Ballantine Books, NY, 1990. Also *Hemp for Victory*, USDA film; 1942.

CANNABIS HERBAL MEDICINES

The secret art of hemp medicine was found effecti as wound healer, muscle relaxant, pain reliever, fev reducer and unparalleled aid to childbirth, not mention hundreds of other medicinal applications.

(Mikuriya, Tod H., M.D., *Marijuana: Medical Papers, 1839-19 Medi-Comp Press, Oakland, CA, 1973; Shultes, R.E., Harva Botanical; Ency. Brittanica; Abel, Ernest, *Marijuana: The Fi 12,000 Years*;. Plenum Press, 1980; Vera Rubin, *Cannabis a Culture*, Institute for the Study of Man; et. al.)

Division of information about this sacred herb a industrial hemp uses was strictly maintained by t priests for thousands of years, up until the last fe centuries. Those outside the priestly class who p sessed drug knowledge were considered (by t priests, of course) to be witches/soothsayers/outla and the ilk, and were often condemned to death.

THE MYSTIC PHILOSOPHERS

Cannabis legend and consumption are fundamental aspects of many of the world's great religions.

For example:

SHINTOISM (Japan)—Marijuana was used for the binding together of married couples, to drive away evil spirits, and was thought to create laughter and happiness in marriage.

HINDUISM (India)—The God Shiva is said "to have brought cannabis from the Himalayas for human enjoyment and enlightenment." The Sardu priests travel throughout India and the world sharing "chillum" pipes filled with cannabis, sometimes blended with other substances. In the Bhagavad-gita, Krishna states, "I am the healing herb" (Ch.9:16), while the Bhagarat-purana Fifth Canto describes hashish in explicitly sexual terms.

BUDDHISTS (Tibet, India and China)—from the 5th century B.C. on—ritually used cannabis; initiation rites and mystical experiences were (are) common in many Chinese Buddhist Sects. Some Tibetan Buddhists and lamas (priests) consider cannabis their most holy plant. Many Buddhist traditions, writings, and belief indicate that "Siddhartha" (the Buddha) himself, used and ate nothing but hemp and its seeds for six years prior to announcing (discovering) his truths and becoming the Buddha (Four Noble Truths, the Eightfold Path).

Regarding the *ZOROASTRIANS* or Magi (Persia, c. eighth to Seventh Centuries B.C. to Third to Fourth Centuries A.D.), it is widely believed by many Christian scholars, commentators, etc., that the three "Magi" or Wise Men who attended the birth of Christ were cult references to the Zoroastrians. The Zoroastrian religion was based (at least on the surface) on the entire cannabis plant, the chief religious sacrament of its priest class, and its most important medicine, (e.g., obstetrics, incense rites, anointing and christening oils), as well as lighting or fire oils in their secular world. The word "magic" is generally considered derived from the Zoroastrians—"Magi."

The *ESSENES* (ancient Israel) used hemp medicinally, as did the *THERAPUTEA* (Egypt), from whom we get the term "therapeutic." Both are believed by some scholars to be disciples of, or in a brotherhood with, the priests/magicians of the Zoroastrians.

SUFIS OF ISLAM (Middle East) are Moslem "mystical" priests who have taught, used and extolled cannabis for divine revelation, insight and oneness with Allah, for at least the last 1,000 years. Many Moslem and world scholars believe the mysticism of the Sufi Priests was actually that of the Zoroastrians who survived Moslem conquests of the 7th and 8th

THE SACRED SMOKE

Pygmy ingesting dagga / marijuana smoke

centuries A.D. and subsequent conversion (change your religion and give up liquor or be beheaded).

Some *COPTIC CHRISTIAN* (Egypt/Ethiopia) sects believe the sacred "green herb of the field" in the Bible ("I will raise up for them a plant of renown, and they shall be no more consumed with hunger in the land, neither bear the shame of the heathen any more." Ezekiel 34:29) and the Biblical secret incenses, sweet incenses and anointing oils to be cannabis.

The *BANTUS* (Africa) had secret Dagga Cults,* societies which restricted cannabis use to the ruling men. The Pygmies, Zulus and Hottentots all found it an indispensable medication for cramps, epilepsy and gout, and as a religious sacrament.

*Their "Dagga" cults believed Holy Cannabis was brought to earth by the Gods, in particular from the "Two Dog Star" system that we call Sirius A and B. "Dagga" literally means "cannabis." Interestingly, the surviving Indo-European word for the plant can also be read as "canna," "reed" and "bi," "two," as well as 'canna,' as in canine; and 'bis,' meaning two (bi)--"Two Dogs."

The *RASTAFARIANS* (Jamaica and elsewhere) are a contemporary religious sect that uses "ganja" as its sacred sacrament to communicate with God (Jah).

"NATURAL MIND"

New United States government funded studies at St. Louis Medical University in 1989 and the National Institute of Drug Abuse in 1990 moved cannabis research into a new realm by confirming that the human brain has receptor sites for in the brain for THC and its natural cannabis cousins which, so far, no other known compounds will bind to.

In order for a chemical to affect the brain it must

bind to a receptor site capable of receiving it.

One reason cannabis is so safe to use is that it does not affect any of the involuntary muscles of breathing and life support. Rather, it affects its own specific receptor cites for motion (movement strategy) and memory (mental strategies).

(Omni, 1989; the Washington Post, 1990; NY Times, July 21, 1990.)

At a cellular level, bits of the compounds fit snugly into the human brain cells' special receivers. This points to an ancient symbiosis between the plant and people, for nothing like THC is made in the body.

Reference to cannabis and other spiritual drug use is often hidden in art during periods of repression. Stylized hemp leaves surround the angels' heads, and their halos resemble the cap of the amanita muscario mushroom in *The Third Day of Creation,* entrance hall of San Marco painted in Venice, Italy. (Sixth to seventh century A.D.)

Although morphine fits the receptor sites of beta-endorphin roughly, and amphetamines correspond loosely to dopamine, these drugs as well as tricyclics and other mood altering drugs present grave danger to the subtle balance of the nerve's vital fluids. Obviously Omni and the NY Times cited no physical dangers in natural cannabis: only the unwanted side-effect of euphoria.

Perhaps these neuronal pathways are the product of pre-cultural symbiosis between man and cannabis. Carl Sagan proposes evidence using the Bushmen of Africa to show hemp to have been the first plant cultivated by man dating to when he was a hunter-gatherer. Some scientists assume that these receptor sites did not evolve for the purpose of getting high: "There must be some kind of neuronal pathway in the brain that developed, whether there were cannabis plants or not," speculated mystified St. Louis University pharmacology professor Allyn Howlett in 1989.

But, maybe not. In his book *Intoxication: Life in Pursuit of Artificial Paradise,* Dr. Ronald K. Siegel, psycho-pharmacologist at UCLA indicates the motivation to achieve altered states of consciousness or moods is a fourth drive akin to hunger, thirst and sex. And humans aren't the only ones to get high. Siegel recorded numerous observations of animals intentionally getting intoxicated.

Cannabis hemp is part of our cultural, spiritual and physiological heritage, and was the backbone of our most stable and long surviving cultures. So, if you

want to know the lon term effects of mari juana use...look in th mirror!

CLOAKED IN SECRECY

The dawn of religiou beliefs for all races an people—Japan, Chin India, Egypt, Pers and Babylon, to Gree Doric, Germanic an European tribes, an even those of Africa an North, South and Cen tral America—derive from accidental disco eries.

There were nea death experiences, d privations— starvatio fasting, breath contro thirst, fever—and u controlled revelry du to accidental fermentation or extraction of wine, bee psilocybe and Amanita mushrooms, cannabis win (Bhang) and other psychoactives which, when con sumed, induced inexplicable, elevated experienc (compared to normal brutish experience). Chemica in these sacred plants and herbs gave our ancesto unexpected, unprepared for, unbelievable visions an journeys into the far corners of incredible consciou ness and, sometimes, universal brotherhood.

Understanding these drug-induced experiences an medications eventually became the most wondrou desirable and necessary spiritual knowledge for eac tribe. Healing! From which extraction? At what dos

Holding this mystical tribal knowledge for futur generations was a priceless task. To know whic plants induced which experiences at what level an mixture meant power!

Thus, this "sacred store" of knowledge was jealous guarded by the herbal doctor/priest, and cryptical encoded in oral and written traditions and myth (e.g., plants with psychoactive powers were embue with human or animal attributes).

To keep their political power, these traditions we deliberately withheld from the "common" tribal men bers (and all other tribes), by the witch doctors an medicine men of the priest/ shaman classes. This als prevented the dangerous "sin" of accidental inge tion, concoction, or experimentation by the childre of the tribe; nor could captured tribal members gi

...p this sacred knowledge to their enemies.

These "old-time" drug and out-of-body religions and rituals, dating back to pre-history, were called "Oriental Mystery Religions" by the Romans from the Caesars' time on.

JUDAIC LINE

Hemp was a major industry in biblical times.

Like other cultures throughout the Middle East, the Hebrew tradition of mysticism (e.g., Cabala) was aware of, and entwined with, regional sects using natural intoxicants in their rituals. As usual, they hid this knowledge behind rituals, symbols and secret codes to protect natural sacraments like "sacred mushrooms" and mind elevating herbs, including cannabis.

Allegro, J.M.; *Sacred Mushroom & the Cross*, Doubleday Co., 1970.

WHAT DOES THE BIBLE SAY?

Finding the encoded references to cannabis and other drugs is made more difficult by the lack of botanical names, discrepancy in translations, use of different "books" by different denominations, commentaries added to original texts, and periodic priestly purges of material considered inappropriate.

About 95% of the people were not allowed to learn Latin, the language of the Bible, which effectively allowed those few priests who could read to interpret the scriptures as they pleased.

However, we find that the use of cannabis is never forbidden or even discouraged in the Bible. Some passages directly refer to the goodness of using herbs like cannabis—and it even predicted prohibition.

"And the Earth brought forth grass and herb-yielding seed after its kind and the tree yielding fruit, whose seed was in itself after its kind: and God saw that it was good." *Genesis: Chapt. 1: Verse 12 (King James Version of the Bible, unless noted).*

"God makes the earth yield healing herbs, which the prudent man should not neglect." *Sirach: 38:4 (Catholic Bible.)*

"Not that which goeth into the mouth defileth a man; but that which cometh out of the mouth defileth a man." *Jesus, quoted: Matt. 15:11.*

"In later times, some shall...speak lies in hypocrisy...commanding to abstain from that which God hath created to be received with thanksgiving of them which believe and know the truth." *Paul: 1 Tim. 1:4*

EARLY CHRISTIANITY

Historians, early artworks, Bibles, manuscripts, Dead Sea Scrolls, Gnostic Gospels, letters from early church fathers, etc., indicate that for the first 300 to 400 years A.D., many early Christian sects were gentle and loving. They were usually open, tolerant and unstructured: a poor man's or slave's religion.

Rome considered Christianity to be simply another bothersome Oriental Mystery cult, like those of Mithra or Isis, then the most popular in the Empire.

THE HOLY ROMAN EMPIRE

Faced with a crumbling empire, political corruption and a series of ruinous wars with barbarians, the old Roman Empire hovered on the brink of disaster. The religious contortions undertaken by the ruling body in Rome to maintain its earthly power led the political leaders to crack down on healthy diversity in the field of individual cults and religions.

To save itself politically, the formerly pantheistic (meaning tolerant of different worships) government of the empire changed its policy.

Starting in 249 A.D., various emperors launched a string of bloody persecutions, which included the troublesome Christians. By 306 A.D., it was clear that this was not working. Emperor Constantine called off the executions and began to patronize the Christian clergy, which promptly adopted a dogma lifted from "Mithraism," among other religions: 'Royal Blood by Birth,' the 'Divine Right to Rule other humans.'

The ambitious Constantine saw that while underground, the church had developed into an intolerant, tightly-knit hierarchy; a well organized network second in influence only to his own. By combining church and state, each was able to double its power and seek out the crimes/sins of all its political rivals and enemies with the full support/blessing of the other.

Columbia History of the World, Harper & Row, NY, 1981.

Constantine soon converted to Christianity and declared one mandatory, monistic, state-empowered religion: the Roman Catholic Church (R.C.Ch.); literally, the Roman Universal Church ("catholic" is latin for "universal"). This was now the absolute and official religion of the empire. In one sweep, all secret societies were outlawed which might have threatened his (and Rome's) mandate to rule the known world, as they had for the previous 400 consecutive years.

CHURCH/STATE ARISTOCRACY

After running from the Roman Empire's police for almost 300 years, Christian Orthodox priests had become their bosses. Starting in the Fourth and Fifth century A.D., pagan religions and all the different Christian sects, beliefs, knowledge, gospels, etc., such as the Essenes and Gnostics, were either incorporated into or edited out of official doctrine and hierarchy.

Finally, in a series of councils, all contrary dogmas (e.g. that the earth was round, and the sun and stars were more than five to 17 miles away) were summarily outlawed and driven underground during the Dark Ages, 400 to 900 A.D. By the early Middle Ages, 10th and 11th centuries A.D., virtually all powers were placed in the hands of the Church and Pope; first, by Germanic conquerors and later by powerful Spanish and French Kings and powerful Italian merchants and nobles (the Borgias, Medicis and other megalomaniacs) probably to protect their trade secrets, alliances and sources of wealth.

All European people were forced to adhere to the "Holy" Roman Empire policy: Zero tolerance by a fundamentalist church/police-state with blind faith in one, unquestioned version of how to worship God...and the Pope's infallibility.

Political rulers aided and abetted the Church in this fraud, as their power now rested only on their new Christian dogma, the patriarchal "Divine right" to rule.

They enacted laws with fantastically vicious punishments for even the slightest infraction or heresy.* Heretics were mercilessly sought out by fanatical, sadistic inquisitors using perverted forms of torture to extract confessions and as punishment.

* Webster's dictionary defines "Her-e-sy (her'e se)" as 1: a religious belief that is opposed to church dogma. 2: any opinion (in philosophy, politics, etc.) opposed to official or established views or doctrines. 3: the holding of any such belief or opinion.

This system kept most of the Western world's inhabitants in a state of constant terror, not only for their own physical safety and freedom, but also for their eternal spirit, with "Hell" lurking mere inches below the surface for those excommunicated by the church.

THE POLITICS OF PAPER

The masses of people, "the commons," were kept in check through a dual system of fear and enforced ignorance: All learning except the most rudimentary was controlled and strictly regulated by the priests.

The commons (about 95% of the people) were forbidden to learn to read or write—not even an alphabet —and often were punished or put to death for doing so.

The people were also forbidden to learn Latin, the language of the Bible. This effectively enabled the few priests who could read to interpret the scriptures any way they pleased for about 1200 years, until the reformation in Europe.

To prohibit knowledge, people were literally kept in the dark, without a piece of paper to write on. The monasteries preserved and guarded hemp's secrets.

They saw that it held two threats to this policy of abslute control: papermaking and lamp oil.

Something had to be done.

CANNABIS MEDICINES FORBIDDEN

While embracing wine as a Sacrament, and tolering beer and hard liquor, the Inquisition outlaw cannabis ingestion in Spain in the 12th century, a France in the 13th. Many other natural remedies we simultaneously banned. Anyone using hemp to co municate, heal or otherwise was belled "witch."

Bird Mask filled with herbs to fend off plague.

Saint Joan of Arc, for exampl was accused in 1430-31 of using variety of herbal "witch" drugs, i cluding cannabis, to hear voices.

LEGAL MEDICINES CONSISTED OF:

Virtually the only legal medic cures allowed the people of Weste Europe by the R.C.Ch. Fathers this time were:

1. Wearing a bird mask (f plague). (See picture.)

2. Bleeding pints and even quar of blood from all flu, pneumonia fever patients (victims) was the most used treatme in Europe and America by doctors until this century. does not work! and did not work for thousands of yea (no matter how much blood they took).

3. Praying to specific Saints for a miraculous cu (e.g. St. Anthony for ergotism, St. Odilla for blindne St. Benedict for poison sufferers, St. Vitus for comed ans and epileptics) was encouraged.

4. Alcohol was legal.

In 1484, Pope Innocent VIII singled out cannab healers and other herbalists, proclaiming hemp an u holy sacrament of the second and third types of satar mass, which lasted for more than 150 years.

Satanic knowledge and masses, according to t Medieval Church, came in three types:

• To Summon or Worship Satan;

• To Have Witch's Knowledge (e.g., herbalists chemists) of making, using or giving others ar unguent or preparation—including cannabis—as me icine or as a spiritual sacrament;

• **The Mass of the Travesty**, which can be liken to the Simpsons, In Living Color, rap music, M Brooks, Second City-TV, Monty Python, or Saturd: Night Live (Father Guido Sarducci-type group) doi irreverent, farcical or satirical take-offs on the dogma

octrines, indulgences, and rituals of the R.C.Ch. mass
nd/or its absolute beliefs.

In other words, because medieval bureaucrats
nought they were sometimes laughed at, ridiculed
nd scorned (often by the most learned monks, clerics
nd leading citizens) under its influence, ingesting
annabis was proclaimed heretical and Satanic.

CONTRADICTIONS

Despite this centuries-long attack by the most power-
al political and religious force in Western civilization,
emp cultivation continued in Northern Europe,
frica and Asia. While the church persecuted cannabis
sers in Europe, the Spanish conquistadors were busy
anting hemp everywhere around the world to pro-
de sails, rope, oakum, clothes, etc.

YET, HEMP ENDURED

The sadistic Ottoman Empire conquered Egypt and,
the 14th century A.D., tried to outlaw cannabis—be-
use Egyptian hemp growers along the Nile were
ading tax revolts. The Turks complained that
annabis use caused Egyptians to laugh and be disre-
pectful to their Sultan and his representatives. In
368, Egypt became the first modern(?) country to out-
w cannabis ingestion, followed in 1910 by South
frica to punish and stop the blacks practicing their
ncient Dagga cults and religions.

In Europe, hemp was widely used both industrially
d medicinally, from the Black Sea (Crimean) to the
ritish Isles, especially in Eastern Europe. The papal
an on cannabis medicines in the Holy Roman Empire
1484 was quite unenforcable north of the Alps, and
this day the Romanians, Czechs and Hungarians
minate world cannabis agronomy.

In Ireland, already world famous for its cannabis
en, the Irish woman who wanted to know whom she
uld eventually marry was advised to seek revelation
rough cannabis.

Eventually, the hemp trades once again became so
portant to the empire builders who followed (in the
e of Discovery/Reason, the 14th to 18th centuries)
at they were central to the intrigues and maneuver-
gs of all the World's great powers.

THE AGE OF ENLIGHTENMENT

The 18th century ushered in a new era of human
ought and civilization; "Life, liberty and the pursuit
happiness!" declared the colonists in America. "Lib-
ty, Fraternity, Equality!" replied their French
usins. The concepts of modern constitutional govern-
ent, guaranteed human rights and separation of
urch and state were unified into a policy designed to
otect citizens from intolerant and arbitrary laws.

ECONOMICS: THE VERY MODEL OF A MODERN INQUISITION

For cannabis-related knowledge, or hundreds of
other "sins"—owning a devil's tool (dinner fork),
reading a sorcerer's book or speaking in tongues
(foreign language), having a different faith, having
the witch's habit (taking a bath or falling into a river), etc.—10% to 33% of the people in Western
Europe were tortured or put to death without trial
during the medieval Roman Catholic Church's 500-
year Inquisition. (11th to 17th centuries.)

While most suffered, some profited handsomely.
The Pope could declare anything "heresy," and use it
as an excuse to legally rob, torture and kill his enemies or anyone else accused. For over 300 years, inquisitors divided up the property forfeited to them by
suspected witches and heretics. Whoever denounced
you else got 1/3 of your property, 1/3 went to the government and 1/3 went to the Papal hierarchy.*

"Beware the scribes which…devour widows' houses." *Jesus, quoted: Luke 20:46*

This perverted prosecution-for-profit model is used
today by state and federal drug warriors just as self-
righteously. Everyone from informant to the prosecutor now share in the bounty of forfeited goods.

In fact, while British common law is the basis for
our modern legal system, forfeiture law relies on the
medieval concept of the cursed object—"deodand"
(from the latin "deo," god and "dare," give; meaning
that any object causing human death was forfeited
to the crown)—is the basis for seizure and confiscation of property rather against persons.

Why? Simple. People have guaranteed legal rights:
property doesn't.

In his landmark essay, *On Liberty,* Ogden Livingston
Mills, whose philosophy shaped our democracy, wrote
that "Human liberty comprises, first, the inward domain of consciousness in the most comprehensive
sense: liberty of thought and feeling, …scientific,
moral or theological, …liberty of tastes and pursuits."

Mills asserted that this freedom of thought or of
"mind" is the basis for all freedoms. Gentleman farmer
Thomas Jefferson's immortal words, "I have sworn
upon the altar of God eternal hostility against every
form of tyranny over the mind of man," are engraved
into the marble of his Memorial in Washington D.C.

Abraham Lincoln was an avowed enemy of prohibition. His wife was prescribed cannabis for her nerves
after his assassination. Virtually every president from
the mid-19th century up until prohibition routinely
used cannabis medicines (See chapter 12: Nineteenth

JEFFERSON'S COMPARISON

Thomas Jefferson wrote and acted on behalf of hemp many times, smuggling rare seeds into America, redesigning the hemp brake, keeping his farm journals and writing this on March 16, 1791:

"The culture (of tobacco) is pernicious. This plant greatly exhausts the soil. Of course, it requires much manure, therefore other productions are deprived of manure, yielding no nourishment for cattle, there is no return for the manure expended....

"It is impolitic. The fact well established in the system of agriculture is that the best hemp and the best tobacco grow on the same kind of soil. The former article is of first necessity to the commerce and marine, in other words to the wealth and protection of the country. The latter, never useful and sometimes pernicious, derives its estimation from caprice, and its value from the taxes to which it was formerly exposed. The preference to be given will result from a comparison of them: Hemp employs in its rudest state more labor than tobacco, but being a material for manufactures of various sorts, becomes afterwards the means of support to numbers of people, hence it is to be preferred in a populous country.

"America imports hemp and will continue to do so, and also sundry articles made of hemp, such as cordage, sail cloth, drilling linnen and stockings.

century use).

More recently, close acquaintances and entertain associates of John Kennedy say he used cannabis reg larly to control his back pain and actually planned legalizing "marijuana" during his second term—a pla cut short by his assassination in 1963.

"How Heads of State Got High," High Times, April, 1980 (see appendi

More recently, former president Gerald Ford's s and Jimmy Carter's son Chip admit to having smok pot in the White House. George Bush's vice preside Dan Quayle had a reputation for smoking grass an using drugs in college. Ronald and even former fir lady Nancy "Just Say No" Reagan are reported to ha smoked pot in the California Governor's mansion.

"Smoke Screen: Inmate Sues Justice Department Over Quayle-Cover-up," Dallas Observer, August 23, 1990. Kelley, Kitty, Nan Reagan: The Unauthorized Biography, Doubleday Co., NY, 1991.

General Footnote/Bibliography:

Hindu Vedas; Shen Nung Pharmacopoeia Herodotus; Abel, Erne Marijuana: The First 12,000 Years;. Plenum Press, 1980; Dead S Scrolls; High Times Encyclopedia; Encyclopaedia Britannic "Pharmacological Cults;" Roffman, Marijuana and Medicine, 198 Ohio State Medical Society, 1860; British Indian Hemp Report, 189 Ungerleider UCLA, 1982; U.S. Army, Edgewood Arsenal, Marylar (Multiples); Shultes, Harvard Botanical; EmBowden, UC Northridg Michael Aldrich, Ph.D.; Vera Rubin, Institute for the Study of Ma Wasson, R. Gordon, SOMA, Divine Mushroom of Immortalit Roffman, Marijuana and Medicine; etymologist Jay Lynn; Allegr J.M., Sacred Mushroom and the Cross, Doubleday & Co., 1970, et al.

NAPOLEON'S EMPIRE • 1810

Chapter Eleven

THE WAR OF 1812 ...
AND NAPOLEON INVADES RUSSIA

This is a piece of history that you may have been a little bit hazy about when they taught it in school:

What the heck were we fighting about, anyway?

We present the events that led up to the Battle of New Orleans, fought three weeks after the war was officially over...

TIME:

1700s AND EARLY 1800s

Cannabis hemp is, as it has been for thousands of years, the biggest business and most important industry on the planet. Its fiber (see chapter 2, "Uses") moves virtually all the world's shipping. The entire world's economy uses and depends upon thousands of different products from the marijuana plant.

1740 ON...

Russia, because of its cheap slave/serf labor, produces 80% of the western world's cannabis hemp, finished hemp products, and is, by far, the world's best-quality manufacturer of cannabis hemp for sails, rope, rigging and nets.

Cannabis is Russia's number one trading commodity—ahead of its furs, timber and iron.

1740 TO 1807

Great Britain buys 90% or more of its marine hemp from Russia; Britain's navy and world sea trade runs on Russian hemp; each British ship must replace 50 to 100 tons of hemp every year or two.

There is no substitute; flax sails, for example, unlike hemp sails, would start rotting in three months or less from salt air and spray.[1]

1793 TO 1799 ON...

The British nobility is hostile toward the new French government primarily because the British are afraid that the 1789-93 French Revolution of commoners could spread, and/or result in a French invasion of England and the loss of its Empire and, of course, its nobility's heads.

1803 TO 1814

Britain's navy blockades Napoleon's France, including Napoleon's allies on the Continent. Britain accomplishes the blockade of France by closing their (France's) English Channel and Atlantic (Bay of Biscay) ports with its navy; also, Britain controls absolute access to and from the Mediterranean and Atlantic, by virtue of its control of the straits of Gibraltar.

(SEE MAP ON FACING PAGE.)

1798 TO 1812

The fledgling United States is officially "neutral" in the war between France and Britain. The United States even begins to solve its own foreign problems by sending its navy and marines (1801-1805) to the Mediterranean to stop Tripoli pirates and ransomers from collecting tribute from American Yankee traders operating in the area. "Millions for Defense—not a penny for Tribute" was America's rallying cry, and the incident came to be memorialized in the second line of the Marine Corps' hymn: "...to the shores of Tripoli."

1803

Napoleon, needing money to press war with Great Britain and pursue control of the European continent, bargain-sells the Louisiana Territory to the United States for $15 million, or roughly two-and-a-half cents per acre.

This area is about one-third of what is now the 48 contiguous states.

TIME:

1803 ON...

The Louisiana Purchase gives rise to some Americans,' mostly Westerners, dreams of "Manifest Destiny"—that is, the United States should extend to the utmost borders of North America: From the top of Canada to the bottom of Mexico and from the Atlantic to the Pacific.

(SEE MAP, NEXT PAGE.)

1803 TO 1807

Britain continues to trade and buy 90% of its hemp directly from Russia.

1807

Napoleon and Czar Alexander of Russia sign the Treaty of Tilset, which cuts off all legal Russian trade with Great Britain, its allies, or any other neutral nation ship acting as agents for Great Britain in Russia.

The treaty also sets up a buffer zone, the Warsaw Duchy (approximately Central Eastern Poland) between Napoleon's allies and Russia.

(SEE MAP.)

Napoleon's strategy—and his most important goal with the treaty—is to stop Russian hemp from reaching England, thereby destroying Britain's navy by forcing it to cannibalize sails, ropes, and rigging from other ships; and Napoleon believes that eventually, with no Russian hemp for its huge navy, Britain will be forced to end its blockade of France and the Continent.

1807 TO 1809

The United States is considered a neutral country by Napoleon, as long as its ships do not trade with or for Great Britain, and the United States considers itself to be neutral in the war between France and Great Britain.

However, Congress passes the 1806 Non-Importation Pact: British articles which are produced in the U.S., but which could be produced elsewhere, are prohibited. Congress also passes the 1807 Embargo Act, to wit: American ships could not bring or carry products to or from Europe.

These laws hurt America more than Europe; however, many Yankee traders ignored the law anyway.

1807 TO 1814

After the Treaty of Tilset cuts off their Russian trade, Britain claims that there are no neutral countries or shipping lanes.

Hence, any ship that trades with Napoleon "Continental System" of allies are the enemy and a subject to blockade.

On this pretext, Britain confiscates American ship and cargo and sends sailors back to the Unite States at American ship owners' expense.

Britain "impresses" some American sailors into se vice in the British Navy. However, England claim that they only "impress" those sailors who are Britis subjects—and whose American shipping companie refused to pay for the sailors' return fares.

1807 TO 1810.

Secretly, however, Britain offers the capture American traders a "deal" (actually a blackma proposition) when they "overhaul"—board and confi cate—an American ship and bring it into an Englis port.

The deal: Either lose your ship and cargos foreve or go to Russia and secretly buy hemp for Britai who will pay American traders with gold in advanc and more gold when the hemp is delivered back.

At the same time, the Americans will be allowed keep and trade their own goods (rum, sugar, spice cotton, coffee, tobacco) to the Czar for hemp —a do ble profit for the Americans.

1808 TO 1810.

Our shrewd Yankee traders, faced with the choi of either running British blockades—and riskin having their ships, cargo and crews confiscated— acting as secret (illegal) licensees for Britain, wit safety and profits guaranteed, mostly choose the la ter.

John Quincy Adams (later to become president who was American Consul at St. Petersburg, in 180 noted:

"As many as 600 clipper ships, flying the America flag, in a two week period, were in Kronstadt" (th Port of St. Petersburg, now called Leningrad, Russi loading principally cannabis hemp for England (ill gally) and America, where quality hemp is also great demand.

(Bemis, *John Q. Adams and the American Foreign Policy*, N York, NY, Alfred A Knopf, 1949.)

The United States passes the 1809 Non-Intercour Act, which resumes legal trade with Europe; exce Britain and France. It is soon replaced with th Macon Bill resuming all legal trade.

1808 TO 1810.

Napoleon insists that Czar Alexander stop all tra with the independent United States traders as th

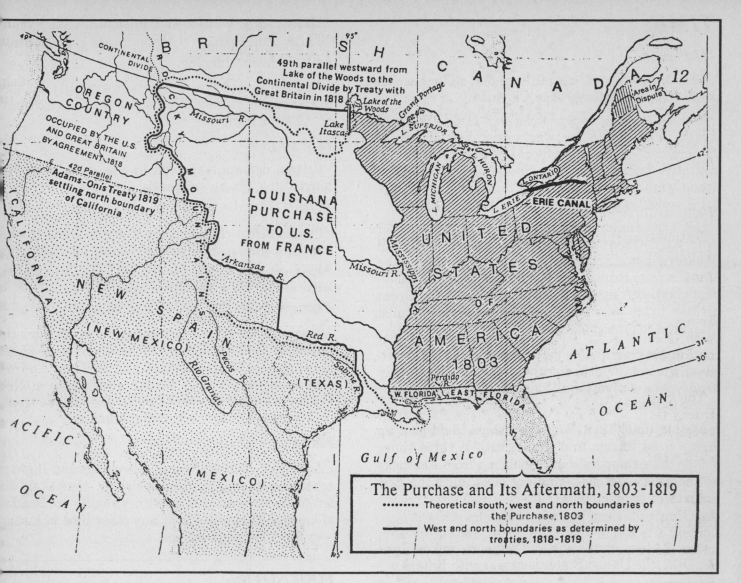

The Purchase and Its Aftermath, 1803-1819

·········· Theoretical south, west and north boundaries of
the Purchase, 1803

————— West and north boundaries as determined by
treaties, 1818-1819

re being coerced into being illegal traders for Great
ritain's hemp.

Napoleon wants the Czar to allow him to place/sta-
on French agents and troops in Kronstadt to make
ure the Czar and his port authorities live up to the
reaty.

TIME:

808 TO 1810.

The Czar says "Nyet!" despite his treaty with
rance, and turns a "blind eye" to the illegal
merican traders, probably because he needs the
opular, profitable trade goods the Americans are
ringing him and his Nobles—as well as the hard
old he is getting from the Americans' (illegal) pur-
hases of hemp for Great Britain.

809.

Napoleon's allies invade the Duchy of Warsaw.

810.

Napoleon orders the Czar to stop all trade with the

American traders! The Czar responds by withdrawing Russia from that part of the Treaty of Tilset that
would require him to stop selling goods to neutral
American ships.

1810 TO 1812.

Napoleon, infuriated with the Czar for allowing
Britain's life blood of navy hemp to reach England,
builds up his army and invades Russia, planning to
punish the Czar and ultimately stop hemp from
reaching the British Navy.

1811 TO 1812.

England, again an ally and full trading partner of
Russia, is still stopping American ships from trading
with the rest of the Continent.

Britain also blockades all U.S. traders from Russia
at the Baltic Sea and insists that American traders
have to now secretly buy other strategic goods for
them (mostly from Mediterranean ports), specifically
from Napoleon and his allies on the Continent who
by this time are happy to sell anything to raise capital.

TIME:

1812

The United States, cut off from 80% of its Russian hemp supply, debates war in Congress.[3]

Ironically, it is representatives of the Western states who argue for war under the excuse of "Impressed" American sailors. However, the representatives of the Maritime States, fearful of loss of trade, argue against war, even though it's their shipping, crews, and states that are allegedly afflicted.

Not one senator from a Maritime State votes for war with Great Britain, whereas virtually all Western senators vote for war, hoping to take Canada from Britain and fulfill their dream of "manifest destiny," in the mistaken belief that Great Britain is too busy with the European wars against Napoleon to protect Canada.

It's interesting to note that Kentucky, a big supporter of the war which disrupted the overseas hemp trade, was actively building up its own domestic hemp industry.

At this time, 1812, American ships could pick up hemp from Russia and return with it three times faster than shippers could get hemp from Kentucky to the East coast over land—at least, until the Erie Canal was completed in 1825.

(SEE MAP.)

The Western states win in Congress, and on June 18, 1812, the United States is at war with Britain.

America enters the war on the side of Napoleon, who marches on Moscow in June of 1812.

Napoleon is soon defeated in Russia by the harsh winter, the Russian scorched-earth policy, 2,000 miles of snowy and muddy supply lines—and by Napoleon not stopping for the winter and regrouping before marching on Moscow, as was the original battle plan.

Of the 450,000 to 600,000 men Napoleon starts with, only 180,000 ever make it back.

1812 TO 1814

Britain, after initial success in war with the United States (including the burning of Washington in retaliation for the earlier American burning of Toronto, then the colonial Canadian capitol), finds its finances and military stretched thin—with blockades, war in Spain with France, and a tough new America on the seas.

Britain agrees to peace, and signs a treaty with the United States in December, 1814. The actual terms of the treaty give little to either side.

In effect, Britain agrees it will never again interfer with American shipping.

And the United States agrees to give up all claim to Canada forever (which we did, with the exceptio of "54-40 or Fight").

1813 TO 1814

Britain defeats Napoleon in Spain and banishe him to Elba, but he escapes for 100 days.

1815

Britain defeats Napoleon at Waterloo (June 18) an banishes him to St. Helena Island off Antarctic where, in 1821, he dies and his hairs and privat parts are sold to the public for souvenirs.

JANUARY 1815

Tragically for Britain, almost three weeks after th December 24, 1814 signing of the Ghent peace treat between the United States and Britain, Andre Jackson defeats a huge British attack force at Ne Orleans (January 8, 1815) while news of the treat slowly makes its way across the Atlantic.

20TH CENTURY

American, British, French, Canadian and Russia schools each teach children their own, completely di ferent versions of history, with virtually no mentio of hemp in this war—or at any other time in histor —in the American versions.

FOOTNOTES

1. Russia—under the Czars' and Russian Orthodox Church's dom nation—continued to have virtual slave/serf/peasant labor for mak ing hemp until 1917.

2. One of America's leading foreign trade deficits, until this centu ry, was to Russia for hemp.

3. Crosby, Alfred, Jr., *America, Russia, Hemp & Napoleon*, Oł State U. Press, 1965.

This situation only began to improve after the 1898 (Spanish American War) conquest and acquisition of the Philippines with it (cheap) coolie labor and manila-hemp (abaca).

AUTHOR'S NOTE:

The author wishes to apologize to history buffs fo all the nuances I have left out from the outline of th 1812 Wars, for example, the Rothschilds, Illuminati stock market manipulations, etc., but I did not wan to write War and Peace. It's been done.

I just want to be sure that our children are taught true comprehensive history in our schools, not wa tered down nonsense that hides the real facts.

Chapter Twelve

CANNABIS DRUG USE IN 19TH CENTURY AMERICA

Although cannabis hemp products for fiber, paper, nautical use, lamp oil, food, etc., were possibly the largest agricultural and industrial business in the world and America in 1839, the hundreds of medical uses of cannabis (known for thousands of years in the Orient and Middle East) were almost entirely unknown in Western Europe and America until 1839 because of the earlier Medieval Catholic Church's suppression.

However, the 19th Century saw a dramatic re-discovery of the benefits of cannabis drugs, which grew in popularity across the U.S., bringing with it healthful elixers and patent medicines, luxuriant Turkish Smoking Parlors and a fountain of literary creativity.

MARIJUANA MEDICINE IN 19TH CENTURY AMERICA

From 1850 to 1937, cannabis was used as the prime medicine for more than 100 separate illnesses or diseases in U.S. pharmacopoeia.

During all this time (until the 1940's) science, doctors, and drug manufacturers (Lilly, Parke-Davis, Squibb, etc.) had no idea of its active ingredients.

Yet from 1842 until the 1890s, marijuana, generally called Cannabis Indica or Indian Hemp extractums, was one of the three items (after alcohol and opium) most used in patent and prescription drugs (in massive* doses, usually by oral ingestion).

* Doses given during the 19th century to American infants, children, youth, adults, women in childbirth, and senior citizens, in one day, were, in many cases, equal to what a current moderate-to-heavy American marijuana user probably consumes in a month or two, using U.S. government's 1983 guidelines for comparison.

Violence was equated with alcohol use; addiction to morphine was known as the "soldiers' illness."

And so, during that era, cannabis gained favor and was even recommended as a way of helping alcoholics and addicts recover.

However, cannabis medicines had been largely lost to the West since the days of the Inquisition. (See Chapter 10, "Sociology.")

Until, that is, W.B. O'Shaugnessy, a 30 year old British physician serving in India's Bengal* province, watched Indian doctors use different hemp extracts successfully to treat all types of illness and disease then untreatable in the West, including tetanus.

* Bengal" means "Bhang Land," literally Marijuana Land.

Papers written by users and doctors using cannabis told straight forward accounts of its usually euphoric, and sometimes disphoric, mind- and time-expanding properties, as well as hilarity and increased appetites.

He then did an enormous (and the first Western) study,* in 1839, and published a 40-page paper on the uses of cannabis medicines. At the same time, a French doctor named Roche was making the same re-discovery of hemp in Middle Eastern medicines.

* O'Shaugnessy used patients, animals, and himself for his research and experiments. Incidentally, O'Shaugnessy went on to become a millionaire and was knighted by Queen Victoria for building India's first telegraph system in the 1850s.

O'Shaugnessy's medical paper and findings on hemp extracts stunned and swept through the Western medical world; in just three years...marijuana was an American and European Super Duper Superstar.

Papers written by first time American users (novices) and doctors using, treating, or experimenting with cannabis, told straight forward accounts of its usually euphoric, and sometimes disphoric, mind- and time-expanding properties for both child and adult, as well as hilarity and increased appetites, especially the first few times they tried it.

Interestingly, during this whole period of time (1840s to 1930s) Lilly, Squibb, Parke Davis, Smith Brothers, Tildens, etc., had no effective way to prolong its very short shelf life and virtually no idea when they had a cannabis extract that worked.

Some temperance organizations even suggest hasheesh as a substitute for (wife beating) "Demon" alcohol.

As noted before, marijuana medicine was so highly regarded by Americans (including some Protestant theologians) during the last century that in 1860, for example, the Committee on Cannabis Indica for the Ohio State Medical Society reported and concluded that, "High Biblical commentators [scholars]" believe "that the gall and vinegar, or myrrhed wine, offered to our Saviour, immediately before his crucifixion, was in all probability, a preparation of Indian hemp [marijuana], and even speak of its earlier use in obstetrics."*

* Reprinted from the transcripts of the 15th annual meeting of the Ohio State Medical Society, at White Sulphur Springs, Ohio, June 12-14, 1860, pg. 75-100.

The main reasons that cannabis medicines fell into disuse in America was the difficulty of identifying and standardizing dosage.

Also, doctors in the late 19th century could not find a way to inject it into humans with their brand new hypodermic needles...and still haven't.

By the 1890s, some of the most popular American marriage guides recommend cannabis as an aphrodisiac of extraordinary powers—no one ever suggested a prohibition law against cannabis. And while there was talk of an alcohol prohibition law, a number of women's temperance organizations even suggested hashish as a substitute for "Demon" alcohol, which they said led to wife beating.

A POPULAR INSPIRATION OF THE 19TH CENTURY LITERARY GREATS

From the early 1800s on, some of the world's foremost romantic and revolutionary writers on individual freedom and human dignity extolled cannabis use. We study their works in school today as 'classics':

Victor Hugo: *Les Miserables*, 1862, *Notre Dame of Paris* (Hunchback of...), 1831.

Alexandre Dumas: *The Count of Monte Cristo* 1844, *The Three Musketeers*, 1844.

Coleridge, Gautier, De Quincy, Balzac, Baudelaire, and John Greenleaf Whittier (Barbara Fritchie), etc.

Cannabis and mushroom imagery influenced Lewis Carroll's *Alice in Wonderland*, 1865, and *Through the Looking Glass*, 1872. (see picture)

In the early 1860s, Mark Twain's best friend and mentor was the already famous best-selling writer and advocate of cannabis, the young (mid-20s) Fitz Hugh Ludlow (*The Hashish Eater*, 1857).

Ludlow extolled hashish eating as a wondrous mind adventure but warned strongly against over-indulgence of it and all drugs.

These authors' stories usually had several things in common:

A complete love of individual freedom; respect for the dignity of each human's search for individual consciousness; and humorous contempt for the establishment, beliefs, bureaucracies and injustices of their day (for example, *Les Miserables*).

The science of psycho-pharmacology started in France circa 1845 with Doctor J.J. Moreau DeTours and cannabis became one of the first drugs used to treat the insane and depressed.

Moreau was best friends with Dumas, Hugo, and Gautier, and in 1845 co-founded with them in Paris the first cannabis club in the Western World: Le Club Des Haschischins.

MAPLE SUGAR HASHISH CANDY

Starting in the 1860s, the "Ganjah Wallah Hasheesh Candy Company" made maple sugar hashish candy which soon became one of the most popular treats in America.

It was sold over the counter and advertised in newspapers by Sears-Roebuck, as well as being listed in its own catalogs, as a totally harmless fun candy for 40 years.

"A SCENE IN ONE OF THE RECENTLY OPENED TURKISH SMOKING PARLORS"
—New York Herald, Sunday, April 28, 1895.

TURKISH SMOKING PARLORS

World Fairs and International Expositions from the 1860s through the early 1900s often featured a popular Turkish Hashish Smoking exposition and concession. Hashish *smoking* was entirely new for Americans, its effects came on much faster, however, smoking hashish was only about one-third as strong, or long lasting as orally ingesting the cannabis extract medicines that even American children were regularly prescribed.

At America's giant 100-year 1876 Centennial Exposition in Philadelphia, fair goers took their friends and family to partake (smoke) at the extremely popular Turkish Hashish Exposition, so as to "enhance" their fair experience.

By 1883, similar hashish smoking parlors were open in every major American city, including New York, Boston, Philadelphia, Chicago, St. Louis, New Orleans, and so on.

The Police Gazette estimated there were over 500 hashish smoking parlors in New York City in the 1880s and it was estimated by the NYPD that there were still 500 or more hashish parlors in N.Y.C. in the 1920s—more of these parlors than there were "speakeasys" during the same 1920s alcohol prohibition period.

AS AMERICAN AS APPLE PIE

By the start of this century almost four generations of Americans had been using cannabis.

Virtually everyone in this country was familiar from childhood on with the "highs" of cannabis extract—yet doctors did not consider it habit forming, anti-social or violent at all after 60 years of use.

This leads us to an important question: If it was not fear of health or social consequences that led to the eventual ban of cannabis use in America (and later forced on the rest of the world), what did?

THE SMEAR CAMPAIGN

What socio-political force would be strong enough to turn Americans against something as innocent as a plant—let alone one which everyone had an interest in using to improve their own lives?

Earlier, you read how the first federal anti-marijuana laws (1937) came about because of William Randolph Hearst's lies, yellow journalism and racist newspaper articles and ravings, which from then on were cited in Congressional testimony by Harry Anslinger as facts.

But what started Hearst on the marijuana and racist scare stories? What intelligence or ignorance, for which we still punish fellow Americans to the tune of 12 million years in jail in just the last 50 years, (500,000 arrested in 1988 alone for marijuana)—brought this all about?

The first step was to introduce the element of fear of the unknown by using a word that no one had ever heard of before: "marijuana."

The next step was to keep the maneuverings hidden from the doctors and hemp industries who would have defended hemp by holding most of the hearings on prohibition in secret.

And, finally, to stir up primal emotions and tap right into an existing pool of hatred that was already poisoning society: racism.

The blackface team of McIntyre and Heath had audiences rolling in the aisles for decades. They repeated this feat in the musical, The Ham Tree.

Chapter Thirteen

PREJUDICE:

MARIJUANA AND THE JIM CROW LAWS

Since the abolition of slavery, racism and bigotry have generally had to manifest themselves in less blatant forms in America.

The cannabis prohibition laws illustrate again this institutional intolerance of racial minorities and show how prejudice is concealed behind rhetoric and laws which seem to have an entirely different purpose.

SMOKING IN AMERICA

The first known* smoking of female cannabis tops in the Western hemisphere was in the 1870s in the West Indies (Jamaica, Bahamas, Barbados, etc.); and arrived with the immigration of thousands of Indian Hindus imported for cheaper labor. By 1886, Mexicans and Black sailors, who traded in those islands, picked up and spread its use throughout all the West Indies and Mexico.

* There are other theories about the first known "smoking" of hemp flower tops, e.g., by American and Brazilian slaves, Shawnee Indians, etc., some fascinating—but none verifiable.

Marijuana smoking was generally used in the West Indies to ease the back-breaking work in the cane fields, beat the heat, and to relax in the evenings without the threat of an alcohol hangover in the morning.

"Negroes, Mexicans and entertainers,"—and their jazz and swing music—were declared an outgrowth of marijuana use.

Given its late 19th century area of usage—the Caribbean West Indies and Mexico—it is not surprising that the first recorded use of marijuana in the U.S. was in the port of New Orleans, in the Black dominated "Storeyville" section frequented by sailors in 1909.

New Orleans' Storeyville was filled with cabarets, brothels, music, and all the other usual accouterments of "red light" districts the world over.

Sailors from the Islands took their shore leave and their marijuana there.

BLACKFACE ...

The Public Safety Commissioner of New Orleans wrote that, "marijuana was the most frightening and vicious drug ever to hit New Orleans," and in 1910 warned that regular users might number as high as 200 in Storeyville alone.

To the D.A. and Public Safety Commissioners and New Orleans newspapers from 1910 through the 1930s, marijuana's insidious evil influence apparently manifested itself in making the "darkies" think they were as good as "white men."

In fact, marijuana was being blamed for the first refusals of black entertainers to wear blackface* and for hysterical laughter by Negroes under marijuana's influence when told to cross a street or go to the back of the trolley, etc.

* That's right, your eyes have not deceived you. Because of a curious quirk in the "Jim Crow" (segregation; apartheid type) laws, black Americans were banned from any stage in the Deep South (and most other places in the North and West also). Negroes had to wear (through the 1920s) blackface—(like Al Jolson wore when he sang "Swanee") a dye which white entertainers wore to resemble or mimic black people. Actually, by "Jim Crow" law, blacks were not allowed on the stage at all, but because of their talent were allowed to sneak/enter through back doors, put on blackface, and pretend to be a white person playing the part of a black person...

...AND ALL THAT JAZZ

In New Orleans, whites were also concerned that black musicians, rumored to smoke marijuana, were spreading (selling) a very powerful (popular) new "voodoo" music that forced even decent white women to tap their feet and was ultimately aimed at throwing off the yoke of the whites. Today we call that new music... Jazz!

Blacks obviously played upon the white New Orleans racists' fears of "voodoo" to try to keep whites out of their lives. Jazz's birthplace is generally recognized to be in Storeyville, New Orleans, and home of the original innovators: Buddy Bohler, Buck Johnson and others (1909-1917). Storeyville was also the birthplace of Louis Armstrong* (1900).

* In 1930—one year after Louis Armstrong recorded "Muggles" (read: "marijuana")—he was arrested for a marijuana cigarette in Los Angeles, California and put in jail for 10 days until he agreed to leave California and not return for two years.

American newspapers, politicians, and police, ha virtually no idea, for 15 years (until the 1920s, an then only rarely), that the marijuana the "darkies and "Chicanos" were smoking in cigarettes or pipe was just a weaker version of the many familiar con centrated cannabis medicines they'd been takin; since childhood, or that the same drug was smoke at the local "white man's" plush hashish parlors.

ANSLINGER'S HATRED OF BLACKS AND JAZZ

After retirement, Harry Anslinger personally delivered his papers from his 30 years as the world's top narc to the University of Pennsylvania.

From the Anslinger papers and the Washington, D.C., DEA Library (containing the old F.B.N. papers and memos), we have this: From 1943 to 1948, Anslinger ordered all his agents throughout the country to watch and keep marijuana criminal files on virtually all jazz and swing musicians; but not to bust them until he could coordinate all the jazz busts on the same night.

Anslinger kept files on Thelonius Monk, Louis Armstrong, Les Brown, Count Basie, Jimmy Dorsey, Duke Ellington, Dizzy Gillespie, Lionel Hampton, Andre Kostelanetz, Cab Calloway, the NBC Orchestra, the Milton Berle show, the Coca-Cola program, the Jackie Gleason show and even the Kate Smith program.

His goal and dream was to bust them all in one giant nationwide sweep! This would garner the front page of every newspaper in America, and make Anslinger more well-known than his chief rival, the famous J. Edgar Hoover. The jazz and swing musicians would be shown to the youth of America for what they really were — "dope fiends."

Anslinger ordered his agents to keep files and constant surveillance on the following "low life" Americans and their bands, singers and comedians: Thelonius Monk, Louis Armstrong, Les Brown, Count Basie, Cab Calloway, Jimmy Dorsey, Duke Ellington, Dizzy Gillespie, Lionel Hampton, Andre Kostelanetz. Also under surveillance were the NBC Orchestra, the Milton Berle show, the Coca-Cola program, the Jackie Gleason program, and even the Kate Smith program. People we think of today as wonderful Americans and musical innovators.

For five years they were watched and the files grew. From 1943 to 1948 the federal agents waited to make their move.

Typical of a "small time" jazz musicians' files is the following: "Defendant is a colored man in Camden, Texas, born ----, is 5'8" tall, 165 lbs., black complexion, black hair, black eyes. He has scars on left forehead, and a tattoo of a dagger and the word----, on his right forearm. He is a musician and plays the trumpet in small 'hot bands.' He has a very large mouth and thick lips which earned him his name of————. He is a marijuana smoker." Other files are just as ridiculous, racist and anti-jazz.

The only reason the big bust of the musicians didn't go down? Anslinger's superior at the Treasury Department, Assistant Secretary Foley, when informed by Anslinger of the nationwide jazz musician round-up, wrote back: "Mr. Foley disapproves!"

Anslinger's longtime and closest departmental associate and probably his best friend, Dr. James Munch*, was interviewed in 1978 about Anslinger's hatred for jazz musicians in the '30s, '40s, and '50s, by Larry Sloman for a book published by Bobbs-Merrill, "Reefer Madness," in 1979.

* Dr. Munch, a chemist for the FBN, was widely touted by the Government and press as America's foremost authority on the effects of marijuana during the 1930's and 40's.

Sloman: "Why did he [Anslinger] want to go after them [the jazz/swing musicians] so much?"

Dr. Munch: "Because the chief effect as far as they [Anslinger, FBN] were concerned was that it lengthens the sense of time, and therefore they could get more grace beats into their music than they could if they simply followed the written [musical] copy..."

Sloman: "What's wrong with that?"

Dr. Munch: "In other words, if you are a musician, you are going to play the thing [music] the way it is printed on a sheet. But, if you're using marijuana, you are going to work in about twice as much music in between the first note and the second note. That's what made jazz musicians. The idea that they could jazz things up, liven them up, you see."

Sloman: "Oh, I see"

Just a few of the marijuana suspects Anslinger had followed for more than five years each in the 1940s.

White racists wrote articles and passed city and ate laws without this knowledge for almost two ecades, chiefly because of Negro/Mexican vicious nsolence"* under the effect of marijuana.

* Vicious Insolence: Between 1884 and 1900, 3,500 documented aths of black Americans were caused by lynchings; between 1900 d 1917, over 1,100 were recorded. The real figures were undoubt- ly higher. It is estimated that one-third of these lynchings were for nsolence," which might be anything from looking (or being accused looking) at a white woman twice, to stepping on a white man's adow, even to looking a white man directly in the eye for more an three seconds, not going directly to the back of the trolley, etc.
It was obvious to whites, marijuana caused Negro and Mexican "vi- ousness" or they wouldn't dare be "insolent"; etc...
Hundreds of thousands of negroes and Chicanos were sentenced om 10 days to 10 years mostly on local and state "chain gangs" for ch silly crimes as we have just listed.
This was the nature of "Jim Crow" Laws until the 1950s and 60s; e laws Martin Luther King, the NAACP, and general public outcry ave finally begun remedying in America.

We can only imagine the immediate effect the Black ntertainers' refusal to wear blackface had on the hite establishment, but seven years later, 1917, toreyville was completely shut-down. Apartheid had s moment of triumph.

No longer did the upright, up-tight white citizen ave to worry about white women going to toreyville to listen to "voodoo" jazz or perhaps be aped by its marijuana-crazed "Black adherents" who howed vicious disrespect (insolence) for whites and heir "Jim Crow Laws" by stepping on their (white en's) shadows and the like when they were high on arijuana.

Black musicians then took their music and mari- uana up the Mississippi to Memphis, Kansas City, t. Louis, Chicago, etc., where the (white) city fa- hers, for the same racist reasons, soon passed local arijuana laws to stop "evil" music and keep white omen from falling prey to Blacks through jazz and arijuana.

MEXICAN-AMERICANS

In 1915, California and Utah passed state laws out- lawing marijuana for the same "Jim Crow" rea- sons—but directed through the Hearst papers at Chicanos.

Mexicans under marijuana's influence were de- manding humane treatment, looking at white women, and asking that their children be edu- cated while the parents harvested sugar beets; and other "insolent" demands.

Colorado followed in 1917. Its legislators cited ex- cesses of Pancho Villa's rebel army, whose drug of choice was supposed to have been marijuana. Which, if true, means that marijuana helped to overthrow one of the most repressive and evil regimes Mexico ever suffered.

The Colorado Legislature felt the only way to pre- vent an actual racial bloodbath and the overthrow of their (whites') ignorant and bigoted laws, attitudes and institutions was to stop marijuana.

Mexicans under marijuana's influence were de- manding humane treatment, looking at white wom- en, and asking that their children be educated while the parents harvested sugar beets; and other "inso- lent" demands. With the excuse of marijuana (Killer Weed) the whites could now use force and rationalize their violent acts of repression.

This "reefer racism" continues into the present day. In 1937, Harry Anslinger told Congress that there were between 50,000 to 100,000* total marijuana smokers then in the U.S. and most of them were "Negroes and Mexicans, and entertainers," and their music, jazz and swing were an outgrowth of this marijuana use. He insisted this "satanic" music and the use of marijuana caused white women to "seek sexual relations with Negroes!"

* Anslinger would flip to know there are 26 million daily marijuana users now, and that rock & roll and jazz are enjoyed by tens of millions who have never smoked marijuana.

SOUTH AFRICA TODAY

In 1910, South Africa* began the outlawing of marijuana for the same reasons as New Orleans: to stop insolent Blacks! And South Africa, along with Egypt, led the international fight (League of Nations) to have cannabis outlawed world-wide.

* South Africa still allowed its Black mine workers to smoke dagga in the mines, though. Why? Because they were more productive!

In fact, in that same year, South Africa influenced Southern U.S. legislators to outlaw cannabis (which many black South Africans revered as dagga their sacred herb).

This is the whole racial and religious (Medieval Catholic Church) basis of where our laws against hemp arose. Are you proud?

Twelve million years so far have been spent in jails, prisons, parole and on probation by Americans for this absurd racist and probably economic reasoning. (See chapter 4, "Last Days of Legal Cannabis.")

Isn't it interesting that in 1985 the U.S. incarcerated a larger percentage of it's people than any country in the world except South Africa? In 1989 the U.S. surpassed South Africa and remains the world's leading prison state to this day.

President Bush, in his great drug policy speech September 5, 1989, promised to double the federal prison population again, after it had already doubled under Reagan.

Remember the outcry in 1979 when former UN Ambassador Andrew Young told the world that the U.S. had more political prisoners than any other nation? (Amnesty International, ACLU.)

LASTING REMNANTS

Even though blackface disappeared as law in the late 1920s, as late as the 1960s, black entertainers (such as Harry Belafonte and Sammy Davis, Jr.) still had to go in the back door of theatrical establishments, bars, etc; by law!

They couldn't rent a hotel room in Las Vegas or Miami Beach—even while being the headline act.

Ben Vereen's 1981 Presidential Inauguration performance for Ronald Reagan presented this country's turn of the century Blackface/Jim Crow laws in a

great story, about black comic genius Bert Williams (circa 1890 to 1920).

Vereen had been invited to perform for the Reagan Inauguration and had accepted only on the condition that he could tell the entire "Blackface" story—but the whole first half of Vereen's show, depicting Bert Williams and blackface, was censored by Reagan's people on ABC TV, contrary to the special agreement Vereen had with the Reagan people.

LATIN DRUG KINGPIN UNMASKED BY POPULAR SCIENCE MAGAZINE

May, 1936

The extent of the marijuana threat in the 1930s is amply illustrated by this photo of an un-named drug smuggler in the years just prior to the enactment of hemp prohibition.

New York state had one narcotics officer at the time.

A Mexican peddler arrested by California narcotic inspectors, with a bale of marijuana, or Indian hemp. Cigarettes are made from leaves and flowers

Chapter Fourteen

A HALF CENTURY OF SUPPRESSION & REPRESSION

1937: Hemp banned. An estimated 60,000 Americans smoke "marijuana," but virtually everyone in the country has heard of it, thanks to Hearst and Anslinger's disinformation campaign.

1945: Newsweek reports that over 100,000 people now smoke marijuana.

1967: Millions of Americans regularly and openly smoke hemp leaves and flowers.

1977: Tens of millions smoke cannabis regularly, with many people growing their own.

1987: One in three Americans have now tried it at least once, and some 10% to 20% of Americans still choose to buy and smoke it regularly, despite urine tests and tougher laws.

Throughout history, Americans have held the legal tradition that one could not give up one's Constitutional rights—and if someone was stripped of these protections, then he or she was being victimized. By 1989, if you sign up for an extracurricular activity in school or apply for a minimum wage job, you could be asked to forego your right to privacy, protection from self-incrimination, Constitutional requirments of reasonable grounds for search and seizure, presumed innocence until found guilty by your peers, and that most fundamental right of all: personal responsibility for your own life and consciousness.

FACTORIES & THE NAVY

The Navy and the other Armed Forces, as well as many civilian factories, will boot you out if you smoke marijuana; even if you smoke it 30 days before testing and while off duty. These tests are done at random and often do not include liquor, tranquilizer or other speed-type drugs. However, according to OSHA and insurance actuarial findings, plus the AFL-ClO, it is alcohol that is involved in 90-95% of drug related factory accidents.

In fact, numerous U.S. Army tests of the effects of cannabis on soldiers (through the 1950s and 60s) at Edgewood Arsenal, Maryland, and elsewhere, show no loss of motivation or performance after two years of heavy (military sponsored) smoking of marijuana.

This study was repeated six more times by the military and dozens of times by universities with the same or similar results. (Also, Panama/Siler study; Jamaican study; British Indian Hemp Report.)

South African gold and diamond mines allowed and encouraged Blacks to use cannabis/Dagga in order to work harder.

(U.S. Government Reports, 1956-58-61-63-68-69-70-76.)

PRIVACY IS A RIGHT

Groups like NORML, HEMP, ACLU, BACH and the Libertarian Party (for example) feel that as long as military personnel (unless on alert) or factory workers do not smoke cannabis while on duty or during the period four to six hours before duty, it's their own business. This is consistent with the conclusions of the U.S. government's own Siler Commission (1933) and Shafer Commission (1972) Reports, as well as the LaGuardia report (1944), the Canadian Government Study (1972) Alaska State Commission (1989), and the California Research Advisory Panel (1989), all of which held that no criminal penalties are in order for its use.

INACCURATE URINE TESTING

Military/factory worker marijuana urine tests are only partially accurate and do not indicate the extent of your intoxication. They indicate only whether you have smoked or been in the presence of cannabis smoke in the last 30 days.

Whether you smoked an hour ago or 30 days ago—and sometimes if you haven't smoked it at all—the test results are the same: Positive.

John P. Morgan, M.D., stated in High Times (February 1989), "The tests are far from reliable. Tampering and high rates of false-positives, false-negatives, etc. are common and further these testing companies are held to no standards but their own."

At 20-50 nanograms (billionths of a gram) per milliliter of THC Carboxy Acid (a metabolite) these

LAROUCHE DECLARES WAR ON ROCK 'N' ROLL

If you thought Anslinger's music craziness was over after he went after jazz in the 1930s and 40s, then consider this:

One of the chief organizations among the 4,000 or so "Families Against Marijuana" type groups today is Lyndon LaRouche's "War on Drugs" committee, supported by Nancy Reagan, Jerry Falwell, Jimmy Swaggart and other right-wing activists.

In January, 1981, this author and five members of the California Marijuana Initiative (CMI) secretly attended the West Coast convention of this organization, whose guest speaker was Ed Davis, former Los Angeles Police Chief, who was at that time a freshman state senator from Chatsworth, California.

As we each walked in separately, we were asked to sign a petition endorsing a Detroit reporter who had written an open letter to the new President, Ronald Reagan, asking him to give immediate presidential clemency and make a national hero of Mark Chapman, who had murdered John Lennon of the Beatles six weeks earlier.

The letter stated that John Lennon had been the most evil man on the planet because he almost single-handedly "turned on" the planet to "illicit drugs." The evils of rock-n-roll are a constant theme of the "War on Drugs" publications.

To keep up with the part we were playing, we signed the petition. (John, forgive us—we were playing a clandestine role: under-cover CMI anti-narc. We remember you for "Give Peace a Chance," "Imagine," and all the rest.)

After we signed the petition, their leaders took us to the back of the room to show us some of the goals that would be achieved when they would come to full power over the next decade.

On five or so long tables set up in the back of the Los Angeles Marriott LAX meeting room were hundreds of recordings of Bach, Beethoven, Wagner, Chopin, Tchaikovsky, Mozart, and others, and dozens of pro-nuclear power publications.

They told us that along with new marijuana laws, they expected to implement their most important goal: anyone in the future playing any disco, rock & roll, or jazz on the radio, on television, in schools, or in concert, or just sold rock & roll records or any other music that wasn't from their approved classical lists, would be jailed, including music teachers, disc jockeys, and record company executives. School teachers, if they allowed such music by students, would be fired. (LA Times; KNBC-TV.)

They were dead serious.

Their magazine "War on Drugs" has always spent more space denouncing music with the "evil marijuana beat" than on heroin, cocaine and PCP combined!

Ed Davis was genuinely shocked and embarrassed about this out-front aspect of their anti-music dogma and said, "Well, I don't believe we could ever get legislation at this time outlawing these other types of music or their lyrics.... But I do believe with the new Reagan Law-and-Order Administration, we are going to be able to pass some new and stronger anti-marijuana paraphernalia laws, even recriminalize marijuana altogether in the states that have decriminalization laws now.... That's the start."

The letter stated that John Lennon had been the most evil man on the planet .

I called his office a few days later and was told by an assistant that Davis had no advance idea of this group's musical fixation and that he had accepted the invitation based solely on the name "War on Drugs." Most of what Davis predicted that day has come about. Those visionaries of a new society, one free from the influence of pot and any mention of it had their way in the 1980s. Remember James Watt and the Beach Boys in 1986?

Since 1981, TV programs have been censored, cut and pulled from the air for having a pro-marijuana connotation or even making jokes about it.

In an episode of Barney Miller, Detective Fish (Abe Vagoda) was told that some brownies he'd been eating all day were laced with pot. He looked forlorn for a moment, then said with a sigh, "Wouldn't you know it, this is the best I ever felt in my life—and it's illegal." This episode has been pulled from distribution.

And screaming comic Sam Kinison stood on the stage of NBC's Saturday Night Live in 1986 and bellowed "Go ahead, you can have the cocaine! Just let us have our pot!" The line has been deleted from audio portion in subsequent re-runs.

The Reagan/Bush drug czar, Carlton Turner, from his position as the White House Chief Drug Advisor quoted to the press passages of "The Rise and Fall of the Roman Empire" and told police and interviewers that jazz musicians and rock singers were destroying the America he loved with their marijuana drug-beat music.

tests can be read as positive or negative—yet results derived from this part of the scale are known to be meaningless. To the untrained eye, any positive indication sends up a red flag. And most testers are untrained and uncertified. Still, the decision to hire, fire, detain, retest or begin drug abuse treatment is made for you on the spot.

"I believe the tendency to read the EMIT [the urine test for THC metabolites] test below the detection limit is one of the important reasons why the test was not often confirmed in published reports," Dr. Morgan said.

In 1985, Milton Wisconsin high school kids were ordered to have urine tests weekly to see if they smoked pot. Local "Families Against Marijuana" type organizations were demanding this testing, but not for liquor, downers or other hazardous drugs.

Hundreds of communities and high schools throughout the country were awaiting the outcome of constitutional challenges in Milton in 1988 before implementing similar testing programs in their own school districts. Testing for high school students participating in extra-curricular activities has since been widely adopted.

For instance, in Oregon the testing of high-school athletes has spread by court order to any and all extra-curricular activity. Band members and majorettes—even debate team members, some debating on the marijuana issue—can now be tested at will.

(NORML reports, High Times, ABC, NBC & CBS News, 1981-1984, Oregonian, October 23, 1989.)

AND ...BABE RUTH

Former Baseball Commissioner Peter V. Ueberroth in 1985 ordered all personnel, except unionized players, to submit to these urine tests. From the owners to the peanut vendors to the batboys, it is mandatory in order to be employed. By 1990, it had been incorporated into all contracts, including ball-players.

Whether you smoked an hour or 30 days ago, the urine test results are the same: Positive.

Aside from the civil liberties questions raised, it is apparently forgotten that "Babe" Ruth would regularly invite reporters to accompany him while he drank 12 beers prior to playing a game, during alcohol prohibition.

Many "dry" organizations and even the League Commissioner implored him to think of the children who idolized him and stop, but the "Babe" refused.

If Peter Ueberroth or his ilk had been in charge of baseball during prohibition, the "Sultan of Swat"

would have been fired in shame and millions of children would not have proudly played in "Babe Ruth Little Leagues."

Lyndon LaRouche's "War on Drugs" committee told us that, along with new marijuana laws, they expected to implement their most important goal: anyone in the future playing any disco, rock & roll or jazz on the radio, on television, in schools, or in concert, or who just sold rock & roll records—or any music that wasn't on their approved classical lists—would be jailed, including music teachers, disc jockeys and record company executives.

Tens of millions of average Americans choose to use cannabis to relax during their time off the job, and therefore risk criminal penalties. Job performance should be the principle criterion for evaluation of all employees, not personal life style choices.

The Babe Ruths of sports, the Henry Fords of industry, the Pink Floyds, Beatles, Picassos and Louis Armstrongs of the arts, and one out of ten Americans have become criminals—and thousands unemployed—for smoking cannabis, even when merely unwinding in the privacy of their own homes.

Robert Mitchum's film career was almost destroyed by a 1948 marijuana arrest. Federal Judge Douglas Ginsburg was on the verge of being appointed to the U.S. Supreme Court in 1987 when it was revealed that he had smoked grass while a university professor, so his name was withdrawn from nomination.

DIVIDING COMMUNITIES ...& SPLITTING UP FAMILIES

"Help a friend, send him to jail," says a billboard in Ventura, California. This is an example of the 'zero tolerance' campaign's inform-on-your-neighbor tactics being used to enforce the laws against the victimless crime of cannabis smoking.

Here's another example from TV. "If you have knowledge of a felony you can earn up to one thousand dollars. Your name will not be used and you will not be required to appear in court."

(Crimestoppers, Ventura, CA, October, 1989.)

One man received a postcard in jail saying, "Our informant received $600 for turning you in. Crimestoppers."

SURVEILLANCE AND SEIZURES

In rural California, where cannabis growing has supported whole communities, the well armed CAMP forces go into a thick forest discovering 15-foot tall, lush, hearty eight-month-old plants.

These are hacked down, piled up and smothered with gasoline and rubber tires. Uncured, they burn slowly.

Elsewhere, a helicopter pilot circles over a neighborhood, peering into a heat sensitive camera pointed at a house. "We're looking for the indoor sun," He explains matter-of-factly.

"We only pursue specific objectives," houses where grow lights have been bought or some other tangible basis exists to suspect 'manufacturing a controlled substance;' a felony.

"Look, there's the light from the house." His thermal-sensitive screen shows heat leaking out from under the eaves of the house. Site confirmed.

Next they obtain a search warrant, raid the property, seize the house under civil proceedings, and prosecute its inhabitants under criminal law.

(48 Hrs., CBS television, "Marijuana Growing in California," October 12, 1989.)

UNAMERICAN POLICIES & POLITICAL EXTORTION

Richard Nixon ordered the FBI to illegally monitor John Lennon 24-hours a day for six solid months in 1971 because Lennon had given a concert in Michigan to free a student (John Sinclair) from five years in jail for possession of two joints.

(L.A. Times, August, 1983.)

The drug and oil and paper and liquor companies want pot illegal forever, no matter whose rights they suppress.

Politicians who are liberal are investigated and, we believe, are blackmailed to keep their mouths shut

PAUL McCARTNEY & HIS BAND ON THE RUN

Timothy White interviewed Paul McCartney, formerly of the Beatles rock group, for a book and developed it into a radio program called "McCartney: The First 20 years." He asked the songwriter to explain his song "Band on the Run," on the album of the same name.

"Well, at the time, bands like us and the Eagles were feeling like and being treated like, outlaws and desperados, you know," replied McCartney.

"I mean, people were getting busted—for pot, that is. And that's about all they were getting popped for. Never anything serious.

"And our argument was that we didn't want to be outlaws. We just wanted to be part of the regular scene, you know, and make our music and live in peace. We didn't see why we should be treated like criminals when all we wanted to do was smoke pot instead of hitting the booze.

"And that's what the song was about; it was my reaction to that whole scene....

*"And the county judge /
who held a grudge /
will search forevermore /
for the band on the run."*

—From "The First 20 Years," broadcast on KLSX 97.1 FM (Los Angeles) and other stations of the Westwood One radio network January 29, 1990.

McCartney also wrote the famous line that got the song "A Day in the Life" banned from British radio: "Had a smoke. Somebody spoke and I went into a dream." A vocal supporter of marijuana legalization, McCartney has repeatedly been arrested and was imprisoned for 10 days during a concert tour of Japan. The government cancelled his tour and banned him from playing in that country, costing him millions of dollars. To his credit, he has continued to speak out for pot smokers.

on this subject and others, or risk being exposed fo some past indiscretion by themselves or members o their families—possibly sexual or drug-related.

POLICE, SECRETS & BLACKMAIL

Los Angeles Police Chief Daryl Gates ordered con stant surveillance of City Councilman Zev Yarslov sky, and of the then-Cit Attorney John Van De Kamp and L.A. Mayo Tom Bradley, among oth ers, a few years ago, mon itoring their private se lives for more than a yea (L.A. Times, August 1983.) J. Edgar Hoover, a Director of the F.B.I., di this for five years t Martin Luther King Ji and, in the most "sick" sit uation, deliberately drov actress Jean Seburg t suicide with terrible ongo ing federal letters and in formation fed to tabloid exposing her pregnancie and private dates with Negroes.

In fact, using the FBI Hoover harassed selecte targets, for as long as 2 years because of their civi rights stands.

The former Director o the FBI and also direc overseer of the DEA, Wi liam Webster, answere questions about th squandering of 50% o federal drug enforcemen money on cannabis en forcement this way: Oh marijuana is an extremel dangerous drug and th proof is now coming i (brain studies, metabolit studies by Heath, Nahas)

Webster then asked fo more money and more un restrained powers to sto pot. (Nightwatch, CBS January 1, 1985.)

PUBLIC HUMILIATION

Entertainers caught with cannabis have had to do "Galileo" type recanting to stay out of jail or to retai heir television, endorsement, or nightclub contracts, tc. Some have had to go on television and denounce narijuana to stay out of jail (e.g., Peter Yarrow of Peter, Paul and Mary" and actress Linda Carter). Our courts and legislators have sold our American guaranteed" Bill of Rights, written on cannabis, to ecure a cannabis-free world.

"Don't suspect your neighbor, turn him in." Any eresy is to be reported. That which revolted us as hildren—the spectre of Nazis asking everyone to spy nd inform on one another; Stalin's secret police; a overnment spreading lies and creating a police tate—has now become our everyday reality. Even in-uisitional torture is allowed under the March, 1991 supreme Court ruling.

And those who dare to stand against the tide of op-ression face the prospect of financial ruin.

SEIZURE: FEUDAL LAW & ORDER

When the federal government seizes cars, boats, noney, real estate and other personal property, the roceedings are set into motion based on laws whose rigins date back to medieval superstition.

English common law of the Middle Ages provided or forfeiture of any object causing a man's death. Known as a "deodand," the object, such as a weapon r run-away ox cart, was personified and declared ainted or evil, and forfeited to the king. Forfeitures ecame the Crown's principle means of tax enforce-nent and added substantially to the Crown's domain.

Forfeitures imposed by the English Crown led to he prohibition of bills of attainder (forfeiture conse-quent to conviction) in the first article of the American Constitution. The main body of the Constitution also forbids forfeiture of estate for trea-on. The very first Congress passed the statute, still aw today, stating that "No conviction or judgement hall work corruption of blood or any forfeiture of es-ate." However, early Americans did incorporate in em procedures under Admiralty and Maritime law, o seize enemy ships at sea and to enforce payment of ustoms duties.

It was not until the outbreak of the Civil War that hese customs procedures were radically changed, in rder to punish Confederate rebels.

The U.S. Supreme Court held that if the Confisca-ion Act of July 17, 1862 was an exercise of the war owers of government and was applied only to ene-nies, then it was Constitutionally allowable in order o ensure a speedy termination of the war.

Today's "in rem" (proceedings against a thing[s] ather than against a person[s]) forfeitures are civil suits against property, which is held guilty and con-demned, as though it were a personality instead of being inanimate and insentient. Relying on analogy to the deodand, through this legal 'personification fic-tion,' the property is the defendant—and the guilt or innocence of the owner is irrelevant.

By applying a civil label to forfeiture proceedings, the government sidesteps almost all the protections offered by the Constitution to individuals. There is no Sixth Amendment guarantee of right to counsel. Innocent until proven guilty is reversed.

Each violation of a constitutional right is then used as the basis for the destruction of another.

The violation of the Fifth Amendment's "innocent until proven guilty" due process standard is used to destroy the prohibition of double jeopardy. Even an acquittal of related criminal charges does not bar re-litigation of the same facts, because the defendant must furnish the proof at the second trial.

Because the Supreme Court holds that the Consti-tution permits in rem forfeiture of property belonging to a person who is completely innocent of criminal ac-tivity and not negligent in his use of the property, lower courts reason that the Eighth Amendment's prohibition of cruel and unusual or excessive punish-ment or fines could not apply to anybody guilty of even a minor drug offense.

If property is seized on navigable waters, there is no right to trial by jury. Unlike civil suits between in-dividuals, the government is immune to counter-suit.

Today, the passions of the "War on Drugs" have caused Congress to once again use in rem proceed-ings to inflict punishment without the nuisance of the protections provided by the Constitution and Bill of Rights. "We have to save our Constitution," says Vickie Linker, whose husband is in prison for two years over a cannabis offense. "We have the truth."

ENTRAPMENT, INTOLERANCE & IGNORANCE

When not enough people seem to be committing crimes, the DEA and police departments often resort to entrapment to make criminals out of unsuspecting and otherwise non-criminal people. Government agents have been caught time after time provoking and participating in drug smuggling and sales.*

* High Witness News department, High Times magazine; "Inside the DEA," Dale Geiringer, Reason Magazine, December, 1986; Christic Institute "La Penca" lawsuit; DeLorean cocaine trial testi-mony and verdict of innocence; Playboy magazine, etc.

This constant fanning of public fears of marijuana turns into demands for more money for a 'war on drugs' (a euphemism for war on certain people who freely choose to use selected substances) and political pressure for the permission to use unconstitutional means to enforce the constantly harsher laws.

In an October, 1989 Louisville, KY address to the Police Chiefs of that state, drug Czar and social drinking nicotine-addict William Bennett announced that marijuana smoking makes people stupid.*

* This is the same man who helped engineer a $2.9 million grant for the Texas National Guard to dress its agents up as cactus to patrol the Mexican border.

He offered no proof, and although crack was not a major issue in Kentucky, proclaimed that more money was necessary for the war on drugs because of this newfound marijuana-induced danger—stupidity! (Which, as far as we know, is still not a crime.)

Bennett was seen to brace himself with a late-morning gin and tonic in December, 1989 as he tried to pitch a similar message to representatives of the broadcast and film industries in Hollywood, CA.

(High Times, February, 1990. See "Booze Brunch" in appendix.)

PDFA: SLICKLY PACKAGED LIES

Another recent development has been the formation of the PDFA (Partnership for a Drug Free America) by the Media PDFA, with primarily in-kind funding from ad agencies and media groups. The PDFA makes available (free of charge to all broadcast and print media) slick public service ads directed primarily against marijuana.

In addition to releasing such meaningless drivel as an ad which shows a skillet ("This is drugs.") on which an egg is frying ("This is your brain. Get it?"), PDFA is not above lying outright in their ads.

Outraged researcher Dr. Donald Blum of the UCLA Neurological Studies center told KABC news that the chart said to show the effects of marijuana actually show the brain waves of someone in a deep sleep—or in a coma.

In one ad, the wreckage of a train is shown. Now, everyone will agree that no one should attempt to drive a train while high on marijuana. But a man's voice says that anyone who tells you that 'marijuana is harmless' is lying, because his wife was killed in a train accident caused by marijuana. This contradicts the direct sworn testimony of the engineer responsible for that disaster; that "this accident was not caused by marijuana." And it deliberately ignores his admissions of drinking, snacking, watching TV, generally failing to pay adequate attention to his job, and deliberately jamming of the train's safety equipment prior to the accident.

In another ad, a sad looking couple is told that they cannot have children because the husband used to smoke pot. This is a direct contradiction both of the clinical evidence developed in nearly a century of cannabis studies and of the personal experiences of millions of Americans who have smoked cannabis and borne perfectly healthy children.

And in yet another ad, the group was so arrogant in putting out lies that it finally got into trouble. The ad showed two brain wave charts which it said showed the brain waves of a 14-year-old "on marijuana."

Outraged, researcher Dr. Donald Blum from the UCLA neurological studies center told KABC TV (Los Angeles) news November 2, 1989, that the chart actually shows the brain waves of someone in a deep sleep—or in a coma.

He said that he and other researchers had previously complained to the PDFA, and added that cannabis user's brain wave charts are much different and have a well-known signature, due to years of research on the effects of cannabis on the brain.

Even after this public refutation, it took the stations and PDFA weeks to pull the spot, and no apology or retraction had yet been offered for the deceit, as this edition of *Emperor* went to press.*

* Groups including the American Hemp Council, the Family Council on Drug Awareness and Help End Marijuana Prohibition (HEMP) have decided to step up their pressure to expose PDFA lies and get their distortions banned from the airwaves or, better yet, replaced with accurate information on the medical, social and commercial uses of hemp.

Perhaps a more valid ad for the PDFA to produce and the networks to run would show a skillet ("This is the PDFA.") and an egg frying ("These are the facts").

DARE: POLICE PROPAGANDISTS

The DARE (Drug Abuse Resistance Education) program, a national program that was initiated in 1983 by Los Angeles Police Chief Daryl Gates, has become yet another tool for disinforming the public on hemp.

Typically, a police department spokesperson will conduct a 17-week course at a local elementary school to promote personal responsible behavior by young people while irresponsibly giving them distorted information and outright lies about cannabis.

Most of the course does not deal with drugs as such, but rather with making choices about how to act when there are opportunities or pressures to drink, smoke, steal, lie, break laws, etc. However, the program's truly useful support for good behavior is undermined by an undercurrent of lies and innuendo about marijuana's effects and users.*

* In an interview, L.A.'s main DARE instructor, Sgt. Domagalski, gave information on the program and made such unsubstan-

ated—and untrue—statements as marijuana leads to heroin, "The [g]uy across the street or next door has been smoking marijuana for [y]ears and there doesn't seem to be anything wrong with him. There [is] something wrong, but it may not be obvious." And, "People in the [S]ixties smoked marijuana and thought there was nothing wrong [w]ith it. Now it's watered and sprayed and pampered—and they're [n]ot concerned what they spray it with, either. But parents don't [k]now this. They got all their information in the Sixties, and they're [n]ot interested in this new information." (Downtown News, July 10, [19]89. Also see letters section, July 31, 1989 for BACH's reply.) See [ch]apter 16, "Debunking" for the facts on his "new information."

[W]hat makes the DARE program uniquely [d]angerous is that it provides some accurate [i]nformation, but undermines itself and [th]e public record by using lies and innuendo [a]bout marijuana.

For example, according to teachers who sit in on [th]e sessions,* the police officer will remark, "I can't [t]ell you that smoking pot causes brain damage, be[c]ause you all know people who smoke pot and they [s]eem pretty normal. But that's what it does. You just [c]an't tell —yet."

* Some of the teachers we talked to find themselves in the uncom[fo]rtable position of knowing the real studies, or have used cannabis [th]emselves and know its effects, but cannot openly present their case [fo]r fear of being urine tested or dismissed.

No supporting evidence is then offered, and the lit[e]rature that goes home with the child (and is poten[ti]ally seen by marijuana-savvy parents) tends to ap[p]ear more balanced, although it refers to mysterious ["n]ew studies" showing the dangers of marijuana.

But throughout the entire course, the police officer [r]efers to lung damage, brain damage, sterility and [o]ther unfounded claims of health damage and death [b]eing caused by marijuana.

Or they report on studies detailing the cardio-pul[m]onary risks of using cocaine, then mention mari[j]uana smoke—unrelated except by context. Or the ['w]ell-intentioned' officer tells anecdotes about people [th]ey claim to know who "started" with marijuana [a]nd ultimately destroyed their lives with hard drugs, [c]rime and depravity; then lumps marijuana in with [g]enuinely dangerous drugs and describes how young[s]ters or their fellow police officers were killed by [th]ese desperate, drug crazed criminals.

Then they encourage the students to "help" their [d]rug using friends and family by becoming a police [i]nformant. These kinds of indirect lies through innu[e]ndo and implication are given in an off-hand man[n]er calculated to leave a strong, permanent impres[s]ion on the sub-conscious mind, without basing it on [a]ny research or other sources that can be objectively [s]tudied or directly challenged—just a lasting, indis[t]inct mental image.

THE ULTIMATE HYPOCRISY

While waging its self-styled "War on Drugs" against Third World peasants and American civilians, the Reagan/Bush/Quayle administrations have encouraged and covered up drug smuggling and distribution by high ranking officials of the U.S. government.

On the one hand, Bush violated international law by invading Panama to bring reputed drug smuggler and long-time Bush/ CIA employee Manuel Noriega to the U.S. to stand trial.

On the other hand, he has refused to extradite Oliver North, John Hull, Admiral Poindexter, General Secord, Lewis Tambs and other Americans to Costa Rica, where they are under indictment by that government for operating a drug smuggling operation there.

(The Guardian, British newspaper, "Cocaine shipped by contra network," July 22, 1989.)

Federal hearings conducted by U.S. Senator John Kerry's (MA) Subcommittee on Terrorism and Narcotics in 1988 and 1989 documented widespread acts by the CIA and National Security Agency (NSA) to block investigations by the Customs Department and FBI into cocaine smuggling by "intelligence operatives" under the guise of national security. No indictments were ever handed down, and witnesses testified under grants of immunity with little media attention.

Special Iran-Contra investigators failed to act on this information or evidence developed by the Christic Institute implicating government complicity in narco-terrorism. And when General Secord was convicted in January, 1990 for crimes related to the Iran Contra drugs-for-arms scandal, he was given a fine of $50 and a brief probation when a federal judge decided that the poor fellow had already "suffered enough."

This from an administration that promotes the death penalty—even beheading—for marijuana dealers.*

* On the Larry King Show in late 1989, drug Czar William Bennett said he had no moral problems with beheading drug dealers...only legal ones.

What makes the DARE program uniquely dangerous is that it provides some accurate information and has genuine value for young people, but undermines itself and the public record by using these irresponsible, underhanded tactics.

If DARE officials want responsible behavior from students, they must also act responsibly. If they have information about marijuana that is hidden from the rest of us, let's see it. But, so far as we know, no DARE organization has yet dared to debate any marijuana legalization advocacy group* or include their literature in its program.

* The Business Alliance for Commerce in Hemp (BACH) issued a standing challenge in early 1989 to publicly debate any DARE representative in the Los Angeles area, which has yet to be taken. It has also offered to provide free and accurate literature on cannabis for DARE's use, but again, has received no response.

THE MEDIA IN A STUPOR

Despite a strong injection of reason and fact into the cannabis debate by the media in the 1960s and 1970s, the national media has largely failed to distinguish marijuana prohibition from the broader "drug war" hysteria, which 'sold more copies' in the 1980s.

Hemp activists have been ignored, their events censored and excluded from calendar listings—even paid advertisements about events or legal, non-smoking hemp products are refused by news sources.

What ever happened to fact checking?

Instead of serving as the probing watchdogs of government and keepers of the public trust, corporate news groups regard themselves as the profit-making tool for forging 'consensus' on national policy.

According to groups like Fairness and Accuracy In Reporting (FAIR) and researchers like Ben Bakdikian and Michael Parenti, these corporations define and protect the "national interest"—often meaning their own vested financial interests and political agendas. It must be remembered that many of the largest publishers have direct holdings in timberland for paper development, and the pharmaceutical drug, petrochemical companies, etc. are among the media's major advertisers.

"Penalties against possession of a drug should not be more damaging to an individual than the use of the drug itself."
—*President Jimmy Carter*
August 2, 1977

In an article published in the L.A. Times Magazine May 7, 1989 entitled "Nothing Works," Stanley Meiseler laments the problem facing schools in drug education programs and inadvertently reveals the news media's own assumptions and bias:

"Critics believe that some education programs have been crippled by exaggerating the dangers of drugs. Principals and teachers, watched closely by city officials, feel pressured not to teach pupils that marijuana, although harmful,* is less addicting than cigarettes.... Failure to acknowledge such information means school programs can lose credibility.

"But more honest programs could be even more harmful." (Emphasis added.)

The harm he predicts is an expected increase in consumption when people learn the health benefits and lack of physical or psychological risks involved with cannabis consumption. Many people decide that they prefer pot (which apparently does not need to advertise) to alcohol and tobacco, for which so many advertising dollars are spent.

* No specific studies showing the alleged harmful effects were cited in the article. In fact, cannabis was barely mentioned except for this reference and a note that detoxification businesses report some success in "breaking a mild dependence on marijuana and alcohol."

ONGOING INJUSTICE

President Jimmy Carter addressed Congress on another kind of harm done by prohibition and the drug issue August 2, 1977, saying that "Penalties against possession of a drug should not be more damaging to an individual than the use of the drug itself.

"Therefore, I support legislation amending federal law to eliminate all federal criminal penalties for the possession of up to one ounce of marijuana."

However, his efforts to apply even this bit of reason to America's marijuana laws were derailed by a Congress determined to show that it is tough on crime, no matter whether an action is criminal or poses any real threat to society, no matter how many people are hurt in the process.

And this attitude of intolerance and oppression has escalated in the post-Carter years.

By 1990, 18 states had established "Special Alternative Incarceration" (SAI) camps where non-violent first time drug offenders are incarcerated in a boot camp-like institution, verbally abused and psychologically worn down to break them of their dissident attitude towards drug use.

The inmates are handled with robotic precision and those who don't conform are subject to incarceration in the state penitentiary. Most of these offenders are in for marijuana. At least 17 more states are considering implementing similar programs.*

* In These Times, "Gulag for drug users," December 20, 1989, pg 4

What has been used to "justify" this anti-American policy? A handful of official government reports and studies that are touted by the DEA, politicians and the media to show that marijuana really is "damaging to an individual."

Next, we look at some of the most famous of these studies.

Chapter Fifteen

THE OFFICIAL STORY

DEBUNKING "GUTTER SCIENCE"

After 15 days of taking testimony and more than a year's legal deliberation, DEA Administrative Law Judge Francis L. Young formally urged the DEA to allow doctors to prescribe marijuana in a September, 1988 judgement. He ruled:

"The evidence in this record clearly shows that marijuana has been accepted as capable of relieving the distress of great numbers of very ill people, and doing so with safety under medical supervision.... It would be unreasonable, arbitrary and capricious for DEA to continue to stand between those sufferers and the benefits of this substance in light of the evidence in this record. In strict medical terms, marijuana is far safer than many foods we commonly consume...marijuana in its natural form is one of the safest therapeutically active substances known to man."

Yet, DEA Administrator John Lawn December 30. 1989 denied this action and continues to deprive people of medical cannabis, based on famous anti-marijuana studies like these:

WASTING TIME, WASTING LIVES

Nearly 100 years has passed since the 1894 British Raj commission study of hashish smokers in India reported that cannabis use was harmless and even helpful. Numerous studies since have all agreed: The most prominent being Siler, LaGuardia, Nixon's Shafer Commission, Canada's LeDain Commission and the California Research Advisory Commission.

Concurrently, American presidents have praised hemp, the USDA amassed volumes of data showing its value as a natural resource and in 1942 the Roosevelt administration even made *Hemp for Victory*, film glorifying our patriotic hemp farmers.

Yet even the humane use of hemp for medicine is now denied. Asked in late 1989 about the DEA's failure to implement his decision quoted above, Judge Young responded that administrator John Lawn was being given time to comply.

More than a year after that ruling, Lawn officially refused to reschedule cannabis, again classing it as a Schedule One "dangerous" drug that is not even allowed to be used as medicine.

Decrying this needless suffering of helpless Americans, the National Organization to Reform Marijuana Laws (NORML) and Family Council on Drug Awareness quickly demanded Lawn's resignation. His successor retains the policy.

What hypocrisy allows public officials to scoff at the facts and deny the truth? How do they rationalize their atrocities? They invent their own experts.

GOVERNMENT DOUBLESPEAK

Since 1976, our federal government (i.e. NIDA, NIH, DEA* and Action), police sponsored groups (like DARE*) and special interest groups (like PDFA*) have proclaimed to public, press and parent group alike that they have "absolute evidence" of the shocking negative effects of marijuana smoking.

* National Institute on Drug Abuse, National Inst. of Health, Drug Enforcement Agency, Drug Abuse Resistance Education, Partnership for a Drug Free America.

All subsequent researchers found Heath's marijuana findings to be of no value, because carbon monoxide poisoning and other factors were totally left out.

When U.S. government sponsored research prior to 1976 indicated that cannabis was harmless or beneficial, the methodology of how each studies was done was always presented in detail in the reports; e.g., read *The Therapeutic Potential of Marijuana* (1976) and you will see exactly what the methodology of each medical study was.

However, when our government bureaucrats deliberately sponsored negative marijuana research, time and time again Playboy magazine, NORML, High Times, etc. had to sue under the new Freedom of Information Act to find out the actual laboratory methodology these "experiments" employed.

What they found *was* shocking.

DR. HEATH/TULANE STUDY, 1974

The Hype: Brain Damage and Dead Monkeys

In 1974, California Governor Ronald Reagan was asked about decriminalizing marijuana.

After producing the Heath/Tulane University study, the so-called "Great Communicator" proclaimed, "The most reliable scientific sources say permanent brain damage is one of the inevitable results of the use of marijuana." (L.A. Times.)

The report from Dr. Heath had concluded that Rhesus monkeys, smoking the equivalent of only 30 joints a day, began to atrophy and die after 90 days.

And ever since, dead brain cells found in monkeys who were forced to smoke marijuana has been given maximum scare play in federal booklets and government sponsored propaganda literature against pot.

Senator Eastland of Mississippi used it throughout the mid 1970s to horrify and stop national legislators from supporting NORML's decriminalization bills in Congress, mostly sponsored by Senator Jacob Javitts of New York.

Reports of the study have also been distributed by the hierarchy of drug rehabilitation professionals as part of their rationalization for wanting to get kids off pot, based on supposed scientific studies. It is used to terrorize parent groups, church organizations, etc., who redistribute it still further.

Heath opened the brains of the dead monkeys, counted the dead brain cells, then took control monkeys who hadn't smoked marijuana, killed them, and counted their dead brain cells. The pot smoking monkeys had enormous amounts of dead brain cells as compared to the "straight" monkeys.

Ronald Reagan's pronouncement was probably based on the fact that marijuana smoking was the only difference in the two sets of monkeys. Perhaps Reagan trusted the federal research to be real and correct. Perhaps he had other motives.

Whatever their reasons, this is what the government ballyhooed to press and PTA, who trusted the government completely.

In 1980, Playboy and NORML finally received for the first time—after six years of requests and suing the government—an accurate accounting of the research procedures used in the famous report:

When NORML/Playboy hired researchers to examine the reported results against the actual methodology, they laughed.

The Facts: Suffocation of Research Animals

The Heath "Voodoo" Research methodology, as reported in Playboy: Rhesus monkeys had been strapped into a chair and pumped the equivalent of 63 Colombian strength joints in "five minutes through gas masks," losing no smoke.

The monkeys were suffocating! Three to five minutes of oxygen deprivation causes brain damage—"dead brain cells." (Red Cross Lifesaving and Water Safety manual).

With the concentration of smoke used, the monkeys were a bit like a person running the engine of his car in a locked garage for 5, 10, 15 minutes at a time ...every day!

The Heath Monkey study was actually a study in animal asphyxiation and carbon monoxide poisoning.

Among other things, Heath had completely (intentionally incompetently?) omitted discussion of the carbon monoxide the monkeys inhaled.

Carbon monoxide is a deadly gas given off by any burning object that also kills brain cells. At that smoke concentration the monkeys were, in effect, like a person locked in a garage with a car engine running for five, 10, 15 minutes at a time every day!

All researchers agree the findings in Heath's experiment regarding marijuana are of no value, because carbon monoxide poisoning and other factors had not been considered in the report. This study and others like Dr. Nahas' 1970s studies, tried to somehow connect the THC metabolites routinely found in the fatty tissue of the human brains, reproductive organs and other fatty areas of the body to the dead brain cells in the suffocated monkeys.

LINGERING THC METABOLITES

The Hype: It Stays in Your System for 30 Days

The government also claimed that since "THC metabolites" stay in the body's fatty cells for up to 30 days after ingestion, just one joint was very dangerous; inferring that the long range view of what these THC metabolites eventually could do to the human race could not even be guessed and other pseudo-scientific double-talk (e.g., phrases like: "might be," "could mean," "possibly," "perhaps," etc.)*

* "May, might, could and possibly are not scientific conclusions" Dr. Fred Oerther, M.D., September 1986.

The Facts: Government's Own Experts Say That Metabolites Are Non-Toxic, Harmless Residue

We interviewed three doctors of national reputation either currently working (or having worked) for the U.S. government on marijuana research:

• Dr. Thomas Ungerlieder, M.D., UCLA, appointed by Richard Nixon in 1969 to the President's Select Committee on Marijuana, re-appointed by Ford, Carter and Reagan, and currently head of California's "Marijuana Medical Program;"

• Dr. Donald Tashkin, UCLA, M.D., for the last 14 years the U.S. government's and the world's leading marijuana researcher on pulmonary functions; and

• Dr. Tod Mikuriya, M.D., former national head of the U.S. government's marijuana research programs in the late 1960s.

In effect, these doctors said that the active ingredients in THC are used-up in the first or second pass

NAHAS' PRESCRIPTION FOR BLOATED POLICE BUDGETS

Incredibly, a famous study which found that cannabis reduces tumors (see chapter 7) was originally ordered by the Federal Government on the premise that pot would hurt the immune system. This was based on the "Reefer Madness" studies done by the disreputable Dr. Gabriel Nahas of Columbia University in 1972.

This is the same Dr. Nahas that claimed his studies showed pot created chromosome, testosterone (male hormone) damage, and countless other horrible effects which suggested the breaking down of the immune system. Nahas background is in the OSS/CIA and later the UN where he worked closely with Lyndon LaRouche and Kurt Waldheim.

Nahas is still the darling favorite of the DEA and NIDA (National Institute of Drug Abuse) yet no anti-marijuana studies of Nahas' have ever been replicated in countless other research attempts. Columbia University specifically disassociated themselves from Nahas' marijuana research in a specially-called press conference in 1975!

Old, discredited Nahas studies are still trotted out by the Drug Enforcement Administration today, and deliberately given to unknowledgeable parents' groups, churches, and PTA's as valid research regarding the evils of pot.

The dissemination of Nahas'* dangerous horror stories is paid for with your tax dollar, even years after the National Institute of Health (NIH) in 1976 specifically forbade Nahas from getting another penny of U.S. government money for cannabis studies because of his embarrassing research in the early 1970s.

*Nahas, in December, 1983, under ridicule from his peers and a funding cut-off from NIDA renounced all his old THC metabolite build-up and unique chromosome petri dish tissue damage studies, conclusions, and extrapolations.

Yet the DEA, NIDA, VISTA, the "War on Drugs," and writer Peggy Mann (in Reader's Digest articles and her book Marijuana Alert, with foreword by Nancy Reagan) have used these discredited studies on parent's groups such as Parents for a Drug Free Youth, etc., often with Nahas as a highly paid guest lecturer, without a word of how his studies are really considered by his peers. This, we assume, is done to scare parents, teachers, legislators and judges, using scientific terminology, bogus non-clinical statistics, ultimately aimed at selling more urine testing equipment and creating more profits for the drug-rehabilitation clinics and their staff of professionals, and to maintain funding for the DEA, local police, judicial, penal, corrections and other government pork barrel, police state interests.

The 'War on Drugs' is big money so the shameless petitioning for more police and more cells continue.

However, we still have thousands of judges, legislators, police, Reader's Digest readers, and parents who have for years used and cited his studies in particular as the prime reasons to continue these unjust laws and to jail millions of Americans over the last decade.

The DEA, after Nahas' 1983 waffling renouncement, consciously and criminally continues to use his studies to polarize ignorant judges, politicians, press, and parent groups, who are unaware of Nahas' renouncement. These groups trust the government to tell them the truth their tax dollars paid for. The media, press, and television commentators still use Nahas' studies as gospel, and much of the frightening folklore and street myths that are whispered around schoolyards spring from this deceitful "scientists" work.

Refuted and never replicated results are still taught, while the honest researcher faces prison if he attempts to test any thoughts about the medical use of cannabis.

In fact, using Nahas' refuted and unreplicated studies on the immune system's reaction from use of synthetic THC in petri-dishes, "hysterical" Families for Drug Free Youth, or "Just Say No" organizations have gotten the press to say marijuana could cause AIDS—which has no basis whatsoever, but the press published all this creating more Reefer Madness!

through the liver. The leftover THC metabolites then attach themselves, in a very normal way, to fatty deposits, for the body to dispose of later, which is a safe and perfectly natural process.

Many chemicals from foods, herbs and medicines do this same thing all the time in your body. Most are not dangerous and THC metabolites show less toxic* potential than virtually any metabolic leftovers in your body of any known to man.

* The U.S. government has also known since 1946 that the oral dose of cannabis required to kill a mouse is about 40,000 times the dose required to produce typical symptoms of intoxication. (Mikuriya, Tod, *Marijuana Medical Papers*, 1976; Loewe, journal of Pharmacological and Experimental Therapeutics, October, 1946.)

THC metabolites left in the body, can be compared to the ash of a cigarette: The inert ingredient leftover after the active cannabinoids have been metabolized by the body. These inert metabolites are what urinary analysis studies show when taken to discharge military or factory or athletic personnel for using, or being in the presence of cannabis within the last 30 days.

LUNG DAMAGE STUDIES

The Hype: More Harmful Than Tobacco

According to the American Lung Association cigarettes and tobacco smoking related diseases kill 434,175 Americans every year. 50 million Americans smoke, and 3,000 teens start each day.

The Berkeley carcinogenic tar studies of the late 1970s concluded that "marijuana is one-and-a-half times more carcinogenic than tobacco."

The Fact: Not One Documented Case of Cancer

There are lung irritants involved in any smoke.

But, while tens of millions of Americans smoke pot regularly, cannabis has *never* caused a known case of lung cancer as of December, 1990, according to America's foremost lung expert, Dr. Donald Tashkin of UCLA. He considers the biggest health risk to the lungs would be a person smoking 16 or more "large" spliffs a day of leaf/bud because of the hypoxia of too much smoke and not enough oxygen.

Tashkin feels there is no danger for anyone to worry about potentiating emphysema "in any way" by the use of marijuana—totally the opposite of tobacco.

Cannabis is a complex, highly evolved plant. There are some 400 compounds in its smoke. Of these, 60 have therapeutic value.

Lab Studies Fail To Reflect the Real World

Virtually all the carcinogens can be removed by using a water pipe system. Our government omitted this information and its significance to the results of such studies when speaking to the press. At the same time politicians outlawed the sale of water pipes, la-

beling them 'drug paraphernalia.'

It has been U.S. government policy to only compar leaf to leaf, even though it knows that 95% to 99% o marijuana smoked by Americans are the flowerin, tops (or buds) of the female plant.

Yet this difference in tar comparisons with tobacc leaf carcinogens gives a totally false interpretation i the public mind of marijuana smoking verses tobacc smoking and the carcinogenic properties of each. Als a tobacco smoker will smoke 20 to 60 cigarettes day, where a heavy marijuana smoker may smok five to seven joints a day.

How Rumors Get Started

In 1976, Dr. Tashkin sent a written report to D Gabriel Nahas at the Rheims, France, Conference o Potential Cannabis Medical Dangers. That report be came the most sensationalized story to come out o this negative world conference on cannabis.

This surprised Tashkin, who had sent the report t the Rheims conference as an afterthought.

What Tashkin reported to the Rheims conferenc was that one of 29 pulmonary areas of the huma lung he studied found marijuana 15 times more a irritant than tobacco—the large air passageway.

(Tashkin, Dr. Donald, UCLA studies, 1969-83; UCLA Pulmonar Studies, 1969-90.)

However, Tashkin notes that tobacco has little ef fect on this area and cannabis has a positive or neu tral effect in most other areas of the lung. (See chap ter 7, "Therapeutic Uses of Cannabis.")

Afterwards, the U.S. government resumed fundin, for ongoing cannabis pulmonary studies which the had cut two years earlier, when Tashkin reported en couraging therapeutic results with marijuana/lun, studies—but now limited the research to the larg air passageway.

We have interviewed Dr. Tashkin numerous times In 1986 I asked him about an article he was prepar ing for the New England Journal of Medicine, indi cating that cannabis smoke caused as many or mor pre-cancerous lesions as tobacco in 'equal' amounts.

Most people do not realize, nor are the media told that *any* tissue abnormality; abrasion, eruption, o even redness is called a pre-cancerous lesion. Unlik lesions caused by tobacco, the THC-related lesion contain no radioactivity.

We asked Tashkin how many people had gone on t get lung cancer in these or any other studies of long term smokers like Rastas, Coptics, etc.

Dr. Tashkin, sitting in his UCLA laboratory, looke at me and said, "That's the strange part. So far n one we've studied has gone on to get lung cancer."

"Was this reported to the press?"

"Well, it's in the article," Dr. Tashkin said. "But no one in the press even asked. They just assumed the worst."

Another Fact: Emphysema Sufferers Benefit

During a later interview, Tashkin congratulated us on the tip that marijuana used for emphysema produced good results among people we knew.

He had presumed that marijuana aggravated emphysema, but after reviewing his evidence found that, except in the rarest of instances, marijuana actually benefitted emphysema sufferers due to the opening and dilation of the bronchial passages.

And so the relief reported to us by cannabis smoking emphysema patients was confirmed.

Marijuana smoke is not unique in its benefits to the lungs. Yerba Santa, Colt's foot, Hoarhound and other herbs have traditionally been smoked to help the lungs.

Tobacco and its associated dangers have so prejudiced people against 'smoking' that most people believe cannabis smoking to be as or more dangerous than tobacco. With research banned, these public health and safety facts are unavailable.

AND SO ON

Most of the anti-marijuana literature we have examined does not cite as much as one single source for us to review. Others only refer to DEA or NIDA. The few studies we have been able to track down usually end up being anecdotal case histories, artificial groupings of data or otherwise lacking controls

Reports of breast enlargement, obesity, addiction and the like all remain unreplicated, and are given little credence by the scientific community. Other reports, like the temporary reduction in sperm count, are statistically insignificant to the general public, yet get blown far out of proportion when presented by the media. Still others, like the handful of throat tumors in the Sacramento area and the high rate of injuries reported in a Baltimore trauma unit are isolated clusters that run contrary to all other statistics.

The spurious results of Heath, Nahas and the pregnant mice and monkey studies at Temple University and UC Davis (where they injected mice with synthetic third-cousin analogues of THC) are now out of the body of scientific and medical literature.

They are not used in scientific discourse, yet hundreds of DEA and pharmaceutical company sponsored literature goes to parent groups, about the long term possible effects of these metabolites on the brain and reproduction.

(Read the 1982 N.I.H.; the National Academy of Science's evaluation on past studies; and the Costa Rican report, 1980.)

RADIOACTIVE TOBACCO: THE UNTOLD STORY

Tobacco smoking kills more people each year than AIDS, heroin, crack, cocaine, alcohol, car accidents, fire and murder combined. Cigarette smoking is as addictive as heroin, complete with withdrawal symptoms, and the percentage of relapses (75%) is the same as for "kicking" cocaine and heroin users.

It is far and away the number one cause of preventable death in the U.S. today. Tobacco smokers have ten times the lung cancer of non-smokers, twice the heart disease and are three times more likely to die of heart disease if they do develop it.

Yet tobacco is totally legal, and even receives the highest U.S. government farm subsidies of any agricultural product in America, all the while being our biggest killer! What total hypocrisy!

In the U.S. one in seven deaths are caused by smoking cigarettes. Women should know that lung cancer is more common than breast cancer in women who smoke and that smoking on the pill increases cancer and heart risks dramatically.

Seven million dollars a day promotes the tobacco business, and it is estimated that the cigarette industry needs about one thousand new smokers a day to replace those who die each day from smoking.

Kentucky's principal business and agriculture for 100 years (until 1890) was the healthful, versatile and useful cannabis hemp. It has since been replaced by non-edible, non-fibrous, soil-depleting tobacco, which is grown by law in soil fertilized with radioactive materials.

U.S. government studies have shown that a pack-and-a half of tobacco cigarettes per day over a year for just one year is the equivalent to your lungs of what some 300 chest x-rays (using the old, slow x-ray film and without using any lead protection) are to your skin.

But while an x-ray dissipates its radioactivity instantly, tobacco has a radioactive half-life that will remain active in the lungs for 21.5 years.

Surgeon General C. Everett Koop said on national television that radioactivity is probably responsible for most tobacco-related cancer.

No radioactivity exists in cannabis tars.

(National Center for Atmospheric Research, 1964; American Lung Assn.; Dr. Joseph R. DiFranza, U. of Mass. Medical Center; Reader's Digest, March 1986; Surg. Gen. C. Everett Koop, 1990.)

OFFICIAL CORRUPTION: CARLTON TURNER

In all the research this author has done about the misapplication of public funds and trusts, nothing, it seems, compares with the either totally ignorant or willful manslaughter of fellow Americans by the bureaucrats and politicians of the following story:

ONE MAN & HIS DRUG SCAMS

The U.S. government policy, starting in the Nixon and Ford administrations and continuing under Carlton Turner* (Drug Czar under Reagan 1981-1986), allowed federal medical marijuana, supplied to the individual state marijuana medical programs, to consist only of the leaf of the marijuana plant, even though it's usually only one-third as strong as the bud and doesn't contain the same whole spectrum of the "crude drug," i.e. the THC and CBNs.

* Prior to becoming Special White House Advisor (read: National Drug Czar) Carlton Turner, from 1971 to 1980, was the head of all U.S. govt. marijuana grown for drugs by reason of his position at the University of Mississippi. The U. of Mississippi Marijuana Research Program is directed by state charter to discover —initiate or sort out the constituents of THC—a "simple" crude Cannabis drug that works as a medicine—then synthesize the substances with beneficial medical properties to attain their full potential for pharmaceutical companies.

For example, the leafs' relief of ocular pressure for glaucoma patients is much shorter lasting and therefore unsatisfactory, compared to the bud. Also, the leaf sometimes gives smokers a headache. The federal government until 1986 used only the leaf. Turner said to the pharmaceutical companies and in interviews, that leaf is all Americans would ever get—although the bud works better.

The reasons given:

• Buds are too hard to roll through a cigarette machine. (Forget the 25 million Americans who do quite well at rolling bud everyday.)

• By extracting compounds from the "crude drug" of the bud, there would be no pharmaceutical patents, therefore no profits. Therefore, his program would have worked against his former employers, the Mississippi University's legislative charter and funding.

(Interviews by Ed Rosenthal for High Times Magazine; Dean Latimer, et al; National Organization for the Reform of Marijuana Laws, or NORML.)

Although buds work better for chemotherapy and glaucoma etc, Turner said they will "never" be given

It also became evident the famous marijuan 'munchies' (appetite stimulation) were not workin for the cancer chemotherapy patients using feder leaf.

And even though no studies have been allowed compare leaf with bud, we know of doctors who und ficially recommend bud and watch their wasting ca cer patients put on weight (NORML).

Poisoning Pot Smokers

In August and September, 1983, Turner went national television to justify the illegal marijuar spraying (by plane) of paraquat in Georgia, Kentuck and Tennessee by the DEA. H said it was a kid's deserve punishment if he died fro paraquat poisoned pot, to tea him a lesson.

Turner was forced to resign after announcing his conclusions in public that marijuana caused homosexuality, the breakdown of the immune system and, therefore, AIDS.

Looking into the therapeut potential of cannabis is th most controlled and discou aged research, but any tes pursuing negative or harmf effects of cannabis are prom ed. Since these tests often bac fire or are inconclusive, even this research is rare.

Turner quoted "The Rise and Fall of the Roma Empire" to show how jazz (rock) singers are erodi the America "he" loves with this hallucinoger drug— marijuana! which he meant to stamp out.

Phony Paraquat Kits

During the 1978 Mexican marijuana paraqu scare, and while still a private citizen working for t State of Mississippi marijuana farm, this sar Carlton Turner called High Times magazine to a vertise a paraquat tester.

Unknown to Turner, High Times was not accepti ads for any paraquat testers because all eviden showed the testers didn't work.

Dean Latimer—then a High Times associate edit

BUSH STRIKES AGAIN

President Ronald Reagan, at the urging of then Vice President George Bush, appointed Carlton Turner as the White House Drug (czar) Advisor in 1981.

At conventions (1981-1986) of pharmaceutical companies and their lobbyist the American Chemical Manufacturers, Turner promised to continue the research ban on the 400 chemical compounds of cannabis.

Bush has managed to continue to direct this effort, simply by not allowing any grants for private or public research with a positive implication to be issued by NIDA or NIH, or approved any recent FDA applications unless they pursue negative results.;.

---

strung Turner along in virtually daily phone conversations for a month, listening to Turner talk about how much money Turner was going to make from sales of the device.

High Times wanted to see a sample. When Turner delivered his prototype version of the paraquat test kit to High Times, it was a total "Rube Goldberg" type rip-off, Latimer wrote in an article published in 1984, "just like the dozen or so phony kits other companies tried to buy ad space for at this time."

Turner apparently never thought High Times was ethical enough to check the contraption out. He assumed they would just take the ad money and run—print the ad and make Turner rich.

He didn't care if some kid lied or was bilked out of money believing in his bogus paraquat test kit.

After this attempted mail fraud, this man became President Reagan's national drug czar in 1981, recommended by George Bush and Nancy Reagan.

A Wanton Disregard For Life

From his own mouth, Turner doesn't even care if hundreds of kids die from smoking pot the federal government has deliberately sprayed with paraquat.

Then at the April 25, 1985 PRIDE conference in Atlanta, Georgia, with Nancy Reagan and 16 foreign First Ladies in attendance (including Imelda Marcos), Turner called for the death penalty for drug dealers.

Turner was, after all, Reagan's, Bush's and the pharmaceutical companies' own hired gun, who saw his entire mission as not against heroin, PCP or cocaine, but to wipe out pot and jazz/rock music...

Carlton Turner was forced to resign after Newsweek magazine excoriated him October 27, 1986 in a large editorial sidebar. His resignation was a foregone conclusion after being lampooned in the Washington Post and elsewhere as no other public

figure in recent memory for his conclusions (in public addresses) that marijuana smoking caused homosexuality, the breakdown of the immune system and therefore, AIDS.

He resigned December 6, 1986. What should have been front page headline news was buried in the back pages during the Iran-contra scandal.

Urine Testing Company

After his resignation. Turner joined with Robert DuPont and former head of NIDA, Peter Bensinger, to corner the market on urine testing. They contracted as advisors to 250 of the largest corporations to develop drug diversion, detection and urine testing programs.

After his resignation. Turner joined with Robert L. Dupont and former head of NIDA, Peter Bensinger, to corner the market on urine testing.

Nancy Reagan recommended, soon after Turner left office, that no corporation be permitted to do business with the Federal government without having a urinary purity policy in place to show their loyalty.

Just as G. Gordon Liddy went into high-tech corporate security after his disgrace, Carlton Turner became a rich man in this growth industry.

This kind of business denies the basic rights of privacy, self-incrimination (Fifth Amendment) rights, unreasonable search and seizure and the presumption of innocence (until proven guilty).

Submission to the humiliation of having your most private body parts and functions observed by a hired voyeur is now the test of eligibility for private employment, or to contract for a living wage.

Turner's new money making scheme demands that all other Americans relinquish their fundamental right to privacy and self-respect.

COMPARISON TO ALCOHOL

There are many terrible drug habits. The worst of which is alcohol, in both numbers of users and the anti-social behavior associated with extreme use. It (alcoholism) is the leading cause of teen-age deaths. 8,000 American teenagers are killed each year and 40,000 are maimed from mixing alcohol and driving. (MADD, Mothers Against Drunk Driving; SADD, Students Against Drunk Driving; NIDA, National Institute on Drug Abuse; etc.)

In fact, U.S. government/police statistics confirm the following strange numbers:

The mortality figures for alcohol use are 100,000 annually, compared with zero marijuana deaths in 10,000 years of consumption.

From 40% to 50% of all murders and highway fatalities are alcohol related. In fact, highway fatalities that are alcohol related might be as high as 90%, according to the Chicago Tribune and L.A. Herald Examiner.

Alcohol is also indicated in the majority (69% to 80%) of all child rape/incest cases; wife beating incidents are in the great majority (60% to 80%) alcohol influenced.

Heroin is indicated in 35% of burglaries, robberies, armed robberies, bank robberies, grand theft auto, etc.

And there were 324,000 arrests for simple marijuana possession in the U.S. in 1988, according to the Uniform Crime Reporting Statistics of the U.S. Department of Justice, Federal Bureau of Investigation.

PEOPLE HAVE PEACEFULLY SMOKED MARIJUANA FOR THOUSANDS OF YEARS

What does it mean to drive a plant species to extinction? Who will forgive us if we allow these greedy tyrants to destroy America and perhaps life on Earth?

At coffee shops like the Bulldog Palace in Amsterdam, one can quietly ponder these issues as you smoke your choice from a wide selection of marijuana and hashish samples.

THE EMPEROR'S NEW CLOTHES

ALTERNATIVES TO PROHIBITION

In conclusion, we see that the government's case against marijuana is woven of transparent lies. In this chapter, we bring to light some research that the government does not like people to know about. Then we talk about some realistic alternatives.

But first, a brief fable:

THE STORY OF THE EMPEROR'S NEW CLOTHES *

There once was a terrible king who heavily taxed s subjects in order to pay for his incredibly fine ardrobe of expensive clothing.

One day, two swindlers, representing themselves as eat tailors from afar, arrived and sought an audi- ce with the king. They told of an amazing new fab- : they had invented, made of a very expensive gold er that only the best, purest and wisest of people uld see. Excited, the king asked to see a sample, d the men brought forth an empty spool. "Ah, isn't lovely," they asked the king.

The king agreed, afraid to admit that he did not see ything because that would mean he was a dull and upid person.

So, to test his ministers the king brought them all to get their opinions. Once the power of the fabric as explained to them, all agreed that this was, in- ed, the finest and most beautiful cloth in the world.

The king ordered a new outfit be made for him, so e tailors took his measurements and ordered the ld from the treasury be given to the tailors to be un into thread. They set about at once working day er day, pretending to cut and sew, while the king d his ministers periodically came by to admire eir handiwork—and to pay the enormous bills the erchants were running up in the course of their ac- ities.

Finally, the big day came when all the people in the nd were ordered gathered to see the king's new tfit, which they had paid so much for and heard so uch about. When he nakedly strode forth, all the people looked in disbelief and said nothing. Then they sang the praises of the miraculous new cloth. "It's the most beautiful work I've ever seen!" "Magnificent!" "I wish I had such lovely fabric!" They all cheered, afraid of being denounced and called stupid if they did otherwise.

And the king proudly paraded in front of his sub- jects, secretly worried—afraid that he would lose the crown if the people knew that he, himself, could not see the cloth that draped his body.

Until he passed a small boy, who in his innocence cried out, "But he has nothing on!"

Suddenly, everyone realized that the king and all the ministers had been tricked by swindlers. Now they realized that the swindlers had not only tricked the king but all their tax money had been wasted on this farce.

* Paraphrased from Hans Christian Andersen's Fairy Tale.

THE LOGICAL ANALOGY

We say the marijuana/hemp laws are the emperor, and he wears no clothes! Like tyrants and prohibi- tionists in the past, this emperor relies on brute force and a police state to maintain his authoritarian, despotic reign while draining the federal treasury and dismantling all vestiges of the Bill of Rights.

This great country was founded on the principles that each person has "inalienable rights" to "life, lib- erty, and the pursuit of happiness," and that each person has the responsibility of maintaining these rights by casting their individual ballot.

It is a criminal offense for officials or executives of the U.S. Government to direct or conspire to wage a deliberate campaign of misinformation, omissions and outright lies with our tax dollars.

George Bush (the Emperor), Nancy Reagan (the Queen of Hearts of Alice In Wonderland—"sentence now, verdict later"), Bill Martinez (the Prime Minister), and their advisors are all wearing the "pure fabric that only the 'purest eyes' may see," woven for them by Anslinger/DuPont/Hearst and their police-state bureaucrats and now maintained by energy, pharmaceutical, drug re-hab professionals, testers and DEA police-state interests.

When a government bureaucrat deliberately acts or conspires this way—be they President, Vice Pres ident, National Drug Czar or head of the FBI, CIA—they should be jailable, at least in an hone American society. Our Federal bureaucracies and th U.S. Supreme Court have taken away more of ou Bill of Rights freedoms (written on hemp paper), u ing marijuana as their principal excuse than all ot er crimes, spies, and wars for the last 200 years con bined! And it is worse in our satellite Central an South American countries, where their leaders hav done this at America's official bidding .

SOME STUDIES THE FEDS DON'T TALK ABOUT

THE COPTIC STUDY (1981)

No Harm to Human Brain or Intelligence

Hemp has been used in virtually all societies since time immemorial as a work motivator and to highlight and renew creative energies.

(Jamaican study; Coptic study; Costa Rican study; Vedas; Dr. Vera Rubin, Research Institute for the Study of Man; et al)

In 1981, a study showed that 10 of America's heaviest pot smokers (from the Coptic religion and residing in Florida) actually believed that using 16 huge high potency spliffs* a day had improved their minds somewhat over a period of 10 years.

They were studied by Drs. Ungerlieder and Shaeffer (UCLA) and showed absolutely no brain differences between them and non-smokers—nor did it confirm any increase in IQ that the Coptics had claimed.

* One spliff is generally equal to five average American joints.

Longer Life, Fewer Wrinkles

Most studies (matched populations, past and present) indicate that—everything else being equal—an average American pot smoker will live longer than his counterpart who does no drugs at all; with less wrinkles, and generally have less stress—thereby having fewer illnesses to upset the immune system, and be a more peaceful neighbor (and if he/she is anything like this writer, have a strong desire to be free, and to listen to good music, and worship as he sees fit).

(Costa Rican and Jamaican Studies.)

JAMAICAN STUDIES (1968-74, 1975)

Definite Benefits For Marijuana Smokers

The most exhaustive study of hemp smoking in its natural setting is probably "Ganja in Jamaica-A Medical Anthropological Study of Chronic Marijuana Use" by Vera Rubin and Lambros Comitas (1975; Mouton & Co., The Hague, Paris/Anchor Books, NY).

"The Jamaica study, sponsored by the Nation. Institute of Mental Health (NIMH) Center fo Studies of Narcotic and Drug Abuse was the fir project in medical anthropology to be undertake and is the first intensive, multi-disciplinary study marijuana use and users to be published."

"No impairment of physiological, sensory and perceptual-motor performance, tests of concept formation, abstracting ability and cognitive style and tests of memory."

"Despite it's illegality, ganja use is pervasive, ar duration and frequency are very high, it is smoke over a longer period in heavier quantities wit greater THC potency than in the U.S. without delet rious social or psychological consequences. The maj difference is that both use and expected behavio are culturally conditioned and controlled by well e tablished tradition." (From the introduction.)

Positive Social Attitudes

The study outlines the positive reinforcement give socially to ganja smokers in Jamaica, the univers: praise for the practice among users, who smoke it a a work motivator. Subjects described the effects smoking making them "brainier" lively, merry, mo responsible and conscious. They reported it was goc for meditation and concentration, and created a ge eral sense of well-being and self-assertiveness.

No Link to Criminal Behavior

Vera Rubin and her colleagues found no relation cannabis to crime (except marijuana busts); no in pairment of motor skills; smokers and non-smoke: had identical extroversion scores with no differen in work records or adjustment. Heavy use of gan; was not found to curtail the motivation to work.

From the psychological assessment the smoke: seemed to be more open in their expressions of fee ngs, somewhat more carefree and somewhat more istractable. There was no evidence of organic brain amage or schizophrenia.

No Physiological Deterioration

Marilyn Bowman, in a battery of psychological tests n chronic cannabis users in Jamaica in 1972 found No impairment of physiological, sensory and perceptual-motor performance, tests of concept formation, bstracting ability and cognitive style and tests of memory." These Jamaicans had smoked anywhere rom six to 31 years (16.6 mean average) and the average age at the first puff was at 12 years and six months.

In the 1975 study; between users and non-users, no ifference was found in plasma testosterone, no difference in total nutrition, slightly higher performance on the intelligence sub-tests (not statistically ignificant) and "A basic measure of cell-mediated mmunity ...was no less vigorous in the users..."

Finally, "Users in our matched pair sample smoked marijuana in addition to as many tobacco cigarettes s did their partners. Yet their airways were, if anything, a bit healthier than their matches.

"We must tentatively conclude either that marijuana has no harmful effects on such passages or hat it actually offers some slight protection against he harmful effects of tobacco smoke. Only further research will clarify which, if either, is the case."

No "Stepping Stone"/Gateway Effect

As to the stepping-stone or gateway drug charges

leveled against cannabis, "The use of hard drugs is as yet virtually unknown among working class Jamaicans—no one in the study (Rubin's) had ever taken any narcotics, stimulants, hallucinogens, barbiturates or sleeping pills..."

COSTA RICAN STUDY (1980)

The Jamaican results were largely confirmed by another Carribean study, the 1980 "Cannabis in Costa Rica—A Study in Chronic Marijuana Use" edited by William Carter for the Institute for Study of Human Issues. (ISHI, 3401 Science Center, Philadelphia.)

Again researchers found no palpable damage to the native population's chronic cannabis smokers. Alcoholic social problems, so evident on neighboring cannabis-free islands, are missing in Costa Rica.

This study makes clear that socially approved ganja use will largely replace the use of alcohol (rum) if available.

THE AMSTERDAM MODEL

Since adopting a policy of tolerance and non-prosecution of cannabis/hashish smokers (it is available in cafes and bars) and rehabilitation and diversion programs for hard drug users, Holland has seen a substantial reduction in cannabis consumption* and a 33% drop in the number of heroin addicts. The strategy of separating cannabis sales from hard drug dealers by bringing pot above-ground has been quite successful. (L.A. Times, August, 1989.)

* " 'Collective Conscience' Breeds Dutch Tolerance" Oregonian, 1989. See appendix.

n Conclusion:

TRUTH & CONSEQUENCES OF PROHIBITION

When DuPont tells you "Better Living Through Chemistry," they don't tell you that it's only for 100 years, then the entire planet dies while they profit.

England and Holland treat their substance abusers s people—keeping them supplied with enough so hey don't disrupt the activities of others. These polies are now firmly established, effective and popular n those countries. Switzerland has begun its own experiments in localized tolerance of public drug use.

So, why should otherwise peaceful hemp growers nd users be labeled and persecuted as lifetime criminals while 35% of all robberies and burglaries are committed by heroin addicts, 40% to 50% of murders, rapes and highway fatalities are alcohol related* and heroin is more available in jail than on the streets?

* FBI Statistics, 1986.

In fact, aside from cannabis usage, take the mob

and the dealers out of heroin and other drugs and you reduce much of the crime that is not alcohol related. The murder rate rose consistently throughout the "Roaring Twenties" era of alcohol prohibition, then dropped every year for the next 10 after its repeal.*

* FBI Statistics.

Let's find another way to deal with drug usage; or be prepared to give up our freedoms, books, songs, and keep our escalating energy bills. Accept the fact that all crime related to drugs decreases if you treat addicts without taking them out of society. Instead, help them be financially productive.

HIGH-TECH REPRESSION

In order for America to be marijuana free, all of us, smokers and non-smokers alike, will have to give up our Bill of Rights...forever! You will have to conform

THE SMITHSONIAN'S SUPPRESSION OF FACTS ABOUT CANNABIS HEMP

It should be noted that, even though 50-80% of all their displayed fibers for paper and cloth from their "Life in America; 1780s to the 1800s" exhibit and "American Maritime Exhibit, 1492-1850" were made of hemp, the Smithsonian Institution has removed all mention of cannabis hemp as it was used in paper and textiles, referring to it only as "other fibers" while cotton, wool, flax, sisal, jute, Manila hemp, etc. are specifically named.

Museum curator Arkadero's response when questioned on this topic was that, "Children don't need to know about hemp anymore, it confuses them," and the director of the Smithsonian said that even though hemp was the primary fiber, "We are not a fiber museum."

He did not mention how they had determined that children *do* need to know about the minor fiber crops in American history.

Were children's innocent questions about hemp and marijuana making the Smithsonian tour guides uncomfortable?

And in a June 20, 1989 letter, Institution secretary Robert McCormic Adams wrote that, "We do not see a cataloging of fibers in early America as part of our task" in presenting these exhibits.

"At times this focus does lead curators to mention fabrics—such as linen, wool or others."

He returned copies of this book and the U.S. government's own 1942 pro-marijuana film, *Hemp for Victory* to us, apparently without reviewing any of the information.

---

to the likes of Lyndon LaRouches, Jerry Falwells Nancy Reagan Edwin Meese and minds of that ridiculous ilk.

The computer that should be our friend will allow the police to finish, today, the job the Roman Catholic Church's Inquisition started because the church could not stand the "commons" laughing at them, or knowing the secrets of, among other things, hygiene, hemp, etc.;* and by blackmailing politicians and judges (and other VIPs) for their private sex lives in order to have more power to bring Orwell's nightmare "1984" to fruition.

* See chapter 11, "Dark Ages."

WASTING OUR TAX MONEY

Yet approximately 50% of all drug enforcement money, federal and state, is directed at marijuana....

Some 70% to 80% of all people in federal, state or county prisons in America, wouldn't be there as criminals until just 60 or so years ago. In other words we, in our (Anslinger inspired) ignorance and prejudices, have approximately 600,000 (of 800,000 total) prisoners in American prisons for crimes that were, at worst, stupid habits, up until the Harrison Act, 1914 (whereby the U.S. Supreme Court in 1924 first ruled that drug addicts weren't sick, just vile criminals).

Hearst's and Anslinger's propaganda and lies have been relentlessly jammed down the throats of all of us—for the last three generations of Americans—as unimpeachable gospel truth...

Some radio and television preachers have called rock music "satanic and voodoo." They want to outlaw rock, burn albums and books, and lock up everyone who doesn't agree with them.

So does Carlton Turner. So does Lyndon LaRouche So does William Bennett.

And virtually every state is in the midst of th biggest prison expansion in its history, while politica vultures demand that we build more prisons and ex pand tax bases to pursue this madness with vigor...

DOUBLE STANDARDS

As an example the physical dependency and menta effects of using opium, morphine, heroin, Dilaudac Placidyl, Quaaludes, et al., are virtually the same.

In essence, they disturb the body's "endorphin (pain-receptors and nullifiers) balance.

However, when U.S. Supreme Court Chief Justic William Rehnquist was "nodding off" in court—an sending other druggies to prison for their habits—h just kept feeding his "eight-a-day" Placidyl habit: th equivalent in dollars, "high," and mental effect of $70 to $125 a-day "street abuser" heroin habit.

Placidyl, quaalude's cousin, is a 'heavy down,' popu lar on the streets for its placid nature.

Rehnquist wasn't seen robbing liquor stores, physi cally injuring his fellow citizens, or doing any of th anti-social behaviors attributed to "junkies."

His habit was easily maintained because th Placidyl was both available and within his normal in come limits. It was also well labeled as to amoun and dosage, while people with outlawed drug habit have to get by on a "dime of tar" or some such dan gerous estimate.

The government also acknowledges that 80% o overdoses by illegal drugs would probably be avoide with accurate labels and appropriate warnings.

POLICIES BASED ON IGNORANCE

While researching this book, we talked with and questioned senators, legislators, judges, police, D.A.s, scientists, historians, Nobel Prize winners, dentists, and M.D.s. All knew little bits and pieces of the history and uses of cannabis, but virtually no one knew any depth about marijuana in its 360 degree entirety except long term medical researchers, such as Ungerlieder, Mikuriya, et al; and writers like Ed Rosenthal, Dean Latimer, Michael Aldrich, et al.

At a large California NORML fundraiser in February, 1983, we spoke privately with then Senate Majority Whip Tom Rutherford, of New Mexico.

He has been a leading pro-marijuana politician for a decade and was then probably the most knowledgeable elected government representative regarding hemp in the United States. We asked him why the government didn't just come out and legalize hemp, especially with everything we knew medically, industrially and historically about hemp.

We were shocked when he replied there really isn't much argument for the legalization of hemp, that he knew—just decriminalization.

So we outlined the entire story of hemp/marijuana to him, figuring he must have heard some of it before. He sat in awe of what was being said. When we finished, he said, "If I had that knowledge outlined for me as you just told it, the government, police and judicial system would be through...on pot.

"But is it true?"

This was in February, 1983 and here were America's politicians who literally didn't know enough about hemp to fill a couple of pages of a book with generalities, yet they left office before they felt they could publicly back marijuana.

But they do know the present laws are unjustifiable and that the government's position on pot is mendacious (false) yellow journalism.

WHAT IS THE LAW?

"All laws which can be violated without doing any one any injury are laughed at." —Spinoza, (c. 1660.)

To control marijuana is to give up our freedoms, for ourselves, our kids, and our kid's kids, forever.

And that, my friends, is called fascism; and simply put, if the laws on cannabis are not overturned immediately, our planet dies at the hands of these ignorant (not-knowing) politicians who think they have a right to pass more and more Draconian laws to fill more and more Draconian jails with some of our most patriotic citizens.

But to truly understand why tens of millions of decent Americans are scared silly of pot after 50 years

of disinformation that continues to this day, consider the character of Los Angeles Police Chief Daryl Gates, who has admitted helping direct a program of squashing accurate hemp information and ordering the arrest and harassment of California Marijuana Initiative workers for doing their civic and Constitutional duty to collect petition signatures.

In January, 1984, Gates was asked by a parent at a San Fernando Valley, CA, public school, "What can I do if I find out my child has used marijuana?" He replied, "It's too late. Once they've smoked one marijuana cigarette, they are lost to us forever!"*

*These exact words were also used by LA County D.A. Ira Reiner in his 1990 campaign for State Attorney General. He lost.

In September, 1983, on television and through a police spokesman, Gates called hemp reform advocates "well-intentioned but terribly naive regarding marijuana and really don't know much about it."

A few months after California attorney general Van de Kamp suppressed the August 17, 1990 report by his own advisory panel that called for hemp re-legalization, Gates testified before the U.S. Senate Judiciary Committee on September 5 that pot smokers should "be taken out and shot." He held to this position for almost a week, until public outcry for his dismissal* forced him to modify his comment to a call for stricter penalties on smokers. A few months later, on March 3, 1991, the world was shocked to see a video of Los Angeles police savagely beating Rodney King, accused of speeding. A urine test later revealed traces of THC....

* Reiner was almost the only official to publicly support Gates.

CONCLUSION

On the basis of the information provided in this book, we demand an end to the enforcement of these prohibition laws. All laws respecting the cultivation of the plant must be stricken from the books, including the UN's Single Convention Treaty of 1961.

We owe an apology to all people who did jail or prison time, had to go through the courts, had their education, families and professions torn apart and their lives, wealth and health often destroyed.

We even owe an apology to honest-but-ignorant police and judges for our willingness to keep them ignorant by letting our government bureaucrats act illegally in censoring or denying the true nature of hemp which has resulted in their deliberate misuse of tax revenues intended for studies to find out the truth of hemp for 60 years now.

WHAT JUSTICE DEMANDS

Nothing but the lifting of all penalties (criminal and civil) and restraint upon the cultivation and use

Hemp / Marijuana rallies: (l) Madison, WI, September, 1989; (r) Ann Arbor, MI, April, 1989. Photos by Andre.

—both smoking and non-smoking—of this remarkable plant will be acceptable.

Prisoners being held for the peaceful possession, sale, transport or cultivation of cannabis hemp must be released immediately. Money and property seized must be returned. Criminal records must be wiped clean, and reparations paid for time served; for these are the real victims of this monstrous crime called the "War on Drugs."

In the end, half measures will not be acceptable.

In the meantime, we must have a moratorium on hemp law enforcement. And we must move swiftly to restore and expand the national archives and historical record on hemp and its valuable uses.

WHAT YOU CAN DO

We think that, now that you've had a good look at our side and the government's side (both as we see it and as the media projects it), you'll want to join us in putting this issue onto the ballots and into the legislatures of this country, where everyone can express their opinions in the straight forward manner set forth in our United States' and individual states constitutions.

Talk about hemp to everyone—all the time. Look for hemp, ask for hemp—buy hemp. And use the information and suggestions included in the appendices at the end of this book.

Write to your elected officials and the news media, to help create a more conscious political leadership and news coverage on marijuana and hemp. Give credit for good votes and coverage, and complain about bad. Register and vote. Run for office.

Demand that our prisoners of conscience be freed and rewarded and honored.

They deserve a hero's welcome, all the veterans

benefits and rights of this 'war on drugs'—not th DEA or police. For if these outlaw citizens had n defied the government and preserved the hemp see our government and its prohibitionist policies woul have eradicated this plant from Earth.

So, our Robin Hood hero is not William Bennett Nancy Reagan, but those who defied them. The must have their life and property returned. Thes people must be remembered for all time by each on of us for defying these tyrannical laws. For the saved the seed that's going to save the planet.

Hemp for Victory.

Let our people go. Let our people grow. And neve let us or our politicians again impose these fanatic prohibition laws against any natural substance in i natural form. We almost lost the seed and knowledg to save the planet.

Democracy doesn't work—ever—unless it is honest.

And if hemp is just one example of the kind of lie with which American police/bureaucrats have bee blackmailing their theoretical bosses—elected polit cians and the public—we are in big trouble!

As the little boy said while watching the parad pass by: "The Emperor wears no clothes."

We have reviewed this "drug war" against cannabi hemp/marijuana as thoroughly as we possibly coul and what we have seen sickens us.

THEREFORE, WE CLAIM THE EMPEROR IS WEARING NO CLOTHES!!
WHAT DO YOUR OWN EYES SEE?

GREEN EARTH
OR
GREENHOUSE EFFECT.

THE CHOICE IS OURS.

NO GREENHOUSE EFFECT
NO SULFURS
NO LEAD

HEMP

"AND THEY SAID WE COULDN'T WIN THE WAR ON DRUGS!"

BIBLIOGRAPHY

"All your children are poor, unfortunate victims of lies you believe.
A plague upon your ignorance which keeps the young from the truth they deserve."

—*Frank Zappa, 1967*

General Source Material

Abel, Ernest A.; *Marijuana, The First 12,000 Years*; Plenum Press, NY, 1980.

Anderson, Patrick, *High in America*, Viking Press, NY, 1981.

Andrews, George & Vinkenaog, Simon, editors; *The Book of Grass*, Grove Press, Inc., NY, 1967.

Cohen, Dr. Sidney & Stillman, Richard, editors, *The Therapeutic Potential of Marijuana*, Plenum Press, NY, 1976.

Colby, Jerry, *Dupont Dynasties*, Lyle Stewart, 1984.

Dewey, Lester, "Hemp Industry in America," U.S. Agriculture Dept. Yearbook, 1913, pg 238.

Dewey, Lester, "Hemp Industry in the U.S.," U.S. Agriculture Dept. Yearbook, 1901.

Dewey, Lester, & Merrill, Jason, *Bulletin #404*, U.S. Dept. of Agriculture, 1916.

Encyclopaedia Britannica; The Encyclopaedia Britannica Company, New York, NY.

Frazier, Jack, *The Marijuana Farmers*, Solar Age Press, New Orleans, LA, 1972.

Goldman, Albert, *Grass Roots*, Harper & Row, NY, 1979.

High Times Magazine, Volume 1, No. 1; The Trans-High Corporation, NY, 1974.

rman, Richard and Fox, Allan, ed., *Drug Awareness*, Discus Books, 1970

Indian Hemp Drugs Commission, *Marijuana, Report of the Indian Hemp Drugs Commission,1893-1894*, T. Jefferson Publishing Co., Silver Spring, MD, 1969.

Kaplan, John, *Marijuana: The New Prohibition*, World Publishing Co., 1970.

Latimer, Dean & Goldberg, Jeff, *Flowers in the Blood*; Franklin Watts, NY, 1981.

Literary Digest, Vol. 76, "Hemp, the Barometer of War," January 27, 1923, pg. 26.

Ibid, Vol. 89, "Our Home Hasheesh Crop," April 3, 1926, pg. 64.

Mikuriya, Tod H., M D., *Marijuana Medical Papers, 1839-1972*, Medi-Comp Press, Oakland CA, 1973.

National Academy of Science, *Marijuana and Health*, evaluation on past studies, Relman, Arnold, M.D., editor, National Academy Press, Washington, DC, 1982.

Novak, William, *High Culture*, Cannabis Institute of America, Boston, MA, 1980.

Oxford English Dictionary, Compact Edition, Oxford U. Press, Oxford, England, 1982.

Scientific American, Vol. 71, "Kentucky Hemp," October 6, 1894, pg. 210.

Ibid, Vol. 79, Dodge, G.R., "Growing Hemp in America," May 15, 1915, pg. 308.

Ibid, Vol. 87, "American Hemp Industry," November 29, 1902, pg. 356.

Ibid, Vol. 116, "Making Paper Pulp From Hemp Hurds," February 3, 1917, pg. 127.

Ibid, Vol. 124, Dacy, G.H., "Revolutionizing an Industry; How modern machinery is minimizing hand labor in hemp production," June 4, 1921, pg. 446.

Ibid, Vol. 158, Anslinger, H.J., "Marijuana More Dangerous Than Heroin or Cocaine," May, 1938, pg. 293.

Silver, Gary & Alderich, Michael, Ph.D. *The Dope Chronicles, 1850-1950*, Harper & Row, Publishers; San Francisco; 1979.

Sloman, Larry, *Reefer Madness, Marijuana in America*, Grove Press, Inc., NY, 1979.

Solomon, David, ed. *The Marijuana Papers*; The Bobbs-Merrill Company, NY, 1966.

Stafford, Peter, *Psychedelics Encyclopedia*, And/Or Press, Berkeley CA, 1977.

U.S. Agricultural Indices: 1916 through 1982.

U.S. Agriculture Dept. Yearbooks.

Warner, Roger, *Invisible Hand: The Marijuana Business*, Morrow & Company/ Beech Tree Books, NY, 1986.

Wolfe, Sidney M., M.D. and Coley, Christopher, *Pills That Don't Work*, Public Citizen Health Researach Group, 1981.

Chapter 1: Historical Overview

Abel, Ernest, *Marijuana: The First 12,000 Years*, Plenum Press, NY, 1980.

Allegro, J.M., *Sacred Mushroom & the Cross*, Doubleday, NY, 1969; Pliny;

Allen, James Lane, *The Reign of Law, A Tale of the Kentucky Hemp Fields*, MacMillan Co., NY, 1900.

Bible; King James edition, et al.

Clark, V.S., *History of Manufacture in United States*, McGraw Hill, NY, 1929, pg. 34.

Cohen, S., & Stillman, R., *Therapeutic Potential of Marijuana*, Plenum Books, N 1976.

Columbia History of the World, Harper & Row, NY, 1981

Garaty, John & Gay, Peter, editors, *Columbia Book of World History*, Harp & Row Pub., Inc., 1972.

Dead Sea Scrolls.

Encyclopaedia Brittanica listing, "Pharmacological Cults."

Gnostic Gospels.

Herndon, G.M., *Hemp in Colonial Virginia*, 1963; *The Chesapeake Colonies*, 1954.

Herodotus, *Histories*, 5th century B.C.

Washington, George & Jefferson, Thomas, Diaries of; also Jefferson's Farm Books, Aug. 7, 1765.

Kaballah, Ginsberg Legends edition, c. 186

L.A. Times, August 12, 1981.

Mikuriya, Tod, M.D., *Marijuana Medical Papers1839-1972*, Medi-Comp Press, C. 1973.

Research of: Schultes, R.E., director, Harvard Botanical; Wm. EmBoden, U. of CA, Northridge; et al.

Roffman, Roger, Ph.D., *Marijuana as Medicine*, Medrone Books, WA, 1982.

Schultes, R.E., & Wasson, R. Gordon, *Plants of the Gods*.

U.S. Census report, May 12-13, 1850.

Wasson, R. Gordon, *Soma, Divine Mushroom of Immortality*.

Chapter 2: Uses of Hemp

Abel, Ernest, *Marijuana: The First 12,000 Years*, Plenum Press, 1980.

Adams, James T., ed. *Album of American History*, Charles Scribner's Sons, NY, 1944, pg. 116.

Bonnie, Richard & Whitebread, Charles, *The Marijuana Conviction*, Univ. of Virginia Press, VA, 1974.

Burbank, Luther, *How Plants Are Trained To Work For Man, Useful Plants*, P. F. Collier & Son Co., NY, Vol. 6, pg. 48.

Cavender, Jim, Professor of Botany, Ohio University, "Authorities Examine Pot Claims," Athens News, November 16, 1989.

ohen, S., & Stillman, R., *Therapeutic Potential of Marijuana*, Plenum Books, NY, 1976.

aughters of the American Revolution (DAR) histories.

ational Narcotics Intelligence Consumers Committee (NNICC) 1988 Report, El Paso, TX, April, 1989.

ewey, Lester, & Merrill, Jason, *Bulletin #404*, U.S. Dept. of Agriculture, 1916.

ncyclopaedia Brittanica, 11th Edition, 1910.

arm Crop Reports, USDA international abstracts.

razier, Jack, *The Marijuana Farmers*, Solar Age Press, New Orleans, LA, 1972.

albraith, Gatewood, *Kentucky Marijuana Feasibility Study*, 1977.

lerndon, G.M., *Hemp in Colonial Virginia*, 1963.

lerodotus, *Histories*, 5th century B.C.

evi-Strauss & Company of San Francisco, CA, Personal communication with Gene McClaine, 1985.

lagoun, Alexander, *The Frigate Constitution*, 1928.

likuriya, Tod, M.D., *Marijuana Medical Papers1839-1972*, Medi-Comp Press, CA, 1973.

xford English Dictionary.

'aine, Thomas, *Common Sense*, 1776.

evolution film with Al Pacino, 1985.

tubin, Dr. Vera, *Jamaican studies*, Institute for the Study of Man, 1968-74.

sloman, Larry, *Reefer Madness, Marijuana in America*, Grove Press, Inc., NY, 1979, pg. 72.

solar Gas, 1980.

'he DuPont Dynasties

J. of KY Agricultural Ext. Service Leaflet 25, March, 1943.

J.S. Agricultural Index, 1916-1982.

J.S. Library of Congress; National Archives; U.S. Mint; etc.

JSDA film, *Hemp for Victory*, 1942.

Chapter 3: "Billion Dollar Crop"

Billion Dollar Crop," Popular Mechanics, February, 1938

'Hemp and Flax," Mechanical Engineering, February, 1938

Chapter 4: Last Days of Legal Hemp

Anslinger, Harry, *The Murderers*, also his own records and writings.

Bonnie, Richard & Whitebread, Charles, *The Marijuana Conviction*, Univ. of Virginia Press, VA, 1974.

Colby, Jerry, *Dupont Dynasties*, Lyle Stewart, 1984.

Congressional Record, Ways and Means Committee "Marijuana Tax" hearing transcripts, 1937.

Dewey, Lester, & Merrill, Jason, *Bulletin #404*, U.S. Dept. of Agriculture, 1916.

DuPont Company, annual report, 1937.

Kimberly Clark production records from its giant French hemp-fiber paper subsidiary, De Mauduit, 1937 through 1984.

Lindsmith, Alfred, *The Addict and the Law*, Indiana U. Press.

Mikuriya, Tod, M.D., *Marijuana Medical Papers1839-1972*, Medi-Comp Press, CA, 1973.

New Scientist, November 13, 1980.

Popular Mechanics magazine, "New Billion-Dollar Crop," February 1938.

Sloman, Larry, *Reefer Madness, Marijuana in America*, Grove Press, Inc., NY, 1979.

U.S. Agricultural Indexes, 1916 through 1982.

U.S. Congressional Records.

Uelmen & Haddox, *Drug Abuse and the Law*, 1974.

Webster's dictionary

Chapter 5: Prohibition

Abel, Ernest, *Marijuana, The First 12,000 Years*, Plenum Press, NY, 1980, p. 73, 99.

Anslinger, Harry, *The Murderers*.

High Times, *The Encyclopedia of Recreational Drugs*, Trans High Publishing, pg. 138.

Latimer, Dean & Goldberg, Jeff, *Flowers in the Blood*; Franklin Watts, NY, 1981.

Lee, Martin & Shlain, Bruce, *Acid Dreams*, Grove Press, NY, 1985.

Research of Dr. Michael Aldrich, Richard Ashley, Michael Horowitz, et al.

Sloman, Larry, *Reefer Madness*, Grove Press, Inc, NY, 1979, pg. 40, 196, 197.

The Oregonian, January 21, 1985.

Chapter 6: Medical Literature

Cohen, S., & Stillman, R., *Therapeutic Potential of Marijuana*, Plenum Books, NY, 1976.

Coptic studies (U.S.), 1981,

Costa Rican studies through 1982.

LaGuardia Marijuana Study, 1938-1944, New York Academy of Medicine.

Medicine: Army Study of Marijuana Smokers Points to Better Ways of Treatment, Newsweek, Jan. 15, 1945, pg. 72.

Medicine: Marijuana and Mentality, Newsweek, November. 18, 1946

Mikuriya, Tod, M.D., *Marijuana Medical Papers1839-1972*, Medi-Comp Press, CA, 1973.

Mother Jones Magazine, 1979, June 1989.

National Academy of Science, *Marijuana and Health*, evaluation on past studies, Relman, Arnold, M.D., editor, National Academy Press, Washington, DC, 1982.

O'Shaugnessy, W.B., monograph on medical cannabis, 1839.

Ohio State Medical Society 15th annual meeting, June 12-14, 1860, transcripts, pg. 75-100.

Omni magazine, September 1982.

Periodical el Tiempo Bogota (Columbia's largest newspaper), 1983.

Research of Dr. Norman Zinberg; Dr. Andrew Weil; Dr. Lester Grinspoon, Dr. Thomas Ungerleider, Dr. Shafer, Dr. Raphael Mechoulam (Tel Aviv/ Jerusalem U.) 1964-84.

Roffman, Roger, Ph.D., *Marijuana as Medicine*, Medrone Books, WA, 1982.

Rubin, Dr. Vera, *Jamaican studies*, Institute for the Study of Man, 1968-74.

Transcripts, Ohio State Medical Society 15th annual meeting, June 12-14, 1860, pg. 75-100.

U.S. Government's Presidential Commission reports, 1969; Shaeffer Commission through 1982.

U.S. military studies since the 1950s and 60s.

Chapter 7: Therapeutic Uses

Carter, Edward W., *Cannabis In Costa Rica - A Study in Chronic Marijuana Use*, 1980-82, Institute for the study of Human Issues, 3401 Science Center, Philadelphia, PA.

Cohen, Dr. S., & Stillman, R, *Therapeutic Potential of Marijuana*, UCLA, 1976; personal interviews with researchers, Washington, DC, November, 1982.

Harvard Medical School Mental Health Letter, Vol. 4, No. 5, November, 1987.

International Farm Crop abstracts.

Life Insurance Actuarial rates, "Life shortening effects of childhood asthma," 1969-1976, 1983.

Medical Cannabis studies: Harvard; Hepler & Frank, UCLA, 1971; Medical College of Georgia; University of North Carolina School of Medicine, 1975; National Eye Institute.

Mikuriya, Tod, M.D., *Marijuana Medical Papers1839-1972*, Medi-Comp Press, CA, 1973, Antibiotic Effect of Cannabis Indica, The, 1952-53-55; Antibacterial Effect of Can. Indica, The, 1955;

Roffman, Roger, Ph.D., *Marijuana as Medicine*, Medrone Books, WA, 1982.

Ruben, Dr. Vera & Comitas, Lambros, *Ganja in Jamaica, A Medical Anthropological Study of Chronic Marijuana Use*, 1975, Moutan & Co., The Hague, Paris

Public Citizen Health Research Group, "Stopping Valium," 2000 'P' St. NW, Wash. DC, 20036.

Tashkin, Dr. Donald, UCLA studies, 1969-83; UCLA Pulmonary Studies, 1969-90.

U.S. Center for Disease Control report that 20% to 40% of "-zine" drug users have or will develop permanent lifetime palsies shakes, Atlanta, GA, November, 1983.

U.S. Pharmacopoeia prior to 1937.

Chapter 8: Food

Australian History books.

Czechoslovakian Tubercular Nutritional Study, 1955.

Loziers, Ralph, testimony on behalf of National Oil Seed Institute, House Ways and Means Committee, 1937.

McKenny, Margaret, *Birds in the Garden*, Reynal & Hitchcock, NY, 1939.

Teramura, Alan, University of MD study, Discover magazine, September, 1989.

Chapter 9: Economy & Ecology

Beatty, A., "Southern Agriculture," C.M. Saxton & Co., NY, 1843, pg. 113.

Brookhaven National Laboratory, 1986.

Dewey, Lester, & Merrill, Jason, *Bulletin #404*, U.S. Dept. of Agriculture, 1916.

Harvard Business School, Report of the Energy Project., *Energy Future*, Random House, NY, 1979, Vintage Press, 1983.

Osburn, Lynn, "Energy Farming in America," BACH publishing, 1989.

Research of Dr. Carl Sagan.

Teramura, Alan, U. of MD study, Discover Magazine, September, 1989.

U. of KY Agricultural Ext. Service Leaflet 25, March, 1943.

U.S. EPA prediction of world-wide disaster in the making within 30 to 50 years, 1983.

Chapter 10: Sociology

Abel, Ernest, *Marijuana: The First 12,000 Years;* Plenum Press, 1980.

Allegro, J.M., *Sacred Mushroom and the Cross.*

British Indian Hemp Commission Report, 1894.

Bible, King James, Genesis Chapter 1, Verse 12; Matthew 15:11; Paul 1 Timothy 1:4; Luke 20:46. Also see Psalm 104 14:15; Isaiah 18:4-5; Isaiah 61:1; Paul: 1 Timothy 4:1-6; Rev 22:1-2; Ezekiel 34:29.

Bible, Catholic, Sirach Chapter 38, Verse 4.

Columbia History of the World, Harper & Row, NY, 1981, pg. 54.

Dead Sea Scrolls.

Dewey, Lyster, *Hemp*, U.S.D.A. Agriculture Yearbook, 1913, p. 283- 293:

Emboden, Wm. A., Jr., et al., *Flesh of the Gods*, Furst, Peter, ed. Praeger Press, NY, 1974.

Encyclopaedia Britannica, listing for "Pharmacological Cults."

Encyclopaedia Brittanica.

Fletcher, John, "Rollo, Duke of Normandy," Act III, scene 3; 1639.

Herodotus, *Histories*.

High Times Encyclopedia.

Hindu Vedas.

"How Heads of State Got High," High Times, April, 1980 (see appendix).

Jefferson, Thomas, *The Writings of Thomas Jefferson*, H.A. Washington, ed, J.B.Lippincotts Co., Philadelphia, PA, 1871.

Mikura, Tod H., M.D., *Marijuana: Medical Papers, 1839-1972*, Medi-Comp Press, Berkeley, CA, 1973.

Mills, Ogden Livingston, *On Liberty* (essay).

Ohio State Medical Society, 1860.

Research of Shultes, R.E., Harvard Botanical Dept.; EmBowden, William, UC Northridge; Michael Aldrich, Ph.D.; Vera Rubin, Institute for the Study of Man; etymologist Jay Lynn, Dr. Thomas Ungerleider (UCLA, 1982).

Roffman, Roger, Ph.D., *Marijuana as Medicine*, Medrone Books, WA, 1982.

Rubin, Dr. Vera, *Jamaican studies*, Institute for the Study of Man, 1968-74.

Shen Nung Pharmacopoeia; Ponts'ao Ching; Han Dynasty classics; et al.

Shushan, E.R.; Grave Matters; Ballantine Books, NY, 1990.

Siegel,Dr. Ronald K., *Intoxication: Life in Pursuit of Artificial Paradise,*

"Smoke Screen: Inmate Sues Justice Department Over Quayle-Pot Cover-up," Dallas Observer (TX), August 23, 1990.

Kelly, Kitty, *Nancy Reagan, The Unauthorized Biography,* Doubleday Co., NY, 1991.

U.S. Army, Edgewood Arsenal (MD), Multiples.

Wasson, R. Gordon, *SOMA, Divine Mushroom of Immortality*.

Chapter 11: War if 1812

Crosby, Alfred, Jr., *America, Russia, Hemp & Napoleon*, OH State U. Press, 1965.

Adams, John Q., Microfilms, Mass. Historical Society, Boston, MA.

National Archives, Dept. of State, Washington DC.

Peabody Museum, Salem, MA.

Chapter 12: Nineteenth Century

Ohio State Medical Society, transcripts of the 15th annual meeting of the at White Sulphur Springs, OH, June 12-14, 1860, pg. 75-100.

O'Shaugnessy, W.B., 'Monograph on Cannabis Medicine,' 1839.

Chapter 13: Prejudice

Anslinger, Harry J., Congressional testimony, July 12, 1937.

Newsweek, "Army Study of Marihuana Smokers," January 15, 1945.

Chapter 14: Debunking

48-Hrs., "Marijuana Growing in California," CBS TV, October 12, 1989.

Carter, President Jimmy, Statement on National Drug Policy, August 2, 1977.

Christic Institute "La Penca" lawsuit depositions.

DeLorean cocaine trial testimony and verdict of innocense.

Downtown News, "Chat With Sgt. Domagaki," Los Angeles, CA, Jul. 10, 1989

Downtown News, L.A. CA, "Letters: DAR to tell the Truth" July 31, 1989.

Geiringer, Dale, "Inside the DEA," Reason Magazine, December 1986.

Guardian, The, "Cocaine shipped by contra network," (British newspaper), July 22 1989.

In These Times, "Gulag for drug user," December 20, 1989, pg. 4.

High Times,"Can Pot Save the World," February, 1989.

High Witness News department, High Tim magazine.

Kerry, Senator John (Mass), Report of the Senate Intelligence Committee Subcommittee on Terrorism and Narcotics, 198

Cockburn, Leslie, *Out of Control*, Atlantic Monthly Press, NY, 1987.

Meiseler, Stanley, "Nothing Works," LA Times Magazine, May 7, 1989.

Warner, Roger, *Invisible Hand*, Beech Tree Books, NY, 1986.

Nightwatch, CBS TV, January 1, 1985.

The Oregonian, October 23, 1989.

Chapter 15: Half Century of Prohibition

Dr. Joseph R. DiFranza, U. of Mass. Medic Center.

Cohen, S., & Stillman, R., *Therapeutic Potential of Marijuana*, Plenum Books, N 1976.

Loewe, journal of Pharmacological and Experimental Therapeutics, October, 194

McCartney, Paul, interview by Timothy White, broadcast on KLSX radio, Los Angeles, CA, January 29, 1990.

Mikuriya, Tod, M.D., *Marijuana Medical Papers1839-1972*, Medi-Comp Press, CA, 1973, National Center for Atmospheric Research reports, 1964.

National Academy of Science, *Marijuana and Health*, evaluation on past studies Relman, Arnold, M.D., editor, National Academy Press, Washington, DC, 1982

Radio Activity--The New Found Danger of Cigarettes, Reader's Digest, March, 19

Chapter 16: The Emperor

Anderson, Hans Christian, *The Emperor's New Clothes*, 19th Century

Morris, David, 'Collective Conscience Bree Tolerance,' The Oregonian, October 19 1989.

Los Angeles Times, "Schultz, New Interest Drug Legalization Debate," November 1989.

Special thanks to Lyster Dewey, U.S. Dept. Agriculture botanist, for all his researc into the characteristics of this amazing plant, and to Dr. W.B. O'Shaughnessy f bringing the herbal and medicinal back to Western science.

— INDEX —

And...

My final dedication, to my old, dear friend, 'Crazy Bill' Rosson, decorated WWII Naval hero of Guadacanal who, in his last words to me, two days before his death in December, 1989 said, "... don't you ever stop going after them [the government], they can't stand up to your information--they'll try to ignore it--get the press to ignore it, but you keep putting it out there and they'll fall. They [the old police-state government] will be over and they will all be remenbered as an old ugly joke. Promise me Jack, no matter what, you'll keep going after them."

APPENDIX

Now that we've had our say, we thought you might want to look over some of the primary source material and evidence yourself. But we know what it can be like, trying to get to the library and all, so we decided to bring the library to you.

You will note that we have not over-organized this information, so that you can explore it at your own leisure. We deliberately set it up to allow you to make new discoveries of your own as you go along. Think of it as a treasure chest where , with the help of a magnifying glass or copier with enlarging capabilities, you might find any kind of amazing thing at any given moment; with every turn of a page. We hope you enjoy reading through it.

PARTIAL LISTING OF SOURCE MATERIALS IN THIS APPENDIX:

Reign of Law: A Tale of the Kentucky Hemp Fields, 1900

Crimping Progress by Banning Hemp, 1988 movie review of "Hemp For Victory"

Hemp, Farmers' Bulletin No. 1935, 1943

"Hemp for Victory," 1942 USDA film narration

Documentation of authenticity for "Hemp for Victory"

The Weed, (the Gene Krupa story), 1943

Hemp Will Be Grown, But Bureau Will Police Areas, 1942

Marihuana: New Federal Tax Hits Dealings in Potent Weed, 1937

Hemp Wood As a Papermaking Material, 1921

Hemp Being Grown in U.S. As War Cuts Off Imports, 1942

Marijuana Found Useful In Certain Mental Ills

War Booms the Hemp Industry, 1942

Can We Have Rope Without Dope?

Hemp Quota Cut, 1944

Hemp Slows Up

Army Study of Marijuana Smokers Points to Better Ways of Treatment, 1945

Marijuana and Mentality, 1946

Marijuana, 1940

Hemp Needs New Uses, 1945'

Fat Solubility' Pot Scare Quietly Put To Sleep, 1982

Marijuana and the Male, 1973

Marijuana Hazards Cited in New Government Study, 1974

Radioactivity: T he New-Found Danger in Cigarettes, 1986

Diazepines (Valium): #1 in Abuse

Drug Charges, 1990

Welcome to the National Health Federation's 35th Annual Health Convention, 1990

The Marijuana Conviction, Part One--The Birth of Prohibition, 1987

Hemp Hurds As Paper-making Material, USDA Bulletin No. 404, 1916

Hearing before a Subcommittee of the Committee on Finance, U.S. Senate, 1937

The Marijuana Tax Act of 1937--Excerpts of Congressional Hearings: Committee on Ways and Means, House of Representatives, 1937

Same campaign, different drug:, 1989

America, Russia, Hemp, and Napoleon--American Trade with Russia and the Baltic, 1783-1812, 1965

Marijuana More Dangerous Than Heroin or Cocaine, 1938

Protect Youth Against Dope

Ecology cover-story collage

Authorities Examine Pot Claims, 1989

Greenhouse effect articles

Marijuana Backers Urge Production of Dioxin-Free Paper Made from Hemp, 1990

Hemp for Fuel, 1989

Marijuana legalization conferences and the environment assorted clippings

THE REIGN OF LAW: A TALE OF THE KENTUCKY HEMP FIELDS

"AS AN INITIATION INTO THE DELIGHTS OF KENTUCKY FICTION THE WORKS OF JAMES LANE ALLEN MAY STILL BE RECOMMENDED ABOVE THOSE OF ANY AUTHOR... THE REIGN OF LAW (1900) IS PERHAPS MR ALLEN'S MOST SIGNIFICANT BOOK, AND IT TO HAS BEEN WIDELY READ. ONE OF THE MOST FAMOUS PASSAGES IN KENTUCKY LITERATURE IS THE FIRST CHAPTER, A DESCRIPTION OF THE ONCE FLOURISHING HEMP FIELDS OF CENTRAL KENTUCKY; BUT THE BROADER SIGNIFICANCE LIES IN THE REALISTIC TALE OF A YOUNG MAN'S SEARCH FOR THE TRUTH AND THE SENSITIVE PORTRAYAL OF THE INTELLECTUAL CLIMATE OF MID AMERICA AROUND THE TURN OF THE CENTURY." KENTUCKY TRADITION L.S. THOMPSON, UK 1977

"THE EARLIEST SOWER OF THE HEMP GOES FORTH INTO THE FIELDS."

(See page 8.)

THE REIGN OF LAW

A TALE OF THE KENTUCKY HEMP FIELDS

BY

JAMES LANE ALLEN

AUTHOR OF "THE CHOIR INVISIBLE," "SUMMER IN ARCADY," "A KENTUCKY CARDINAL," ETC.

WITH ILLUSTRATIONS BY

HARRY FENN AND J. C. EARL

New York

THE MACMILLAN COMPANY

LONDON: MACMILLAN & CO., LTD.

1900

3

THE REIGN OF LAW

HEMP

THE Anglo-Saxon farmers had scarce conquered foothold, stronghold, freehold in the Western wilderness before they became sowers of hemp—with remembrance of dear ancestral Britain. Away back in the days when they lived with wife, child, flock in frontier wooden fortresses and hardly ventured forth for water, salt, game, tillage—in the very summer of that wild day-light ride of Tomlinson and Bell, by comparison with which, my children, the midnight ride of Paul Revere, was as tame as the pitching of a rocking-horse in a boy's nursery—on that history-making twelfth of August, of the year 1782, when these two backwoods riflemen, during that same Revolution, the Kentuckians then fighting

---

a branch of that same British army, rushed out of Bryan's Station for the rousing of the settlements and the saving of the West—hemp was growing tall and thick near the walls of the fort.

Hemp in Kentucky in 1782—early landmark in the history of the soil, of the people. Cultivated first for the needs of cabin and clearing solely; for twine and rope, towel and table, sheet and shirt. By and by not for cabin and clearing only; not for tow-homespun, fur-clad Kentucky alone. To the north had begun the building of ships, American ships for American commerce, for American arms, for a nation which Nature had herself created and had distinguished as a sea-faring race. To the south had begun the raising of cotton. As the great period of shipbuilding went on—greatest during the twenty years or more ending in 1860; as the great period of cotton-raising and cotton-baling went on—never so great before as that in that same year—the two parts of the nation looked equally to the one border plateau

---

lying between them, to several counties of Kentucky, for most of the nation's hemp. It was in those days of the North that the *Constitution* was rigged with Russian hemp on one side, with American hemp on the other, for a patriotic test of the superiority of home-grown, home-prepared fibre; and thanks to the latter, before those days ended with the outbreak of the Civil War, the country had become second to Great Britain in her ocean craft, and but little behind that mistress of the seas. So that in response to this double demand for hemp on the American ship and hemp on the southern plantation, at the close of that period of national history on land and sea, from those few counties of Kentucky, in the year 1859, were taken well-nigh forty thousand tons of the well-cleaned bast.

What history it wrought in those years, directly for the republic, indirectly for the world! What ineffaceable marks it left on Kentucky itself, land, land-owners! To make way for it, a forest the like of

---

which no human eye will ever see again was felled; and with the forest went its pastures, its waters. The roads of Kentucky, those long limestone turnpikes connecting the towns and villages with the farms—they were early made necessary by the hauling of the hemp. For the sake of it slaves were perpetually being trained, hired, bartered; lands perpetually rented and sold; fortunes made or lost. The advancing price of farms, the westward movement of poor families and consequent dispersion of the Kentuckians over cheaper territory, whither they carried the same passion for the cultivation of the same plant,—thus making Missouri the second hemp-producing state in the Union,—the regulation of the hours in the Kentucky cabin, in the house, at the rope-walk, in the factory,—what phase of life went unaffected by the pursuit and fascination of it. Thought, care, hope of the entire farmer oftentimes throughout the entire year! Upon it depending, it may be, the college of his son, the accomplish-

---

ments of his daughter, the luxuries of his wife, the house he would build, the stock he could own. His own pleasures also: his deer hunting in the South, his fox hunting at home, his fishing on the great lakes, his excursions on the old floating palaces of the Mississippi down to New Orleans—all these depending in large measure upon his hemp, that thickest gold-dust of his golden acres.

With the Civil War began the long decline, lasting still. The record stands that throughout the one hundred and twenty-five odd years elapsing from the entrance of the Anglo-Saxon farmers into the wilderness down to the present time, a few counties of Kentucky have furnished army and navy, the entire country, with all but a small part of the native hemp consumed. Little comparatively is cultivated in Kentucky now. The traveller may still see it here and there, crowning those ever-renewing, self-renewing inexhaustible fields. But the time cannot be far distant when the industry there

---

will have become extinct. Its place in the nation's markets will be still further taken by metals, by other fibres, by finer varieties of the same fibre, by the same variety cultivated in soils less valuable. The history of it in Kentucky will be ended, and, being ended, lost.

Some morning when the roar of March winds is no more heard in the tossing woods, but along still brown boughs a faint, veil-like greenness runs; when every spring, welling out of the soaked earth, trickles through banks of sod unbarred by ice; before a bee is abroad under the calling sky; before the red of apple-buds becomes a sign in the low orchards, or the high song of the thrush is pouring forth far away at wet pale-green sunsets, goes forth into the fields.

Warm they must be, soft and warm, those fields, its chosen birthplace. Upturned by the plough, crossed and re-crossed by the harrow, clodless, levelled,

---

deep, fine, fertile—some extinct river-bottom, some valley threaded by streams, some table-land of mild rays, moist airs, alluvial or limestone soils—such is the favorite cradle of the hemp in Nature. Back and forth with measured tread, with measured distance, broadcast the sower sows, scattering with plenteous hand those small oval-shaped fruits, gray-green, black-striped, heavily packed with living marrow.

Lightly covered over by drag or harrow, under the rolled earth now they lie, those mighty, those inert seeds. Down into the darkness about them the sun rays penetrate day by day, stroking them with the brushes of light, prodding them with spears of flame. Drops of nightly dews, drops from the coursing clouds, trickle down to them, moistening the dryness, closing up the little hollows of the ground, drawing the particles of maternal earth more closely. Suddenly—as an insect that has been feigning death cautiously unrolls itself and starts into action—in each seed the great miracle of life begins. Each awakens as from a sleep, as from pretended death. It starts, it moves, it bursts its ashen woody shell, it takes two opposite courses, the white, fibril-tapered root hurrying away from the sun; the tiny stem, bearing its lance-like leaves, ascending graceful, brave like a palm.

Some morning, not many days later, the farmer, walking out into his barn lot and casting a look in the direction of his field, sees—or does he not see?—the surface of it less dark. What is that uncertain flush low on the ground, that irresistible rush of multitudinous green? A fortnight, and the field is brown no longer. Overflowing it, burying it out of sight, is the shallow tidal sea of the hemp, ever rippling. Green are the woods now with their varied greenness. Green are the pastures. Green here and there are the fields: with the bluish green of young oats and wheat; with the gray green of young barley and rye: with orderly dots of dull dark green in vast array—the hills of Indian maize. But as the eye

sweeps the whole landscape undulating far and near, from the hues of tree, pasture, and corn of every kind, it turns to the color of the hemp. With that in view, all other shades in nature seem dead and count for nothing. Far reflected, conspicuous, brilliant, strange; masses of living emerald, saturated with blazing sunlight.

Darker, always darker turns the hemp as it rushes upward: scarce darker as to the stemless stalks which are hidden now; but darker in the tops. Yet here two shades of greenness: the male plants paler, smaller, maturing earlier, dying first; the females darker, taller, living longer, more luxuriant of foliage and flowering heads.

A hundred days from the sowing, and those flowering heads have come forth with their mass of leaves and bloom and earliest fruits, elastic, swaying six, ten, twelve feet from the ground and ripe for cutting. A hundred days reckoning from the last of March or the last of April, so that it is July, it is August. And now,

borne far through the steaming air floats an odor, balsamic, startling: the odor of those plumes and stalks and blossoms from which is exuding freely the narcotic resin of the great nettle. The nostril expands quickly, the lungs swell out deeply to draw it in: fragrance once known in childhood, ever in the memory afterward and able to bring back to the wanderer homesick thoughts of midsummer days in the shadowy, many-toned woods, over into which is blown the smell of the hemp-fields.

Who apparently could number the acres of these in the days gone by? A land of hemp, ready for the cutting! The oats heavy-headed, rustling, have turned to gold and been stacked in the stubble or stored in the lofts of white, bursting barns. The heavy-headed, rustling wheat has turned to gold and been stacked in the stubble or sent through the whirling thresher. The barley and the rye are garnered and gone, the landscape has many bare and open spaces. But separat-

ing these everywhere, rise the fields of Indian corn now in blade and tassel; and —more valuable than all else that has been sown and harvested or remains to be—everywhere the impenetrable thickets of the hemp.

Impenetrable! For close together stand the stalks, making common cause for soil and light, each but one of many, the fibre being better when so grown—as is also the fibre of men. Impenetrable and therefore weedless; for no plant life can flourish there, nor animal nor bird. Scarce a beetle runs bewilderingly through those forbidding colossal solitudes. The field-sparrow will flutter away from pollen-bearing to pollen-receiving top, trying to beguile you from its nest hidden near the edge. The crow and the blackbird will seem to love it, having a keen eye for the cutworm, its only enemy. The quail does love it, not for itself, but for its protection, leading her brood into its labyrinths out of the dusty road when danger draws near. Best of all winged creatures it is

loved by the iris-eyed, burnish-breasted, murmuring doves, already beginning to gather in the deadened tree-tops with crops eager for the seed. Well remembered also by the long-flight passenger pigeon, coming into the land for the mast. Best of all wild things whose safety lies not in the wing but in the foot, it is loved by the hare for its young, for refuge. Those lithe, velvety, summer-thin bodies! Observe carefully the tops of the still hemp: are they slightly shaken? Among the bases of those stalks a cotton-tail is threading its way inward beyond reach of its pursuer. Are they shaken violently, parted clean and wide to right and left? It is the path of the dog following the hot scent—ever baffled.

A hundred days to lift out of those tiny seed these powerful stalks, hollow, hairy, covered with their tough fibre,—that strength of cables when the big ships are tugged at by the joined fury of wind and ocean. And now some morning at the corner of the field stand the black

"LET THESE MEN BE THE STRONGEST."

(See page 15.)

men with hooks and whetstones. The hook, a keen, straight blade, bent at right angles to the handle two feet from the hand. Let these men be the strongest; no weakling can handle the hemp from seed to seed again. A heart, the doors and walls of which are in perfect order, through which flows freely the full stream of a healthy man's red blood; lungs deep, clear, easily filled, easily emptied; a body that can bend and twist and be straightened again in ceaseless rhythmical movement; limbs tireless; the very spirit of primeval man conquering primeval nature—all these go into the cutting of the hemp. The leader strides to the edge, and throwing forward his left arm, along which the muscles play, he grasps as much as it will embrace, bends the stalks over, and with his right hand draws the blade through them an inch or more from the ground. When he has gathered his armful, he turns and flings it down behind him, so that it lies spread out, covering when fallen the same space it filled while standing. And so he crosses the broad acres, and so each of the big black followers, stepping one by one to a place behind him, until the long, wavering, whitish green swaths of the prostrate hemp lie shimmering across the fields. Strongest now is the smell of it, impregnating the clothing of the men, spreading far throughout the air.

So it lies a week or more drying, dying, till the sap is out of the stalks, till leaves and blossoms and earliest ripened or unripened fruits wither and drop off, giving back to the soil the nourishment they have drawn from it; the whole top being thus otherwise wasted—that part of the hemp which every year the dreamy millions of the Orient still consume in quantities beyond human computation, and for the love of which the very history of this plant is lost in the antiquity of India and Persia, its home—land of narcotics and desires and dreams.

Then the rakers with enormous wooden rakes; they draw the stalks into bundles, tying each with the hemp itself. Following

the binders, move the wagon-beds or slides, gathering the bundles and carrying them to where, huge, flat, and round, the stacks begin to rise. At last these are well built; the gates of the field are closed or the bars put up; wagons and laborers are gone; the brown fields stand deserted.

One day something is gone from earth and sky: Autumn has come, season of scales and balances, when the Earth, brought to judgment for its fruits, says, "I have done what I could—now let me rest!"

Fall!—and everywhere the sights and sounds of falling. In the woods, through the cool silvery air, the leaves, so indispensable once, so useless now. Bright day after bright day, dripping night after dripping night, the never-ending filtering or gusty fall of leaves. The fall of walnuts, dropping from bare boughs with muffled boom into the deep grass. The fall of the hickory-nut, rattling noisily down through the scaly limbs and scattering its hulls among the stones of the brook below.

The fall of buckeyes, rolling like balls of mahogany into the little dust paths made by sheep in the hot months when they had sought those roofs of leaves. The fall of acorns, leaping out of their matted green cups as they strike the rooty earth. The fall of red haw, persimmon, and pawpaw, and the odorous wild plum in its valley thickets. The fall of all seeds whatsoever of the forest, now made ripe in their high places and sent back to the ground, there to be folded in against the time when they shall arise again as the living generations; the homing, downward flight of the seeds in the many-colored woods all over the quiet land.

In the fields, too, the sights and sounds of falling, the fall of the standing fatness. The silent fall of the tobacco, to be hung head downward in fragrant sheds and barns. The felling whack of the corn-knife and the rustling of the blades, as the workman gathers within his arm the topheavy stalks and presses them into the bulging shock. The fall of pumpkins into

the slow-drawn wagons, the shaded side of them still white with the morning rime. In the orchards, the fall of apples shaken thunderously down, and the piling of these in sprawling heaps near the cider mills. In the vineyards the fall of sugaring grapes into the baskets and the bearing of them to the winepress in the cool sunshine, where there is the late droning of bees about the sweet pomace.

But of all that the earth has yielded with or without the farmer's help, of all that he can call his own within the limits of his land, nothing pleases him better than those still, brown fields where the shapely stacks stand amid the deadened trees. Two months have passed, the workmen are at it again. The stacks are torn down, the bundles scattered, the hemp spread out as once before. There to lie till it shall be dew-retted or rotted; there to suffer freeze and thaw, chill rains, locking frosts and loosening snows—all the action of the elements—until the gums holding together the filaments of the fibre

rot out and dissolve, until the bast be separated from the woody portion of the stalk, and the stalk itself be decayed and easily broken.

Some day you walk across the spread hemp, your foot goes through at each step, you stoop and taking several stalks, snap them readily in your fingers. The ends stick out clean apart; and lo! hanging between them, there it is at last—a festoon of wet, coarse, dark gray riband, wealth of the hemp, sail of the wild Scythian centuries before Horace ever sang of him, sail of the Roman, dress of the Saxon and Celt, dress of the Kentucky pioneer.

The rakers reappear at intervals of dry weather, and draw the hemp into armfuls and set it up in shocks of convenient size, wide flared at the bottom, well pressed in and bound at the top, so that the slanting sides may catch the drying sun and the sturdy base resist the strong winds. And now the fields are as the dark brown camps of armies—each shock a soldier's tent. Yet not dark always; at times snow-

covered; and then the white tents gleam for miles in the winter sunshine—the snow-white tents of the camping hemp.

Throughout the winter and on into early spring, as days may be warm or the hemp dry, the breaking continues. At each nightfall, cleaned and baled, it is hauled on wagon-beds or slides to the barns or the hemphouses, where it is weighed for the work and wages of the day.

Last of all, the brakes having been taken from the field, some night—dear sport for the lads!—takes place the burning of the "hempherds," thus returning their elements to the soil. To kindle a handful of tow and fling it as a firebrand into one of those masses of tinder; to see the flames spread and the sparks rush like swarms of red bees skyward through the smoke into the awful abysses of the night; to run from gray heap to gray heap, igniting the long line of signal fires, until the whole earth seems a conflagration and the heavens are as rosy as at morn; to look far away and descry on the horizon an

array of answering lights; not in one direction only, but leagues away, to see the fainter ever fainter glow of burning hempherds—this, too, is one of the experiences, one of the memories.

And now along the turnpikes the great loaded creaking wagons pass slowly to the towns, bearing the hemp to the factories, thence to be scattered over land and sea. Some day, when the winds of March are dying down, the sower enters the field and begins where he began twelve months before.

A round year of the earth's changes enters into the creation of the hemp. The planet has described its vast orbit ere it be grown and finished. All seasons are its servitors; all contradictions and extremes of nature meet in its making. The vernal patience of the warming soil; the long, fierce arrows of the summer heat; the long, silvery arrows of the summer rain; autumn's dead skies and sobbing winds; winter's sternest, all-tightening frosts. Of none but strong virtues is it the sum. Sickness

or infirmity it knows not. It will have a mother young and vigorous, or none; an old or weak or exhausted soil cannot produce it. It will endure no roof of shade, basking only in the eye of the fatherly sun, and demanding the whole sky for the walls of its nursery.

Ah! type, too, of our life, which also is earth-sown, earth-rooted; which must struggle upward, be cut down, rotted and broken, ere the separation take place between our dross and our worth—poor perishable shard and immortal fibre. Oh, the mystery, the mystery of that growth from the casting of the soul as a seed into the dark earth, until the time when, led through all natural changes and cleansed of weakness, it is borne from the fields of its nativity for the long service.

"Hemp for Victory:" Government's Best Film to Date on Marijuana Use in America

Crimping progress by banning hemp

By Alan W. Bock

I've just finished watching a film made in 1942 for the US Dept. of Agriculture. "Hemp for Victory" was made to encourage US farmers to grow hemp and showed in detail how to grow, harvest, and process it. According to the film, "patriotic farmers, at the government's request, planted 36,000 acres of seed hemp" in 1942, and the goal was 50,000 acres in 1943. The government also exulted over 14,000 acres of fiber hemp in 1942 and urged farmers to go for 300,000 acres in 1943.

Did you read about any of this in your government school history books?

Hemp, of course, is marijuana. The federal campaign to stamp out marijuana began in 1937. Why the 1942 glamorization of this plant which, as the film put it "was already old in the service of mankind" thousands of years ago?

The reason, of course, was World War II. The Japanese held the Philipines (source of Manila hemp, made from a different plant) and much of eastern Asia (source of hemp and other fibers). The Navy needed rope and the Army needed thread for shoes and boots. Hemp was also used for fire hoses, parachute webbing, tents, and backpacks. Chances are when George Bush bailed out over the South Pacific, he relied on a parachute webbing made from a marijuana plant.

It turns out that hemp is one of the most useful and versatile plants around, and people have known this for thousands of years. For centuries all the ships that sailed the Western seas were rigged with hempen rope and sails. (The very word "canvas" is derived from the Greek and Latin words for hemp, "cannabis." Check any decent dictionary.) Most of the linen made before 1937 was made from hemp, rather than flax. The prairie schooners that opened the West were covered with hempen canvas; the Bibles the pioneers carried were probably printed on hemp paper. The first two drafts of the Declaration of Independence were written on hemp paper; the final version went onto parchment.

Thomas Jefferson and George Washington were required by law to grow hemp, because every part of the plant is useful. The seeds are al-

Since 1937, about half the forests in the world have been cut down to make paper. If hemp had not been outlawed, most would still be standing, oxygenating the planet.

most as good a source of protein as soybeans and are much cheaper; oil from the seeds was widely used for paints and varnishes.

All this is not too hard to discover. The Encyclopaedia Britannica has most of it if you check cross-references for a couple of hours. But hardly any American knows any of it, and most Americans will find it incredible. The history and useful aspects of hemp have been shoved down the American memory hole almost as effectively as knowledge was suppressed in the Dark Ages or erased in Orwell's 1984.

Most history books, if they discuss useful fibers in our early history, will refer to cotton, wool, flax, jute, sisal, manila, and "other fibers." "Other fibers" means hemp, which was, in fact, the dominant fiber crop in the US until about 1840. It began to be displaced by cotton after the invention of the cotton gin, which enormously reduced the cost of removing the seeds from the usable fiber. Hemp fiber had to be beaten out of the stalks by hand, a physically wearing and labor-intensive job.

As US farmers became more affluent and farming more mechanized, hemp cultivation gradually died out here, surviving in countries with very large, poorly paid peasant work forces.

In 1916, the US Dept. of Agriculture (Bulletin No. 404) announced a new method for making paper from hemp "hurds" or pulp, and predicted that if a machine for stripping hemp were developed, it would be unnecessary to cut down forests to make paper. By the mid-1930s, state-of-the-art stripping and pulp-saving machinery was available. According to an article in the February 1938 *Popular Mechanics* magazine, this new technology should have opened up a hugely profitable new crop that didn't compete with domestic crops but displaced imports.

"Fish nets, bow strings, canvas,

strong rope, overalls, damask tablecloths, fine linen garments, towels, bed linen, and thousands of other everyday items can be grown on American farms." said *Popular Mechanics*. "The paper industry offers even greater possibilities. As an industry it amounts to over $1 billion a year, and of that 80 percent is imported. But hemp will produce every grade of paper, and government figures estimate that 10,000 acres devoted to hemp will produce as much paper as 40,000 acres of average pulp land."

The magazine knew about federal regulation of hemp as a drug, but hoped that "if federal regulations can be drawn to protect the public without preventing the legitimate culture of hemp, this new crop can add immeasurably to American agriculture and industry."

That hope turned out to be empty. Not only did Harry Anslinger of the post-prohibition Bureau of Narcotics bully Congress into outlawing hemp with his campaign of lies and hardly veiled bigotry, almost all knowledge of the unequivocally useful aspects of the plant was suppressed. The government still knew about them in 1942, and may still know. It doesn't want you to know.

Since 1937, about half the forests in the world have been cut down to make paper. If hemp had not been outlawed, most would still be standing, oxygenating the planet. Hemp pulp could be used for methanol at competitive prices; hempseed oil would be used instead of petrochemicals for hundreds of uses, meaning less pollution. We might not be facing the Greenhouse Effect.

Outlawing hemp has been an agricultural, industrial, and environmental disaster. What punishment fits this crime against humanity? I would recommend clemency myself, but it would be unmitigated folly to continue this misguided effort at prohibition.

Reprinted from the *Orange County Register*, the second largest newspaper in California, October 30, 1988.
Bock is the *Register's* senior columnist.

946.
41 min., 16 mm. (? ...ery, no. 1)
Order no. ...16.
Summary: D... ...ibes pathologic, ...ostic, and thera]... ...
emothorax and other disorders . the pleura and pleural cavity.
medical personnel.
Pleura—Diseases. 1. U. S. War Dept. (Series)
616.25 Fi E 52–2221
U. S. Office of Education. Visual Education Service

367

1. Ford, Henr'
Leaders of An'

Eye Ga'

1

Hemp for victory (*Motion picture*) U. S. Dept. of Agriculture, 1942.
14 min., sd., b&w, 16 mm.
Summary: Explains that the war cut off the supply of East Indian coarse fibers, and stresses the need for American-grown hemp for military and civilian uses. Portrays farm practices of hemp growers in Kentucky and Wisconsin.
—— Another issue. 35 mm.
1. Hemp—U. S. 1. U. S. Dept. of Agriculture.
633.53 Fi E 53–370
U. S. Office of Education. Visual Education Service

H'
P'
1952
20 n.
Summ
ers can do
Republican
canvassing;
techniques.
Credits
H. Wolf
Cast: J'
1. '
cal
Ne

It

Hen hop (*Motion picture*) National Film Board of Canada, Ottawa, 1944. P' leased in the U. S. by International Film Bureau.
5 min., sd., c'
Warnercol'
*Summar'
Simple go
a hen v
Rock
c'

h French-Canadian bar'
built up rhythmically

Henry
Tele
Lond
...

WHEN THE U.S. GOVERNMENT SAID "THERE'S NO SUCH FILM" WE PROVED THEM WRONG

2

HELP ELIMINATE MARIJUANA PROHIBITION

H.E.MP 5632 Van Nuys #210, Van Nuys, CA 91401 (818) 377-5886

Dear Friend,

For the last fifteen years, the United States Department of Agriculture's 1942 film, "Hemp For Victory", was given to every facet of the media (newspapers, magazines, TV, etc.) by the California Marijuana Initiative, the Oregon Marijuana Initiative, NORML, etc., as part of our proof of hemp's history and the incredible potential for mass-producing hemp by harvesting it mechanically (see "Popular Mechanics" Feb. 1938 article, "New Billion Dollar Crop", enclosed).

And for the last fifteen years the USDA, its library, and the Library of Congress have told or written the media and all other interested parties (e.g., see enclosed letter to Jim Evans) that no such movie was _ever_ made by the USDA or any branch of the US government.

In May of 1989, Maria Farrow, Carl Packard, and myself, Jack Herer, were in Washington D.C., going through the Library of Congress' motion pictures and filmstrips records, and the records at the USDA library at Bettsville, Maryland. After being told by their librarians that it simply couldn't have disappeared from the card catalogs, files, and electronic searches of all our major libraries if the US government had indeed made it, we looked until we were beat, and we quit.

Then we decided to try once more at the Library of Congress. We asked for the film catalogs of thirty to forty years ago, and after all those government searches denying its existence, we found it! (See enclosed certification from the Library of Congress) We donated two VHS copies of "HFV" into the Library of Congress, and they were accepted on May 19, 1989.

Jack Herer

3

United States
Department of
Agriculture

Agricultural
Stabilization and
Conservation Service

Oregon State Office
1220 SW 3rd Ave, Rm 1524
Portland, OR 97204

June 19, 1989

Mr. Jim Evans
1565 Siskiyou, #32
Ashland, OR 97520

Dear Mr. Evans:

We contacted the Washington DC office of the Department of Agriculture and also the Federal Audio Center and have been unable to locate any film with the title "Hemp for Victory" that was produced by any department of the federal government.

If you have any further information as to when or where you learned of this film, or any other title it might have been produced under, we will be glad to make another attempt at locating it for you.

Sincerely,

John Van Calcar
John Van Calcar,
Information Officer

JVC/BE

4

THE LIBRARY OF CONGRESS
WASHINGTON, D.C. 20540

PHOTODUPLICATION SERVICE

I hereby certify that I am the Chief of the Photoduplication Service at the Library of Congress and that there is now in the collections of the Library of Congress a publication entitled *The National Union Catalog, Volume 28 Motion Pictures and Filmstrips, 1953–1957*

I further certify that the attached photocopies are true copies of *title page and page 367*

made from said publication.

In testimony whereof I hereunto subscribe my name and cause the seal of the Library of Congress to be affixed hereon this *12th* day of *July* 19 *79*

Acting *Mary Ann Ferrara*
Chief, Photoduplication Service

5

THE LIBRARY OF CONGRESS CATALOGS

The National Union Catalog

*A Cumulative Author List Representing
Library of Congress Printed Cards
and Titles Reported by Other American Libraries*

COMPILED BY THE LIBRARY OF CONGRESS
WITH THE COOPERATION
OF THE COMMITTEE ON RESOURCES OF AMERICAN LIBRARIES
OF THE AMERICAN LIBRARY ASSOCIATION

1953-1957

VOLUME 28
MOTION PICTURES AND FILMSTRIPS

Hemp for victory (*Motion picture*) U. S. Dept. of Agriculture, 1942.
14 min., sd., b&w, 16 mm.
Summary: Explains that the war cut off the supply of East Indian coarse fibers, and stresses the need for American-grown hemp for military and civilian uses. Portrays farm practices of hemp growers in Kentucky and Wisconsin.
—— Another issue. 35 mm.
1. Hemp—U. S. 1. U. S. Dept. of Agriculture.
633.53 Fi E 53–370
U. S. Office of Education. Visual Education Service

J. W. EDWARDS, INC
ANN ARBOR, MICHIGAN
1958

Hemp Machines

FROM 150 YEARS OF INTERNATIONAL HARVESTER *
CRESTLINE PUBLISHING
© 1981

An early photo from the IH Archives shows a reaper at work in a field of hemp. The fiber derived from hemp has long been of value for rope and cordage. Cyrus Hall Mc-Cormick and his father invested heavily in time and money trying to perfect a hemp brake during the 1830's. Hemp harvesting by mechanical means remained an unsolvable problem until the early 1900's.

During World War One, there was a renewed interest in domestic hemp. Wartime demands for rope and cordage exceeded a limited overseas supply, and the possibility existed that even these sources might be lost. The International hemp harvester was designed to cut the hemp and leave it nicely placed for retting. This natural process separated the usable fiber from the woody material in the stems.

After retting, a hemp gathering machine tied the material into bundles for further curing and an eventual trip to the hemp mill. During the 1918-20 period, International Harvester Company devoted considerable attention to hemp machinery, and perfected a hemp brake, hemp harvester, hemp scutcher, and hemp tow cleaner. With the end of military hostilities, enthusiasm for domestic hemp declined.

Responding to wartime needs, International Harvester Company developed a new hemp gatherer-binder by 1943. The cut material shown here underwent a suitable retting period. This ranged from two to six weeks, depending on the weather conditions. The basic design of this hemp gatherer-binder differed little from the 1918 machine.

A closeup view of the International hemp binder shows the travel of loose hemp over the front of the machine. An ordinary grain binder knotter was used to tie the bundles. This machine was being operated on the Axel Anderson farm near Mason City, Iowa. A hemp mill was located at that city, under the auspices of the War Hemp Industries, Inc., a Government-owned organization. Some 4,000 to 5,000 acres of hemp was planted in the area surrounding each mill. Forty two such installations were built across the United States.

Long ago when these ancient Grecian temples were new, hemp was already old in the service of mankind. For thousands of years, even then, this plant had been grown for cordage and cloth in China and elsewhere in the East. For centuries prior to about 1850 all the ships that sailed the western seas were rigged with hempen rope and sails. For the sailor, no less than the hangman, hemp was indispensable.

A 44-gun frigate like our cherished Old Ironsides took over 60 tons of hemp for rigging, including an anchor cable 25 inches in circumference. The Conestoga wagons and prairie schooners of pioneer days were covered with hemp canvas. Indeed the very word canvas comes from the Arabic word for hemp. In those days hemp was an important crop in Kentucky and Missouri. Then came cheaper imported fibers for cordage, like jute, sisal and Manila hemp, and the culture of hemp in America declined.

But now with Philippine and East Indian sources of hemp in the hands of the Japanese, and shipment of jute from India curtailed, American hemp must meet the needs of our Army and Navy as well as of our industry. In 1942, patriotic farmers at the government's request planted 36,000 acres of seed hemp, an increase of several thousand percent. The goal for 1943 is 50,000 acres of seed hemp.

In Kentucky much of the seed hemp acreage is on river bottom land such as this. Some of these fields are inaccessible except by boat. Thus plans are afoot for a great expansion of a hemp industry as a part of the war program. This film is designed to tell farmers how to handle this ancient crop now little known outside Kentucky and Wisconsin.

This is hemp seed. Be careful how you use it. For to grow hemp legally you must have a federal registration and tax stamp. This is provided for in your contract. Ask your county agent about it. Don't forget.

Hemp demands a rich, well-drained soil such as is found here in the Blue Grass region of Kentucky or in central Wisconsin. It must be loose and rich in organic matter. Poor soils won't do. Soil that will grow good corn will usually grow hemp.

Hemp is not hard on the soil. In Kentucky it has been grown for several years on the same ground, though this practice is not recommended. A dense and shady crop, hemp tends to choke out weeds. Here's a Canada thistle that couldn't stand the competition, dead as a dodo. Thus hemp leaves the ground in good condition for the following crop.

For fiber, hemp should be sewn closely, the closer the rows, the better. These rows are spaced about four inches. This hemp has been broadcast. Either way it should be sewn thick enough to grow a slender stalk. Here's an ideal stand: the right height to be harvested easily, thick enough to grow slender stalks that are easy to cut and process.

Stalks like these here on the left yield the most fiber and the best. Those on the right are too coarse and woody. For seed, hemp is planted in hills like corn. Sometimes by hand. Hemp is a dioecious plant. The female flower is inconspicuous. But the male flower is easily spotted. In seed production after the pollen has been shed, these male plants are cut out. These are the seeds on a female plant.

Hemp for fiber is ready to harvest when the pollen is shedding and the leaves are falling. In Kentucky, hemp harvest comes in August. Here the old standby has been the self-rake reaper, which has been used for a generation or more.

Hemp grows so luxuriantly in Kentucky that harvesting is sometimes difficult, which may account for the popularity of the self-rake with its lateral stroke. A modified rice binder has been used to some extent. This machine works well on average hemp. Recently, the improved hemp harvester, used for many years in Wisconsin, has been introduced in Kentucky. This machine spreads the hemp in a continuous swath. It is a far cry from this fast and efficient modern harvester, that doesn't stall in the heaviest hemp.

In Kentucky, hand cutting is practicing in opening fields for the machine. In Kentucky, hemp is shucked as soon as safe, after cutting, to be spread out for retting later in the fall.

In Wisconsin, hemp is harvested in September. Here the hemp harvester with automatic spreader is standard equipment. Note how smoothly the rotating apron lays the swaths preparatory to retting. Here it is a common and essential practice to leave headlands around hemp fields. These strips may be planted with other crops, preferably small grain. Thus the harvester has room to make its first round without preparatory hand cutting. The other machine is running over corn stubble. When the cutter bar is much shorter than the hemp is tall, overlapping occurs. Not so good for retting. The standard cut is eight to nine feet.

The length of time hemp is left on the ground to ret depends on the weather. The swaths must be turned to get a uniform ret. When the woody core breaks away readily like this, the hemp is about ready to pick up and bind into bundles. Well-retted hemp is light to dark grey. The fiber tends to pull away from the stalks. The presence of stalks in the bough-string stage indicates that retting is well underway. When hemp is short or tangled or when the ground is too wet for machines, it's bound by hand. A wooden bucket is used. Twine will do for tying, but the hemp itself makes a good band.

When conditions are favorable, the pickup binder is commonly used. The swaths should lie smooth and even with the stalks parallel. The picker won't work well in tangled hemp. After binding, hemp is shucked as soon as possible to stop further retting. In 1942, 14,000 acres of fiber hemp were harvested in the United States. The goal for the old standby cordage fiber, is staging a strong comeback.

This is Kentucky hemp going into the dryer over mill at Versailles. In the old days braking was done by hand. One of the hardest jobs known to man. Now the power braker makes quick work of it.

Spinning American hemp into rope yarn or twine in the old Kentucky river mill at Frankfort, Kentucky. Another pioneer plant that has been making cordage for more than a century. All such plants will presently be turning out products spun from American-grown hemp: twine of various kinds for tying and upholster's work; rope for marine rigging and towing; for hay forks, derricks, and heavy duty tackle; light duty firehose; thread for shoes for millions of American soldiers; and parachute webbing for our paratroopers. As for the United States Navy, every battleship requires 34,000 feet of rope. Here in the Boston Navy Yard, where cables for frigates were made long ago, crews are now working night and day making cordage for the fleet. In the old days rope yarn was spun by hand. The rope yarn feeds through holes in an iron plate. This is Manila hemp from the Navy's rapidly dwindling reserves. When it is gone, American hemp will go on duty again: hemp for mooring ships; hemp for tow lines; hemp for tackle and gear; hemp for countless naval uses both on ship and shore. Just as in the days when Old Ironsides sailed the seas victorious with her hempen shrouds and hempen sails. Hemp for victory. ✦

TRANSCRIPT OF THE ORIGINAL USDA FILM:

HEMP FOR VICTORY

— 1942 —

Reprinted from High Times, October 1989

Hemp

FARMERS' BULLETIN No. 1935

Caution

THE HEMP PLANT contains the drug marihuana. Any farmer planning to grow hemp must comply with certain regulations of the Marihuana Tax Act of 1937. This involves registration with the farmer's nearest Internal Revenue Collector and the payment of a fee of $1. Although the fee is small, the registration is mandatory and should not be neglected, as the penalty provisions for not complying with the regulations are very severe. The registration must be renewed each year beginning July 1. This so-called "license" permits a farmer to obtain viable hemp seed from a registered firm dealing in hemp, to plant and grow the crop, and to deliver mature, retted hemp stalks to a hemp mill.

Washington, D. C.

Issued January 1943
Slightly Revised April 1952

HEMP

By B. B. Robinson, Senior Agronomist

*Division of Cotton and Other Fiber Crops and Diseases
Bureau of Plant Industry, Soils, and Agricultural Engineering
Agricultural Research Administration*

HEMP is a fiber used in making twines and light cordage. It is also used as an extender for imported cordage fibers, particularly abaca, sisal, and henequen, when supplies of these are not adequate to meet domestic demands. The size of the hemp industry, therefore, is greatly influenced by the availability of imported cordage fibers.

Hemp is not a hard crop to grow. It should be planted on the most productive land on the farm—land that would make 50 to 70 bushels of corn per acre.

The crop is planted with a grain drill and harvested with special machinery rented from hemp mills.

It is allowed to lie on the ground until the outer part of the stalks has rotted, freeing the fibers. This process is called dew retting.

The most important step in hemp farming is to stop the retting process at the proper time. (See pp. 12 and 13.)

This bulletin tells how to grow and harvest hemp. For more information write to the Bureau of Plant Industry, Soils, and Agricultural Engineering, United States Department of Agriculture, or to your State experiment station, or consult your county agent.

What it is

Hemp is an annual plant that grows from seed each year, and therefore it can be brought readily into production. It produces twice as much fiber per acre as flax, the only other fiber that is its equal in strength and durability and that is known to be suitable for culture and preparation on machinery in this country.

When hemp seed is sown thickly for fiber production, the plants usually grow from 5 to 8 feet tall. However, when the plants are thinly spaced in rows for seed production, they may, under favorable conditions, reach a height of 12 to 16 feet. If the plants are not crowded, they become much branched and are bushy. Uniform stems approximately ⅜ inch in diameter and 5 to 8 feet long are especially desired for fiber production, because they can be handled well by the harvesting and processing machinery available in this country.

Hemp is a dioecious plant, that is, the staminate (male) and pis-

hemp plants, containing much of the plant nutrients removed from the soil, fall off during the growth and maturing of the plant. The remaining leaves may drop off in the field during the process of retting. Further, the plant stems lose about 20 percent in weight of soluble and decomposed materials, which leach out upon the fields, and the stubble may be plowed under. The plant in this manner returns to the land a large part of the plant nutrients that it removes during its growth.

Commercial fertilizers may be used to advantage on soils that are not well supplied with organic matter. Ordinarily, the best fertilizer for hemp is barnyard manure, but commercial fertilizer can be used to advantage to supplement manure. Lime applications may be supplied on acid soils to advantage. Consult your county agent for recommendations as to amounts of fertilizer and lime to apply.

Seed

The period of flowering of the hemp plant may extend over several weeks, and as a result the seed does not all mature at one time. Hemp seed for sowing frequently contains some immature green to yellowish-green seeds that may not germinate well. Good hemp seed for sowing should be relatively free of such seeds and should germinate 90 percent or better. As the oil content of hemp seed usually ranges between 29 and 34 percent, the seed should be kept cool and dry, as it spoils rapidly under warm and damp conditions. Hemp seed seldom retains its germinating power well enough to be used for seed after 2-years' storage.

When to Plant

Hemp should be planted in the spring just before corn. In a program calling for small spring grains and corn, the farmer should plan to plant his hemp between the time he plants his small grains and the corn.

Seeding

Hemp grown for seed production should be sown in rows or hills. The hills are commonly spaced 5 by 5 feet, with 6 to 10 seeds to the hill, planted not more than ½ inch deep. The plants are thinned to 3 to 5 to a hill. If care is taken to save seed, about 1½ pounds will sow an acre. Most farmers use more seed, and frequently the crop is replanted because of late floods or failure to obtain good stands.

Hemp grown for fiber should be sown with a broadcast seeder or with a grain drill. A drill with 4 inches between drill tubes is preferred to one with 6 inches or more. The seed should not be planted deeper than 1 inch, and a depth of ½ inch is preferred. If the seed is planted deep, the hemp seedling is not capable of pushing its way to the surface of the ground. A slight crust on the ground frequently results in a poor stand. If the seedbed is loose, disks on a seed drill may cut too deep into the soil and the seed will be sown more than 1 inch deep. In such cases, to make certain that the disks do not cut too deep into the seedbed, they should be tied to the seed box.

A standard bushel of hempseed weighs 44 pounds. The rate of seeding hemp for fiber production ranges between 3 and 5 pecks of seed per acre. In Kentucky, where hemp is hand-broken, it has been the practice to sow 3 pecks (33 pounds) per acre. However, when the hemp is to go to the mill, 1 bushel per acre gives a product that is better suited to milling. Wisconsin and other Corn Belt farmers have commonly sown 5 pecks per acre. The lighter rate of seeding in Kentucky produces larger stalks. These stalks are easily broken, and the fiber is easily prepared by the hand breaking methods that have been used there since colonial days. Machine methods of breaking and scutching to prepare the fiber are used in Wisconsin, and

It grows well in the Corn Belt

Hemp is recommended as a good crop for the Corn Belt States, because of their favorable climatic and soil conditions.

Most fiber-producing varieties of hemp require a frost-free growing season of 5 months or longer to produce seed and approximately 4 months for fiber production. Hemp will endure light frosts in spring and survive frosts in the fall better than corn. It grows best when well supplied with moisture throughout its growing season, and especially in its early stages of growth. Drought conditions, if accompanied by high temperatures, appear to hasten maturity before the plants are fully grown.

The vegetative growth of hemp should be uniform. This growth is noticeably affected if the soil is flooded or saturated with moisture too long a period. The leaves turn yellow, and the plants die. Rainfall, well distributed during the growing season, is, therefore, desirable for uniform vegetative growth. Hemp should be planted only on well-drained soils and not on flat, heavy, impervious soils.

Climate is important not only in the growth of the plant but also in the preparation of the crop after harvest. It influences the method used in handling the crop and the labor requirements, which determine the cost of production. In the United States the common practice (known as dew retting) is to cut the crop and let it lie on the ground. Exposure to the weather causes the fiber in the outer part of the stem to separate. Light snows and alternate freezing and thawing seem to improve or make the retting more uniform.

How to grow it

Soils and Fertilizers

Hemp should not be grown on poor soils. To obtain good yields and fiber of high quality, it is necessary to have a growth of uniform stalks 6 to 8 feet long. Short stalks, from poor nonfertile soils, seldom produce a high-quality fiber.

Fiber hemp grows successfully on soils of the Clarion, Tama, Carrington, Maury, Hagerstown, and Miami series, which, in general, are deep, medium-heavy loams, well-drained, and high in organic matter. Artificially drained areas of the Webster, Brookston, and Maumee series also give satisfactory yields. These soils are among the most productive soils of the Corn Belt. They produce average yields of 50 to 70 bushels or more of corn per acre. If land will not produce from 50 to 70 bushels of corn per acre, it should not be planted to hemp for fiber production.

Muck or peat soils are not recommended for the production of high-quality hemp fiber. The quantity of fiber produced per acre on these soils may be very high, but experience has demonstrated that the fiber lacks strength, which is the first requirement of hemp fiber for good cordage.

The inexperienced farmer usually gets advice from an experienced hemp-mill superintendent in the selection of the right soil. In fact, the farmer's contract to grow hemp usually specifies the exact field that it has been mutually agreed should be used for the hemp crop. This type of supervision by the company contracting for hemp has helped to prevent many crop failures.

Hemp should not be grown continuously on the same soil, for the same reasons that many other crops are not adapted to such practices. In Wisconsin, fields previously used for a cultivated crop are selected for hemp planting in preference to ones upon which small grains have been grown. In Kentucky, bluegrass soil, if obtainable, is selected. Old pastures plowed up are well suited for hemp culture. Fields previously cropped to soybeans, alfalfa, and clover are excellent for hemp. A good rotation is to follow corn with hemp, and in Kentucky a fall cereal may follow the hemp.

Although hemp requires a rich soil, it does not remove from the farm an excess of plant-food material. Nearly all the leaves on the

The flowers of the two types of plants are different, but the male plant is easily distinguished from the female, as the anthers are about the size of a wheat kernel. The male plants die soon after discharging their pollen; this is usually about 3 to 5 weeks before the female plants mature seed and die.

The fiber of commerce ranges from 4 to 8 feet in length and has the appearance of a flat, fine ribbon. It lies very close to the epidermis or skin of the plant. Spinners desire the fiber ribbon 1/16 inch or less in width. The long strands of fiber are called "line" fiber to distinguish them from "tow" fiber, which consists of shorter, broken, tangled pieces.

PISTILLATE STAMINATE

tillate (female) flowers are borne on separate plants, rather than both on one plant.

recently to some extent in Kentucky. The machines will handle finer stems, and the sowing of 5 pecks is advisable where hemp is to be prepared by machine.

A good practice in planting hemp for fiber production is to sow around the edge of the field next to the fence a 16- to 18-foot width of small grains, which may be harvested before the hemp. Space is thus provided for the harvester to enter the field and begin cutting without injuring the hemp. It also prevents hemp plants at the edge from growing too rank. Uniform plants are necessary for uniform fiber quality.

Culture

Fall plowing in Wisconsin gives better results with hemp than spring plowing.

Hemp for fiber production requires little or no cultivation or care after planting until the harvest; but if, after seeding and before the seedlings emerge, the ground crusts badly it may be advisable to roll the field to break the crust. Hemp for seed production should be cultivated the same as corn; that is, sufficiently to keep back the weeds. Spudding out Canada thistles where they appear in dense stands in hemp fields should be done when the hemp is only a few inches high. In most cases hemp will compete well with weeds, if the hemp gets off to a good start.

Varieties to grow

The fiber hemp grown in the United States by the early colonists was of European origin; but our present hemp, commonly known as Kentucky or domestic hemp, is of Chinese origin. Few importations of hempseed have been made in recent years for commercial plantings, as imported seed has not proved as productive under domestic conditions as Kentucky hemp.

Enemies

In the United States there are no hemp diseases of economic importance, and hemp has not been seriously attacked by insects. The European corn borer and similar stem-boring insects occasionally kill a hemp stem. However, they have not proved important, perhaps because hemp has not been grown to any extent in the sections of the United States where the European corn borer is a serious pest. Seedling plants are frequently attacked by cutworms and white grubs after spring plowing of sod land.

Broom rape is a small weed 6 to 15 inches high that is parasitic on the roots of hemp, tobacco, and tomatoes. It usually grows in clumps and has purple flowers, which produce many very small seeds. These adhere to the waxy flower parts surrounding the hempseed and are distributed in this manner. Broom rape can be very serious on hemp if proper control measures are not followed. Only well-cleaned hempseed and seed from fields containing no broom rape should be sown.

Hemp has been recommended as a weed-control crop. Its dense, tall growth helps to kill out many common weeds. The noxious bindweed, a member of the morning-glory family, is checked to some extent by hemp. Unfortunately, bindweed and several other species of morning-glory have seeds so near the same size and weight of hemp seed that mixtures obtained in producing hempseed are carried to the field planted for fiber production. In growing hemp for seed all vine weeds of this type found on the hemp stalks should be removed before the hemp plants begin to produce seed.

Harvesting

Time to Harvest

Hemp is harvested for seed production when the plant on being shaken sheds most of its seed. This occurs when the seeds are fully mature on the middle branches. The seeds will mature on the lower branches first and on the top of the plant last. The common method

of harvesting hemp for seed production is to cut it by hand and shock it to permit more seed to mature and cure before threshing. The harvesting should be in the early morning or on damp days when the seeds do not shatter so much as they do in the warmer and drier part of the day. Threshing of the seed hemp should be done on dry afternoons. In threshing, the seed shocks should be placed on large canvas cloths 24 by 24 feet and then be beaten with long sticks to remove the seed.

Hemp is harvested for fiber production when the male plants are in full flower and are shedding pollen. By harvesting before the male plants die, the retting of both male and female plants is more uniform, as both types of plants are still green and growing. The harvesting period may extend for 2 weeks or longer. Very early harvested hemp may produce a finer and softer fiber than that harvested later, but it is usually weaker. The fiber from hemp that has been harvested so late that many seeds have matured does not possess so good cordage and textile characteristics as fiber from hemp harvested earlier. Hemp stalks should be relatively free of leaves except a few at the very top before harvesting. This is important when hemp is shocked after harvest, as it makes the top of the shock smaller so that less rain can enter the shock.

Machinery

Harvesting methods vary with locality and climate. In Kentucky hemp may grow to a height of 15 feet or more. These long stalks are difficult to handle with machinery. Self-rake reapers (see below) have been used in harvesting hemp for many years, and they probably do better work with very tall hemp than any other machine now available. A modified rice binder, which cuts and

binds the hemp into bundles, is also available, although difficulty in handling the very tall hemp may be experienced. This latter type of machine can be used for short hemp in areas, such as Kentucky, where hemp must be shocked within a few days after harvest to avoid sunburn.

In the northern part of the Corn Belt the hemp usually does not grow so tall and can be handled more easily with machines. During the first World War hemp-harvesting machinery was developed. These harvesters (see above) in one operation cut an 8- or 9-foot swath and elevate the stalks to a quarter-circle platform where they are turned automatically and dropped or spread on the ground for retting. The butts of the stems all lie in the same direction and are relatively even. The thickness of the layer of stalks in the swath influences the speed and uniformity of the dew retting. Machines of this type, because of their labor economy, are recommended for use in the Northern States, where hemp can be safely spread for retting when harvested.

Hemp harvesters are usually owned by the hemp mills. They are rented to the individual farmers, who usually furnish the motive power and the labor to run the harvesters.

Retting

Retting is the partial rotting of the hemp stalk. It permits the fiber in the stalk to separate easily in long strands from the woody core. The fiber strands break if unretted stems are bent or broken.

In this country the usual practice is to ret hemp by allowing it to lie on the ground, where it is exposed to rain and dew. This method is called dew retting.

Dew retting is dependent upon dews and rains to furnish the moist conditions necessary for the growth of the molds that cause the retting. In warm, moist weather the retting may require 1 to 2 weeks, but usually 4 to 5 weeks is required for retting in Kentucky and Wisconsin. Hemp has remained spread under snow in Wisconsin until spring without serious injury, but more often hemp left spread under snow all winter is overretted and ruined.

Underretting and Overretting

If hemp stalks are lifted from the ground before they are sufficiently retted, the fiber will not separate easily from the woody hurds (small pieces of the woody core of the plant) in milling. However, if the retting is permitted to go too far, the fiber separates very readily from the core, but the adhesive substance between the individual fiber cells in the long strand breaks down and the fiber is weak. Hemp further overretted produces mostly short broken strands of fiber called tow fiber, which is less valuable than the long parallel strands of fiber called line fiber.

Nowhere in the growing or processing of hemp is good judgment more needed than in determining the time to end the ret. Experience and good judgment are necessary to determine just when the hemp stalks should be lifted from the field and shocked. The lifting and shocking stops the retting action. The value of the fiber can be cut in half or entirely lost by several days' overretting in warm weather.

Sunburning

In Kentucky, hemp spread immediately to ret after harvest is apt to sunburn, or sunscald. It is common belief that the hot, bright days in August and September in some way cause deterioration of the fiber if spread for retting. Sunburned fiber is uneven in color, usually has less strength, and possibly is drier and more harsh than fiber not sunburned. In order to avoid sunscalding, the hemp is shocked after being harvested and not spread for retting until the cooler days of November. In locations having climatic conditions similar to those prevailing in Wisconsin, sunscald of hemp is rare.

Turning Stalks

In dew retting the spread stalks should be turned once or more during the retting period. This aids in bleaching the stalks and results in fiber of more uniform color and quality. The turning is

done by workmen using bent poles approximately 8 to 10 feet in length. The poles are pushed under the head ends of stalks in the swath, and the stalks are turned over without moving the butt ends.

In turning the straw the workmen start in the middle of the field, turning the first swath into vacant center space. The second swath will be turned to lie where the first swath had been, and so on.

Care should be exercised in turning to prevent the stalks from tangling. The more hemp is handled, the more tangled the stalks may become. Tangled hemp is more difficult to process and produces a high proportion of tangled, short tow fiber.

WELL RETTED

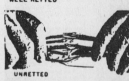

WELL RETTED

UNRETTED

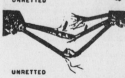

UNRETTED

Testing the End Point of the Ret

A few days too long in the field may make the difference between retting and rotting. Therefore, it is most important that inexperienced farmers obtain the assistance of the hemp-mill superintendent or an experienced grower in determining when to stop the retting.

Dry hemp stalks should be tested when possible to determine the degree of retting. Three to six stalks are taken in both hands and bent back and forth to perform the break test. If properly retted the fiber should fall free of the woody core when the woody core breaks. The hurds should fall free of the fiber in the breaking and shaking between one's hands. If the hemp is only partly retted, some hurds will adhere to the loosened fiber. Unretted hemp fiber is usually green or light yellow. Dew-retted hemp is usually slate gray or black.

After the fiber is broken free, its strength should be tested by break

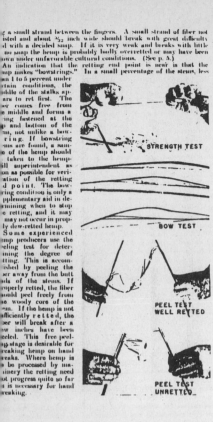

g a small strand between the fingers. A small strand of fiber not
isted and about ³⁄₃₂ inch wide should break with great difficulty
d with a decided snap. If it is very weak and breaks with little
no snap the hemp is probably badly overretted or may have been
own under unfavorable cultural conditions. (See p. 5.)

An indication that the retting end point is near is that the
mp makes "bowstrings." In a small percentage of the stems, less
an 1 to 5 percent under
rtain conditions, the
ddle of the stalks ap-
ars to ret first. The
er comes free from
e middle and forms a
ing fastened at the
p and bottom of the
m, not unlike a bow-
ring. If bowstring
ms are found, a sam-
e of the hemp should
taken to the hemp-
ll superintendent as
on as possible for veri-
ation of the retting
d point. The bow-
ring condition is only a
pplementary aid in de-
rmining when to stop
e retting, and it may
may not occur in prop-
ly dew-retted hemp.

Some experienced
mp producers use the
eling test for deter-
ning the degree of
tting. This is accom-
ished by peeling the
er away from the bu-
of the stems. If
perly retted, the fiber
ould peel freely from
woody core of the
m. If the hemp is not
ficiently retted, the
er will break after a
w inches have been
led. This free peel-
stage is desirable for
eaking hemp on hand
eaks. Where hemp is
be processed by ma-
nery the retting need
t progress quite so far
s necessary for hand
eaking.

STRENGTH TEST

BOW TEST

PEEL TEST WELL RETTED

PEEL TEST UNRETTED

Picking Up the Retted Stalks

Hemp stalks may be picked up by hand. This method has been
used from early times and is satisfactory where labor is plentiful.
However, in this country it is being replaced by machine pick-up
binders.

In picking up the straw by hand, small sticks about 3 feet long
with a single steel or wooden hook on the end are used. The hemp
is raked into bunches with these implements, and usually tied.
Hemp-fiber bands are used in tying the bundles. An inexpensive
"buck" (see above) may be used to bunch the hemp, or it may
be bunched with a pitchfork.

The most efficient method is to use the pick-up binder. These
machines, drawn by tractors, cover about an acre an hour. They

pick up the retted hemp stalks and tie them into bundles in one
operation. The machines are part of the modern hemp-mill equipment and are rented to farmers.

Dew-retted hemp is usually shocked after being picked up. The
hemp remains in the shock until it is transported to the mill.

Extra Care Insures Extra Profits

The farmer's job is done when he delivers the hemp to the mill.
All further processing to prepare the fiber is part of the milling operation. However, it is of interest to both farmers and mill operators
to attempt to keep the hemp stalks and fiber well butted. This
means keeping the butt ends of the stalks or fiber in a bundle all
even. Every time the hemp stalks are handled, care should be taken
to see that this is done. If the hemp stalks are well butted in the
bundle when processed, the milling operations can be carried out
more economically. Tangled, uneven bundles are more difficult and
require more time to handle. The yield of high-value long-life fiber
is much greater if the stalks are well butted.

Hemp stalks are considered most desirable if they are less than
half an inch in diameter. The thickness of a pencil is frequently
used to illustrate the size of desirable stalks. The larger diameter
stalks have a lower percentage of fiber than finer stems, are harder
to break, and produce more tow fiber.

Hemp stalks grown on unproductive soil usually contain a lower
percentage of fiber, and this fiber may be coarse, harsh, and of low
strength, so that it breaks into tow in milling.

Stalks underretted frequently must be run through the mill
breaker a second or third time to remove the remaining hurds. This
increases the milling labor costs, and the resultant fiber may be reduced to a low grade. On the other hand, overretted hemp must
be milled as little as possible, with less pressure exerted on the rollers
and a slower speed of the scutcher wheel to keep from making an ex-

Yields

Hemp yields have been extremely variable when this crop has been
planted in new areas by inexperienced farmers. In Wisconsin and
Kentucky, where only experienced farmers have grown the crop in
recent years, the yields have not varied a great deal. The crop has
been reasonably dependable and has not often been injured by storms
or droughts.

The average yields per acre for experienced farmers are approximately 2¼ to 2½ tons of air-dry retted hemp stalks; 850 pounds
total fiber. Under the Wisconsin machine-milling system the yields
may average 450 pounds line fiber and 400 pounds tow fiber; under
the Kentucky hand-breaking system they may average 775 pounds
Kentucky rough and 75 pounds tow.

If hemp is planted for seed production, the average yields per acre
are approximately 15 bushels or 660 pounds, on bottom land, and 12
bushels on uplands.

OCT. 13, 1921 PAPER TRADE JOURNAL, 50TH YEAR

MARIHUANA: New Federal Tax Hits Dealings in Potent Weed

Cannabis sativa, scraggly tramp of the vegetable world, grows with equal ease alongside Chinese railroad tracks, in Indianapolis' vacant lots, and on Buenos Aires ash dumps. Birdseed manufacturers harvest the mature plant, thresh out the seeds, and use them to restore molting pigeons to health. The plant's fiber is twisted into rope and woven into cheap cloth.

It was neither of these legitimate uses that impelled Representative Robert L. Doughton of North Carolina to introduce a bill imposing a transaction tax on commerce in the weed; he was interested in *Cannabis sativa* because it is a dangerous and devastating narcotic—known to the Orient as hashish, to the Occident as marihuana.

Through Turkish water pipes Indians and other Orientals for centuries have inhaled the acrid, tarry smoke of hashish. About a decade ago Negro musicians in New Orleans began drying and crushing the plant's leaves and rolling them into cigarettes. Known variously as bennys, reefers, Mary Warners, and muggles, these cigarettes spread over the United States; shoestring peddlers market them for a dime apiece. Recently, Negro bandmen have introduced them to London's smart Mayfair.

Nearly every State has enacted legislation curbing production, and enforcement agents have discovered cultivated plots growing in Maryland, in Brooklyn, N.Y., and even in the San Quentin prison lot. But curbing the traffic without Federal aid has proved all but impossible. Since few policemen know enough botany to recognize the weed, arrests for cultivation and sale are made almost entirely by narcotics squads of big-city police forces. Doughton's measure—which became law last week when President Roosevelt signed it—imposes a tax on all transactions; since no peddler would be foolish enough to pay such a tax, he is instantly liable to a $2,000 fine or a five-year jail term, or both.

Inhaling the smoke—which is held in the lungs as long as possible—impels some users to lassitude, others to violence. Generally, however, subjective reactions stick to one well-defined track:

Half an hour after smoking a reefer, the subject becomes jovial, carefree, and capable of rare feats of strength. Hallucinations follow: space expands and time slows down; a minute seems like a day and a room looks like a place viewed from the large end of a pair of binoculars. This phase is valuable to hot-band players—time distortion slows down everything and gives opportunity to crowd in a dozen cornet notes where previously there was only time for one. The third stage of intoxication is the dangerous one. The weed acts as a powerful aphrodisiac and renders users capable of various acts of violence; a

© NEWS-WEEK August 14, 1937

HEMP WOOD AS A PAPERMAKING MATERIAL

ABSTRACTED BY C. J. WEST

If the composition of hemp wood as reported by Schwalbe and Becker in *Z. angew. Chem.* 32, 127 (1919) is correct, it should be a very promising raw material for paper mills. They reported a surprisingly high content of pure cellulose, namely, 51.7 per cent, while Heuser and Haug (*Z. angew. Chem.* 31, 99, 103, 166, 172 (1918) found only 43 per cent for the cellulose content of straw. Since straw has lately become an important raw material for the manufacture of pulp, it must be supposed that hemp wood, because of its higher cellulose content, would be even more suitable for this purpose.

Because of the importance of the question, B. Rassow and Alfred Zschenderlein (*Z. angew. Chem.* 34, 204-206 (1921) have re-investigated the question of the composition of wood from hemp. The material used in the investigation consisted, first, of the product as obtained in the ordinary process of retting (from the Deutschen Hanfbaugesellschaft), and second, of a product prepared by the method of Krais (*Z. angew. Chem.* 32, 25, 160, 326; 33, 102) in which tenth normal sodium bicarbonate solution is used.

Krais' method (the "Sicherheitsröste," as Krais calls it) for the digestion of the bast fibers is readily applicable to hemp. The bast fibers dissolve completely in from three to three and a half days when the air-dry stalks are treated with a tenth normal sodium bicarbonate solution at 35 to 37° C and the resulting product shaken with hot water.

The first step in determining the suitability of the hemp wood for pulp manufacture was a study of the chemical composition of the two products. Schwalbe's scheme of analysis (*Z. angew. Chem.* 31, 50, 193; 32, 125) was used; the results were as follows:

Table I—Composition of Hemp Wood Shavings

	Hemp prepared by retting		Hemp prepared by Krais' method		Schwalbe's results	
	Air-dry	Water-free	Air-dry	Water-free	Air-dry	Water-free
Water	10.52		8.86		12.59	
Ash	1.15	1.28	1.39	1.51	1.05	1.20
Fat and wax	2.55	2.85	3.88	4.26	1.96	2.23
Furfural	12.70	14.18	13.09	14.37	11.39	13.03
Pentosan	21.63	24.16	22.31	24.47	19.43	22.15
Crude cellulose	46.63	52.09	47.51	52.11	62.39	71.38
Per cent of pentosan	22.12		22.41		27.57	
Pure cellulose	36.32	40.57	36.86	40.43	45.19	51.70
Lignin	20.89	23.34	20.21	22.08	26.34	30.13

The figures in the last two columns are the results obtained by Schwalbe and Becker. It must be remembered that these values cannot be compared in the same way that results from inorganic analysis are compared, since the methods employed do not have the same degree of precision.

The two samples analyzed by Rassow and Zschenderlein have practically the same composition. This is of great practical importance, since it indicates that the composition is independent of the method of preparation. Hemp wood resembles ordinary wood in composition, as shown by the figures obtained by Schwalbe and Becker (*Z. angew. Chem.* 32, 230) and König and Becker (*Z. angew. Chem.* 32, 157.) It resembles in particular the deciduous trees, which is seen by examining the values for pentosans and lignin, the two values which are characteristic for the difference between deciduous and coniferous trees.

Comparison of the values in the above table shows that the figures obtained by Schwalbe for crude cellulose, cellulose pentosans and pure cellulose vary considerably from those reported by Rassow and Zschenderlein. Even though the cellulose determination is not a very exact one, this fact can scarcely explain the difference between the two values for crude cellulose: 52.09 and 71.38 per cent. In attempting to explain these differences, the various methods for determining cellulose were compared with each other. Approximately the same results were found when vary-

ing amounts of chlorine and different methods of washing were used. The supposition that Schwalbe and Becker used an entirely different material was ruled out by analyzing some of the original material which they used, and obtaining results comparable with the lower ones here reported.

A comparison of the figures reported by Schwalbe and Becker for various woods with those of other investigators, such as König and Becker or Heuser and Sieber (*Z. angew. Chem.*, 26, 801) showed that, while a part of the numbers agreed fairly well, the values for crude cellulose, cellulose pentosans and pure cellulose were consistently higher. The only explanation of this is that the crude cellulose of Schwalbe and Becker is not completely chlorinated and therefore contains considerable amounts of lignin.

Three experiments were carried out in order to determine the influence of the velocity of the chlorine stream: (1) 1 bubble in ½ second; (2) ½ bubbles per second, and (3) a lively stream. The method of Cross and Bevan as modified by Heuser and Haug was used, in which the products formed during the chlorination are washed out with 1 per cent sodium hydroxide. Hydrochloric acid is formed in the chlorination process, which, according to Heuser and Sieber, is a measure of the reactivity of the chlorine. The chlorinated product is washed with warm water (not higher than 30° C) until the filtrate is chlorine-free. The combined filtrate is warmed carefully to drive off free chlorine, and the solution of hydrochloric acid made up to volume and titrated with tenth normal sodium hydroxide. The results show that the yield of crude and pure cellulose is the same, but that the course of the reaction depends upon the velocity of the chlorine stream.

Table II

	Chlorine stream I	II	III
First chlorination	5.89	8.76	11.74
Second "	4.17	6.05	4.37
Third "	3.64	0.57	0.19
Fourth "	2.08	0.22	0.13
Total	15.78%	15.62%	16.53%

These results indicate that, in order to prepare a lignin-free crude cellulose, the fourth chlorination is necessary. They also show that even by the use of a rapid chlorine stream, as in III, there is little if any oxycellulose formed, since Heuser and Haug have shown that the amount of hydrochloric acid formed increases with the formation of oxycellulose. On the other hand, three chlorinations are not sufficient, since the results show that in I, 2.08 per cent hydrochloric acid is formed on the fourth chlorination, a proof that the product still contained lignin. A fifth chlorination is not necessary because the product from the fourth dissolves to a clear solution in concentrated sulphuric acid.

The determination of crude cellulose in hemp wood, as well as in other woods, straw, flax, etc.—since these all have a similar composition—requires four chlorination periods of half an hour each, using a gas stream of 1 to 2 drops per second. By this procedure it is certain that the crude cellulose contains no lignin and at the same time, is free of oxycelluloses. One may follow the course of the chlorination by the change in color of the cellulose material. As long as it contains lignin, it will have an orange color. Pure cellulose is not changed in color by the action of chlorine.

The second problem related to the method of washing the chlorinated product. Experiments were carried out with Heuser and Haug's method, using 1 per cent sodium hydroxide, and with Renker's method, in which sodium sulphite solution was used. The results indicated that slightly better results were obtained by

(Continued on page 48)

HEMP WOOD AS PAPERMAKING MATERIAL
(Continued from page 46)

the first method, and it is recommended that the method be used in all cellulose determinations.

Finally, experiments were undertaken to determine the value of the hemp wood for the preparation of pulp. Cooking with water gave a product which might find use as a kraft pulp. Digestion with sodium hydroxide and sulphite liquor gave a pulp of good appearance, but containing large amounts of pentosans. The soda pulp contained as high as 20 per cent, while sulphite pulp, depending upon the manner of cooking, may contain up to 10 per cent. The Ritter-Kellner method is the most suitable. Cooking for 12—13 hours at 140—150° with about 4 per cent sulphite liquor gives a pulp which, unbleached, contains 93—94 per cent crude cellulose, of which about 10 per cent is pentosans. It is not necessary to use a stronger sulphite liquor, since experiments showed that a 6 per cent liquor gave no better results.

California man decapitated his best friend while under the violent spell of the smoke, and a Florida youngster put the ax to his mother and father.

No one can guess how widespread use of the narcotic is. Sensational press stories about its use in grade and high schools generally prove unfounded. New York, the nation's biggest consumer, jailed 42 users and sellers last year and has collared 37 so far this year. Main concern of narcotics squads, however, are the marihuana rings, wholesalers to agents.

SCIENCE NEWS LETTER

THE WEEKLY SUMMARY OF CURRENT SCIENCE.

May 30, 1942

A SCIENCE SERVICE PUBLICATION

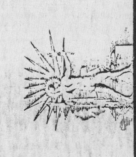

For All American Rope

Science Service

AGRICULTURE

Hemp Being Grown in U. S. As War Cuts Off Imports

See Front Cover

WHEN they hang Adolf Hitler on a sour-apple tree, there'll be a good rope of American-grown hemp ready for the job. After a lapse of a couple of generations, hemp is again being cultivated in the United States, to make good the cutting off of our Asiatic import sources for cordage. You can't run a modern steel-and-steam Navy, not even a modern Navy, without hemp rope. The Army needs a lot, too, and war-essential industries also have their hemp demands.

The U. S. Department of Agriculture has bought and distributed about 3,000 bushels of hemp seed, enough to plant some 35,000 acres. Most of the planting will be done in Kentucky, where hemp cultivation started in 1775 and has survived on a small scale ever since. Hemp will also be grown in Wisconsin, Minnesota, and Illinois. That acreage may be expanded into other states in 1943.

With the hemp seed was in the warehouse it was guarded by soldiers. Hemp is the source of very troublesome narcotic drugs.

Science News Letter, May 30, 1942

CURING THE STRAW

After the hemp stems come from the drier, it is fed into a hemp brake which thoroughly crushes it. Then the hemp is cleaned by beating and brushing in a hand machine. That process, which removes the woody, pithy portion, called hurds and sends the fiber out clean, is shown in the picture on the front cover of this week's SCIENCE NEWS LETTER. Both photographs are official pictures of the U. S. Department of Agriculture by Forsythe.

"The patient was in a better frame of mind, his spirits elevated, his physical condition was rapidly rehabilitated and he expected a wish to return to his occupation sooner," Dr. Allentuck reported. He concluded: "There is no evidence to suggest that the continued use of marihuana is a stepping stone to the use of opiates. Prolonged use of the drug does not lead to physical, mental or moral degeneration, nor have we observed any permanent deleterious effects from its continued use. Quite the contrary, marihuana and its derivatives and allied synthetics have potentially valuable therapeutic applications which merit future investigations."

Science News Letter, May 30, 1942

Effect of the drug on 77 volunteers from New York's prison population had previously been studied by a special research group appointed by Mayor La Guardia. These studies showed marihuana was something like alcohol in that it did not create a "new" personality but, by lowering inhibitions, accentuated all traits, both harmful and beneficial.

Used to combat withdrawal symptoms of narcotic drug addicts who were being taken off their drug, marihuana lessened the severity of the withdrawal symptoms or eliminated them sooner.

This spinning machine spins loose strands of American hemp into fine yarns. U.S.D.A. photograph by Forsythe.

breakdowns in the face of difficulties which are not the common experience of man. But it is a well-known fact that the majority of these combat casualties can be returned to useful civilian occupations if treated early enough.

The trouble is that naval casualties occur in widely scattered areas and a long time, sometimes weeks, may elapse before they reach a naval hospital.

Among British casualties and American, there are some who go into a deep stupor like that in some cases of the mental disease schizophrenia. But in the case of the battle casualties, it has been found that prompt treatment results in quick and relatively complete improvement. This peculiar form of psychiatric battle casualty seems to be much more common in this war than in any before.

Science News Letter, May 30, 1942

MEDICINE—PSYCHIATRY

Marihuana Found Useful In Certain Mental Ills

MARIHUANA, often blamed for crime and insanity among its users who smoke it in "reefers," "muggles" or "good-butts," was reported as a drug of potentially "great usefulness in the treatment of drug addicts" and patients suffering from mental depressions and other nervous disorders.

This new and favorable picture of marihuana appeared in a report by Dr. Samuel Allentuck, of New York City, to the American Psychiatric Association meeting in Boston.

Dr. Allentuck used the drug experimentally in cases of mental depression and nervous disorders characterized by listlessness and lack of appetite. The drug was found to increase the appetite, and induce calmness and relaxation in those previously greatly agitated.

Newsweek Oct. 15, 1942

War booms the hemp industry: Fresh-cut straw is made into sturdy fibers

Hemp: Part of the cargo on the Mayflower was hemp seed. And, being the raw material for making rope and burlap, it was an important crop in this country all during the sailing-ship era. But about the turn of the century it was replaced by imports of Manila hemp, sisal, and jute from Africa and the Orient.

Long-range planners now are looking to the future even though present stockpiles will last until about 1944. Already the government has contracted for almost all the Haitian output of sisal, and that little republic is increasing its production. Last week the War Production Board approved plans for planting in the United States 300,000 acres of hemp (the only one of the fibers which will grow in this climate) and for building 71 processing mills. Plantings will be concentrated in Kentucky, Indiana, Illinois, Wisconsin, Minnesota, and Iowa, with the processing plants in approximately the same areas.

This program should assure an adequate supply by the time stocks run out, for hemp is normally only a four-month crop. Farmers like it, too, because it helps control weeds, needs no tending until harvest time, and leaves the soil in good condition. It is expensive, however. The seed is high, and it can't be harvested without ex-

Hemp Quota Cut

CCC will subsidize only 60,000 acres this year, because the current supply is sufficient to carry through 1945.

Corn Belt farmers have received the bad news that the Commodity Credit Corp. will contract for only 60,000 acres of hemp straw this year, as compared with 168,000 acres under contract in 1943.

● **Surplus of Seed**—No seed at all will be grown under contract, since the current supply (some 500,000 bu.) is more than ample through 1945 (BW—Oct. 23'43, p40). The surplus of seed will be available for canary birds—at a cost of $5,000,000 to the government.

Growers aren't pleased over the cutback in hemp production. They thought hemp was to be a permanent, government-subsidized, postwar industry. At $30 to $50 a ton for the straw, the 1943 crop competed favorably with the re-

Business Week ● January 22, 1944   29

Hemp Slows Up

WPB is cool to domestic product now that imports have improved, but CCC and DPC have $25,000,000 at stake.

A $25,000,000 hemp headache is beginning to beat upon the financial temples of the Commodity Credit Corp. and the Defense Plant Corp.

● **The Chill**—It comes from the cooling of the War Production Board's ardor for domestic hemp, as imports of hemp and sisal from Central and South America increase, as prospects for importations of Italian hemp rise, and as jute from India goes increasingly into cordage.

Hot for hemp a year ago, WPB promoted a big expansion program. CCC guaranteed domestic producers $30 to $50 a ton for hemp straw. DPC financed the erection of 42 hemp mills at $360,000 a mill. Financing of harvesting and milling equipment runs the total beyond $25,000,000.

● **Seed Failure**—Both corporations, however, would have more at stake were it not for a partial failure of the 1942 crop of hempseed in Kentucky. This was wanted for planting to straw this year of 300,000 acres, mostly in the Corn Belt, to yield enough fiber to keep 71 mills busy. Due to the Kentucky seed failure, only 175,000 acres were planted to straw.

The project has been ill-starred.

First, the Kentucky seed growers complained that CCC's buying price for 1942 seed ($8 a ton) was too low, and its selling price ($11 a ton for the same seed cleaned) too high.

Kentucky straw growers complained that they were stuck without buyers for straw the government had induced them to grow last year.

● **Price Increased**—CCC upped the buying price for 1943 seed to $10 a ton and agreed to buy the 1942 straw.

These difficulties resolved, the Agricultural Adjustment Administration rushed out its men to sign up Corn Belt acreage for 1943.

Twenty thousand farmers signed, but later their dreams of $200-an-acre hemp (four tons to the acre at $50 a ton) faded when storms flattened part of the crop.

Can we have rope without dope?

We need hemp—lots of it—for cordage, but hemp means marijuana, too. Can scientists take the drug menace out of this useful plant?

By ALDEN P. ARMAGNAC

CO-OPERATING with the U. S. Department of Agriculture, American farmers will produce 75,000 tons of hemp fiber this year, and probably more than twice as much in 1944. The record-shattering crops will replace Manila fiber from the Philippines and sisal from the Dutch East Indies, which are now cut off by the war.

The result will be a boon to users of cordage—and a headache for law-enforcement officers. A Jekyll-and-Hyde plant, hemp provides twine and rope urgently needed for military purposes. But it also yields marijuana, a drug that makes depraved creatures of its addicts. What can be done to keep these enormous new supplies, from which there almost inevitably will be "leaks," out of their twitching hands?

"Drugless hemp" is the bold proposal of the Department of Agriculture for solving the problem. In short, it is attempting to breed a strain of hemp of good fiber quality, but containing a negligible amount of the baneful marijuana drug. For aid, it has enlisted the expert services of Dr. H. E. Warmke, at the Cold Springs Harbor, N. Y., experimental station of the Carnegie Institution.

First of Dr. Warmke's problems has been to develop a method of determining reliably the amount of marijuana in individual hemp plants. With undesirables weeded out, he then cross-pollinates and breeds the desirable, or relatively drug-free, plants. Only a little more time will be needed to learn whether he can establish a pure, self-perpetuating race of them.

Fish serve as test animals for determining the potency of marijuana extracts.

RACISM DISGUISED AS SCIENCE
...Gutter Science, That Is

MEDICINE

(handwritten: NEGROES WERE SEGRAGATED IN MILATARY with only WHITE OFFICERS 1945)

Army Study of Marihuana Smokers Points to Better Ways of Treatment

"You get hot and you feel that you're going to freeze. You like to go to one of those freaky dens where you can look at bodies sprawled out. You want to listen to the frantic tom-tom of the Duke . . ."

The soldier's face wore an ecstatic expression. In a low, dreamy whisper, he continued: "The Army's all right as long as I keep my stuff on hand. I can't live without it."

Doctors diagnosed the case as drug addiction (Cannabis sativa, or marihuana) and confined the man to the Army Air Forces Regional Station Hospital, March Field, Calif. There he became one of a group of 35 confirmed marihuana smokers, subjects of an intensive seven-month Army medical study. This was probably the first intimate scientific investigation, either of a civilian or military nature, of the cause and treatment of this little-understood habit.

Last week in the magazine War Medicine, two of the hospital's psychiatrists, Capt. Eli Marcovitz and Capt. Henry J. Myers, made their first official report on the experiment. It added up to the fact that marihuana smoking, a notoriously troublesome civilian problem,* becomes even more serious when combined with military service. "In effect," the doctors reported, "the soldiers felt and acted like enemy aliens toward society."

The Reefer Men: Of the experimental group 34 were Negroes and one was white. They were referred to the hospital's neuropsychiatric service because of (1) chronic physical complaints, chiefly headaches; (2) intoxication, with uncontrolled behavior or a state of near-stupor; (3) open demands to superior officers that they be given passes to go out for marihuana; (4) violence or self-mutilating action (mainly wrist-slashing) in the guard house.

As a group, the soldiers had civilian histories packed with adverse family, social, and economic factors. Only five had graduated from high school. For 24 there were records of arrests and sentences to reform schools and jails. The offenses ranged from assault to burglary, drunkeness, vagrancy, and carrying concealed weapons.

Of 32 subjects seventeen were single and fifteen married. Ten of the fifteen married men were either separated or divorced. In most cases, sexual activity began as early as 13 or 14 years.

Many of the soldiers had never worked at all. Some were supported by their women friends and some by gambling or drug peddling. One had had twenty jobs in three years. Another, who had never held a job longer than a month, said: "I ain't for working."

The Marihuana Personality: Unlike alcoholics, these marihuana users showed no sense of guilt or remorse. They were indifferent to opinion, and they frequently tried to persuade the doctors that they and other "squares" (non-users) ought to try marihuana because they were missing "the greatest thing in life."

A great many of them attempted to form a compensatory image of themselves as superior people. "I could be a general like MacArthur," one asserted. "He looks smooth—like he's high all the time."

Toward women their attitude combined indifference with extreme promiscuity. Most of them said they would take marihuana instead of girls if they had to make a choice. On the other hand, some spoke glowingly of the "reefer pads" (marihuana dens) and the "freakish women" there—women who, with or without drugs, were uninhibited sexually. Some said frankly that marihuana increased their feeling of sexual potency. "After you smoke it," said one, "you feel that no woman can resist you."

In civilian life the men were unable to stand frustration, deprivation, or authority. Their response to such situations was "explosive aggression." Even though some began their Army service with attempts to be good soldiers, the old patterns reasserted themselves. Either their "smoking" increased or they ran into trouble with their superiors.

Bad Soldiers: In addition to inadequate performance, there was the problem of discipline in the marihuana group. Many could not stand being reprimanded. Commanding officers' reports included these quotes: "A potentially dangerous man, under constant observation for untoward behavior." "It is difficult to assign him to a duty which he will fulfill without continued prodding."

The Way Out: In the hospital these men revealed "the usual behavior of the outlaw who rejects and rebels against the authority from which he really wants love and of which he longs to be a part."

After a few weeks of sedatives, certain freedoms, and sympathetic encouragement, "hostility diminished and they showed evidence of better rapport." They were still not able or willing to do any useful work in the wards. But there was sufficient change in their attitude to make it seem reasonable that a patient, long-term therapeutic program carried out under favorable conditions might help to rehabilitate the majority of the group.

How to deal with this problem stumped Army officials. Only rarely does a marihuana addict develop a chronic psychotic state calling for medical discharge. Only a few behave so aggressively that they are court-martialed and sentenced to long confinement where a rehabilitation program might have good effect.

Because the marihuana smokers interfere with Army efficiency, separation from the service eventually becomes necessary. But this solution, according to the March Field doctors, "merely releases the addict to civilian life where he can continue to have his difficulties. Also, he tends to foster the use of marihuana by others."

Instead of discharge the officers conducting the March Field survey recommended the creation of special government institutions to which these men can be committed. "Such therapy must include not only psychotherapy," they concluded, "but the provision of a social situation, a community in which the individual is given the opportunity to take his place as a productive normal member of society. Only after succeeding in such a situation should he be discharged from custody."

◉ Newsweek, November 18, 1946

Marijuana and Mentality

Although only 700 to 800 persons are arrested each year in the United States for using marijuana, the drug's reputation as a public menace has touched off a bitter medical controversy.

When a marijuana committee appointed by former Mayor Fiorello H. La Guardia of New York City announced in 1945 that the drug's dangers were greatly overrated, the American Medical Association called the report "thoroughly unscientific" and charged it with doing "great damage." Acting as umpire, the Treasury's Bureau of Narcotics admitted that the use of marijuana had fallen off slightly since 1940 (18,500 marijuana reefers were confiscated in 1940, 17,000 in 1945), but warned that the drug was still "an important cause of crime."

Last summer, the United States Public Health Service decided to conduct its own marijuana experiment at the USPHS hospital at Lexington, Ky. Six addicts, ranging in age from 24 to 33, were allowed to smoke a daily average of 17 reefers supplied by the Bureau of Narcotics for a period of 39 days.

* Rough estimates say there are 100,000 addicts in the United States, mainly high-school students, Negro and white jazz musicians, Harlem habitues, and criminals.

At first, the marijuana smokers showed extreme exhilaration. They talked, laughed, and pranced about the room. Later they began to complain of headaches, dry mouths, irritated throats, and swollen eyelids. After a few days, they grew lethargic and careless about personal hygiene. None became violent, but most of them sulked when subjected to exhaustive mental and physical tests.

From the USPHS experiment came these significant medical facts:

❡ The senses of touch, smell, and sight were not affected by marijuana.

❡ Body temperature and pulse rate decreased; weight increased slightly.

❡ Although mental vigor increased, intelligence ratings fell.

❡ Musical ability was not improved, although most patients thought so while under the drug's influence. This confirms other medical opinions on the effect of marijuana on musical talent (NEWSWEEK, Oct. 28, 1946).

❡ After the first burst of exhilaration, patients lost interest in work and spent most of their time sleeping.

❡ With prolonged usage of the drug patients developed a tolerance to it but gave no definite proof that it is habit-forming.

As for the relation of marijuana to crime and insanity, the Public Health Service officials pointed out last week to NEWSWEEK: "Although the drug lessens inhibitions, it does not incite normally law-abiding people to crime. Most addicts are people with unstable backgrounds—poverty, broken homes, or criminal records—and for them, marijuana may increase the chance for crime. The drug is more harmful than habit-forming opium in inducing fits of temporary insanity, but it seldom leads to permanent derangement."

In the various studies, no definite conclusion seems to have been reached on the aphrodisiac qualities of marijuana. The general opinion indicates that the drug causes a release of all inhibitions, similar to that of alcohol though more intense. In other words, marijuana may not actually stimulate the sex centers. But it dulls the higher centers which control sexual behavior and, in many cases, sex activity of a perverse nature results.

October 1940

MARIHUANA

By S. R. WINTERS

MARIHUANA, according to the Bureau of Narcotics, United States Treasury Department, is the government's most formidable and versatile criminal outlaw. It has, like most criminals, a variety of aliases collected from world wide travel, but is best known on the Western Hemisphere as Marihuana, a euphonious name of Spanish-Mexican origin. In botanical circles it is known as *Canabis sativa,* while in pharmocopeia it is referred to as *cannabis.* Nontechnically, this "coquette of drugdom" is known all over the world as hemp or Indian hemp.

The Indian government permits drugs of hemp origin to be smoked, eaten and drunk in moderation. These drugs, known in India for over thirty centuries, are widely used there for social and religious functions. But the name that betrays the real character of this outlaw culprit is hasheesh, commonly spelled hashish. About this there is a story:

Hassan ben Sabah, a boyhood friend of Omar Khayyam, after unsuccessfully plotting for dictatorial power in 1090, was exiled from Persia to Egypt. Incensed, he introduced "purging" or the secret murder of enemies. According to medieval folklore, the Old Man of the Mountains organized youths in a group known as Devoted Ones, who were stupefied with hashish before being sent forth to avenge him. The word "assassin" is derived from the Arabian term *hashhashin*, meaning a hashish eater. Supremacy of this secret murder ring lasted until the middle of the thirteenth century, but today marihuana assassins still run amuck. And consumption of this drug is still supplied throughout the world by illicit traffic.

Marihuana is especially difficult to control because, like a weed, it grows wild, matures rapidly and requires no attention to grow profusely. It was known in America as early as 1630, but its use as a narcotic did not become prevalent until the last decade. In 1937 the Marihuana Tax Act was passed, providing for the control of cannabis and its derivatives, and required any one dealing with the drug to register and pay a special tax. Violations are punishable by either a $2,000 fine or 5 years in prison, or both.

Another complication in controlling the use of marihuana is that the fibers of this plant are used legitimately by industries to manufacture rope, twines, hats, and paper. The plant's long fibers are also used to make textiles and plastics, but when the stalk is cut before the plant reaches maturity, little or no resin, from which the narcotic substance is made, has been able to develop. The seeds of the plant are used for bird foods; the oils obtained from the seeds are used in the preparation of pharmacal emulsions, paints, varnishes, soap and linoleum. The residue of the hempseed, after pressing, is used for both a livestock feed and a fertilizer.

NEW YORK CITY

Dr. Gabriel Nahas of Columbia University here, who for over 20 years has conducted a heroic political campaign against marijuana ("Cannabis," Dr. Nahas once told the Moonie paper *News World*, "is the greatest plot the East has against the West"), has proven that "fat soluble" marijuana by-products do *not* accumulate in the brain and reproductive organs over continued periods of use.

This determination necessarily invalidates whole reams of "drug education and prevention" literature that for years warned that grass end products *must* pile up in the brain and reproductive system, threatening mental and reproductive functions over a long term. Ironically, the original source of these shock speculations were cronies of Nahas's and the various political "antidrug" organizations with which he has been affiliated, such as the American Council on Marijuana, in Washington, and Lyndon LaRouche's bizarre National Anti-Drug Coalition.

"Fat solubility" was the media code for the reefermadness notion that marijuana residues must accumulate messily in brain and genital tissues. The active components of grass—cannabinoids, such as delta-9 THC—are known to be "lipophilic": attracted to fatty tissues in the body. Lipophilic substances like THC (and certain vitamins) are very slowly released from fatty tissues. Since the brain, testicles and ovaries are largely composed of fat, it's easy to induce unsophisticated people to leap to the alarming conclusion that THC must accumulate steadily in these vital organs with continued pot smoking, remaining there for long periods of time, exerting there all sorts of toxic effects.

However, it has long been known that the body appears to naturally process and dispose of lipophilic vitamins by trapping and neutralizing them in fatty acids in the digestive system, prohibiting their access to the brain and gonadal system, where they might otherwise have toxic effects. But since cannabinoids aren't vitamins, it was speculated that they might escape this natural defense

NAHAS TO THE RESCUE:

'FAT SOLUBILITY' POT SCARE QUIETLY PUT TO SLEEP

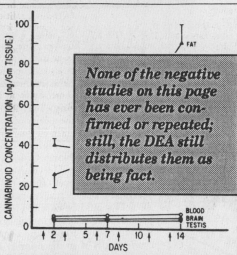

None of the negative studies on this page has ever been confirmed or repeated; still, the DEA still distributes them as being fact.

These rats got the equivalent of the THC in 140 joints of grass regularly, for the equivalent of six months, by rodent body time. But do you see the slightest hint of a rise in those lines labeled "brain" and "testis"?

This means no, marijuana end products don't pile up in your brains and balls and ovaries.

system—until Dr. Nahas's paper, "Kinetics of Cannabinoid Distribution and Storage with Special Reference to Brain and Testis," appeared in the August–September 1981 issue of the *Journal of Clinical Pharmacology*.

Working at Columbia, in conjunction with Dr. Colette Leger at the Hospital Fernand Widel in Paris, the Nahas group shot up rats with intramuscular doses of radioactively labeled THC and measured the residual accumulations of the labeled THC in various organs, after "sacrificing" the animals at various intervals after administration. Several interesting data emerged.

For one thing, it was shown that THC hardly enters the reproductive organs at all; THC concentrations in testes and ovaries were the lowest of any body organs, barely achieving one nanogram (one-*billionth* of a gram) per gram of tissue, and were almost entirely eliminated

within 24 hours after a single dose. The THC concentration in the brain was only slightly higher, and was eliminated at an even more rapid rate. Most THC was trapped and neutralized in the liver and digestive system, just like vitamins.

As to accumulation of THC in the body over a period of regular ingestion, it was found that it does *not* accumulate in brain or reproductive tissues at all. "Cannabinoid concentration in the brain and testis…did not reflect any significant increase in storage in these tissues," the paper noted. "Concentrations of cannabinoids in brain and testis remained lower than that in blood and did not reflect any significant accumulation of the drug in those tissues." Accumulation occurred in the liver and "neutral fat," as would be expected of any other lipophilic substance.

Considering that cannaboids like THC are indeed strongly attracted to body fat, their rapid elimination from brain tissue and their failure to enter testes and ovaries is quite remarkable. The Nahas group therefore concludes that further investigations into this phenomenon may well turn up new clues to how the body naturally protects itself from a broad variety of potentially toxic substances.

"These data illustrate the efficiency of the blood-brain barrier and the blood-testicular barrier in limiting the access and accumulation of this highly lipophilic substance into brain and testis," the researchers conclude. "The mechanisms which limit the storage of cannabinoids in these organs deserve additional investigation."

In layspeak, what this means is that no, marijuana end products *don't* pile up in your brain and balls and ovaries, sitting there for weeks after a single joint, snapping nerves and deforming sperm and egg cells. Drug-abuse counselors who are still saying it does these awful things should be respectfully referred to this fresh-off-thepress 1981 study conducted by Dr. Gabriel Nahas of the College of Physicians and Surgeons at Columbia University, or to the National Council on Marijuana, which provided partial support for the study.

Marijuana And The Male

by Charles Peterson

On Nov. 2, 1972, The *New England Journal of Medicine* carried an article entitled, "Gynecomastia in Marijuana Users" by two members of the Harvard Medical School faculty, Drs. Menelaos Aliapoulios and John Harmon, both surgeons.

Gynecomastia is the medical term for enlarged breasts in the male.

The surgeons pointed out in their article that they had treated three young men in the 22-26 age group for gynecomastia and that all three turned out to be heavy pot smokers.

Since then, Drs. Aliapoulios and Harmon have treated 10 more young men with the same affliction and have come to the conclusion that there is a positive correlation between heavy marijuana use and breast enlargement.

"There is a strong similarity," Dr. Aliapoulios said "between an ingredient of marijuana, delta ninetetrahydrocannabinol, and the female hormone, estradiol. Young men who smoke pot heavily, and by that I mean one or two hours per day or two to three hours, three or four times a week, such men stand a very good chance of developing gynecomastia.

1973
PARADE • MAY 13, 1973

"Not only do their breasts enlarge and swell painfully but their nipples begin to discharge a white, milky liquid. Obviously marijuana contains a feminizing ingredient.

"We are fairly sure that heavy marijuana smoking will cause breast enlargement in females, but in females it is much more difficult to detect. In males it is easy, because gynecomastia is virtually unheard of in young men, aged 22 to 26."

Dr. Aliapoulios, who was graduated from The Johns Hopkins University Medical School in 1959, has written more than 40 papers on various aspects of breast cancer. "But not until we wrote this article for the New England Journal of Medicine on pot smoking and breast enlargement," he reports, "have we had any lay publicity. Since that one came out we have been written up in college newspapers, interviewed on the radio, consulted by news magazines."

'A risk in overdoing'

Dr. Aliapoulios and Dr. Harmon believe that the full side effects of marijuana are as yet unrecorded and that people who smoke the drug heavily are taking unnecessary risks.

"We know," says Dr. Harmon, "that the side effects of excessive alcohol are far more deleterious than the side effects of pot. But nevertheless there's a risk in overdoing anything. We have operated on three young men, reduced the size of their breasts, because they smoked too much pot. And in another three cases where the men have stopped pot smoking, their breasts have receded in size. So obviously, if someone suffers from gynecomastia, it is easier to remedy the case by staying off pot than submitting to surgery."

All young men who smoke pot heavily, will not, of course, develop breast enlargement. Some, however, will, and swollen breasts in young men are particularly painful and psychologically harmful.

BLOW UP OR GET OUT YOUR **MAGNIFYING GLASS**…

---

8 **Tues., Nov. 19, 1974   THE DAILY OKLAHOMAN**

Marijuana Hazards Cited In New Government Study

WASHINGTON (AP) — Laboratory studies suggest that marijuana smoking may interfere with reproduction, disease resistance, and basic biological processes, according to a new government report released Monday.

But the report, "Marijuana and Health," also speculated that marijuana may sometime in the future prove useful in treating tumors and in preventing rejection of transplanted organs.

The National Institute on Drug Abuse, which prepared the report for Congress, cautioned that its research findings were speculative since they involved, for the most part, studies on animals and tissue in test tubes.

Dr. Robert L. DuPont, the institute's director who admitted trying marijuana "a number of years ago," said the preliminary findings give "cause for concern and caution."

"For now it would seem the possible adverse effects should lead marijuana smokers or potential smokers to question whether it is worth the risk," he said.

DuPont, who is also director of the White House Special Action Office for Drug Abuse Prevention, said that if he had known as a younger man what the latest report disclosed, "I think it might very well have deterred me" from marijuana experimentation.

WHY WE ARE EASY PREY FOR SPIES
PAGE 49

MIRACLES OF COURAGE
PAGE 39

Surgeon General C. Everett Koop said this is probably the reason cigarette smokers get lung cancer...

THE LIFE OF
A FLYING
FORTRESS

March 1986 $1.75

Reader's Digest

...magazine
...guages bought monthly   ★

Chemical carcinogens have been widely publicized as health hazards for smokers. Now research focuses on . . .

Radioactivity:
The New-Found Danger in Cigarettes

By Lowell Ponte

IN THE EVENING, after a hard day of work, a smoker lights up. For years he has done this, enjoying the puff and the smoke and the glow, though dimly aware of publicity about chemical hazards. But if his eyes could detect what scientific instruments can, he would see radioactivity coming from his cigarette and from his body—from his lungs, liver, kidneys, pancreas, sex glands and even from the bones of his skeleton.

Cigarettes contain so much radioactivity, according to Dr. Thomas H. Winters, director of an occupational health center in North Quincy, Mass., and Dr. Joseph R. DiFranza of the University of Massachusetts Medical Center, that a pack-and-a-half-per-day smoker gets a yearly dose of radiation in parts of his lungs equal to what his skin would be exposed to in about 300 chest X rays. Scientists are only beginning to discover how much harm the radioactive isotopes in cigarettes do. Estimates vary dramatically as to the number of cases of lung cancer in smokers that are caused by radiation in cigarettes. Dr. DiFranza, however, believes that "radiation alone could account for about half of all lung cancers in smokers." (In 1985, 180,000 Americans are estimated to have died

123

from smoking-related cancers—most from lung cancer.)

Radioactive Footprints. How did radioactive elements get into cigarettes? T. C. Tso, a former researcher for the U.S. Department of Agriculture, tracked these radioactive footprints to the fields where tobacco is grown. For many decades, farmers have fertilized tobacco crops with phosphates rich in uranium. By decay, this uranium generates radium-226, which in turn spawns radon-222, and eventually lead-210 and polonium-210. Tobacco plants readily absorb radioactive elements from the fertilizer and from naturally occurring radiation in the soil, air and water. Breezes and farm equipment whip these dangerous elements into the air, where they are absorbed by the sticky resin tips of hairs that grow on each tobacco leaf.

When a smoker lights up, the heat of the cigarette's glowing tip fires the hair tips of the tobacco into insoluble particles, which, incorporating the radioactive isotopes, are then inhaled deep into the smoker's lungs. Inside the lungs the airways branch out into smaller and smaller passageways. It is especially at each branching, many scientists claim, that the particles in the inhaled smoke tend to accumulate, much as floating river debris piles up on sand bars.

As a smoker consumes cigarette after cigarette, these particles may be deposited at the same points in the lungs. According to Edward A. Martell, a specialist in radiochemistry at the National Center for Atmospheric Research, these points become "hot spots" of radioactivity. Martell believes it is no coincidence that most lung cancers begin at these branch points where radioactive debris gathers.

A healthy body's defenses are usually able to clear away the smoke, ash and poison-gas pollution from a single cigarette within hours. But the accumulated smoke particles are much harder to remove from the moist protective coating of lung tissues, the bronchial epithelium, and remain in the lungs usually for three to six months—in some instances for many years—emitting radiation.

Eventually the body's immune-system cells clean these particles from the lungs, but in the process the radioisotopes are carried into the bloodstream and to other parts of the body—the liver, pancreas, kidneys, lymph nodes, thyroid and bone marrow. Here, too, the radioactive particles accumulate year after year, emitting radiation that can damage nearby cells.

Martell notes that the calcified plaques in the blood vessels of smokers suffering atherosclerosis (hardening of the arteries) show high levels of lead-210 and polonium-210, the same radioactive isotopes inhaled with tobacco smoke—and he speculates that the radiation in cigarettes may also be a contributing factor in smokers' developing atherosclerosis, which itself can

124

lead to early coronaries and also to strokes.

Dangerous Interaction. How long does such radioactivity persist in a smoker's body? Radioactive lead-210 has a half-life of 21.4 years. Beverly S. Cohen and Naomi H. Harley of the New York University Medical Center discovered that smokers who quit still had, five years later, almost as much lower-lung radioactivity from lead-210 as did active smokers. And most smokers do not quit permanently. Indeed, each year the average smoker in the United States consumes more than 11,000 cigarettes.

The most harmful radiation in cigarettes, however, comes not from lead-210, which emits the relatively weak beta radiation, but from its radioactive "granddaughter," polonium-210, which emits highly localized, ionizing alpha radiation, the same sort given off by the plutonium of atom bombs. Alpha radiation smashes into atoms, turning them into ions that can readily damage the genetic blueprint of living cells, killing them or turning them into cancer cells. Scientists have recognized the danger to living things in beta radiation, but alpha radiation can be 20 times as damaging.

The human body evolved on a planet with low levels of natural radioactivity from such sources as cosmic rays, and therefore it has some ability to heal radiation injury. But with each cigarette, a smoker inhales almost as much polonium-210 as he would get from natural sources in 24 hours. Thus the average smoker exposes himself each day to about 30 times more of this long-lived radioactive element than do most non-smokers.

For more than 20 years, Dr. John B. Little and his colleagues at the Harvard University School of Public Health studied the effect of polonium-210 on the lungs of laboratory animals and humans. They found that alpha radiation from inhaled polonium-210, at doses the same as those inhaled by long-time smokers, can cause lung cancer. Uranium miners on the job inhale short-lived radon daughters as well as polonium-210 and other alpha-emitting isotopes, and some studies have shown that those miners who also smoke tend to get lung cancer five to ten years sooner than non-smoking co-workers do.

Can this radioactivity in cigarettes cause cancer in humans by itself, as it can in laboratory animals? Scientists are not yet sure. Many researchers suspect, however, that it can combine with *other* factors to cause cancer. When a smoker lights up, he inhales more than 4000 chemicals with his first puff. Some, such as the polycyclic aromatic hydrocarbon benzo(a)pyrene, are powerful carcinogens. When Dr. Little and his Harvard colleagues exposed animals sequentially to alpha radiation from polonium-210 and to benzo(a)pyrene, they found that the two substances together acted synergistically and

125

caused malignant lung tumors at "about twice the rate expected from the simple additive effect" of polonium-210 and benzo(a)pyrene.

Radioactive elements in cigarette smoke can also accumulate in areas important to a body's immune defenses. There is evidence indicating that smoking can undermine the body's ability to fight off poisons, cancer and other diseases.

Menace in the Home. Recently scientists discovered another deadly mixture in smoking. Soil gives off small amounts of radon, a radioactive gas derived from radium. New weather-sealing technologies to help conserve energy in our homes can also trap and concentrate this dangerous gas indoors.* The Environmental Protection Agency estimates that up to 20,000 Americans each year may be dying from lung cancer caused by inhaling radon in homes and work places.

But when indoor air already polluted with invisible, odorless radon gas is also polluted with cigarette smoke, something even more frightening happens. In clean air the radon's short-lived daughters tend to attach themselves to walls, rugs and draperies. But with tobacco smoke in the air, the radon daughters condense onto smoke particles and remain aloft to be inhaled by smokers and those who breathe secondhand smoke. As a result, the combination of indoor radon pollution and indoor ciga-

*See "The Menace of Indoor Pollution," Reader's Digest, February '83.

126

rette-smoke pollution may create yet another synergy deadlier than each of the pollutants separately.

Even without radon, those who breathe smoke-clouded air will be dosed with radioactivity from tobacco. At least 50 percent of the radioactive isotopes in cigarette smoke wind up in the air, and a smaller percentage of this and other elements in the smoke are inhaled by those around the smoker. Dr. Takeshi Hirayama of the Institute of Preventive Oncology in Tokyo studied records of more than 91,000 women and found that non-smoking wives of heavy smokers had more than double the risk of dying from lung cancer than did the non-smoking wives of non-smokers.

NOTHING CAN REMOVE all the radioactivity from cigarettes, but steps can be taken to reduce this hazard:
- Tobacco growers could switch to fertilizers low in radioactivity and to tobacco-plant hybrids with less tendency to concentrate radioactive elements in their leaves. Denser planting also seems to reduce the radioactivity in each leaf.
- Cigarette companies should be encouraged to continue improving their filters so that even more radioactivity is removed.
- Since polonium-210 seems to be the single element in smoke that causes cancer by inhalation in lab animals, the Surgeon General should add a new warning on cigarette labels to alert smokers to this peril.
- Smokers can educate them-

selves to the hazards of radioactivity in tobacco. Smoking more frequently and inhaling deeply, for example, expose them to much more danger from the volatile radioactive elements in smoke. Many believe that filtered "light" cigarettes are safer, but research shows that smokers tend to inhale these more deeply and to smoke a larger number of them.
- More funds should be made available to researchers so that they may investigate further the effects on human health of the radioactivity in cigarettes.

With all that scientists have learned about radioactivity in cigarettes, however, the best way to protect yourself is not to let tobacco smoke into your lungs at all.

> For information on reprints of this article, see page 222

DIAZEPINES (VALIUM): #1 IN ABUSE

Crack and coke and heroin kill and hurt people and get talked about in the news media, but they're not the biggest drug abuse problem in the U.S. Street dope is the biggest *illegal* drug abuse problem. In 1985, emergency room admissions for cocaine-related problems added up to 13,501; there were 14,696 for morphine and heroin combined; but 18,492 were admitted for the number one drug abuse problem in the country—benzodiazepines, a prescription tranquilizer family best known by the best seller Valium (23 million prescriptions filled in 1985, of a total of 81 million for these types of sedatives).

Many people are addicted to benzodiazepines; stop taking them and you get nervous, agitated. Physicians, however, routinely prescribe these drugs for long-term use, without a full understanding of long-term effects. Many people don't need Valium and could benefit more by understanding the cause of anxiety, by counseling, and perhaps by just a brief treatment with the drug.

For more information, see *Stopping Valium*, a Health Research Group book about Valium and similar drugs. Send $3 to PCHRG, 2000 P St. NW, Washington, D.C. 20036. For more consumer information on health issues of all kinds, see the monthly *Health Letter*, $18 a year, c/o address above.

Whole Life Times,
Mid-April/May 1985

Would You Still Rather Fight Than Switch?

In spite of recent government moves to make the warnings on cigarette packages stronger the new findings that second-hand smoke is also hazardous to your health, many smokers and non-smokers alike are still unaware that the main cause of lung cancer in smokers is probably not tar and nicotine, but radioactivity. "Americans are exposed to far more radiation from tobacco smoke than from any other source," according to Dr. R. T. Ravenholt, former director of World Health Surveys at the Center for Disease Control.

A pack-and-a-half-day smoker absorbs a daily dose of radiation equal to the amount he would have received standing downwind of the Three Mile Island nuclear reactor for 21 hours after the infamous accident. A regular smoker absorbs more radiation annually than the maximum exposure allowed nuclear-power-plant workers.

Tobacco in any form emits alpha radiation from polonium-210, a radioactive isotope linked to a variety of ailments, including cancer, premature aging, and artherosclerosis. The polonium-210 is the end result of several radioisotopes naturally present in air and soil, which collect on the sticky tobacco leaves and come through the plant's roots. The phosphate fertilizers used to grow tobacco contain especially high concentrations of these radioisotopes.

There is enough polonium-210 in cigarettes to cause at least 95% of the lung cancer reported in smokers, according to Dr. Edward Martell, a radiochemist with the National Center for Atmospheric Research (published in *Proceedings of the National Academy of Science, Biophysics, and Biological Science*, March 1983). The radiation circulates in the bloodstream and also contributes to cardiovascular degeneration.

Radioactivity in cigarette smoke might explain why, oddly smokers of low-tar and nicotine cigarettes have the same death rate from lung cancer as smokers of other cigarettes. Studies show that 50% of the radiation in tobacco is discharged into the air. This could explain why non-smokers married to heavy smokers have an increased risk of lung cancer-as do subjects whose mothers smoked according to a 1983 National Institute of Health (NIH)

study (*Lancet*, September 1983; also see "Thumbs Down on Second Hand Smoke," *Newsviews*, September 1984).

More than 20 chemical compounds in tobacco have also been identified as carcinogens. But even the most potent one, benzopyrene, is only present in quantity sufficient to account for 1% of the cancer found in smokers.

The presence of radioactive isotopes in tobacco has been known for 20 years. Research at top institutions-Harvard University, the U.S. Centers for Disease Control, New York University-repeatedly confirm its existence, yet the public remains unaware of the danger. The press has largely ignored the subject, perhaps, as Elizabeth Whelan, executive director of the American Council on Science and Health, charges, for fear of offending its biggest advertiser, the tobacco industry. Magazines that accept tobacco advertising, she found in a recent study, give the health hazards of smoking almost no coverage. She strongly suspects *Newsday* of watering down a recent 18-page supplement so as to delete all negative references to smoking.

The major cancer-research institutions focus their efforts on chemical hazards in tobacco; the National Cancer Institute, for example, with a yearly budget of $986 million, allocated nothing for radiation research last year. The U.S. Surgeon General in his 1981 and 1982 reports acknowledged that polonium is present in tobacco but dismissed it as a minor risk.

A Harvard researcher, Vilma Hunt, originally discovered polonium-210 in tobacco in 1964. Network news picked up the story; headlines screamed "Radioactivity in Tobacco." On the day of the announcement, Hunt recalls, it seemed that every chemist and physicist she knew quit smoking. "They understood immediately the implication," she recounts. "They said, 'If there's ionizing radiation in this stuff, that's it. I'm finished.'"

The Marijuana Conviction, Part One
The Birth of Prohibition

A History of Marijuana Prohibition in the United States
by Richard J. Bonnie and Charles Whitebread II

Condensation published by permission of University Press of Virginia

(In 1937 Congress passed the Marihuana Tax Act, which levied a "prohibitive" tax of $100 an ounce for transfer to an unregistered person, effectively making sale or possession of marihuana a federal crime. Part one of this condensation of The Marihuana Conviction describes how the Marihuana Tax Act came to be.)

In the days before marihuana became a political issue in the United States, policy was rarely voiced to the long-standing social policy vehemently opposed to its use and to the harsh legal policy of jailing its users. This consensus has been shattered, but an alternative one is not yet in view.

The pivotal issue in the current debate is which of the nation's contradictory policies toward intoxicant use will be applied to marihuana. Proponents of change never fail to raise in their behalf the relative dangers of alcohol use and inevitable repeal of its prohibition, predicting a similar fate for present marihuana policy. Opponents of change dismiss the comparison, asking whether this society should be satisfied with the consequences of repeal, and linking marihuana instead to a public consensus opposed to "narcotics" and "drug abuse."

The practices of smoking marihuana and of growing it for that purpose filtered into the United States from the south in the early years of the twentieth century. Transported by Mexicans and West Indians, the plant and its intoxicant use encountered in the ensuing quarter-century, criminal prohibitions appeared on the statute books of nearly every state where the drug was used. Well into the 1930's, however, marihuana-smoking attracted little concerted attention from the national policy and opinion apparatus, which was deeply engaged in drug matters of much wider social impact than the limited, regional use of this new drug.

It has become fashionable in recent years to attribute the illegal status of marihuana to the Federal Bureau of Narcotics and its long-time head, Harry J. Anslinger. Such a theory has been particularly popular among those seeking to alter the existing public policy since it implies that what was done by one man is not entitled to the deference which a more broadly based policy would enjoy.

However, the recent public policy emerged in a more subtle, less controversial fashion. Although the federal narcotics bureaucracy, with Commissioner Anslinger at the the helm, was to become marihuana's leading antagonist in the mid-thirties, a restrictive public policy toward the drug was well rooted locally before that time. During the "local" phase of marihuana prohibition, lasting roughly from 1914 to 1931, twenty-nine states, including seventeen west of the Mississippi, prohibited use of the drug for non-medical purposes. (Four more states did so in 1933.)

The most important feature of this initial prohibitory phase is that marihuana was inevitably viewed as a "narcotic" drug, thereby invoking the broad consensus underlying the nation's recently enunciated anti-narcotics policy. This classification emerged primarily from the drug's alien character. Although the use of some drugs - alcohol and tobacco - was indigenous to American life, the use of "narcotics" for pleasure was not. Evidently, drugs associated with ethnic minorities and with otherwise "immoral" populations were automatically viewed as "narcotics." The scientific community shared this social bias and therefore had little interest in scientific accuracy.

From this instinctive classification of marihuana with opium, morphine, heroin, and cocaine flowed the entire set of factual supports on which narcotics prohibition rested. Marihuana was presumed to be addictive, its use inevitably tending to excess. Since its users - Mexicans, West Indians, blacks, and underworld whites - were associated in the public mind with crime, particularly of a violent nature, the association applied also to marihuana, which had a similar reputation in Mexican folklore. Since the nation was preoccupied during the twenties with lawlessness, especially among the foreign born, this association was a strong one.

To the idea of an alien cancer in the social organism was added the inevitable fear that it would spread. In New Orleans, Denver, and Chicago the specter of a doped school population was the cornerstone of the prohibitory effort. In short, marihuana prohibition was a predictable phenomenon. In states where either Mexicans or the weed had appeared, suppressing its use required no public clamor or citizen's movement; soon after being apprised of its presence, local lawmakers invoked the criminal law, and some also turned to Washington for assistance.

The first cry to Washington for help in suppressing marihuana came from El Paso. In 1914 the deputy sheriff decided that Mexicans should no longer be permitted to bring any more "loco weed" across the Rio Grande. He had little difficulty persuading local

(continued on page 14)

(continued from page 13)

representatives of the federal government to recommend the only available administrative action: a declaration by the secretary of agriculture that importations of cannabis "were being used for purposes other than in the preparation of medicines and that, unless used in medicinal preparations, this drug is believed to be injurious to health." Upon such a declaration, the Secretary of the Treasury was authorized under the Food and Drug act of 1906 to deny importation of the drug if it was not intended for medical purposes. In addition, the commissioner of Internal Revenue, in his 1915 report, recommended the inclusion of cannabis in the Harrison Act (regulating opiates and cocaine). This proposal went virtually unnoticed.

The Harrison Narcotic Act was drafted as a tax law rather than an outright regulatory or prohibitory statute in order to accomplish indirectly what Congress believed, probably correctly, it could not do directly - that is, to regulate the possession and sale of narcotics. That the Supreme Court upheld the act as an exercise of taxing power by a slim five-to-four margin in 1919 had a significant bearing on the federal response to marihuana during the ensuing twenty years. In 1930 the narcotics area of the Prohibition Bureau's responsibilities was extracted (from the Treasury Department) and transferred to a separate Bureau of Narcotics.

Despite the propaganda released by the law enforcement community in the early thirties, the general public was probably largely unaware of the drug, its use, or its alleged effects. Contrary to the picture of a marihuana epidemic conveyed by the propagandists in the early thirties, use at this time probably had stabilized both geographically and demographically. It was still a regional, ethnic phenomenon. Commissioner Anslinger himself observed in late 1937 that "ten years ago we only heard about (marihuana) throughout the Southwest . . . (It has only become a national menace in the last three years."

As Anslinger's comment suggests, there seems to have been a change around the end of 1934. It is hard to determine whether use increased or whether public opinion makers - including the press, the FBN, and various other groups - succeeded in increasing public awareness. Whatever its cause, this increased awareness played a significant role in passage of a Uniform Narcotic Drug Act by the states and in the decision of

The Idol of Both

national politicians to seek federal legislation.

After the bureau initiated a marihuana strategy in late 1934, sufficient attention was aroused among organized moralist groups to incite legislative adoption of the Uniform Act. Interest in marihuana was still regional, although transient interest had now been aroused elsewhere. Viewed nationally, apathy was the norm. Most of the public which had heard at all of marihuana would have concurred in Anslinger's own characterization of the drug in April 1937: "If the hideous monster Frankenstein came face to face with the monster Marihuana , he would drop dead of fright."

Apprehensions about the constitutionality of federal action and the political influence of the pharmaceutical industry deterred the FBN from seeking federal legislation in 1930 and 1931. The bureau chose to concentrate its energies instead on securing adoption of the Uniform Act, including the cannabis provision (classifying it as a "narcotic,") by the state legislatures. Even so, however, Commissioner Anslinger had not ruled out federal legislation "at the appropriate time".

That "future date" may have come sooner than even Anslinger had hoped or desired. The occasion was the request, in 1935, for a Treasury Department position on a pair of bills, S. 1615 introduced by Senator Hatch of New Mexico and H.R. 6145 introduced by Congressman Dempsey of New Mexico, to prohibit the shipment and transportation of cannabis in interstate or foreign commerce. This legislation had been part of a three-pronged approach which had been suggested by Anslinger in 1930.

Despite reluctance on the part of the FBN, the tide had turned. Although the Hatch and Dempsey bills did not reach the floor, the "appropriate time" for federal legislation was drawing near. Why? We can only surmise that political pressure was building for federal action because the state and its private army had generated a climate of fear in order to secure passage of the Uniform Act - but the bureau had done its job too well. Whether or not Anslinger concurred with (Treasury) on the desirability of federal legislation, he undoubtedly preferred to wait until they could work out a full statutory scheme which would not endanger the Harrison Act.

There were two constitutional problems with "regulating" marihuana by use of the taxing power, which Congress had used in the Harrison Act to regulate the opiates and cocaine. First, because the drugs covered by the Harrison Drug Act by the states and in the decision of

(continued from page 15)

imported, the constitutional objection that Congress was regulating production, a local activity, was not germane; instead the main constitutional difficulty under the Harrison Act was that Congress was regulating the medical profession. Marihuana, however, was growing widely as a roadside weed or in gardens and fields all over the country; under these circumstances, effective control would require intensive regulation and/or the prohibition of production, either of which would go well beyond the Harrison Act. The taxing power might not suffice as a shield in this case.

Second, legitimate production of marihuana for medical purposes was decreasing, and the cost of controlling illegitimate growth under the Harrison scheme would far exceed revenue which might be derived. In such an event - a net loss to the government - the court would not be likely to accept Congress' word that it was exercising the taxing power and probably would not close its eyes to Congress' real motive.

A Trap for a Mad Dog

By the fall of 1936 Herman Oliphant (general counsel to the Treasury Department) had decided to employ the taxing power, but in a statute modeled after the National Firearms Act and wholly unrelated to the Harrison Act. Oliphant himself was in charge of preparing the bill. Anslinger directed his army to turn its campaign toward Washington.

The key departure of the marihuana tax scheme from that of the Harrison Act is the notion of the prohibitive tax. Under the Harrison Act a non-medical user could not legitimately buy or possess narcotics. To the dissenters in the Supreme Court decisions upholding the act, this clearly demonstrated that Congress' motive was to prohibit conduct rather than raise revenue. So in the National Firearms Act, designed to prohibit traffic in machine guns, Congress "permitted" anyone to buy a machine gun but required him to pay a $200 transfer tax and carry out the purchase on an order form. The Firearms Act, passed in June 1934, was the first act to hide Congress' motives behind a "prohibitive" tax. The Supreme Court unanimously upheld the anti-machine gun law on 29 March 1937. Oliphant had undoubtedly been awaiting the Court's decision, and the Treasury Department introduced its marihuana tax bill two weeks later, on 14 April 1937.

It is important to understand that these legal intricacies were the essence of the marihuana "issue." There was a recognized need for the federal government to take action forbidden to it under the prevailing constitutional doctrine. The legal reality of the marihuana issue was of significantly more interest to the bureaucracy and to the Congress than the scientific and social realities of marihuana use.

Marihuana was condemned without a trial. The decision makers did not insist on accurate information, and the policy-making process reflects only the trappings of science. The assumptions that marihuana caused addiction, insanity, and crime were not without serious attack even then; yet the federal narcotics bureaucracy made no serious effort before the decision to seek federal legislation to find out what the drug's effects really were.

Many members of the scientific community who were skeptical of the claims against marihuana were nevertheless willing to tolerate "a certain necessary degree of sensationalism" to propel enactment of criminal legislation. But social, not scientific, thinking dictated their policy judgements.

Assistant Surgeon General Walter Treadway's report for the Cannabis Subcommittee of the League of Nations Advisory Committee in early 1937 indicates the scientific perspective:

Cannabis indica does not produce a dependence such as in opium addiction. In opium addiction there is a complete dependence and when it is withdrawn there is actual physical pain which is not the case with cannabis. Alcohol more nearly produces the same effect as cannabis in that there is an excitement or a general feeling of lifting of personality, followed by a delirious stage, and subsequent narcosis. There is no dependence or increased tolerance such as in opium addiction. As to the social or moral degradation associated with cannabis it probably belongs in the same category as alcohol. As with alcohol, it may be taken a relatively long time without social or emotional breakdown. Marihuana is habit-forming, although not addicting, in the same sense as alcohol might be with some people, or sugar or coffee.

The sociological perspective in its most blatant form can be seen in Dr. A. E. Fossier's influential 1931 piece: "The debasing and baneful influence of hashish and opium is not restricted to individuals but has manifested itself in nations and races as well. the dominant race and most enlightened countries are alcoholic, whilst the races and nations addicted to hemp and opium, some of which once attained to heights of culture and civilization have deteriorated both mentally and physically."

The excising of marihuana use from the social organism was seen quite clearly as a means of rooting out idleness and irresponsibility among deviant minorities. The assertion of the Protestant ethic required drastic measures for marihuana, but not for alcohol, because the sociological, if not pharmacological,

(continued on page 18)

reasons the use of marihuana inevitably tended to excess while "civilized" use of alcohol was characteristic of the American middle class. Especially during the depression era, public health experts were apprehensive that increased idleness would spawn increased marihuana use, which in turn would perpetuate further idleness. And since "the vice still flourishes in every country in which it has once been established," early, decisive action was required.

The Treasury Department went to Capitol Hill to secure passage of the Marihuana Tax Act with an open-and-shut case. Anslinger and his colleagues stressed four points in their testimony before the House Ways and Means Committee and a subcommittee of the Senate Finance Committee: marihuana was a disastrous drug; its use was increasingly alarming and had generated public hysteria; state legislation had proved incapable of meeting the threat posed by the weed, and federal action was therefore required; and, the government might best act through separate legislation rather than through an amendment to the Harrison Act.

For five mornings in the House and one morning in the Senate, the legislators and bureaucrats convinced one another of the need for this legislation. Of primary interest was the question of federal responsi-

Still a Menace.

bility. The New Deal Congress had been flexing its muscles for four years and resented any suggestion that any "national" problem was beyond its competence. If the Treasury "experts" contended that marihuana was a national menace, then the United States Congress was committed in principle to federal action. The threat of invalidation by the Supreme Court posed the only restraint, and even that issue was rapidly becoming one only of form.

The narcotics bureaucracy had no definitive scientific study of the effects of marihuana to present to the Congress. Even so, one might have thought the Treasury Department would have submitted a synthesis of available scientific information, or perhaps would have summoned a number of private investigators or the government's own public health experts to testify about the drug's effects. None of these things were done. No statement was submitted by the Public Health Service. Neither of the government's own public health experts, Drs. Walter Treadway and Lawrence Kolb, testified, nor did Drs. Walter Bromberg and J.F. Siler who had recently published scientific articles on the effects of cannabis in humans.

Instead, the scientific aspects were summarized briefly by the FBN, a law enforcement agency.

The act passed Congress with little debate and even less public attention. Although the Federal Bureau of Narcotics had not sought legislation, the bureau's efforts on behalf of the Uniform Narcotic Drug Act had created a climate of fear which provoked insistent cries for a federal remedy, particularly by a few state law enforcement agents hoping to get federal support for their activities. As a result, the law was tied neither to scientific study nor to enforcement need. The Marihuana Tax Act was hastily drawn, heard, debated, and passed. It was a paradigm of the unconstitutional law.

It has been postulated by some researchers that the FBN's own desire to expand its jurisdiction ignited passage of the Marihuana Tax Act. Conversely, there is some evidence that Anslinger resisted federal legislation in order to protect his bureaucracy. In any event, the act did increase significantly the bureau's area of responsibility. In fact, as Dr. Woodward (of the AMA) pointed out to the Ways and Means Committee, the bureau was economically incapable of securing full enforcement of the act. Hemp growing wild all over the country would have to be eradicated. Since medical distribution of the drug had all but disappeared, the contorted revenue-related devices employed in the act (written order forms, registration) bore no relation to the real world; the net effect was that simple possession now became a federal crime. Similarly, all non-medical transfers, whatever the amount, circumstances, or geographical nature, were also federal crimes. In a sense the Marihuana Tax Act blanketed existing state and local offenses with a coextensive range of federal offenses, all of these governing the same conduct.

Given the breadth of this statutory mandate, what did the bureau do? Anslinger began an enforcement policy that even today is the foundation of anti-marihuana efforts. The tenets of this policy was, and is, control of cultivation and eradication of wild growth, education of the judiciary towards strict application of the law, and allocation of federal enforcement resources toward major trafficking rather than petty offenses.

IN THE NEXT ISSUE OF COMMON SENSE FOR AMERICA, PART TWO OF *THE MARIJUANA CONVICTION*: 'MARIHUANA, FROM THE JAZZ THREAT TO THE ERA OF DECRIMINALIZATION'

UNITED STATES DEPARTMENT OF AGRICULTURE

BULLETIN No. 404

Contribution from the Bureau of Plant Industry
WM. A. TAYLOR, Chief

Washington, D. C.   PROFESSIONAL PAPER   October 14, 1916

HEMP HURDS AS PAPER-MAKING MATERIAL.

By LYSTER H. DEWEY, *Botanist in Charge of Fiber-Plant Investigations,* and JASON L. MERRILL, *Paper-Plant Chemist, Paper-Plant Investigations.*

CONTENTS.

In preparing the report on the manufacture of paper from hemp hurds it became evident that a short discussion of the agricultural aspects of this material should be included in the publication. Such an article was prepared, therefore, and the two reports are here presented together.

THE PRODUCTION AND HANDLING OF HEMP HURDS.

By LYSTER H. DEWEY, *Botanist in Charge of Fiber-Plant Investigations.*

WHAT HEMP HURDS ARE.

The woody inner portion of the hemp stalk, broken into pieces and separated from the fiber in the processes of breaking and scutching, is called hemp hurds. These hurds correspond to shives in flax, but are much coarser and are usually softer in texture.

NOTE.—This bulletin should be useful to all persons who are interested in the economic phases of paper making, especially to print and book paper manufacturers. It also should be of interest to scientific investigators and chemists.

81017°—Bull. 404—16——1

UNITED STATES DEPARTMENT OF AGRICULTURE

BULLETIN No. 404

Contribution from the Bureau of Plant Industry
WM. A. TAYLOR, Chief

Washington, D. C.   PROFESSIONAL PAPER   October 14, 1916

LIBRARY

HEMP HURDS AS PAPER-MAKING MATERIAL

By

LYSTER H. DEWEY, Botanist in Charge of Fiber-Plant Investigations, and JASON L. MERRILL, Paper-Plant Chemist, Paper-Plant Investigations

This bulletin is printed on paper manufactured from hemp hurds (run No. 143, which is recorded on page 20

CONTENTS

WASHINGTON
GOVERNMENT PRINTING OFFICE
1916

BULLETIN 404, U. S. DEPARTMENT OF AGRICULTURE.

The hemp stalk grown in a broadcast crop for fiber production is om one-eighth to three-eighths of an inch in diameter and from 4 to feet tall. The stalk is hollow, with a cylindrical woody shell, thick ar the base, where the stalk is nearly solid, and thinner above, where e hollow is relatively wider.

In the process of breaking, the woody cylinder inside of the fiber-aring bark is broken into pieces one-half of an inch to 3 inches long d usually split into numerous segments. The thicker lower sec-ons are split less than the thin-shelled upper ones, and they are often ft quite solid.

PITH, WOOD, AND FIBER.

The inner surface of the hurds usually bears a layer of pith, consisting thin-walled cells nearly spherical or angular, but not elongated. he are more or less crushed and torn. They are probably of little alue for paper, but they constitute less than 1 per cent of the weight the hurds. The principal weight and bulk consist of slender elon-ated woody cells. The outer surface is covered with fine secondary bers composed of slender elongated cells, tougher than those of the ood but finer and shorter than those of the hemp fiber of commerce. o method has been devised thus far which completely separates om the hurds all of the long fiber. From 5 to 15 per cent of the eight of the hurds consists of hemp fiber, in strands from 3 inches 8 feet in length. Some fragments of the bark, made up of short ubical cells, usually dark in color, cling to the strands of fiber.

CHARACTER OF HURDS AFFECTED BY RETTING.

Nearly all of the hemp in the United States is dew retted. The alks are spread on the ground in swaths, as grain is laid by the cradle. he action of the weather, dew, and rain, aided by bacteria, dissolves nd washes out the green coloring matter (chlorophyll) and most of e gums, leaving only the fibrous bark and the wood. The plants in is process lose about 60 per cent of their green weight, or about 40 er cent of their air-dry weight.

The stalks are sometimes set up in shocks to cure before retting, nd after retting they are set up in shocks to dry. Each time the alks are handled they are chucked down on the ground to keep the utts even. In these operations sand and clay are often driven up to the hollow at the base of the stalks, and this dirt, which often ings tenaciously, may constitute an objectionable feature in the use hemp hurds for paper stock.

In Italy and in most localities in Russia and Austria-Hungary here hemp is extensively cultivated, it is retted in water, but water tting has never been practiced in the United States except to a mited extent before the middle of the last century. Hurds from

HEMP HURDS AS PAPER-MAKING MATERIAL. 3

water-retted hemp are cleaner and softer than those from dew-retted hemp.

The fiber is sometimes broken from dry hemp stalks without retting. The hurds thus produced contain a small percentage of soluble gums, chiefly of the pectose series. Comparatively little hemp is prepared in this manner in America.

Process retting by means of weak solutions of chemicals or oils in hot water is practiced to a limited extent. The hurds from these processes may contain traces of the chemicals or oils and also soluble gums in greater degree than those of the dew-retted or water-retted hemp.

PROPORTION OF HURDS TO FIBER AND YIELD PER ACRE.

The yield of hemp fiber varies from 400 to 2,500 pounds per acre, averaging 1,000 pounds under favorable conditions. The weight of

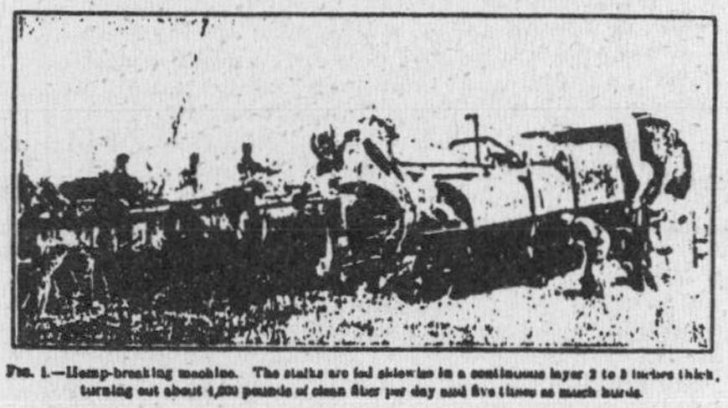

FIG. 1.—Hemp-breaking machine. The stalks are fed sidewise in a continuous layer 2 to 3 inches thick, turning out about 4,000 pounds of clean fiber per day and five times as much hurds.

hurds is about five times that of the fiber, or somewhat greater from hemp grown on peaty soils. A yield of 2½ tons of hurds per acre may be taken as a fair average.

HURDS AVAILABLE FROM MACHINE-BROKEN HEMP.

Hemp hurds are available only from hemp which is broken by machines, when the hurds may be collected in quantity in one place (figs. 1 and 2). Most of the hemp in Kentucky is still broken by hand brakes. These small brakes are moved from shock to shock, so that the hurds are scattered all over the field in small piles of less than 50 pounds each, and it is the common practice to set fire to them as soon as the brake is moved. It would be difficult to collect them at a cost which would permit their use for paper stock.

Where machine brakes are used, the hemp stalks are brought to the machine as grain is brought to a thrashing machine, and the hurds accumulate in large piles, being blown from the machine by wind stackers.

Machine brakes are used in Wisconsin, Indiana, Ohio, and California, but to only a limited extent in Kentucky. Five different kinds of machine brakes are now in actual use in this country, and still others are used in Europe. All of the best hemp in Italy, commanding the highest market price paid for any hemp, is broken by machines. The better machine brakes now in use in this country prepare the fiber better and much more rapidly than the hand brakes, and they will undoubtedly be used in all localities where hemp raising is introduced as a new industry. They may also be used in Kentucky when their cost is reduced to more reasonable rates, so that they may compete with the hand brake. Hemp-breaking machines are being

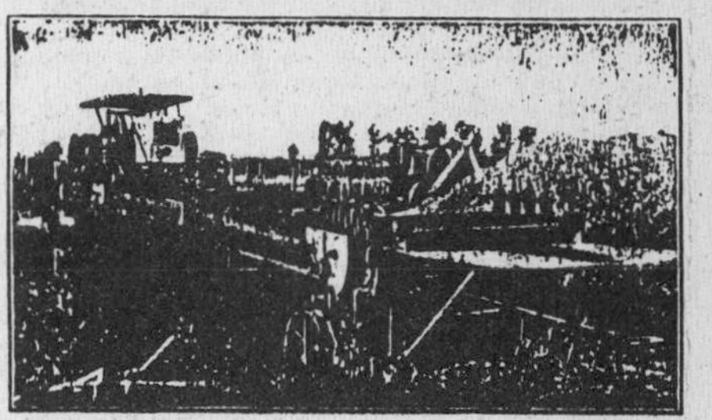

FIG. 2.—Machine brake and hemp hurds. Hemp hurds from machine brakes quickly accumulate in large piles.

improved and their use is increasing. The hemp-growing industry can increase in this country only as machine brakes are developed to prepare the fiber. A profitable use for the hurds will add an incentive to the use of the machine brake.

PRESENT USES OF HEMP HURDS.

Hemp hurds are used to a limited extent for barnyard litter and stable bedding, as a substitute for sawdust in packing ice, and, in rare instances, for fuel. They are not regarded as having a commercial value for any of these uses, though they are doubtless worth at least $1 per ton on the farm when used for stable bedding. They are a waste product, without value for other purposes which might compete with their use for paper stock.

PRESENT SUPPLIES OF HURDS AVAILABLE.

During the last season, 1915, about 1,500 acres of hemp have been arvested outside of Kentucky and in regions where machine brakes re used. Estimating the yield of hurds at 2½ tons per acre, this hould give a total quantity of about 3,750 tons. Large quantities of emp from the crop of 1914, which are still unbroken in these areas, nd large piles of hurds undisturbed where the machines have been sed during the last two or three years, increase the total to more han 7,000 tons. Hemp is now grown outside of Kentucky in the vicinity of McGuffey, east of Lima, Ohio; around Nappanee, Elkhart County, and near Pierceton, in Kosciusko County, Ind.; about Waupun and Brandon, Wis.; and at Rio Vista and Stockton, Cal.

In Kentucky, hemp is grown in most of the counties within a radius of 50 miles of Lexington. No accurate statistics of the acreage are collected, but the crop harvested in 1915 is estimated at 7,000 acres. A machine brake will probably be used in Bourbon County and also n Clark County, but most of the hemp in Kentucky will be broken on hand brakes.

BALING FOR SHIPMENT.

The hurds will have to be baled to facilitate handling in transportation and to economize storage space at the paper mills. The bales will need to be covered with burlap or some material to keep them from shaking out. They may be baled in the same presses that are used for baling hemp fiber, but care must be exercised to avoid breaking the press, for the hurds are more resistant than hemp fiber. A bale of hemp 2 by 3 by 4 feet weighs about 500 pounds. A bale of hurds of the same size will weigh about one-third less, or approximately six bales per ton.

Rough hemp fiber as it is shipped from the farm is not covered; therefore, the covering material must be purchased especially for the hurds. A piece of burlap about 36 by 48 inches placed on either side of the bale will be sufficient, but these pieces, weighing about 3 pounds each, cost about 40 cents a pair. Baling rope, in addition to jute covering, will cost at least 5 cents per bale, making the total cost of covering and ties $2.70 or more per ton. Possibly chip board, costing about $33 per ton, or not more than 5 cents for the two pieces for each bale, may be used in place of burlap. Chip board, burlap, and also rope ties may all be used for paper stock. Burlap covers might be returned, to be used repeatedly until worn out, but chip board could not be used more than once.

COST OF BALING.

If burlap covers are used the cost of baling, including covering, ties, use of baling press, power, and labor will amount to at least 60 cents per bale, or about $3.75 per ton. If chip board can be used the cost

6 BULLETIN 404, U. S. DEPARTMENT OF AGRICULTURE.

may be reduced to about $2 per ton. The cost of hauling and loading on the cars will vary from $1 to $3 per ton, depending upon the distance and the roads. The farmer must therefore receive from $4 to $6 per ton for the hurds, baled, on board cars at his home station.

SUMMARY.

Hemp hurds are the woody inner portion of the hemp stalk, broken into pieces in removing the fiber.

They are not used at present for any purpose that would compete with their use for paper.

Hurds are available only from machine-broken hemp, for the cost of collecting them from the hand brakes would be too great.

About 7,000 tons are now available in restricted localities in Ohio, Indiana, Wisconsin, and California.

The quantity is likely to increase as the use of machine brakes increases.

The hurds may be baled in hemp-fiber presses, with partial burlap covers like those on cotton bales, or possibly chip-board covers.

It is estimated that the farmers may deliver the bales on board cars profitably at $4 to $6 per ton.

BLOW UP OR GET OUT YOUR MAGNIFYING GLASS...

THE MANUFACTURE OF PAPER FROM HEMP HURDS.

By JASON L. MERRILL, *Paper-Plant Chemist, Paper-Plant Investigations.*

INTRODUCTION.

The purpose of this paper is to report upon preliminary tests which were conducted to determine the paper-making value of hemp hurds, a crop waste of the hemp-fiber industry.

The search for plant materials capable of being utilized in paper manufacture is a comparatively recent but world-wide activity which has for its object the husbanding of present sources of paper-stock supply by the substitution of new materials for some of those which are rapidly becoming less plentiful and more costly.

The abstract idea of utilizing that which is at present a waste can play no important rôle in such activities, the successful commercial outcome of which must be based on the three fundamental factors—market or demand for product, satisfactory raw material, and cost.

Since hemp hurds are to be treated in this report as a raw material for the manufacture of book and printing papers, the qualities, supply, probable future, and cost of the material will be considered in comparison with wood, with which it must compete. There seems to be little doubt that the present wood supply can not withstand indefinitely the demands placed upon it, and with increased scarcity economy in the use of wood will become imperative. This effect is already apparent in many wood-using industries, and although the paper industry consumes only about 3 per cent of the total forest cut, it is probable that it will be affected through this economy. Our forests are being cut three times as fast as they grow, and as wood becomes more expensive proper growing and reforesting will receive more attention. Thus, naturally, a balance will be established between production and consumption, but as this condition approaches its limiting values the price of wood may rise to such levels that there will be a demand for other raw materials.

The use of waste paper in conjunction with chemical wood pulp has increased to enormous proportions, and it is probable that the increase will continue. Although it is a cheaper raw material than wood, it is reasonable to suppose that as the wood supply decreases and the price of wood pulp advances, the price of waste paper will advance somewhat proportionately.

In view of these conditions it is advisable to investigate the paper-making value of the more promising plant materials before a critical situation arises. To be of substantial value the investigations should include not only a determination of the quality and quantity of pulp and paper which the material is capable of producing, but should embrace a consideration of such relevant factors as agricultural conditions, farm practice, assembling conditions, transportation, and probable future supply.

Certain cultivated plants seem particularly promising, because in the harvesting of the regular crop that portion which might be utilized for paper manufacture necessarily is either wholly or partially assembled. To this class of plants belong corn, broom corn, sorghum, sugar cane, bagasse, flax, hemp, and the cereal straws.[1]

It is generally conceded that the employment of different raw materials would probably yield products of a somewhat different quality than those now prevailing in the markets, but the qualities of papers and the public demands are so diversified and numerous that this possible objection should not be serious. Ten years ago sulphite manufacturers would not accept consignments of spruce logs if they contained over 5 per cent of fir, while to-day many manufacturers tolerate 50 per cent. Rope papers are found to contain not only jute, but when this raw material is not plentiful, chemical pulp of various kinds. "Linen paper" is often no more than a trade term. Not long ago printing papers were made entirely from chemical wood pulp, but to-day if it is desired to secure paper which is free from ground wood the specifications must so stipulate. Writing papers, formerly made entirely from rags, now are likely to contain either chemical or even ground-wood pulp unless the specifications prohibit it. Without doubt, many paper manufacturers have maintained certain papers up to a fixed standard for a long series of years, but it is equally true that competition has lowered the standard of a great many papers, some of which had acquired a distinctive recognition. The employment of plant fibers will not necessarily lower the present quality of papers, but if their employment does result in products whose qualities are somewhat different from our so-called standard papers it does not necessarily follow that such papers will not find a ready market.

FACTORS JUSTIFYING AN INVESTIGATION OF HEMP HURDS.

Hemp hurds form a crop waste, in that they necessarily are produced in the raising and preparation of hemp fiber, and their present use and value are comparatively insignificant.

The assembling of the hurds may be effected with economy, since the area in which hemp is handled with the use of machine brakes is restricted. Although it must be stated that the present annual

[1] For descriptions of investigations of some of these crops, see the list of publications at the end of this bulletin.

supply would not be sufficient to justify the installation of a pulp mill nor would its transportation to existing mills appear feasible, it is expected that the available annual tonnage, especially in certain general sections, will increase, due to the increased use of the machine brake. The present tonnage per annum is approximately as follows: In the region of Ohio and Indiana, 2,500 tons; in the Wisconsin section, 1,000 tons; in the California region, 1,400 tons.

In years of adverse weather conditions there are often large areas of hemp which are not harvested on account of its poor quality; there are also large areas of cut hemp which become overretted, due to inclement weather. It has been suggested by some of the hemp raisers that this large amount of material might be utilized as a paper stock. In these cases the cost of the whole material would probably be somewhat higher than that of the hurds, because either all or part of the cost of harvesting and the total cost of breaking would have to be borne by the paper maker. Moreover, the quality of this material would be so very irregular and the supply so uncertain that it probably would not appeal to the paper manufacturer.

Without doubt, hemp will continue to be one of the staple agricultural crops of the United States. The wholesale destruction of the supply by fire, as frequently happens in the case of wood, is precluded by the very nature of the hemp-raising industry. Since only one year's growth can be harvested annually the supply is not endangered by the pernicious practice of overcropping, which has contributed so much to the present high and increasing cost of pulp wood. The permanency of the supply of hemp hurds thus seems assured.

The favorable location geographically of the hemp regions in relation to the pulp and paper industry is a factor of considerable importance. The Kentucky region is not at present in a position to supply hurds, as machine methods have not been adopted there to any appreciable degree. The Ohio and Indiana region, which at present has the greatest annual tonnage, with the prospect of an increase, is situated south of the Wisconsin and Michigan wood-pulp producing region and at a distance from the eastern wood-pulp producing regions; therefore, it is in a favorable position to compete in the large Ohio and Indiana markets. Since, as will be shown, the hurd pulp acts far more like soda poplar stock than sulphite stock, competition would be strongest from the eastern mills; in fact, the hurd stock might very possibly meet with favor as a book-stock furnish in the Michigan and Wisconsin paper mills, which are within the sulphite fiber-producing region. Because of its very close proximity to paper mills, this latter possibility applies with far greater force to the Wisconsin hemp region, where a considerable extension of the hemp industry is anticipated.

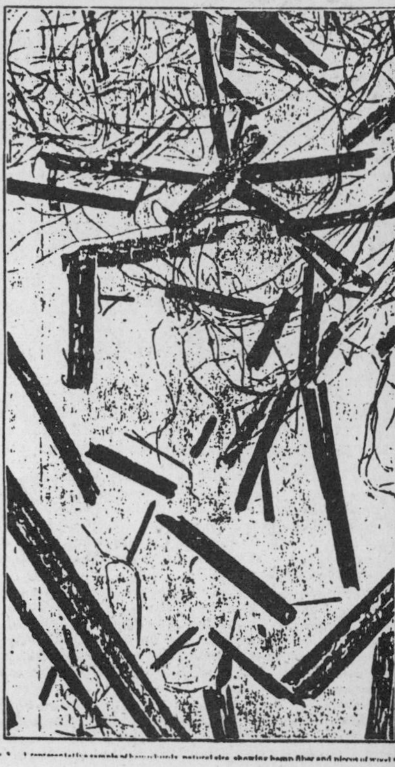

Fig. 3.—A representative sample of hemp hurds, natural size, showing hemp fiber and pieces of wood

CHARACTER OF THE MATERIAL.

As received from Pierceton, Ind., the hurds consisted of a mixture of tangled hemp bast fibers and pieces of broken wood of the hemp stalk. (Fig. 3.) No reliable data were secured as to the proportion of bast fiber in the total shipment of 4 tons, although two hand separations of small representative samples gave results averaging 8 per cent. The chemical character of the material was such and the quantity was so small that any appreciable variation of the proportion should not affect materially the treating processes finally adopted, yet its presence in varying proportions undoubtedly would

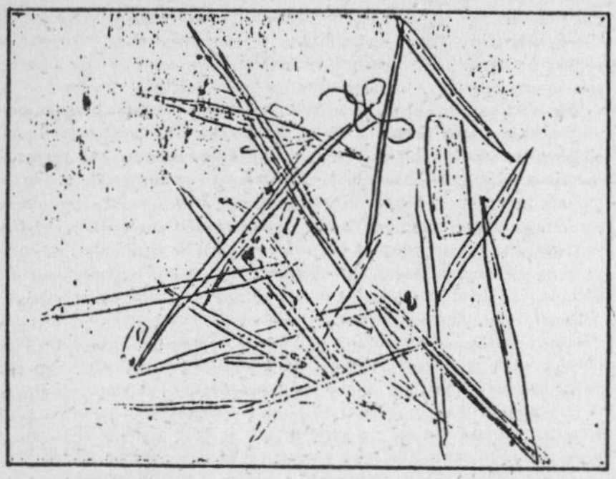

Fig. 4.—Fiber derived from the woody portion of the hurds. × 75. From a microphotograph.

modify to some extent the quality of the resulting paper product. Since the length of the ultimate bast fiber averages about 22 mm. and the length of the ultimate hemp wood fiber averages 0.7 mm., it is natural to assume that the bast fiber would tend to increase the strength of paper produced from the hurds. (Fig. 4.)

The broken pieces of wood contained in the hurds varied in length from mere particles which were somewhat finer than sawdust to pieces about 3½ inches long, exceptional pieces being found which measured 6 inches in length. The majority of the long pieces were between 2 and 3 inches in length. In thickness the pieces ranged from one-eighth of an inch, in case they were derived from the base of the hemp stalks, to about one sixty-fourth of an inch in those pieces which were derived from the top and branches of the stalks. In cross section the

pieces often were found to be a quarter or half of the rounded rectangular woody shell of the stalk, although there appeared to be no regularity in this respect.

From the pulp-maker's standpoint the great irregularity in thickness, length, and mass of the woody pieces militates decidedly against economy in pulp production. The smaller pieces reduce by chemical treatment sooner than the larger fragments and are thereby overtreated, which results in a lower yield of cellulose fiber and a product composed of undertreated and overtreated fibers, the production and use of which are not satisfactory or economical. It probably would be found more satisfactory, therefore, to screen or sort the hurds and treat the various sizes separately and differently.

Associated with the hurds was a small quantity of chaff and dirt, composed chiefly of sand, soil, particles of hemp leaves and flowers, and other extraneous matter. The sand and soil were present because of the practice of placing the stalks in shocks in the field, the butts of the stalks being in contact with the soil. It is a simple matter, however, to remove the chaff and dirt by sieving, and this practice was followed in most of the paper tests conducted with this material.

CHARACTER OF THE TESTS.

Because of the similarity of hemp hurds to other materials which have been tested by the Office of Paper-Plant Investigations, semicommercial tests were conducted in cooperation with a paper manufacturer without preliminary laboratory tests. Laboratory pulp and paper tests are regarded only as a preliminary to semicommercial tests and therefore are not employed unless the material in question presents new features which should receive investigation before large-sized tests are undertaken.

The advantages of cooperative mill tests are many, among which may be mentioned the counsel and advice of the mill management and employees, the services of specialized and skilled labor, facilities for comparing the processes and the results of tests with commercial processes and results, and the use of commercial or semicommercial types and sizes of machinery. Tests conducted in this manner and on this scale are of a different quality than is possible in those conducted in a laboratory, and the results are susceptible of commercial interpretation with a fair degree of reliability. It is found, in general, that the cost of securing such equipment and service for a complete and comprehensive test does not exceed $500, while the installation of an equally satisfactory equipment alone would cost at least $50,000 and in many cases very much more. Tests conducted in this manner constitute a direct demonstration to the manufacturer, and the results obtained are found to carry more weight when presented to other manufacturers for consideration.

It is well known that the method of conducting tests necessa varies with the size of the test. In the matter of yield determinat for example, laboratory tests may be on such a small scale that weighing and sampling of the resulting cellulose fibers may be c ducted by means of chemical laboratory apparatus and analyt balance, while in tests involving a matter of 5 to 10 pounds of mate larger and different types of equipment are necessary. W the tests are so increased in size as to employ 300 or 400 poun still other types of equipment are necessary for the treatment the material and for a determination of the yield of fiber. tests involving tons of material the equipment involves the use machines. Accuracy in degree of control and in results will v materially with the size of the test. As the size of the test increa certain factors will vary in a beneficial manner, while others will v in a detrimental manner, so it is a question for each investigator decide, after taking all factors into consideration, as to the size test which will give the most satisfactory results. In work of t nature it is found, on the whole, that better results are obtained large tests, although the control of the factors and the determinat of the yield of fiber are more difficult than in smaller tests.

In the tests described in this bulletin, the Department of Agric ture employed a rotary digester of its own design,[1] comprising a sl 5 feet 5 inches in length by 4 feet in diameter, capable of hold about 300 pounds of air-dry hurds. It is believed that a test of t size is large enough to give satisfactory results and that the resu are susceptible of commercial interpretation, while at the same ti they are sufficiently small for complete control and to afford fib yield figures which are both accurate and reliable. Two such rota charges gave enough fiber for one complete paper-making test.

OPERATIONS INVOLVED IN A TEST.

A complete test on hurds comprises seven distinct operations, a the method will be described, operation by operation, in the or in which they were conducted.

Sieving.—The hurds for the first test were not sieved to remo sand and dirt, but the resulting paper was so dirty that sieving v practiced in all subsequent tests. The hurds were raked along horizontal galvanized-iron screen, 15 feet long and 3 feet wide, w 11½ meshes per linear inch, the screen being agitated by hand fr below. Various amounts of dirt and chaff could be removed, depe ing on the degree of action, but it was found that if much more th 3 per cent of the material was removed it consisted chiefly of fi pieces of wood with practically no additional sand or dirt; in most the tests, therefore, the material was screened so as to remo

[1] For a description of this rotary digester, see Brand, C. J., and Merrill, J. L., Zacaton as a pa making material, U. S. Dept. Agr. Bul. [illegible], p. [illegible], 1915.

approximately 3 per cent. It became apparent that a finer screen would probably serve as well and effect a saving of small but good hurds.

Cooking.—Cooking is the technical term for the operation by which fibrous raw materials are reduced to a residue of cellulose pulp by means of chemical treatment. In these tests about 300 pounds of hurds were charged into the rotary with the addition of a caustic-soda solution, such as is regularly employed in pulp mills and which tested an average of 109.5 grams of caustic soda per liter, or 0.916 pound per gallon, and averaged 85 per cent causticity. Sufficient caustic solution was added to furnish 25 or 30 per cent of actual caustic soda, calculated on the bone-dry weight of hurds in the charge. After closing the rotary head, it was started rotating at the rate of one-half revolution per minute, and in about five minutes steam at 20 pounds per square inch was admitted at such a rate that the charge was heated in one hour to 170° C., which is the theoretical equivalent of 100 pounds of steam pressure per square inch. It was found, however, that when the temperature reached 170° C. the pressure was usually 115 or 120 pounds instead of 100 pounds, due to air and gases inclosed in the rotary. At this point the rotary was stopped and steam and air relieved until the pressure dropped to 100 pounds, or a solid steam pressure. The temperature was maintained at this point for the number of hours required to reduce the hurds, which was found to be about five, after which the rotary was stopped and steam relieved until the pressure was reduced to zero, when the head was removed and the stock was emptied into a tank underneath, measuring 5½ by 6 by 2 feet deep, where it was drained and washed. Samples of waste soda solution or "black liquor," which were taken from some of the "cooks" for analysis, were drawn while the stock was being thus emptied into the drainer.

Determination of yield.—For determining the yield of cellulose fiber the stock in the drain tank was washed with water until free from waste soda solution, when, by means of a vacuum pump communicating with the space between the bottom and the false perforated bottom, the water was sucked from the stock, leaving the fiber with a very uniform moisture content throughout its entire mass and in a condition suitable for removing, sampling, and weighing for a yield determination. Tests have shown that it is possible to sample and calculate the yield of bone-dry fiber within 0.05 per cent of the actual amount.

It has been found that stocks from different materials vary greatly in their ability to mat in the drain tank, thereby enabling a good vacuum to be obtained, some stocks permitting a 25-inch vacuum to be obtained, while others will not permit more than 5 inches. For this reason the moisture content of the stock will vary from 65 to 85 per cent.

Washing and bleaching.—Washing and bleaching were performed for the purpose of bleaching the brown-colored cooked stock to a white product, since it was regarded as highly probable that the fiber would be suitable for book-paper manufacture. The colored stock was charged into a 400-pound beating and washing engine of regular construction and washed about one hour, the cylinder washer being covered with 60-mesh wire cloth in order to remove fine loose dirt and chemical residues. The washer was then raised, the stock heated by steam to about 40° C., and a solution of commercial bleaching powder was added in the quantity judged to be necessary, after which the stock was pumped to a large wooden tank, to remain and bleach over night. If the stock was bleached sufficiently white it was drained and washed from bleach residues, and if not more bleach was added until a good color was obtained. The bleaching powder used was estimated to contain 35 per cent of available chlorin, as this is the commercial practice, and the amount required was calculated to the bone-dry weight of the unbleached stock. More bleach is required for undercooked stock than for stock which is properly cooked or overcooked; therefore, the percentage of bleach required is an indication of the quality of the cooked stock. Since bleaching is usually more expensive than cooking, it is desirable to cook to such a degree that the consumption of bleach will be held within certain limits, depending on the raw materials used and the quality of paper to be produced. In these tests it was desirable so to cook the hurds that the consumption of bleach would not be over about 10 per cent of the fiber.

Furnishing.—Furnishing is the operation of charging the beating engine with the desired kind or kinds of fiber in the proper proportion and amount and the adding of such loading and sizing agents as may be necessary. As shown in the record of results, the furnish in these tests consisted of hurd stock alone and of various proportions of hurds, sulphite fiber, and soda fiber. The percentages to be given in the record of the furnishes refer to the percentage of the total fiber furnish, and this likewise applies to the loading and sizing agents. In case sulphite or soda fiber was used, the commercial product in the dry state was charged into the beating engine and disintegrated, after which the hurd stock was added in the wet condition.

Beating.—Beating is that operation concerning which the paper makers often say "there is where the paper is really made," and although the statement may not be literally true it contains a great deal of truth. It is the operation whereby the fibers are separated from each other, reduced to the proper lengths, and put in such a physical or chemical condition that they felt properly and form into a satisfactory sheet. It is probable that the quality of the sheet depends more upon the proper beater action than upon any other single operation. The action consists in drawing a water suspension of the fiber between two sets of rather blunt knives, one set being

located in the bottom of a circulating trough and the other set on the periphery of a roll revolving just above the former set of knives. It is during this operation that the loading and sizing agents are incorporated and the whole furnish is tinted either to produce a satisfactory white or the desired color.

The term "paper making," as used in this publication, means the operation of forming the finished sheet of paper from stock which has been furnished and prepared in the beater. In these tests a 30-inch Fourdrinier machine of regular construction was used, a machine which often is used for the production of paper for filling regular commercial orders. The machine is designed to cause the water suspension of fibers to flow on to a traveling wire cloth, whereby the water drains away. More water is removed by passing the wet sheet through a series of press rolls, after which the sheet is dried on steam-heated drums and passed through polished iron rolls, which impart a finish to the sheet. A Jordan refining machine was employed in conjunction with the machine to improve further the quality of the fiber, and a pulp screen was used in order to remove coarse and extraneous materials from the fiber.

DESCRIPTION OF TESTS.

The nature of each complete paper test and the dependence of each operation on the others were such that it does not seem advisable to submit the results of the seven tests in tabular form. The numerous cooks, however, which furnished the pulp for the paper tests are presented in Table I in all essential detail.

TABLE I.—*Data on cooking hemp hurds.*

Cook No.	Caustic soda used (percentage of bone-dry hurds).	Strength of caustic soda (grams per liter).	Causticity of soda solution.	Cooking.		Yield of bone-dry fiber (percentage of bone-dry unsieved hurds).
				Time (hours).	Temperature (°C.)	
293	20.6	100	75.3	3	166	....
294	21	100	75.3	3	166	....
295	21.6	100	75.3	3	166	....
296	20.3	100	75.3	3	166	....
301	21.0	100	82.5	4	166	(¹)
302	24.4	100	82.5	4	166	....
303	24.3	100	84.3	4	166	44.1
304	25	100	84.3	4	170	39.5
305	25	100	84.3	5	170	39.4
306	27.8	107.8	84.3	4	166	36.5
307	26.7	107	84.4	5	170	36.1
308	28	107	84.4	5	170	37.5 (308–309)
309	27.3	107	84.4	5	170	
310	27.1	107	84.4	6	170	37.0
311	27.3	107	84.4	6	170	36.8
312	28.5	116.5	85.5	5	170	36.9
313	29.1	113.1	84.9	5	170	34.3 (313–314)
314	29.1	109	83.9	5	170	
315	29.4	109	83.9	5	170	34.9
316	30	109.5	84.9	5	170	37.2
317	29.6	109.5	84.9	5	170	37.0
318	29.6	107	84.5	5	170	37.7
319	29.4	107.5	84.3	5	170	36.6 (319–320)
320	29.5	107.5	84.3	5	170	

¹ Stock not used; dirty.

Discussion of the various cooks will be given in connection with the descriptions of those paper tests in which the stocks from the cooks were used, since a stock and its cooking condition can be judged adequately only after it has been put through the various processes and into the finished sheet of paper.

The first test consisted in making four separate cooks, Nos. 293, 294, 295, and 296, of approximately 300 pounds each, dividing the total stock into two parts and making two separate paper tests. The first test was made primarily in order to learn some of the qualities and characteristics of the stock and to get the machinery equipment adjusted properly. The yield of fiber was not determined in this preliminary test, since the knowledge of it was not essential at this stage of the work. The cooked stock which was emptied into the drainer to be washed free from black liquor was composed largely of whole pieces of hurds, but only slight pressure between the fingers was required to crush the pieces. In the case of wood, this condition ordinarily would indicate undercooking, but might not in the case of hurds. Further observation on the action of the cooked stock during subsequent processes was necessary in order to judge of its quality or the suitability of the cooking conditions. The total cooked stock, about 500 pounds, was divided into two portions of 200 and 300 pounds, respectively, and work was continued on them separately. The 200-pound test, designated as run No. 135, was put into a 350-pound washing engine, washed one hour, and given a total light brush of 2½ hours. The washing removed a great amount of dirt, but the engine did not reduce the hurd stock as much as was desired. After heating the stock in the beater to 40° C., it was bleached with bleaching-powder solution, 94 gallons at 0.418 pound bleach per gallon, equivalent to 19.7 per cent of the fiber. This percentage of bleach is regarded as too high for stock intended for book-paper manufacture, and subsequent cooks therefore were given harder treatment in order to reduce this figure. After draining and washing free from bleach residues, the stock was furnished in the beater with 13 per cent of clay, 1 per cent of resin size, and 2.5 per cent of alum, was tinted blue, given one hour's light brush, and pumped to the stock chest. When running it on the paper machine, the Jordan refiner seemed to have little effect in reducing shives of undertreated wood, which indicated further the necessity of harder cooking. The furnish acted well on the paper machine at 70 feet per minute, but appeared somewhat too "free" on the wire. The paper produced from this test is of very low quality, due to the improper preparation of the stock, lack of sufficient bleach, the use of too small an amount of blue tinting, and the presence of an excessive amount of dirt, sand, and shives. The excessive amount of dirt and sand suggested the sieving of the hurds before cooking, and this was performed in all subsequent cooks.

The finish of the sheet is very poor, due to the fact that the calender stack was composed of very light rolls which did not have a satisfactory surface, yet the stack is known to be able to produce better finishes if the proper stock is employed.

Run No. 136 was made on the 300-pound portion of stock from cooks Nos. 293, 294, 295, and 296, and in essentially the same manner as run No. 135. The stock was washed one hour, but given a brush of three hours, and this brush was harder than in run No. 135. Bleach to the extent of 19.8 per cent of the fiber was used, assisted by 1 pint of oil of vitriol, and the resulting color was an improvement over that of run No. 135. After adding 13.5 per cent of clay and sizing with 1.1 per cent of resin size, the furnish was given one-half hour's light brush, tinted, and run on the machine, which was set at 70 feet per minute. This stock acted better on the wire and gave no trouble on the machine, but it still seemed to be impossible to reduce the wood shives by manipulation of the Jordan refiner. The resulting sheet is an improvement over that produced by No. 135, but is far from satisfactory.

Run No. 138 was made from hurds which, as in all subsequent tests, were sieved on a 11½-mesh wire screen until practically all the loose dirt and sand was removed, which operation caused a loss averaging 3 per cent of the hurds. Stock from cooks Nos. 302 and 303 was used for this run and the increased amount of caustic soda and the increase in the time of cooking gave a stock of better appearance than those of preceding tests.

The stock, amounting to 231 pounds dry weight, was washed and at the same time given a light brush for one hour only, after which it was bleached with 17 per cent of bleach without the addition of acid. Since the preceding paper appeared somewhat weak and had a low tearing quality, it was decided to use a furnish of 15.7 per cent bleached sulphite and 84.3 per cent bleached hemp-hurd stock. After loading with 13.1 per cent of clay and sizing with 1.1 per cent of resin size, the furnish was given a medium brush for one hour, tinted, and run on to the machine at 70 feet per minute. The stock gave no trouble on the machine, but it was impossible to judge the effect of the Jordan refiner, because through an oversight the machine chest had not been cleaned since previous use on an unbleached yucca material. It is believed, however, that sheet No. 138 shows improvement in the preparation of the hurd pulp.

Run No. 139 was made from stock of cooks Nos. 304 and 305, in which still more caustic soda was employed and the time and temperature of cooking were increased, giving a yield of total fiber of 40.7 per cent of the sieved or 39.4 per cent of the unsieved hurds. The cooked stock still seemed to be undertreated, but it must be remembered that in working with any new raw material it is impos-

sible to know in advance how the properly treated material should appear. A washing of one hour was given while the roll was lowered from a light to a medium brush, after which the stock was bleached with 17.1 per cent of bleach without the aid of acid. Since sulphite stock improved the previous paper, this bleached stock was used in a furnish of 16.6 per cent sulphite and 83.4 per cent hurds, loaded with 16.7 per cent clay, sized with 1.4 per cent resin size, given a medium brush of two hours, tinted, and run on to the machine at 70 feet per minute. The Jordan refiner seemed to have little effect in reducing shives and was therefore left "just off." No trouble was experienced with the stock on the machine, and the sheet is an improvement over previous samples.

Run No. 140 was made from cooks Nos. 306 and 307, in which more caustic soda was employed than in any previous cooks and at a higher concentration, the fiber yields of which averaged 37.3 per cent of the unsieved hurds. Not much improvement was apparent in the cooked stock, in spite of the increased severity of cooking. The stock was washed and given a medium brush for one hour, bleached with 11.9 per cent of bleach, assisted with one-half pint of oil of vitriol, and made into a furnish of 14.9 per cent sulphite and 85.1 per cent of the hurd stock. After loading with 14.7 per cent of clay and sizing with 1.28 per cent of resin size, the furnish was given two hours' medium brush, tinted, and run on to the paper machine at 70 feet per minute. Again the Jordan refiner did not seem to reduce the wood shives sufficiently, and it was left "just off." No trouble which could be attributed to the stock was experienced on the paper machine. The color of the resulting paper is due to the use of too little blue in tinting and probably in some measure to the use of too low a percentage of bleach.

Run No. 141 was made from the stock of cooks Nos. 308 and 309 in practically the same manner as run No. 140. The stock was washed and brushed one hour, bleached (the record of the amount of bleach was lost), made into a furnish of 14.7 per cent of sulphite and 85.3 per cent of hurd stock, loaded with 14.9 per cent of clay, sized with 1.26 per cent of resin size, given one hour at a medium brush, tinted, and run on to the machine. The Jordan refiner was able to reduce the wood shives to a somewhat greater degree than in previous runs and was held at a medium brush. The stock acted well on the machine and produced a sheet of better quality than any preceding, with the exception of the color, which was due to using too small a quantity of blue.

Among the cooks made for run No. 142 are Nos. 312 and 313, in which the concentration of the caustic soda was raised to 113 and 116 grams per liter and the percentage employed was also increased. In spite of these increases the stock from these two cooks did not show any appreciable improvement when dumped from the rotary. Stock from cooks Nos. 310, 311, and 312 was given a medium brush and washing of one hour, bleached with 10.95 per cent of bleach, made into a furnish consisting of 15.2 per cent of sulphite and 84.8 per cent of hurd stock, loaded with 15.2 per cent of clay, sized with 1.28 per cent of resin size, given a medium brush for one hour, tinted, and pumped to the stock chest. Stock from cooks Nos. 313 and 314 was treated in exactly the same manner, except that 11.4 per cent of bleach was used. It was pumped to the stock chest and mixed with the furnished stock from cooks Nos. 310, 311, and 312. A medium Jordan brush was given the stock and it acted well on the paper machine, which was speeded to 75 feet per minute. There seems to be a tendency in the hurd stock to crush a little at the "dandy roll," and although the marks are not removed by the calender stack which was employed in those tests it was found that one "nip" on the supercalenders renders them practically imperceptible and it is believed that the proper size and weight of calender stack would entirely remove these marks. All of the papers produced up to this point are somewhat lacking in the bulk desired in a book paper; therefore, in the two following runs soda-poplar stock was included in the furnishes.

In run No. 143 stock from cooks Nos. 315 and 316 was given a medium brush and washing for one hour and was medium brushed for one hour more, bleached with 11.3 per cent of bleach assisted with one-half pint of oil of vitriol, made into a furnish of 16.5 per cent of sulphite, 22.3 per cent of soda poplar, and 61.2 per cent of hurd stock, loaded with 22 per cent of clay, sized with 1.38 per cent of resin size, given a hard brush for one hour, tinted very strongly, and pumped to the stock chest. This stock was beaten to a greater extent than in previous runs. The stock was run on the paper machine at a speed of 75 feet per minute, using a medium Jordan brush, and no trouble whatsoever was experienced. Not over 2 pounds of "broke" was produced during the whole run, and that was in the "threading" of the machine. The color of the sheet is entirely satisfactory for many uses. The wood shives apparently were reduced to a satisfactory degree. Experienced paper makers commented very favorably on the running of this furnish and the quality of the paper produced.

Run No. 144 was intended as a duplicate of run No. 143. Stock from cooks Nos. 317 and 318 was given a medium brush and washing for one hour and a further medium brush of one hour, bleached with 11.4 per cent of bleach, and made into a furnish composed of 15.5 per cent of sulphite, 23.5 per cent of soda poplar, and 61 per cent of hurd stock, loaded with 21.4 per cent of clay, sized with 1.17 per cent of resin size, hard brushed for one hour, tinted by the expert colorer

of the company, and pumped to the stock chest. Stock from cooks Nos. 319 and 320 was treated in exactly the same manner except that the stock was bleached with 12.1 per cent of bleach and pumped to the stock chest to mix with the former furnish. The stock acted very well on the machine, which was speeded to 75 feet per minute, with the Jordan refiner set at a medium brush. The sheet is as good, if not better, than that of run No. 143, and it is also a good illustration of the extent to which proper tinting will enhance the general appearance of a paper. The poor appearance of the samples of previous runs is due largely to lack of proper tinting. Various degrees of whiteness, however, are demanded by the trade.

COMPARISON OF THE TESTS AND COMMERCIAL PRACTICE.

In work of this nature and on this scale it is practically impossible to arrive at a cost figure which would be susceptible of commercial interpretation, and in this preliminary publication nothing will be attempted beyond a comparison of the process used with the hurds with that process commercially applied to poplar wood. The process last used with the hurds should not be regarded as final, satisfactory, or most suitable, as it has been shown that progress was being made up to the conclusion of the work.

In comparing the method of using hurds with the method of handling poplar wood, a difference is apparent on the delivery of raw material at the mill. Ordinarily, poplar is received at the mill in the form of logs about 4 feet in length, which may be stored in piles in the open. Hurds very likely would be received baled, and it would seem advisable to store them under cover for the following reasons: (a) Baled hurds would probably absorb and retain more water during wet weather than logs of wood, thereby causing excessive dilution of the caustic liquor; (b) prolonged excessive dampness might create heating and deterioration unless the hemp were properly retted; (c) wet hurds could not be sieved free from sand and chaff. Should further work show that the first two reasons need not be taken into consideration, the third objection might be overcome by sieving the hurds before baling. Even then, it is probable that baled hurds stored in the open would accumulate and retain considerable dirt from factory chimneys, locomotives, and wind. Checked pulp wood exposed in the open invariably suffers from these causes.

In the preparation of the raw material for the digesters there is likewise considerable difference between hurds and poplar wood. The former apparently requires only a moderate sieving to remove sand and chaff, which operation doubtless would require only a small amount of labor and the installation of some simple machinery of low power consumption. In preparing poplar for digestion, the

4-foot logs are chipped by a heavy, comparatively expensive chipp of high power consumption, after which the chips are sorted sieving, the large pieces being rechipped. There would be a no worthy difference in the installation, operating, and depreciati costs of the two equipments, and this difference would counterb ance to a considerable extent the difference in cost of raw mater storage.

It is possible that in the use of the chip loft more care would ha to be exercised in using hurds because of the tendency of the b fiber to cause lodgments, but this should not be considered a serio difficulty.

The weight of hurds which are capable of being charged into rotary is a decidedly unfavorable factor. The weight of a cu foot of hurds varies somewhat with the proportion of bast fib but averages about 5.4 pounds, which, compared with a cubic fo of poplar chips at 8.93 pounds, represents a digester charge of 6 per cent of the weight of a poplar-wood charge, or, in terms of fib capacity, the hurds charge would yield 38.6 per cent as much fib as the wood charge. The hurds upon being baled for transport tion may be broken and crushed to such a degree that the weig of the charge may be increased, and it might be found possible increase the charge weight by steaming or by the employment tamping devices. This small weight of charge constitutes one of t most serious objections to the use of hurds in paper manufacture.

In those tests in which the most satisfactory results were obtaine the cooking conditions were 29.5 per cent of caustic soda at a conce tration of 107 grams per liter and a causticity of 84.0 per cent acti at a temperature of 170° C. for five hours, or a total time of seve hours. The steam condensation in the rotary used for these tes was abnormally high, due to the fact that the steam supply pipe w uncovered for a considerable distance and the rotary was entirel uncovered. It is believed, therefore, that a larger amount of caust was necessary than would otherwise have been the case. Th belief is strengthened by the quality of the waste liquor from one the later cooks, which gave on analysis 16.85 grams per liter of fr caustic soda and showed a causticity of 27.75 per cent. These dat show that only 67.3 per cent of the total caustic employed was actu ally consumed in the cooking operation, which percentage is lowe than obtains in practice. The stock from this cook was bleach with 11.5 per cent of bleach. But even as the figures stand, th comparison with poplar cooking practice is as follows: 29.5 per cen caustic soda used as against 22 to 25 per cent; 107 grams per lite as against 100 to 110; 84 per cent causticity is little different tha obtains in practice; 170° C. is about commercial practice; five hour at pressure as against four to six hours; seven hours' total time a

against possibly six to eight hours; 11.5 per cent bleach as against 8 to 10 per cent. Thus, it is evident that the cooking conditions employed were slightly more severe and expensive than those in commercial use with poplar wood.

The yield of total fiber obtained from the hurds may be placed at 35 per cent of bone-dry fiber calculated on the bone-dry weight of hurds used, or 33.1 per cent of air-dry fiber calculated on air-dry hurds. The yield of bleached fiber was not determined in this preliminary work, but may be safely estimated as 30 per cent, which is low when compared with a yield of about 47 per cent of bone-dry bleached fiber from bone-dry poplar wood. It is believed quite possible that satisfactory cooking conditions may be found which will give a higher yield than was obtained during these tests. The stock should be classed as easy bleaching, and 11.4 per cent of bleach is a satisfactory figure, although a little high.

As to beating cost, in the last two and most satisfactory tests the total washing and beating time was three hours, which may be about an hour more than ordinarily is used in making papers of this grade, although the practice varies to a considerable extent.

In regard to furnish, there is such a diversity of practice that it is difficult to make a comparison, but if the hurd stock can be produced as cheaply as soda-poplar stock, the furnish used in these last two tests should be regarded as satisfactory to the book and printing paper manufacturer.

The finish of the paper was not all that might be desired, but that was due almost entirely to the calender stack available for the work, which was composed of nine light rolls, many of which were about 6 inches in diameter and which had not been reground for some time. From a small test on a large calender stack it was readily shown that the paper produced is capable of taking a satisfactory finish.

This comparison, satisfactory in many respects, develops two factors which are decidedly unfavorable to hemp hurds, namely, raw-material storage and digester capacity, and they must be taken into full account in considering the paper-making value of this material, although it should be recognized that investigation may result in the material improvement of these conditions. Moreover, it is not at all improbable that further investigation would develop more satisfactory treating conditions and more suitable furnish compositions, and the belief in this possibility is strengthened by the fact that material progress was being made at the conclusion of this preliminary work.

Calculations on the raw material and acreage for a permanent supply for a pulp mill producing 25 tons of fiber a day for 300 days per annum, or 7,500 tons per annum, give the comparison between hurds and wood shown in Table II.

TABLE II.—*Comparison between wood and hemp hurds.*

Material.	Pulp yield.	Raw material required per year.	Annual growth per acre.	Acres required for sustained supply.	
				For 25-ton mill.	For 1 ton of fiber per year.
Wood	Two cords yield 1 ton of fiber.	15,000 cords	0.37 cord (about 0.55 ton).	40,500	5.4
Hemp hurds	One ton yields 600 pounds of fiber.	25,000 tons	2.5 tons	10,000	1.33

The most important point derived from this calculation is in regard to areas required for a sustained supply, which are in the ratio of 4 to 1. Every tract of 10,000 acres which is devoted to hemp raising year by year is equivalent to a sustained pulp-producing capacity of 40,500 acres of average pulp-wood lands. In other words, in order to secure additional raw material for the production of 25 tons of fiber per day there exists the possibility of utilizing the agricultural waste already produced on 10,000 acres of hemp lands instead of securing, holding, reforesting, and protecting 40,500 acres of pulp-wood land.

The annual growth per acre, although decidedly in favor of hurds, has little bearing on the project, because the utilization of the hurds is subordinate to the raising of hemp, and the paper manufacturer probably could afford to use only hurds resulting from the hemp industry.

PHYSICAL TESTS OF THE PAPERS PRODUCED.

Samples of paper produced in the seven tests were submitted to the Leather and Paper Laboratory of the Bureau of Chemistry. The report of that bureau on its tests is given in Table III.

TABLE III.—*Report of the Leather and Paper Laboratory of the Bureau of Chemistry on papers manufactured from hemp hurds.*

Laboratory No.	Run No.	Ash.	Weight of 500 sheets.		Thickness, 1/10000.	Strength (Mullen).			Strength factor (25 by 40, 500).	Folding endurance.	
			25 by 38.	25 by 40.		Average.	Maximum.	Minimum.		Longitudinal.	Transverse.
		Per ct.	Pounds.	Pounds.							
31570	144	13.9	48	50½	33	15.0	17.0	11.0	0.30	5	3
31571	142	14.6	49	51½	33	14.0	14.0	13.0	.28	4	4
31572	143	9.5	49½	52	33	19.0	20.0	18.0	.37	8	6
31573	141	16.9	48	50½	33	16.5	18.0	11.0	.33	10	8
31574	140	11.4	42	44	30	14.5	16.0	13.0	.33	7	6
31575	139	13.4	53	55	40	18.5	20.5	17.0	.34	8	6
31576	138	16.4	56	60	40	25.0	28.5	19.5	.34	25	15

There is no system of numerically recording the general appearance and "look through" of a paper, but it can be stated that only papers

Nos. 143 and 144 are satisfactory in these respects, the other samples being more or less thickly specked with shives. The general character and tests of these papers correspond very closely with No. 1 machine-finish printing paper, according to the specifications of the United States Government Printing Office, which call for a sheet not exceeding 0.0035 inch in thickness, strength not less than 12 points, free from unbleached or ground wood pulp, and ash not over 10 per cent. The strength factor of such papers is about 0.28. The ash should not be over 10 per cent for this grade of paper, but in spite of the larger amount used the physical tests are sufficiently high. It is to be noted that the physical tests of samples Nos. 138 to 142, inclusive, are higher than in Nos. 143 and 144, in which 23 per cent of soda poplar was used, which shows clearly that hemp-hurd stock imparts strength and folding endurance to a greater extent than does soda-poplar stock. From these preliminary tests it would be concluded, therefore, that hemp-hurd stock acts similarly to soda-poplar stock, but will produce a somewhat harsher and stronger sheet and one of higher folding endurance. Undoubtedly, there is more dirt in the samples than would be tolerated by the trade, but this was to be expected, since in this preliminary work the raw material was sieved by hand screens instead of by automatic machines which would sieve more thoroughly.

CONCLUSIONS.

There appears to be little doubt that under the present system of forest use and consumption the present supply can not withstand the demands placed upon it. By the time improved methods of forestry have established an equilibrium between production and consumption, the price of pulp wood may be such that a knowledge of other available raw materials may be imperative.

Semicommercial paper-making tests were conducted, therefore, on hemp hurds, in cooperation with a paper manufacturer. After several trials, under conditions of treatment and manufacture which are regarded as favorable in comparison with those used with pulp wood, paper was produced which received very favorable comment both from investigators and from the trade and which according to official tests would be classed as a No. 1 machine-finish printing paper.

THE MARIJUANA TAX ACT OF 1937

Excerpts of Congressional Hearings:

Committee on Ways and Means
House of Representatives
75th Congress

First Session on H.R. 6385
April 27-30, May 4, 1937

TRANSCRIPTS OF ACTUAL HOUSE HEARINGS ON THE MARIJUANA TAX ACT

ALEXANDER DUNETZ
Jan. 15, 1979

- page 1 -

(Committee comes to order, -general shot-

NARRATOR: In April 1937 the U.S. House Committee on Ways and Means of the 75th Congress held hearings for the proposed legislation on the control of marijuana through prohibitive taxation.

Committee Chairman, Robert L. Doughton of North Carolina.

CHAIRMAN: The Committee will come to order. The meeting this morning has been called for the purpose of considering H.R. 6385, introduced by me on April 14, 1937, a bill "to impose an occupational excise tax upon certain dealers in marijuana, to impose a transfer tax upon certain transfers in marijuana and to safeguard the revenue therefrom by registry and recording."

(Chairman holds up report, hands over to page, committee shuffles around.)

CHAIRMAN: This bill was introduced by me at the request of the Secretary of the Treasury. Representatives of the Treasury Department are here this morning to explain the bill.

Mr. Hester, assistant general counsel for the Treasury Department will be the first witness to be heard in behalf of the proposed legislation.

NARRATOR: Clinton Hester is an Assistant General counsel for the Department of the Treasury.

(Chairman swears in Hester.

HESTER: We Chairman and members of the Ways and Means Committee, for the past two years the Treasury Department has been making a study of the subject of marijuana, a drug which is found in the flowering tops, seeds, and leaves of Indian hemp, and is now being used extensively by high-school

MARIJUANA TAX ACT OF 1937

CAST . . . . ;

Narrator

Committee members:

Robert L. Doughton, North Carolina, Chairman
Fred M. Vinson, Kentucky
David J. Lewis, Maryland
Daniel A. Reed, New York
John D. Dingell, Michigan
John W. McCormack, Massachusetts

Witnesses:

Clinton M. Hester, Assistant General Counsel for
Department of the Treasury
Dr. H. J. Anslinger, Commissioner of Narcotics,
Department of the Treasury
Raymond G. Scarlett, Wm. G. Scarlett & Co., Baltimore, MD.
Dr. William C. Woodward, legislative counsel, American
Medical Association, Chicago, Ill.

- page 2 -

children in cigarettes. Its effect is deadly.

I would like to say at this point that we have with us this morning Commissioner Anslinger, of the Bureau of Narcotics, who has had charge of the enforcement of the Harrison Narcotic Act, and who will have charge of the enforcement of this act, if this bill is enacted into law. We also have with us a pharmacologist who is prepared to testify as to the effect of the drug on human beings. We also have an expert chemist, and one of the outstanding botanists in the country, who are prepared to testify with reference to the bill, if you desire to hear them.

The leading newspapers of the United States have recognized the seriousness of this problem and many of them have advocated Federal legislation to control the traffic in marijuana. In fact, several newspapers in the city of Washington have advocated such legislation. In a recent editorial, the Washington Times stated:

The marijuana cigarette is one of the most insidious of all forms of dope, largely because of the failure of the public to understand its fatal qualities.
The Nation is almost defenseless against it, having no Federal laws to cope with it and virtually no organized campaign for combatting it.
The result is tragic.
School children are the prey of peddlers who infest school neighborhoods.
High-school boys and girls buy the destructive weed without knowledge of its capacity for harm, and conscienceless dealers sell it with impunity.
This is a national problem, and it must have national attention.

The purpose of House Resolution 6385 is to employ the Federal taxing power not only to raise revenue from the marijuana traffic, but also to discourage the current and widespread undesirable use of marijuana by smokers and drug

- page 3 -

addicts and thus drive the traffic into channels where the plant will be put to valuable industrial, medical, and scientific uses. In accomplishing this general purpose, two objectives should dictate the form of the proposed legislation. First, the development of a scheme of taxation which would raise revenue and which would also render virtually impossible the acquisition of marijuana by persons who would put it to illicit uses without unduly interfering with the use of the plant for industrial, medical, and scientific purposes; and second, the development of an adequate means of publicizing dealings in marijuana in order that the traffic may be effectively taxed and controlled.

In order to obviate the possibility of an attack upon the constitutionality of this bill, it, like the National Firearms Act, permits the transfer of marijuana to nonregistered persons upon the payment of a heavy transfer tax.

The bill would permit the transfer of marijuana to anyone.
But it would impose a $100 per ounce tax upon a transfer to a person who might use it for purposes which are dangerous and harmful to the public, just as the National Firearms Act permits a transfer of a machine gun to anyone but imposes a $200 tax upon a transfer to a person who would be likely to put it to an illegal use.

Although the $100 transfer tax in this bill is intended to be prohibitive, as is the $200 transfer tax in the National Firearms Act, it is submitted that it is constitutional as a revenue measure.

This bill would permit anyone to purchase marijuana, as was done in the National Firearms Act in permitting anyone to buy a machine gun, but he would have to pay a tax of $100 per ounce of marijuana and make his purchase on an

- page 4 -

official order form. A person who wants to buy marijuana would have to go to the collector and get an order form in duplicate, and buy the $100 tax stamp and put it on the original order form there. He would take the original to the vendor if, the person who purchases the marijuana from his has to do the same thing and pay the $100 tax. That is the scheme that has been adopted to stop high-school children from getting marijuana.

VINSON: What is the fair market value, per ounce, of marijuana?

HESTER: In its raw state it is about a dollar per ounce, as a drug.

VINSON: I notice in your statement - and I want to say it is a good statement; the gentleman does not have any other kind of a statement when he comes before our committee.

HESTER: I thank you.

CHAIRMAN: Through what channel or agency is this drug in its deleterious form dispensed or distributed? Is it sold by druggists, or at grocery stores?

HESTER: I will answer your question, but I hope you will ask the same question of Mr. Anslinger, because he can speak more authoritatively on that phase of the subject.
The flowered tops, leaves, and seeds are smoked in cigarettes.

CHAIRMAN: Is it carried generally by druggists?

HESTER: I do not think so, for this reason. It is very variable. It may affect you in one way and affect me in another way, and then, too, there are very many better substitutes.

CHAIRMAN: And a deleterious use?

HESTER: The smoking of it, yes. You can take the leaves, tops, and seeds and fix them in a way somewhat similar to tobacco.

- page 5 -

It is just about the same as tobacco; you can smoke it like tobacco.

CHAIRMAN: Just as an illustration, suppose I were in the market for some of this drug; where would I find it?

MESTER: There are about 10,000 acres under cultivation by legitimate producers.

CHAIRMAN: I want to know where it could be bought; where is it being sold?

LEWIS: Where do the victims get it?

REED: I think what the chairman wants to know is how high-school children are able to get it. Is it not true that there are illicit peddlers who hang around the high-school buildings, and as soon as they find out that there is some boy to whom they think they can sell it, they make his acquaintance?

MESTER: Yes. I read in the newspapers not long ago that a place on Twelfth Street was raided, where a lady was selling marijuana.

LEWIS: Do legitimate companies make these cigarettes, or are they made in an illicit manner, like bootleg whiskey used to be made? Do reputable firms make these cigarettes?

MESTER: I would like to refer that question to Commissioner Anslinger.

REED: I would like to make a statement at this point in reference to this question. Some years ago the committee of the House of which I happened to be chairman held a hearing going into the narcotic problem. That was at the time when there was a great deal of talk about heroin, and we devoted a good deal of the time of that hearing to that subject.

We had experts there from New York and other parts of the country. At that time they were selling heroin through

- page 6 -

peddlers to high-school students, particularly to athletes. The peddler was usually a man of some personality, and he would sell the heroin to these tired boys as they came off of the athletic training field. They would say to these boys, "Here is something that will put the pep in you." They soon had a lot of these boys in these schools developed into addicts. I assume you have the same thing here.

(Committee is rather inattentive during Reed's statement, Mester has assembled his documents and leaves, Anslinger replaces him and commences to be sworn in, -camera pans-

NARRATOR: We have just heard testimony from Clinton Mester of the Treasury Department. The following witness is Harry J. Anslinger, who is currently the federal government's chief drug law enforcer.

CHAIRMAN: Mr. Anslinger, the committee will be glad to have a statement from you at this time. Will you state your full name and the position you occupy in the Treasury Department?

ANSLINGER: Mr. Chairman, my name is H.J. Anslinger; I am Commissioner of Narcotics in the Bureau of Narcotics, in the Treasury Department.

Mr. Chairman and distinguished members of the Ways and Means Committee, this traffic in marijuana is increasing to such an extent that it has become the cause for the greatest national concern.

In medical schools the physician-to-be is taught that without opium medicine would be like a one-armed man. That is true, because you cannot get along without opium.

But here we have a drug that is not like opium. Opium has all of the good of Dr. Jekyll and all the evil of Mr. Hyde. This drug is entirely the monster Hyde, the harmful effect of which cannot be measured.

DINGELL: I want to be certain what this is. Is this the same weed that

- page 7 -

grows wild in some of our Western States which is sometimes called the loco weed?

ANSLINGER: No, sir; that is another family.

DINGELL: That is also a harmful drug-producing weed, is it not?

ANSLINGER: Not to my knowledge; it is not used by humans.

CHAIRMAN: In what particular sections does this weed grow wild?

ANSLINGER: In almost every state in the Union today.

REED: What you are describing is a plant which has a rather large flower?

ANSLINGER: No, sir; a very small flower.

REED: It is not Indian hemp?

ANSLINGER: It is Indian hemp. We have some specimens here.

(Anslinger raises stalks from adjacent chair and places them on the table, -long close-up -

VINSON: When was this brought to your attention as being a menace among our own people?

ANSLINGER: About ten years ago-

VINSON: Why did you wait until 1937 to bring in a recommendation of this kind?

ANSLINGER: Ten years ago we only heard about it throughout the Southwest. It is only in the last few years that it has become a national menace. It has grown like wildfire, but it has only become a national menace in the last three years. It is only in the last two years that we have had to send reports about it to the League of Nations.

McCORMACK: What are its first manifestations, afeeling of grandeur and self-exaltation, and things of that sort?

ANSLINGER: It affects different individuals in different ways. Some individuals have a complete loss of a sense of time or a sense of value. They lose the sense of place. They have an increased feeling of physical strength and power.

- page 8 -

Some people will fly into a delirious rage, and they are temporarily irresponsible and may commit violent crimes. Other people will laugh uncontrollably. It is impossible to say what the effect will be on any individual. Those research men who have tried it have always been under control. They have always insisted upon that.

McCORMACK: Is it used by the criminal class?

ANSLINGER: Yes, it is. It is dangerous to the mind and body, and particularly dangerous to the criminal type, because it releases all of the inhibitions.

DINGELL: What is the price of marijuana?

ANSLINGER: The addict pays anywhere from 10 to 25 cents per cigarette. It will be sold by the cigarette. In illicit traffic the bulk price would be around $20 per pound. Legitimately, the bulk is around $2 per pound.

DINGELL: How does that compare with the price of opium or morphine? Do the class of people who use this drug use it because it is cheaper than the other kinds?

ANSLINGER: That is one reason; yes, sir. To be a morphine or heroin addict it would cost you from $5 to $8 a day to maintain your supply. But if you want to smoke a cigarette you pay 10 cents.

McCORMACK: Just one of them will knock the socks off of you.

ANSLINGER: One of them can do it.

McCORMACK: Some of those cigarettes are sold much cheaper then 10 cents, are they not? In other words, it is a low-priced cigarette, and that is one of the reasons for the tremendous increase in its use.

ANSLINGER: Yes; it is low enough in price for school children to buy it.

McCORMACK: And they have parties in different parts of the country that they call "reefer parties."

ANSLINGER: Yes, sir; we have heard of them, and know of them.

McCORMACK: Another thing is that they will not be able to get other kinds of dope, but they do have an opportunity to get this marijuana, which causes it to be so much sought after and used in the community.

ANSLINGER: That is true, and the effect is just passed by word of mouth, and everybody wants to try it.

CHAIRMAN: Mr. Anslinger, at this time the committee would like to thank you for your time and call upon another witness before our adjournment today. I will, however, ask for you to be available to this committee for any further testimony during the remainder of hearings on this matter.

(Anslinger nods and proceeds to assemble his visual aids, Chairman engages in hand gesturing while the rest of the hearing room shuffles about, - general pan shots -

CHAIRMAN: The committee will be in order. Yesterday the chairman was informed there was some disagreement in connection with some of the provisions of the bill, by the people engaged in the processing of seed or some objection to parts of the bill we have under consideration.

The chairman suggested to Mr. Mester that we have a conference with the people representing that industry to see if it was possible to reach an agreement and remove the objection they had by some change or modification of the bill, but which would warrant them in withdrawing their objection.

We will be glad to hear any statement from representatives of this industry at this time.

(Chairman looks impatiently into the chamber, witness approaches to be sworn,

NARRATOR: The committee will now hear testimony from Raymond G.

- page 10 -

SCARLETT: Mr. Chairman, our company handles a considerable quantity of hempseed annually for use in pigeon feeds. That is a necessary ingredient in pigeon food because it contains an oil substance that is a valuable ingredient of pigeon feed, and we have not been able to find any seed that will take its place.

If you substitute anything for the hemp, it has a tendency to change the character of the squabs produced; and if we were deprived of the use of hempseed, it would affect all of the pigeon producers in the United States, of which there are upwards of 40,000.

CHAIRMAN: Does that seed have the same effect on pigeons as the drug has on individuals?

(The chairman's questions draws laughs and smirks throughout the chamber, chairman looks impatiently at his watch, pounds his gavel, -close-up shot on the witness

SCARLETT: I have never noticed it. It has a tendency to bring back the feathers and improve the birds.

We are not interested in spreading marijuana, or anything like that. We do not want to be drug peddlers.

CHAIRMAN: Well, at this time the committee will adjourn until 10:00 tomorrow morning. We will continue our discussion with Mr. Scarlett at that time.

(Chairman pound gavel, chamber files out, -general shots with close-ups on committee members conferring with each other, and close-up on Chairman waving Scarlett over -

NARRATOR: That will conclude today's proceedings on the Marijuana Tax Act.

(Camera break)

We now continue hearings with Dr. William C. Woodward,

CHAIRMAN: The committee will be in order. The meeting this morning is for the purpose of continuing hearings on House Resolution 6385.

Dr. Woodward, will you come forward and give your name and address and the capacity in which you appear.

WOODWARD: Mr. Chairman and gentlemen, my name is Dr. William C. Woodward, representing the American Medical Association. The address is 535 North Dearborn St., Chicago, Illinois.

CHAIRMAN: Do you appear in the capacity of a medical expert, a legal expert, or a legislative expert, or in all three capacities?

WOODWARD: My profession is that of a practitioner of medicine and of legal medicine. I have combined the two. If you want to class me as an expert, you might class me as a medical-legal expert. I have lectured on legal medicine as a lawyer and doctor.

CHAIRMAN: Thank you, Dr. Woodward, please continue.

(pause, as Woodward organizes

WOODWARD: There is nothing in the medicinal use of Cannabis that has any relation to Cannabis addiction. I use the word "Cannabis" in preference to the word "marijuana", because cannabis is the correct term for describing the plant and its products. The term "marijuana" is a mongrel word that has crept into this country over the Mexican border and has no general meaning, except as it relates to the use of Cannabis preparations for smoking. It is not recognized in medicine, and hardly recognized even in the Treasury Department. Marijuana is not the correct term. It was the use of the term "marijuana" rather then the use of the term "Cannabis" or the use of the term "Indian hemp" that was responsible, as now realized, probably a day or two ago, for the

- page 12 -

this bill with their business until rather late in the day. So, I shall use the word "Cannabis", and I should certainly suggest that if any legislation is enacted, the term used be "Cannabis" and not the mongrel word "marijuana".

I say the medicinal use of Cannabis had nothing to do with Cannabis or marijuana addiction. In all that you have heard here thus far, no mention has been made of any excessive use of the drug by any doctor or its excessive distribution by any pharmacist. And yet the burden of this bill is placed heavily on the doctors and pharmacists of the country; and I may say very heavily, most heavily, possibly of all, on the farmers of the country.

My interest is primarily, of course, in the medical aspects. We object to the imposing of an additional tax on physicians, pharmacists, and others, catering to the sick; to require that they register and reregister; that they have special order forms to be used for this particular drug, when the matter can just as well be covered by an amendment to the Harrison Narcotic Act.

If you are referring to the particular problem, I object to the act because it is utterly unsusceptible of execution, and an act that is not susceptible of execution is a bad thing on the statute books.

CHAIRMAN: If the use of marijuana as a dope has increased until it has become serious and a menace to the public, as has been testified here - and the testimony here has been that it causes people to lose their mental balance, causes them to become criminals so that they do not seem to realize

taking into consideration the growth in its use so far as any beneficial and its diminution in its use so far as any injurious effect is concerned, you realize, do you not, that some good may be accomplished by this proposed legislation?

WOODWARD: Some legislation; yes, Mr. Chairman.

CHAIRMAN: If that is admitted, let us get down to a few concrete facts. With the experience in the Bureau of Narcotics and with the State government trying to enforce the laws that are on the State statute books against the use of this deleterious drug, and the Federal Government has realized that the State law are ineffective, don't you think some Federal legislation necessary?

WOODWARD: I do not.

CHAIRMAN: You do not?

WOODWARD: No. I think it is the usual tendency to —

CHAIRMAN: I believe you did say in response to Mr. Cooper that you believed that some legislation or some change in the present law would be helpful. If that is true, why have you not been here before this bill was introduced proposing some remedy for this evil?

WOODWARD: Mr. Chairman. I have visited the Commissioner of Narcotics on various occasions.

CHAIRMAN: That is not an answer to my question at all.

WOODWARD: I have not been here because —

CHAIRMAN: You are here representing the medical association. If your association has realized the necessity, the importance of some legislation — which you now admit — why did you wait until this bill was introduced to come here and make mention of it? Why did you not come here voluntarily and suggest to this committee some legislation?

WOODWARD: I have talked these matters over many times with the —

CHAIRMAN: That does not do us any good to talk matters over. I have talked over a lot of things. The states do not seem to be able to deal with it effectively, nor is the Federal Government dealing with it at all. Why do you wait until now and then come in here to oppose something that is presented to us. You propose nothing whatever to correct the evil that exists.

Now, I do not like to have a round-about answer to that question.

WOODWARD: We do not propose legislation directly to Congress when the same end can be reached through one of the executive departments of the government.

CHAIRMAN: You admit that it has not been done. You said that you thought some legislation would be helpful. That is what I am trying to hold you down to. Now, why have you not proposed any legislation? That is what I want a clear, definite, clean-cut answer to.

WOODWARD: In the first place, it is not a medical addiction that is involved and the data do not come before the medical society. You may absolutely forbid the use of Cannabis by any physician. disposition of Cannabis by any pharmacist in the country, and you would not have touched your Cannabis addiction as it stands today, because there is no relation between it and the practice of medicine or pharmacy. It is entirely outside of those two branches.

CHAIRMAN: If the statement that you have just made has any relation to the question that I asked, I just do not have the mind to understand it; I am sorry.

WOODWARD: I say that we do not ordinarily come directly to Congress if a department can take care of the matter. I have talked with the Commissioner, with Commissioner Anslinger.

- page 15 -

interested in, or that the AMA is interested in, but all of the people are interested in it. Incidentally, I would like to ask how many doctors are members of the AMA.

WOODWARD: Approximately 100,000.

DINGELL: That many are members of the AMA?

WOODWARD: Yes, sir.

DINGELL: How many doctors are there in the United States?

WOODWARD: Probably 140,000 or 150,000, or there may be 160,000.

DINGELL: Are we to understand that the medical men of the state of Michigan, or the medical profession in Wayne County, or the the medical association of Detroit, are opposed to this legislation?

WOODWARD: I do not know. No medical man would identify this bill with a medicine until he read it through, because marijuana is not a drug.

DINGELL: Please tell me this: What effort has been made in my state through the medical association to protect the school children and the unfortunate people who are falling victims to this habit? I ask that question since we are talking about controlling it through the state. I want to know what has been done by the State of Michigan and the members of the medical profession to give protection intended by this bill.

WOODWARD: It is, of course, impossible for me to say just what has been done in any particular state; but in the Michigan laws of 1931, chapter 173, they do regulate the production and distribution of Cannabis indica.

DINGELL: What kind of regulation is that?

WOODWARD: I do not have the law here.

- page 17 -

DINGELL: Can you tell me whether that legislation was at that time sponsored by the medical association of my state?

WOODWARD: I do not know. I cannot carry all of those details in my mind. You understand that marijuana is simply a name given Cannabis. It is a mongrel word brought in from Mexico. It is a popular term to indicate Cannabis, like "coke" is used to indicate cocaine, and as "dope" is used to indicate opium.

DINGELL: We know that it is a habit that is spreading, particularly among youngsters. We learn that from the pages of the newspapers. You say that Michigan has a law regulating it. We have a state law, but we do not seem to be able to get anywhere with it, because, as I have said, the habit is growing. The number of victims is increasing each year.

WOODWARD: There is no evidence of that.

DINGELL: I have not been impressed by your testimony here as reflecting the sentiment of the high-class members of the medical profession in my state. I am confident that the medical profession in the state of Michigan, and in Wayne County particularly, or in my district, will subscribe wholeheartedly to any law that will suppress this thing, despite that fact that there is a $1 tax imposed.

WOODWARD: If there was any law that would absolutely suppress the thing, perhaps that is true, but when the law simply contains provisions that impose a useless expense, and does not accomplish the result —

DINGELL: That is simply your personal opinion. That is kindred to the opinion you entertained with reference to the Harrison Narcotics Act.

-page 18-

WOODWARD: If we had been asked to cooperate in drafting it —

DINGELL: You are not cooperating in this at all.

WOODWARD: As a matter of fact, it does not serve to suppress the use of opium and cocaine.

DINGELL: The medical profession should be doing its utmost to aid in the suppression of this curse that is eating the very vitals of the nation.

WOODWARD: They are?

McCORMACK: Are you not simply piqued because you were not consulted in the drafting of the bill?

WOODWARD: That is not the case at all. I said, in explaining why I was here, that the measure should have been discussed and an expression of opinion obtained before the Treasury Department brought the bill before the Congress of the United States, so that it would be in a form that would be acceptable, with as few differences of opinion as possible.

McCORMACK: With all due respect to you and for your appearance here. Is it not a fact that you are peeved because you were not called in and consulted in the drafting of the bill?

WOODWARD: Not in the least. I have drafted too many bills to be peeved about that.

McCORMACK: There is no question but that the drug habit has been increasing rapidly in recent years.

WOODWARD: There is no evidence to show whether or not it has been.

McCORMACK: In your opinion, has it increased?

WOODWARD: I should say it has increased slightly. Newspaper exploitation if the habit has done more to increase it than anything else.

McCORMACK: It is likely to increase further unless some effort is made to suppress it.

- page 19 -

WOODWARD: I do not know. The exploitation tempts young men and women to venture into the habit.

McCORMACK: At any event, it is a drug; yes.

WOODWARD: Cannabis indica is a drug.

(During the course of Woodward's testimony, committee members present have become impatient and restless over witness' calm resistance)

CHAIRMAN: The public authorities dealing with this evil, the state authorities and Federal authorities, say that they need further legislation in order to protect the people from its insidious influence and effects. Under those conditions, do you not believe that Congress should try to do something?

WOODWARD: I think something should be done, but it is only a question of what should be done.

CHAIRMAN: You stated a while ago that you believed this law would be ineffective. Of course, the law against carrying concealed weapons, designed to protect people against criminals is not entirely effective, but you would not advocate the repeal of the law. The law against prostitution and murder are not entirely effective, but without legislative control we would be at the mercy of the criminal class, and we would have no civilization whatever.

(Chairman looks disgustedly at witness, --close-up, backing away.

We thank you for your appearance before the committee. We will now take a recess to meet tomorrow at 10:00 in executive session.

(Chairman pounds gavel, committee members glare at Woodward, reminder of chamber files out slowly. --360 shot-

- page 20 -

NARRATOR: The House Ways and Means Committee approved the Marijuana Tax Act and sent it to a Senate Subcommittee, which after one day of hearings also approved it.

On June 14, 1937, the bill came before the full House. Only four congressmen asked for explanation of the bill's provisions. What they received was an account of the criminal acts perpetrated by marijuana use from a member of the Ways and Means Committee. The act passed without a roll call. The question of whether the American Medical Association agreed with the bill was answered by Congressman Vinson.

VINSON: (voice only) Our committee heard testimony of Dr. William Wharton who not only gave this measure his full support, but also the approval from the American Medical Association which he represented as legislative counsel.

NARRATOR: The act passed Congress with little debate and even less public attention.

It stands today as a monument to uncontroversial law.

TRANSCRIPTS OF ACTUAL SENATE HEARINGS ON THE MARIJUANA TAX ACT

HEARING

BEFORE A

SUBCOMMITTEE OF THE COMMITTEE ON FINANCE UNITED STATES SENATE

SEVENTY-FIFTH CONGRESS

FIRST SESSION

ON

H. R. 6906

AN ACT TO IMPOSE AN OCCUPATIONAL EXCISE TAX UPON CERTAIN DEALERS IN MARIHUANA, TO IMPOSE A TRANSFER TAX UPON CERTAIN DEALINGS IN MARIHUANA, AND TO SAFEGUARD THE REVENUE THEREFROM BY REGISTRY AND RECORDING

JULY 12, 1937

Printed for the use of the Committee on Finance

UNITED STATES
GOVERNMENT PRINTING OFFICE
7785 WASHINGTON : 1937

COMMITTEE ON FINANCE

PAT HARRISON, Mississippi, Chairman

WILLIAM H. KING, Utah
WALTER F. GEORGE, Georgia
DAVID I. WALSH, Massachusetts
ALBEN W. BARKLEY, Kentucky
TOM CONNALLY, Texas
JOSIAH W. BAILEY, North Carolina
BENNETT CHAMP CLARK, Missouri
HARRY FLOOD BYRD, Virginia
AUGUSTINE LONERGAN, Connecticut
HUGO L. BLACK, Alabama
PETER G. GERRY, Rhode Island
JOSEPH F. GUFFEY, Pennsylvania
ROBERT J. BULKLEY, Ohio
PRENTISS M. BROWN, Michigan
CLYDE L. HERRING, Iowa
ROBERT M. LA FOLLETTE, Jr., Wisconsin
ARTHUR CAPPER, Kansas
ARTHUR H. VANDENBERG, Michigan
JOHN G. TOWNSEND, Jr., Delaware
JAMES J. DAVIS, Pennsylvania

FELTON M. JOHNSTON, Clerk

SUBCOMMITTEE ON H. R. 6906

PRENTISS M. BROWN, Michigan, Chairman

CLYDE L. HERRING, Iowa
JAMES J. DAVIS, Pennsylvania

CONTENTS

TAXATION OF MARIHUANA

MONDAY, JULY 12, 1937

UNITED STATES SENATE,
SUBCOMMITTEE OF THE COMMITTEE ON FINANCE,
Washington, D. C.

The subcommittee met, pursuant to call, at 10 a. m., in the Senate Finance Committee room, Senate Office Building, Senator Prentiss M. Brown presiding.

Present: Senators Brown (chairman), Herring, and Davis.

(The subcommittee had under consideration H. R. 6906, which is as follows:)

[H. R. 6906, 75th Cong. 1st sess.]

AN ACT To impose an occupational excise tax upon certain dealers in marihuana, to impose a transfer tax upon certain dealings in marihuana, and to safeguard the revenue therefrom by registry and recording

Be it enacted by the Senate and House of Representatives of the United States of America in Congress assembled, That when used in this Act—

(a) The term "person" means an individual, a partnership, trust, association, company, or corporation and includes an officer or employee of a trust, association, company, or corporation, or a member or employee of a partnership, who as such officer, employee, or member, is under a duty to perform any act in respect of which any violation of this Act occurs.

(b) The term "marihuana" means all parts of the plant Cannabis sativa L., whether growing or not; the seeds thereof; the resin extracted from any part of such plant; and every compound, manufacture, salt, derivative, mixture, or preparation of such plant, its seeds, or resin; but shall not include the mature stalks of such plant, oil or cake made from the seeds of such plant, any compound, manufacture, salt, derivative, mixture, or preparation of such mature stalks (except the resin extracted therefrom), oil, or cake, or the sterilized seed of such plant which is incapable of germination.

(c) The term "producer" means any person who (1) plants, cultivates, or in any way facilitates the natural growth of marihuana; or (2) harvests and transfers or makes use of marihuana.

(d) The term "Secretary" means the Secretary of the Treasury and the term "collector" means collector of internal revenue.

(e) The term "transfer" or "transferred" means any type of disposition resulting in a change of possession but shall not include a transfer to a common carrier for the purpose of transporting marihuana.

SEC. 2. (a) Every person who imports, manufactures, produces, compounds, sells, deals in, dispenses, prescribes, administers, or gives away marihuana shall (1) within fifteen days after the effective date of this Act, or (2) before engaging after the expiration of such fifteen-day period in any of the above-mentioned activities, and (3) thereafter, on or before July 1 of each year, pay the following special taxes respectively:

(1) Importers, manufacturers, and compounders of marihuana, $21 per year.

(2) Producers of marihuana (except those included within subdivision (1) of this subsection), $5 per year.

(3) Physicians, dentists, veterinary surgeons, and other practitioners who distribute, dispense, give away, administer, or prescribe marihuana to patients upon whom they in the course of their professional practice are in attendance, $1 per year or fraction thereof during which they engage in any of such activities.

(4) Any person not registered as an importer, manufacturer, producer, or compounder who obtains and uses marihuana in a laboratory for the purpose of re-

BLOW UP OR GET OUT YOUR MAGNIFYING GLASS...

search, instruction, or analysis, or who produces marihuana for any such purpose, $1 per year, or fraction thereof, during which he engages in such activities.

(5) Any person who is not a physician, dentist, veterinary surgeon, or other practitioner and who deals in, dispenses, or gives away marihuana, $3 per year: *Provided,* That any person who has registered and paid the special tax as an importer, manufacturer, compounder, or producer, as required by subdivisions (1) and (2) of this subsection, may deal in, dispense, or give away marihuana imported, manufactured, compounded, or produced by him without further payment of the tax imposed by this section.

(b) Where a tax under subdivision (1), (2), or (5) is payable on July 1 of any year it shall be computed for one year; where any such tax is payable on any other day it shall be computed proportionately from the first day of the month in which the liability for the tax accrued to the following July 1.

(c) In the event that any person subject to a tax imposed by this section engages in any of the activities enumerated in subsection (a) of this section at more than one place, such person shall pay the tax with respect to each such place.

(d) Except as otherwise provided, whenever more than one of the activities enumerated in subsection (a) of this section is carried on by the same person at the same time, such person shall pay the tax for each such activity, according to the respective rates prescribed.

(e) Any person subject to the tax imposed by this section shall, upon payment of such tax, register his name or style and his place or places of business with the collector of the district in which such place or places of business are located.

(f) Collectors are authorized to furnish, upon written request, to any person a certified copy of the names of any or all persons who may be listed in their respective collection districts as special taxpayers under this section, upon payment of a fee of $1 for each one hundred of such names or fraction thereof upon such copy so requested.

SEC. 3. (a) No employee of any person who has paid the special tax and registered, as required by section 2 of this Act, acting within the scope of his employment, shall be required to register and pay such special tax.

(b) An officer or employee of the United States, any State, Territory, the District of Columbia, or insular possession, or political subdivision, who, in the exercise of his official duties, engages in any of the activities enumerated in section 2 of this Act shall not be required to register or pay the special tax, but his right to this exemption shall be evidenced in such manner as the Secretary may by regulations prescribe.

SEC. 4. (a) It shall be unlawful for any person required to register and pay the special tax under the provisions of section 2 to import, manufacture, produce, compound, sell, deal in, dispense, distribute, prescribe, administer, or give away marihuana without having so registered and paid such tax.

(b) In any suit or proceeding to enforce the liability imposed by this section or section 2, if proof is made that marihuana was at any time growing upon land under the control of the defendant, such proof shall be presumptive evidence that at such time the defendant was a producer and liable under this section as well as under section 2.

SEC. 5. It shall be unlawful for any person who shall not have paid the special tax and registered, as required by section 2, to send, ship, carry, transport, or deliver any marihuana within any Territory, the District of Columbia, any insular possession, or the Canal Zone, or from any State, Territory, the District of Columbia, any insular possession of the United States, or the Canal Zone, into any other State, Territory, the District of Columbia, insular possession of the United States, or the Canal Zone: *Provided,* That nothing contained in this section shall apply to any common carrier engaged in transporting marihuana; or to any employee of any person who shall have registered and paid the special tax as required by section 2 while acting within the scope of his employment; or to any person who shall deliver marihuana which has been prescribed or dispensed by a physician, dentist, veterinary surgeon, or other practitioner registered under section 2, who has been employed to prescribe for the particular patient receiving such marihuana; or to any United States, State, county, municipal, District, Territorial, or insular officer or official acting within the scope of his official duties.

SEC. 6. (a) It shall be unlawful for any person, whether or not required to pay a special tax and register under section 2, to transfer marihuana, except in pursuance of a written order of the person to whom such marihuana is transferred, on a form to be issued in blank for that purpose by the Secretary.

(b) Subject to such regulations as the Secretary may prescribe, nothing contained in this section shall apply—

(1) To a transfer of marihuana to a patient by a physician, dentist, veterinary surgeon, or other practitioner registered under section 2, in the course of his professional practice only: *Provided,* That such physician, dentist, veterinary surgeon, or other practitioner shall keep a record of all such marihuana transferred, showing the amount transferred and the name and address of the patient to whom such marihuana is transferred, and such record shall be kept for a period of two years from the date of the transfer of such marihuana, and subject to inspection as provided in section 11.

(2) To a transfer of marihuana, made in good faith by a dealer to a consumer under and in pursuance of a written prescription issued by a physician, dentist, veterinary surgeon, or other practitioner registered under section 2: *Provided,* That such prescription shall be dated as of the day on which signed and shall be signed by the physician, dentist, veterinary surgeon, or other practitioner who issues the same: *Provided further,* That such dealer shall preserve such prescription for a period of two years from the day on which such prescription is filled so as to be readily accessible for inspection by the officers, agents, employees, and officials mentioned in section 11.

(3) To the sale, exportation, shipment, or delivery of marihuana by any person within the United States, any Territory, the District of Columbia, any of the insular possessions of the United States or the Canal Zone, to any person in any foreign country regulating the entry of marihuana, if such sale, shipment, or delivery of marihuana is made in accordance with such regulations for importation into such foreign country as are prescribed by such foreign country, such regulations to be promulgated from time to time by the Secretary of State of the United States.

(4) To a transfer of marihuana to any officer or employee of the United States Government or of any State, Territorial, District, county, or municipal or insular government lawfully engaged in making purchases thereof for the various departments of the Army and Navy, the Public Health Service, and for Government, State, Territorial, District, county, or municipal or insular hospitals or prisons.

(5) To a transfer of any seeds of the plant Cannabis sativa L. to a person, registered as a producer under section 2, for use by such person for the further production of such plant, or to a person, registered under section 2 as a manufacturer, importer, or compounder, for use by such person for the manufacture of birdseed or for the manufacture of seed oil, seed cake, or any compound, manufacture, salt, derivative, mixture, or preparation of such oil or cake.

(c) The Secretary shall cause suitable forms to be prepared for the purposes before mentioned and shall cause them to be distributed to collectors for sale. The price at which such forms shall be sold by said collectors shall be fixed by the Secretary, but shall not exceed 2 cents each. Whenever any collector shall sell any of such forms he shall cause the date of sale, the name and address of the proposed vendor, the name and address of the purchaser, and the amount of marihuana ordered to be plainly written or stamped thereon before delivering the same.

(d) Each such order form sold by a collector shall be prepared by him and shall include an original and two copies, any one of which shall be admissible in evidence as an original. The original and one copy shall be given by the collector to the purchaser thereof. The original shall in turn be given by the purchaser thereof to any person who shall, in pursuance thereof, transfer marihuana to him and shall be preserved by such person for a period of two years so as to be readily accessible for inspection by any officer, agent, or employee mentioned in section 11. The copy given to the purchaser by the collector shall be retained by the purchaser and preserved for a period of two years so as to be readily accessible to inspection by any officer, agent, or employee mentioned in section 11. The second copy shall be preserved in the records of the collector.

SEC. 7. (a) There shall be levied, collected, and paid upon all transfers of marihuana which are required by section 6 to be carried out in pursuance of written order forms taxes at the following rates:

(1) Upon each transfer to any person who has paid the special tax and registered under section 2 of this Act, $1 per ounce of marihuana or fraction thereof.

(2) Upon each transfer to any person who has not paid the special tax and registered under section 2 of this Act, $100 per ounce of marihuana or fraction thereof.

(b) Such tax shall be paid by the transferee at the time of securing each order form and shall be in addition to the price of such form. Such transferee shall be liable for the tax imposed by this section but in the event that the transfer is made in violation of section 6 without an order form and without payment of the transfer tax imposed by this section, the transferor shall also be liable for such tax.

(c) Payment of the tax herein provided shall be represented by appropriate stamps to be provided by the Secretary and said stamps shall be affixed by the collector or his representative to the original order form.

(d) All provisions of law relating to the engraving, issuance, sale, accountability, cancelation, and destruction of tax-paid stamps provided for in the internal-revenue laws shall, insofar as applicable and not inconsistent with this Act be extended and made to apply to stamps provided for in this section.

(e) All provisions of law (including penalties) applicable in respect of the taxes imposed by the Act of December 17, 1914 (38 Stat. 785; U. S. C., 1934 ed., title 26, secs. 1040–1061, 1383–1391), as amended, shall, insofar as not inconsistent with this Act, be applicable in respect of the taxes imposed by this Act.

SEC. 8. (a) It shall be unlawful for any person who is a transferee required to pay the transfer tax imposed by section 7 to acquire or otherwise obtain any marihuana without having paid such tax; and proof that any person shall have had in his possession any marihuana and shall have failed, after reasonable notice and demand by the collector, to produce the order form required by section 6 to be retained by him, shall be presumptive evidence of guilt under this section and of liability for the tax imposed by section 7.

(b) No liability shall be imposed by virtue of this section upon any duly authorized officer of the Treasury Department engaged in the enforcement of this Act or upon any duly authorized officer of any State, or Territory, or of any political subdivision thereof, or the District of Columbia, or of any insular possession of the United States, who shall be engaged in the enforcement of any law or municipal ordinance dealing with the production, sale, prescribing, dispensing, dealing in, or distributing of marihuana.

SEC. 9. (a) Any marihuana which has been imported, manufactured, compounded, transferred, or produced in violation of any of the provisions of this Act shall be subject to seizure and forfeiture and, except as inconsistent with the provisions of this Act, all the provisions of internal-revenue laws relating to searches, seizures, and forfeitures are extended to include marihuana.

(b) Any marihuana which may be seized by the United States Government from any person or persons charged with any violation of this Act shall upon conviction of the person or persons from whom seized be confiscated by and forfeited to the United States.

(c) Any marihuana seized or coming into the possession of the United States in the enforcement of this Act, the owner or owners of which are unknown, shall be confiscated by and forfeited to the United States.

(d) The Secretary is hereby directed to destroy any marihuana confiscated by and forfeited to the United States under this section or to deliver such marihuana to any department, bureau, or other agency of the United States Government, upon proper application therefor under such regulations as may be prescribed by the Secretary.

SEC. 10. (a) Every person liable to any tax imposed by this Act shall keep such books and records, render under oath such statements, make such returns, and comply with such rules and regulations as the Secretary may from time to time prescribe.

(b) Any person who shall be registered under the provisions of section 2 in any internal-revenue district shall, whenever required so to do by the collector of the district, render to the collector a true and correct statement or return, verified by affidavits, setting forth the quantity of marihuana received or harvested by him during such period immediately preceding the demand of the collector, not exceeding three months, as the said collector may fix and determine. If such person is not solely a producer, he shall set forth in such statement or return the names of the persons from whom said marihuana was received, the quantity in each instance received from such persons, and the date when received.

SEC. 11. The order forms and copies thereof and the prescriptions and records required to be preserved under the provisions of section 6, and the statements or returns filed in the office of the collector of the district under the provisions of section 10 (b) shall be open to inspection by officers, agents, and employees of the Treasury Department duly authorized for that purpose, and such officers of any State, or Territory, or of any political subdivision thereof, or the District of Columbia, or of any insular possession of the United States as shall be charged with the enforcement of any law or municipal ordinance regulating the production, sale, prescribing, dispensing, dealing in, or distributing of marihuana. Each collector shall be authorized to furnish, upon written request, copies of any of the said statement or returns filed in his office to any of such officials of any State or Territory, or political subdivision thereof, or the District of Columbia, or any insular possession of the United States as shall be entitled to inspect the said statements or returns filed in the office of the said collector, upon the payment of a fee of $1 for each 100 words or fraction thereof in the copy or copies so requested.

SEC. 12. Any person who is convicted of a violation of any provision of this Act shall be fined not more than $2,000 or imprisoned not more than five years, or both, in the discretion of the court.

SEC. 13. It shall not be necessary to negative any exemptions set forth in this Act in any complaint, information, indictment, or other writ or proceeding laid or brought under this Act and the burden of proof of any such exemption shall be upon the defendant. In the absence of the production of evidence by the defendant that he has complied with the provisions of section 2 relating to registration or that he has complied with the provisions of section 6 relating to order forms, he shall be presumed not to have complied with such provisions of such sections, as the case may be.

SEC. 14. The Secretary is authorized to make, prescribe, and publish all necessary rules and regulations for carrying out the provisions of this Act and to confer or impose any of the rights, privileges, powers, and duties conferred or imposed upon him by this Act upon such officers or employees of the Treasury Department as he shall designate or appoint.

SEC. 15. The provisions of this Act shall apply to the several States, the District of Columbia, the Territory of Alaska, the Territory of Hawaii, the Canal Zone, and the insular possessions of the United States, except the Philippine Islands. In Puerto Rico the administration of this Act, the collection of the special taxes and transfer taxes, and the issuance of the order forms provided for in section 6 shall be performed by the appropriate internal-revenue officers of that government, and all revenues collected under this Act in Puerto Rico shall accrue intact to the general government thereof. The President is hereby authorized and directed to issue such Executive orders as will carry into effect in the Canal Zone and the Virgin Islands the intent and purpose of this Act by providing for the registration with appropriate officers and the imposition of the special and transfer taxes upon all persons in the Canal Zone and the Virgin Islands who import, manufacture, produce, compound, sell, deal in, dispense, prescribe, administer, or give away marihuana.

SEC. 16. If any provision of this Act or the application thereof to any person or circumstances is held invalid, the remainder of the Act and the application of such provision to other persons or circumstances shall not be affected thereby.

SEC. 17. This Act shall take effect on the first day of the second month after the month during which it is enacted.

SEC. 18. This Act may be cited as the "Marihuana Tax Act of 1937."

Passed the House of Representatives June 14, 1937.

Attest:

SOUTH TRIMBLE, *Clerk.*

Senator BROWN. The committee will be in order. The hearing is on H. R. 6906. We will first hear from Mr. Hester, the Assistant General Counsel of the Treasury Department.

STATEMENT OF CLINTON M. HESTER, ASSISTANT GENERAL COUNSEL, TREASURY DEPARTMENT

Mr. HESTER. The purpose, Mr. Chairman, of H. R. 6906 is to employ the Federal taxing power to raise revenue by imposing occupational and transfer taxes upon dealings in marihuana and to discourage the widespread use of the drug by smokers and drug addicts.

The flowering tops, leaves, and seeds of the hemp plant contain a dangerous drug known as marihuana. The drug is used only to a negligible extent by the medical profession. In fact, last year only 4 out of every 10,000 prescriptions contained marihuana. The drug is prescribed as a sedative, but it is used very rarely by the medical profession because the effect of the drug is so variable that a physician cannot tell how his patient will react to the drug and because there are so many better substitutes.

The plant also has many industrial uses. From the mature stalk fiber is produced which in turn is manufactured into twine, and other

2785—37——2

fiber products. From the seeds, oil is extracted which is used in the manufacture of such products as paint, varnish, linoleum, and soap. From hempseed cake, the residue of the seed after the oil has been extracted, cattle feed and fertilizer are manufactured. In addition the seed is used as special feed for pigeons.

Marihuana is also used illicitly by smoking it in crudely prepared cigarettes, which are readily procurable in almost all parts of the country at prices ranging from 10 to 25 cents each. Under the influence of this drug the will is destroyed and all power of directing and controlling thought is lost.

Senator DAVIS. Do you mean that the cigarettes cost 25 cents each?

Mr. HESTER. They are manufactured illicitly, and that is the price that the peddlers generally get for them.

Senator DAVIS. That is per cigarette, and not per package?

Mr. HESTER. That is per cigarette.

Senator DAVIS. For one cigarette?

Mr. HESTER. That is right.

Inhibitions are released. As a result of these effects, many violent crimes have been and are being committed by persons under the influence of this drug. Not only is marihuana used by hardened criminals to steel them to commit violent crimes, but it is also being placed in the hands of high-school children in the form of marihuana cigarettes by unscrupulous peddlers. Its continued use results many times in impotency and insanity.

Two objectives have dictated the form of H. R. 6906, first, the development of a plan of taxation which will raise revenue and at the same time render extremely difficult the acquisition of marihuana by persons who desire it for illicit uses, and second, the development of an adequate means of publicizing dealings in marihuana in order to tax and control the traffic effectively.

This bill is modeled upon both the Harrison Narcotic Act and the National Firearms Act, which were designed to accomplish these same general objectives with respect to opium and coca leaves, and firearms, respectively.

Under the provisions of this bill all legitimate handlers of marihuana are required to pay occupational taxes as follows: Manufacturers, compounders, and importers, $24 per year; producers, $5 per year; dealers, $3 per year; practitioners (doctors, dentists, veterinaries, and other of like character), and persons who use marihuana for experimental purposes, $1 per year. These persons, in addition to paying the occupational tax, must register with the collector of internal revenue and file information returns as to their dealings in marihuana.

However, as an additional means of bringing the traffic in marihuana into the open, the bill requires all transfers of marihuana to be made in pursuance of official order forms issued by the Secretary of the Treasury, upon which the details of the transaction are set forth. In order to raise additional revenue and to prevent transfers to persons who would use marihuana for undesirable purposes, a transfer tax is imposed upon each transfer of marihuana. Upon transfers to registered persons, this tax is $1 per ounce, while, upon transfers to nonregistered person, who under ordinary circumstances will be the illicit users of marihuana, a heavy tax of $100 per ounce is imposed. Heavy criminal penalties are provided for manufacturing, producing, or dealing in marihuana without registering and paying the special taxes, for transferring marihuana not in pursuance of an order form, and for acquiring marihuana without payment of the transfer tax.

Thus, the bill is designed, through the occupational tax and the order form procedure, to publicize legitimate dealings in marihuana and through the $100 transfer tax to prevent the drug from coming into the hands of those who will put it to illicit uses.

The production and sale of hemp and its products for industrial purposes will not be adversely affected by this bill. In general, the term "marihuana" is defined in the bill so as to include only the flowering tops, leaves, and seeds of the hemp plant and to exclude the mature stalk, oil, and meal obtained from the seeds of the plant, and sterilized seed, incapable of germination.

Under this definition of "marihuana" the hemp producer will pay a small occupational tax but his fiber products will be entirely exempt from the provisions of the bill, including the order form and transfer tax provisions.

Senator BROWN. That means the farmer will pay $5?

Mr. HESTER. That is right.

Senator BROWN. That is all he will have to pay?

Mr. HESTER. That is all he will have to pay.

Senator BROWN. And it makes no difference how extensive his acreage is?

Mr. HESTER. No; $5 is the limit.

Senator BROWN. It is $5 whether he cultivates an acre or 10 acres?

Mr. HESTER. That is right.

The same is true of seed produced by the hemp grower for sale for the further production of the plant, for the manufacture of oil or for birdseed, except that such transfers will be made subject to regulations designed to prevent diversion of the seed for illegal uses.

Similarly, the manufacturers of oil and the byproducts of seed, such as hemp seed cake and meal, will pay an occupational tax, but their purchases of seed and sales of such oil, cake, and meal will be entirely exempt from the provisions of the bill except that purchases of such seed will be subject to regulations designed to prevent diversion.

Manufacturers of birdseed will also pay an occupational tax, but their purchases of seed will be exempt from the transfer tax and order form provisions of the bill, if carried out in accordance with regulations. Further, under the definition of marihuana, the bill will not apply to their sales of birdseed, if the hemp seed contained therein is sterilized so as to be incapable of germination.

I might say at this point that this provision with respect to the birdseed was worked out with the birdseed people, and those who appeared before the Ways and Means Committee approved that provision.

Now, this is an important provision, this particular provision right here that we are discussing.

Notwithstanding, as already shown, that under the bill the producers of hemp will only pay a small occupational tax and make their purchases and sales of seed subject to regulations, some suggestion has been made that the producers be entirely eliminated from the bill. Such an exemption, however, is believed to be impossible.

The imposition of an occupational tax enables the Government constitutionally to make it illegal to engage in the occupation without payment of the tax. Thus, unless the Congress in this bill imposes an occupational tax upon the producers of hemp, Congress cannot make the production of hemp for illicit purposes illegal. Hence, if the occupational tax is not imposed upon producers, marihuana may be legally produced for illicit purposes. Furthermore, the imposition of an occupational tax enables the Government to require the taxpayer to furnish information in connection with the business taxed. This would permit the Government to ascertain where the legitimate production of hemp is being carried on, and, having this information, it can stamp out the illicit production more effectively. Obviously, therefore, the legitimate producers of hemp cannot be further exempted from the provisions of the bill. Otherwise, the bill cannot be enforced.

Aside from the reasons stated as to why it is believed to be impossible to further exempt the producers of hemp from the provisions of the bill, attention is invited to the fact that the primary purpose of this legislation is to raise revenue.

That completes my statement, and we have witnesses present.

Senator DAVIS. Do I understand you to say that the primary purpose of the bill is to raise revenue?

Mr. HESTER. The primary purpose of this legislation must be to raise revenue, because we are resorting to the taxing clause of the Constitution and the rule is that if on the face of the bill it appears to be a revenue bill, the courts will not inquire into any other motives that the Congress may have had in enacting this legislation.

This bill is modeled on the Harrison Narcotics Act and the National Firearms Act. The Harrison Narcotics Act has been sustained by the Supreme Court, the first time by a 5-to-4 decision, and a second time by a 6-to-3 decision. The Supreme Court in March of this year sustained the constitutionality of the National Firearms Act, insofar as it related to the occupational tax.

Senator DAVIS. The Harrison Narcotics Act you say was before the Supreme Court twice. Was there a change in the judges between the time of the first decision and the time of the second decision?

Mr. HESTER. I do not know whether there was a new judge placed upon the bench at that time or not, but the vote was 6 to 3 the second time. That was some years later.

Senator DAVIS. What was the date of the 6-to-3 decision?

Mr. HESTER. 1927.

Senator DAVIS. Justice Stone went on the Court at that time?

Mr. HESTER. He went on the Court in the Coolidge administration.

Senator DAVIS. That is right.

Mr. HESTER. Yes; he was on.

Senator DAVIS. When was the first decision?

Mr. HESTER. The first decision was about 1918. I think it was about that time.

Senator BROWN. Mr. Hester, will you give us a summary of the history of State legislation respecting marihuana?

Mr. HESTER. Every State in the Union has legislation regulating the traffic in marihuana.

Senator BROWN. Is there fairly uniform law on the subject among the States?

Mr. HESTER. Yes; it is fairly uniform. In some States they prohibit entirely all production of marihuana. I think there are six States that prohibit the production of marihuana, and it probably could be constitutionally done by the Congress.

Senator BROWN. That is, there could be a prohibition?

Mr. HESTER. That is right. But you would have to prohibit it entirely, and of course you would put all of these legitimate industries out of business. The Supreme Court has held that where on the face of act it appears to be a taxing measure, the fact that it happens to be prohibitive in character will not affect the constitutionality of it. But we have tried throughout this measure not to interfere materially with the production of marihuana, but to permit it, and to do it in a manner which will enable the Government to stamp out this illicit traffic in the sale of it.

Senator BROWN. Say you are in this situation: You have a plant that produces several articles that are valuable commercially.

Mr. HESTER. That is right.

Senator BROWN. At the same time, as a byproduct the leaves and the seeds can be used for marihuana?

Mr. HESTER. That is right.

Senator BROWN. That is the deleterious part of it.

Mr. HESTER. That is correct.

Senator BROWN. As Senator Davis suggests, I think it would be valuable if you would summarize the state legislation, first informing us as to what the fairly uniform general legislation is upon the subject, and then giving us the names of the States that have prohibited the use of marihuana.

Mr. HESTER. May we prepare a memorandum for inclusion in the record on that because we really do not have that at the moment?

Senator BROWN. Yes.

(Mr. Hester later prepared and submitted for the record the following memorandum summarizing legislation upon the subject of marihuana among the States:)

State laws relating to marihuana

Controls (or licenses) production	Controls possession	Controls sale
Alabama.[1]	Alabama.	Alabama.
Arizona.[1]	Arizona.	Arizona.
Arkansas.[1]	Arkansas.	Arkansas.
	California.	California.
Colorado.[1]	Colorado.	Colorado.
Connecticut.[1]	Connecticut.	Connecticut.
Delaware.[1]	Delaware.	Delaware.
Florida.[1]	Florida.	Florida.
Georgia.[1]	Georgia.	Georgia.
Idaho.[1]	Idaho.	Idaho.
Illinois.[1]	Illinois.	Illinois.
Indiana.[1]	Indiana.	Indiana.
Iowa.[1]	Iowa.	Iowa.
Kansas.[2]	Kansas.	Kansas.
	Kentucky.	Kentucky.
Louisiana.[1]	Louisiana.	Louisiana.
		Maine.
Maryland.[1]	Maryland.	Maryland.
Massachusetts.	Massachusetts.	Massachusetts.
Michigan.	Michigan.	Michigan.
Minnesota.	Minnesota.	Minnesota.
Mississippi.[1]	Mississippi.	Mississippi.
Missouri.[1]	Missouri.	Missouri.
Montana.[1]	Montana.	Montana.
Nebraska.[2]	Nebraska.	Nebraska.
Nevada.[1]	Nevada.	Nevada.
		New Hampshire.
New Jersey.[1]	New Jersey.	New Jersey.
New Mexico.[1]	New Mexico.	New Mexico.
New York.[1]	New York.	New York.
North Carolina.[1]	North Carolina.	North Carolina.
	North Dakota.	North Dakota.

[1] Denotes States which control marihuana under the uniform narcotic drug law.
[2] Denotes State which prohibit cultivation of marihuana.

State laws relating to marihuana—Continued

Controls (or licenses) production	Controls possession	Controls sale
Ohio.[1]	Ohio.	Ohio.
Oklahoma.[1]	Oklahoma.	Oklahoma.
Oregon.[1]	Oregon.	Oregon.
	Pennsylvania.	Pennsylvania.
Rhode Island.[1]	Rhode Island.	Rhode Island.
South Carolina.[1]	South Carolina.	South Carolina.
South Dakota.[1]	South Dakota.	South Dakota.
	Tennessee.	Tennessee.
Texas.[1]	Texas.	Texas.
Utah.[1]	Utah.	Utah.
		Vermont.
Virginia.[1]	Virginia.	Virginia.
	Washington.	Washington.
		West Virginia.
Wisconsin.[1]	Wisconsin.	Wisconsin.
Wyoming.[1]	Wyoming.	Wyoming.

[1] Denotes States which control marihuana under the uniform narcotic drug law.
[2] Denotes State which prohibit cultivation of marihuana.

Mr. HESTER. We have with us this morning Commissioner Anslinger, of the Bureau of Narcotics, who is in charge of the enforcement of the Harrison Narcotics Act, and who will have charge of the enforcement of this act if this legislation should be enacted into law. He is prepared to testify on the necessity of the legislation and the practical situation.

Senator BROWN. All right. Thank you, Mr. Hester. We will hear Mr. Anslinger.

STATEMENT OF H. J. ANSLINGER, COMMISSIONER OF NARCOTICS, BUREAU OF NARCOTICS OF THE TREASURY DEPARTMENT

Mr. ANSLINGER. Mr. Chairman and distinguished members of the committee, we are having a great deal of difficulty. Last year there were some 338 seizures of marihuana in some 31 States involving several hundred tons of growing plants, bulk marihuana and cigarettes.

The States are asking for help. We are trying to give it to them, but we are rather limited in our ability at the present time.

I have made a statement before the Ways and Means Committee, which is in the record, but since that time I want to point out to the committee an incident which occurred on June 28 at Abingdon, Va. There was a marihuana farm at that point, and the man who was growing those plants had been connected with a family that was engaged in smuggling narcotic drugs into Atlanta Penitentiary some years ago. When we heard Dewey Doss was engaged in the production of marihuana, we went after him, and we got the State officers to make a case against him. We could not do anything about that, although the information came to us first.

A month or so ago, down in Texas, a man was arrested on a Missouri Pacific train going north with a quantity of cannabis, and another man was arrested in the vicinity of this place, called Raymondsville, Tex., They both had stripped the plants on a hemp farm.

Senator BROWN. You mean they had taken the leaves off?

Mr. ANSLINGER. They had taken the leaves off and the flowering tops.

I received this letter from an attorney at Houston, Tex., just the other day. That case involves a murder in which he alleges that his client, a boy 19 years old, had been addicted to the use of marihuana.

Senator Brown. Shall we have this read into the record?

Mr. Anslinger. Yes, sir; I shall be very glad if you will.

(The letter is as follows:)

Houston, Tex., July 7, 1937.

H. J. Anslinger,
United States Commissioner of Narcotics,
Washington, D. C.

Dear Sir: Your article on Marihuana appearing in the July issue of the American is very useful as well as interesting.

This subject strikes close to home because of a client I have who not so long ago murdered in a brutal way a man who had befriended him in giving him a ride. This client is a boy 20 years of age and he explained to me he had been smoking marihuana for several years. I would like to have about 15 copies of your article, and will gladly pay any necessary charges. I would appreciate an early reply.

Yours truly,
Sidney Benbow.

Mr. Anslinger. I have another letter from a prosecutor at a place in New Jersey.

It is as follows:

The Interstate Commission on Crime,
Charles Schwarz,
Washington, D. C. March 18, 1937.

My Dear Mr. Schwarz: That I fully appreciate the need for action, you may judge from the fact that last January I tried a murder case for several days, of a particularly brutal character in which one colored young man killed another, literally smashing his face and head to a pulp, as the enclosed photograph demonstrates. One of the defences was that the defendant's intellect was so prostrated from his smoking marihuana cigarettes that he did not know what he was doing. The defendant was found guilty and sentenced to a long term of years. I am convinced that marihuana had been indulged in, in that the smoking had recurred, and the brutality of the murder was accounted for by the narcotic, though the defendant's intellect had not been totally prostrate, so the verdict was legally correct. It seems to me that this instance might be of value to you in your campaign.

Sincerely yours,
Ricard Hartshorne.

Mr. Hartshorne is a member of the Interstate Commission on Crime.

We have many cases of this kind.

Senator Brown. It affects them that way?

Mr. Anslinger. Yes.

Senator Davis (viewing a photograph presented by Mr. Anslinger). Was there in this case a blood or skin disease caused by marihuana?

Mr. Anslinger. No; this is a photograph of the murdered man, Senator. It shows the fury of the murderer.

Senator Brown. That is terrible.

Mr. Anslinger. That is one of the worst cases that has come to my attention, and it is to show you its relation to crime that I am putting those two letters in the record.

Senator Brown. The first letter is also very interesting.

Mr. Anslinger. This first letter was from an attorney at Houston.

In June of this year, at Geneva, an international committee of experts in going over the reports received from all over the world said that the reports thus far indicate that the medical value of the cannabis

---

12   TAXATION OF MARIHUANA

derivatives is very doubtful. There is another report here from Dr. Paul Nicholas Leech:—

Senator Brown. That is, to make it perfectly clear, its medical value is not very great, and there are many other drugs that may be used in place of it that are fully as good if not better?

Mr. Anslinger. Yes, sir; it is not indispensable.

Senator Brown. I think some medical men say that if we had no such drug at all the medical profession would not be very greatly handicapped. That is, medical science would not be very greatly handicapped.

Mr. Anslinger. I think they are pretty generally in agreement that its use could be abandoned without any suffering.

I have a few cases here that I would just like to tell the committee about. In Alamosa, Colo., they seem to be having a lot of difficulty. The citizens petitioned Congress for help, in addition to the help that is given them under the State law. In Kansas and New Mexico also we have had a great deal of trouble.

Here is a typical illustration: A 15-year-old boy, found mentally deranged from smoking marihuana cigarettes, furnished enough information to the police officers to lead to the seizure of 15 pounds of marihuana. That was seized in a garage in an Ohio town. These boys had been getting marihuana at a playground, and the supervisors there had been peddling it to children, but they got rather alarmed when they saw these boys developing the habit, and particularly when this boy began to go insane.

In Florida some years ago we had the case of a 20-year-old boy who killed his brothers, a sister, and his parents while under the influence of marihuana.

Recently, in Ohio, there was a gang of very young men, all under 20 years of age, every one of whom confessed that they had committed some 38 holdups while under the influence of the drug.

In another place in Ohio a young man shot the hotel clerk while trying to hold him up. His defense was that he was under the influence of marihuana.

Senator Brown. When a person smokes the cigarette, how long does the influence of the drug continue?

Mr. Anslinger. From reports coming to me, I think it might last as long as 48 hours before the effects of the drug fully wear off.

Senator Brown. I do not know whether it was your article I read, or an article from some other source, but I understand that experiments have been conducted, in which the persons smoking the marihuana have been kept under control after taking the drug. Do you know whether or not that demonstrated how long the effect would be felt?

Mr. Anslinger. As I remember it, the effects in those cases were something like 48 hours, before they fully returned to their normal senses.

Here is a case in Baltimore, where a young man committed rape while under the influence of marihuana. He was hanged for it. Last fall, about September, we uncovered a field of several acres, growing right outside the city limits of Baltimore. Those men were selling it to New York; sending it all over the country, at $20 a pound.

Senator Davis. And how many pounds to the acre?

[TAXATION OF MARIHUANA]

Mr. Anslinger. That all would depend, Senator. If they just took the flowering tops the yield would not be so big, but some of them strip off the leaves and the flowering tops and grind them up.

Senator Davis. Do the leaves have the same effect as the flowering top?

Mr. Anslinger. Yes, sir; one of the Treasury's chemists is here, who can verify that, sir. It has been proved by experts in other countries, who have analyzed the leaves. They find that the resin is also present in the leaf. Our experiments have not shown the presence of any drug in the mature stalk, though. At one time we thought that the dangerous principle was only in the flowering top, but that is not true. What led us to the study as to whether there was resin in the leaves was the fact that we had seen so much of this stuff rolled up. In some cases only the leaves had been crushed, and they seemed to be giving the effect. In New Mexico officers sent us about 4 or 5 pounds of nothing but leaves, and some of that particular shipment had been the cause of the killing of a police officer, and also the killing of a man within the ring. Every day we have such seizures reported.

Senator Brown. Is the cigarette that is made from the flowering top more potent than the one made from the leaves?

Mr. Anslinger. Yes, sir; it would be, because the tops have the resin concentrated.

Senator Brown. Do I understand that the seed is ground up, too, and used to any extent?

Mr. Anslinger. Well, we have heard of them smoking the seed.

Senator Brown. Does it produce the same effect?

Mr. Anslinger. I am not qualified to say. We have not made any experiments as to that, but we do know that the seed has been smoked. I think that the proposition of the seed people sterilizing the seed by heat and moisture will certainly do a lot to kill this traffic. I think that that one thing might cut this traffic in half, because much of the trouble we encounter is due to the trafficker going to a feed store and buying the birdseed and planting cannabis, and also due to birdseed being scattered during the winter. Hempseed is thrown out in the garden or in the vacant lot. The following year you have a growth of cannabis. That is what happened in Baltimore, and particularly in Philadelphia. I know of a case there where the State officers got over 200,000 pounds of growing plants, as the result of dissemination by birdseeds. A lot of that growth was being used illicitly. The traffickers knew where to get it. The plant reseeded itself.

The action that will be taken under this bill by the birdseed people in sterilizing the seed should have a remarkable effect in killing this traffic.

Senator Brown. The sterilized seed will not reproduce?

Mr. Anslinger. It will re-seed itself.

Senator Brown. I am referring to the birdseed. What are they going to do to the birdseed?

Mr. Anslinger. They are going to kill the germinating power.

Senator Brown. When the seed is then thrown out, what will happen?

Mr. Anslinger. Nothing will happen.

Senator Davis. Will it be of any use as a birdseed?

Mr. Anslinger. Oh, yes. It will still have food properties.

2785—37——3

---

14   TAXATION OF MARIHUANA

Senator Brown. The birds will sing just the same?

Mr. Anslinger. There is some question about that. Sterilization is a voluntary action by the birdseed people.

Senator Brown. That is not in this bill?

Mr. Anslinger. It is not in there. They voluntarily agreed to do that under this act.

Mr. Hester. Yes, it is in the bill.

Senator Brown. I want to bring out one fact that you have not touched upon yet. As I understand it marihuana is not a habit-producing drug, at least to the same extent that opium is, for instance. It is somewhat easier to break the habit in the case of marihuana than it is in the case of opium smoking?

Mr. Anslinger. Yes, you have stated that correctly, Senator. It is a very difficult matter to break the opium habit. However, this habit can be broken. There is some evidence that it is habit-forming. The experts have not gone very far on that.

Senator Brown. There is the impression that it is stimulating to a certain extent? It is used by criminals when they want to go out and perform some deed that they would not commit in their ordinary frame of mind?

Mr. Anslinger. That was demonstrated by these seven boys, who said they did not know what they were doing after they smoked marihuana. They conceived the series of crimes while in a state of marihuana intoxication.

Senator Davis. How many cigarettes would you have to smoke before you got this vicious mental attitude toward your neighbor?

Mr. Anslinger. I believe in some cases one cigarette might develop a homicidal mania, probably to kill his brother. It depends on the physical characteristics of the individual. Every individual reacts differently to the drug. It stimulates some and others it depresses. It is impossible to say just what the action of the drug will be on a given individual, or the amount. Probably some people could smoke five before it would take effect, but all the experts agree that the continued use leads to insanity. There are many cases of insanity.

Senator Brown. Is it every type of hemp that contains this drug, or is it just some particular type?

Mr. Anslinger. There is only one species.

Senator Herring. There is only one species of hemp?

Mr. Anslinger. Yes, sir; there are different forms, but only one species.

Senator Brown. This thought has impressed me: I read with care the supplemental statement which you placed in the record before the Ways and Means Committee, in which you brought out quite clearly that the use, which will be "illicit" if we may describe it that way, in the event this bill becomes a law, has been known to the peoples of Europe and Mexico and the United States for centuries.

Mr. Anslinger. That is right.

Senator Brown. Do you think that the recent great increase in the use of it that has taken place in the United States is probably due to the heavy hand of the law, in its effect upon the use of other drugs, and that persons who desire a stimulant are turning to this because of enforcement of the Harrison Narcotics Act and the State laws?

Mr. Anslinger. We do not know of any cases where the opium user has transferred to marihuana. There is an entirely new class of

---

people using marihuana. The opium user is around 35 to 40 years old. These users are 20 years old, and know nothing of heroin or morphine.

Senator Brown. What has caused the new dissemination of it? We did not hear anything of it until the last year or so.

Mr. Anslinger. I do not think that the war against opium has very much bearing upon the situation. That same question has been discussed in other countries; in Egypt particularly, where a great deal of hashheesh is used, they tried to show that the marihuana user went to heroin, and when heroin got short he jumped back to hashheesh, but that is not true. This is an entirely different class.

I do not know just why the abuse of marihuana has spread like wildfire in the last 4 or 5 years.

Senator Brown. Could you give us any estimate of the number of persons that are engaged in this illicit traffic? Please state that as nearly as you can.

Mr. Anslinger. I can only give you what our records show, Senator. There were about 400 arrests throughout the States in the year.

Senator Brown. That is for violations of State law?

Mr. Anslinger. For violations of State law. That would not include the arrests in California, where I understand they have several hundred a year; but the figure I am giving you of 400 arrests would be about the average number that are being picked up now, under just a noncoordinated enforcement policy, every State doing its own work, and bringing us in occasionally. When they run into "dope" we go down and say, "It is marihuana and you take the case."

The State of Ohio recently seized what we call a "plant." It was a seizure of marihuana. These people had a mailing list of 6,000 customers scattered throughout the States.

Senator Davis. How were they dispensing it?

Mr. Anslinger. They were selling it in lots from a pound down, just selling it by mail.

Senator Brown. There was nothing in the law to prevent a man in Columbus, Ohio, using the mail in selling it to a person in Louisville, Kentucky?

Mr. Anslinger. No; they are doing it every day.

Senator Davis. Is there anything in the present bill to prevent them using the mail?

Mr. Anslinger. Under this bill it would have to be tax-paid, and all of that would be illicit, sir.

Senator Herring. You say there are several hundred arrests in California alone, and about that same number throughout the rest of the United States?

Mr. Anslinger. There are about that same number in the rest of the United States.

Senator Herring. How do you account for that? Is it because of their State law?

Mr. Anslinger. It is because they have a State enforcement agency there. They vigorously enforce the law. I might say that Pennsylvania is doing important work also.

Senator Herring. It might be just as prevalent in other States, but for the fact that we do not have the law enforced as efficiently?

---

16   TAXATION OF MARIHUANA

Mr. Anslinger. I would not say it is as prevalent, but certainly the use has increased in the last few years. In Pennsylvania the enforcement people are very active today, particularly at Pittsburgh and Philadelphia, and they are constantly calling upon us.

Senator Davis. Are they enforcing the Harrison Narcotics Act in a manner satisfactory to you?

Mr. Anslinger. Yes, sir; that is satisfactory, but they are asking us for help now and then when they run into a rather large situation.

Senator Brown. I think that while you are on that point you had better make clear the need for Federal legislation. You say the States have asked you to do that. I presume it is because of the freedom of interstate traffic that the States require this legislation?

Mr. Anslinger. We have had requests from States to step in because they claimed it was not growing in that State, but that it was coming in from another State.

Senator Brown. And they could not touch that?

Mr. Anslinger. And they could not touch it and we could not touch it.

There is need for coordinated effort. We are required to report to the League of Nations, under a treaty arrangement, all of the seizures of marihuana made throughout the United States. It is rather difficult to get, I would say, half of them. One particular reason and one primary reason for this is—usually these complaints come to us first—that there is "dope" being used in a certain place, and that there is a supply of it on a certain street. Our men go and investigate it, and they find it is marihuana. Well, we have to call in the State officers, and there is a lot of lost effort. Very often by the time the State officer comes the case is gone. I would say in most of these cases we get the information first and turn it over to the State officer. Now, we want to coordinate all of that work throughout the States. By State and Federal cooperation we can make a good dent in this traffic.

For instance, all States had narcotic laws before the enactment of the Harrison Narcotics Act, but until the Federal Government stepped in no substantial progress was made.

Senator Brown. What have you to say about the extent of the production of hemp? May it be produced in practically any State in the Union?

Mr. Anslinger. Yes, sir; it can be produced.

Senator Brown. There is climatically no reason why it could not be produced everywhere in the United States?

Mr. Anslinger. No.

Senator Brown. Growing as a weed, could take place anywhere?

Mr. Anslinger. Anywhere; yes, sir. That has been demonstrated.

Senator Davis. A moment ago I asked you what was the yield per acre, and you then told me so much of the flower and so much of the leaves. What is the combined yield per acre of both the flower and the leaves?

Mr. Anslinger. I would not be able to say, sir. That would be impossible.

Senator Davis. Is there any way of getting that information?

Mr. Anslinger. We are growing an experimental crop over here on the Agricultural Farm. We can find out that way, or we can take nt and strip the leaves and the flowers, and find out how many ts there were to the acre and multiply it. I think that would a reasonably accurate estimate. I think I can find that out.

nator DAVIS. I wish you would.

nator BROWN. Now, Commissioner Anslinger, I do not know her you are the best man to answer this question, or Mr. Hester. t dangers, if any, does this bill have for the persons engaged in egitimate uses of the hemp plant?

r. ANSLINGER. I would say they are not only amply protected er this act, but they can go ahead and raise hemp just as they have ys done it.

nator BROWN. It has been represented to me that the farmer at hesitate to grow hemp when he is not only subjected to a $5 out also to the supervision by the Government, or what you might the "nosing" of the Government into his business. What have to say as to that proposition?

r. ANSLINGER. Well, I would say the answer to that is the fact they are already controlled under State legislation.

nator BROWN. In practically every State in the Union.

Ir. ANSLINGER. Not all the States, but certainly in a lot of hemp-ving States they are controlled. In most of the States cultivation rohibited, but in some States they are regulated by license.

nator BROWN. Administratively, it seems you have charge of the inistration of the tax and the collection of the tax?

Ir. ANSLINGER. Yes, sir.

nator BROWN. Just what would happen? We will take a farmer g the other side of Alexandria, over in Virginia. Just what ld happen to him if he wanted to grow 2 acres of hemp? What ld he have to do?

Ir. ANSLINGER. He would go down to the collector of internal nue and put down his $5 and get a registration, a stamp tax. t would permit him to grow under the act, and at the end of the —

nator BROWN. That is a stamp tax similar to the one a doctor who uses a narcotic?

Ir. ANSLINGER. Yes, sir; the same kind of a tax.

enator BROWN. He would hang that up in his house?

Ir. ANSLINGER. Yes, sir. At the end of the year we would just him how much he grew.

enator BROWN. Would you not go down and look his field over, to ertain whether or not he was making any illicit use of the otherwise thless byproduct? As I understand it, there is no legislation ut the use of the petals or the flower or of these leaves.

Ir. ANSLINGER. So far very few of these hemp people have been olved. Well, they have not been involved in the illicit traffic at This case in Texas is the only case I know of. We were not ng to supervise his crop. It would not be possible.

enator BROWN. I do not mean that, but suppose that some fellow nes along and says, "I will give you $100 to let me go in and strip r leaves and top flowers from your hemp crop." How would you er that? How would you meet a situation of that kind?

Ir. ANSLINGER. Certainly under the act, if the farmer agreed to t, they would both be guilty of conspiracy to violate the act.

enator BROWN. But you would exercise no particular supervision r the growing of that crop?

Mr. ANSLINGER. The exercise would be in this way: If we see Mr. Dewey Doss, the photograph of whose place I showed you, go in and pay $5 to the collector, we would watch that. We would be very careful to see what disposition he made of that, but we would certainly know the sheep from the goats without any close general supervision.

Senator BROWN. I do not think you would have any trouble with legitimate manufacturers, because they are dealing with the Government; but the farmer himself might be a little disposed not to grow the hemp, knowing of the illicit use that might be made of a part of his crop.

Mr. ANSLINGER. It is just an information return. That is all we would be interested in, unless he would conspire with someone else to have the crop stripped. But one saving feature about this whole thing so far as the farmer is concerned is that the crop is cut before the resin reaches the nth state.

Senator BROWN. Before it reaches its greatest potency?

Mr. ANSLINGER. In other words, before it reaches its greatest potency. There is some resin that comes up through the plant, but if he is a legitimate hemp producer he will cut it down before the resin makes its appearance.

Senator BROWN. You had before the Ways and Means Committee two samples of the plant. Do you happen to have any of those samples here?

Mr. HESTER. We do not have them here this morning. We can get those samples for you.

Mr. ANSLINGER. The plant which I have in my hand now can be easily distinguished as you are going along the road.

Senator DAVIS. You can see that along all the highways of the country.

Mr. ANSLINGER. Well, Senator Davis, that will grow up 16 feet.

Senator DAVIS. How high?

Mr. ANSLINGER. Sixteen feet.

Senator DAVIS. Sixteen feet?

Mr. ANSLINGER. Sixteen feet. Of course, when they are small like that you cannot distinguish them.

Senator BROWN. At what height are they usually harvested?

Mr. ANSLINGER. About 14 or 16 feet.

Senator BROWN. At that height?

Mr. ANSLINGER. Not for hemp production. That is for resin.

Senator BROWN. I mean for hemp production.

Mr. ANSLINGER. Oh, for hemp production, I would say around 10, 12, 14 feet; but it is certainly before the resin gets up there to do the damage.

Senator BROWN. Are there any other questions that any member wants to ask Mr. Anslinger?

Mr. ANSLINGER. What is the return to the farmer per acre?

Mr. ANSLINGER. I do not know. The hemp people here could tell you what the return is, but I understand it is around $30.

Senator BROWN. Does it require intensive cultivation?

Mr. ANSLINGER. I do not think so.

Senator HERRING. It is a reed that will grow, is it not?

Mr. ANSLINGER. It will grow without any trouble. In fact, a lot of these illicit traffickers will try to hide their field with corn. They will grow corn all around it. Well, the hemp will shoot right up above the corn, and will grow 4 or 5 feet higher.

Mr. HESTER. Before we complete our case I think we ought to say one word on the regulations, if I may?

Senator BROWN. Yes; we shall be glad to have that.

Mr. HESTER. From time immemorial it has been the policy of Congress in imposing taxes and in providing for exemptions under certain conditions from the imposition of those taxes, to provide that the exemptions will be made under regulations to be prescribed by the Commissioner of Internal Revenue.

Take for example in this particular case, in the Revenue Act of 1932 they provided that automobile parts and accessories should be exempt from taxes if the manufacturer sells them to a manufacturer who is going to make a complete automobile or truck.

In order to get that exemption the manufacturer who is going to sell that part of an automobile or truck to the other manufacturer, who is going to make a completed truck, cannot get that exemption except under regulations to be prescribed by the Commissioner of Internal Revenue.

The Commissioner merely requires him to obtain a certificate from the other manufacturer that this part is to be used in the manufacture of a completed truck.

In this particular we have exactly the same situation here, and we are simply following the practice, I say, that Congress has followed for time immemorial in revenue acts. The farmer here will not even have to go to the Collector's office. All he will have to do will be merely to mail in his $5, and they will send him the stamp tax and the registration. At the end of the year he will make an information return as to how much land he has under cultivation and what disposition he has made of it.

When he wants to sell his crop of seeds all he will have to do under the regulations of the Treasury Department will be to obtain some evidence from the person to whom he sells it, that that person is entitled to the exemption.

That is the situation with respect to the seed, which is the important item involved here so far as the domestic interests are concerned. Of course the fiber products are entirely out of the bill.

That completes our case.

Senator BROWN. Mr. Hester, what are you going to do with respect to the large number of farmers who are not going to know about this law in its earlier stages of enforcement? It seems to me that with the lack of dissemination of information, a great many of them are going to engage perhaps in a legitimate production of it, not knowing of this law. Are you rather harsh toward those fellows, or can you be reasonable and generous toward them?

Mr. HESTER. No, the bill will not become effective for 60 days, and there are not a great many of these hemp producers in the United States. Of course the Treasury Department would do everything it possibly could to notify these people. There would be no hardship imposed upon them. This would be administered exactly as any other revenue act is administered, and frequently there are excise taxes imposed where the ordinary individual does not know anything about it.

Senator BROWN. What legitimate uses are now made of the hemp plant in the United States. That is, what causes the farmer to raise it?

Mr. HESTER. Some raise it for seeds.

Senator BROWN. Do you mean birdseeds?

Mr. HESTER. Yes. They raise the seeds for use in the manufacture birdseed. They make oil out of it. Most of the seed, however, at is used in the manufacture of oil is imported from Manchuria, it it may develop in this country.

Then after the seed is used for the making of oil, they take that seed d crush it, and make meal and meal cake, and that is sold to cattle isers.

The oil is used in the manufacture of varnish and paint and soap nd linoleum, and then in the case of the mature stalk they use that r making fiber and fiber products. Of course, they are entirely itside the bill.

Senator DAVIS. While primarily you are placing a tax, it is for the ole purpose of getting an enforcement of the law, and getting a plan r enforcing it?

Mr. HESTER. That is correct.

Senator DAVIS. If it should be $1, what difference would that make?

Mr. HESTER. Well, the situation is simply this——

Senator DAVIS. I am only talking now of the farmer's point of view, f charging him $1 instead of $5.

Mr. HESTER. I am glad you raised that point, Senator Davis. When the Harrison Act was first before the Supreme Court the ccupational tax was only $1, and the vote was 5 to 4. In other ords, the Supreme Court said, "This is a revenue measure", although e tax was only $1. But the vote was 5 to 4. After that Congress aised the occupational tax and then when the case came before the upreme Court the vote was 6 to 3, and the Court said, "We now have ore reason to sustain the constitutionality of this act than we had efore, because it is more of a revenue act than it was then."

In the case of producers, under the Harrison Narcotics Act, although ere are no poppies grown in this country, there is a classification in e Harrison Narcotics Act for producers. The rate is $24. If rmers raise poppies in this country, if they could develop it so that ey could raise poppies, so that they could get opium from it, the rmer would have to pay $24; but in this case the producer only ays $5.

We have left the practitioner at $1, because that was the situation f the Harrison Narcotics Act, and that is the real reason why the gures are set in this bill at $24, $5, $3, and $1, so that we can have a al revenue-raising measure.

Senator DAVIS. You charge $5 an acre under this?

Mr. HESTER. Oh, no—a year.

Senator DAVIS. I meant to say this: You charge $5, whether he roduces on 1 acre or on 1,000 acres?

Mr. HESTER. That is right.

Senator BROWN. Have you worked out the Canal Zone matter with he Department?

Mr. HESTER. We have. They wish to be exempted, and they have greed not to propose their amendment providing for direct regulation f marihuana in the zone because as I pointed out to you the other ay it might indicate on the face of the bill that it is a regulatory easure, but they wish to be exempted, and we have no objection. We are preparing to change that.

Senator BROWN. Just one or two more matters. Why should they be exempted?

Mr. HESTER. There is no legitimate business in the Canal Zone, and they say that they have sufficient control over the marihuana problem in the zone at this time under existing legislation, and they object to general legislation being applied.

Senator BROWN. It would probably be considerable duplication of effort down there.

Mr. HESTER. There might be some. The Harrison Narcotics Act applies to the Canal Zone, and that is the reason why it was included in this bill. But the Treasury Department has no objection if the Canal Zone goes out.

Senator BROWN. Will this entail any considerable increase in personnel for the Department?

Mr. HESTER. No, I do not think so.

Mr. ANSLINGER. No, sir.

Senator BROWN. I understand this measure has the approval of the Treasury Department.

Mr. HESTER. Yes. Oh, yes; it is strongly recommended by the Treasury Department.

Senator BROWN. Is there anything further from the Government? Do you desire to have a chemist testify?

Mr. HESTER. I think we have finished our case.

Senator BROWN. Very well. Thank you, Mr. Hester and Commissioner Anslinger.

The next witness on my list is Mr. Rens, of the Rens Hemp Co., of Brandon, Wis. We would be glad to hear from him.

STATEMENT OF MATT RENS, REPRESENTING RENS HEMP CO., BRANDON, WIS.

Mr. RENS. We have no objection whatever to controlling narcotics. Personally I am a producer, a farmer, and also a mill owner, a hemp mill owner, and we grow this hemp solely for the purpose of fiber. It is American hemp, which we sell to the Navy and to other industrials in the East, the spinning companies.

We have prepared an interpretation of this bill as we see it, and also a general summary of the discussion and suggested changes and reasons for these changes. This is quite lengthy. I do not know as you want to take the time for me to read it. We might have it in the record and give it to you folks.

Senator BROWN. We would be glad to have you present the statement and put it in the record.

(The memorandum presented by Mr. Rens is as follows:)

INTERPRETATION OF H. R. 6906—MARIHUANA (HEMP) BILL

This attempt to interpret H. R. 6906 is intended to help legitimate hemp producers and processors to understand those provisions in H. R. 6906 that directly affect them.

RELATION TO PRODUCERS

There are in the United States two rather distinct classes of hemp producers; one produces hemp for seed; and the other produces hemp for the fiber that is in the stalks. The same person may produce for both purposes, yet the usual situation is for persons to produce for one or the other purpose only. The bill, H. R. 6906, affects each class of producers alike so far as taxes and registrations are concerned.

Occupational registration of producers: Each producer of hemp, regardless of whether he is producing for seed or for fiber, is required to register with the internal revenue collector in the district in which the producer is located. While the specific procedure is not stated in the bill; it is assumed that the producer will obtain the required forms for occupational registration, and that he will execute these forms and deliver them to the collector of internal revenue; that when this is done and the required tax is paid, the producer is then registered (sec. 2a–5e).

There is nothing in H. R. 6906 to indicate the exact procedure; such as whether the forms must be purchased; whether the producer himself must make application for the forms; whether they may be obtained by mail; or whether they must be obtained in person. Neither is there any indication of the specific information that must be supplied; such as acreage grown, or to be grown; intended disposition of the harvested crop; or the like.

Transfer registration of producers: The producer of hemp seed can transfer the seed which he produced to any other registered producer without additional registration or tax, or without an order from the purchaser (sec. 6b-5). The producer of hemp seed can also transfer to any nonproducer, who is a registered dealer, upon the presentation of an official (written) order form; or he may sell to an unregistered dealer on the presentation of a properly executed official order form (sec. 6a).

The producer can deliver his mature hemp straw (stalks) to any person without any additional registration or tax and without any order on an official form from the purchaser of the straw (stalks) (sec. 1b).

Producer's taxes: Any person who grows hemp plants, regardless of the purpose for which they are grown—whether for seed or for fiber—must pay a tax (sec. 2a–2). The tax is paid to the collector of internal revenue of the district in which the crop is grown and the amount as now provided in the bill is $5 per year for each producer (sec. 2a–2).

RELATION TO DEALERS

There are several classes of dealers, including registered producer-dealers, registered dealers, who are not producers, and dealers who are neither registered as producers nor registered as dealers. Also there are dealers in seed, and dealers in hemp straw (mature stalks). Dealers in hempseed will be affected by the proposed legislation, while dealers in hemp straw (mature stalks) are exempted.

Occupational registration of dealers: A dealer in hempseed who is also a registered producer of hempseed, is not required to register (reregister) as a dealer (sec. 2a–5). Those not registered as producers, who wish to deal in hempseed, must register as a dealer (sec. 2a–5).

Transfer registration of dealers: All dealers who purchase hempseed, except registered producers, are required to use official order forms (register each purchase) (sec. 6b–5).

The foregoing means that if anyone, who is not a registered producer, wishes to purchase seed, he must execute an official blank for each purchase which he makes (and pay a tax in each case). This applies, regardless of whether or not the person from whom the seed is purchased is a registered producer. The official forms (order blanks) are bought from the collector of internal revenue and must be prepared (filled out) by the collector (not by the dealer) (sec. 6d).

The foregoing indicates that dealers, not registered as producers, who wish to purchase hempseed, must visit the internal-revenue collector, supply him with whatever information is required, and the collector must enter this information on the order form.

Dealer's occupational tax: Any person dealing in hempseed, who is not a registered producer, must pay an occupational tax of $3 per year. This is paid in connection with his registration (sec. 2-5).

Dealer's transfer tax: Any person who deals in hempseed and who is not a registered producer pays a transfer tax. This is in addition to his occupational tax. The amount of the transfer tax is $1 per ounce.

The foregoing means that anyone, who is not a registered producer and who wishes to purchase (transfer) hempseed, is required to pay a tax of $1 per ounce.

It is also provided in the bill that any person, who is not registered either as a producer or as a dealer, can purchase hempseed from a registered producer or dealer by presenting an official and properly executed order form, and by paying a tax of $100 per ounce.

GENERAL SUMMARY AND DISCUSSION

The utilization of hemp for fiber is an old, well established, and legitimate industry in the United States. Every person engaged in the hemp industry would be affected by the proposed legislation. The farmer-producer of hemp for fiber—the person who plants, grows, and harvests the fiber crops—would be obliged to register as a producer and to pay the producer's occupational tax. He would probably register and pay the tax at the time he obtains the seed. The seed would be distributed to him by the hemp milling company. The producer of hemp for fiber would be obliged to submit to no other registration, nor pay any additional tax, in order to distribute all of his hemp straw (mature stalks) to the hemp company; thus the procedure for growing and handling the crop for fiber is reasonably clear cut and understandable.

Hemp companies in order to obtain the seed and distribute it to the farmer-growers would be obliged either to qualify as a producer or as a dealer. To qualify as a producer, the hemp company would be obliged to grow hemp on its own account and to register as such and to pay the producer's occupational tax. To qualify as a dealer, a hemp company would be obliged to register and pay the dealer's occupational tax, and in addition sell only against properly executed order forms.

Relative to the requirements concerned with producing, distributing, and purchasing hempseed, the proposals in the bill are decidedly complicated and involved. In an attempt to trace the procedure from the producer of hempseed to the final consumer, who plants the seed for fiber purposes, we arrive at the following: The person who grew hempseed would be obliged to register and pay an occupational tax of $5. As a registered producer, he could sell seed to any other registered producer without any further registration, or payment of taxes for the crop year concerned. If he were to sell to any person other than a registered producer, then the person to whom he sells would be obliged to present a properly executed order form (a form filled out by the collector of internal revenue). This purchaser would have to register and pay a dealer's occupational tax of $3, and in additional pay a tax of $1 per ounce for the seed purchased. This of course means that no one, except those registered as producers, could do business in hempseed. In other words, this means that the only persons, who could buy and sell hempseed, would be those registered as producers; thus a registered fiber hemp grower in Illinois or Wisconsin would be obliged to buy his hempseed from a registered hempseed grower in Kentucky. This would exclude all legitimate dealers in hempseed other than those who are producers as well as dealers. It would also exclude hemp milling companies from acting as dealers unless they were to qualify as producers.

Relative to the proposed tax on producers, there appears to be no good reason why the amount should be $5 per year for each producer. Such a tax would force all small producers out of business of growing hemp and the proportion of small producers is considerable. The tax should not be more than $1 per year for each grower.

SUGGESTED CHANGES IN H. R. 6906

These suggestions are proposed in the interests of those persons only who are connected with the legitimate hemp industry in the United States, including hemp fiber milling and processing companies, farmers who produce hempseed, and farmers who produce hemp for fiber.

1. In every instance in which the term "marihuana" is used in H. R. 6906, the term "Cannabis" should be substituted.
2. Viable hempseed should be excluded from the definition of Cannibis (marihuana); thus excluding all transfers of hempseed, but not excluding producer of hemp for seed (sec. 1b).
3. The definition of "producer" should be clarified so that there can be no misunderstanding as to what persons are producers (sec. 1c).
4. The occupational tax for producers should be reduced from $5 per year to $1 per year (sec. 2–2).

REASONS FOR PROPOSED CHANGES

1. As used in the bill (H. R. 6906) the term "marihuana" is synonymous with true hemp, the scientific name of which is *Cannabis sativa L.* The chemical substance found in hemp which produces the narcotic effect has been officially termed "Cannabis indica", and is known throughout the world as Cannabis indica. Since botanists now recognise hemp as consisting of only one specie, the term "indica" should be discontinued; thus in referring to hemp in a narcotic sense, the term "Cannabis" is most appropriate and more universally understood. There can be no good reason for using the term marihuana, which is purely a localized term of Mexican (Indian) origin, and has no more general significance

and is no more universally recognized than "bhang", "hashish", and similar local terms. Furthermore, in all national narcotic acts and in all State narcotic acts the term Cannabis is used. Also in the Senate bill (S. 325), introduced in the Seventy-fifth Congress on January 25, 1937, the term "Cannabis" is used.

2. By excluding hemp seed from the definition of cannabis (marihuana) no registration or tax will be necessary by those who transfer, import, or otherwise deal in either viable or sterilized hemp seed. No evidence has been obtained, either by scientific investigation or by practical observation to indicate that hemp seed, as handled in the trade, contains an appreciable proportion of the chemical substances which cause the narcotic effect. The substances producing the narcotic effect have never been specifically isolated or discovered. No one knows what specific chemical compound or compounds produce the narcotic effect. Biological tests on experimental animals are therefore necessary. A recent and thorough-going inquiry indicates that there are no biological tests or other researches which show that narcotic-producing substances are present in the seeds themselves in a sufficient proportion to be harmful, in fact, there is nothing that shows that true seeds cause any of the narcotic effects.

The technical evidence given in the hearings on H. R. 6385 shows that the seed does not contain an appreciable proportion of the narcotic substances. The hearings also show that the seed was considered so harmless as to warrant omitting sterilized hemp seed from the definition of marihuana; thus in H. R. 6906 sterilized hemp seed is excluded (compare sec. 1 b, H. R. 6385 with sec. 1 b, H. R. 6906). There is also no evidence, either practical or technical, to show that hemp seed has ever been used to produce the drug effect.

All the foregoing indicates very clearly that hemp seed as such is not a source of marihuana. The requiring of registration and tax payment by producers who transfer hemp or dealers who trade in hemp seed must be construed as for the sole purpose of obtaining information concerning where and by whom hemp as a plant is being grown. It seems reasonable to assume that little or nothing would be accomplished by registering and taxing the transfer of hemp seed; that seed that would thus be registered and taxed is not the source from which illegitimate producers or handlers would obtain their supply; that those who use hemp for illicit use would not report transactions nor is it likely that any transactions that such persons would make would be detectable through the registering and taxing of legitimate dealers in hemp seed. Illicit producers and handlers either carry over the seed from year to year, or obtain it from others who deal in the same traffic, or obtain it from plants that grow in a wild state in practically all sections of the United States. Another thing, hemp plants are noticeably conspicuous. They are large and readily observable, and thus wild patches and all other areas can be rather easily detected if any attempt is made to do so, and it seems reasonable to assume that the use of Cannabis as an illicit drug will not be controlled unless there is a thorough-going surveillance of the growing plant.

In consideration of the foregoing, it is sincerely contended that any tax or registration required of those who transfer or deal in hemp seed to be used for legitimate purposes would not reduce to any extent whatever the use of hemp for producing Cannabis (marihuana).

3. The term "producer" as defined in H. R. 6906 includes both the persons who cultivate and grow the plants as a crop, and also those who transfer (sell or deal in) use, compound, process, or consume Cannabis (marihuana).

In the definition there is no distinction between a true producer and a dealer, yet the tax on a producer is different than that on a dealer and the whole set-up of the bill rather definitely distinguishes between the producer and the dealer.

It is urged therefore that the term "producer" be limited to include only those persons who plant, cultivate, harvest, or in any way facilitate the natural growth of marihuana. There should be no mention in connection with the term "producer" of such functions as transferring, or making use of the plant. If it seems proper to include volunteer hemp (which grows without planting), then the definition should specifically include such hemp (sec. 4 b).

4. In H. R. 6906 it is proposed to tax each producer of hemp (Cannabis or marihuana) $5 per year. The tax proposed for dealers is $3 per year, and the tax proposed for physicians, dentists, and the like is $1 per year. Now there does not seem to be any good reason why a producer should be taxed any more than a physician, dentist, and the like. It cannot be contended that a tax of $5 would be necessary in order to finance the enforcement of the bill because the income obtained, if producers were taxed $5 per year, would not be greater than $3,500 per year. A reasonably accurate estimate of the number of producers in the United States in 1937 shows that there are approximately 300 in Illinois, 120 in Wisconsin, 50 in Minnesota, 200 in Kentucky, and 10 in Texas—a total of 680,

which if taxed $5 each, would provide an annual revenue of $3,400. Now, t
clearly indicates that, as a source of revenue, a tax of $5 per grower would be
little consequence. On the other hand, individual growers would in many ca
be severely taxed, for in some sections it is common practice for farmers to g
very small acreages.

In the Kentucky river bottoms, where hemp is grown for seed, an acreage
grower of less than 1 acre, and as little as one-fourth acre, is not unusual. Also
Wisconsin, where hemp is grown for fiber only, farmers may grow as little a
acre and they frequently grow as little as 4 acres. For such small growers,
tax would amount to from $1.25 per acre to as much as $20 per acre. Thus
bill, if enacted, would eliminate all small growers. Thus it seems reasona
fair, and in every way in keeping with the intention of the proposed legislat
that the occupations tax for producers of hemp should not be more than $1
year per individual producer.

CONCLUDING STATEMENT

It is maintained that the foregoing proposed changes would in nowise de
the purpose of the bill or weaken its effectiveness. Sufficient authority is c
tained in section 10a to allow the Treasury Department to prescribe legisla
covering reports, records, and the like. In addition the proposed change
made would permit those now engaged in the legitimate phases of the hemp
dustry to continue as heretofore without any serious disturbance.

Senator Brown. With the general purposes of the bill you are
agreement?

Mr. Rens. Yes.

Senator Brown. You suggest a few modifications to it?

Mr. Rens. Yes, sir.

Senator Brown. Have you discussed that with Mr. Hester or a
one in the Treasury Department?

Mr. Rens. We have written to Mr. Anslinger, and we have sen
copy of this to Mr. Edwards, of the Division of Cotton and Ot
Fibers, of the Bureau of Standards. He has a copy of this a

Senator Brown. Mr. Rens, unless you have something else
present, you are excused and we thank you.

Mr. Rens. No, not particularly. I think this covers it. A
farmer I am interested.

Senator Brown. We will take this into consideration.

Mr. Rens. The reason I would state for reducing this fee from
to $1 in this, that there are so many farmers in Kentucky especi
that grow this. That is where we get our seed, in Kentucky. T
have perhaps one-eighth or a quarter of acre. It would discour
those farmers from growing hemp.

Senator Brown. How much would they get say from an eighth
an acre, by way of total return?

Mr. Rens. Perhaps 12 or 14 bushels.

Senator Brown. What would that be worth?

Mr. Rens. They may get $2 or $3 a bushel. I do not think t
get more. We have to pay more. We have to pay the man o
there, the dealer.

Senator Brown. That is all he would get at his farm?

Mr. Rens. Yes. And another thing, the fiber, our farmers
hesitate. It will hurt us in getting the acreage for the mill. We h
000 acres, personally; that is, the mill has; and we have some
growers. Now, the tax I think we will have to pay for the gro
will come to one man. The grower will hesitate.

Senator Brown. Mr. Hester, do you hear what he says to the eff
that farmers in Kentucky that produce for his mill, some of th
grow as small an amount as one-eighth of an acre, and their t
return at the farm would be somewhere from $12 to $15?

Mr. Rens. Bushels—bushels per acre.

Senator Brown. How much in dollars?

Mr. Rens. Sometimes the yield will be less—maybe from $20 to $30.

Senator Brown. $20 to $30?

Mr. Rens. An acre; yes.

Senator Brown. Well, of course, taking $5 out of $20—is a high percentage.

Mr. Hester. They would just have to add that $5 tax onto the price that this gentleman would pay for it.

Mr. Rens. Then you have first the price of the seed, and then you have your transfer again. Another thing is the transfer of this. If the man that buys it from Kentucky is a dealer, and not a producer, that will mean $1 an ounce. That man is out of business.

Senator Brown. I do not follow you there.

Mr. Rens. As we see this bill, the interpretation of that is that the dealer, who is not a producer——

Mr. Hester. Let me say this. I think I can save the committee time on that. We did not know until you have just made the statement there, and I think Mr. Johnson brought it to our attention, that there are some dealers in this country who act as a broker for seeds. Now, we have no objection to an amendment in this that would take care of that situation.

Senator Brown. Exempting them?

Mr. Hester. Yes, so there will not be any transfer tax.

Senator Brown. Will you take care of that?

Mr. Hester. Yes. We will take care of that so they will save that.

Mr. Rens. I see no reason why growers should be charged $5 and the dentists or the doctors $1. They use the drug which you are trying to prohibit, which you are trying to control.

Now, we harvest our hemp in the State when it is still green, with no seed in it, and we field-wet it. All these leaves are gone. There is no marihuana drug there, in the way we handle it in Wisconsin, and still the grower must pay. We often have growers that only have, say two or three acres or hemp.

Senator Brown. Do you think, Mr. Hester, an arrangement whereby you would cut that $5 down $1 for fractions of an acre would be any serious impediment?

Mr. Hester. Just how do you mean, Senator Brown?

Senator Brown. Suppose you made it $5 for an acre or more, or something like that, and $1 for fractional parts of an acre.

Mr. Hester. The question would arise then as to whether that would be a proper classification under the due process clause of the Constitution.

Senator Brown. Will you give that consideration?

Mr. Hester. We will be very glad to look into that.

Senator Brown. I can see something in your point there.

Mr. Rens. Personally I have grown 100 acres or better. Well, that is $5. But I have men that have 2 acres or 3 acres.

Senator Brown. If is the fellow as you said who has a quarter or one-eighth of an acre, who has a small amount, who will have to bear a proportionately heavier burden.

Mr. Rens. The real purpose of this bill is not to raise money, is it?

Senator Brown. Well, we are sticking to the proposition, that it is.

Mr. Rens. It will cost a million.

Senator Brown. We thank you, Mr. Rens.

The next witness will be M. G. Moksnes.

STATEMENT OF M. G. MOKSNES, REPRESENTING THE AMHEMPCO CORPORATION, DANVILLE, ILL.

Mr. Moksnes. I happen to be the superintendent of the Amhempco Corporation, at Danville, Ill.

Senator Brown. I want to say that Congressman Meeks wrote me about your problem.

Mr. Moksnes. This company was organized 3 years ago by Bell Bros., of Muncie, Ind., and the Sloan Interests, who are textile people in New York. They had in mind developing a process whereby a fiber that is now being used for rope and cordage could be further processed to go into textiles, and also that the hurd or the woody part could be processed and made into plastics. Three years ago we planted 4,200 acres, last year 1,200 acres, and this year 7,000 acres, and we are in operation. The capacity of the plant is 15,000 acres.

We have to contract our seed from the growers in Kentucky, that was covered by Mr. Rens, and their acreage runs anywhere from a quarter of an acre up, and we have no objection to the bill. In fact, any attempt to prevent the passage of a bill to protect the narcotic traffic would be unethical and un-American. That is not the point, but we do believe that a tax of $5 is going to be prohibitive for the small dealer as well as the man that grows the hemp; not only the seed dealer, but the man that grows the crop, because he will average—I do not know what the average will be, but they raise as little as 2 acres.

Senator Brown. As I understand it, Mr. Hester can take care of the dealer.

Mr. Hester. The dealer; yes.

Senator Brown. That will be generally agreed, that he will be exempted from that tax.

Mr. Hester. From the transfer tax. He will be exempted from the transfer tax.

Mr. Moksnes. That is the deal. That is the transfer tax, but how about the grower of seed?

Senator Herring. The man who only grows one-eighth of an acre with a $20 or $25 crop cannot be harmed much. He does not have much at stake.

Mr. Hester. He would just have to add the occupational tax on to the price that he sells to the dealer in the city.

Senator Herring. Of course, that would make it pretty difficult for him to compete with the producer who had 10 or 15 acres.

Mr. Moksnes. You see we are dependent on the small growers down in the Kentucky River bottoms to furnish our seed. They are small growers who probably do not have over 10 or 15 acres of land, distributed among several crops. If he has to pay $5 an acre——

Mr. Hester. Not $5 an acre—$5 a year.

Mr. Moksnes. I mean $5 a year, and he only has a quarter or half an acre, that tax is going to be prohibitive, we are going to lose the small growers, and it is the combination of growers that we have to depend on.

Senator Brown. According to my understanding the Treasury will endeavor to see if they can cover that problem, and we will do our best about it. We are not certain what we can do about it, but we will do the best we can.

salt, derivative, mixture, or preparation of such plant, its seeds, or resin; but sh
not include——

Senator Brown. Mr. Johnson, as I understand it the petals of t
flower are the most dangerous.

Mr. Johnson. Yes; which eventually become the seeds. T
flower becomes seed.

Senator Brown. It is used, as I understand it, as a petal. Is it n
ground up?

Mr. Johnson. The leaves.

Senator Herring. Is not the bloom used the same as the leaves?

Mr. Hester. Oh, yes; the flower on the tops.

Mr. Johnson. The flower and the seeds.

Senator Brown. It seems to me you did not cover the flowers.

Mr. Johnson. I tried to copy in detail the words now in the bil
I am copying the bill at this time, except as to the insertion of th
word "such" where they say "all" in the first line. They have n
said "flowers", so I did not say "flowers."

Senator Brown. "All parts of the plant" would include the flower

Mr. Johnson. Then "flowers" could be inserted.

Senator Brown. I think so.

Mr. Johnson. "The leaves or flowers of the plant"; I concede tha
because I have wanted to cover it all [reading]:

> Such * * * plant, its seeds, or resin; but shall not include oil or ca
> made from the seeds of such plant, any compound, manufacture, salt, derivativ
> mixture, or preparation of mature stalk, oil or cake or the sterilized seed which
> incapable of germination.

And then for the purpose of clarification I wanted to insert this:

> Specifically excluded are mature stalks known as hemp stalks, which contai
> no resin or harmful properties, which are used for various legitimate commercia
> purposes, and which are grown by producers under contract with licensed proce
> sors or manufacturers.

Now, getting down to the practical part of this measure, no on
has any business growing this hemp in any quantity whatever excep
under contract with someone who is using it for a legitimate busines
They have no more business growing it on one-tenth of an acre tha
I have growing sweetpotatoes on my front lawn. Anyone who use
the seed or who uses the stalk—the hurd—or uses the fiber is a manu
facturer, a processor, who will contract to pay a man a good price t
grow it for him; and these other people ought to be simply barred
and I am in favor of licensing them. I think the small producer i
going to be eliminated, this man that sticks in one-tenth of an acre
And why shouldn't he be? He is doing no good to himself or anybody
else. But here is a great industry where men will put in 10, 20, 30, 40
one gentlemen who will put in 100 acres, and the people I represen
have planted 2,200 acres and expect to plant 20,000 acres.

This has been experimented with in South Carolina, in Oregon
and all over the country, because these big industries that use th
fiber and use the hurd have to take into consideration crop failures
and therefore cannot confine themselves to just Minnesota or to South
Carolina or to Oregon. Some of these people have already expende
$300,000 in the last few years, trying to work out in big industries th
use of this fiber, and they feel that it should be so stated in the law
that the farmer who is growing the stalk and growing the fiber know
definitely that he is not growing anything that has marihuana in it.

Me does not want to grow marihuana, and yet we might lose in industry purely by the phraseology of the measure.

I think I have said all I could say on that. I could say much more, but I have stated it in a few words.

Now, on this question of the tax, and the constitutionality of the law, I am firmly convinced that the farmers' can be reduced to $1 and this law be sustained. This is not the sort of measure that people are saying it is, a regulatory measure under the guise of a tax measure. We do not need to run around the corner to the hemp industry in order to stop the sale of the flower or of the leaves. It can be taxed like the automobile industry, like the cosmetic industry, like the fur industry, and we do not need to use any legal sophistry in this to sustain this statute because hemp is produced in the United States; and I would say in the presence of this committee that I am sure and would almost guarantee that Mr. Hester and Mr. Tipton could go before the Supreme Court and get a unanimous decision, if they would argue along the lines I am suggesting. This is not like narcotics, where there are no poppies grown, nothing like it. In my judgment a $1 tax on the farmer is sufficient. To my mind this industry is going to be more affected by the regulations, but I have no doubt Mr. Anslinger and the gentlemen associated with him, with their wide experience and with their desire to do justice, will work out regulations far more important than the law which will be fair to industry and the farmer.

Now, I want to say further a little more on this industry itself. If there are abuses by this legitimate producer——

Senator Brown. Just let me ask you one question there. You say you want the farmer to be made to realize that he is not growing marihuana?

Mr. Johnson. In the stalk and fiber.

Senator Brown. In the stalk and fiber, but of course he cannot grow the stalk and fiber without growing the resin plant?

Mr. Johnson. That is right.

Senator Brown. How are you going to leave that out? I do not see.

Mr. Johnson. Because he is going to have to sell his product. He will have to sell this to a manufacturer. Now, as a matter of fact the people making paper, and the finest grades of paper, which you cannot make in this country without the use of hemp at the present time, and which is being imported—even a great deal of the paper that goes into our money is being imported—must have hemp fiber. It is just a ridiculous situation, because it can be made out of our local products in this country. The paper manufacturer, when he gets the plant, simply blows these leaves away. They disappear when dried. They are gone. As a matter of fact these people in Minnesota did not know until 2 months ago that the hemp which they grew there contained marihuana. Until this agitation came up they did not dream of it, and they were as much surprised as anyone else.

Now, they will have some difficulties, just as the liquor people had some difficulties, eventually, and the man who does not recognize that, the producer or manufacturer, is going to be put out of business in my judgment, because there is a problem with marihuana. I will concede these licenses are right, but I do think that the farmers' license fee ought to be reduced to $1. I have no fear whatever but

what the law will be declared constitutional. I would like to see such amendments in there.

Senator Brown. Of course, you must have a situation where the farmer is made to realize, it seems to me, just the opposite of what you say. He has got to be made to realize that in growing this legitimate product and fiber it can be put to illegitimate uses. Therefore I think the bill should place in the farmer a knowledge of that fact. Otherwise he will be just as your clients were, ignorant of the fact that he is growing on his farm a decidedly dangerous and deleterious product.

Mr. Johnson. Mr. Chairman, do you not think though that that section 2 could be rewritten so it would say definitely that "in the flower, in the leaves", and so forth, there is a harmful product?

Senator Brown. Yes; that is all right.

Mr. Johnson. So that it is clear, make it clear to him, then, but also make it clear in the bill that there is no harmful product, which is agreed to by everyone, in the hurd, fiber, and in the stalk. In other words, I do not think that this could be worked out so we could do exactly what the committee wants to do, and that there would be no opposition whatever to this bill, except a desire on the part of everyone to strengthen it and make it stronger in every possible way against the illegitimate use of this hemp.

Mr. Hester. If I may say a word there, we will be very happy to sit down with you, Mr. Johnson. I am not sure that if you should ask our recommendation on his amendment that we would agree to recommend it, but we would be very happy to sit down and study it with him.

Senator Brown. Is that all, Mr. Johnson?

Mr. Johnson. That is all, and I thank the committee very much.

Senator Brown. We have Mr. Olman, I think, as the only remaining witness.

STATEMENT OF O. C. OLMAN, REPRESENTING JUNEAU FIBRE CO., JUNEAU, WIS.

Mr. Olman. From what I have heard here, and from what has been remarked by Mr. Hester, I do not know as I shall take any time of the committee at all, because I am in the same boat that Mr. Mokenes is, and Mr. Johnson is.

I would like to mention just one or two things, Mr. Chairman, and that will be all, but I think we can iron it out with Mr. Hester, for instance, the discussion as to what is a mature plant. Now, we cut the plant before that, in the pollen stage. They are not mature according to our understanding.

This is one point I would like to ask Mr. Hester. Another point, of course, is the definition of "producer", so we can qualify as a producer. We are "dealers" under the bill, but we would like to qualify as "producers."

Then another thing is that for instance, a farmer wants to grow 2 acres or 4 acres of hemp, and he has to go before the collector of internal revenue and give such information as is wanted, and then get his permit. Now, I think that can be ironed out. If he has to do that, 60 or 70 of our farmers will have to drive 70 miles to Milwaukee.

Senator Brown. I think you can work that out.

Mr. Hester. No; they just write a letter to the collector, that is all.

Mr. Olman. And of course we were not afraid of the transfer tax, and so on.

I was interested in the question you asked the doctor, Mr. Chairman, and that was with reference to that in growing of hemp. I believe that we are in a position to give the Government a great deal of help in supervising and inspecting and reporting the growth of hemp.

Senator Brown. For your producers?

Mr. Olman. In our vicinity. I thank you.

Mr. Hester. Fine.

Senator Brown. How long a time will you gentlemen want, to submit to the committee such representations as may be agreed upon? Would Wednesday morning be about right?

Mr. Hester. That would be fine.

Senator Brown. Suppose, Senator Herring, we agree on 10 o'clock Wednesday morning for an executive session on this measure, unless there is a serious disagreement. If there is you gentlemen, who are in disagreement, can come in.

Mr. Olman. I am sure there will not be.

Mr. Hester. Thank you very much, Mr. Chairman.

Senator Brown. Before we adjourn, I desire to place in the record a letter regarding the pending bill addressed to Senator Harrison by Dr. William C. Woodward, of the American Medical Association, Chicago, Ill.

AMERICAN MEDICAL ASSOCIATION,
BUREAU OF LEGAL MEDICINE AND LEGISLATION,
Chicago, July 10, 1937.

Hon. PAT HARRISON,
Chairman, Committee on Finance, United States Senate,
Washington, D. C.

SIR: I have been instructed by the board of trustees of the American Medical Association to protest on behalf of the association against the enactment in its present form of so much of H. R. 6906 as relates to the medicinal use of cannabis and its preparations and derivatives. The act is entitled, "An Act to impose an occupational excise tax upon certain dealers in marihuana, to impose a transfer tax upon certain dealings in marihuana, and to safeguard the revenue therefrom by registry and recording."

Cannabis and its preparations and derivatives are covered in the bill by the term "marihuana" as that term is defined in section 1, paragraph (b). There is no evidence, however, that the medicinal use of these drugs has caused or is causing cannabis addiction. As remedial agents they are used to an inconsiderable extent, and the obvious purpose and effect of this bill is to impose so many restrictions on their medicinal use as to prevent such use altogether. Since the medicinal use of cannabis has not caused and is not causing addiction, the prevention of the use of the drug for medicinal purposes can accomplish no good end whatsoever. How far it may serve to deprive the public of the benefit of a drug that on further research may prove to be of substantial value, it is impossible to foresee.

The American Medical Association has no objection to any reasonable regulation of the medicinal use of cannabis and its preparations and derivatives. It does protest, however, against being called on to pay a special tax, to use special order forms in order to procure the drug, to keep special records concerning its professional use and to make special returns to Treasury Department officials, as a condition precedent to the use of cannabis in the practice of medicine in the several States, all separate and apart from the taxes, order forms, records, and reports required under the Harrison Narcotic Act with reference to opium and coca leaves and their preparations and derivatives.

If the medicinal use of cannabis calls for Federal legal regulation further than the legal regulation that now exists, the drug can without difficulty be covered under the provisions of the Harrison Narcotic Act by a suitable amendment. By

such a procedure the professional use of cannabis may readily be controlled as effectively as are the professional uses of opium and coca leaves, with less interference with professional practice and less cost and labor on the part of the Treasury Department. It has been suggested that the incorporation of cannabis into the Harrison Narcotic Act would jeopardize the constitutionality of that act, but that suggestion has been supported by no specific statements of its legal basis or citations of legal authorities.

Respectfully,
WM. C. WOODWARD,
Legislative Counsel.

(Whereupon, at 11:35 a. m., Monday, July 12, 1937, the subcommittee adjourned.)

BLOW UP OR GET OUT YOUR MAGNIFYING GLASS...

SCIENTIFIC AMERICAN

Same campaign, different drug: A Repeal Prohibition campaign car begins its 1932 trip from Wilmington, Del., to Seattle.

Hagley Museum and Library, Wilmington, Del.

MARIHUANA MORE MAY · 1938
DANGEROUS THAN
HEROIN OR COCAINE

MARIHUANA is "a more dangerous drug than heroin or cocaine." Authority for this statement is United States Commissioner of Narcotics H. J. Anslinger. Mr. Anslinger's statement was made as part of a report on narcotics appearing in the bulletin of the Federal Bureau of Investigation.

"I am surprised to learn that certain police officers have been inclined to minimize the effects of the use of marihuana," *Science Service* quotes Mr. Anslinger. "These officers should review some of the cases that are reported to the Bureau. They would, I am sure, be convinced that the drug is adhering to its Old World traditions of murder, assault, rape, physical demoralization, and mental breakdown. A study of the effects of marihuana shows clearly that it is a dangerous drug, and Bureau records prove that its use is associated with insanity and crime."

Effects of marihuana, according to an authority quoted by Mr. Anslinger, are as follows:

"1. Feeling of unaccountable hilarity.

"2. Excitation and a disassociation of ideas; the weakening of power to direct thoughts.

"3. Errors in time and space.

"4. Intensification of auditory sensibilities, causing profound dejection or mad gayety.

"5. Fixed ideas; delirious conviction. This is a type of intellectual injury so frequent in mental alienation. The user imagines the most unbelievable things, giving way to monstrous extravagances.

"6. Emotional disturbance during which the user is powerless to direct his thoughts, loses the power to resist emotions, and may commit violence which knows no bounds when disorders of the intellect have reached a point of incoherence. During this dangerous phenomenon, evil instincts are brought to the surface and cause a fury to rage within the user.

"7. Irresistible impulses which may result in suicide.

"The illusions are those of sight, hearing, and sense. The mind loses all idea of space and extent, and tends to exaggeration in all things; the slightest impulse or suggestion carries it away."

[handwritten:] Typical Hearst Marijuana Diatribe Of The 1930s

---

America, Russia, Hemp, and Napoleon

American Trade with Russia and the Baltic, 1783–1812

BY ALFRED W. CROSBY, JR.

[handwritten:] Ohio State Univ Press 1965

Ohio State University Press

Bibliography

PRIMARY SOURCES

A *Manuscript Sources* *

Essex Institute, Salem, Massachusetts

This institution owns innumerable log books and letterbooks written by men in the Baltic, at St. Petersburg and at Archangel, all of which were valuable to me. Particularly valuable was the log of the ship "Susan," 1806–7, because this ship was in Danish waters when the bombardment of Copenhagen began.

Massachusetts Historical Society, Boston, Massachusetts

The utterly indispensable Adams microfilms are issued by this society. The letterbook of John March, one of my best sources on Gothenburg, and a private letter written by Erving to Madison from Copenhagen in June, 1811, my best source on the peculations of Joy, are owned by this institution.

National Archives, Department of State, Washington, D.C.

Without the consular reports from Copenhagen, Gothenburg, St. Petersburg, Stockholm, and Archangel, and the ministerial

* Without information sent to me by Messrs. Mikoletzky, of the Austrian State Archives, and Svend Aakjaer and Aage Rasch, of the Danish State Archives, some of the essential pieces of my jigsaw puzzle of a book would still be missing.

287

Bibliography

Journals of the House of Commons. Vols. LXV, LXVII, and LXVIII.

These volumes contain most of the statistics I use about British trade.

Papers Relating to the License Trade. Ordered to be printed by the House of Commons, 26 February 1812.

Contains a few oblique hints as to clandestine English trade with Russia.

"Report Relative to the Trade with the East Indies and China from the Select Committee of the House of Lords, Appointed to Inquire into the Means of Extending and Securing the Foreign Trade of the Country . . . ," *Parliamentary Papers,* 1821. Vol. VII.

Contains a reference to land trade between Russia and China in English woolens and tea.

C. Public Documents, United States

American State Papers. Documents, Legislative and Executive, of the Congress of the United States . . . Selected and Edited under Authority of Congress. Washington, D.C.: Gales & Seaton, 1832–61.

Class I: Foreign Relations Vols. I–III.

Little on relations with Russia and Sweden, but quite a lot on relations with Denmark.

Class II: Commerce and Navigation Vols. I–II.

Contains all the available statistics on exports to and imports from the Baltic nations. Any conclusions drawn from these statistics should be very carefully examined. The statistics in these volumes were compiled on the basis of a year that ended, not on 31 December, but on 30 September. Therefore, American statistics on the Russian trade are particularly deceptive because the Baltic and Archangel shipping season ran from winter to winter, and 30 September fell right in the middle of that shipping season. Most American exports to Russia in a given year arrived there by 30 September, so the *American State Papers'* statistics on exports to Russia are somewhat dependable. However, only one-half or so of imports from Russia in a given year arrived in America by 30 September. For instance, if in the astronomical year of 1800, America imported 100,000 hundredweight of hemp from Russia, and in the year 1811, only 50,000, the statistics in the *American State Papers* would show an importation of approximately 75,000 hundredweight of hemp for each of the two years.

Class VI: Naval Affairs Vols. I–III.

Contains very interesting notes on the quality of American hemp and flax as compared with Russian, and an essay on the Russian method of hemp cultivation and processing by John Quincy Adams.

The Diplomatic Correspondence of the United States of America from the Signing of the Definitive Treaty of Peace 10th September 1783, to the Adoption of the Constitution, March 4, 1789. Washington, D.C.: Francis Preston Blair, 1833–34.

This work is indispensable for coverage of relations with Europe during the Confederation. Also, this work contains letters written by John Paul Jones from Russia and Denmark.

Journals of the Continental Congress, 1774–89. Washington, D.C.: Library of Congress.

Contains a few remarks on Dana's mission.

Message of the President of the United States, Transmitting List of Vessels Permitted to Depart from the United States since December, 1807. Washington, D.C.: Roger Chew Weightman, 1808.

This mentions one vessel permitted to clear for Russia during the embargo.

Protect Youth
Against Dope

THE Hearst newspapers, which have crusaded unceasingly against the NARCOTIC EVIL in all its vicious forms, are gratified to know that Narcotic Education Week is centering attention upon the MARIHUANA PROBLEM.

Legal authorities, while increasingly vigilant against other habit-forming drugs, have permitted the marihuana cigarette to become a NATIONAL MENACE.

One of the consequences, according to Ethel Schiller, sociologist of the Chicago Women's Court, is that SIXTY PER CENT of all juvenile delinquents are victims of the drug.

* * *

ADMIRAL RICHMOND P. HOBSON, President of the World Narcotic Defense Association, says:

"The warfare on the dope ring has made much progress. At the same time the enemy has developed a very dangerous new field, the exploitation of marihuana cigarettes, which is especially menacing and destructive for our youth."

The marihuana cigarette is one of the most INSIDIOUS of all forms of dope, largely because of the failure of the public to understand its fatal qualities.

The nation is almost defenseless against it, having no Federal laws to cope with it and virtually no organized campaign for combatting it.

The result is tragic.

High school boys and girls buy the destructive weed without knowledge of its capacity for harm, and conscienceless dealers sell it with impunity.

* * *

THIS is a NATIONAL PROBLEM, and it must have national attention.

The fatal marihuana cigarette must be recognized as a DEADLY DRUG and American children must be PROTECTED AGAINST IT.

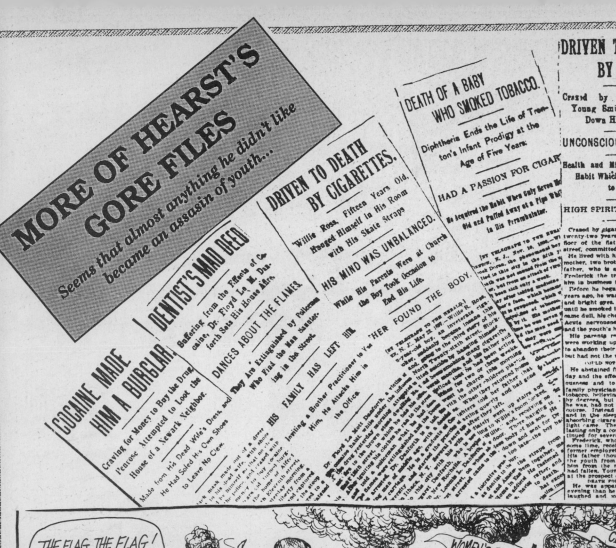

GREENPEACE

VOLUME 14 · NUMBER 3 · MAY/JUNE 1989 · BI-MONTHLY · $1.50

THE HEAT IS ON:

PLANET OF THE YEAR

TIME

Endangered Earth

CHOLESTEROL ANXIETY
Is It Worth All the Worry?

Newsweek

THE ALASKA SPILL
What Exxon Leaves Behind

EXXON VALDEZ

TIME

Our Filthy Seas

GORBACHEV'S FREE-FOR-ALL
Moscow's Historic Party Conference

Newsweek

The Greenhouse Effect

HUD: Silent Sam Speaks

TIME
Torching the Amazon
Can the rain forest be saved?

OMNI

ENVIRONMENTAL SPECIAL

SAVE THE PLANET
A 16-PAGE ACTIVIST'S PRIMER TO
HEALING AN AILING EARTH

KIDS SPEAK OUT
ON DRUGS, WAR AND ILLITERACY

$3.50

In Global-Warming Debate, Skeptics Corral Bush With a Policy of Inaction

■ **Environment:** A small group of conservative scientists tell the President there is no problem; a substantial body of scientific testimony argues otherwise.

By Donella H. Meadows

PLAINFIELD, N.H.

What's happening to the Earth's climate is not certain. What's happening to U.S. policy on global climate change is becoming clear. Last week President Bush ducked yet another opportunity to exert even minimal leadership on the issue. His speech Monday to the U.N. Intergovernmental Panel on Climate Change was a resolute call for more study.

Last November the United States and Japan blocked an international agreement on climate change by refusing to discuss specific reduction of greenhouse gas pollutants by any target date. At that meeting, too, Bush's team supported only further study.

That do-nothing stance is the result of a White House power struggle being won by conservatives led by Chief of Staff John H. Sununu. Sununu is greatly aided by a group of conservative scientists who have turned technical uncertainties about the greenhouse effect into pseudo-scientific politicking. They argue, to the distress of many of their colleagues, that there may not *be* any global warming.

The greenhouse skeptics, according to Science magazine, "number less than a dozen . . . . Most have not specialized in greenhouse research and have only recently entered the fray." But they are sought out and quoted liberally by anyone who wishes the greenhouse effect would go away—by Forbes magazine, for example, in a recent cover article titled "The Global Warming Panic: A Classic Case of Overreaction."

Three skeptics—William A. Nierenberg, director emeritus of Scripps Institution of Oceanography; Robert Jastrow, former director of the Goddard Institute for Space Studies, and Frederick Seitz, president emeritus of Rockefeller University—have produced a 35-page report widely circulated in the White House. The report says, basically, that there is no evidence for global warming now, no certainty that there ever will be and even a possibility of cooling in the next century.

That's half the argument that Sununu is putting into the President's mouth. The other half, advanced by conservative economists, is that anti-greenhouse measures will be so expensive that only the greatest scientific certainty could justify them.

And in the opposite corner we have James E. Hansen, current Goddard director, who also produced scientific shock waves by testifying before Congress that, "with 99% confidence," greenhouse warming is already here. We have Steve Schneider of the National Center for Atmospheric Research, who puts the confidence level at 80%, and who has written a blistering critique of the Nierenberg/Jastrow/Seitz report.

Donella H. Meadows is an adjunct professor of environmental and policy studies at Dartmouth College.

The do-nothing stance results from a White House power struggle being won by conservatives led by Chief of Staff John H. Sununu.

We have Amory Lovins of the Rocky Mountain Institute, who calculates that the cost of reducing greenhouse gases through energy-efficiency measures could be *negative*—saving so much money and reducing so many other kinds of pollutants that the measures could pay for themselves. And a distinguished array of the nation's ecologists—George Woodwell, Paul Ehrlich, E.O. Wilson and others—are convinced that greenhouse warming is one of the most serious threats to the Earth's ecosystems.

The primary action necessary to combat a greenhouse effect is to use fossil fuels much more efficiently. Whether there is a greenhouse effect or not, energy efficiency would improve the environment, the balance of payments and the general economy. But it would greatly inconvenience the oil, coal, electricity and automobile industries, among others. Hence the eagerness in some political camps not to believe in the greenhouse effect, and to cite only the side of the argument that feeds such bias.

Some scientists play directly into that political eagerness. Like the rest of us, they have genes, glands, emotions, values, whatever predisposes people to prefer nature to oil companies or vice versa.

Many of the protagonists in the greenhouse debate have been combating one another for decades. Whether the issue is nuclear energy or nuclear winter, population policy or global warming, they are arrayed predictably, some advocating social reform, others defending the current order. The last time Nierenberg, Jastrow and Seitz made a public statement, it was to promote the Strategic Defense Initiative. Schneider, Ehrlich, and Lovins have never taken anything but a dim view of the environmental effects of untrammeled industrial society.

That does not make them wrong or manipulative or insincere, it makes them human. Their fault comes only when they pass off their values as science.

Suppose (a large supposition indeed) we had an administration or citizenry that wanted to sort out whatever truth there is in the scientific brouhaha, and choose the wisest course of action for the whole society. Would that be possible?

It would. The way to separate values from science is to do what Sununu is not doing—listen openly and critically to all sides. Listen for agreement (scientific certainty, as far as it goes) and disagreement (scientific uncertainty, all mixed up with values).

In the case of global warming, there is absolute agreement that human activities are rapidly increasing greenhouse gases in the atmosphere. There is near-agreement that more greenhouse gases mean a climate warmer than it would otherwise be. There is no agreement about what it would otherwise be. Other forces besides greenhouse gases—such as the sun's energy and wobbles in the Earth's orbit—also affect the climate. Those other forces could be moving in a warming direction just now, or they could be about to plunge us into an ice age. That we don't know.

We also don't know what feedbacks warming might set off. A hotter Earth would evaporate more water, which could make more clouds, which could cool the Earth again. Or a hotter Earth could release methane locked in frozen tundra—methane is a greenhouse gas; that would make the Earth still hotter. The computerized climate models, from which most greenhouse forecasts derive, include few of these feedbacks, which could bring on the greenhouse effect much faster than we expect, or much slower.

In short, we know we are doing something that, all else equal, will lead to warming. Whether all else will be equal, how fast a climate change could happen, what it would mean for rainfall and sea levels, droughts and hurricanes, ecosystems and human settlements, all that *we don't know.*

Therefore we know almost nothing about costs. I have yet to see a cost estimate on this matter done honestly—which is to say, done by comparing what greenhouse gas reductions would cost versus what it would cost to endure a global warming. The job is virtually impossible. But I believe that every anti-greenhouse policy—energy efficiency, solar energy, forest preservation and reforestation, chlorofluorocarbon reduction, population control—is worth pursuing in its own right, even if there is no greenhouse effect.

So here we are, causing large changes in our atmosphere and highly uncertain about the consequences. The dynamics of the planet are such that if we wait for certainty, it will be too late to do anything—if anything ought to be done. Our choice boils down to a judgment about the value of the current society, whose blessings and faults we know, versus an attainable alternative society that could be better, or worse, or better for some and worse for others.

Who gets to define better and worse? Where should the burden of our uncertainty be placed? On a few sectors of the human economy, on the Earth's ecosystems or to some extent on both? Sununu and Bush are letting the ecosys-

Please see INACTION, M8

BLOW UP OR GET OUT YOUR MAGNIFYING GLASS...

THE OREGONIAN, MONDAY, JANUARY 22 1990

Marijuana backers urge production of dioxin-free paper made from hemp

By BILL GRAVES and DAVID HOGAN
of The Oregonian staff

If government will not let Americans grow marijuana to smoke, it should at least let them cultivate it commercially for products such as dioxin-free white paper, speakers at a marijuana activists conference said Saturday.

Most in the group of about 30 attending the Marijuana Activists Regional Conference at Lewis and Clark College wish the government would allow both uses. But one panel on the second day of the three-day conference focused on various commercial uses of marijuana, also known as hemp.

Hemp can be used to produce fuel, linenlike fiber for fabric and pulp for various grades of paper, the speakers said. Most of the paper used in China is made from hemp, and it lasts four to five times longer than paper made from wood, said Paul Stanford of Portland, who imports Chinese hemp products.

Further, cellulose-rich hemp can be made into white paper using hydrogen peroxide rather than the chlorine-bleaching process used by U.S. pulp mills, said Jim Evans, 35, an Ashland education student who hopes to plant commercial hemp crops in the Willamette Valley this spring.

The chlorine procedure leaves traces of dioxin in white paper products and in waste discharges. The Oregon Department of Environmental Quality has proposed forcing three Oregon pulp mills to cut their dioxin emissions.

Jack Herer of Los Angeles, head of a political action group seeking to make marijuana legal, said the mills can eliminate dioxin and save forests by switching to hemp.

"You can make every grade of paper from toilet paper to newspapers at one-fourth the cost," said, Herer, wearing a brown hemp shirt and holding a book about hemp made of hemp.

Mary O'Brien, a Eugene scientist for the Northwest Coalition for Alternatives to Pesticides, said hemp is worth considering as a paper source, particularly if there are species free of the substance that makes people high.

"The question of hemp as paper just adds to this interesting ferment of ideas as to multiple ways to make papers for multiple purposes," O'Brien said.

Chris Conrad of Los Angeles, director of the Business Alliance for Commercial Hemp, said he expects to see hemp legalized for commercial use within five years. Evans thinks he has found a legal path through the Internal Revenue Service that will allow him to grow hemp commercially this year.

The discussion among marijuana activists came against the backdrop of a report Thursday in Portland by Doug McVay, projects director for the National Organization for the Reform of Marijuana Laws. McVay predicted illegal marijuana production will continue to increase in the United States in the 1990s, with Oregon remaining one of the top growers.

He said Oregon's marijuana crop led all states in 1987 and 1988, based on reports from growers, government agencies and the media. No estimates were available for last year.

Estimates of Oregon's marijuana crop range from $600 million to $1 billion annually, placing Oregon among the three leading states for marijuana growing, U.S. Attorney Charles H. Turner and Multnomah County District Attorney Michael Schrunk said in a report last year.

McVay claimed the Oregon crop is worth as much as $1.5 billion a year, not counting plants seized by police.

Oregon Marijuana Initiative is collecting signatures in hopes of placing an initiative to legalize marijuana on the November 1990 ballot.

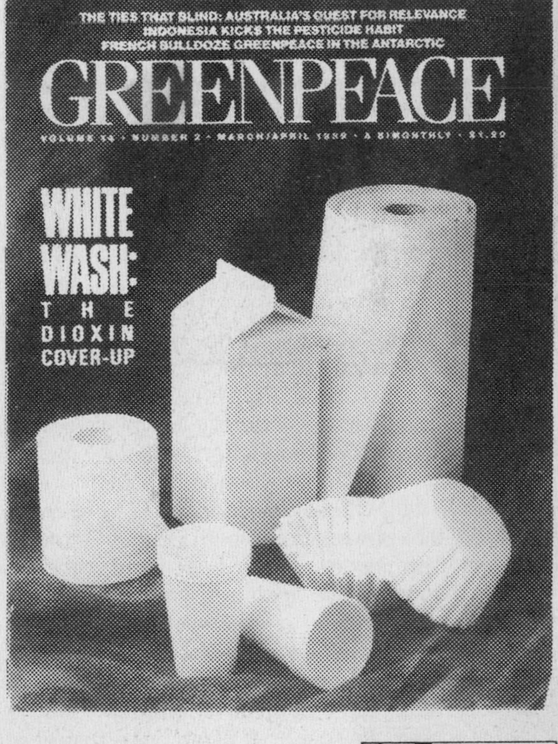
THE TIES THAT BLIND: AUSTRALIA'S QUEST FOR RELEVANCE
INDONESIA KICKS THE PESTICIDE HABIT
FRENCH BULLDOZE GREENPEACE IN THE ANTARCTIC
GREENPEACE
WHITE WASH: THE DIOXIN COVER-UP

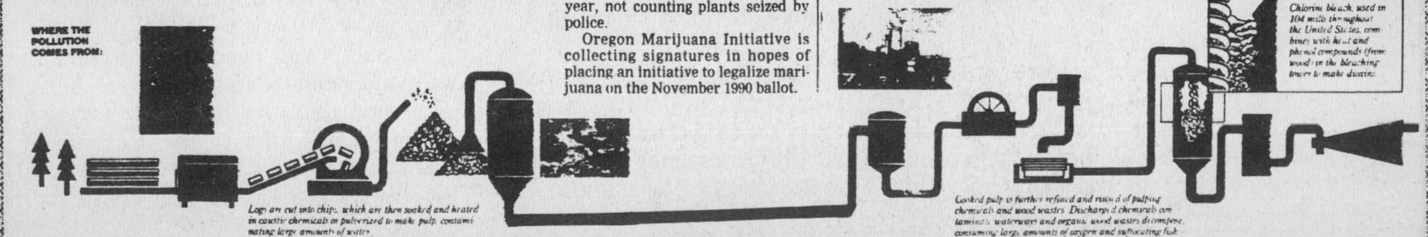
WHERE THE POLLUTION COMES FROM:
Logs are cut into chips, which are then soaked and heated in caustic chemicals or pulverized to make pulp, contaminating large amounts of water.
Cooked pulp is further refined and rinsed of pulping chemicals and wood wastes. Discharged chemicals contaminate waterways and organic wood wastes decompose, consuming large amounts of oxygen and suffocating fish.
Chlorine bleach, used in 104 mills throughout the United States, combines with heat and phenol compounds (from wood) in the bleaching tower to make dioxins.

HEMP FOR FUEL

Excerpted from *Energy Farming in America,* by Lynn Osburn

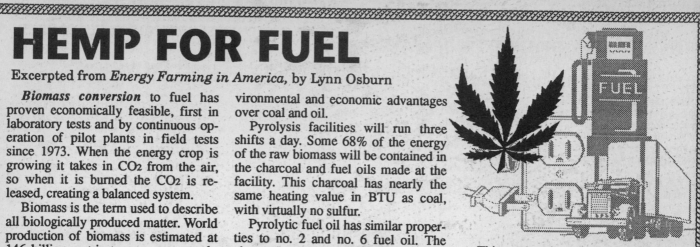

Biomass conversion to fuel has proven economically feasible, first in laboratory tests and by continuous operation of pilot plants in field tests since 1973. When the energy crop is growing it takes in CO_2 from the air, so when it is burned the CO_2 is released, creating a balanced system.

Biomass is the term used to describe all biologically produced matter. World production of biomass is estimated at 146 billion metric tons a year, mostly wild plant growth. Some farm crops and trees can produce up to 20 metric tons per acre of biomass a year. Types of algae and grasses may produce 50 metric tons per year.

This biomass has a heating value of 5000-8000 BTU/lb, with virtually no ash or sulfur produced during combustion. About 6% of contiguous United States land area put into cultivation for biomass could supply all current demands for oil and gas.

The foundation upon which this will be achieved is the emerging concept of "energy farming," wherein farmers grow and harvest crops for biomass conversion to fuels.

Pyrolysis is the technique of applying high heat to organic matter (lignocellulosic materials) in the absence of air or in reduced air. The process can produce charcoal, condensable organic liquids (pyrolitic fuel oil), non-condensable gasses, acetic acid, acetone, and methanol. The process can be adjusted to favor charcoal, pyrolytic oil, gas, or methanol production with a 95.5% fuel-to-feed efficiency.

Pyrolysis has been used since the dawn of civilization. Ancient Egyptians practiced wood distillation by collecting the tars and pyroligneous acid for use in their embalming industry.

Methanol-powered automobiles and reduced emissions from coal-fired power plants can be accomplished by biomass conversion to fuel utilizing pyrolysis technology, and at the same time save the American family farm while turning the American heartland into a prosperous source of clean energy production.

Pyrolysis has the advantage of using the same technology now used to process crude fossil fuel oil and coal. Coal and oil conversion is more efficient in terms of fuel-to-feed ratio, but biomass conversion by pyrolysis has many environmental and economic advantages over coal and oil.

Pyrolysis facilities will run three shifts a day. Some 68% of the energy of the raw biomass will be contained in the charcoal and fuel oils made at the facility. This charcoal has nearly the same heating value in BTU as coal, with virtually no sulfur.

Pyrolytic fuel oil has similar properties to no. 2 and no. 6 fuel oil. The charcoal can be transported economically by rail to all urban area power plants generating electricity. The fuel oil can be transported economically by trucking creating more jobs for Americans. When these plants use charcoal instead of coal, the problems of acid rain will begin to disappear.

When this energy system is on line producing a steady supply of fuel for electrical power plants, it will be more feasible to build the complex gasifying systems to produce methanol from the cubed biomass, or make synthetic gasoline from the methanol by the addition of the Mobil Co. process equipment to the gasifier.

Farmers must be allowed to grow an energy crop capable of producing 10 tons per acre in 90-120 days. This crop must be woody in nature and high in lignocellulose. It must be able to grow in all climactic zones in America.

And it should not compete with food crops for the most productive land, but be grown in rotation with food crops or on marginal land where food crop production isn't profitable.

When farmers can make a profit growing energy, it will not take long to get 6% of continental American land mass into cultivation of biomass fuel —enough to replace our economy's dependence on fossil fuels. We will no longer be increasing the CO_2 burden in the atmosphere. The threat of global greenhouse warming and adverse climactic change will diminish.

To keep costs down, pyrolysis reactors need to be located within a 50 mile radius of the energy farms. This necessity will bring life back to our small towns by providing jobs locally.

Hemp is the number one biomass producer on planet earth: 10 tons per acre in approximately four months. It is a woody plant containing 77% cellulose. Wood produces 60% cellulose.

This energy crop can be harvested with equipment readily available. It can be "cubed" by modifying hay cubing equipment. This method condenses the bulk, reducing trucking costs from the field to the pyrolysis reactor. And the biomass cubes are ready for conversion with no further treatment.

Hemp is drought resistant, making it an ideal crop in the dry western regions of the country. Hemp is the only biomass resource capable of making America energy independent. And our government outlawed it in 1938.

Remember, in 10 years, by the year 2000, America will have exhausted 80% of her petroleum reserves. Will we then go to war with the Arabs for the privilege of driving our cars; will we stripmine our land for coal, and poison our air so we can drive our autos an extra 100 years; will we raze our forests for our energy needs?

During World War II, our supply of hemp was cut off by the Japanese. The federal government responded to the emergency by suspending marijuana prohibition. Patriotic American farmers were encouraged to apply for a license to cultivate hemp and responded enthusiastically. Hundreds of thousands of acres of hemp were grown.

The argument against hemp production does not hold up to scrutiny: hemp grown for biomass makes very poor grade marijuana. The 20 to 40 million Americans who smoke marijuana would loath to smoke hemp grown for biomass, so a farmer's hemp biomass crop is worthless as marijuana.

It is time the government once again respond to our economic emergency as they did in WWII to permit our farmers to grow American hemp so this mighty nation can once again become energy independent and smog free.

For more information on the many uses of hemp, contact the Business Alliance for Commerce in Hemp, Box 71093, LA, CA 90071-0093

ON-WOOD PLANT FIBERS AS A SOURCE OF RAW MATERIAL FOR PULP INDUSTRY

Anon.
: PAP/79/7, Ronze: UN Food & Agriculture Organization,
r. 1979, 12pp. (in English) (PM 5785)

part I of this report the main non-wood fibers used or considered for pulping
d papermaking are reviewed under three main group headings: agricultural
idues from sugar, cereal or fibre corps; grasses and reeds; and bast and hemp
nt fibers. Also, statistical information on world non-wood fiber pulping capaci-
n 1977 and an estimate for 1982 is presented. In Part II of the report, a ne-
cted non-wood fiber supply is considered, namely sesbania aculeata. The dis-
ution and agricultural aspects of this plant are described and its potential use
he pulp and paper industry is outlined. Tests carried out indicate a similarity
ween sesbania aculeata pulp and birch pulp.

OMPLETE UTILIZATION OF HEMP THROUGH ALKALI-OXYGEN & CHEMI-MECHANICAL PROCESSES

A. Bosia and D. Nisi
eprints 17th EUCEPA Conf., Vienna, Oct. 1977,
cent developments in pulp and papermaking, Book 1,
77-86 (in English) (PM 4132B)

tails are given of work done by ENCC in Italy on the use of hemp in paper
anufacture. Studies were carried out on the use of hurds fibers, as opposed to
e long fiber fraction, with the aim of producing a pulp to replace hardwood. A
v process for separating the hurds from the bark long fibers is described, and
rk on mechanical or chemi-mechanical pulping of the hurds is summarized.
ygen-alkali pulping of the long fibers is also discussed.

ROBLEMS OF RAW MATERIALS AND SHORT AND EDIUM TERM PROSPECTS OF THE ITALIAN PAPER NDUSTRY

F. Nardi)
l. Carta, vol. 15, no. 7, July 1977, pp. 262-271
Italian)

e problem of fibrous raw material supply in the Italian paper industry is dis-
ssed. It is suggested that raw material consumption could be reduced by: in-
eased recycling of waste paper; greater use of semi-chemical, chemi-mechanical
d thermo-mechanical pulps; and more use of fibers such as straw, hemp, waste
od, young and unbarked wood

ARIATION IN THE CONTENT OF CELLULOSE DUR-NG THE VEGETATIVE PERIOD OF HEMP

R. Becietti and N. Ciaralli
llulosa Carta, Vol. 27, no. 3, Mar. 1976, pp. 27-30
Italian); Abstr. Bull. Inst. Pap. Chem., vol. 47, no. 5, Nov. 1976, p. 518

emical analysis of hemp (Cannabis sativa) shows that the cellulose content of
th the bark and the woody core increases as the plant matures, while the ex-
actives, ash, and lignin contents decrease. Thus, one can conclude that better
lping yields will be obtained by delaying, weather permitting, the harvesting of
e hemp as long as possible.

INFLUENCE OF NITROGEN FERTILIZATION AND HARVESTING TIME ON THE PRODUCTION OF FIBER AND CELLULOSE BY CULTIVARS AND HYBRIDS OF HEMP. NOTE 1.

F. Basso and C. Ruggiero
Cellulosa Carta, vol. 27, no. 3, Mar. 1976, pp. 17-26
(in Italian); Abstr. Bull. Inst. Pap. Chem., vol. 47, no. 5, Nov. 1976, p. 518

Results are reported on a two-year test conducted in the Volturno river plain
(Italy) on cultivars and hybrids of hemp, with the aim of investigating the effects
of two levels of N fertilization (80 and 160 kg/ha), two application methods) solid
and liquid), and two harvesting times (full bloom and mature seed) on cellulose
fiber yields. Better results as regards cellulose fiber yields were obtained when
harvesting was conducted on plants with mature seeds.

ANNUAL CROPS: RENEWABLE SOURCE FOR CELLULOSE

D. L. Miller
J. Appl. Polymer Sci. (Appl. Polymer Symp.), no. 28,
1975, pp. 21-28; Abstr. Bull. Inst. Pap. Chem., vol. 47, no. 2, Aug. 1976, p. 175

Cellulose materials from annual crops have been historically of major industrial
importance, predating the use of wood for paper by centuries. Pressed sheets
from papyrus were made in Egypt as early as 500 B. C. Paper making techniques
related to present processes were based primarily on annual fibers such as cotton, flax, and hemp. Cellulose is commercially available from annual fiber crops,
by-products, residues. Typical crops are cotton, reeds, esparto grass, jute, hemp,
and kenaf; they may be cultivated or of natural growth. By-products include cereal straws, bagasse, oilseed stalks, and similar cellulosic materials associated with
principal agricultural wastes. Annual crops have increasing potential as renewable raw materials to meet future requirements of cellulose or cellulose-based
chemicals

NEW RAW MATERIALS FOR PAPER: MECHANICAL PULP FROM "HURDS" (WOODY CORE OF HEMP)

A. Bosia
Papel, Vol. 36, Mar. 1975, pp. 43-47 (in Portuguese);
Abstr. Bull. Inst. Pap. Chem., vol. 46, no. 3, Sept. 1975, p. 300

Studies were carried out at ENCC concerning the hardwood, Paulownia fortunei,
with respect to general characteristics, fiber dimensions, chemical composition,
and suitability to NSCC and sodium bisulphite pulping and to refiner ground-
wood production, and concerning the woody core of hemp (Cannabis sativa) with
respect to chemical composition and suitability to mechanical and thermomechanical pulping. The hardwood species is shown to be well suited to NSCC and
bisulphite pulping, giving pulps with breaking lengths of up to 9400 m. Refiner
groundwood obtained form the species had a breaking length of 2200 m, a tear
factor of 0.2, a burst factor fo 35.3, and a GE brightness of 70. Data from refiner
groundwood and thermomechanical pulp production using the woody core of
hemp indicate that this material should also be of commercial interest as a papermaking raw material. Breading length ran as high as 3620 m; GE brightness,
as high as 64.5 (bleached thermomechanical pulp).

DROUGHT HELPS HEMP

The Official Record, USDA, December 25, 1930, p. 3
This year's drought has had a good effect on
e crop at least. Hemp grown in Kentucky, Illinois,
d Wisconsin, in fields that were well prepared and
anted early, is giving a remarkable yield of fiber of
cceptionally good quality, say the fiber plant spe-
alists of the department. Some of Wisconsin's 1930
op show a yield of about 1,000 pounds of fiber an
re; the average yield in that State for the preced-
g 10 years was about 800 pounds an acre.

USDA Bulletin 404: Hemp Hurds as Paper-Making Material
United States Department of Agriculture, October 14, 1916, p.25

CONCLUSIONS: There appears to be little doubt that under the present system of forest use and
consumption the present supply cannot withstand the demands placed upon it. By the time improved
methods of forestry have established an equilibrium between production and consumption, the price of
pulp wood may be such that a knowledge of other available raw materials may be imperative

Semicommercial paper-making tests were conducted, therefore, on hemp hurds, in cooperation with
a paper manufacturer. After several trials, under conditions of treatment and manufacture which are
regarded as favorable in comparison with those used with pulp wood, paper was produced which received very favorable comment both from investigators and from the trade which according to official
test would be classed as a No. 1 machine finished printing paper.

New Bibliographic Sources for the 1991 edition:

Encyclopedia of Textiles, 3rd edition
By the editors of American Fabrics and Fashions Magazine
William C. Segal, Publisher
Prentice-Hall, Inc.
Englewood cliffs, N.J.
1980

"Chemical characteristics - Like other bast fibres, hemp breaks down into cellulose, water, ash, fat wax and gum. In this case cellulose is about 77% of the composition.
"Characteristics - The hemp fibre runs 40 to 80 inches in length, is generally yellowish-brown in color and fairly lustrous. It has good breaking strength and looks very much like flax in general appearance.
"History and production- Hemp , like flax, is a prehistoric fiber and is thought to have been used first in Asia. It was also known in ancient China and Persia and Japan."

PAPER TRADE JOURNAL
Technical Association Section
May 15, 1930
"Physical and Chemical Characteristics of Hemp Stalks and Seed Flax Straw"
By E.R. Schafer and F. A. Simmonds
Presented before the Division of Cellulose Chemistry at the 78th meeting of the American Chemical Society, Minneapolis, Minn., Sept. 9 to 13, 1929 published in Ind. Eng. Chem. 21, 1241 (Dec., 1929.)

"Chemical Characteristics - The bast fiber of hemp may be noted from Table 1 to consist of relatively pure cellulose associated with materials easily dissolved in organic solvents, dilute alkaline solutions, and water; whereas the hurds, although containing a large amount of material soluble in dilute alkali, contain a relatively smaller amount of cellulose, which is closely combined with larger amounts of lignin and pentosans in proportions similar to that found in wood. In these general characteristics hemp fiber and hurds are similar to flax fibres and shives."

A Statistical View of the Commerce of the United States (1816)
Reprints of Economic Classics
Augustus M. Kelley Publishers
New York
1967

Amounts of hemp imported from Petersburgh, Russia 1783-1805, domestic production of goods in early America also chronicled.

"The Fabric Catalogue"
Martin Hardingham
Pocket Books
1978

"Canvas-Canvas has become the generic term to describe many types of heavy, closely -woven cotton and linen fabrics. The name canvas comes from the Early English work canevas which derives from the Latin for hemp: cannabis. It was from hemp and flax that early, heavy closely -woven fabrics were made for tents and sails."

A History of Agriculture and Prices In England
1259-1793
Compiled entirely from original and contemporaneous record by James E. T. Rogers, M.A. Professor of Political Economy, Oxford
MDCCCLXVL

"Hemp and Flax. Note. Hemp is sold by the petra, the garb, the bundle, the stater, and the pound. Flax, which has only been found once, by the garb (concerning the period from 1278-1376).

Agrarian Kentucky
University Press of Kentucky
Bicentennial Bookshelf

Kentucky hemp was valued at $500,000 in 1817.

Matthews' Textile Fibers 6th Edition
by H.R. Mauersberger
John Wiley and Sons Inc., N.Y.
Chapman and Hall, Ltd. London
1954

"Individual (hemp fibre) cells are quite long, ranging, according to Vetillart , from 0.20 to 2.16 in., and averaging 0.59 to 0.98 in."

CIBA REVIEW Volume 5 numbers 49-60
1945-47
by Gustav Schaefer, Basle
Pages 1779-1794
"In Japan hemp is considered to be the oldest cultivated textile plan

CIBA REVIEW
1961-62
The Hemp Plant
by Luigi Castellini
Director of the "Centro Difesa Canapa"
Milan Italy
p 2-31
"The following is a short list of the principal applications, with an indication of their respective contributions to total production of retted fibre of Italian origin:
· 50%: household textiles, dress materials, fabrics for interior decorating (soft furnishings), and baggage linings;
30%: industrial fabrics such as drills, waterproof tarpaulins, webbing, belting, carrier straps, filters, waterhose, netting, and twin and sewing thread for industrial and craft uses.
20% : string, rope, and cable, especially for marine purposes.
All products made from hemp benefit from the natural advantag which the hemp fibre offers the processing industries. Its most notable feature is the strikingly high level of tensile strength which unequalled by any natural fibre and only surpassed by the strongest synthetics. To this must be added other intrinsic advantages such a permeability to evaporated perspiration, and absorbency, which the

hemp industry is showing great ingenuity in exploiting to meet the demands of modern living."

1977 Report to the Ontario , Canada, Department of Agriculture. Unattributed, but generally informative, we only have a retyped photocopy of this text.

The paper outlines the history of Canadian hemp farming and points out potential value of Canada domestically producing denim and twine.
"Canada is bound with 67 other nations to the 1961 Single International Convention on Narcotics. This agreement dictates outmoded terms concerning cultivation of the cannabis plant in all it's forms, fibre and oil seed production is under needless restrictions because of the S.I.C. Act."

Popular Mechanics Magazine :
June, 1939 "From the Test Tube to You"
by Lammot DuPont, President of Dupont, Inc.
"Consider our natural resources. The chemist has aided in conserving natural resources by developing products to supplement or wholly replace natural products....Synthetic plastics find application in fabricating a wide variety of articles, many of which in the past were made from natural products."

Popular Mechanics Magazine
December, 1941 "Pinch-Hitters for Defense"
"When Henry Ford recently unveiled his plastic car, result of twelve years of research, he gave the world a glimpse of the automobile of tomorrow, it's tough panels molded under hydraulic pressure of 1,500 pounds per square inch from a recipe that calls for 70 percent of cellulose fibers from wheat straw, hemp and sisal plus 30 per cent resin binder."
Also in the same article : "Yesterday you lived in the age of metals. Today metal is yours only to the point where your need encroaches on that of your country's defense; for the moment, it is an age of substitutes. Tomorrow—the post-war tommorrow—those substitutes may have proved superior; the plastics and synthetic yarns and new chemicals and molded wood products and other substitutes invented ·

Athens newspapers tried to disprove that "hemp can save world" and went to Ohio U. Botany Dept. Professors, who report back that hemp can probably do every thing we said, and that what we claimed for hemp was probably not overblown

The Athens NEWS
Volume 13 Issue 92
Thursday, Nov. 16, 1989

Authorities examine pot claims

By Jim Phillips
Athens NEWS Writer

At last week's "Just Say Know" conference in Athens, members of the National Organization to Reform Marijuana Laws (NORML) and other groups took a new tack on the pot-legalization question. While few of them abandoned their advocacy of the drug as a recreational substance, they raised another argument for making it legal — the marijuana plant's alleged usefulness as a fiber and energy crop.

Drawing on the research of author Jack Herer, they claimed that the hemp plant — the source of marijuana — could be no less than an ecological panacea. Planted in bulk, they contended, the sturdy, fast-growing hemp plant could provide a better source of clothing and paper fiber than cotton, as well as plentiful biomass (a fancy name for "organic stuff") and a potential source of chemicals, proteins and cheap, clean fuel.

In the vision of those who called for widespread hemp cultivation, running the country on renewable hemp-derived fuel would go a long way toward eliminating the dangerous pollution associated with burning petroleum.

Some continue to question the motives of those who present hemp as an answer toward environmental sanity. An Ohio University botany professor, however, said Monday that for the most part, the claims being made on hemp's behalf are probably not overblown.

"It's a big crop in some parts of the world," confirmed Professor Jim Cavender. "They used to use it for rope and clothing. Hemp was your predominant fiber in some parts of the world ... it's a very useful plant."

In his writings and speeches, Herer has maintained that hemp is far and away the best plant choice for producing biomass, as it grows faster and bigger than most plants, and does well in a variety of conditions.

"He could be right there," mused Cavender. "I haven't seen any data." The botanist did confirm, though, that hemp "produces a lot of mass in one growing season — it produces a lot of bulk," and added, "at this latitude there probably wouldn't be anything to compete with it ... It's a pretty vigorous plant. It grows like a weed. It doesn't have too many enemies."

Herer has said also that hemp is much preferable to cotton as a source of fiber for clothing, being softer and stronger, and causing very little depletion of the soil in which it grows.

"It is a good fiber," Cavender acknowledged. "I think it's a little rougher (than cotton) ... Of course, cotton is the worst, as far as effect on the soil is concerned. About one-half of the chemicals used in American agriculture are used on cotton. Someday we may have to get away from cotton, and hemp might be an alternative."

In what may come as sad news to those at NORML, Cavender added that hemp grown for fiber and energy need not be worth much rolled in a joint. Attaining a high concentration of the plant's active drug ingredient requires selective cultivation and specific growing procedures, he said.

"The stuff that grows wild in India is no good (as a drug)," he noted. "And I think the stuff that used to grow wild here (in the United States) was no good ... It could be grown with a very low drug content, and I think that probably would be a very good idea, if this were permitted."

Athens Police Capt. Clyde Beasley suggested that the entire environmental angle on pot may be just one more facet of a public-relations push on the drug's behalf by dealers and users.

"If you're a user, you're going to be for it, right?" he asked. "It's just like politics — you hire people to be your lobbyist ... You know why NORML's doing what it's doing."

Beasley said of legalization that he would "hate to see it come about. What's it going to do for society? ... You legalize it ... you make it more readily accessible. Now there are some restraints."

One argument made in support of marijuana — especially in this area, known as a major cultivation spot — is the amount of economic activity pot growing generates. (By some estimates, marijuana is the nation's number two cash crop; in places like Athens and Meigs counties, it may be number one.) Beasley, however, contended that any local monetary benefit from pot is illusory.

"I've never seen any of that money stay in this area," he declared. "It goes to people in the *business*. It goes out of here in grocery sacks or whatever. It doesn't help pump up the economy out here."

The Ohio University Ecology Club co-sponsored the "Just Say Know" conference with NORML. Ecology Club treasurer Craig Goldstein said Wednesday that his group does not support the use of hemp as a drug, but would like to see the plant utilized for its many useful properties.

"We've gone through some incredible evidence" regarding hemp's potential as a fuel, Goldstein said, adding that if the facts he has read are true, "I'm against anything that would prevent further research." According to the research, he added, hemp produces 40 times the biomass of other plants, such as corn, that have been proposed as energy sources. By a process called pyrolysis, he explained, the plant is turned into methanol, which could be used to run engines — including those in cars.

Among other sources, Goldstein cited a paper by Lynn Osburn, "Energy Farming in America." In that paper, Osburn points out that "hemp grown for biomass makes very poor grade marijuana. The 20 to 40 million Americans who smoke marijuana would be loath to smoke hemp grown for biomass."

State Rep. Mary Abel, D-Athens, who attended a senate subcommittee hearing on drug legislation at which Herer pitched the hemp-for-energy idea, cautiously praised the "diversity of opinion" heard at the session. However, she added that she feels the dangers of marijuana as a drug may outweigh any value it has environmentally.

"People are concerned that drugs like marijuana really become a gateway drug," Abel said. "We know we've got an abuse that is growing. Changing the category of what is legal is not going to help the problem."

LOS ANGELES TIMES ★ FRIDAY, DECEMBER 15, 1989

Congress to Host Meeting on Global Warming Issue

■ **Environment:** Senators say it's time to act on pressing issues. But they deny seeking to upstage the Administration.

By WILLIAM J. EATON
TIMES STAFF WRITER

WASHINGTON—Getting a jump on the Bush Administration, Congress announced Thursday that a first-ever conference of legislators from 33 nations will be convened in Washington next spring to consider global warming and other environmental issues.

While it will precede by six months an international meeting on global warming to be hosted by President Bush, Senate sponsors of the April 29-May 2 meeting said it is intended to spur international cooperation, not to upstage the President.

"We believe the time for action is now," said Sen. Albert Gore Jr. (D-Tenn.), chairman of the Senate delegation to the conference. "We are ready to move."

Gore insisted that the conference was not an exercise in one-upmanship. "This is in no way partisan," he said. "We are not taking an adversarial position against the Administration."

Others in the seven-member Senate delegation said the meeting would give the United States a chance again to assume leadership on worldwide environmental issues that had been lost during the Reagan Administration. A House delegation will be named later.

□

Congressional sources said the conference of lawmakers—authorized by legislation approved last August—reflected a bipartisan concern that Bush was not responding fast enough to serious global problems despite his call for a major overhaul of the nation's clean-air laws.

About 250 legislators—including some from the Soviet Union, Poland and Hungary, but none from China—were invited to the spring conference. The participants will seek consensus on a new set of environmental goals to deal with global warming and other major concerns.

Gore said climate change, deforestation, the spread of deserts, depletion of the ozone layer, vanishing species, the impact of population growth and prospects for sustainable development would be the leading issues before the conference of lawmakers.

"The global ecological crisis we face demands unprecedented responses such as this—the first-ever gathering of the legislators ultimately responsible for ... policies needed to change our future and the course of our world for generations to come," Gore said.

Sen. John H. Chafee (R-R.I.) said the United States should take the lead on global environmental problems. By the time the conference is held, Chafee predicted, the Senate will have approved a clean-air bill that would eliminate production of chlorofluorocarbons by the year 2000 and reduce carbon dioxide emissions from cars.

Sen. John Kerry (D-Mass.) said the conference would enable the United States to regain its pre-eminent position on environmental issues. Sen. John Heinz (R-Pa.) contended that the federal government was lagging behind the states and individual citizens on these issues.

□

"Environmental isolationism must be a way of the past," Senate Majority Leader George J. Mitchell (D-Me.) said in a statement. "Our planet has become too small to insist on acting alone or to insist on acting only if everyone adopts the same policy."

President Bush had initially resisted calls for an international conference on global warming. During his Malta talks with Soviet President Mikhail S. Gorbachev, however, Bush reversed himself and announced that the United States would host such a meeting next fall.

The Administration was criticized at a meeting in the Netherlands last month when it opposed efforts by virtually all other industrialized nations to limit gases that contribute to the greenhouse effect.

In February, two months before the congressional conference, an International Panel on Climate Change composed of scientists and other experts will meet in Washington to consider new evidence on global warming and devise ways to

Greenhouse Effect Tied To Possible Disease Hike

THE ASSOCIATED PRESS

WASHINGTON — Changes in the Earth's climate could encourage the spread of diseases like encephalitis and rabies, while at the same time damaging the human body's ability to fight them, a conference on climate and health was told Tuesday.

Potential problems stem both from the increase in ultraviolet radiation, as the protective ozone layer in the stratosphere is damaged, and from climate warming that many scientists believe is occurring in a so-called greenhouse effect.

Ultraviolet radiation, already known to cause skin cancer, also has a major effect in reducing the response of the human immune system, said Dr. Raymond Daynes of the University of Utah.

"There is really no advantage to sunbathing. Your skin is really not meant to withstand ultraviolet radiation," Daynes told the conference on "Global Atmospheric Change and Public Health."

SUNDAY, FEBRUARY 11, 1990 LOS ANGELES TIMES

Hot Air and the Greenhouse Effect

It doesn't take a degree in meteorology to see that the White House is cooling off on global warming. The question is: Why?

If this reflects only President Bush's customary caution, there is no harm done. Even if it reflects skepticism about being able to come up soon with precise measurements of anything as vast as the planetary atmosphere, there is no real cause to strip Bush of his environmental epaulets.

But if it represents a backing away from concern that man-made carbon dioxides are forming an envelope around the Earth that eventually will raise temperatures in strange places by trapping heat that now escapes into space, then the environmentalists are right to worry.

Few scientists question the validity of the theory that various gases, most of them generated by burning fuels for energy, are creating a monster greenhouse effect. They just want more information before they are ready to join the handful who think they know enough now to say when heat will cause oceans to rise and glaciers to melt.

Bush was right to ask Congress for one thing that is essential to answer questions like those: money. His new budget would increase this country's Global Change research program by 60%, to more than $1 billion.

Caution on the greenhouse also can cause little trouble as long as Bush does not slow down programs that could retard global warming because they make sense on other grounds, such as making electrical generators and automobiles more efficient and saving tropical rain forests.

But the President was on rather shaky ground when he talked of making absolutely certain that future efforts to deal with the greenhouse effect are consistent with sound principles of economics. Nearly a century ago, a British economist, A. C. Pigou, developed the now widely held theory that industries could not expect to pay hard cash for raw materials, land, labor and the rent of money and then use air and water as if they were free goods. Principles of economics don't get any more sound or venerable than that.

How Our Heads of State Got High

High Times April, 1980

May 12–13: sowed hemp at muddy hole by swamp.

August 7: began to separate the male from the female hemp —rather too late.

While it is unlikely that George Washington, who penned these diary notes 200 years ago, smoked any of the scraggly rope-dope he was growing on his Mount Vernon plantation, he certainly dreamed of hemp as a cash crop. After all, it had a solid foreign market and was perfect for cottage industry, basketmaking and such. He won over Thomas Jefferson, who began importing hemp seeds to Monticello, but failed to win the support of early American farmers, who favored tobacco cultivation. If, by some historical quirk, they had instead followed Washington's advice, early U.S. history might have been considerably headier.

As it turned out, not until the 19th century did Americans —including presidents—really turn on. The patent-medicine boom in the mid 1800s was largely responsible: Virtually everyone sampled various opium-, cannabis- and cocaine-based remedies and elixirs. If the president had the flu, a stomach ache, piles or a hangover, the prescribed remedy was tincture of opium: laudanum. Also prescribed for all manner of "female complaints," laudanum found its way into first ladies' medicine chests too. A century before Betty Ford got strung out on Valium and vodka, Mary Todd Lincoln was portrayed by presidential biographer William H. Herdon as a virtual patent-medicine junkie.

On the whole, however, records of bummers on these 19th-century elixirs are far outweighed by the good trips. Ulysses S. Grant, burned out by years of boozing, was miraculously revitalized near the end of his life by daily doses of Mariani tea, one of chemist Angelo Mariani's delightful cocaine-based products. It so bolstered the aging ex-president that he was able to put in hours of work a day on his memoirs, valued as one of the finest accounts of the Civil War.

During the 1880s, coca wine, another Mariani tonic, enjoyed unsurpassed popularity on the patent-medicine market. The enterprising Mariani eventually rounded up glowing endorsements from the prince of Wales, the czar and czarina of Russia, the kings of Norway and Sweden, and Pope Leo XIII. In the United States, Pres. William McKinley's secretary noted that a case of Vin Ma-

JFK's most effective space program was the one he conducted on himself.

riani had received an enthusiastic reception from the president.

All this came to an end—sort of —with the election of Theodore Roosevelt in 1901, under whose "progressive" administration the first federal controls on what people drank, swallowed and smoked were instituted and the stage was set for Prohibition. Still, the rough-riding, trust-busting Teddy may not have been the straight arrow he claimed to be. One day in 1912, according to the account of one Herford Cowling, a 91-year-old retired newsreel cameraman, the retired president halted a motorcade on its way to the Roosevelt Dam when he spotted a stand of "cactus fruits" growing in the middle of the Arizona desert. According to Cowling, reporters watched bewildered as he rushed to the site and commenced "pulling off the little green bulbs and eating them."

Still, by the time Teddy Roosevelt left office in 1909, the nation's first antidrug campaign was really rolling. First came the Harrison Narcotics Act of 1914, prohibiting over-the-counter sales of opiates and cocaine. However high-minded their pitch to save children from Mother Baily's Soothing Syrup and other kiddie narcotics, and to regulate the quality of medicine, some of the prohibitionists concealed darker motives. This country's first official drug policy was instituted against a background of Hearst-syndicate "yellow peril" journalism, portraying Chinese as shifty, no-good dope fiends. The hidden objective was racial and financial: to halt the flood of Chinese immigrants into the U.S. labor pool. Racism also underscored cocaine prohibition, as characterized by Dr. Christopher Koch's statement before Congress in 1910 that "most attacks upon white women in the South are the direct result of a cocaine-crazed Negro brain."

Hysteria and hypocrisy have all too often characterized drug policy since then. The Volstead

Act (passed 1919, repealed 1933) banned alcohol, but didn't prevent Pres. Warren Harding from hosting regular booze parties. And 50 years later, Richard Nixon launched his "war on drugs" while the CIA was actually running shotgun for opium traders in Southeast Asia to prevent the well-armed opium dealers from supporting the Communists. There was a reassuring note of cosmic justice as the curtain fell on Tricky Dick, stoned on downs, talking to the presidential portraits in the White House. Even his spiritual adviser, Billy Graham, had to lament that it was "sleeping pills and demons" that caused Nixon's decline and fall in 1974 (see HIGH TIMES, "The High & Mighty," August '79).

Among other recent presidents, chemical preferences have been varied. According to William Burroughs, Dwight Eisenhower swore by the rejuvenative qualities of placenta serum, a compound 'rich in endorphins (natural body opiates) derived from the placentas of sheep.

John Kennedy's favorite tonics are by now widely documented. He received regular injections of megavitamins and amphetamines from Dr. Max Jacobson ("Dr. Jake"), who has since—many ex-patients feel, unfairly—been barred from practice. According

to other accounts, JFK was also fond of the procaine-novocaine derivative "gerovital" (CH_3), which advocates tout as a dandy antidepressant, libido stimulator and longevity drug. (The Food and Drug Administration has yet to approve it for general use.) And in 1962, according to Judith Exner's account, he became the first president to smoke dope in the White House.

No less enlightened was brother Bobby. Psychedelic pioneer Dr. John Beresford (writing in the introduction to Peter Stafford's Psychedelic Encyclopedia) notes that in the spring of 1963, Bobby was known to be taking LSD or psilocybin and providing psychedelic entertainment for foreign dignitaries. This at a time when the CIA was organizing its own secret acid tests.

Once upon a time none of this would have been considered at all shocking. Among primitive peoples, the heads—shamanic healers and prophets—have always been among the most highly regarded tribal members. The pharaohs revered opium so much they took jarfuls of it with them on their journeys to the land of the dead. Not only were the leaders in ancient Greece familiar with the many healing and mind-expanding properties of drugs, their gods and goddesses turned on too: According to Greek myth, Demeter was the first opium eater. And in the 11th century, Hasan-i-Sabah, the Old Man of the Mountain, rose to lead the Moslem faithful against the Crusaders. According to legend, his fabled Assassins (Hashashans) topped off their battle-weary days by smoking hashish in lovely pleasure gardens. So why not presidents?

The point is simply this: While attitudes regarding specific highs may change, the turn-on goes on, right on up to the top.

—*Jeff Goldberg*

Los Angeles Times 10-8-89 p. 15

Iran Executes Over 30 Drug Traffickers

From Associated Press

NICOSIA, Cyprus—Iran executed more than 30 drug traffickers Saturday under tough new laws passed as part of an anti-narcotics campaign, according to Iranian news reports.

The smugglers were tried by

Islamic revolutionary courts, which are charged with carrying out the anti-drug campaign, the official Islamic Republic News Agency said.

It is believed that about 950 convicted smugglers have been executed under the new laws.

IRNA said 10 traffickers, including a woman, were hanged Saturday in Tehran's Qasr prison. Tehran Radio said 21 others, including another two women, went to the gallows in eight other Iranian cities.

High Times July 1980

A High & Mighty SPECIAL REPORT

Paul's Pot-Bust Shocker Makes Him Jailhouse Rocker

January 16, 1980: Beatle Paulie makes unscheduled appearance at Japanese public prosecutor's office praying for a ticket to ride.

by Harry Wasserman

"I think we could decriminalize marijuana, and I would like to see a really unbiased medical report on it," said pop singer Paul McCartney after being deported from Japan for bringing almost half a pound of marijuana into Tokyo for an 11-concert Wings tour that had to be cancelled.

"I spent my time [in the Tokyo jail] making a mental list of all those drugs which are legal but dangerous. We're all on drugs—cigarettes, whiskey and wild, wild women. Society thinks alcohol is terrific, yet it kills. Cigarettes can kill. They are worse than marijuana. It is just not true that marijuana can kill. What about all the little old ladies on Valium? Think of aspirin's danger to the stomach."

McCartney said he preferred the limited decriminalization of pot in the United States to Japan's harsh drug laws, under which he had faced up to seven years of imprisonment and a possible fine of up to $2,000.

The former Beatle's stand on pot first surfaced in the beady days of *Sgt. Pepper* and the Summer of Love. McCartney helped pay for a full-page advertisement in the London *Times* of July 24, 1967, that called for legalization of pot possession, release of all prisoners on possession charges and government research into marijuana's medical uses. The ad, sponsored by a group called Soma, was signed by 65 Britishers including all four Beatles, their manager Brian Epstein, author Graham Greene, psychologist R.D. Laing, 16 doctors and two members of Parliament.

McCartney used to be an active supporter of the Legalise Cannabis Campaign, the British NORML, whose current sponsors include rock star Commander Cody, actress Julie Christie and classical guitarist John Williams.

Prior to the mishap in Japan, McCartney was busted three times for pot. He paid a $2,000 fine for smuggling hashish into Sweden in 1972, was fined for pot possession in Scotland that same year and was fined $240 for growing pot on his Scottish Highlands farm in 1973. His wife Linda was arrested in Los Angeles for pot possession in 1975, but the charges were dropped.

These busts had resulted in Japan denying McCartney admission to the country on previous occasions, but Japanese Immigration Bureau officials changed their minds after continual pressure from music promoters such as Udo Music, which eventually booked the Wings tour. McCartney's arrival in Tokyo was his first visit since a Beatles tour there in '66, and Japanese police confirm that he was a marked man because of his past busts.

On January 16, McCartney was arrested by Japanese customs officials at Tokyo International Airport when they found two plastic bags in his suitcases containing 219 grams of marijuana (approximately 7.7 ounces).

"I didn't try to hide [the pot]," says McCartney. "I had just come from America and I still had the American attitude that marijuana isn't that bad. I did not realize how strict the Japanese attitude is."

McCartney was taken in handcuffs to a government office while Japanese officials decided what action to take. There is no immediate bail in Japan. Customs officials quoted Paul's first admission of smuggling after five hours of questioning: "I brought some hemp for my smoking." He spent the night in the Tokyo jail.

The next day, says Paul, "I was taken to the narcotics headquarters, handcuffed and a rope tied around me, led along like a dog." While McCartney was interrogated for six hours, 200 fans held a vigil outside the bureau, some weeping, others screaming "Paul! Paul!" Linda and other Wings members were also questioned but not charged. Narcotics officials say McCartney was "relaxed and cooperative," insisting to the narcs that he brought the pot into Japan for his own use.

Flashback: Venus and Mars learn they're busted for pot possession in 1972.

After the interrogation, narcotics agents tried to return McCartney to jail but were forced back into the bureau by hundreds of screaming fans who blocked the way in a hysteria reminiscent of early '60s Beatlemania. Riot police were called in to restore order, and McCartney was eventually taken away.

On January 18, the Tokyo District Court permitted the public prosecutor's office to detain McCartney for up to ten days for questioning.

"At first I thought [the jail] was barbaric," McCartney said. "But underneath their inscrutable exterior the guards were quite warm. We joked and had sing-songs, songs like 'Baby Face' and 'Red Red Robin.' I also got a few requests for 'Yesterday.' I would sing, they clapped. It was a bit of a laugh."

He described a typical day in jail: "I was woken at six in the morning, then had to sit cross-legged for roll call. It was like *Bridge on the River Kwai*: They shouted out '22' [his prison number] and I had to shout back 'Hi.' But I did it. I wasn't going to go against the system."

After inspection, he was given a bowl of seaweed and onion soup—"not the greatest thing in the morning if you're used to cornflakes." Breakfast was followed by 20 minutes of exercises. Lunch was bread and jam. In the afternoon came questioning by narcotics agents.

At night he read in his cell, but lights went out at 8 P.M. He said he tried to sleep on a thin mattress and admitted, "I like a soft bed. But I have no complaints. All in all I was very well treated."

McCartney was denied a request for his guitar but was allowed to have his entourage bring him extra blankets, clothes and hot food. He made friends with two fellow prisoners, one doing time for murder and the other on a similar pot charge.

Paul's lawyer, Lee Eastman, was flown into Tokyo to plan the defense with the help of Japanese lawyer Tasuko Matsuo. The prosecutor, Keiji Yonezawa, was discussing the case with D.W.F. Warren-Knott, a first secretary at the British embassy, on January 19 when a call came in from Sen. Edward Kennedy back in the States. "Senator Kennedy said that he wanted to inquire about McCartney's case," says Warren-Knott, "because McCartney and his rock group, Wings, might be giving a concert in the U.S." If McCartney had been convicted, he could have been refused a U.S. visa under current immigration laws.

McCartney was finally released and deported on January 25. When asked why he was turned loose, McCartney balked, "Don't ask me, ask them. They just told me I could get out." Japanese authorities said they decided against the jail sentence because of his ignorance of their strict laws. "We always give some weight to clear signs of repentance," one official added.

The incarceration cost McCartney the revenue from the canceled Wings dates, plus an additional £200,000 to cover losses incurred by Udo Music, as well as £10,000 a day expenses for his lawyers and family.

This was McCartney's second deportation. His first occurred nearly 20 years ago, when he and George Harrison were expelled from West Germany after starting a fire in a Hamburg rock club by igniting a condom.

Japanese teens clutch their now-useless Wings tickets.

John and George Know How It Feels

On October 18, 1968, John Lennon and Yoko Ono were arrested in Ringo's basement apartment by the Scotland Yard Drug Squad for unlawful possession of cannabis resin (a lump of hash). John pleaded guilty; charges against Yoko were dropped. Lennon was fined £150 plus 20 guineas court costs. In March 1973 Lennon was ordered to leave the United States by immigration officials due to the prior bust, but in October 1975 the U.S. Court of Appeals overturned the deportation order, ruling that the British law under which Lennon was convicted is unjust by U.S. standards.

1968: "They're gonna crucify me!"

1968: George and Patti [illegible]

In March 1968 George Harrison and wife Patti were arrested in their London home following a raid by police whose dope-sniffing dogs allegedly dug up 570 grains of marijuana—enough for 120 joints, claimed the cops. George and Patti were fined £600. Harrison told reporters that the dope had been planted by the police and that he never would have buried it: "I'm a tidy sort of bloke. I kept records in the record rack, tea in the tea caddy, and pot in the pot box. Those who think this is a lowdown dirty thing to smoke pot will be further convinced they're right and we're wrong. But it will strengthen the others who follow us."

National Enquirer, July 1970

John Lennon Reveals . . .

The Beatles Were 'High' on Marijuana When Queen Elizabeth Decorated Them At Buckingham Palace

GEORGE HARRISON
1970

JOHN LENNON
1970

BLOW UP OR GET OUT YOUR MAGNIFYING GLASS...

By THOMAS KNOWLES

The Beatles smoked marijuana right under the staid noses of the British royal family — in Buckingham Palace.

"We smoked a 'joint' in the lavatory of the palace because we were nervous about meeting the Queen," admitted John Lennon, the group's most outspoken member, in an interview in Paris.

The incident took place in 1965 when the Beatles were invited to the official residence of Queen Elizabeth and her family to receive an honor award, the MBE.

Lennon's recent "pot in the palace" confession has outraged the conservative British almost as much as the original announcement that the long-haired pop group would receive the decoration.

QUEEN ELIZABETH
Awarded medals

HONORED: Happy Beatles (from left) Ringo Starr, John Lennon, Paul McCartney and George Harrison display medals presented to them by Queen Elizabeth.

PAUL McCARTNEY
1970

RINGO STARR
1970

The MBE — Member of the Order of the British Empire — is traditionally awarded by the reigning monarch for distinguished service to the country.

"When we heard we had been recommended for the MBE, I took it as a joke and at first we wanted to laugh," Lennon said.

"But once it happens, when you actually receive your decoration you don't make jokes any longer.

"But we giggled all the same — you see, we had just smoked a joint (marijuana cigarette) in the lavatory at Buckingham Palace. We were high and so nervous . . ."

Lennon said the four Beatles were overawed by the lavish surroundings, and at coming face-to-face with the Queen.

"Even if you don't believe in royalty you can't help being impressed," he said.

Lennon said he wanted to refuse the MBE at first but was talked into accepting the prestige award by their manager. Lennon has since sent his back. Lennon recalled that the Beatles were using drugs when they made their film, "Help."

"The best scenes were those when we were sprawling on the floor unable to say a word.

"We'd just started to smoke marijuana and we were stoned."

He admitted also that the Beatles were on "acid" or LSD when they cut their best-selling LP, "Sergeant Pepper."

After making these admissions the 29-year-old Lennon said he no longer believed in taking drugs.

"The ideal is to have no drugs at all, no coffee, no cigarettes, no drinks. I gave up cigarettes but I started again, it was too hard to go without.

"But I'm against drugs, I really am."

POLICE STATES: PROHIBITION THROUGH THE AGES

16th century	Coffee banned in Egypt and supplies of coffee burned—use spreads rapidly.
17th century	The czar of Russia executes tobacco users.
c. 1650	Tobacco prohibited in Bavaria, Saxony, Zurich; the Ottoman sultan zealously executes smokers to no avail.
1736	The Gin Act fails to halt consumption in England.
1792	The penalty for opium selling in China is strangulation.
1845	New York bans the public sale of liquor—repeals law two years later.
1875-1914	27 states and cities ban opium smoking—opium smoking increases sevenfold.
1914	Passage of Harrison Narcotics Act controlling opium and cocoa derivatives.
1914	Czar bans alcohol—Bolsheviks lift ban in 1924.
1914-70	Congress passes 55 laws to strengthen Harrison Act.
1918	Special Committee studies Harrison Act effects—widespread smuggling and increased use of narcotics—and calls for stricter enforcement.
1919	Eighteenth Amendment banning alcohol is passed—repealed in 1933.
1919-1933	Use of marijuana, ether, and coffee increases.
1921	Cigarettes are illegal in 14 states.
1924	Congress bans heroin completely—after law passed, heroin replaces morphine in black market.
1937	First federal law against marijuana.
1949	Law enforcement crackdown on non-prescription barbiturates—use increases 800% 1942-69.
1955	Shah of Iran bans opium—ban partially repealed in 1969.
1956	U.S. Narcotic Drug Control Act provides for death penalty for selling heroin to minors.
1958	Soviet premier Khruschchev raises alcohol prices 21 to reduce consumption—he later deems the program failure.
1959	Campaign against glue-sniffing begins—causes " boom in cocaine smuggling" by 1969.
1962	FDA halts legal production of LSD—LSD use skyroc ets by 1970.
1965	Amphetamine enforcement intensifies—causes "a boo in cocaine smuggling" by 1969.
1968	Campaign against marijuana use among U.S. troops Vietnam—soldiers switch to heroin.
1969	New York City increases drug arrests by 9000—no ir pact on drug availability noted.
1971	All-out campaign against heroin use in Vietnam fails.
1971	900 pounds of heroin seized in New York City—no i crease in price occurs.
1971	President Nixon declares drugs "America's public en my No. 1."
1972	The House passes a $1 billion anti-drug bill.
1972	President Nixon declares drugs "America's public en my No. 1"—again.
1973	Rockefeller's tough drug bill is passed in New York.
1973	President Nixon announces, "We have turned the co ner on drug addiction in America."
1975	Malaysia enacts death penalty for drug trafficking.
1975	Singapore enacts death penalty for drug trafficking— few years later, to drug official says, "Heroin seems be more widely used than ever."
1977	Bar Association committee concludes that Rockefell drug law had no effect on heroin use.
1980	300,000 youths in Malaysia are using illegal drugs.
1983	Malaysia toughens death penalty for drug traffickin Soviets crack down on alcohol consumption.
1986	Moscow officials lower taxes on alcohol.
1987	Malaysia's 12-foot-high, double-barbed-wire securit fence protecting 32 miles of border with Thailand fai to halt drug traffic.
1987	Soviets increase penalties against moonshining.
1987	Legal alcohol production down 50% in Soviet Unio hard liquor moonshining up 40%; homemade wine pr duction up 300%; 200,000 prosecuted for illegal hom brewing.
1987	Soviets launch "Operation Black Poppy" to stop opiu use—2,000 poppy fields destroyed.
1987	The Russian city of Murmansk bans sale of men cologne (containing alcohol) until 2 p.m., when liqu stores open.
1987	Glue-sniffing doubles among high school students i Soviet Union.
1988	U.S. Senate adds $2.6 billion to federal anti-drug e forts.
1988	Title of Tampa Tribune feature article: "The Jok Among Federal Agents: 'We've Turned the Corner o Drugs.'"
1989	President Reagan declares victory in War on Drugs a being a major achievement of his administration.
1989	Secretary of State James A. Baker III reports that th global war on narcotics production "is clearly not bein won."

— Courtesy of the Cato Institute

Reprinted from SECURITY magazine, June, 1989.

SECURITY WRAP-UP: DRUG USE

From 1989 to 1987, beer consumption among Americans dropped 7%, wine use fell 14% and consumption of distilled spirits sharply decreased 23%. The use of distilled spirits fell from 3.02 gallons per person in 1980 to 2.32 gallons in 1987.

And the membership in Alcoholics Anonymous more than doubled between 1977 and 1987, from 612,000 to 1.6 million.

A number of trends make drinking less appealing to Americans. An increased emphasis on workplace productivity and the hazards of drunken driving has decreased liquor consumption.

And more people are substituting liquor and cigarettes with rowing machines and weights.

Health insurance coverage for drug treatment is spreading. It's now required in 13 states. Up to 80% of workers are now covered under benefit plans.

New rules for government contractors require a good faith effort to ensure a drug-free workplace. There will be no contracts for those who do not comply.

Undercover drug investigators are being used by many companies.

Posing as regular employees they can identify both users and sellers to develop the necessary evidence.

This year the Supreme Court will decide on mandatory drug tests for transportation workers and random testing of federal government employees.

The court's ruling may affect all types of employees.

Condemned to Repeat Department

H.R. 4079 AND ITS PARALLELS WITH NAZI GERMANY

GERMANY • 1924-1939	UNITED STATES • 1990
1) May 27, 1924: Motion in Riechstag to place all Jews under "special legislation."	1) H.R.-4079 Legislation in Congress places drug users under special legislation.
2) March 21, 1933: "Enabling Act" gives government power to promulgate emergency legislation that deviates from constitution.	2) H.R. 4079 gives government power to promulgate emergency legislation that deviates from constitution.
3) March 22, 1933: Dachau concentration camp opened to place people who "cannot be allowed to remain free as they continue to agitate and cause unrest."	3) H.R. 4079 creates provisions to set up camps for drug users to "...meet the extraordinary threat to the nation by the use and trafficking of illegal drugs."
4) March 26, 1933: Anti-Jewish boycott goes into effect.	4) "Operation Green Merchant" and new legislation concerning drug paraphenalia has basically forced boycott of merchants by disallowing the sale of the goods that they would be selling.
5) March 31, 1933: Jewish judges replaced with NSDAP judges.	5) H.R. 4079 sets up provisions to monitor judges' sentencing patterns to be sure that they comply with the bill. Removes judges that are soft on drugs by not allowing them to sentence people according to their opinons.
6) April 1933: Jewish people prohibited from employment in government, teaching, newspapers. orchestras.	6) 4079 imposes drug testing to guarantee termination from ALL jobs for drug users.
7) April 21, 1933: Jewish ritual of slaughtering animals for food banned.	7) April 17, 1990: Supreme Court ruling #88-1213: Peoples' peyote ritual is now illegal.
8) April 25, 1933: Non-aryans excluded from public schools.	8) 4079 demands drug testing, resulting in expulsion of drug users from school.
9) July 14, 1933: Annulment of citizenship of "undesirables."	9)4079 takes away Constitutional rights of drug users, makes them subjects of republic as opposed to citizens of democracy.
10) October 26, 1939: Random seizures of Jews for forced labor starts after decree is issued making "forced labor compulsory for all Jews between the ages of 14 and 60."	10) 4079 makes labor mandatory for ALL prisoners unable to prove 100% disability.
11) Art deemed "objectionable" banned from public viewing and confiscated. (Before burned, art put on display with derogatory statements placed under them. Art show had largest attendance in German history.)	11) U.S.Government continues to try to impose censorship by going after material that is deemed objectionable by the general population.
12) "Operation Green", Hitler's invasion of Czechoslovakia, despite existing non-agression pact.	12) "Operation Just Cause", Bush's invasion of Panama was conducted without regard for U.N. treaties.
13) Hitler assures Germany he "wanted only peace."	13) Bush assures U.S. we will have "A Kinder, Gentler Nation."

Research by P. A. Fuzsi/PORTLAND FREE PRESS

U.S. jails more people than any other nation

America hurdles S. Africa during '80s

WASHINGTON (AP) — With more than 1 million people behind bars, the United States imprisons a bigger share of its population than any other nation, a private group said Friday.

The high U.S. incarceration rate results from a high crime rate and increasingly harsh public attitudes toward dealing with lawbreakers, said the report by The Sentencing Project, a non-profit research organization that promotes sentencing reforms and alternatives.

More than 1 million Americans are in jail or prison, either awaiting trial or serving time, the report said. It said that 426 of every 100,000 U.S. residents are incarcerated, at an annual cost of $16 billion. For black American men, the rate is 3,109 per 100,000.

South Africa has the world's second-highest imprisonment rate, with 333 people imprisoned per 100,000 residents, the report said. Its incarceration rate for black males is 729 per 100,000.

The Soviet Union ranks third in overall incarceration with 268 per 100,000 residents.

Incarceration rates in Europe generally range from 35 to 120 per 100,000 residents and in Asian countries from 21 to 140 per 100,000, the report said.

Marc Mauer, assistant director of The Sentencing Project, who wrote the report, said it shows that "the same policies that have helped make us a world leader in incarceration have clearly failed to make us a safer nation."

"We need a fundamental change of direction, towards proven programs and policies that work to reduce both imprisonment and crime," Mauer said.

Commenting on the report, Rep. John Conyers, D-Mich. and chairman of the House Government Operations Committee, said:

"We've got to stop jailing and start rehabilitating. ... We can build all the jails we think we need and slam the doors down on thousands of people, but it won't make a bit of difference until we address the fundamental causes of crime."

The U.S. incarceration rate jumped ahead of South Africa's and the Soviet Union's over the last decade as states and the federal government adopted mandatory minimum sentences, tightened parole eligibility criteria and otherwise relied more on imprisonment and less on alternatives, the report said.

IMPRISONED

- 426 of every 100,000 U.S. residents are incarcerated.
- 333 South Africans are imprisoned per 100,000 residents.
- 268 per 100,000 Soviet Union residents are incarcerated.

It acknowledged that the U.S. crime rate is higher than in many countries. The nation's murder rate is at least seven times higher than in most European countries. There were six times as many robberies and three times as many rapes in the United States as in West Germany prior to unification with East Germany.

The report noted that the overall U.S. crime rate has fallen 3.5 percent since 1980, while the nation's prison population doubled.

Forty-six states now have laws requiring prison time for some offenses. The U.S. Sentencing Commission says new sentencing guidelines and tougher penalties for drug-law violations may result in a 119 percent increase in the federal prison population from 1987 to 1997, the report said.

The proportion of criminals sentenced to prison jumped 54 percent from 1980 to 1987, the report said. In 1980, the rate was 196 offenders imprisoned for every 1,000 arrests for serious crimes. The 1987 rate was 301 per 100,000.

Drug-related crime is the biggest cause of the prison population explosion and helps explain the disproportionately high rate of black male incarceration, the report said. Thirty-eight percent of the people arrested on drug charges in 1988 were black, up from 30 percent in 1984.

In Michigan, drug arrests have doubled since 1985 while drug-related arrests of blacks have tripled.

"With the war on drugs primarily waged through the criminal justice system and disproportionately targeting inner-city drug users, the end result is an increasing number of prisoners and an even larger share of black male inmates," the report said.

Alternative punishments are less costly than imprisonment, the report said. A 1989 Delaware study found that the annual cost of imprisoning a criminal was $17,761, while putting the person on probation cost only $569 a year.

For every drug offender sentenced to prison, three could be treated in an inpatient program and 16 could be treated as outpatients, the study said.

BAKERSFIELD CALIFORNIAN
JAN. 5, 1991

THE CHEMISTRY OF REEFER MADNESS

MIND

By Leah Wallach

It makes *Homo sapiens* hungry, horny, drowsy, and glad—or anxious. It dulls pain, inhibits movements, lowers body temperature, fools time. It sets memory chasing its own tail and turns thought and perceptual processes awry. Why?

For decades there were as many theories of how people got high on pot as there were researchers interested in testing the 421 compounds found in marijuana's serrated green leaves. Some scientists thought the weed's active compounds just dissolved into the membranes surrounding brain cells. Others believed the compounds worked through receptors, specialized areas on the membranes that fit lock-and-key style with specific molecules. One prominent neurochemist confessed to three notebooks of experiments that had failed to find a neuronal lock for a *Cannabis sativa* key. No one was able to figure out exactly how marijuana really did work until last year.

In the fall of 1988 pharmacology professor Allyn Howlett and her group at St. Louis University Medical School announced that they had found the receptor for a major cannabinoid molecule.

The story of Howlett's discovery began in the Sixties, when Rafael Mechoulam of the Hebrew University in Jerusalem determined that the main psychoactive compound in extracts of marijuana was a substance called delta-9-tetrahydrocannabinol (THC). Although not especially potent, THC represented a new class of compounds structurally different from those found in other psychoactive drugs. Drug companies were intrigued. "If you look in an old pharmacology text from, say, the Twenties, before the *Reefer Madness* business," Howlett explains, "extracts of cannabis were about the only compounds that could be used for pain relief and anxiety." Subsequently pharmacologists began synthesizing THC analogs called cannabinoids, which were chemicals structurally and biologically similar to the naturally occurring chemicals but more powerful.

In the mid-Seventies Ross Johnson and Larry Melvin worked with synthetic cannabinoids at Pfizer, a Connecticut-based pharmaceutical company. They were trying to develop a THC-like analgesic. The problem, Melvin explains, was that they couldn't detach the painkilling from pot's psychoactive properties. They developed several compounds 100 times more potent than THC, but the animal (and, in one case, human) subjects were zonked. This meant the drugs could be used only in hospitals, where opiates had already cornered the painkiller market. In the early Eighties Pfizer stopped the research project. The academic community took over and began studying the Pfizer cannabinoids.

When a compound locks into its receptor on a cell membrane, it changes the activity of structures in the membrane, which in turn alters the way the cell processes information. Howlett wanted to see if the Pfizer cannabinoids worked the way some other analgesics do: by affecting a molecule called cyclic AMP (cAMP). Cyclic AMP is a "second messenger": It regulates the way the inside of the cell responds to messages received at the membrane.

Howlett found that the Pfizer cannabinoids—especially the potent Levonantradol—affected cAMP production in cultured mouse neurons by inhibiting a key enzyme. The more effectively the compound inhibited cAMP in the test tube, the more effectively it killed pain in animals. Howlett's next step was to see if the cannabinoids actually attached to neuronal membranes. She labeled the compounds radioactively, and by tracking the radioactivity, she was able to show that the cannabinoid molecules bound tightly to the membranes. "The compounds that bound most strongly were the ones most active at the cellular level, and in the animals. And that," she says, "is what really defines a receptor." She also found—potheads might be interested to know—that the cannabinoids did not hurt the cells. After exposure for several hours, however, the cells no longer responded to the drug. That suggests, despite what ganja smokers might say, that it takes increasingly large doses to get the same buzz.

Billy Martin, a cannabinoid researcher at the Medical College of Virginia, tested the Pfizer cannabinoids on a variety of animals to see if alterations in cAMP production were related to painkilling power alone or to the panoply of behavioral effects that make up a THC high. "It looks as though the structure of the compounds might be correlated with other behavioral effects besides analgesia," Martin says carefully. In the words of another researcher, "Probably we've seen people at parties who were like these animals: out to lunch."

If the investigators could prevent THC effects by stopping up the cell receptor sites, they would be able to prove conclusively that the binding of cannabinoids to cell membranes causes the high. "We need an antagonist," Martin explains. (An antagonist is a chemical key that fits into the same receptor lock as the drug but will not trigger the same response—in this case, getting stoned.) Antagonists could provide a power tool for drug research: By selectively blocking some, but not all, cannabinoid effects, they could help scientists tease apart THC's complex activities.

Antagonists and analogs might also have therapeutic value. Scientists might discover more refined versions of the cannabinoid compounds now being used to treat glaucoma and decrease nausea during chemotherapy. The compounds could be used for brain research as well. "It has been noted in people who use marijuana that they can't remember later things they learned while high," says Howlett. "You see something similar in the dementia of aging or the first stages of Alzheimer's." THC analogs, she speculates, might be used as a model for studying what happens in Alzheimer's. And an antagonist might help treat the disease. "We also could learn more about pain mechanisms and pathways," she continues. "This receptor suggests that opioids are not the only drugs involved in the regulation and processing of the pain response in the central nervous system."

Miles Herkenham of the National Institute of Mental Health has used autoradiography—a technique allowing precise location of binding sites—to map the distribution of the Pfizer analogs in the brain. Noting the arrangement of binding sites in areas associated with movement, he wonders if THC analogs and antagonists can relieve symptoms of movement disorders such as Parkinson's disease and Huntington's chorea.

If THC analogs or antagonists prove to have therapeutic properties, it will be because they mimic or block the action of natural endogenous substances that use these pathways. Howlett's next project is to look for the brain chemical that normally binds to the cannabinoid receptor. She has ruled out all known neurotransmitters. Scientists presume these receptors did not evolve so that animals could get stoned. "There must be some kind of neuronal pathway in the brain that developed whether there were cannabis plants or not," she says.

"We looked at hormones, steroids, glucocorticoids, peptides, and found nothing else that would bind to the site," notes Howlett, who found the same response in chickens, turtles, frogs, and trout. "Cannabinoid binding sites in their brains

CONTINUED ON PAGE 64

were nearly as dense as in later-evolved mammals. We even found some in fruit flies." In rats Howlett found the highest density of cannabinoid receptors in the cortex and hippocampus (areas of the brain associated with memory, perception, and cognition) and in the cerebellum and striatum (both areas associated with movement).

Miles Herkenham found that the pattern of distribution Howlett saw in rats also characterized the human brain. The receptor sites were densest in the hippocampus, cerebral cortex, and areas of the cerebellum. "What really struck me," he says, "was the front-brain loading. It's sort of a high-brow receptor." Herkenham was also impressed by the sheer quantity of receptors. "The binding sites are incredibly numerous compared with other neurotransmitter systems," he says, "which suggests they are receptors for an important, ubiquitous transmitter."

Unraveling the mystery of this ubiquitous not transmitter will help us understand how humans and other vertebrates manage the extraordinary juggling act of living. The chemistry of reefer madness will give us another way to look inside the hungry, horny, drowsy, excitable, glad, anxious, musing, giggly, cogitating, perfectly sober brain.∞

Pro-pot police teacher

GAINESVILLE, Fla. (AP) — The head of a police academy in North Florida says he smokes marijuana and would like it legalized for home use. But he admits his stand may cost him his job.

"It's just a pleasurable experience that I and everybody else ought to be able to enjoy if they want to," said Bob Phillips, coordinator of Sante Fe Community College's Police Academy.

Phillips, 39, has participated in training many police officers in a 14-county area the past three years and has been in law enforcement for 15 years.

"I've never known a policeman destroyed by marijuana, but I've seen a lot of them destroyed by alcoholism," said Phillips, who called himself a reformed alcoholic.

He said he uses pot like some people use cocktails to relax after work. "I've enjoyed it and I've smoked it off and on for 2½ years," he said.

Police Chief Nolen W. Freeman, informed of Phillips' statements, said Phillips' position as top man at the academy should be reviewed.

"I feel if it is against the law and the man is going to teach people to enforce the law, he should abide by it himself," said Freeman. "If he wants the law changed, he should work toward that, not violate it."

Phillips said private use of marijuana should be decriminalized but the drug should not be legalized totally. He suggested laws to permit personal production and consumption of marijuana patterned after laws which allow small amounts of beer and wine to be produced for personal use.

Phillips said he expects some friction because of his statements, but he said he will not resign his post. However, he added that he may be pressured out of the job.

OK City Times 9-13-75

Teens can use yet not abuse drugs — maybe

USA 10-15-86 TODAY

By Karen S. Peterson
USA TODAY

Teen drug users aren't necessarily drug abusers, says the author of a controversial government-sponsored study.

And the best way to deal with kids who use drugs may be to focus on those who get in trouble at school or elsewhere — and leave the rest alone, says Harvey Joanning, associate professor of family therapy at Texas Tech University at Lubbock.

"If left to their own devices, adolescents who use drugs recreationally and are still functional will tend to grow out of it," says Joanning, who has worked with about 130 kids ages 8-20 under a four-year, $500,000 grant from the National Institute on Drug Abuse.

He presents his approach to drugs and therapy Oct. 23 at the four-day American Association for Marriage and Family Therapy in Orlando, Fla.

He expects the hotly debated topic will "raise some eyebrows."

Charles Schuster, NIDA director, already is alarmed.

"It is very risky to talk about drug use among adolescents as OK as long as it doesn't become abuse," he warns. "The minute we adopt that attitude we expose a number of kids to drug abuse."

Joanning disagrees. He says that many youngsters using drugs like marijuana and beer are fully functional and shouldn't be labeled abusers.

"We should not assume that any kid using drugs is an abuser and needs treatment," he says. "In many instances use does not equal abuse."

Joanning's research team of 11 has been working two years. Their focus: finding out why some kids can use some drugs safely and others get into trouble; and finding an effective way to help.

The key, Joanning says, may be working with parents, peers and the community — a kid's total environment.

He says that approach is effective two-thirds of the time in helping a teen quit drugs or move to "appropriate use."

"We have learned the hard way that if you want to reach kids, you can't say: 'We want you to stop using drugs,' " Joanning says. "They will tune you out. You say, 'We know you are going to keep using them. Let's talk about how.' "

But, says Schuster, "The simple fact is we can't predict now who is going to go on to use drugs in a destructive fashion and who will walk away unscathed.

"Any kid who starts experimenting with drugs may be the one who finds the experience so compelling that his whole life will revolve around (it).

"It is simply not normal for a 12-year-old to be smoking marijuana," Schuster adds. "We can't afford to condone it."

THE WASHINGTON POST 8-9-1990

Marijuana Receptor Exists in Brain, Study Confirms

Scientists Predict Discovery Will Lead to New Drugs That Mimic Medicinal Effects

By William Booth
Washington Post Staff Writer

Researchers have confirmed the existence of a receptor in the brain that serves as a target for marijuana, a discovery that could lead to new drugs that mimic marijuana's medicinal powers while avoiding some of its mind-altering effects.

The finding, reported today in the scientific journal Nature, implies that the body may produce a natural marijuana-like substance that acts on the brain. The existence of these natural cannabinoids, as they would be called, is still uncertain, but researchers suspect they must exist because a receptor for them exists in the brain. The discovery is expected to spark a race to find the substances.

The discovery should help researchers understand how marijuana affects the brain.

The research reported today by Lisa Matsuda and her colleagues at the National Institute of Mental Health deals with the cloning of the marijuana receptor, which sits on the outside of brain cells and is shaped specifically to grab molecules of the active ingredient in marijuana, delta-9-tetrahydrocannabinol or THC, and produce a specific reaction within the brain cell. Until now, the putative existence of a specific marijuana receptor was controversial and considered by many researchers to be unproven.

"I'd say it's one of the most important discoveries in marijuana research," said Solomon Snyder of Johns Hopkins University, the neuroscientist who almost two decades ago helped discover that the brain harbors receptors for opiates such as heroin and morphine, as well as natural brain opioids such as the endorphins, which produce the oft-touted "runner's high."

Lewis Judd, director of the National Institute of Mental Health, where the research was accomplished, said, "Now scientists may be able to develop drugs that possess marijuana's positive medicinal effects without its negative effects, such as an intoxicated feeling, disorientation, and impaired preception and memory."

Marijuana is legendary among recreational users for its mood-altering effects, which can include feelings of calm and giddiness and can shift preceptions of time and space. But among physicians and researchers, marijuana is also known to prevent nausea, reduce blood pressure, stimulate appetite, kill pain and suppress convulsions. But efforts to create synthetic versions of the drug have been frustrated by a poor understanding of how marijuana works in the brain.

Traditionally, the study of marijuana has been limited to relatively few researchers. With the latest advance—finding and cloning the gene for the marijuana receptor—scientists say they now have a powerful tool for understanding how the drug operates in the brain and for designing more sophisticated versions of therapy.

"I bet the field will explode," Snyder said.

The work ends a long-running debate over marijuana's method of action in the brain. Ever since the active ingredient in marijuana was discovered by Raphael Mechoulam in 1965, most researchers have assumed marijuana affects brain cells by sticking to the surface of cells in an indiscriminate way and somehow

will pay our farmers for not farming their land; while we spend tens of billions of dollars every year to buy foreign oil..."

95th. Congress U.S. Industry Public Witness Panel Testimony

Inter-Industry Emission Control Program (Ford, ARCO, Mobil, and Standard Oil companies):

"Gasoline From Methanol
...Several engineering problems have been identified in this paper that will require solutions before methanol can be used reliably as an automotive fuel. Another approach, which would circumvent the engineering problems, is conversion of methanol to gasoline. ...Using a zeolitic catalyst nearly 90% yields of product with the composition, octane number, boiling range, and other specifications of high-quality gasoline can be obtained."

"Methanol From Synthesis Gas -
[Mobil Oil Co., John J. Wise]: "Today, I would like to tell you about a new process invented by Mobil scientists to convert methanol into high-octane gasoline.
"The gasoline is 96 octane, unleaded, and chemically similar to gasoline made from crude oil. It contains no sulfur, nitrogen, or other impurities... What the Mobil process does essentially is to wring out the water and rearrange the remaining hydrogen and carbon atoms into the concentrated, high energy fuel we know as gasoline. Each gallon of gasoline has 95% of the energy contained in the 2 gallons of methanol it was made from.
"Our process is relatively simple, and uses equipment of the general type used routinely in the oil industry.
"...We estimate that 2 barrels 84 gallons of gasoline can be made from 1 ton of raw Wyoming subbituminous coal. "The final scale up could be to a commercial-size facility, which could require another 6 years to get on stream. The technology is so well advanced, however, that the lead time could be considerably shortened if necessary.
[Sen. Bayh] "You go directly from methanol to gasoline?"
[Wise] "Yes; essentially, senator, our argument is that there is no need to put alcohol into gasoline ... we have a process that effectively converts alcohols into gasoline with 95% thermal efficiency...
"We believe the type of alcohol that would be the cheapest is methanol made from coal..."
[Bayh] "...one thing we can be certain of is that as the quantity of petroleum gets less, the cost is going to go up. There has been a very close relationship, has there not, in the increased cost of coal and the increased cost of petroleum? If you take the escalating cost of petroleum and the escalating cost of the coal and compare that with grain or farm produce, there really hasn't been the same history... Do you get rid of the sulfur problem and by-products?"
[Wise] "Yes; sulfur and all the impurities are...scrubbed out."
[Bayh] "Is it cleaner burning gasoline than we have now or would we have the same exhaust problem?"
[Wise] "It is actually cleaner burning but you would still need the catalytic converter to clean it up."

95th. Congress Agriculture Public Witness Panel Testimony

William C. Burrows, Senior Staff Scientist, John Deere & Co.:
"Energy Development From Biomass -
Agricultural residues, surplus agricultural production, forest residues and the plant material growing on marginal lands are the largest portion of what is collectively referred to as biomass. It represents a sizable and renewable energy resource, equivalent to a part of total U.S. petroleum use.
"We consider that biomass will be used as an energy source in the future. Machinery is currently in production and available to processors to handle the growing and harvesting of biomass for energy.
"Maybe I should emphasize that a little more because it is easy to pass over this in the testimony. We think the technology, the machinery for using this material is here now. It can be bought in the marketplace..."

Donald N. Duvick, Director, Dept. of Corn Breeding, Pioneer Hybrid International, Johnston, Iowa:
[Sen. Bayh questioning Mr. Duvick] "Is it fair to assume that if the Nation determines that it is in the national interest to develop an alternative source of energy that is not petroleum-based, to take advantage of the productive capacity of the American farmer that, whether it is agriculture research or university research, that it is entirely possible that a product can be grown that has significantly higher cellulosic content than even alfalfa?"
[Duvick] "It may well be [but] cultivation has been pointed towards almost anything except cellulose. I think it could well be by either looking into the crops that we now grow or perhaps by looking toward new crops that we have not yet considered we would find things which could produce much more cellulose per acre."

George T. Tsao, Professor at Purdue University:
"Recently, we at Purdue University have worked out a new process which gives 100% yield of glucose from available cellulose at a low cost...solvent A is first used to remove the third major component of cellulosic materials, besides cellulose and lignin, called hemicellulose. The solid residue containing cellulose and lignin is then treated with another solvent B which dissolves cellulose but not lignin. This approach which is simple in concept will obviously remove the two major obstacles to cellulose conversion.
"Glucose can be fermented by yeast to produce alcohol and can also be processed to produce many chemicals replacing petroleum....
"Some of these are direct consumer products and some of these are industrial intermediates which in turn can be processed into even a larger number of products. From the other two major components of cellulosic materials, namely hemicellulose and lignin, one can also make a large number of petroleum sparing products...complete processing industries can be developed based upon the ultimate raw material, cellulosic materials, which is a valuable renewable resource.
"The 'land set aside' program costs our government large sums of tax money. The acreage can be used for producing cellulosic materials sold at $30 per ton. ...Our country is blessed with the largest and the richest land mass in the world. It is a shame to all of us, today we

TO GET A GLIMPSE OF GOVT. AT ITS WORST READ

BUSH/LILLY SIDE - BAR (page 29) THEN READ page 147

New York Times

CNESDAY. MAY 19. 1982

h Tried to Sway Tax Rule Change ıt Then Withdrew

By JEFF GERTH

Special to The New York Times

HINGTON, May 18 — Vice ent Bush, in an unusual move, in-ed with the Treasury in March in tion with proposed rules that have forced pharmaceutical nies to pay significantly more

al weeks later, Mr. Bush with-om involvement in the tax issue e, he said, he felt "uncomfort-bout the "appearance" of a con-interest. When Mr. Bush took of-owned $145,000 worth of drug y stocks, and he had been a di-f Eli Lilly & Company from 1977

rnment documents show that e President initially signed a echnical letter to Treasury Sec-Donald T. Regan, urging that the y alter plans to modify a section ax law that has allowed drug ies to avoid billions of dollars in n income earned by their opera-Puerto Rico.

rding to Mr. Bush's counsel, who awyer and lobbyist for a drug y before joining the Adminis-the letter was written by a staff r who formerly headed the

CONT.→

THE NEW YORK TIMES, WEDNESDAY, MAY 19, 1982

The New York Times

Bush Intervenes on Tax but Withdraws

Continued From Page A1

Puerto Rican agency that screened tax exemptions for companies. On April 14 Mr. Bush signed another letter to Mr. Regan, saying he "must now disengage" from any further discussion of the matter because he felt "uncomfortable about the appearance of my active, personal involvement in the details of a tax matter directly affecting a company with which I once had a close association."

Meantime, however, the Treasury had begun to revise its proposed regulations in response to the complaints of the Vice President and the drug companies, according to Government officials.

Data Provided by Staff

Mr. Bush declined to respond personally to questions about his involvement in the tax issue, although members of his staff provided documents and granted interviews.

Under Section 936 of the Internal Revenue Code, American companies that operate in United States possessions are sheltered from Federal taxes. This tax benefit is used mostly by drug companies operating in Puerto Rico, according to Treasury documents, and is intended to encourage economic development there.

But critics such as the Senate Budget Committee chairman, Pete V. Domenici, Republican of New Mexico, say Section 936 is an unnecessary loophole that helps only big corporations and costs the Treasury $1.5 billion a year. And the Internal Revenue Service contends that some drug companies have abused the provision by improperly shifting taxable income from the United States mainland to Puerto Rico. The companies deny this.

The Treasury documents show that Mr. Bush's letter focused on the crucial issue in the court cases. Aside from the drug industry, most American companies were satisfied, according to Treasury officials and business executives, with the modifications in the tax law planned by the Treasury Department.

Help From Specialists

Mr. Bush's press secretary, Peter Teeley, and his counsel, C. Boyden Gray, said the Vice President was not familiar with the technical issues he raised with Secretary Regan. Mr. Teeley said the letter was written by Rafael V. Capo, a deputy counsel who had dealt with tax issues when he worked for the Puerto Rican government.

The Vice President's involvement, his aides said, resulted from his long-standing interest in Puerto Rico and from a request for his assistance by the White House chief of staff, James A. Baker 3d. Mr. Bush has rarely become personally involved in the details of agency regulations.

Section 936, enacted in 1921 to help the Philippines, then a United States possession, is little known to the public but arouses strong emotions among people familiar with it.

Supporters of Section 936 include drug company executives, some Puerto Rican officials and supply-side theorists such as Norman B. Ture, Under Secretary of the Treasury for Tax and Economic Affairs. They argue that Section 936 is the key to long-range economic development in Puerto Rico. Many of these supporters, including Mr. Bush, say the best way to help Puerto Rico — where unemployment is 23 percent and where more than 50 percent of the population receives food stamps — is to give tax breaks to corporations that invest there rather than to give direct Government payments to needy Puerto Ricans.

Critics of Section 936 cite a 1980 Treasury report to Congress showing that pharmaceutical companies in Puerto Rico have their taxes reduced by more than $43,000 a year for every job they create in Puerto Rico and that the average salary of these jobs is $13,000. That report also showed that in 1978 drug companies accounted for half the claims of the more than $800 million in Section 936 tax savings.

The Reagan Administration's 1981 report on Section 936 was required by law to be submitted last June, but it has not been filed. According to Treasury oficials, Mr. Ture has objected to the draft report's analysis of the impact of the law.

The Internal Revenue Service has accused several drug companies of abuse of Section 936, according to records on file with the Securities and Exchange Commission and the United States Tax Court. The I.R.S. is seeking hundreds of millions of dollars from such companies as G. D. Searle & Company and Eli Lilly.

Taxable Income at Stake

The Revenue Service says the companies, in their accounting procedures, improperly shifted taxable income in the mid-1970's from the United States mainland to tax-sheltered subsidiaries in Puerto Rico. The companies are contesting these charges in court.

The I.R.S. cases underlie the attempt by the Treasury Department, begun last fall, to draft regulatory guidelines limiting the amount of income that could be shifted to Puerto Rico. It is these draft guidelines, finished in March, that the drug companies and Mr. Bush have objected to.

Mr. Bush's involvement included a March 29 letter to Secretary Regan in which he complained that the guidelines failed to deal with the key technical issue in the pending tax court cases — the transfer to Puerto Rico of trademarks and trade names, such as those that apply to drugs.

In addition to drafting the letter, according to Mr. Teeley, Mr. Capo, the highest-ranking Puerto Rican in the Administration, also talked to Mr. Ture about the letter.

Bush's Holdings Noted

In his April 14 letter, in which he withdrew from involvement in the tax issue, Mr. Bush denied any actual conflict of interest, saying he had sold his holding of 1,500 Eli Lilly shares in 1978. However, according to his 1981 financial disclosure statement and qualified blind trust agreement, the Vice President still owned the Eli Lilly stock upon taking office. It was his most valuable stock holding. At yesterday's closing price of 58⅞ on the New York Stock Exchange, 1,500 Eli Lilly shares would be worth almost $90,000.

"My letter is factually inaccurate," acknowledged Mr. Gray, who said he had drafted the April 14 letter. "I should have done more checking."

An examination of Mr. Bush's 1981 financial records shows that his 12 stock holdings also included more than $50,000 worth of shares of the Bristol-Myers Company, another drug concern that operates in Puerto Rico. Under Mr. Bush's trust arrangement, it is not known whether he still holds the drug company stocks.

Mr. Gray also said he had personally objected to the April 14 letter because "I was nervous about him calling attention to something like this" in light of the fact that his "regulatory relief task force deals with a lot of drug company stuff."

Mr. Bush is head of the Presidential Task Force on Regulatory Relief, which, according to its documents, has already helped eliminate a Federal Drug Administration regulation that the drug industry opposed.

Task Force Operations

Mr. Gray said that Mr. Bush had not personally been involved in task force matters relating to the drug industry but that he might "recuse" himself from future actions in this area.

Federal laws prohibit officials from participating in Government actions in which they have a "personal financial interest," but the President and Vice President are immune from prosecution, Federal officials say.

The strongest proponents of Section 936 have been businessmen promoting economic development, beginning with enactment of the tax exemption in 1921 at the urging of Americans doing business in the Philippines and continuing through a liberalization of the exemption in 1976.

During Congressional debate in the mid-1970's about repealing Section 936, supporters of the exemption argued that it would cost the Government only $285 million a year in lost tax revenues.

Apparently accepting these arguments, Congress, in the Tax Reform Act of 1976, voted to retain the section and even made it easier for American companies to distribute tax-free profits from a Puerto Rican subsidiary to the corporate parent on the mainland.

Annual Report Required

The 1976 act, however, also required the Treasury Department to submit an annual report on the effect of Section 936. Reports were issued in June 1978, 1979 and 1980.

The findings of these reports, according to Treasury officials, underlie the delay in the publication of the 1981 report. The findings include these:

¶The revenue loss, predicted in 1976 to be $285 million a year, is more than $1 billion and is expected soon to reach $1.5 billion a year.

¶Puerto Rican unemployment rose sharply in the 1970's as investments shifted from job-producing industries, such as textiles, to capital-intensive industries, such as drug companies.

¶In 1978, the latest year for which figures are available, the exemption cost the Treasury an average of $43,261 for each employee of the drug companies in Puerto Rico. Nine companies received tax benefits that year of more than $100,000 an employee. But more traditional labor-intensive companies averaged less than $3,000 an employee in lost revenues.

Edgar G. Davis, Eli Lilly's vice president for corporate affairs, defends Section 936, saying that the drug companies provide "quality" jobs. Lilly, according to Mr. Davis, opposes any reduction in tax benefits and has made its views known to White House officials.

Most Puerto Rican officials support the concept of Section 936. One supporter, Ariel L. Mendez, general counsel for Puerto Rico's Washington office, said that Puerto Rico would prefer more "labor-intensive industries" but that the commonwealth did not want to lose the capital-intensive industries already there. Nelson Famadas, head of the Puerto Rican Governor's Economic and Financial Council, suggested that a tightening of Section 936 would only cause drug companies to invest abroad.

An examination of documents on file in the United States Tax Court shows how some drug companies have put the section to use. In a case involving Eli Lilly, the documents show, the parent company handed over to Puerto Rican subsidiaries the patents and trademarks, sometimes called marketing intangibles, to its most successful products, including the popular painkiller Darvon and its Elizabeth Arden cosmetics line.

Back Taxes in Dispute

While the parent company, based in Indianapolis, claimed most of the marketing expenses, which were deducted against Federal taxes, the tax-exempt Puerto Rican subsidiary claimed most of the income, the documents indicate. The revenue service has reallocated Eli Lilly's income and expenses between its mainland and Puerto Rican subsidiaries between 1971 and 1975 "in order to prevent evasion of taxes," the documents show.

The company is contesting more than $50 million in back taxes sought by the I.R.S. for the years 1971 to 1975. The company contends it acted properly and relied in part on earlier I.R.S. rulings it says allowed the transfers.

The I.R.S. crackdown on Section 936, begun during the Carter Administration, led to Treasury Department discussions last fall to construct a formula for allocating future income and expenses under the secion between the United States mainland and Puerto Rico. The discussions were led by Mr. Ture; John Chapoton, Assistant Secretary of Treasury for Tax Policy, and Roscoe L. Egger Jr., the I.R.S. Commissioner, and were intended to limit income shifting to Puerto Rico.

Drug Companies' Objections

In March a draft proposal was completed, according to Treasury officials involved in the talks who wished to remain anonymous. These proposals were acceptable to most companies operating in Puerto Rico, but not some drug companies, according to Treasury and company officials. The drug companies objected to the fact that the proposals did not deal with the issue of marketing intangibles.

About this time, according to Mr. Gray, Vice President Bush became involved in the discussions, protesting the failure of the proposals to deal with the issue of marketing intangibles. In addition to the pressure from Vice President Bush, opposition came from Puerto Rican officials.

Mr. Regan asked Deputy Treasury Secretary R. T. McNamar to help revise the guidelines and try to forge a "consensus" between Mr. Ture, who supports Section 936, and Mr. Egger and Mr. Chapoton, who are less supportive, Government officials say.

THOUSAND OAKS CA.
8-17-90

Panel will pay to publish call for legal marijuana

SAN FRANCISCO (AP) — The vice chairman of a state advisory committee plans to pay to publish the panel's recommendation to legalize marijuana because the attorney general's office refused to publicly issue those findings.

"I think at the moment, the reaction (to the panel's recommendation) has just been hysterical," said Dr. Frederick H. Meyers, vice chairman and professor of pharmacology at the University of California-San Francisco.

Meyers has been on the Research Advisory Panel since its inception in 1969.

It said the Legislature should legalize cultivation of marijuana for personal use, consider decriminalization of other drugs on an individual basis and legalize possession of hypodermic needles.

Compiled by *The Californian* Business staff

Philip Morris has most ads

NEW YORK — Food and tobacco giant Philip Morris Cos. was the heaviest U.S. advertiser in 1989 for the third consecutive year, the trade publication Advertising Age reported.

Philip Morris, the New York-based manufacturer of Marlboro cigarettes, Miller beer, Maxwell House coffee and Kraft foods, spent $2.07 billion on advertising last year, up from $2.06 billion in 1988, the magazine reported.

Procter & Gamble Co., the consumer products maker that was displaced in 1987 after a longstanding run atop the ad spending list, came in second once again at $1.79 billion.

Sears, Roebuck & Co., the Chicago-based retailer, moved up one spot on the list to third place at $1.43 billion while the auto giant General Motors Corp. slipped one spot to fourth place at $1.35 billion.

Fifth was Grand Metropolitan PLC, the British owner of Pillsbury Co. and Burger King Corp., at $823.3 million.

Rounding out the Ad Age list of the top 10 U.S. advertisers and their spending totals were: Pepsico Inc., $786.1 million; McDonald's Corp., $774.4 million; Eastman Kodak Co., $718.8 million; RJR Nabisco, $703.5 million, and Kellogg Co., $611.6 million.

Overall, the top 100 U.S. advertisers spent $33.9 billion in 1989, up 6.4 percent from $32.2 billion in 1988, Ad Age said.

'Just Say Enough' may be best option

Study: Some drug use may be healthy

SAN FRANCISCO (AP) — Teens provide behavioral clues in early childhood that they'll become drug users, and adolescents who experiment with drugs tend to be better adjusted than abstainers or abusers, a University of California study says.

The findings by Berkeley psychologists Jonathan Shedler and Jack Block might fly in the face of the "Just Say No" anti-drug campaign, but their peers agreed Tuesday that casual drug experimentation often is part of having a healthy personality and doesn't always lead to addiction.

"This may be hard for some people to take, but the real issue is knowing when to put the brakes on," said Shirley Feldman, deputy director of the Stanford University's Center for Study of Family, Children and Youth. "There's a whole big world out there and, psychologically speaking, experimentation· is healthy in most youths."

Shedler, perhaps nervous about the study being misinterpreted, said his and Block's careful research that tracked 101 San Francisco

youths from age 3 to age 18, doesn't advocate illegal drug experimentation.

"These findings absolutely do not mean drug experimentation is ·something that is beneficial," he said. "But it does mean that some limited drug experimentation may not be catastrophic. It could be a sign of trouble to come or simply a sign ·of normal adolescent exploration."

Brian Flay, director of drug prevention research in the public health department of the University of Illinois, said, "The 'Just Say No' campaign has always been off the mark."

"We can't stop kids from trying everything," Flay said. "The 'Just Say No' campaign is extremely simplistic. It should be, 'learn how to moderate your behavior, learn how to resist the pressure to go overboard.' "

Psychologists, including Shedler, said a more effective anti-drug effort would identify children who have traits that signal possible drug problems later in life, and then counsel those "at risk" youths.

Australians Want to Make Paper From Pot

BY WILSON DA SILVA

Sydney

A GROUP of Australian farmers and environmentalists want to make paper without cutting down trees. Problem is, they want to replace wood with marijuana, a plant they say is superior to wood and more environmentally friendly.

Researchers agree, but marijuana's narcotic properties have authorities in Australia's island state of Tasmania worried.

"I'm sure we would become a very popular state if we started growing Indian hemp legally and on a large scale," said Ian Colvin of the Tasmanian premier's office.

The consortium, Hemp for Paper, submitted a proposal to Tasmania's government in early February to plant 37,000 acres of marijuana and produce 100,000 tons a year of pulp for making paper.

"Hardwood is not needed for paper. Any fiber high enough in cellulose will do, and hemp is one of the best," said Patsy Harmsen, a spokes-

woman for the 12-member consortium.

"It's been used for paper for hundreds of years. Forestry companies are afraid of what this could do to them. It's cheaper for them to cut down existing forests for next to nothing than to grow their own fiber," she said from Hobart.

Tasmanian development authorities are studying the proposal. The state is already home to the country's only legal farms for opium poppy, a plant grown for pharmaceutical uses in Tasmania but used elsewhere for the manufacture of heroin.

An Australian authority on non-wood fibers for making paper, Ian Wood of the Commonwealth Scientific and Industrial Research Organization, says a lot of the world's paper and rope was made from hemp until about 1850.

Today 93 percent of the world's paper is made from wood, and only 29 percent of the paper is recycled. Some 7 percent of paper is made from bamboo, grasses, bagasse sugar residue and even wheat stalks left after harvesting. Some 226 million tons of wood were pulped for paper in 1988, and at current rates of demand

growth, this will triple by 2020.

Hemp paper has a life-span of hundreds of years, compared with only 25 to 80 years for the many grades of wood paper. It can be recycled seven times, compared with wood paper's three, and does not need environmentally damaging bleaching.

Harmsen, a psychologist and land owner, says hemp as a rotation crop would suppress weeds, improve soil, need no herbicides or pesticides and would not damage soil fertility. Researcher Wood says hemp, when grown in temperate climates like that of Tasmania, would yield low amounts of the alkaloid resin that gives the plant its narcotic qualities.

"You'd probably have to smoke 100 kilos (220 pounds) of it to get high, and you would probably just end up with a sore throat," Wood said from Brisbane, where he studies non-wood production at the Commonwealth Research Organization's division of tropical crops.

But grow hemp in a tropical climate, Wood says, and it becomes a potent narcotic.

One plant very similar to marijuana, known

Marijuana-Fueled Power Suggested

SYDNEY, Australia (AP) — A top state official claims his idea of burning marijuana to generate electricity is far from a pipe dream.

New South Wales state Minerals and Energy Minister Neil Pickard told Parliament on Tuesday that he had asked the Electricity Commission to examine the possibility of burning confiscated pot crops to ·generate electricity.

"Marijuana burns at extremely high temperatures and gives off considerable heat energy," he said.

Pickard's comments were greeted with uproarious laughter, but he said it was a serious proposition.

He said burning marijuana would be cheaper than coal and produce about as much energy. The Electricity Commission would look into what modifications would be needed for power stations to handle marijuana as well as coal, Pickard said.

SUNDAY PUNCH/MARCH 24, 1991   MONDAY, FEBRUARY 5, 1990 ★

Los Angeles Times

Drug Charges

Now that we have captured Panamanian Gen. Manuel Noriega to stand trial here on drug charges, it would seem to be the appropriate time to send Col. Oliver North, John Hull, John Poindexter and their lot down to Costa Rica, where they are facing cocaine-trafficking charges.

CHRIS CONRAD
Long Beach

MIAMI HERALD 12-12-90

Among the companies that have "bribed" physicians, Wolfe alleged, were these:

■ Wyeth Ayerst Laboratories, of Radnor, Pa., which from 1986 to 1989 offered doctors 1,000 frequent-flier bonus points on American Airlines flights for each prescription they wrote for a long-acting version of the heart drug Inderal. A spokesman for the firm could not be reached for comment Tuesday.

Wolfe said the program was discontinued, and the company paid a fine of $195,000, after a state of Massachusetts investigation.

■ Sandoz Pharmaceuticals of East Hanover, N.J., which offers doctors $100 to use Sandimmune, an immune-suppressing drug, to treat psoriasis, even though it was not FDA-approved for that ailment. A company spokesman said in a telephone interview Tuesday the offer was intended to pay doctors for their time in return for providing data that could be used in an FDA application.

Popular Mechanics Magazine

REGISTERED IN U. S. PATENT OFFICE AND CANADA

WRITTEN SO YOU CAN UNDERSTAND IT

Vol. 76   **DECEMBER, 1941**   **No. 6**

uto Body Made of Plastics Resists Denting Under Hard Blows

Car with plastic body hints possible end of steel bodies

After twelve years of research, the Ford Motor Company has completed an experimental automobile with a plastic body. Although its design takes advantage of the properties of plastics, the streamline car does not differ greatly in appearance from its steel counterpart. The only steel in the hand-made body is found in the tubular welded frame on which are mounted 14 plastic panels, ³⁄₁₆ inch thick. Composed of a mixture of farm crops and synthetic chemicals, the plastic is reported to withstand a blow 10 times as great as steel without denting. Even the windows and windshield are of plastic. The total weight of the plastic car is about 2,000 pounds, compared with 3,000 pounds for a steel automobile of the same size. Although no hint has been given as to when plastic cars may go into production, the experimental model is pictured as a step toward materialization of Henry Ford's belief that some day he would "grow automobiles from the soil."

POPULAR MECHANICS

PINCH HITTERS *for* DEFENSE

above, quarter-scale model of Ford plastic r and its welded tubular steel frame

st year Westinghouse recovered 60,000 → allons of paint that "missed" in spraying

OVER in England it's saccharine for sugar; on the continent 's charcoal "gasogenes" in the umble seat instead of gasoline in he tank. Here in America there's lenty of sugar, plenty of gasoline. et there's an industrial revolu- on in progress just the same, a evolution in materials that will ffect every home.

Here is the auto Henry Ford "grew from the soil." Its plastic panels, with impact strength 10 times greater than steel, were made from flax, wheat, hemp, spruce pulp

3
↑

When Henry Ford recently unveiled his plastic car, result of 12 years of research, he gave the world a glimpse of the automobile of tomorrow, its tough panels molded under hydraulic pressure of 1,500 pounds per square inch from a recipe that calls for 70 percent of cellulose fibers from wheat straw, hemp and sisal plus 30 percent resin binder. The only steel in the car is its tubular welded frame. The plastic car weighs a ton, 1,000 pounds lighter than a comparable steel car. Manufacturers are already talking of a low-priced plastic car to test the public's taste by 1943.

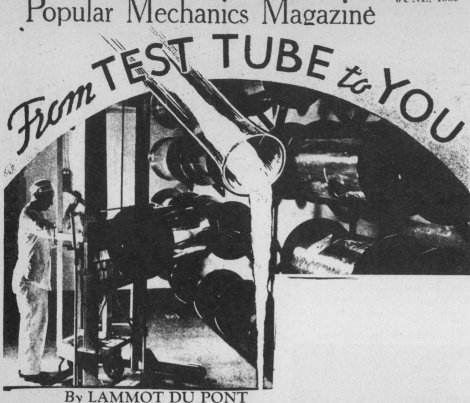

From TEST TUBE to YOU

By LAMMOT DU PONT

President, E. I. du Pont de Nemours & Company

Synthetic plastics find application in fabricating a wide variety of articles, many of which in the past were made from natural products. The synthetic plastics are used in making toiletware, costume jewelry, ash trays, unbreakable tableware, electrical appliances, lighting equipment, dental plates, buttons and buckles, scuffless shoe heels, mouthpieces for pipes and cigarette holders, windows for airplanes, motion-picture film, radio cabinets, automobile accessories and reflectors which contribute to safe driving at night by clearly outlining the highway for a half-mile or more.

Most of us are aware that the chemist has produced new products and has improved existing products. We are conscious of beautiful chemical plastics, the durable lacquer finishes on the automobile and refrigerator, the gleaming transparent wrapping material, the rainbow of man-made colors from coal tar, and fabrics fashioned from rayon.

But what of the significance of these things to the nation?

Consider our natural resources. The chemist has aided in conserving natural resources by developing synthetic products to supplement or wholly replace natural products.

Today, American chemical industry and industries based on chemistry have become so important that they employ one-fifth of all factory workers and one-fourth of all industrial capital investments.

Chemistry underlies not only such patently chemical industries as the manufacture of acids, alkalis, dyestuffs, explosives, and plastics, but also such giant industries as leather tanning, petroleum refining, pulp and papermaking, the smelting of metals, and soapmaking.

How does chemistry work? If you expect magic, you will be disappointed. Rather, the chemist pursues his work methodically, carefully investigating one possibility after another, much as a salesman calls on a list of prospective customers.

Day after day, perhaps month after month, he seemingly makes no progress. Finally, he comes upon an idea that seems worth while. It is only an idea, however, proved solely in the test tube. The idea must be developed on progressively larger scales, until it can be operated as a factory process. Supplies of raw material must be assured; outlets determined; and the product introduced to the public.

THE
American Peoples
ENCYCLOPEDIA
1953

DU PONT, THOMAS COLEMAN, 1863-1930, American financier, was born in Louisville, Ky., and educated at Massachusetts Institute of Technology. He was promoting street railways when, through the insistence of his cousin, ALFRED I. DU PONT, he headed the reorganized Du Pont business and engineered the moves by which the firm became the largest manufacturer of explosives in the United States. He sold his interests in 1914. Appointed U.S. senator in 1921 to fill an unexpired term, he was elected in 1924 and resigned in 1928 because of ill health.

DUPONT, borough, NE Pennsylvania, Luzerne County, on the Lackawanna and Wyoming Valley Railroad, near the Susquehanna River about midway between Wilkes-Barre and Scranton in a coal mining region. The borough was founded in 1917 and named for the du Pont family which operated a powder plant near by. Pop. (1950) 4,107.

DU PONT (E. I. DU PONT DE NEMOURS & CO., INC.). This company was founded in 1802 as a manufacturer of black powder by ELEUTHÈRE IRÉNÉE DU PONT de Nemours, a student of Lavoisier. Thomas Jefferson urged the founding of the company on the young French refugee to provide the struggling new nation with powder for hunting, land clearance, mining, quarrying, and defense. It operated as a partnership until 1899 at which time it became a corporation.

Until 1857, Du Pont made only black powder when Lammot du Pont developed "soda powder," with a sodium nitrate base, for blasting. In 1880 Du Pont began the manufacture of nitroglycerin and dynamite. Du Pont's development of smokeless powder from cellulose launched the company into research on other cellulose products. In 1904, Du Pont began producing special nitrocellulose for lacquers, belt cement, leather finishes, and the like. "Artificial leather" was added in 1910, "pyroxylin" or nitrocellulose plastics in 1915, and rubber-coated textiles in 1916. Next year, Du Pont entered the acids, heavy chemicals, pigments, dry colors, mixed paints and lithopone fields, and became interested in dyestuffs to release America from dependence upon German sources for coal-tar products. In World War I, Du Pont turned out 40 per cent of the smokeless powder fired by Allied guns, but at the end of that war terminated all its military explosives activities except for two small plants working for the government security program.

The ammonia department's fixation of atmospheric nitrogen helped relieve the nation of its dependence on Chile for nitrates for explosives and fertilizers, and developed processes for manufacturing methanol, glycol, urea, higher alcohols, and other chemicals.

Du Pont spent $43,000,000 before receiving any profit on its coal tar developments, but out of them came such products as CELLOPHANE (1920's), NYLON (1930's), ORLON (1940's), and DACRON (1950's). Nitrocellulose lacquers and neoprene synthetic RUBBER were Du Pont developments. Du Pont became a leader in such diverse industries as paints, rayon, plastics, electrochemicals, photographic film, insecticides, and agricultural chemicals.

Du Pont was entrusted with a principal role in the development of atomic energy, thus taking the company into the field of nuclear physics. Du Pont designed, constructed, and operated the Hanford, Wash., Engineer Works, producing plutonium, the fissionable material of the "Nagasaki-type" ATOMIC BOMB. Work on this project, involving by far the biggest plant Du Pont ever built or operated, involved an expenditure of $350,000,000 for which the company received a profit of only one dollar and agreed to the return of all patent rights to the government. Construction of the plant was begun in June, 1943, and operation of the first of the three "piles" began in September, 1944. In 1950, when the government decided to build its first plant for the manufacture of materials to be used in the hydrogen bomb, Du Pont was again chosen to design, build, and operate the plant on the Savannah River in South Carolina, at a fixed fee of one dollar. See CAROTHERS, WALLACE HUME; NIEUWLAND, JULIUS; and biographies of various members of the Du Pont family.

JAMES COLVIN

MAKING FOSSILS OF FOSSIL FUELS

Plant-based plastics and fuels can provide environment-friendly alternatives

Plant-based products, many of which were first developed before World War II, are being given a second look.

L iving in a hydrocarbon economy where much of what we come in contact with each day has been made from petrochemicals, it's easy to forget that it hasn't always been this way. Two hundred years ago plant matter, not fossil fuels, provided our tools, houses, clothing, fertilizers, paints, dyes, machines, and energy.

While low prices and political machinations caused the demise of many plant-based products, some old techniques are resurfacing and new technologies—from soy ink to plastics made from sugar—are arising. Advocates say the future could bring far more advances, such as sugar cane paper, that could aid farmers here and abroad as well as lessening damage to the environment.

The simple fact is that anything made from a hydrocarbon can also be made from a carbohydrate (not so difficult to understand since fossil fuels are, as their name connotes, the densely compacted remains of living matter), and at one time or another, it was.

In the 1880s, the first plastics were made from the cellulosic fibers of cotton. Its name reflected its feedstock: celluloid. Twenty years later much stronger plastics were made from wood. Post-World War I car radios were made from this material, called bakelite. The first synthetic fiber was not nylon, but wood-derived rayon. The first film plastic is still familiar: cellophane.

Hydrocarbons, first coal, then petroleum and natural gas,

achieved supremacy over carbohydrates because they were cheaper to produce, easier to transport, and more convenient to use. But one might argue that politics, not economics, was the deciding factor in the competition between plant matter and fossil fuels. As I have pointed out in the **St. Paul Pioneer Press** (Dec. 3, 1990), one of the ironies of materials history is that we turned a blind eye to the poisons generated by a hydrocarbon economy, while imposing considerable obstacles on carbohydrates because they can give us physical pleasure.

The tortuous path of fuel alcohol illustrates the point. In 1860, ethanol (made from plants) was a widely used and economically competitive fuel for lighting and solvent for industrial uses. Two years later, as the first oil wells began operating, the federal government imposed a stiff tax on liquor to pay for the Civil War. Ethanol, being liquor, suffered the tax, but its competitor kerosene (a byproduct of petroleum) did not. The tax, not lifted until 1906, priced ethanol out of the emerging liquid fuel markets. A May 22, 1906, *New York Times* editorial insisted, "It is only the heavy tax imposed by the United States that has prevented the use of a large number of vegetable products for the manufacturing of an exceedingly cheap and available alcohol." In 1919, with ethanol again poised to compete with gasoline, Prohibition descended on the na-

tion. (For more information see *Forbidden Fuel: Power Alcohol in the 20th Century* by Hal Bernton, William Kovarik, and Scott Sklar, Boyd-Griffin, New York, 1982.)

Hemp, the world's number-one crop in the 19th century, suffered the same kind of discrimination. Jack Herer provides the historical overview in his monumental book *The Emperor Wears No Clothes* (available from HEMP, 5632 Van Nuys Blvd., Suite 210, Van Nuys, CA 91401). For hundreds of years hemp oil was used to make paints, and hemp fibers and "hurds" (a by product of this fiber-stripping process) were made into clothing, rope, and canvas (derived from the word *cannabis*). In 1914 the Department of Agriculture praised hemp as a possible source of paper. But hemp's potential was limited by the lack of a machine like the cotton gin to separate the fibers from the rest of the plant. Such a machine was invented in 1937, and in February 1938 *Popular Mechanics* predicted a billion-dollar market for hemp. That same year prohibition was imposed on the hemp flower, marijuana.

In the last 20 years we've taken off our blinders when it comes to the environmental costs of hydrocarbons. Acid rain, global warming, air and water pollutants of all kinds result primarily from the use of fossil fuels. We've begun to realize the cost of this pollution, and the resulting rise in the price of hydrocarbon-derived products and fuels, coupled with the increasing ability to improve biological processing technologies, gives new hope for a carbohydrate economy.

Phasing out leaded gasoline opened up a market for octane-enhancing ethanol. Ethanol production increased 50-fold between 1980 and 1991. Similarly, phasing out ozone-depleting chlorofluorocarbons (CFCs) created the opportunity for one small Florida firm to make a solvent for cleaning semiconductor boards out of citrus fruits; the citrus solvent is cheaper than CFC-based solvents. A federal threat to impose pollution costs on petroleum-based printing inks galvanized the farm community to develop soybean-based inks that have already captured one-third of the colored ink market among newspapers. Vegetable paints are making a comeback. (For an analysis of commercial opportunities for using plant matter, done for the state of Nebraska, see "Substituting Agricultural Materials for Petroleum-Based Industrial Products," Institute for Local Self-Reliance, 1986.)

And yes, plant-matter-based plastics are back. **Popular Science** (April 1990) reports that a number of companies are producing degradable plastics with 6 to 12 per-

cent starch. The British chemical giant ICI makes a high-quality plastic that is produced by a bacteria that feeds on sugar. This plastic is now used in making bottles.

Plant matter seems poised once again to wage a serious struggle for supremacy with hydrocarbons, and there is also competition among crops themselves. Since the 1850s we have been making paper primarily from slow-growing trees. Gar Smith in **Earth Island Journal** (Fall 1990) argues for treeless paper. Why make paper out of 100-year-old trees that grow at the rate of a ton per acre per year, he asks, when equivalent-quality paper can be made from annual crops like hemp or kenaf or sugar cane that grow to maturity in one season and produce three to five times more yield per acre than trees?

A plant-matter-based economy might revive the hopes of Third World countries blessed with long growing seasons and abundant sunlight. **The Biomass Users Network Newsletter** (May/June 1990) notes that a 25-acre sugar cane research project in Puerto Rico has achieved yields of more than 45 tons of dry matter per acre, five times more than fast-growing tree varieties in the United States.

—David Morris

Seizure & Forfeiture Laws:
TAKE YOUR HANDS OFF MY ASSETS

by Judy Osburn

When the federal government seizes cars, boats, money, real estate and other personal property, the proceedings, are set into motion based on laws whose origins date back to medieval superstition.

These "in rem" forfeitures are a civil suit against the property itself. The property is held guilty and condemned, as though it were a personality instead of being inanimate and insentient.

Through this legal 'personification fiction,' the property is the defendant—and the guilt or innocence of the owner is irrelevant. By applying a civil label to forfeiture proceedings, the government sidesteps almost all the protections offered by the Constitution to individuals.

There is no Sixth Amendment guarantee of the right to counsel. Twenty days after seizure, the property is automatically forfeited, without review by a judge or jury—unless the owner has the resources available to intervene in the proceedings.

Civil attorneys' retainers are high, and those with knowledge in this area of law are few.

Those who are able to halt the automatic non-judicial forfeiture process find themselves in a "Through the Looking Glass" world of law, where the property is presumed guilty until proven innocent; the innocence of the owner (now claimant) is not a defense; heresay is admissible to prove the property "guilty," but not admissible in its defense; and the government's claim to the property "relates back" to the time of the illegal act, so that anyone with a subsequent interest in the property is subject to the government's prior claim of forfeiture.

This "relation-back doctrine" is used not only against unknowing purchasers and lien holders of the "tainted" property, but also against fees paid to defense counsel. Property is subject to forfeiture through its "intended use" to facilitate a drug offense, extending the law from the regulation of action to the regulation of thought.

Each violation of a constitutional right is then used as the basis for the destruction of another.

The violation of the Fifth Amendment's "Innocent until proven guilty" due process standard is used to destroy the prohibition of double jeopardy. Even an acquittal of related criminal charges does not bar re-litigation of the same facts, because the defendant must furnish the proof at the second trial.

Because the Supreme Court holds that the Constitution permits in rem forfeiture of property belonging to a person who is completely innocent of criminal activity and not negligent in his use of the property, lower courts reason that the Eighth Amendment's prohibition of

cruel and unusual of excessive punishment or fines could not apply to anybody guilty of even a minor drug offense.

The right to a jury trial is automatically waived unless demand is made within the specified time. It the property was seized on navigable waters, there is no right to trial by jury.

An incarcerated claimant does not necessarily have the right even to be present at the forfeiture proceeding. If the property is valued under $100,000 or is a conveyance accused of transporting contraband, the right to trial must be purchased through a 'cost bond' equal to 10% of the value of the property. The government retains custody of the property and is not responsible for its deterioration.

Unlike civil suits between individuals, the government as plaintiff is immune from counter-suit.

English common law of the middle ages provided for forfeiture of any object causing a man's death. Known as a deodand, the object, such as a weapon or run-away ox cart, was personified and declared tainted or evil, and forfeited to the king. Forfeitures became the Crown's principle means of tax enforcement. Forfeiture of the estates of traitors and felons added substantially to the Crown's domain.

Forfeitures imposed by the English Crown led to the prohibition off bills of attainder (forfeiture consequent to conviction) in the first article of the American Constitution.

The main body of the Constitution also forbids forfeiture of estate for treason. The very first Congress passed the statute, still law to-

day, stating that "No conviction or judgeme[nt] shall work corruption of blood or any forfe[i]ture of estate."

However, early Americans did incorpora[te] in rem procedures under Admiralty an[d] Maritime law, to seize enemy ships at sea an[d] to enforce payment of customs duties.

It was not until the outbreak of the Civ[il] War that these customs procedures were rad[i]cally changed, in order to punish Confedera[te] rebels.

Opponents of the Confiscation Act of Ju[ly] 17, 1862 called the use of in rem proceeding[s] "no more than 'hocus pocus,' designed [to] avoid the Constitutional requirements [of] criminal trial," and predicted that if it we[re] passed, "a total revolution [will be] wroug[ht] in our criminal jurisprudence...despite all t[he] safeguards of the Constitution."

The Act did pass, and was soon challenged.

The Kentucky State Supreme Court held unconstitutional, stating, "These [in rem] pr[o]ceedings may today be the engines of punis[h]ment to the rebels but, in the future, they ma[y] be the instruments of oppression, injustice an[d] tyranny."

But the Supreme Court held that, if the A[ct] was an exercise of the war powers of gover[n]ment and was only applied to enemies, then [it] was Constitutionally allowable, in order to e[n]sure a speedy termination of the war.

Today, the passions of the "War on Drugs" have caused Congress to once again use i[n] rem proceedings to inflict punishment witho[ut] the nuisance of the protections provided b[y] the Constitution and Bill of Rights.

Drug Legalization: Interest Rises in Prestigious Circles

By STANLEY MEISLER
TIMES STAFF WRITER

WASHINGTON—Hours before the Stanford-Notre Dame football game Oct. 7, a relaxed and candid George P. Shultz, wearing a Stanford-red polo shirt, outlined some of his philosophical ideas to a group of alumni of the Stanford Business School at Memorial Auditorium in Palo Alto.

"Now that I am out of government I can say this," the former secretary of state began, speaking thoughtfully. Then, in a suggestion that would astound and infuriate former colleagues in the government, he told the alumni: "We need at least to consider and examine forms of controlled legalization of drugs."

"I find it very difficult to say that," Shultz said. "Sometimes at a reception or a cocktail party I

advance these views and people head for somebody else. They don't even want to talk to you." He screwed up his face in mock imitation of the shock he has caused, drawing a roar of laughter from the alumni.

But no one ever associated wild and wooly ideas with the cautious and conservative Shultz when he served more than six years as secretary of state in the Ronald Reagan Administration and two years as secretary of the Treasury in the Richard M. Nixon Administration.

And Shultz's current position on drugs does not put him in deepest left field. Interest is mounting in academic and scientific circles in the idea of legalizing drugs, and the number of those willing to be counted is increasing markedly.

Aside from Shultz, the list of

Please see DRUGS, A18

George P. Shultz

'We're not really going to get anywhere until we can take the criminality out of the drug business and the incentives for criminality out of it.'

Continued from A1

those advocating at least a study of some form of controlled legalization now includes Nobel Prize-winning economist Milton Friedman, conservative columnist William F. Buckley, Baltimore Mayor Kurt L. Schmoke, former New York Police Commissioner Patrick V. Murphy, astronomer Carl Sagan, Executive Director Ira Glasser of the American Civil Liberties Union and a significant number of psychiatrists, doctors and political scientists.

To them, making drugs illegal merely fosters crime and violence while failing utterly to stop drug use, just as Prohibition of alcohol failed in the 1920s.

Opposition Exists

The Bush Administration, however, regards the arguments for legalizing drugs as anathema. "There is even a question [among Administration officials] that the discussion in itself is a little risky."

—Enforcing the drug laws succeeds only in driving prices up and thus aggravating the violence bred by the heavy profits earned by dealers.

"If the marijuana, cocaine and heroin markets were legal, state and federal governments would collect billions of dollars annually in tax revenues," Nadelman said. "Instead, they expend billions in what amounts to a subsidy of organized criminals."

—The government has no moral right to treat drugs differently from alcohol and tobacco.

"Enforcement of drug laws makes a mockery of an essential principle of a free society, that those who do no harm to others should not be harmed by others and particularly not by the state," Nadelman wrote. "Most of the 40 million Americans who illegally consume drugs each year do no direct harm to anyone else; indeed, most do relatively little harm even to themselves."

Glaucoma Victim Pushes Legal Use of Marijuana

By BRIAN MURPHY, *Associated Press*

HOLLYWOOD, Fla.—Elvy Musikka begins most days as she ends them—smoking a legal joint and hoping others like her can some day do the same.

Either rolled like a cigarette or baked into brownies, marijuana has been in Musikka's life for more than 12 years as she tried to lessen the effects of glaucoma, which has left her with only 10% of her sight.

But she clearly sees herself as a crusader for the thousands of glaucoma victims throughout the United States denied legal use of the drug that reduces the high eye pressure caused by the disease.

"I think people have every right to sue the government for keeping them from what could be their one hope left of keeping their sight," said Musikka, 44, one of three people given government-grown marijuana for medical reasons.

"I am constantly haunted by the idea there are others who will never see the stars again or look upon their children because they were denied a simple plant."

Musikka's application for legal

marijuana was approved [by] U.S. Food and Drug Administration in October, two months a[fter] Broward Circuit Court jud[ge] persuaded to clear her of m[ari]na-growing charges.

Each month, Musikka re[ceives] 300 marijuana cigarettes shi[pped] Bascom Palmer Eye Instit[ute] Miami.

If she smokes, it's a joint [every] three hours. "But actually I [do] to eat it," Musikka said. "Y[ou're] less stoned and it lasts longe[r if] eat some pot brownies and g[o] 12 hours. Also, your throat [doesn't] get so raspy. But that's OK [if you] want to sing some blues."

Musikka has turned to [music] since her limited sight kee[ps her] from working. She now [travels] throughout Florida disc[ussing] marijuana treatment for gla[ucoma] and promoting her newly re[corded] four-song record album p[artly] funded by a $6,000 grant fr[om the] state Division of Blind Servi[ces.]

The songs—two in Engli[sh,] two in Spanish—are among

Please see MARIJUANA, [](#)

Administrative Judge Urges Medicinal Use of Marijuana

DEA Expected to Reject Call for Limited Legalization

Washington Post 9-7-88 p. 42

By Michael Isikoff
Washington Post Staff Writer

A Drug Enforcement Administration administrative law judge, calling marijuana "one of the safest therapeutically active substances known to man," recommended yesterday that the drug be made legally available for some medical purposes, including treatment of cancer patients.

If adopted, the opinion by Judge Francis L. Young would mean that doctors could prescribe marijuana—a fundamental change in the drug's legal status that some specialists said could aid tens of thousands of patients suffering from nausea-inducing chemotherapy and muscle spasms of multiple sclerosis.

The opinion is not likely to have any immediate effect because DEA Administrator John C. Lawn is considered almost certain to reject Young's conclusions. Nevertheless, coming after a 16-year legal battle, the 69-page ruling marks the first time a government official has accepted a medical role for the country's mostly widely used illicit drug.

"The evidence in this record clearly shows that marijuana has been accepted as capable of relieving the distress of great numbers of very ill people, and doing so with safety under medical supervision," Young wrote. "It would be unreasonable, arbitrary and capricious for DEA to continue to stand between those sufferers and the benefits of this substance in light of the evidence in this record."

The long-awaited ruling was immediately criticized by DEA lawyers and antidrug groups who said it would send a confusing message at a time the federal government is attempting to wage a war on drugs. DEA officials also said the ruling ran counter to the body of accepted medical opinion.

"This totally ignores the bulk of the medical evidence," said Stephen E. Stone, associate counsel of DEA, which had fought changing marijuana's classification. "The judge seems to hang his hat on what he calls a 'respectable minority of physicians.' What percent are you talking about? One half of 1

percent? One quarter of 1 percent?

"From our point of view, marijuana has not been established as a safe and effective drug," Stone added.

Young's ruling, which cites medical researchers from Harvard, New York University and other leading medical schools, comes in the form of a recommendation to Lawn to change the status of marijuana under the 1970 Controlled Substance Act. Ever since the act was passed, marijuana has been classified with heroin and LSD as a Schedule I controlled substance, which means it is an illegal drug with no known medical use.

Young recommends that Lawn use discretionary authority to make marijuana a Schedule II substance. This means it would become a drug—like morphine and cocaine—that, while still unavailable to the general public, can be prescribed by doctors for limited purposes.

A DEA spokesman said yesterday that Lawn would not comment on the ruling until he has a chance to review it. Even if he rejects the recommendation, however, lawyers for the National Organization for the Reform of Marijuana Laws (NORML) and other pro-marijuana groups said Young's ruling would provide a powerful evidence to overturn a rejection in federal court.

"This is the most significant victory that one can imagine," said Robert C. Randall, president of the Alliance for Cannabis Therapeutics, a group that joined with NORML and the Drug Policy Foundation in petitioning DEA for the ruling. "For the first time in over half a century, the federal government is viewing marijuana in a rational context . . . not just saying it's something evil."

In his opinion, Young cited a number of medical experts and patients as a basis for his conclusion that marijuana's medical use was "clear beyond any question." Their testimony showed that marijuana helped suppress nausea and vomiting experienced by chemotherapy patients, was a "highly successful appetite stimulant" and was widely—if illicitly—used in some hospitals.

"This successful use of marijuana has given many cancer chemotherapy patients a much more positive outlook on their overall treatment," Young wrote, adding that smoking marijuana was far more effective than taking pills with synthetic THC, the active ingredient in the drug.

Young found similar benefits for using marijuana to control muscle spasms suffered by patients with multiple sclerosis, spasticity and hyperparathyroidism, a painful horomonal disorder that causes bone spurs. But Young rejected permitting marijuana for treatment of glaucoma, saying there is insufficient evidence that many physicians support such a move.

At the core of Young's ruling, however, was his conclusion that the dangers of marijuana do not outweigh its medical benefits. While agreeing that marijuana "can be harmful" and "abused," he noted there is still not a documented death caused by the drug. "In strict medical terms, marijuana is far safer than many foods we commonly consume," he wrote.

TUESDAY, DECEMBER 19, 1989   LOS ANGELES TIMES

AIDS Patient to Get Legal Marijuana for Pain Relief

From United Press International

WASHINGTON—The federal government for the first time has approved the legal use of marijuana for an AIDS patient to test reduction of nausea, vomiting and pain caused by the disease and its treatment, officials said Monday.

Under the license, approved Wednesday by the Food and Drug Administration, a 33-year-old Texan, identified only as Steve because of patient confidentiality rules, will receive prescription marijuana from the government's stock, controlled by the National Institute on Drug Abuse.

He joins a handful of other patients with cancer, glaucoma and

multiple sclerosis who have obtained medical access to the drug in order to treat elements of their diseases or alleviate harsh effects of therapy.

"This is a significant breakthrough for persons afflicted with AIDS and for all those seeking legal, medically supervised access to prescription marijuana," said Robert Randall, president of the Alliance for Cannabis Therapeutics, the Washington-based group that disclosed the approval.

FDA spokesmen said they did not know of the approval, but officials at the National Institute of Drug Abuse, which must ship the marijuana to the patient's doctor, confirmed that the FDA had ap-

CALIFORNIA HEMP INITIATIVE '92

Name, Summary & Analysis of the Measure:*

HEMP: RESTORATION & REGULATION

Restores the right to farm and use hemp as a natural resource for paper, textile, fabrication, construction, seed, fuel, seed oil and medical industries, etc., in competition with the petroleum, timber and other industries. Makes herbal hemp and medicinal extracts available to people with arthritis, asthma, cancer, AIDS, glaucoma, etc. Protects the privacy of home and family.

Sets 21-year age limit on consumption of hemp intoxicants (called grass, reefer, marijuana, pot, etc.) and regulates them like the California wine industry. Restricts consumption in public and driving while intoxicated. Limits drug testing. Sets $10 fee for clearing out-of-date police records. Requires a one-year study to consider feasibility of settling grievances.

Financial Impact Analysis:

Tremendous benefit. Potentially up to $100 billion in new hemp industries brought into the state, along with thousands of jobs. Tens of billions of dollars in tax savings, which the legislative analyst predicts will be used to fight violent crime. Cost of study offset by savings and billions of dollars in new tax revenue paid into the state general fund, which is used to fund schools, public transit, trauma centers, etc. A more just, speedy and efficient legal system. Less prison crowding without more prison bonds.

Environmental Impact Analysis:

A drought resistant, environmentally friendly cash crop for California. Every 1,000 acres of hemp used for paper or construction saves 4,100 acres of trees from being cut. A cleaner source of fuel than petroleum, without oil spills or offshore drilling. Offers new biodegradable alternatives to plastic and synthetic fibers. Uses fewer chemical pesticides and fertilizers than crops like corn, tobacco and cotton, so it reduces water pollution from contaminated runoff. Less dioxin, air pollution, acid rain, etc.

* Notice: This is a full, accurate and honest description of the hemp initiative. Proponents are challenging the state Attorney General for distorting the intent of the measure, using lies and prejudicial language in his official title and summary, which legally must appear on the petitions. Signers should be aware that the title and summary assigned to this initiative are misleading. Please read the text of the initiative.

Contact: H.E.M.P., 5632 Van Nuys Blvd., Suite 210, Van Nuys CA 91401 • 213/ 392-1806

AN ACT TO AMEND THE HEALTH AND SAFETY CODE OF CALIFORNIA

Add Section 11357.5 to the Health and Safety Code of California, any laws or policies to the contrary not withstanding:

(1) Persons, 21 years or older, shall not be prosecuted, be denied any right or privilege, nor be subject to criminal or civil penalties for the cultivation, transportation, distribution, or consumption of:

(a) Industrial hemp products. Hemp farmers and manufacturers of industrial hemp products shall not be subject to any special zoning or licensing fees that are discriminatory or prohibitive.

(b) Hemp medicinal preparations.

(c) Hemp products for nutritional use.

(d) Hemp products for personal use in private. No permit or license may be required for non-commercial cultivation, transportation, distribution, or consumption of any hemp product.

(2) Definitions:

(a) The term "hemp" means hemp, cannabis, or marijuana, or any part or preparation of the plant cannabis sativa, cannabis indica, cannabis americana, or any variety of cannabis.

(b) The term "industrial hemp products" means all products made from hemp, cannabis, or marijuana, that are not designed or intended for human consumption, and includes, but is not limited to: paper, fiber, fuel, plastics, paint, seed for cultivation, animal feed, veterinary medicine, oil, plants used for crop rotation, erosion control, or weed control.

(c) The term "hemp medicinal preparations" means all products made from hemp, cannabis, or marijuana, that are designed, intended, or used for human consumption, for the treatment of any disease, the relief of pain, or for any healing purpose including the treatment or relief of asthma, glaucoma, arthritis, anorexia, migraine, multiple sclerosis, epilepsy, nausea, stress, for use as an antibiotic, an antiemetic, or as any healing agent, or as an adjunct to any medical procedure or herbal treatment.

(d) The term "hemp products for nutritional use" means the use of any hemp product intended for human consumption as food, for example, but not limited to: seed protein, seed oil, seed cake, or gruel, or any preparation thereof.

(e) The term "personal use" means the use of any product or preparation of hemp, cannabis, or marijuana, intended for any relaxational, ritual, spiritual, or other personal purpose.

(f) The term "hemp intoxicating products" means any hemp product other than industrial hemp products, hemp medicinal preparations, or hemp products for nutritional use.

(3) Hemp medicinal preparations are hereby restored to the available list of medicines in California. Licensed physicians shall not be penalized for or restricted from prescribing hemp preparations for medical purposes to patients of any age.

(4) Hemp intoxicating products shall be regulated according to California's wine industry model. For the purpose of distinguishing personal versus commercial production, under Section 23000 et seq. of the Business and Professions Code of California, one half ounce of cured hemp flowers and/or leaves shall be considered equivalent to one gallon of dry wine.

(5) The manufacturing, marketing, distribution, or sales between adults of equipment or accessories designed or marketed for use in the planting, cultivation, harvesting, curing, processing, packaging, storing, analyzing, consumption, or transportation of hemp, industrial hemp products, hemp medicinal preparations, hemp products for nutritional use, or hemp products for personal use shall not be prohibited.

(6) The enactment of this initiative is to be retroactive in its application to include amnesty and clearing of all criminal records for all cannabis/marijuana related acts which are hereby no longer illegal. The Attorney General, within 60 days of the passage of this act, shall develop and distribute a one page application, providing for the destruction of all criminal records in California for cannabis/marijuana related acts which are no longer illegal. Such forms shall be distributed to district and city attorneys and all police departments in the state of California, and made available to persons hereby affected. Upon filing such form with the Attorney General and payment of a fee no greater than $10.00, all pertinent records anywhere in the state of California relating to the application shall be destroyed. Such persons may truthfully state that they have never been convicted of cannabis/marijuana related acts which are no longer illegal.

II. The legislature is authorized to enact legislation, using reasonable standards to determine impairment, to regulate or prohibit persons under the influence of hemp from operating a motor vehicle, heavy machinery, or otherwise engaging in conduct which may affect public safety. Testing for inert cannabis metabolites shall not be required for employment or insurance, nor be considered in determining impairment.

III. The legislature is authorized to enact legislation, using reasonable standards, limiting the use of hemp intoxicating products in public places.

IV. No California law enforcement personnel or funds shall be used to assist enforcement of federal cannabis/marijuana laws governing cannabis/marijuana related acts which are no longer illegal in the state of California.

V. The legislature, the Governor, and the Attorney General are directed to challenge federal cannabis/marijuana prohibitions which conflict with this act.

VI. Severability: If any provision of this act, or the application of any such provision to any person or circumstance, shall be held invalid by any court, the remainder of this act to the extent it can be given effect, or the application of such provision to persons or circumstances other than those as to which it is held invalid, shall not be affected thereby, and to this end the provisions of this act are severable.

VII. If any rival or conflicting initiative regulating any matter addressed by this act receives the higher affirmative vote, then all non-conflicting parts of this act shall become operative.

VIII. Within 120 days following the passage of this act the legislature shall fund, from law enforcement savings hereby generated, an advisory panel to study the feasibility and methods of making restitution to all persons who were imprisoned, fined or had private properties forfeited as a result of criminal or civil actions for cannabis/marijuana related acts which are hereby no longer illegal. Said restitution could only be paid from a portion of the tax revenues created by the re-introduction of the hemp industries. This advisory panel shall consist of thirteen members to be appointed in the following manner: one appointed by the Governor, one appointed by the State Attorney General, one appointed by the State Controller, two appointed by the Speaker of the Assembly, two appointed by the President Pro-tem of the Senate, and the remaining six to be chosen from the private sector: three by the Secretary of State and three by the State Treasurer. The advisory panel will hold a minimum of six meetings which will be open to the public. A preliminary report shall be submitted to the legislature within six months of the formation of the advisory panel. A final report shall be submitted to the legislature and the public within one year of the formation of the advisory panel.

IX. Purpose of Act: Construction

This act is an exercise of the police powers of the State for the protection of the safety, welfare, health and peace of the people and the environment of the State, to allow for the industrial and medicinal type uses of hemp, to eliminate the evils of unlicensed and unlawful cultivation, selling and dispensing of hemp, and to promote temperance in the consumption of hemp as an intoxicant. It is hereby declared that the subject matter of this act involves in the highest degree, the economic, social and moral well-being and the safety of the State and of all its people. All provisions of this act shall be liberally construed for the accomplishment of these purposes.

SOCIAL PROBLEMS, Vol. 31, No. 1, October 1983

JURY NULLIFICATION IN POLITICAL TRIALS*

STEVEN E. BARKAN
University of Maine, Orono

Judges in the United States usually do not tell juries of their historic power to nullify the law by acquitting defendants who are guilty according to the evidence. This fact may affect the fortunes of political defendants and their protest movements. This paper looks at the history of jury nullification in political trials in England and the United States and the ideological consequences of the refusal of many judges in trials of Vietnam War protesters to inform jurors of their power to nullify. Had jurors been so informed, more acquittals or hung juries would probably have resulted, presenting a serious challenge to the government's conduct of the war. I also address the theoretical and research implications of my analysis.

Political protesters have faced criminal prosecution throughout the history of the United States. From the tax and mercantile protests of the colonial era to the demonstrations against nuclear power and nuclear weapons of the 1970s and 1980s, tens of thousands of U.S. citizens have been arrested, prosecuted, and often imprisoned for dissent. This use of the courts has affected the fate of many social movements. In several periods of protest, the courts have provided effective vehicles of social control for government officials and other antagonists. In 1917 and 1918, for example, federal and state prosecutions of some 2,000 socialists, anarchists, and other radicals under laws forbidding virtually all criticism of the First World War stifled dissent and helped destroy the Industrial Workers of the World (Chafee, 1941). In other times, though, the legal system has enabled insurgents to mobilize needed resources and gain other important advantages. Colonial law and legal proceedings, for example, proved a "creative force" (Teachout, 1981:198) in the struggle against English rule. Despite this rich history of political justice, however, sociologists have paid little attention to the impact of the legal system, and especially the criminal courts, on social movements.

Courts are some of the many "third-party" resources (McCarthy and Zald, 1977; Oberschall, 1939) which may help achieve or obstruct the goals of social movement organizations (Barkan, 1980c; Handler, 1978).[1] In this framework, political trials are especially important.[2] Government officials may use criminal charges and prosecutions to discredit a movement and compel its members to spend time, money, and energy avoiding conviction and punishment. A movement may in turn use the court proceedings to convince the public of the justness of its cause and the unfairness of the prosecution (Allen, 1974; Becker, 1971; Hakman, 1972; Kirchheimer, 1961). The jury's verdict thus has a crucial effect on both sides. Conviction advances the prosecution's goals of social control; acquittal frustrates the labeling of the movement's beliefs and conduct

* The larger study from which this paper is derived would not have been possible without the advice and encouragement of the late Forrest Dill. This is a revised version of a paper presented at the annual meeting of the American Sociological Association, San Francisco, September 6-10, 1982. The author thanks Steven Cohn, John Gilmore, and Michael Schwarz for their comments. Correspondence to: Department of Sociology and Social Work, 221 East Annex, University of Maine, Orono, Maine 04469.

1. A number of political scientists have examined the strategies of interest group litigation and analyzed factors which influence the incidence and outcomes of such litigation (Cortner, 1968; Hahn, 1973; O'Connor, 1980; Vose, 1959, 1972). Except for Handler (1978), however, these analysts have not generally been informed by the broader social movement theory of sociologists. Further, in focusing on civil litigation, they have neglected the use of criminal courts in social movement conflict.

2. As other analysts have recognized (Becker, 1971; Belknap, 1981), the definition of "political trial" is elusive. Elsewhere, I have distinguished two kinds of political trials. The first involves defendants who have deliberately broken the law with acts of civil disobedience. The second involves the use by government officials of "trumped-up" charges as a means of harassing individuals and groups felt to be politically dangerous (Barkan, 1980c).

---

38   BARKAN

Dyke, 1977:278). Still another judge, interviewed anonymously by Bannan and Bannan (1974:278), maintained, "I don't think that is what our form of government was ever intended to set up, that there should be—whenever there is a jury trial—that the question of the morality of law would come into play."

The real reasons underlying such statements are impossible to discern; judges will not readily admit to deliberate attempts at social control. Many judges were no doubt sincerely concerned about possible harm to the rule of law should jurors be informed of their power to nullify. In light of the history of nullification, however, it is not inconceivable that their opposition also derived in large part from their lack of sympathy for the antiwar movement. At the very least, Vietnam-era judges must have realized that refusing to have jurors informed of their power to nullify would help ensure convictions, even if their own purpose in preventing jurors from being so informed was to uphold the rule of law. Another judge interviewed anonymously by Bannan and Bannan (1974:194) recognized both these consequences:

The question becomes . . . has the defendant violated the law, or hasn't he, by his conduct. And this, of course, by its very process avoids a great many of the arguments the defendants attempt to raise which go to the legality of the Vietnam war. . . . I think it misplaces the jury's functions to attempt to have the jury pass upon that morality.

In a way, the question of the real motives of judges who opposed informing juries in antiwar cases of their power to nullify is moot, for the ideological, social-control function of their opposition was the same nonetheless. Mannheim (1936) stressed the unwitting, unintentional nature of ideological statements; thus, the refusal of Vietnam-era judges to let juries know of nullification was ideological even if it could be shown that their intent was to uphold the rule of law and not to impede antiwar goals. As Merton (1968:120) has pointed out, we need not assume that the reasons given by people for their behavior are the same as the actual consequences of their behavior. These consequences may be unintended, or latent, and in their study lies "the distinctive intellectual contributions of the sociologist."

CONCLUSIONS AND IMPLICATIONS

In political trials, the jury's verdict often helps determine the repercussions of the proceedings for social movement efforts. The jury's decision reflects not only the wider public view of the defendants and their movement, but also the extent to which judges allow defense arguments into evidence, permit defense teams to urge juries to use their conscience, and instruct juries on their power to disregard the law. As a result, the likelihood of a jury acquittal may vary not only from case to case and year to year within the same movement, but from one movement to another. It would thus be useful to examine prosecutions of political activists in periods not covered by this paper, as well as in other nations where jury trials are less available or juries themselves are more controlled by the judge.

Jury acquittals in the colonial, abolitionist, and post-bellum eras of the United States helped advance insurgent aims and hamper government efforts at social control. Widespread jury acquittals or hung juries during the Vietnam War might have had the same effect. But the refusal of judges in trials of antiwar protesters to inform juries of their power to disregard the law helped ensure convictions, which in turn frustrated antiwar goals and protected the government from the many repercussions that acquittals or hung juries would have brought. Juries have, of course, nullified in political and conventional cases even without being informed in court of their power to do so. But this paper has argued that nullification is more likely if juries are told of their power. Where juries feel strongly one way or the other about protest actions and goals, nullification instructions would probably not make much difference. But in trials where jurors' feelings are not strong enough to overcome the judge's charge to follow the law, nullification information may have a significant impact.

NOW YOU CAN HELP REINSTATE THE JURY AS THE CITIZENS' SAFEGUARD OF LIBERTY

FIJA CALIFORNIA NEEDS YOUR HELP TO GUARANTEE EVERY JUROR KNOWS THE TRUTH!

"I consider trial by jury as the only anchor yet imagined by man, by which a government can be held to the principles of its constitution."-- Thomas Jefferson (1789)

The Fully Informed Jury Amendment to the California State Constitution has now been filed as an initiative measure. FIJA requires judges resume the practice of informing jurors about their inherent right and responsibility to judge whether a law is unjust or unjustly applied in a particular case. FIJA requires that defendants motives be admissible as evidence, and would reaffirm the jury's authority to acquit or convict according to the dictates of conscience.

"Jury nullification of the law" is a traditional right dating back to the Magna Carta and was intended by America's founding fathers as the final test a law must pass before it gains the authority to punish violators.

John Adams, our nation's second president, in 1771 said of the jury, "it is not only his right, but his duty...to find the verdict according to his own best understanding, judgment, and conscience, though in direct opposition to the direction of the court. (74, *Yale Law Journal*, 1964:73)

In a historic Supreme Court civil forfeiture jury trial, first Chief Justice John Jay instructed the jury that the facts of the case had been determined and the only judgment remaining for the jury to make was upon the law itself. "The jury has the right to judge both the law as well as the fact in controversy." *Georgia vs. Brailsford*, 1794:4.)

The trial jury's veto power continues to be recognized by the state Constitutions of Maryland and Indiana. And, "[the jury has an] unreviewable and irreversible power...to acquit in disregard of the instruction on the law given by the trial judge...The pages of history shine on instances of the jury's exercise of its prerogative to disregard instructions of the judge; for example, acquittals under the fugitive slave law." (U.S. Court of Appeals, 1972, 473 F.2d, 1130.)

Jury veto power decided the seditious libel trial of Peter Zenger in 1735, and is celebrated as a hallmark of freedom of the press in America. Colonial juries' refusal to enforce forfeitures under the English Navigation Acts is another example. And jury nullification in liquor law trials was a major contributing factor in ending alcohol prohibition.

Informed juries provide ever-evolving feedback to legislatures and protect minorities from, in James Madison's words, "the body of the people, operating by the majority against the minority." Even in an era of a hysterical majority empowered juries will assure that the government can exercise no powers over the people without the unanimous consent of twelve jurors.

Due to special interest pressure, juries have been misinformed of their right to judge law as well as fact for almost 100 years. Jurors now swear in their oaths to judge only the facts of the case according to the the law as dictated to them by the judge. No officer of the court is allowed to tell jurors of their power to say no to unjust laws. In most cases juries are no longer allowed to hear the defendant's motives.

Trial by jury is trial by the people. When juries are not allowed to judge the law it becomes trial by government. If juries are not allowed to judge the the justice of the law they can not protect the people from the oppressions of government because, as history has shown, government may authorize any oppression by law.

"If a juror accepts as the law that which the judge states then that juror has accepted the exercise of absolute authority of a government employee and has surrendered a power and right that once was the citizen's safeguard of liberty, -- for the saddest epitaph which can be carved in memory of a vanished liberty is that it was lost because its possessors failed to stretch forth a saving hand while there was time." [2 *Elliots Debates*, 94, Bancroft, History of the Constitution, 267, 1788.]

Join these patriots who defended jury rights: William Penn, John Hancock, John Adams, first Chief Justice John Jay, Alexander Hamilton, Samual Chase, Thomas Jefferson, Thomas Paine...

Initiative Measure to be Submitted Directly to the Voters

SECTION I. PURPOSE OF ACT: CONSTRUCTION.

The purpose of this Act is to assure that jurors are made aware of:

(a) The jurors' inherent right to judge whether the law or laws applicable to the case being tried are unjust or misapplied.

(b) The jurors' traditional right to vote according to conscience.

To this end, juries affected by this Act shall be allowed to hear evidence concerning the defendant's motives. This Act shall be construed liberally to effect its purposes.

SECTION II. Article I of the Constitution of the State of California is amended by adding a Section 29 that reads:

"JURY RIGHTS AND RESPONSIBILITIES Section 29

Whenever state or local government is one of the parties in any trial by jury, the court must inform the jurors that in addition to their responsibility to judge the facts of the case, they have the inherent right to judge the law itself."

ANSWER TO ED
An open letter from Jack Herer and Lynn Osburn,
April 15, 1991

In the May, 1991 issue of *High Times*, Ed Rosenthal interviewed David Gold, author of Solar Gas. His title for the interview was, "Hemp & Biomass vs Fossil Fuels."

We do not understand why Ed would ask numerous questions pertaining to hemp as a fuel resource when Mr. Gold's area of expertise was small scale ethyl (sugar) alcohol production from grains and fruit. He clearly stated that he was not an expert on methanol (wood alcohol) fuel production, nor had he done any research on methanol production pertaining to hemp as a fuel resource.

David Gold's research was important to our 1985-86 hypothesis, in the original "Emperor," that hemp could be a major biomass resource for fuel production. Since that time our investigations into hemp for fuel have lead into a different direction than that persued by Mr. Gold. We believe Mr. Gold's work to be of great value to biomass fuels research. His use of solar power to overcome the low fuel-to-feed efficiency that plagues ethanol fuel development is quite ingenious and was one of the inspirations for our initial hemp-for-energy investigations.

However, we must agree with scientific testimony given at the 1978 Senate Commission on Alcohol Fuels, that ethyl alcohol fuel produced by biological digestion (fermentation) methods cannot hope to meet the demand for gasoline in the USA, though it would certainly help. The fuel and method most promising to replace US gasoline use is methanol made from biomass through thermochemical decomposition. This method is called pyrolysis and has a 95.5% fuel-to-feed efficiency. ("Pyrolysis of Wood Residues with a Vertical Bed Reactor," J.A. Knight, Georgia Institute of Technology, Academic Press, NY 1979)

Ed Rosenthal says in the opening line to the interview, "Since the world has gone to war over energy sources, the idea of growing hemp for fuel has gained credibility. But how realistic is it?" His last statement in the opening papagraph before the interview actually begins is, "And though he [Gold] agrees that hemp could be an important crop for energy production, he says there's one that's even better." On page 44 of Rosenthal's High Times interview the reader finally comes to find out the plant Ed has insinuated to be better than hemp for energy production is cattails!

Cattails, according to *Funk and Wagnals Encyclopedia*, is a perennial with a creeping rootstock that primarily grows in fresh water swamps in both tropical and temperate climates and is occasionally cultivated along pond borders and bog gardens. These growing conditions are not found in many places in the U.S. David Gold never said in the interview that be believed cattails could out-do hemp for energy production. Why did Ed Rosenthal put those words into David Gold's mouth?

As for Ed's contention that cattails are better suited than hemp for erosion control—soil erosion occurrs on sloped land—there are no bogs, that we know of, existing on slopes, and any use of cattails for erosion control must be limited to the formation of new ponds or bogs.

Ed Rosenthal states in the side bar to his interview of David Gold: *"Hemp proponents often claim it could be grown on marginal land and would not affect the production of other crops. This is simply not true. Hemp needs a rich fertile soil for high productivity. This limits it's production to areas which are already being farmed."*

Our answer to Ed is: of course most plants will achieve maximum productivity when grown on rich, fertile soil, including hemp. The fertile soils of Kentucky will produce top quality fiber, commanding a much higher price per pound than hemp grown for biomass. The meaning of marginal land is land that is not profitable for growing standard cash crops, such as wheat, corn, rye, hay, etc. Here is what *The Paper Trade Journal*, May 15, 1930 had to say about hemp growth on land "that has little value for the production of other crops:"

"The growing of hemp for paper-making manufacture on drained peat marsh land *that has little value for the production of other crops* has been suggested. There are 10,000 such acres of such land, *known to be suitable for hemp production* in Wisconsin alone. The actual area is undoubtedly much larger. The fiber production would be somewhat inferior for textile uses and therefore would not command so high a price as that produced for tex-

tiles. The average yield of hemp fiber from this land is about 900 pounds per acre, therefore, the total production possible from Wisconsin marsh land would be at least 4500 tons [fiber] annually." [22,500 tons of cellulose rich hurds would also be produced by the hemp crop on that marginal Wisconson land.] (*Paper Trade Journal*, Technical Association Section, May 15, 1930. "Physical and Chemical Characteristics of Hemp Stalks and Seed Flax Straw," E.R. Schafer and F.A. Simmonds, presented to the American Chemical Society, Division of Cellulose Chemistry, Sept. 1929. *Emphasis added.*)

And here is what the Illustrated Historical Gazetteer of Missouri had to say about hemp production on marginal land:

"I have resided in this county for some twelve years, and have been raising hemp every year... I think on good land the Chinese hemp will yield, on a average, 1120 [fiber] pounds per acre; 1500 pounds has been raised per acre on a crop of thirty-five acres.

"...I can raise on my land hemp for twelve of fifteen years in succession without manure or rest. In regards to wheat, I think our soil is not so well adapted to that product as it will be after it [hemp] has been cultivated for some years. Owing to our light soil rye does better than wheat." ("Platte County. The Hemp Culture," Nathan Parker, *Illustrated Historical Gazetteer of Missouri*, J.B. Lippincott & Co., Philadelphia, 1867. *Emphasis added.*)

Hemp fiber has approximately the same value and per acre production a cotton fiber. Hemp will grow and produce profits on marginal land. This is not only simply true, it is definitely true. When hemp is grown on any land 83% of the harvest is high cellulose hurds. Because hemp hurds are 77% cellulose they are the ideal raw resource for the cellulose polymer industry whic includes rayon, celluloid, cellophane, plastics, explosives and according to Popular Mechanics Magazine, 1938, 1941, twenty-five thousand other products.

Ed contends that hemp's value as a fuel lies mainly in the oil pressed from hemp seed. In order for a resource to qualify as a fuel, not only must it burn, it must be cheap to produce. Hemp seed oil has far greater value as a paint and varnish drying agent, chemical feedstock and a cooking oil. Hemp seed oil as a fuel will never be as cheap to produce as pyrolytic fuel oils made from cracking hemp biomass in a fractional still (destructive distillation) because too much energy goes into pressing the oil from the seed. Nor can any seed crop produce enough oil to meet U.S. fuel oil demands.

The per acre yield reported in the two pre-prohibition articles cited above are typical reports from the era. The yields refer to fiber harvest, which is according to USDA Bulletin 404, 1916, one sixth the harvest of fiber and hurds combined. At a competitive fuel resource price of $30 per ton, hemp stalks grown for biomass production will fetch the farmer $300 per acre on land which farmers cannot make a profit growing anything else.

Judging from the conclusion to his sidebar, Ed seems to be unaware that when hemp is grown for a seed crop total biomass production is a fraction of that when grown for fiber because the plants are grown five to ten feet apart t facilitate branching in order to produce more seeds per plant. When hemp is grown for fiber, seed is planted two to four inches apart to gain the highest fiber yield. It is not reasonable to expect maximun fiber and hurd production as well as a maximun seed yield from the same stand of hemp because the planting and growing techniques are different.

Hemp is tremendously important to future world economy and ecology because of the diversity of end products that result from altered cultivation methods. Hemp for medicine and intoxication, hemp for fiber and hurds, hemp for seed, and hemp for biomass are all hemp industry resources requiring different crop management techniques to produce the desired quality end products. These hemp industries per acre yields cannot be added together to achieve a total field crop yield, as Ed did in his article, anymore than adding apples to oranges will give a useful total for anything but fruit salad.

We are disturbed that *High Times* editors when answering a letter in the front of the May issue would tell the reader "Turn to page 39 for our most extensive hemp article to date." Page 39 is the page Ed Rosenthal's interview begins on. Ed Rosenthal's article is one of the worst cases of misunderstanding about hemp that we have ever seen in the pages of *High Times*. Perhaps Ed Rosenthal may still be the guru of ganja, but he is not yet hep to hemp, though we all share the same goal—to learn from each other and work to end hemp prohibition.

Sincerely,

Jack Herer and Lynn Osburn

Oregonian 10-19-89

'Collective conscience' breeds Dutch tolerance

By DAVID MORRIS

Holland. Every conservative's nightmare come true. Legal prostitution. Coffeehouses that sell marijuana to teen-agers. Free abortions on request. Free needles for heroin addicts. Special rooms for prisoners to conduct liaisons with outside partners, even of the same sex. Euthanasia in hospitals.

To Americans, such policies represent a moral breakdown. They are a prescription for social anarchy: promiscuity, drug addiction, family breakdown, AIDS. To Amsterdam Judge Frits Ruter, such policies are "above all, pragmatic and undogmatic." You cannot solve social problems "by making them taboo," he insists.

The Dutch don't drive their human weaknesses underground. Amsterdam's Utopia coffeehouse, where you can choose among 10 kinds of hashish and grass for about $6 a gram, is five doors from the neighborhood police station. The Royal Symphony Hall backs into a red-light district that houses not only prostitutes in well-lit windows, but also sex shops that would make Hugh Hefner blush.

The minister of justice of Holland's conservative government explains: The aim is to "prevent as much as possible a situation in which more harm is caused by criminal proceedings than by the (activity) itself."

Legalization allows the government much more flexibility than criminalization. Prostitutes must undergo regular health examinations. One result is an astonishingly low rate of AIDS infection: less than 1 percent, compared to 30 percent to 40 percent among America's illegal but probably equally plentiful hooker population. Clean needles for intravenous drug users slows AIDS transmission among a group that now accounts for half the AIDS population in New York. Allowing prisoners sex with loved ones reduces prison tension and curbs aggressive in-prison homosexuality.

As for drugs, allowing the sale of marijuana gives the government much more credibility when it warns the young about the dangers of hard drugs. Indeed, says the Dutch secretary of drug policy, "Cannabis used to be the symbol of the youth culture — it was attractive because it was forbidden. Our aim was to turn it into an unsensational item." It worked. The proportion of Dutch teen-agers using marijuana has dropped substantially. It is a fraction of U.S. use. Crack is virtually non-existent.

David Morris, an author, lecturer and consultant, writes for the St. Paul Pioneer Press Dispatch. He spent a week in the Netherlands this fall.

All Dutch schools teach sex education. A year's worth of birth control pills costs about $10. Yet Dutch girls are no more sexually active than American girls. And 90 percent of those teen-agers who are active use contraceptives. Holland's teen-age pregnancy rate is one-seventh that of America's. American teen-agers have 12 to 14 times more abortions than Dutch teen-agers.

The Dutch treat prostitutes, drug addicts, teen-age pot smokers and the terminally ill with respect. Not surprisingly, respect breeds responsibility, not license. The heroin addict uses a clean needle. The prostitute does not transmit disease. The teen-ager uses birth control. Doctors assist a patient's death only after a long, close relationship with that patient.

Where does this sense of mutual respect and collective responsibility come from? Historian Simon Schama looks to Dutch history in "The Embarrassment of Riches."

In the 1600s, tiny Holland was the most prosperous nation on earth. Riches bred a "collective conscience" that demanded generosity for the needy and tolerance for those with different religions and different habits. Obligations to community, to society came first.

Today the Dutch continue that 300-year tradition. They know the most fertile breeding ground for irresponsible behavior is the slum. Thus they offer the world's most comprehensive social support programs. Medical care is free; child care plentiful. Unemployment insurance is nearly forever.

Amsterdam suffers a housing problem incomprehensible to U.S. urban planners. Sufficient housing exists for those of modest means, but there's not enough for the rich.

Such generosity of spirit and purse has not undermined Dutch prosperity. They live longer than Americans. Their economy is robust, their businesses competitive.

This prosperous country of 14 million has much to teach us, for tolerance has never been an American trait. We have a long history of demanding moral purity of our neighbors and eagerly locking them up if they transgress. We rely on force to solve our social problems, not wisdom.

Why we do so is up to the historians and sociologists to ponder. That we do so seems not to be in question. Today America imprisons a larger proportion of its citizens than any country except South Africa, and President Bush now vows to double the number of federal prisoners.

The Dutch watch in amazement our descent into social anarchy. They cannot understand why a nation would willfully destroy itself to control its citizens' personal behavior.

OPINION

o.c. Register, January 1990

There's no solution to drugs or 'the war'

Legalization would force us to face a serious problem in a realistic way

By William F. Buckley Jr.

The release last month by Judge Robert Sweet of New York of his opinions on drug policy brought on a furious response from most quarters, who roiled at his suggestion that we would be better off under a program of legalization than under the auspices of our present war on drugs.

He did find support here and there; columnist Earl Caldwell, without exactly endorsing Judge Sweet's opinions, found them responsible, serious, and worth considering; Ann Landers and Dear Abby, once again without committing themselves, asked the question, "Is legalization the answer? Lord knows that what we are doing now isn't working."

George Crockett of Detroit became the first congressman to come out for legalization. In doing so, he did not cite the speech of Judge Sweet, but he used most of Sweet's arguments. Columnist Richard Cohen summarized his views by writing: "The cries for legalization may reflect an irrational impatience with the unsuccessful war on drugs. Possibly, though, they reflect some sound thinking — an alternative route that might work and save lives. Not even to consider such an option — given the carnage in the inner city — is not wise. Worse, it may even be what drug czar William Bennett calls legalization proposals: 'morally scandalous.'"

What strikes the eye of one observer of the drug controversy is a point or two not conventionally raised. The *Wall Street Journal*, in an agitated reply to Judge Sweet and others, made the point, interesting in itself, that people should stop comparing drugs such as crack and heroin with cigarettes and alcohol. We must concede what we have no alternative than to concede, namely that tobacco (270,000-320,000 deaths per year) and alcohol (50,000-150,000) shouldn't be compared with the hard stuff for the following reason, namely that when people sit down to light up or to have a drink they do not become psychologically or emotionally deranged, which is a good point and true.

When the average social drinker orders a margarita, he anticipates a light elevation of the spirit. When the crack user smokes a rock, he wants the equivalent of what the man who ordered a margarita would want if instead of ordering one at the bar, he ordered 20 — clearly intending to pass out. In doing so, he desires a kind of escapism that we never associate with the cigarette smoker, the rational functioning of whose mind is unaffected by cigarettes, never mind the biological attrition he is inviting.

The exercise reminds us that it is difficult to compare any experience to any other experience, because all of them are in some way different. Assuming that the only consideration was how many deaths does it cause, then unquestionably the first drug to be outlawed would be tobacco. But the tobacco people would counter by pointing out precisely the differences here outlined, namely that tobacco users don't go about dropping out, and sometimes causing mayhem.

Where some legalizers make a mistake is in suggesting that legalization might constitute a "solution" for the drug problem. That is careless, given that there is no solution to the drug problem. Conservative philosophy, by the way, rejects absolutely the use of the word "solution" except in narrow situations. One can correctly speak of the solution to the smallpox problem, one of the great boons of science. Science will never come around with a packaged solution to the search for escapism.

The person who takes drugs because for a few moments he is made psychologically free of the awful impositions of life in the ghetto, is indulging an impulse which, *mutatis mutandis*, is not unrelated to that of the woman who picks up a volume of poems to relieve her of preoccupation with quotidian concerns. The drives are not unrelated: watching a soap opera on television, reading a thriller, smoking a cigarette, taking a drink, smoking a crack rock have in common the desire to remove oneself from the immediate scene. The differences that engage our attention have to do with the effect of the one form of escapism on the individual, compared to other forms of escapism.

There is no "solution" to the problem in legalization. What legalization advocates seek is a heavy mitigation of the concomitant consequences of the war on drugs: crime, the pre-emption of the energies of the justice system, and the engagement of society in a futile exercise. Legalization advocates are saying not that they have a solution to the drug problem, but that they are better off facing the situation that would eventuate after legalization than what they face today as drug warriors.

HARPER'S INDEX (December, 1989, Excerpted)

* Rank of the Tobacco Institute, among the groups that paid members of Congress the most in honoraria last year: 1

* Percentage of U.S. companies that have a policy against hiring smokers: 6

* Chances that a first-time cigarette smoker will become addicted: 9 in 10

* Chances that a first-time user of cocaine will become addicted: 1 in 6

* Percentage of Americans who say that "lack of opportunity due to poverty" is a main cause of teen-age violence: 50

* Percentage who say that "rock music lyrics that glorify sex and violence" are a main cause of teen-age violence: 52

VOICES FOR LEGALIZATION

Opposite page, clockwise from top left: Jerry Garcia (Paul Miller/Blackstar), Kurt Schmoke (AP/Wide World), George Shultz (A/P Wide World), Lou Reed (courtesy of Warner Bros.), and Milton Friedman (Charles Csavossy/Blackstar).

"In the years to come, the rhetoric of Dope War will replace the rhetoric of Cold War as the justification for foreign military intervention. Instead of sending in the marines, Washington will send in the narcs."
--"Dope Dictators: The Vietnamization of Mexico, Jamaica, Colombia and the Third World," HIGH TIMES, March 1977

"We're in a war we shouldn't be in and can't win. The police are victims of this war just as soldiers were the victims in Vietnam."
--Wesley A. Pomeroy, a lifelong police officer who served as assistant director to the White House's Office of Drug Abuse Policy under President Carter.

"What we ought to do is try to get at the source of this problem, which is poverty and disillusion, and put our resources behind that and turn it around. I suggest it is time to abolish the prohibition--to cease treating indulgence in mind-alteration as a crime. The result would be the elimination of the profit motive, the gangs, the drug dealers. Obviously, the model is the repeal of Prohibition and the end of Al Capone and Dutch Schultz."
--US District Judge Robert W. Sweet, in a speech at the Cosmopolitan Club in New York City, December 12, 1989

Urine tests! Our pioneer ancestors would piss in their graves at the thought of urine tests to decide whether a man is competent to do his job. The measure of a man's competence is performance. In the good old days a man's personal habits were personal and private. Now even a citizen's blood and urine are subject to arbitrary seizure and search.

"What may lurk behind this colossal red herring of the war against drugs? A war neither likely nor designed to succeed. In politics, if something doesn't work, that is the best reason to go on doing it. If something looks like it might work, stay well away. A thing like that could make waves, and the boys at the top, they don't like waves."
--"Just Say No To Drug Hysteria," by William S. Burroughs, from the album, Like a Girl, I Want You To Keep Coming (Giorno Poetry Systems Records)

"A small group of drug criminals now probably launders tax-free sums of over $100 billion a year, more than the GNPs of 150 of the 170 nations of the world."
--The Economist, April 2, 1988

"Forget the war on drugs. It's over. Drugs won. There was no way to win it in the first place... Now poor William Bennett is being asked to play the lead in the latest episode of the situation tragedy known as The War on Drugs. He must know the enterprise is doomed... If Bennett has courage, he will come to one dreadful conclusion: we must end the war by legalizing drugs."
--Pete Hamill, NY Post, March 14, 1989

"It has quickly become received wisdom even in the middlebrow press that the vaunted War on Drugs is a failure, with an admission of futility only a step away. That step would be to call in the entire armed forces, a move the Pentagon has long resisted. Failing full militarization, only one other step remains: rethinking the whole mess in terms of legalization."
--Charles Paul Freund, The New Republic

"What if Bill Bennett should look at the problem hard in the face and conclude that prudent policy calls for licensing the sale of the drugs side-by-side with a massive national effort to warn against their consumption? If one were to remove from the price of drugs the overhead of sneaking it into the United States, killing or bribing all who stand in the way of this operation, and all who stand in the way of merchandising the drugs in the streets, then the price of it would certainly collapse, and there would be no profit in its sale, save the modest profit of paying the licensed dispenser."
--William F. Buckley, in his syndicated column

"In the '60s, legalizing drugs could be fairly regarded as another indulgence by a self-indulgent generation. Today, it can be considered as not only pragmatic but necessary. It at least deserves an airing."
--Thomas Collins, syndicated columnist, from Newsday

"Any serious approach to this problem (as opposed to the present one) demands a recognition of complexity and ambiguity. We have to compromise between social reality and the dream of a drug free society. We may have to acknowledge that the use of drugs and alcohol has benefits as well as dangers. The main obstacle to thinking about any serious alternative to present policies is that no one in government wants to give up the symbolism of the criminal law or the commitment that has been made over the last 70 years, not only in the United States but all over the world, to treating drugs as a criminal problem."
--Lester Grinspoon, MD, Associate Professor of Psychiatry, Harvard Medical School, "The Harmfulness Tax," Drug Policy 1989-1990: A Reformer's Catalogue

"Body counts don't really matter. In the end, we're just fighting a holding action. We're taking a lot of prisoners, but we're not winning the war."
--US Attorney Gene Anderson of Seattle, Washington, quoted in the Reader, November 18, 1988

"It is ridiculous going to jail for marijuana. In Pima County, about 75 percent of people between the ages of 20 and 40 smoke grass. It is just like Al Capone and prohibition; they do it anyway."
--Joe Brewster, unsuccessful candidate for Pima County sheriff, quoted in the Tucson Citizen, April 23, 1988

"It's a joke. Greed and the desire to take drugs are two separate things. If you want to separate the two, the thing you do is make drugs legal. It's the obvious solution. Accept the reality that people do want to change their consciousness, and make an effort to make safer, healthier drugs."

--Jerry Garcia, *Rolling Stone*, November 30th, 1989

"Have we failed to consider the lessons of the Prohibition era? Now is the time to fight on the only terms the drug underground empire respects -- money. Let's take the profit out of drug trafficking."
--Kurt L. Schmoke, mayor of Baltimore, at a meeting of the US Conference of Mayors, April 25, 1988

"This plea comes from the bottom of my heart. Every friend of freedom, and I know you are one, must be revolted as I am by the prospect of turning the United States into an armed camp, by the vision of jails filled with casual drug users and of an army of enforcers empowered to invade the liberty of citizens on slight evidence. A country in which shooting down unidentified planes 'on suspicion' can be seriously considered as a drug war tactic is not the kind of United States that either you or I want to hand on to future generations."

--Milton Friedman, Hoover Institution, Stanford University, "An Open Letter to Bill Bennett," *The Wall Street Journal*, Sept. 7, 1989

"Think what you could do with all the money they spend trying to fight drugs. Legalize it.

"Tax it, make it pure, stop the disease, the killing, the crime. I mean, they can't stop it 'cos the market for it is so gigantic. That's the bottom line. If they took the illegal profit out of it, that'd hurt them.

"Imagine it--big deal, there's a drug store. It'd be cheap too. OK, some drugs, I personally think, you should only be able to get when you're over 50. If you live past 50, you can try Ecstasy or whatever the hell you want. But legalize the shit. Take the taboo and glamour out of it."

--Lou Reed, *New Musical Express* (UK), June 10, 1989

"It seems to me we're not really going to get anywhere until we can take the criminality out of the drug business and the incentives for criminality out of it.... We need at least to consider and examine forms of controlled legalization of drugs."
--Former Secretary of State George P. Shultz

continued on page 58

Fairbanks Daily News-Miner, Fairbanks, Alaska, Tuesday, October 30, 1990

Dangers of asthma drug being hidden, group says

By BRIGID SCHULTE
States News Service

WASHINGTON—A group of lawyers and medical experts today warned that a widely prescribed asthma drug may lead to brain damage and death in certain instances, and charged that drug companies have hidden its dangers.

Experts acknowledged that the drug, theophylline, is vitally important to the 10 million Americans who suffer from chronic asthma and lung disease. But if taken when an asthma sufferer has a high fever or the flu, the drug becomes toxic and can result in seizures and permanent injuries.

In a letter sent last week, the American Trial Lawyers' Association (ATLA) is asking the U.S. Food and Drug Adminstration to ban five over-the-counter asthma drugs, including Primatene Tablets, Bronkotabs, Bronkolixir and Bronkaid Tablets, that contain theophylline.

"Theophylline is one of the top three medicines that are most difficult for physicians to use," said Dr. Howard Zeitz, an allergist at Grant Hospital in Chicago. "Neither of the other two are in over-the-counter-drugs."

Drug manufacturers, on the other hand, say the lawyers are launching a "publicity campaign aimed at alarming asthma patients."

"Properly used, under physician supervision and in accordance with approved labeling, serious theophylline side effects have been very rare," said officials at the New Jersey-based pharmaceutical Schering-Plough Corp. "Our products have been prescribed approximately 60 million times since 1985 alone, and in that time the reported incidence of serious adverse drug events . . . has been only 1.3 per 100,000 prescriptions."

While the drug, which occurs commonly in tea, has been used for nearly 50 years to relieve breathing problems, the trial lawyers charged that the 40 U.S. manufacturers of theophylline have known of its dangers for at least a decade and have failed to adequately warn doctors.

The life of Jennifer Pollock, a 7-year-old from Everett, Wash., will never be the same because of the deadly combination of the drug and high fever, her father told reporters at a press conference here—a combination that her physician was not aware of.

"Theophylline was a big help to Jennifer when she needed it to help her breathing," Jeffry Pollock said. "But it also caused severe brain damage that Jennifer will never be able to fully overcome."

When Jennifer caught the flu as a three-year-old, her doctor gave her an additional dose of theophylline to help her breathe, Pollock said. Soon after, the child suffered convulsions and permanent brain damage. She now functions as if a 6-month-old child.

"I just don't want this to happen to other families," Pollock said when asked about the nationwide theophylline awareness campaign. "It shouldn't have to happen."

Pollock sued and settled with Jennifer's doctor, James Kripcera, who in turn successfully sued the Fisons Corp. for failing to warn him of the drug's dangers.

Dr. Peter Young, senior vice president at the Fisons Corp., a British pharmaceutical company headquartered in Rochester, N.Y., said the company will no longer manufacture theophylline.

"For commercial reasons, we've either stopped or are in the process of discontinuing products with theophylline," he said. "We can't add any other comment to that."

In 1989, more than 6,500 cases of theophylline overdose were reported to poison control centers across the country, according to ATLA. Nearly 100 of those cases resulted in serious injury, and 34 in death. Not all of these cases are in litigation, lawyers said.

Lawyers are asking that drug companies and the FDA make all doctors and patients aware of the potentially harmful side effects of theophylline. While the Physicians Desk Reference mentions that theophylline is difficult to eliminate from the body during high fevers, that information not listed under the "Warning" section, but rather in general information of the make-up of the drug.

"I firmly believe that what ATLA is doing is of vital importance," said Paul Luvera, Pollock's attorney. "Just as a result of our case, we heard from physicians, some of whom were taking the drug themselves or giving it to their children, that they didn't know of the dangers either."

MUSIC

The Weed

One of the more nervous heroes of hot jazz, Gene Krupa, went to California's San Quentin Prison this week to serve a sentence of one to six years. Drummer Krupa had been sentenced on two counts. The first was a felony: employing a minor, one John Pateakos, to transport narcotics. The second and lesser count was a misdemeanor: possession of the drug marijuana, a violation which, if it could be universally detected, would land a great many jazz musicians behind prison bars. It is no secret that some of the finest flights of American syncopation, like some of the finest products of the symbolist poets, owe much of their expressiveness to the use of a drug. But the nature and effects of marijuana, specifically, are a good deal more of a secret than they need be.

To its users, the drug has many names —many of them evasive. Marijuana may be called muggles, mooter, Mary Warner, Mary Jane, Indian hay, loco weed, love weed, bambalacha, mohasky, mu, moocah, grass, tea or blue sage. Cigarets made from it are killers, goof-butts, joy-smokes, giggle-smokes or reefers. The word marijuana is of Mexican origin and means "the weed that intoxicates." It is made from the Indian hemp plant, a spreading green bush resembling sumac. Known to the pharmacopoeia as *Cannabis sativa*, it is a source of important paint ingredients and rope fiber as well as narcotics. It can be grown easily almost anywhere, hence tends to be inexpensive, as drugs go. Its recent prices (10¢ to 50¢ a cigaret) have placed it beneath the dignity of big-time racketeers. But its furtive preparation and sale afford a modest living to thousands.

In most U.S. cities the marijuana salesman peddles his cigarets to known clients in public places. He is known to his clients as a "pusher." His clients are known as "vipers." Etiquette between pushers and vipers is necessarily delicate. When he wants to buy, the viper sidles up to the pusher and inquires "Are ya stickin'?" or "Are ya layin' down the hustle?" If the answer is affirmative, the viper says, "Gimme an ace" (meaning one reefer), "a deuce" (meaning two), or "a deck" (meaning a large number). The viper may then quietly "blast the weed" (smoke). Two or three long puffs usually suffice after a while to produce a light jag. The smoker is then said to be "high" or "floating." When he has smoked a reefer down to a half-inch butt, he carefully conserves it in an empty match box. In this condition it is known, in Mexican, as a *chicharra*, or in English, as a "roach."

Around the Piccolo. Some pushers run establishments known as "tea pads." The tea pad may be anything from a rented room to a suite in a fashionable hotel. Usually it is dimly lighted with colored lamps and recks of incense burned to cover the telltale, bonfire-like odor of burning marijuana. Most tea pads are supplied with a juke box (known in marijuanese as a "piccolo"). Clients who have assembled to "have a pad" may smoke their own reefers. But commonly they blast a goof-butt collectively, passing a single reefer around from mouth to mouth like a pipe of peace. Next morning, enjoying a heavy sensation very much like an alcoholic hangover, they are said to be "down."

The effects of marijuana smoking somewhat resemble those of alcohol. Within half to one hour the viper's eyes redden, his pupils dilate, his tongue gets parched. If he is a novice, he frequently breaks into uncontrollable laughter, or vomits. But an hour or so later he is "high." He

GENE KRUPA, DRUMMING
Curious things happen to time.

has a sensation of floating on air, or falling softly on waves. His ears ring sweetly, his head swims pleasantly, his limbs are languorously heavy, his hunger grows, especially for sweets. Curious things happen to his perceptions of space and time. Objects a mile outside the window may seem within easy reach. A lazy minute may seem like an hour. Curiously, the power of mental concentration appears to increase rather than diminish. Some specialists find that marijuana stimulates their capacity for thought.

The association of marijuana with hot jazz is no accident. The drug's power to slow the sense of time gives an improper the illusion that he has all the time in the world in which to conceive his next phrases. And the drug also serves to heighten the hearing—so that, for instance, chord formations are easier to analyze under marijuana. Jazz-playing vipers may be outnumbered by "lushes" (alcoholics)—who almost never smoke reefers. Today, among all dance musicians (including those of the "sweet" bands), the percentage of marijuana smokers probably does not exceed 20%. But among hot jazz players there are few (except the confirmed lushes) who do not occasionally smoke.

Old Persian Practice. In some form, hemp has been smoked since long before the beginning of the Christian Era. It was familiar to the ancient Hindus and Persians. It is smoked widely by the Arabs. Eminent European vipers have included De Quincey, Baudelaire (who once, under the influence, sketched a self-portrait, with the Colonne Vendôme in hashish perspective—*see cut, p. 54*), Dumas, Gautier. The U.S. vogue, precisely coincident with the vogue for hot jazz, began in New Orleans a generation ago, moved up the Mississippi to Chicago, thereafter spread east and west.

Despite its lurid reputation, marijuana seems no more harmful than alcohol. Though habitual criminals often use it, psychiatrists and police narcotic experts have never been able to prove that it induces criminal tendencies in otherwise normal people. It is less habit-forming than tobacco, alcohol or opium. The most confirmed vipers have no particular craving for the drug. They just enjoy its effects. Like alcohol, of course, it can raise hell with orderly living, release bad as well as good personality traits. But in spite of the legends, no case of physical, mental or moral degeneration has ever been traced exclusively to marijuana.

Because of its non-habit-forming character, doctors have recently been experimenting with the drug as an aid in curing opium addiction. In the world of hot jazz, marijuana's relatively benign effects are attested by long experience. Lushes often die young from cirrhosis of the liver or apoplexy, often spend their final days in delirium tremens. But vipers frequently live on to enjoy old age. In *You Rascal You*, a viper addresses an imaginary lush: "I'll be standing on the corner high when they bring your body by."

---

for April 29, 1944

PSYCHOLOGY
Tests Show Marihuana Does Not Help

▶ MUSICIANS, especially members of dance orchestras, may think marihuana improves their musical ability, but psychological tests with a synthetic marihuana-like chemical show it does not. Dr. C. Knight Aldrich, U. S. Public Health Service, reports. (*Public Health Reports,* March 31.)

The tests were made with 12 healthy white male patients who volunteered for the experiment. All were serving prison sentences for violation of the Marihuana Tax Act and had used the drug for an average of nine and one-half years. Of the 12, two were professional musicians and two had musical ambitions.

The Seashore tests, played on phonograph records, were used "because they seemed to offer the most carefully standardized tests available of musical capability."

Each man was given the test three times at intervals of one week. The first two were given without any drug, the third four and one-half hours after the drug. The dose and time interval produced a "kick" comparable to a satisfying amount of marihuana in most cases.

When asked whether they noticed any differences in their own performances on the tests, eight said they felt sure they had improved with the drug, three felt they remained the same, and one "couldn't say."

Actually, however, nine of the 12 had lower scores on the tests after the drug than on the second trial without it.

"The Seashore test," Dr. Aldrich points out, "measures only sensory musical capacity and leaves out of account such factors as motor-speed and coordination, release of inhibitions and fatigability, which could conceivably influence the playing of present-day music."

CHARLES BAUDELAIRE, SMOKING
Curious things happen to space.
TIME July 19, 1943

PUBLIC HEALTH—RESOURCES
Hemp Will Be Grown, But Bureau Will Police Areas

HEMP growing in the United States, which the U. S. Bureau of Narcotics has tried to stop in order to prevent marijuana addiction, is now apparently going to be allowed and even encouraged as a result of the war.

This is seen from a War Production Board order prohibiting the use of domestically produced hemp seed for any purpose except the growing of hemp fiber or the growing of additional hemp seed. The officially stated reason is to conserve and increase the domestic hemp supply. In the past the bulk of this country's hemp requirements for rope and sacking have come from the Philippines.

The Bureau of Narcotics, however, will police the areas where the hemp is produced, Commissioner H. J. Anslinger states. He believes that through cooperation with federal, state and local authorities, it will be possible to control the hemp growing so that none will be diverted to the making of "reefers" or any other form in which it could contribute to narcotic drug addiction.

SCIENCE NEWS LETTER *for February 7, 1942*

Nancy Reagan enlists John Paul II in campaign against drug addiction

HAPPY MOOD — Nancy Reagan joins Pope John Paul II after flying Saturday to Rome for a special audience in the Vatican.

Associated Press

VATICAN CITY (AP) — First lady Nancy Reagan brought her anti-drug campaign to the Vatican in a 30-minute audience Saturday with Pope John Paul II, who deplored the "tragic and debilitating" effects of drug abuse.

The Vatican and Italian security officials cleared half of St. Peter's Square of pilgrims and tourists to let the Reagan motorcade pass through an arch adjoining the largest church in Christendom.

At the start of the meeting, the 64-year-old pope handed Reagan a three-page speech in English in which he lauded her "participation in the fight against drug abuse and in the rehabiliation of those whose lives have been affected by this social evil."

A Vatican spokesman, Monsignor Giulio Nicolini, said the pontiff did not read the speech in order to be able to devote more time to talking to Reagan.

The undelivered speech, distributed by the Vatican while the audience was under way, called drug abuse "a great social evil" and said "the consequences for the family and for society in general are tragic and debilitating."

It called on world leaders to cooperate "with a view to arresting, and eventually eliminating, this great social evil."

In an exchange of gifts, Reagan gave the pope the book "Scribes and Sources," described as a scholarly work by A.S. Osley, and a rectangular crystal box with the White House and Reagan's signature etched on the top.

Reagan was given a silver and mother-of-pearl rosary by the pontiff.

After the audience, the pope and the first lady walked out of the library hand in hand, and the pope was overheard saying: "God bless you. Thank you very much for your visit."

After the audience, she toured the Sistine and Pauline chapels for 20 minutes. Reagan flew back to Bonn in the afternoon to rejoin President Reagan for a state visit to West Germany.

THE OREGONIAN, WEDNESDAY, APRIL 17, 1985

Court gives CIA power to cloak sources in secrecy

By PHILIP HAGER
LA Times-Washington Post Service

WASHINGTON — The Supreme Court ruled Tuesday that the Central Intelligence Agency has sweeping authority to maintain the secrecy of its far-ranging sources of intelligence data.

The court said that even when disclosure would not affect national security, the CIA may refuse requests under the Freedom of Information Act for the names of scientists, researchers and others who provide intelligence for the books, journals and other documents the agency analyzes.

"Congress intended to give the director of central intelligence broad power to protect the secrecy and integrity of the intelligence process," Chief Justice Warren E. Burger wrote for the court. "The reasons are too obvious to call for enlarged discussion; without such protections the agency would be virtually impotent."

The justices overturned a federal appeals court ruling that said the CIA could withhold the identity of only those sources who provided information that could not be obtained without guaranteeing confidentiality. They said the forced disclosure of any intelligence source could have a "devastating impact" on the agency.

Two justices, while agreeing in a concurring opinion that the appellate ruling had been too restrictive, argued that the Supreme Court had gone too far.

Justice Thurgood Marshall, joined by Justice William J. Brennan Jr., said the justices' broad grant of authority to the CIA will "mangle,

seriously," congressional efforts to balance the public's interest in information with the government's need for secrecy.

The decision also was denounced by a lawyer representing a group that had sought the names of private researchers and institutions involved in a controversial CIA drug experiment begun in the 1950s.

"This comes close to being a complete exemption of the CIA from the Freedom of Information Act," said Paul Alan Levy of the Public Citizen Litigation Group of Washington. "It is a severe setback for the public's right to learn about abuses by national security agencies."

Levy said the ruling would enable the CIA and, perhaps, other intelligence-gathering agencies not only to refuse to reveal sources of information but also to "hide _ne details of almost any program that it would prefer the public not know about — so long as it claims disclosure of the information might lead to disclosure of the persons who provided it."

The ruling came in a case (CIA vs. Sims, 83-1075) involving an attempt by the Ralph Nader Public Citizen Health Research Group to obtain the names of 185 college professors and other researchers and 80 institutions that participated in CIA project involving mind-altering drugs. The government said the program was instituted to counteract Soviet and Chinese advances in brainwashing and interrogation techniques.

In another action Tuesday, the justices on an 8-0 vote struck down a post-Reconstruction provision of the Alabama Constitution that denied the right to vote to persons convicted of

misdemeanors involving "moral turpitude" — a term the state defined as an act "immoral in itself."

The court, in an opinion by Justice William H. Rehnquist, concluded that the 84-year-old law had been enacted with the aim of preventing blacks from voting — and that its impact was being felt even today.

Rehnquist cited testimony in the case indicating that in some Alabama counties blacks were nearly twice as likely as whites to be barred from voting on the grounds they had committed such misdemeanors.

While many state constitutions deny convicted felons the right to vote, few still bar persons convicted of misdemeanors — minor crimes ordinarily punishable by fines or jail terms of less than a year.

DOONESBURY By Garry Trudeau

— 165 —

U.S. Smoking Toll Put at $52 Billion

■ Health: Illness and productivity losses average about $1 billion per state annually, the government reports. The California cost is $5.8 billion.

By MARLENE CIMONS
TIMES STAFF WRITER

WASHINGTON—Health care expenses and productivity losses associated with smoking-related disease cost the nation more than $52 billion every year, according to a government report released Tuesday.

The Department of Health and Human Services, in a national status report to Congress, estimated that illnesses caused by smoking impose an average economic burden of $1 billion per state, although some states run much higher tabs than others.

California, the most populous state, has the highest estimated smoking cost, $5.8 billion, the report said. Alaska was lowest, with $82 million annually. Following California, in order, were New York, Texas, Pennsylvania, Illinois, Ohio and Michigan.

The annual expenses of smoking-related disease average $221 for every man, woman and child in the nation, ranging from a low of $56 a person in Utah to $284 in Rhode Island, the report said.

Meanwhile, congressional sponsors of a law banning smoking on virtually all domestic airline flights vowed Tuesday to fight for no-smoking rules on other forms of transportation and to attack U.S. trade policies that encourage tobacco exports.

Sen. Frank R. Lautenberg (D-N.J.) and Rep. Richard J. Durbin (D-Ill.) said that they would next press their campaign to apply to Amtrak train service and other transportation.

The airline smoking ban, which begins Sunday, will apply to domestic flights of six hours or less. Longer flights, charter flights and overseas flights are exempt.

The law expands and extends a temporary smoking ban on short domestic flights that was adopted in 1987.

The HHS report said that expenses related to smoking are borne indirectly by all Americans in the form of higher private and public insurance premiums and the increased burden on publicly supported health care facilities and personnel.

"Each and every American, including those who don't even smoke, is paying a hidden tax . . . for the consequences of smoking," HHS Secretary Louis W. Sullivan said in testimony before a Senate committee considering anti-smoking legislation.

"My view," Sullivan said, "is straightforward and simple: no smoking."

The report was immediately assailed by the Tobacco Institute, which said that "to assume that smokers impose a cost on society is a misapplication of a valid economic theory."

Brennan Dawson, a spokeswoman for the industry group, said that "smokers pay their own [insurance] premiums, so they cover their own costs. And, just because they file a claim, it doesn't mean it's a smoking claim."

Further, she said, "if people are less productive, that's not a cost to society—they bear the burden through lower pay, less frequent job promotions or getting fired."

The report said that smoking causes more premature deaths than cocaine, heroin, alcohol, fire, automobile accidents, homicide and suicide combined.

Sullivan said that smoking kills nearly 400,000 Americans each year and is responsible for more than one of every six deaths in the United States. In addition, he said, smoking is becoming increasingly concentrated among low-income, less-educated Americans.

"I am especially concerned that we make more progress in reaching young people, women, minorities and blue-collar workers with accurate and compelling information about smoking and its devastating impact on their health," he said in a statement.

Dr. Ronald M. Davis, director of the HHS Office on Smoking and Health, said that deaths caused by smoking have increased during the last 20 years, despite a dramatic decline in the number of smokers. In 1965, 40% of all U.S. adults were cigarette smokers, compared to 29% in 1987, he said.

Nevertheless, "it takes a good 20 to 25 years after the smoking rates go down before we begin to see a decrease in smoking-related deaths and costs," he said in an interview.

Sullivan recently criticized plans by R.J. Reynolds Tobacco Co. to test-market in Philadelphia a new cigarette, called Uptown, targeted at black smokers. The firm quickly announced that it had canceled the marketing campaign.

Sullivan told members of the Senate Labor and Human Resources Committee that he was just as upset by the company's plan to introduce another new cigarette, called Dakota, reportedly aimed at young blue-collar women.

"I'm outraged," he said when questioned about Dakota. "No one believes the tobacco companies when they say they are not targeting young people."

In 1985, the average number of deaths attributed to smoking was 6,097 per state, ranging from 271 in Alaska to 28,533 in California.

ANNUAL REPORT 1937

In all business units, large and small, throughout all industry, plans for replacement and expansion will be deferred or abandoned, expenditures for construction and research will be avoided or less freely undertaken, and even the ordinary rate of daily manufacture and sales will be curtailed, if the prospect is not sufficiently clear and stable to give reasonable assurance that the opportunity will continue for the efficient enterpriser to earn a profit upon the capital that he must risk. The smaller the business unit, the more pronounced this tendency must be. Today, industry's forward pathway is blanketed with a fog of uncertainties more retarding to progress than any burden industry must carry.

With respect to taxation, of which the direct burden upon your company in 1937 was approximately $18,900,000, the future is clouded with uncertainties, not only as to the amount and form of future imposts but also as to the extent to which the revenue-raising power of government may be converted into an instrument for forcing acceptance of sudden new ideas of industrial and social reorganization. The funds for the development of new industries or for the expansion of established lines must be provided out of savings—either a prudently withheld part of the

25

LA Times Feb. 20, 1990

Paroled Felons Returning in Large Numbers

■ Corrections: Prison crowding and the release of inmates have doubled the number of convicted criminals coming back to L.A.

By RALPH FRAMMOLINO
TIMES STAFF WRITER

SACRAMENTO—Led by an unprecedented return of convicted drug dealers, the number of felons paroled to Los Angeles County has increased more than 100% in the last five years, according to statistics released last week by the state Department of Corrections.

According to civil libertarians and some parole officials, the rising tide of parolees in the county, as well as elsewhere in California, may prove ominous news for law-and-order advocates like Gov. George Deukmejian, who found strong public support in pushing mandatory prison sentences and appointing hard-line judges.

As convicts sent off in record numbers to overcrowded state prisons over the last decade return home, observers say, experience is showing that more than half of the parolees will be incarcerated again for using drugs or committing other crimes.

"The result of the Deukmejian get-tough-on-crime approach is now coming home to roost. It's now coming back to haunt us," said John Hagar, staff attorney for the American Civil Liberties Union in Los Angeles.

"Prosecutors told the public that if we put people away for longer sentences in our clean, modern, safe prisons that you—the public—will be safe," said Hagar, who has represented inmates in lawsuits against the state. "That wasn't true. To put people away for longer periods of time in overcrowded institutions . . . made those people

Please see FELONS, B9

By controlling all three axes of synthetics production—oil, coal, processed wood pulp (i.e. a preponderance of the intermediate and finished products of all three)—GM/Du Pont in effect *nullified* its nearest competitor, Ford. So what if old man Ford kept fields of hemp as part of his scheme to build an alternative automobile, independent of the oil industry. The Duponts were able to use their control of the *entire sphere of the auto industry* to keep out incompatible technologies. When Morgan and the Rockefellers blocked them from taking over U.S. Steel in 1926, they simply started substituting more and more plastics in their GM models. And when used in their car's fuel line—say the carburetor—these plastics *melt* if you try to run on a fuel mix containing methanol!

Chapter 3
PIERRE'S NOBLE EXPERIMENT

The only thing the family couldn't get its *mitts on* was Prohibition. In its old age, populism—which started out as an anti-capitalist movement of little farmers against the Railroads and the Banks—turned cranky, "progressive," and concerned with "reforming morals," and bequeathed upon us Prohibition, William Jennings Bryan prosecuting the Scopes Monkey Trial, and racist media fads like the resurgent Ku Klux Klan and Reefer Madness.

The Duponts disdained the KKK, a bunch of hillbilly Protestant Drys crazed by a movie, running around in bedsheets. The Duponts were upper-crustic Wets. For a little union or red-bashing, they preferred the more respectable American Legion, organized by Big Business after World War I to beat up Communists and lynch the Wobblies.**

Their own wine cellars behind the high walls of family country manors were never raided by Prohibition agents. But to Catholics like the Duponts, Prohibition must have smacked of sacrelijion...as French Aristocrats, the whole affair was an imposition by the Protestant Yahoos of the West.

Pierre Dupont, Chairman of Du Pont, was a public leader of the wets. His pet idea: replace his income taxes with a heavy federal liquor tax. He sincerely argued

---

Meanwhile, "The House of Butterflies" continued its output of other deadly gases, seldom releasing its casualty reports. As one former Du Pont physician once remarked, "but why make all this fuss about extra lead? The Du Pons make other poisons in there and in even *greater* quantity which kill a man like that(," (he snapped his fingers,) "and those plants are still going full blast." (pps. 245-250)

Du Pont *never closed* any operation down if they could help it, because their wealth was all in equipment and plant—*investments the minute idled*—and equipment mean—*troubles*—they would be stuck with a quickly expanding *pool* of toxic chemical feed-stuffs 'that would only become toxic pollution unless they could turn it into something saleable. (Company policy since 1802 has been to turn potential pollutants into profitable products—or dump. But *never* neutralize toxics or clean up pollution at a loss.)

- With its conquest of chemicals—Du Pont made an interesting discovery. Horizontal trusts were illegal under Sherman Anti-Trust. Vertical trusts less so. (Du Pont ownership of GM was the classic vertical trust, with the monopoly progressively buying up and insuring its semi-trolling *all* chemicals or *ill* auto production.)

By adding control of the petrol *tars (we-tetra-lead) to coal tars (the German chemical patents), and their original axis of production, nitrated cellulose (*or graph 1), altogether new and higher development of capitalism: the Spherical Trust, control of the rapidly expanding sphere of synthetics via these 3 key axes of production. And with it the preponderant direction of 20 Century technology. The Spherical Trust enabled Du Pont to subjugate the *internal markets* of the Developed West to a degree of regimentation comparable to the systematic hyper-exploitation they had already imposed on labor.

It took the U.S. Justice Dept. 40 more years to force the divestiture of General Motors by Du Pont, Inc. [to various Dupont family members]; and the law has never *settled* the *entire inter-related sphere of industrial processes and output Du Pont possess in order to maintain the market monopoly of each particular product Du Pont possess or produce.*

For example, from 1922 to the present-day, more than half the American cars on the road have been built by

---

PART V
MARIJUANA vs. DRUG FASCISM

Foreword

The people behind pothibition may be the Dukes of Delaware, the Prince Pretenders of Louisiana, but they cannot rest until one of their number takes the seat of President, and becomes King. Unfortunately, these are dismal times for Royalists. As Victor Emmanual discovered in Italy, sometimes the only people who will work with you are the *fascisti*.

Maintaining the fascist house that Anslinger built has always required its proprietors to find collaborators. But the link running through the War on Drugs between America's Royalists and out-right neo-Nazis goes a lot deeper than the Dupont scion who was committed to keep him from handing everything over to Lyndon La Rouche.

The fact is that the most "reputable" figures of the War on Drugs—men like Drs. Robert S. Dupont, Carlton Turner, Gabriel Nahas—never talk about their 40-year association with neo-Nazi cult-leader Lyndon La Rouche. Precisely because they share his pro-nuke, anti-jazz obsessions and more, they are particularly concerned lest his current legal problems compromise certain mutual, extremely long-range plans...

Today, in the sunset of the Reagan years, the explosion of crack in the midst of a total disappearance of marijuana has created a terrible crisis on the streets of America which, unbeknownst to the general public, is actually the work of a small group of extremist former OSS/CIA men and "drug experts", who did it on purpose.

Chapter 1
THE SPIDER IN THE WEB

The Lyndon LaRouche clique successfully infiltrated U.S. drug enforcement at the highest levels on behalf of Pothibition after of the 1978 firing of marijuana decrim advocate Dr. Peter Bourne as Carter's chief drug adviser.

Utilizing sophisticated expertise on the likely social impact of changing America's illicit drug-of-choice.

DuPont Company and the
NUCLEAR WEAPONS INDUSTRIAL COMPLEX

BENDIX — Kansas City, Missouri

GENERAL ELECTRIC — Pinellas, Florida

KIRKLAND AIR FORCE BASE (Factories) — Albuquerque, New Mexico

SANDIA CORPORATION (WESTERN) (ELECTRIC) — chemical parts & missile warheads

LOS ALAMOS SCIENTIFIC LABORATORY — Los Alamos, New Mexico

DU PONT + Nuclear Regulatory Commission — SAVANNAH RIVER PLANT — WEAPONS GRADE PLUTONIUM — nuclear components and materials

NUCLEAR WEAPONS ASSEMBLY — Pantex, Texas — MASON & HANGER— SILAS MASON CO., INC.

MONSANTO — Miamisberg, Ohio

ROCKWELL INTERNATIONAL — Rocky Flats, Colorado

UNION CARBIDE — Oak Ridge, Tennessee

LIVERMORE LABORATORIES — Livermore, California

PENTAGON — Department of Defense — Washington, D.C.

WHITE HOUSE — WASHINGTON, D.C.

(connecting labels: electrical/mechanical weapons components; electrical components; components; nuclear components; nuclear materials; nuclear materials and components; design; chemical parts & missile warheads)

MORE DANA BEAL PIECES

Chapter 2
BEHIND THE WALDHEIM COVER-UP

The controversy over charges of nepotism at the U.N. involving Waldheim—that he corruptly advanced his daughter's career as a U.N. bureaucrat once in office—have received no play in the U.S. press compared to Europe, where the Swiss paper *Weltwoche* ran a series of articles ventilating the details.

Even less attention has been focused on the implication that LaRouche, Nahas and others derived the political leverage from this ongoing coverup of Waldheim's war crimes necessary to entrench Dr. Nahas in the UN narcotic control bureaucracy for a whole decade—long enough to reverse worldwide momentum for liberalization on cannabis.

The early '70s were a bad time for marijuana prohibition. As has been noted, resistence to the Anslinger/La Rouche line was so intense in Academia and the federal bureaucracy, that Columbia University in 1975 specifically staged a press conference to dissociate itself from Nahas' U.N. studies; even though Nahas remained a tenured Columbia Professor.

But on the U.N. level, Nahas was operating unchallenged, letting out grants to chosen colleagues whose "research" gave indications of finally proving lung, brain, and reproductive organ damage from marijuana . . . the famous Monkey experiment, the pictures of spermatozoa supposedly pitted by exposure to hash oil . . . After 5 years he was ready to showcase these "new studies," proving conclusively that marijuana was the worst drug threat of all, at a symposium in May of '78, at his alma mater in Rheims, France.

Did Waldheim Cover-up Secure Nahas' U.N. Position?

Then in July of 1978, Dr. Peter Bourne, Carter's White House drug czar whose goal was to decriminalize marijuana and "make cocaine expensive and hard to get," was busted for writing phony quaalude scripts, as result of a set-up involving a Virginia drug control agent who "just happened" to be in the pharmacy where the prescription was being filled. Then Bourne was exposed as having used cocaine at a NORML party. In a twinkling, anti-decrim hardliner and DEA head Peter Bens- Hitler, the Allies then classified all documents not part of the bare bones public record.

For one of these fighters, Robert Gungk, who had worked in another OSS section, planning post-War de-Nazification, this turn of events was especially frustrating. For him de-Nazification was personal, and he would become Dr. Behr's main source for much of this. Gungk had lost his father, the chief Rabbi of Prague, because the old man refused to leave when the Nazis occupied Bohemia. He knew, among just a few in post-War Austria, the truth about Kurt Waldheim's past. But U.S. Intelligence had classified all the documents which would impeach Waldheim's version of events for 30 or 40 years.

The year was 1946.

Meanwhile, Lyndon LaRouche and a young Frenchman named Gabriel Nahas were also working for the OSS, in other departments—LaRouche at a desk in Washington, Nahas in Burma in 1943, and subsequently in the Southern European theatre. They didn't meet each other until after the war, however, in Washington, D.C. In 1948 they began a collaboration which deepened as they both moved on to Columbia University in the '50's—LaRouche to spy on the Socialist Workers Party and ultimately form his own neo-fascist version of SDS, Nahas to make his name by planting hysterical scare stories about marijuana in the press at a time when the general weight of scientific opinion was moving in the other direction.

It was not until the early '60's, [under a pot-head President, Kennedy], that Nahas and LaRouche happened to meet Waldheim through the OSS old boys' network . . . old boys ready to work together on new projects. In his autobiography, Waldheim records his excitement at being the new Ambassador from a country which had just been re-united after being partially occupied by the Russians, especially at meeting "such great scientists as Gabriel Nahas and Edward Teller."

Ever the opportunist, Waldheim was eager to implement the agenda of the cabal around LaRouche when opportunity later knocked, with those World War II records conveniently shelved so that an ex-Nazi could become UN Secretary General in 1970. [The few who wanted to expose the truth, like Robert Gungk, stood by helplessly, unable to substantiate any charges until relevant documents were de-classified, starting in the late

Waldheim perpetuate his coverup. But by that time the public relations war, as well as 1980 election, had been won by recrim forces. Without some one of Bourne's stature, committed by his own policies to stepping forward and denouncing Nahas' pseudo-science immediately, Carter's last two years in office saw an anti-marijuana blitz sweep the country, abetted by cocaine incidents involving Carter staffers, conveniently turned up by Bensinger's DEA. By November of 1980, whatever credibility decrim and Carter once possessed had been leached away.

Chapter 3
THE TRUTH ABOUT NAHAS, LAROUCHE & WALDHEIM

With Reagan's takeover, Bensinger and Dupont, who left federal government to form a company making urinalysis tests, were replaced as drug policy heavies by Carlton Turner and Ed Meese. But Lyndon LaRouche embarked on the most respectable period of his career, with his candidates running unchallenged as neo-conservative Democrats right through the early '80's.

According to researcher Dennis King, LaRouche early on gained unique access to the Reagan White House, providing weekly briefings on supposed terrorist plots against Administration figures. Although White House interest flagged after a year or two, as the spurious nature of these false alarms became apparent, LaRouche's policy access through the DEA has continued unimpeded to this day. In 1983, LaRouche was officially cleared to meet with Reagan in the White House by the FBI, despite evidence that he might be in violation of the foreign agents' registration act for accepting millions of dollars from shadowy Latin American sources. The Attorney General declined to send the case to a Grand Jury.

But by '83, the Administration had already implemented the current model marijuana eradication program, committing 80 per cent of its enforcement budget to wiping out domestic growing as well as the flow from Columbia and Mexico. Critics soon were pointing out that this policy was encouraging the Columbians to shift, en masse, to smuggling cocaine. A cocaine glut was inevitable.

The view of many feds involved was that with the success of a model marijuana program, they would be able to go back to the taxpayers and get appropriations

---

The Du Ponts built three rayon plants in this decade. All were in the South: near Richmond, Virginia: at the Old Hickory plant site in Tennessee; and at Waynesboro, Virginia: the site of eight production units worth 46 million and employing 6,400 workers, all non-union. From the Richmond (actually, Ampthill, Virginia) site, the Du Pont Engineering Company built a special concrete roadway to the Richmond-Petersburg Turnpike to facilitate the marketing of manufactured rayon. By 1927, rayon workers in the South were producing one-third of Du Pont's total income. Du Pont's 3.3 million in research was soon returning over 5 million in profits every year.[!] (pp. 229-30)

Chapter 2
THE BIRTH OF THE SPHERICAL TRUST

Inasmuch as they virtually controlled the Republican Party, having moved from the smoke-filled back rooms to political respectibility with the election of Warren G. Harding, the Duponts indeed were soon able to force through massive tariffs on foreign sylhetics. The New Era was staunchly pro-Big Business, and the family concentrated on polishing up its act, with newspaper campaigns to supplant the greedy, monopolistic, warmongering union-busters in people's minds with paens to the top Duponts as "20th Century Heros" of road-building and education. It was an era of Reaganomics, with their banker, Mellon, who happened to be Treasury Secretary, fueling a speculative boom with supply-side tax breaks for the rich . . .

With their new grasp of the entire emerging synthetics industry, Du Pont didn't have to own an industry outright to acheive control and profits. Every car in the country needed an additive called tetra-ethyl lead, acquired by Du Pont in 1922, to keep it from knocking. Soon oil companies were adding this vital Dupont product to virtually all their gasoline, just to compete.

"Deepwater's Silent Terror"

On the southern edge of New Jersey, situated along the banks of the Delaware, was one of the strangest cities in the United States. Although nightly it cast a vast 6-square mile panorama of blinking lights, this city had no mayor, no legal government at all. Although it was one of the country's busiest ports, it was not listed on the nautical maps. Press releases were issued in its name, yet it had no post office.

This was Deepwater, a Du Pont "dyes" plant that had, not dyes, but poison gas as its main product. For some of its workers, however, between 1923 and 1925 its main product was death.

Deepwater was the result of a collaboration between Du Pont and General Motors, or, to be more precise, Irenee du Pont, president of Du Pont, and Pierre du Pont, president of General Motors and chairman of both companies. In 1922 General Motors researchers discovered that tetraethyl lead, when added to gasoline, could supposedly make one gallon do the work of two. But before G.M. even filed its patent application, Pierre

BLOW UP OR GET OUT YOUR MAGNIFYING GLASS...

informed Irenee of the discovery. By October 6 the brothers had signed an exclusive contract handing over the manufacture of its no-knock compounds to Du Pont, which was already producing the appropriate gases. Deepwater, publicly billed as a dye works, had become a complex of poison gas plants, producing phosgene and chlorine gases and the deadly benzol series. Already, strange rumors had begun to circulate in the area of "the House of Butterfies," the five-story brick building where workmen drew pictures of winged insects on the walls and used to snatch at the empty air. On September 2, 1923, these rumours were capped by terror. Frank Durr, a 37-year-old man who had worked for Du Pont since he had been a lad of 12, suddenly died at his home in nearby Penns Grove, New Jersey. Listed by Du Pont as a "dyeworker," he, like many of his co-workers, had been recently plagued by frightful nightmares, and he died in a straight jacket like a madman.

Yet there was silence, the kind of silence known only in a company town. Durr's wife was given a small $17.00 a week pension for only four years and Deepwater continued its deadly production without interruption, constantly striving to keep up with the new demands of Standard Oil's Bayway plant to the north.

Standard Oil joined Pierre's General Motors to form the Ethyl Gasoline Corporation in 1924. A fifty-fifty alliance, Ethyl Gasoline marketed the new "no knock" power fuel treated with tetraethyl lead supplied by Du Pont. This arrangement created a boom in Du Pont's tetraethyl lead production. Just as Pierre was anticipating profits from the new firm, he was hit in October by screaming headlines. Five workers in Standard Oil's Bayway plant had suddenly gone violently insane, dying in raving delirium. Their deaths were attributed to fumes from Du Pont's tetraethyl lead, which the newspapers promptly condemned as "looney gas."

Efforts were quickly made to point out that only the year before the Bureau of Mines had given tetraethyl a clean bill of health. Then, to Pierre's embarrassment, it was revealed that General Motors had financed the Bureau's investigations. Furthermore, the deaths by poisoning of two workers at G.M.'s Canton, Ohio, plant were also exposed.

The country was in a furor. New York City health authorities forbade all ethyl gasoline sales, and cities across the country followed suit. Yet the spotlight only fell on Bayway and the Standard Oil/G.M. alliance. Deepwater, although the subject of many queries, escaped exposure. But when the discoverer of tetraethyl lead, Thomas Midgely, commented that "The Du Ponts have been having trouble too," Irenee decided a statement was in order. "Tetraethyl lead is poisonous," he conceded, "and its manufacture involves risk, but no more so than many chemicals manufactured and used in enormously greater amounts. The Du Pont Company, during the experimental period, experienced much trouble with men becoming poisoned, even to the extent of fatalities. During the past year of production, when more than 100 men have been employed continuously, the difficulty has deminished steadily. In the past several months, under full production, only slight difficulties have been encountered."

Irenee's "slight difficulties" assertion came just one week after the third death at Deepwater in three months: Joseph Cianci, a 24 year-old "dyeworker" and operator, had died on July 30, 1924; Frank Hanley, a 28 year old "dyeworker," had died on August 12; and Simm Jones, a 47 year old janitor, died on October 20. All died with the same "looney gas" symptoms; all died in Salem Memorial Hospital, which was [illegible] a 20 minute ambulance run from Deepwater.

Yet word of the deaths were not publicized until the following year. Wilmington's three daily newspapers, all owned by Pierre and Irenee's Christianas Security, failed to report the deaths. Salem was also silent. The editor of its major new[illegible] was also the president of Salem's hospital, which, by be[illegible] a public tax-free institution, owed its electric laundry system and a good part of its revenue to the Du Ponts. The Du Ponts made donations annually and often paid for the treatment of patients from budget; the budget, in turn, allegedly recieved as much as 50 percent of its tax revenue from the Du Ponts. No one in Salem, therefore, questioned why a DuPont executive from Deepwater was also on Salem Memorial Board of Managers. Nor did anyone question why no coroner's [illegible] test was ever held about Deepwater's strange deaths. Dr. E. C. Lyon, Salem's county physician, between praises of the Du Ponts' care for their men explained why to a national magazine writer: "No, it was not an accident—It was an occupational disease [illegible] there is no occasion to call in the coroner."

Another such case of "occupational disease" was John Demesse. Demesse, a plumber, died with "looney gas" symptoms at Delaware Hospital in Wilmington after doing some work in the Deepwater plants. The hospital listed the death as typhoid. Mrs. Mary Casey, a cousin, who spoke with the attending doctor, recalled that "He said that there were typhoid germs in the body, but that John's poisoning didn't help him any." Efforts by *Nation's* investigating reporter to reach the physician, Dr. Lawrence J. Rigney, were futile. Curiously enough, it was not he, but a member of the hospital staff, Dr.

YEARBOOK

OF THE

UNITED STATES DEPARTMENT OF AGRICULTURE

—

1913

WASHINGTON
GOVERNMENT PRINTING OFFICE
1914

INTRODUCTION OF CHINESE HEMP INTO AMERICA.

In 1857 the first Chinese hemp seed was imported. It met with such favor that some of this seed is said to have brought $10 per quart.[1] Since that time the common hemp of European origin has given place in this country to the larger and better types from China.

GEOGRAPHICAL DISTRIBUTION.

The original home of the hemp plant was in Asia, and the evidence points to central Asia, or the region between the Himalayas and Siberia. Historical evidence must be accepted rather than the collection of wild specimens, for hemp readily becomes naturalized, and it is now found growing without cultivation in all parts of the world where it has been introduced. Hemp is abundant as a wild plant in many localities in western Missouri, Iowa, and in southern Minnesota, and it is often found as a roadside weed throughout the Middle West. De Candolle[2] writes of its origin as follows:

> The species has been found wild, beyond a doubt, south of the Caspian Sea (De Bunge); in Siberia, near the Irtysch; and in the Desert of Kirghis, beyond Lake Baikal, in Dahuria (Government of Irkutsk). It is found throughout central and southern Russia and south of the Caucasus, but its wild nature here is less certain. I doubt whether it is indigenous in Persia, for the Greeks and Hebrews would have known of it earlier.

Hemp is now cultivated for the production of fiber in China, Manchuria, Japan, northern India, Turkey, Russia, Austria-Hungary, Italy, France, Belgium, Germany, Sweden, Chile, and in the United States. It is grown for the production of the drugs bhang, ganja, kif, marihuana, hashoosh, etc., in the warm, arid, or semiarid climates of India, Persia, Turkey, Algeria, central and southern Africa, and in Mexico, and for the production of seed for oil in China and Manchuria.

In the United States hemp is now cultivated in the bluegrass region of Kentucky within a radius of 50 miles of Lexington; in the region of Waupun, Wis.; in northern Indiana; near Lima, Ohio; and at Lerdo and Rio Vista, Cal. There are numerous small experimental plats in other places.

The principal countries producing hemp fiber for export are Russia, Italy, Hungary, and Roumania. China and

[1] Moore, Brent. The Hemp Industry in Kentucky, pp. 60–61, 1905.
[2] De Candolle, Alphonse. Origin of Cultivated Plants, p. 148, 1885.

Japan produce hemp fiber of excellent quality; but it is nearly all used for home consumption. Hemp is not cultivated for fiber in the Tropics or in any of the warm countries.

The historical distribution of hemp, as nearly as may be traced from the records, and the areas where hemp is now cultivated are indicated in the accompanying map, figure 6.

VARIETIES.

Hemp, cultivated for three different products—fiber from the bast, oil from the seeds, and resinous drugs from the flowers and leaves—has developed into three rather distinct types or groups of forms. The extreme, or more typical, forms of each group have been described as different species, but the presence of intergrading forms and the fact that the types do not remain distinct when cultivated under new conditions make it impossible to regard them as valid species.

There are few recognized varieties in either group. Less than 20 varieties of fiber-producing hemp are known, although hemp has been cultivated for more than 40 centuries, or much longer than either cotton or corn, both of which now have hundreds of named varieties.

CHINA.

The original home of the hemp plant was in China, and more varieties are found there than elsewhere. It is cultivated for fiber in nearly all parts of the Chinese Republic, except in the extreme south, and over a wide range of differences in soil and climate with little interchange of seed, thus favoring the development and perpetuation of varietal differences.

The variety called "ta-ma" (great hemp) is cultivated chiefly in the provinces of Chekiang, Kiangsu, and Fukien, south of the Yangtze. In the rich lowland soils, often in rotation with rice, but not irrigated, and with a warmer and longer growing season than in Kentucky, this hemp attains a height of 10 to 15 feet. The seed is dark colored, usually well mottled, small, weighing about 1.2 grams per hundred. The internodes of the main stem are 6 to 10 inches long; the branches long and slender, usually drooping at the ends the leaves large; and the pistillate flowers in small clusters

---

The American Midland Naturalist

Published Quarterly by The University of Notre Dame, Notre Dame, Indiana

Vol. 93   JANUARY, 1975   No. 1

An Ecological Study of Naturalized Hemp (Cannabis sativa L.) in East-Central Illinois

ALAN HANEY and BENJAMIN B. KUTSCHEID
Department of Botany, University of Illinois, Urbana 61801

ABSTRACT: Naturalized populations of hemp (*Cannabis sativa* L.) on a range of sites in E-central Illinois were intensively studied. Fifty-one independent (site) and 26 dependent (plant) parameters were quantified from 101 randomly selected stands. All site variables that could be quantified were examined statistically. These included soil physical and chemical properties, competition, physical site characteristics and stand histories. Correlations between dependent parameters and linear relationships between dependent and independent parameters were examined prior to multiple correlation analysis of each dependent variable. Extreme variation was found in most dependent variables. In only a few instances could a significant portion of the variance in a dependent variable be partitioned by multiple regression. Regression did permit an evaluation of the relative importance of each specific independent variable to any given dependent variable and to the overall ecology of hemp. Those parameters were particularly important that influenced seed production in this annual plant whose seeds do not long retain viability in the soil. Important parameters that influenced seed production were interspecific competition, especially from grasses, exposure to sunlight, soil disturbance the previous year, soil aeration and available phosphorus and potassium. Viable seed production ranged from 0 to 34,433 per sq m, with a mean of 4555. Two important agents effected some degree of biological control. *Alternaria alternata* (Fr.) Keissler, a common fungal pathogen of many plants, destroyed an average of 20.5% of developing seeds, while larvae of *Grapholitha tristrigana* Clemens (Lepidoptera: Tortricidae) destroyed 7.1%. Although a few stands had no damage by the insect, every stand suffered attack from the fungus which destroyed up to 45.5% of seeds in extreme cases.

INTRODUCTION

Cannabis, generally considered a monotypic genus, is one of the most widely distributed plants. Probably originating in Asia, numerous ecotypes and cultivars now are found throughout most of the temperate and tropic regions of the world. Use of hemp for food, fiber and drug, which to a great extent led to its widespread distribution, is well documented with evidence suggesting that this is one of the oldest cultivated plants. Literature on origin, nomenclature and uses of *Cannabis* was summarized most recently by Schultes (1970).

Hemp may have been introduced into United States as early as 1629 (Boyce, 1900). In North America, the plant grows from Quebec to British Columbia in Canada and S throughout the United States and Mexico. Based on botanical collections, a study by Haney and Bazzaz (1970) found naturalized hemp to be rare in United States south of 37° N. latitude. Although widely cultivated, hemp apparently has

---

not become naturalized in Mexico, an observation that seems to apply to most of the tropical and subtropical areas where it is grown, although Arnold (1968) reported that hemp is escaped in Hawaii.

Commercial fiber production from hemp was established in Virginia soon after the original introduction in New England, and in Kentucky by 1775. From Kentucky seed sources, hemp plantations were established in Missouri about 1835, in Illinois in 1875, in Nebraska in 1887 and in California by 1912 (Dewey, 1913). Doubtlessly, settlers carried seeds with them prior to these dates. Crop improvement, through selection of superior plants, was conducted over many decades to increase hemp fiber yield and quality. Eventually, introduction, both accidental and intentional, occurred in every state, especially during the early part of World War II. Although abuse of the plant for drugs, paucity of trained labor for fiber production, and development of competitive fibers led to the discontinuation of hemp cultivation in United States by 1955, hemp had escaped and become well established in waste areas, particularly in the Midwest. De Schweinitz (1836) noted that "naturalized *Cannabis sativa* is very common in eastern United States." Brendel (1887), in an account of the vegetation of one area in N-central Illinois, wrote that *Cannabis sativa* was "perfectly naturalized and common around Peoria in the year 1852."

Haney and Bazzaz (1970) suggested that the naturalized populations of hemp in United States still were expanding. The study reported here was undertaken to learn more of the ecology of naturalized hemp such that a better prediction could be made of the rate of spread and habitat preferences of hemp in the Midwest.

We wish to express our appreciation to W. R. Boggess and Gary L. Rolfe, Department of Forestry, Univ. of Illinois, for their advice in soil analyses and for instruments loaned for this study; to T. R. Peck, of Illinois' Department of Agronomy, for arranging our use of the Kjeldahl laboratory; to Robert W. Poole, Illinois State Natural History Survey and Bruce P. Hanna, of the university's Center for Advanced Computation, for advice and suggestions on statistical methods; to Charles J. Sheviak and F. A. Bazzaz, Department of Botany at the university, for suggestions and critical review of methods and interpretations; and to the landowners, law enforcement officers and interested persons who provided information and cooperated in this study.

REVIEW OF PERTINENT LITERATURE

No attempt will be made here to summarize exhaustively the literature pertaining to the ecology of naturalized hemp. The interested reader is referred to Joyce and Curry (1970), Eddy (1965) and Waller and Denny (1971) for more complete summaries.

Hemp is an annual, dioecious forb; hermaphroditic flowers and polygamomonoecious plants rarely were present in our populations. The ratio of male to female plants reportedly is decreased by ultraviolet light exposure of seeds (Montemartini, 1926), increased by

---

Vanishing Amphibians: Why They're Croaking

Scientists this week moved closer to figuring out why certain species of frogs, toads and salamanders have taken a nose dive in recent years and why some have already sung their swan song. At a National Research Council conference in Irvine, Calif., researchers presented strong evidence linking acidic rain and snow—usually viewed as an eastern phenomenon — to salamander deaths in the western United States. Others argued that global climate changes may play a role in the amphibian deaths now plaguing such diverse habitats as the open woodlands of southeastern Australia, the mountain country of northern Colorado and the tropical forests of Costa Rica and Brazil.

Behind the mysterious decline, which apparently began 10 to 20 years ago but only recently received unified attention, lies the possibility that the dying animals are an ominous indicator of human-made environmental problems. "There are some things about [amphibians] that make them a very good 'canary in the coal mine,'" asserts zoologist Henry Wilbur of Duke University in Durham, N.C., referring to the traditional mining practice of detecting toxic gases through their deadly effect on canaries. Amphibian skin readily absorbs chemicals present in soil and water, he says, and the insects these animals eat may harbor other toxic compounds. Moreover, water

evaporates quickly from the porous skin, suggesting amphibians may be especially vulnerable to droughts. Wilbur adds that "frogs naturally have great fluctuations in population size" — perhaps reflecting an inherent sensitivity to environmental changes. The key to explaining the scattered distribution of decline among various regions and species, he maintains, is that many amphibians, particularly frogs, need access to several interconnected habitats in order to survive, jumping from pond to pond or from tree to tree when the going gets tough. When alternative dwellings are destroyed, often by human activities, frogs may become sitting ducks for other environmental assaults.

Habitat isolation might help explain the demise of the golden toads that virtually carpeted a small rain forest reserve near Monte Verde, Costa Rica, as recently as 1983, says biologist Marc Hayes of the University of Miami. These creatures, he notes, have an unusual characteristic: They lay eggs only during a 10-day "window" between rainy and dry seasons. Recent fluctuations in that interval could have disrupted the golden toad's life cycle, Hayes suggests. Similarly, rapid melting of acidic snow in the Colorado Rockies can severely damage tiger salamander eggs during a critical five-day period in development, reports John Harte of the University of California, Berkeley.

Hayes and others say stocking lakes with game fish that prey on tadpoles has contributed substantially to the decline of frogs in many U.S. lakes. This, he suggests, might help explain why certain frog species long accustomed to fish-free lakes are the hardest hit in the West.

"The interaction [causing the decline] may differ from region to region, but there is clearly a global problem of some kind—some kind of climate effect," Hayes adds. Researchers point to several interrelated trends: a worldwide warming, increased atmospheric carbon dioxide and methane, and a slight increase in ultraviolet light due to thinning of stratospheric ozone. But they admit that no one really knows how such trends might affect amphibian survival, or whether several small factors added together can devastate an existing population.

For now, says biologist Harold J. Morowitz of George Mason University in Fairfax, Va., the decline may serve as an environmental rallying point for both scientists and the public. "Who cares if 1,000 arachnids become extinct in an Amazon rain forest? That's dynamite to a scientist," he says, "but the public can relate better to Kermit." — R. Cowen

"Low level" radioactive waste not worthy of concern

WASHINGTON, DC—Radioactive waste could soon join the old tires, banana peels and coffee grounds in America's landfills if the U.S. Nuclear Regulatory Commission the Environmental Protection Agency (EPA) go through with a policy treating nuclear waste as though it were not radioactive.

The NRC in 1986 developed a policy called Below Regulatory Concern (BRC) for deregulating radioactive waste. Although the policy has not yet been implemented, an application for implementation is expected this spring from the Nuclear Utilities Management and Resource Council.

Once the application is approved, more than 30 percent of the nation's currently regulated "low level" nuclear power-plant waste could be dumped as ordinary non-nuclear trash. Under the BRC label, loads of radioactive waste would travel with regular garbage on highways, railways and rivers and could be emptied in landfills and sewers, burned

in incinerators and spread in the form of radioactive sludge on farmlands. The EPA has also included the BRC deregulation policy in its proposed radioactive-waste dump standards.

The deregulation plan does not provide for notification of haulers, waste handlers or other workers. Several unions have opposed the plan. When the proposal surfaced several years ago, the United Steelworkers of America stopped recycling radioactive metal. In addition, there will be no monitoring once the waste leaves the nuclear power-plant site and communities will not be informed that they are receiving radioactive waste.

The major rationale behind deregulation is to save nuclear power-plant owners money. The EPA estimates that the industry's disposal costs will be reduced by $620 million over the next 20 years if one-third of the waste is deregulated. The EPA also notes the human cost—one death per 10,000 people exposed to deregulated waste.

The Illinois Department of Nuclear Safety has severely criticized the EPA for its proposed exposure levels. "Any level of exposure to deregulated nuclear waste is too much,

because there is no plan to verify or enforce that the level won't be exceeded," says Michael Mariotte, director of the Nuclear Information and Resource Service. "There is no safe level of exposure to radiation, so waste should be isolated for as long as it remains hazardous."

Some of the waste that could be deregulated—including irradiated piping, sewage sludge, sandblasting grit, soils, oils, resins and evaporator bottoms from filtering radioactive water—could remain hazardous for centuries. If the material is burnable, it could be incinerated. If it's water soluble, it could go down the drain. Solid waste could go to landfills, and recyclable metals could be melted down for reuse.

Several important questions remain unanswered: why add radioactive waste to already crowded landfills? How will the public know when and where radioactive waste is being burned or dumped? How will abuses, such as dumping more radioactive waste than permitted, be prevented?

For more information on BRC waste, contact the Nuclear Information and Resource Service at (202) 328-0002, 1424 16th St. NW, Suite 601, Washington, DC 20036.

—Leigh Hauter & Diane D'Arrigo

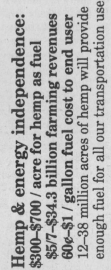

No. 22

FREEDOM NETWORK NEWS

June/July 1989

A GRASS HOUSE IN YOUR FUTURE?

By Vincent H. Miller

Karl Hess shows us his Pyramod home in West Virginia.

A problem facing much of the world today is the availability of decent, affordable housing. We at L.I. have observed this first hand in the 3rd world and in areas like the South African black townships -- and even in the 1st world where great numbers of people are coming to realize that, after taxes, owning a home is becoming an increasingly more hopeless dream.

Happily there are some rays of hope on the horizon, thanks to L.I. member Bob Glassco and Mansion Industries Inc. of Industry, California, USA.

A VISIT WITH KARL AND THERESE

A few weeks ago we had the pleasure of visiting with our dear friends Karl and Therese Hess in the hills of West Virginia: 1. to help Karl celebrate his 66th birthday and, 2. to see the Hess's new "straw" house!

Straw as a construction material of course is not unknown. It has been used since ancient times and is known for its toughness and durability. But for a modern 21st century family like the Hess's with a modern office full of Macintosh computers?? Rest assured this is not the same straw construction that in mythology has been huffed and puffed away by malevolent wolves. Glassco and his company have used modern technology and combined a number of unique concepts to produce a practical, inexpensive . . . and yes, revolutionary elegant product.

THE RIGHT COMBINATION

The secret of the success of this form of construction is based on specially compressed and heated pre-formed panels (a process called *Envirocor*) and on a uniquely strong pyramidal construction design called *Pyramod*.

The panels are constructed of agricultural fibres such as rice or wheat straw -- although sugar cane rind can also be used when properly separated from the pulp. These fibres are heated to 400 degrees F (205 degrees C), compressed under extremely high pressure in special machines and bonded with heavy kraft paper with a plastic adhesive. The resultant 4.75 inch (12cm) thick panels, are then cut to finished dimensions, including window, door, skylight cutouts, etc. with a diamond saw. According to specification sheets provided by Mansion Industries, these panels are remarkably strong, and have the highly desirable characteristic of being able to act as primary load bearing structural materials. They are highly flame resistant, have good insulating qualities and are immune to termite infestation. They are also more resistant to mold and decay than wood and will not emit toxic fumes.

Probably the most interesting aspect of the straw house is that construction with the precut panels can be done very quickly and inexpensively by relatively unskilled labor. No wooden framing is

Libertarian International is an association of individuals and organizations dedicated to building a free and peaceful world, respect for individual rights and liberties, and an open and competitive economic system based on voluntary exchange and free trade.
Members and affiliated organizations pursue this goal through independent action, using their freely chosen strategies. The association exists to promote the exchange of information and ideas, to study diverse strategies and to foster fellowship.

Published by LIBERTARIAN INTERNATIONAL, 9308 Farmington Dr., Richmond, VA 23229   Phone: (804) 740-6932

Envirocor house panels being erected in Guatemala.

required and the panels fit together precisely, requiring only the application of adhesive and tape. The interior may be painted or wallpapered and a number of finishes may be applied to the exterior, including inexpensive fibreglass matting saturated with a special acrylic latex compound which can be applied with a roller. Standard systems for water, electrical and climate control are easily incorporated into the floor design. The end result is quite strong and features outstanding resistance to the the type of shock forces encountered during earthquakes and hurricanes.

Very important, however, is the fact that the finished product is quite aesthetic. The modern pyramidal vaulted ceilings are not only beautiful but give a great sense of space. We were impressed and think that this process should have huge potential around the world -- particularly in developing areas like black African states and 3rd world areas.

Several model homes have been constructed: Karl and Therese's home in West Virginia; one in Guatemala (now being used by an architectural firm); one at the Mansion plant in California; and another in the Philippines.

Mr. Glassco is now busily marketing the production process in various countries around the world. If any of L.I. members are interested in pursuing this further or know of individuals who might be interested in raising the capital to erect such a factory in their area of the world, please contact Bob Glassco at the following address and be sure to mention that you read about it in the *Freedom Network News.*

MANSION INDUSTRIES, INC.
14425 E. Clark Ave., P.O. Box 2220,
Industry, California 91746 USA
Phone: (818) 968-9501
Fax: (818) 330-3084
Telex: 283859 MIND UR

Controlled Substance and the Tarbaby

This work livicated to Bruddah Jim Carner and Bruddah Jacob Miller.

by Lindsey Bradshaw

Controlled Substance," shrieked the mad judge behind the stand.
He looked weary with the gavel in his hand.
"Controlled Substance, yes, this is it," nodded the cops,
"On with the trial," they yelled, "Let's pull out the stops."
"Controlled Substance!' said the jailer with great relief.
"Controlled Substance?" asked the farmer in disbelief.

"Guilty," screamed the judge, "I know how to handle that,
I'll take an eye for an eye, and a tit for a tat.
Guilty, I'll do my damnedest to see you in jail,
Guilty, I'll do my damnedest to up your bail.
Guilty, why, I may take your land,
Maybe even your children. Wouldn't that be grand?
Guilty, I'll do my damnedest to up your taxes,
And if all these fail, I've many such axes."

There was such a ruckus, and such a commotion,
You would have thought that Moses had just parted the ocean.
This kangaroo court, held with such a lack of love,
Caught the attention of Saint Michael above.
St. Mike thought to himself, "They think it's about weed,
Freedom is the issue! Controlled Substance, indeed!"
Mike said, "We must do something, and do it right now,
Why, I'll get some friends, we'll find out just what and how.
He called for Ms. Liberty, and Bogg the Cosmic Clown.
They said, "They're at it again, Let's go down!"

At this, the jury was possessed. They said, "We want out.
Controlled substance, indeed!" they beagan to shout.
Bogg the Clown got the judge with a pie in the face.
"Your honor," said mike, "You, sir, are a disgrace."
Ms. Liberty let loose with a seltzer bottle,
A bus of stonekey cops came in at full throttle.
The ringmaster appeared and said, "Ain't this dandy,
The only thing this place lacks is cotton candy."
This circus has lions, freaks, liars, and geeks. It is too loud.
It is on fire! But don't you dare say so in a crowd.
This circus has plowshares, nowshares, a doubled-edged sword,
And David dancing naked on the altar of the Lord.

"Order in the court," babbled the judge in a fit,
"You want order?" said the clown. "Why? You started this shit."
"So you want order? We'll give you some real quick."
"Ms. Liberty," he asked, "Please now, show us a trick."

She jumped high into the air and did a somersault,
Saying, "Whenever or wherever I land is not my fault."
Controlled Substance, Controlled Substance, indeed," said she.
And half way down she turned into a tarbaby.

The tarbaby landed in the judges lap, by heck.
Tarbaby had a sign hanging around her neck.
The sign read "Marijuana" unmistakably.
The sign read "Marijuana, what about me?"
The judge was too slippery to keep her for long,
So like Pontius Pilate, he threw her to the throng.

But the tarbaby flew high into the air, and did a spin.
She uprighted herself and landed with a grin.
Lightly, the baby sat down with the PTA.
She said, "Keep up the good work, I'm not here to stay.
Your wisdom will tell you, you've bigger problems with booze.
Keep kids off pot? Sure, but let adults choose."

"Tarbaby, tarbaby, what do you have to say?"
Tarbaby answered, "I'm here to do what I may."
"Tarbaby, tarbaby, what do you have to do?"
"Only," said the baby, "to answer the question "Who?"
Tarbaby born in blood, tarbaby made of mud.
She was conceived in fire, in the image of God.
Tarbaby flew high, flew high into the sun.
"Let's put," she said, "the beasts of hell on the run."

The tarbaby landed on the doctor's chest.
Doc tried to give her a urinalysis test.
Tarbaby said, "Sorry, but my body is mine."
Doc said, "You're right. I'll now pass you on down the line."
Ol' tarbaby landed in a lawyer's chair
His first thought was, "Get this out of my hair,
Although, I think I'll be ready for you some day,
I'm just bringing home the bacon, and you don't pay."

This tarbaby is smart, and free, and oh so cool.
This poor innocent baby makes the gangster drool.
The gangster said, "I'm the kind that does as I please,
I like you baby, but I'm gonna put you in a squeeze."
Baby said, "I've met your kind, I know where you are at."
She looked at him. He turned into a vampire bat.

The tarbaby landed on the face of the law.
Poor man, with a gun, a star, was dumbstruck with awe.
The sheriff said, "This case is just down my line,
I'll get more men, increase the axes, up the fine."
Baby said, "I'm just being. It's you who fights.
I demand my inalienable rights."
"But," said the sheriff, "it's my time to play John Wayne,
Though, John didn't say it would be such a pain."
Sheriff found dealing to the baby very hard.
"Well, hot dam" he said, "I need the National Guard!"

The guard came in shooting, as they dropped from the skies.
They came in rooting, but started to drop like flies.
They thought they were strong, lean and mean, or right, at least.
But they were met by the front line generals of the armies of peace.
The generals' backs were against the wall, it was do or die.
"Freedom, now or never," they knew. "Let's let the fur fly."

"Order," whimpered the judge, "I want order in this court."
The clown lit a joint with the procurator's torte.
The jury and the coppers began to rumble.
No doubt, the ol' whorehouse began to crumble.
Now, walking on the ceiling the tarbaby pranced.
All over the courtroom the tarbaby danced.
She said sweetly, "Whatever goes up must come down."
She jumped high into the air and turned herself around.
She did a stretch and a great big yawn,
"Look around you," she said, "'Tis the time of dawn.
Wake up, wake up, oh gracious, wake up from your nap."
Ain't this bodacious, she just landed in your lap."

Thursday, May 3, 1990   The Orange County Register

The environmental impact of the laws against marijuana

By Alan W. Bock

Earth Day has come and gone, with little if any attention being given to a single step that, more than any other, could contribute on a large scale to reducing environmental degradation. The idea — making it legal once again to grow hemp for fiber — is controversial, to be sure, but as Jack Herer, founder of the organization Help Eliminate Marijuana Prohibition keeps saying: "Prove us wrong." So far nobody has been able to do so.

The attempt to eradicate marijuana, or hemp, has not been successful, by a long shot. But it has ensured that hemp will only be grown for its buds, which contain the mild hallucinogen, tetra hydra cannabinol (THC). If hemp were legal, it would be grown for a wide variety of other purposes.

The stalk of the hemp plant has been used for fiber for thousands of years. The seeds are a source of oil that has been used for paint, varnish, and fine lubricating oils, as well as protein suitable for human and animal consumption. Neither contains THC. Since the hemp plant has been effectively unavailable for these uses since about 1937, we have turned to other resources, many non-renewable. Using them has been far more damaging to the environment.

For example, hemp fiber is at least 10 times stronger than cotton. Hemp has not only been used to manufacture canvas (the word is derived from "cannabis"), but linen, rope, and thread. Cotton replaced hemp as the dominant fiber in this country after the cotton gin, which mechanically separated

According to the USDA, 0,000 acres planted in hemp will yield as much paper as 40,000 acres planted in trees. Fewer caustic or toxic chemicals are required to make paper from hemp than to make paper from trees.

the usable fibers from the seeds, was invented. Getting the fibers out of hemp took hard manual labor; it wasn't until the 1930s that machines for separating usable fibers from hemp stems were perfected.

Hemp has few if any natural enemies; that's one reason some call it "weed." Cotton, by contrast, can be grown commercially only with lots of fertilizers and pesticides, and growing it exhausts the soil. About half the pesticides used in the world are used on cotton — which also requires lots of water. If it were legal to cultivate hemp for fiber, we would be using far fewer pesticides.

About half the forests in the world have been cut down since the 1930s to make paper. A US Department of Agriculture bulletin in 1916 explained how paper could be made from the pulpy "hurds" in the hemp stalk, and predicted that if machinery were developed to separate the hurds from the fibers, a thriving domestic paper industry could be developed based on hemp cultivation. The machinery developed in the 1930s did just that.

According to the USDA, 10,000 acres planted in

hemp will yield as much paper as 40,000 acres planted in trees. Fewer caustic or toxic chemicals are required to make paper from hemp than to make paper from trees.

The hemp seed was long used as a base for paints, varnishes, and other finishes — items for which we routinely use petrochemicals or synthetics. In 1935, 116 million pounds of hempseed were used in America for paint and varnish. The seed is also the second richest plant source of protein, and is much cheaper to cultivate than soybeans, the richest source. Hempseed protein could be processed and flavored any way soybean protein can. It could feed most of the earth's domestic animals.

A favorite enthusiasm of environmentalists is alternative fuels produced from biomass. Corn, sugarcane, and kenaf are the plants most often used, because they grow so much in a single season that they produce lots of biomass to be refined and processed into methane or methanol. But they are still more expensive than petroleum-based fuels.

Hemp, however, is the world's champion photosynthesizer. It converts the sun's energy into bio-

mass more efficiently than any other plant, with at least four times the biomass/cellulose potential of corn or kenaf. It could compete economically with petroleum-based fuels.

Coal and petrochemicals got their energy from the sun, thousands of years ago, storing energy as the plants decayed. When they are burned, they release pollutants into the atmosphere. Biomass fuel releases fewer pollutants, and the fuel source spends the growing season removing carbon dioxide from the atmosphere through photosynthesis; biomass fuels contain no sulfur.

The environmental impact of banning hemp, then, has been the use of far more environmentally damaging alternatives. If hemp were legal, it could become an economically viable and low-polluting source of fuel, paints and varnishes, textiles and fabrics, paper, and even food. Hemp might replace trees as raw material for press-board or particleboard construction material. You could even make PVC pipe from hemp.

In 1988, the chief administrative law judge of the Drug Enforcement Administration wrote: "There is no record in the extensive medical literature describing a proven, documented cannabis-induced fatality.... In strict medical terms, marijuana is far safer than many foods we commonly consume." The dangers of hemp are far from overwhelming. Relegalizing hemp could be the single most important environmental reform we could undertake. Prove me wrong? Sure, if you can do it with facts.

Mr. Bock is the Register's *senior columnist.*

Hemp a source of energy

Group wants pot legalized

United Press International

ALBANY — Marijuana plants could produce paper, cloth and energy cheaply and cleanly, but alcohol, pharmaceutical and synthetic fiber companies stand in the way of its legalization, marijuana advocates said Monday.

Members of Help End Marijuana Prohibition held a rally on the steps of the state Capitol as part of a 60-city tour calling for its legalization.

Calling marijuana prohibition "a crime against the American farmer," group spokesman Shan Clark said an acre of hemp, or marijuana, will yield as much paper as four acres of trees or as much energy as 25 barrels of oil and called it "one of the safest therapeutically active substances known to man."

"I say there is no public health danger associated with legalization at all," Clark said.

"I've smoked it for years and I can see no ill effects," he said, adding, "I represent 30 (million) or 40 million Americans."

Hemp grows in more soils and climates than any other commercial crop and is naturally resistant to insects and weeds, making herbicides and pesticides unnecessary, Clark said.

He said hemp was an important cash crop until the late 1930s, and its prohibition was urged by alcohol and synthetic fiber companies.

The paintings of the masters, the U.S. Constitution and the Declaration of Independence are all on hemp, and the USS *Constitution* was rigged with 60 tons of it in its sails, Clark said.

He said marijuana is also a safe stress reliever, and called the Partnership for a Drug-Free America the "partnership for no competition on the drug market," saying the group's support from alcohol and pharmaceutical companies has been reported in the New York *Times*.

Ron Coffman, a professor of plant breeding and international agriculture at Cornell University, agreed that hemp had agricultural value as recently as World War II, when farmers received government incentives to grow it in the "Hemp for Victory" program.

"Definitely, hemp was, and perhaps in some parts of the world still is, a widely used source of fiber," Coffman said.

State Division of Substance Abuse Services spokesman Louis Ganim said that despite its possible agricultural value, marijuana should not be legalized.

Albany Times-Union Aug. 26 1990
Albany, New York

— 177 —

Pro-pot forces rally, argue it's hip to grow hemp

Legalization is said to hold commercial, environmental hope

By Adam Gelb
Staff writer

Frustrated since the reefer-mad 1960s in its efforts to end pot prohibition, the marijuana legalization movement has turned green.

At rallies from Atlanta to California, marijuana enthusiasts have softened their emphasis on individual liberty and taken to extolling the environmental and commercial virtues of the hemp plant, the stalk that grows marijuana leaves.

Pot smokers are touting hemp as the answer to everything from rescuing family farms to beating dependence on foreign oil — a natural way to save the planet and escape from it at the same time.

"There's more people in Georgia now who know the hemp information than knew it in the whole country five years ago," said Jack Herer, founder of the Los Angeles-based group Help End Marijuana Prohibition (HEMP) and author of the hemp bible, "The Emperor Wears No Clothes." "We have a grass-roots movement — no pun intended — and it's going to be one hell of a movement."

On Saturday, the occasional whiff of pungent pot smoke floated through Piedmont Park at the second annual Great Atlanta Pot Festival, sponsored by the National Organization for the Reform of Marijuana Laws (NORML). Organizers attributed the sizable turnout, estimated at 3,500, in part to city officials who initially banned the rally, saying it wasn't a legitimate political event, then agreed to allow it after NORML filed suit.

The colorful crowd danced, cooked barbecue and burned incense to tunes from three bands, and cheered its speak-

Kimberly Smith/Staff

The Great Atlanta Pot Festival continued the traditional connection between marijuana and rock music but played down legalization advocates' old focus on individual liberties. Arthur "Skip" Gantt dances to the music Saturday.

ers, including lawyer Michael R. Hauptman, who filed the suit for NORML, and Walker Chandler, the Libertarian Party candidate for lieutenant governor last year. Atlanta police kept a close eye but made no arrests.

Supporters in California have launched the first serious effort since the 1970s to get a marijuana legalization initiative on a statewide ballot.

In West Virginia, National Guardsmen threatened to stop a hemp rally at an armory March 27, but a federal judge decided it could continue.

Until it was outlawed in 1937, cannabis hemp was widely grown and made into rope, fabric, paper and other products. Advocates say it can make paper and save trees and be used as an alternative to plastics and petroleum. It doesn't need to be sprayed with dangerous pesticides like other crops, they add.

A favorite argument is that hemp made up part of the parachute that saved young Navy pilot George Bush's life when he bailed out over the Pacific during World War II. A short film

produced by the U.S. Department of Agriculture in 1942, called "Hemp for Victory," urged farmers to plant hemp for various war-related purposes, including parachute riggings.

The Drug Enforcement Administration, a bitter opponent of relaxing marijuana laws, declined to comment on the hemp issue. A spokeswoman in Washington said the agency couldn't discuss the issue because of a case pending in federal appeals court over the medical uses of the drug.

Another nemesis of the lega-

lizers, the Atlanta-based Parents' Resource Institute for Drug Education (PRIDE), said the hemp strategy is clever, especially because it is likely to appeal to increasingly environmentally conscious youths.

"I think this new environmental effort is coming about because they've failed miserably on the health, safety and legal issues," said Marsha Keith Shuchard, PRIDE co-founder. "There are all kinds of plants that can do exactly what they say marijuana can do without the hallucinogenic ingredient. It's pretty ridiculous."

SOME SOURCES OF LEGAL, NON-SMOKING HEMP PRODUCTS

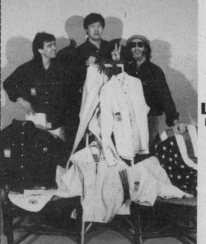

BOOKMARKS

Jack Herer, left, a critic of laws against marijuana, at the annual U-M Hash Bash on Sunday.

JOHN LUKE/Detroit Free Press

Rebel with an illegal cause

By MIKE DUFFY
Free Press Staff Writer

Forget reefer madness, says Jack Herer, it's time for reefer gladness.

Hemp heaven on earth is nigh, if only we'd just wise up and take a hit of reality, says Herer, 50, author of "The Emperor Wears No Clothes: The Authoritative Historical Record of the Cannabis Plant, Hemp Prohibition, and How Marijuana Can Still Save the World."

Save the world?

Absolutely, argues Herer, who is the founder and national director of Help End Marijuana Prohibition (HEMP) and has been fighting for the legalization of marijuana for 17 years.

"The laws on marijuana are based totally on disinformation," Herer said during a Monday phone interview, after participating in a marijuana legalization debate at the University of Detroit. "We have outlawed the world's premier plant."

By premier plant, Herer means not only the controversial, outlawed weed that produces a narcotic high. He also means the plant

Author calls hemp a miracle plant

that produces hemp.

And hemp, Herer argues passionately and exhaustively in his book and in interviews, is the most environmentally sane source for making "all the paper, fiber and fuel the world needs."

In other words, he asserts, we could wipe out the greenhouse effect.

We could stop cutting down trees for paper, Herer says, because hemp "produces four times as much pulp with five to seven times less pollution." What's more, Herer claims, hemp could be a primary, totally biodegradable source of textiles and fabrics, paints and varnishes, lighting oil, methanol and building materials.

Besides all of that, Herer says, you can still have a good, safe time smoking the stuff.

"It actually seems that people live longer if they use it," he argues, citing various studies he says prove his point. "If you substi-

tute marijuana for tobacco and alcohol, you'll add eight to 24 years to your life."

So far, Herer hasn't any luck at all in convincing the governmental establishment or substance abuse experts of the truth and wisdom of his claims. He knows he's an outsider, a rebel with crusading cause.

"How can you justify legalizing tobacco and alcohol, petrochemicals and chemicals, but make the world's most benign and friendly plant illegal? You cannot make a law against natural things."

A father of six, each of whom has tried pot with pop, Herer didn't smoke marijuana until he was 30.

"I didn't think it would work. I was above it," Herer said. And the first couple times, nothing did happen. "But the third time, I heard music in colors. And then I made love and it was the most gracious, beautiful experience I've ever had. And I said, 'This is Illegal?'"

(The Emperor Wears No Clothes' can be ordered by writing to HEMP, 5632 Van Nuys, Van Nuys, Calif. 91401. The book costs $12.95, plus $2 for postage and handling.)

Get Your Own Crisp, Clean VHS Copy of

HEMP FOR VICTORY

the 1942 USDA Pro-marijuana film.

along with a button Hemp for Victory & 2 Bumper stickers
plus documentation for the movie.

Only **$20***

Or, for **$35*** you'll get the Silver Membership:

all this, plus a complimentary copy of

The Emperor Wears No Clothes

and membership in H.E.M.P.

* Plus $2 shipping & handling charges